SOURCES AND DOCUMENTS OF

UNITED STATES CONSTITUTIONS

SOURCES AND DOCUMENTS OF

UNITED STATES CONSTITUTIONS

SOURCES AND DOCUMENTS OF
UNITED STATES CONSTITUTIONS

9

SOUTH DAKOTA
TENNESSEE • TEXAS
UTAH • VERMONT

Edited and Annotated

by

WILLIAM F. SWINDLER
John Marshall Professor of Law
College of William and Mary

1979
OCEANA PUBLICATIONS, INC.
DOBBS FERRY, NEW YORK

Library of Congress Cataloging in Publication Data (Revised)

Swindler, William Finley, comp.
    Sources and documents of United States constitutions.

    Includes bibliographies.
    CONTENTS: 1. Alabama. Alaska. Arizona. Arkansas.
California. — 2. Colorado, Connecticut. Delaware.
Florida. Georgia. — 3. Hawaii. Idaho. Illinois.
Indiana. Iowa. [etc.]
    1. Constitutions, State — United States — Sources.
I. Title.
KF4530.S94   342'.73'024   73-170979
ISBN 0-379-16175-3 (series)
ISBN 0-379-16185-0 (vol. 9)

Manufactured in the United States of America

Sources and Documents of United States Constitutions is an annotated collection of the fundamental instruments recording the historical development of constitutional government in each state in the Union. It thus complements the collection of current state constitutions prepared by the Legislative Drafting Research Fund of Columbia University and published under the title, *Constitutions of the United States, National and State,* as well as the Fund's *Index-Digest of State Constitutions.* The analytical indexes for each state in the present collection follow the editorial plan of the *Index-Digest,* and in other respects the present collection has been prepared to be used together with the Columbia University collection of current constitutions, thus providing a comprehensive reference series on state constitutional documents.

STATES IN THE ORDER OF ADMISSION
(Bold indicates states in this volume)

Delaware
December 7, 1787

Pennsylvania
December 12, 1787

New Jersey
December 18, 1787

Georgia
January 2, 1788

Connecticut
January 9, 1788

Massachusetts
February 6, 1788

Maryland
April 28, 1788

South Carolina
May 23, 1788

New Hampshire
June 21, 1788

Virginia
June 25, 1788

New York
July 26, 1788

North Carolina
November 21, 1789

Rhode Island
May 29, 1790

Vermont
March 4, 1791

Kentucky
June 1, 1792

Tennessee
June 1, 1796

Ohio
March 1, 1803

Louisiana
April 30, 1812

Indiana
December 11, 1816

Mississippi
December 10, 1817

Illinois
December 3, 1818

Alabama
December 14, 1819

Maine
March 15, 1820

Missouri
August 10, 1821

Arkansas
June 15, 1836

Michigan
January 26, 1837

Florida
March 3, 1845

Texas
December 29, 1845

Iowa
December 28, 1846

Wisconsin
May 29, 1848

California
September 9, 1850

Minnesota
May 11, 1858

Oregon
February 14, 1859

Kansas
January 29, 1861

West Virginia
June 20, 1863

Nevada
October 31, 1864

Nebraska
March 1, 1867

Colorado
August 1, 1876

North Dakota
November 2, 1889

South Dakota
November 2, 1889

Montana
November 8, 1889

Washington
November 11, 1889

Idaho
July 3, 1890

Wyoming
July 10, 1890

Utah
January 4, 1896

Oklahoma
November 16, 1907

New Mexico
January 6, 1912

Arizona
February 14, 1912

Alaska
January 3, 1959

Hawaii
August 21, 1959

OUTLINE OF VOLUME IX

For detailed contents for each state, consult the individual tables of contents at the beginning of the collection of sources and documents for that state.

INTRODUCTORY ESSAY

I

The first collection of American state constitutions was printed in French, "in Philadelphia, and sold in Paris," in 1778, evidence of the great interest aroused in Europe by the independence movement and perhaps stimulated by Benjamin Franklin, American minister to France, to whom this edition was dedicated. Two years later the Continental Congress adopted a resolution on December 29, 1780, "that a committee of three be appointed to collect, and cause to be published, two hundred correct copies, of the Declaration of Independence, the Articles of Confederation and perpetual union, the alliance between the United States and His Most Christian Majesty (the King of France), with the constitutions or forms of government of the several States."

The committee -- Thomas Bee of South Carolina, John Witherspoon of New Jersey and Oliver Wolcott of Connecticut -- proceeded to collect the documents and have them printed at Philadelphia the following year. Another French translation, this time officially negotiated by Franklin with the Duke de la Rochefoucauld, was published in Paris in 1783. Later in the same year the Philadelphia edition was reprinted in Glasgow, a reflection of the considerable Scottish interest in the progress of American affairs. Indeed, the Glasgow printer was moved to insert, by way of a preface, some "Verses on the Constitutions," indifferent in literary quality but articulating the conviction of many people that these unique documents were evidence of a new era in politics. A few stanzas illustrate the viewpoint:

> Most human forms of government were made
> For low ambition's more than virtue's aid.
> Some barb'rous warrior, hast'ning to a throne,
> And deeming what he conquer'd all his own,
> Devis'd a set of laws for ruling men
> That suits the savage monsters of the den...
>
> But now, behold, a set of newborn states,
> (Their western shores the vast Atlantic beats)
> Whose constitutions have no other plan
> Nor aim than this, the happiness of man.

This small volume of 257 pages contained, among other things, the constitutions which had been adopted by eleven of the states in response to a Congressional call in 1776 urging that they take appropriate steps "for the maintenance of internal peace and the defense of their lives, liberties or properties." Also included were the colonial charters under which Connecticut and Rhode Island elected to continue for the immediate future. In 1783, the first comparative study of the new state constitutions was published in London under the title, *A View of the Constitution of the British Colonies...at the Time the Civil War Broke Out on the Continent of America.* The author, Anthony Stokes, was the former royal chief justice of the colony of Georgia, who prepared the book because, as he wrote, there were "not any two States in which the forms of Government agree in every particular."

In 1791 came another Congressional publication, including the new Constitution of the United States and the first ten Amendments, as well as the constitution of the fourteenth state, Vermont. Reprintings of this edition quickly appeared in London and Paris, and by 1796 the first American comparative study was published, edited by Congressman William Loughton Smith of South Carolina. Smith, a scholarly lawyer who had studied at the Middle Temple in London and later at Geneva, wrote that his work -- entitled, *A Comparative View of the Constitutions of the Several States With Each Other, and With That of the United States* -- was intended, "by comparing them one with another, and by referring at the same time to the various degrees of order and prosperity, and to the state of society and morals, of each particular state, (to make) a tolerably correct estimate...of the relative perfection or imperfection of those constitutions." While this was an overly ambitious objective, the basic value of the book lay in what it did accomplish: "Those of our fellow citizens who may, from time to time, be delegated to revise these constitutions will be furnished with a work, which will assist them in the discharge of their duty, and greatly facilitate their labours."

For the sixteen states then in the Union, Smith's work, consisting of a series of tables outlining the features of the governmental structure in each state, afforded a clear and concise panorama of constitutional machinery. The only comparable work of this general period was prepared by James Mercer Garnett, legislator and planter, for the Virginia state constitutional convention of 1829-1830, under the title, *Constitutional Charts; or, Comparative Views of the Legislative, Executive and Judiciary Departments, in the Constitutions of All the States in the Union.* By that time there were twenty-three states in the Union, and the problem of comparisons was substantially more challenging. Periodically new collections of the current constitutions -- as new states were admitted and older states adopted new instruments -- were prepared by official or private sources: Congress authorized new compilations from time to time throughout the first half of the nineteenth century, and there were occasional independent editorial projects like J. R. Bigelow's *The American's Own Book; or, The Constitutions of the Several States in the Union,* published in 1849.

The study of trends in state constitutionalism entered a more sophisticated phase in the generation following the Civil War. Amid a steady succession of new charters which came into being in this period, Judge Thomas M. Cooley of Michigan in 1868 published the first edition of *A Treatise on the Constitutional Limitations which Rest upon the Legislative Powers of the States of the American Union.* Complementing this, in 1877, came the first historical collection of documents in *Federal and State Constitutions, Colonial Charters, and Other Organic Laws of the United States,* prepared by the printing clerk of the Senate, Ben: Perley Poore, with the aid of a committee of jurists and historians. Between them, these works broadened the study of state constitutions into three dimensions: the comparison of contemporary documents in the manner of the Smith and Garnett volumes of fifty to seventy-five years before; the comparison of historical documents now brought together in Poore's collection; and the interpretation of basic constitutional principles as adjudicated by the courts of the several states, which was the objective of Cooley's treatise.

In the introduction to his first edition, Cooley confessed that "he had written in full sympathy with all those restraints which the caution of the fathers had imposed upon the exercise of the powers of government." His conservative premises, indeed, made his work a basic reference for the burgeoning industrialism and *laissez-faire* capitalism of the last quarter of the nineteenth century, and it was powerfully corroborated by two other works of the period which gained equal positions of influence -- *Limitations on Police Power,* by Professor Christopher Tiedemann of Missouri, and *Law and Jurisprudence in England and America,* by Judge John F. Dillon of Iowa. These works, published in 1886 and 1894 respectively, completed a powerful trilogy of legal authorities favorable to the free enterprise system of the day; and Cooley's profound work, running through twelve editions to 1928, carried on the dogma almost to the end of the era of *laissez-faire* itself.

Poore's collection continued to be the standard reference for the documentary historian for three decades, until it was succeeded in 1909 by the seven-volume collection prepared for Congress by Professor Francis Newton Thorpe of the University of Pennsylvania. For more than sixty years, this work on *American Charters, Constitutions and Organic Laws* has been the most recent and most regularly cited source of historical information on the subject. In 1915 a comparative study of contemporary state constitutions was prepared by the Legislative Drafting Research Fund of Columbia University for the New York State Constitutional Convention Commission and published in a massive 1500-page volume as the *Index-Digest of State Constitutions.* This had been preceded in 1910 by a monographic study on *The Revision and Amendment of State Constitutions,* by Walter F. Dodd and published by the John's Hopkins University, and followed in 1918 by another study for the New York commission by Charles Kettleborough, *The State Constitutions and the Federal Constitution and*

Organic Laws of the Territories and Other Colonial Dependencies of the United States of America. Another compilation of contemporary state constitutions was made for the New York commission of 1938.

II

The ultimate need for a periodically updated collection of current state constitutions was met in 1962 with the publication of the two volumes of *Constitutions of the United States, National and State,* prepared by the Legislative Drafting Research Fund of Columbia University. Supplementing this was an equally needed second edition of its *Index-Digest of State Constitutions,* published in 1959 and kept up to date with pocket supplements. Between these two valuable publications, it will probably be unnecessary for other scholars or institutions to undertake the formidable task of keeping current on the constitutional structure of each of the states. Together with the numerous studies of the National Municipal League, whose *Model State Constitution* was first drafted and published in 1933, and the annual reports on state constitution making in the Council of State Governments' *Book of the States,* contemporary state constitutional developments are now adequately surveyed.

Meantime, Thorpe's reference has become out of date as well as out of print. Although the editor was one of the leading students of American constitutionalism in his day, later documentary inventories and a small but authoritative bookshelf of scholarly works within individual states have made it increasingly urgent that a new collection, edited with the aid of these fresh materials, be prepared. One major resource which now may be drawn upon is the multi-volume *Territorial Papers of the United States,* begun in 1934 under the editorship of Clarence Carter of the State Department and now being continued under the National Archives. Even more useful, for the purposes of the present work, are the constitutional materials in the State Records Microfilm Project carried on between 1941 and 1951 by the University of North Carolina and the Library of Congress, under the general direction of Dr. William Sumner Jenkins.

These available resources have made possible an editorial plan for the present collection which it is hoped will make the documents considerably more useful and, by correlating with the volumes of contemporary state constitutions of the Legislative Drafting Research Fund, will provide a definitive reference series on the subject. For each of the states there will be (1) one or two tables, as the case may be, summarizing the historical sequence of major developments in the constitutional history of the state, and comparing the provisions of succeeding constitutions or organic laws in the course of this development; (2) a general background note on the pre-territorial or pre-colonial period of the state; (3) an introductory note for each of the documents reproduced in the territorial and statehood periods respectively; (4) such editorial commentary as may be necessary to clarify the meaning or significance of specific passages within each document; (5) typographic treatment, explained at the beginning of the section for each state, to indicate the major differences between the language of one constitutional document and its predecessor or successor; (6) a selected bibliography on the constitutional history of each state; and (7) an index-digest, more modest in character but similar in purpose and structure to the *Index-Digest* of the Legislative Drafting Research Fund, for the constitutions of that state.

Wherever possible, all documents used in this collection have been reproduced from the best available primary sources, even though, in instances of constitutions published under primitive frontier conditions, the original printing left something to be desired. The commentary upon each document has been based upon the editor's own researches over a period of more than a decade, corroborated through correspondence with various authorities in each of the states. State archivists and historians, attorneys general and secretaries of state, private practitioners and scholars too numerous to mention individually are herewith recognized collectively for their years of assistance and encouragement.

Because the current collection has been planned to correlate with the Columbia University collection already mentioned, the current constitution of the states has been omitted from the present collection in most instances. The full text of that constitution, with its amendments to date, appears in the Columbia volumes; the purpose of the present collection is served, except in a few instances where only one constitution has been adopted by a state, by summarizing the basic provisions of the current instrument in order to complete the tracing of the development of specific provisions through succeeding constitutions in the state's history. While there will occasionally be gaps – as when a state subsequently adopts a new constitution – it is believed that on the whole these two collections will complement each other by this editorial plan.

State constitutions are, of course, judicially interpreted and legislatively implemented. Out of these supplemental sources of state constitutional law will emerge – once the documentation for the fifty states has been completed – the functions of government which Cooley saw in terms of limitations and the modern age sees as powers and duties. The present editor has sought to keep separate the essentially subjective matter of interpretation and implementation, and the objective matter of assembling and explaining, in terms of historical fact, the documents by which constitutional government in each of the states was developed. The first step is the establishing of the documentary record. Whether this editor or some other will undertake the second step is something for the future to determine. If, within the continuum of the historical constitutional documents and the continually updated collection of the contemporary constitutions, a complete reference shelf on constitutionalism in the states of the Union is produced, the editors of both collections will be satisfied.

William F. Swindler

Williamsburg, Virginia

South Dakota

Fortieth State

November 2, 1889

EDITORIAL NOTE

North and South Dakota were admitted virtually simultaneously, with the other states in the "omnibus bill" of 1889, which disposed of much of the remaining territory from the original Louisiana Purchase and the Congressional administration thereof throughout the period of Western settlement. The documents and general history for North Dakota, appearing in Volume VII, is relevant here as well.

SOUTH DAKOTA CONTENTS

SOURCES OF DOCUMENTS

No. 1   12 Stat. 239

No. 2   <u>South Dakota Constitutional Conven-</u>
         <u>tion... 1885</u> (Huron, S.D., 1907), I,
         p. 9

No. 3   25 Stat. 676

No. 4   6 Thorpe, 3357

No. 5   26 Stat. 1549

CONSTITUTION OF SOUTH DAKOTA

Contents

PREAMBLE

ARTICLE I. NAME AND BOUNDARY
Sec. 1. Name of state
Sec. 2. Boundaries of state

ARTICLE II. DIVISION OF THE POWERS OF GOVERNMENT

ARTICLE III. LEGISLATIVE DEPARTMENT
Sec. 1. Bicameral legislature; initiative; referendum
Sec. 2. Size of legislature; sessions
Sec. 3. Qualifications of legislators; dual office holding
Sec. 4. Disqualification from office
Sec. 5. Apportionment
Sec. 6. Terms of office; compensation; length of regular session
Sec. 7. Date and place of session
Sec. 8. Oath of office
Sec. 9. Rules of procedure
Sec. 10. Vacancies
Sec. 11. Privileges of legislators
Sec. 12. Dual office holding; interest in government contracts
Sec. 13. Journal
Sec. 14. Voting in legislature
Sec. 15. Public sessions

Sec. 16. Adjournment
Sec. 17. Reading of bills
Sec. 18. Style of enacting clause; passage of bills
Sec. 19. Signing of bills
Sec. 20. Origin of bills
Sec. 21. Title of bills
Sec. 22. Effective date of acts
Sec. 23. Private or special laws prohibited
Sec. 24. Obligations to state
Sec. 25. Games of chance
Sec. 26. Delegation of legislative powers
Sec. 27. Suits against the state
Sec. 28. Bribery and corrupt solicitation; self-incrimination
Sec. 29. Continuity of government

ARTICLE IV. EXECUTIVE DEPARTMENT
Sec. 1. Governor; lieutenant governor
Sec. 2. Qualifications
Sec. 3. Election
Sec. 4. Powers and duties of governor
Sec. 5. Pardons
Sec. 6. Succession to governorship
Sec. 7. Powers and duties of lieutenant governor; succession to governorship
Sec. 8. Vacancy in office

BACKGROUND NOTE

Much of early development of South Dakota is included in the history of the territory before its division into northern and southern parts in 1889 (see Volume VII). French explorers passed through the region from Canada in 1743, and half a century later other French traders came upriver from St. Louis to establish the first settlements on the upper Missouri River. In 1804-06 the Lewis and Clark Expedition passed through the area on both its outward and returning treks. Soon thereafter the fur trade began a rapid growth, and the economic and strategic resources of the region were valued sufficiently to lead the American government to employ a special agent, Manuel Lisa, to discourage Indian considerations of British overtures during the War of 1812.

In 1817 the first permanent settlement, eventually named Fort Pierre (for Pierre Chouteau), was founded. In 1831 the beginning of regular steamboat service on the upper Missouri substantially encouraged settlement, although the competition of rival land settlement societies in Iowa and Minnesota held up agricultural development. Another obstacle was the long period of limbo in which the Dakota region was left after Minnesota became a state in 1854, and Nebraska was organized as a separate territory in 1858. As in the case of Oregon (see Volume VIII), local efforts were made to set up provisional governments, but the sparseness of population made this impractical.

In one of the final acts of his administration President Buchanan signed the territorial act of March 2, 1861 (Doc. No. 1), incorporating an enormous expanse of territory east of the Rocky Mountains and north of Nebraska--but with less than two thousand settlers. The first territorial legislature which met the following year recorded nine members in the upper chamber and thirteen in the lower. In 1874 the discovery of gold in the Black Hills brought waves of prospectors and repetition of the familiar maneuver to oust the Indians who had been promised perpetual title to the hills. Meantime, a separate territorial organization for Montana in 1864 and Wyoming in 1868 had reduced Dakota to a more practical size, and in 1883 a draft constitution and petition for

statehood for the southern half was drawn up and
forwarded to Congress. It died in committee, as
did a virtually identical version in 1885 (Doc.
No. 2).

Although by now it had been agreed that the
northern and southern parts of Dakota were to be
admitted as sister states, the Democratic majority
in Congress opposed the addition of four presum-
ably Republican Senators, and further action had
to await the return of Republicans to power in
1889. Thereupon an enabling act was passed (Doc.
No. 3), a convention at Sioux Falls on July 4,
1889 adopted another constitution (Doc. No. 4) and
on November 4 the Dakotas were admitted to the
Union (Doc. No. 5).

[Doc. No. 1]

Territorial Act of March 2, 1861

— *An Act to provide a temporary Government for the Territory of Dakota, and to create the Office of Surveyor General therein.*

Be it enacted by the Senate and House of Representatives of the United States of America in Congress assembled, That all that part of the territory of the United States included within the following limits, namely: commencing at a point in the main channel of the Red River of the North, where the forty-ninth degree of north latitude crosses the same; thence up the main channel of the same, and along the boundary of the State of Minnesota, to Big Stone lake; thence along the boundary line of the said State of Minnesota to the Iowa line; thence along the boundary line of the State of Iowa to the point of intersection between the Big Sioux and Missouri rivers; thence up the Missouri river, and along the boundary line of the Territory of Nebraska, to the mouth of the Niobrara or Running Water river; thence following up the same, in the middle of the main channel thereof, to the mouth of the Keha Paha or Turtle Hill river; thence up said river to the forty-third parallel of north latitude; thence due west to the present boundary of the Territory of Washington; thence along the boundary line of Washington Territory, to the forty-ninth degree of north latitude; thence east, along said forty-ninth degree of north latitude, to the place of beginning, be, and the same is hereby, organized into a temporary government, by the name of the Territory of Dakota: *Provided*, That nothing in this act contained shall be construed to impair the rights of person or property now pertaining to the Indians in said Territory, so long as such rights shall remain unextinguished by treaty between the United States and such Indians, or to include any territory which, by treaty with any Indian tribe, is not, without the consent of said tribe, to be included within the territorial limits or jurisdiction of any State or Territory; but all such territory shall be excepted out of the boundaries and constitute no part of the Territory of Dakota, until said tribe shall signify their assent to the President of the United States to be included within the said Territory, or to affect the authority of the government of the United States to make any regulations respecting such Indians, their lands, property, or other rights, by treaty, law, or otherwise, which it would have been competent for the government to make if this act had never passed: *Provided, further,* That nothing in this act contained shall be construed to inhibit the government of the United States from dividing said Territory into two or more Territories, in such manner and at such times as Congress shall deem convenient and proper, or from attaching any portion thereof to any other Territory or State.

SEC. 2. *And be it further enacted*, That the executive power and authority in and over said Territory of Dakota, shall be vested in a governor, who shall hold his office for four years, and until his successor shall be appointed and qualified, unless sooner removed by the President

Margin notes:

March 2, 1861.
1863, ch. 70, § 4.
Post, p. 701.
Territory of Dakota.

Boundaries.

Rights of the Indians not impaired.

Indian Territory excepted out of said boundaries.

Territory may be divided

Executive.

Governor—term of office, powers, and duties.

of the United States. The governor shall reside within said Territory, shall be commander-in-chief of the militia thereof, shall perform the duties and receive the emoluments of superintendent of Indian affairs, and shall approve all laws passed by the legislative assembly before they shall take effect; he may grant pardons for offences against the laws of said Territory, and reprieves for offences against the laws of the United States until the decision of the President can be made known thereon; he shall commission all officers who shall be appointed to office under the laws of said Territory, and shall take care that the laws be faithfully executed.

Secretary — term, powers, and duties.

SEC. 3. *And be it further enacted,* That there shall be a secretary of said Territory, who shall reside therein, and hold his office for four years, unless sooner removed by the President of the United States; he shall record and preserve all the laws and proceedings of the legislative assembly hereinafter constituted, and all the acts and proceedings of the governor, in his executive department; he shall transmit one copy of the laws, and one copy of the executive proceedings, on or before the first day of December in each year, to the President of the United States, and, at the same time, two copies of the laws to the Speaker of the House of Representatives and the President of the Senate, for the use of Congress; and in case of the death, removal, or resignation, or other necessary absence of the governor from the Territory, the secretary shall have, and he is hereby authorized and required, to execute and perform all the powers and duties of the governor during such vacancy or necessary absence, or until another governor shall be duly appointed to fill such vacancy.

Legislative power.

Assembly.

Council.

SEC. 4. *And be it further enacted,* That the legislative power and authority of said Territory shall be vested in the governor and a legislative assembly. The legislative assembly shall consist of a council and house of representatives. The council shall consist of nine members, which may be increased to thirteen, having the qualifications of voters as hereinafter prescribed, whose term of service shall continue two years.

House of Representatives.

The house of representatives shall consist of thirteen members, which may be increased to twenty-six, possessing the same qualifications as prescribed for members of the council, and whose term of service shall continue one year.

Apportionment.

An apportionment shall be made, as nearly equal as practicable, among the several counties or districts for the election of the council and house of representatives, giving to each section of the Territory representation in the ratio of its population, (Indians excepted) as nearly as may be; and the members of the council and of the house of representatives shall reside in, and be inhabitants of, the district

Census.

for which they may be elected, respectively. Previous to the first election, the governor shall cause a census or enumeration of the inhabitants of the several counties and districts of the Territory to be

First election.

taken; and the first election shall be held at such time and places, and be conducted in such manner, as the governor shall appoint and direct; and he shall, at the same time, declare the number of the members of the council and house of representatives to which each of the counties or districts shall be entitled under this act. The number of persons authorized to be elected, having the highest number of votes in each of said council districts, for members of the council, shall be declared by the governor to be duly elected to the council; and the person or persons authorized to be elected having the greatest number of votes for the house of representatives, equal to the number to which each county or district shall be entitled, shall be declared by the governor to be elected members of

Proviso.

the house of representatives: *Provided,* That in case of a tie between two or more persons voted for, the governor shall order a new election, to supply the vacancy made by such tie. And the persons thus elected to the legislative assembly shall meet at such place and on such day as the governor shall appoint; but thereafter, the time, place, and manner of holding and conducting all elections by the people, and the apportioning the representation in the several counties or districts to the council and house of representatives, according to the population, shall be prescribed by law, as well as the day of the commencement of the regular sessions of the legislative assembly : *Provided,* That no one session shall exceed the term of forty days, except the first, which may be extended to sixty days, but no longer. *(margin: Subsequent elections.)* *(margin: Length of sessions.)*

SEC. 5. *And be it further enacted,* That every free white male inhabitant of the United States above the age of twenty-one years, who shall have been a resident of said Territory at the time of the passage of this act, shall be entitled to vote at the first election, and shall be eligible to any office within the said Territory; but the qualifications of voters and of holding office at all subsequent elections shall be such as shall be prescribed by the legislative assembly: *Provided,* That the right of suffrage and of holding office shall be exercised only by citizens of the United States and those who shall have declared on oath their intention to become such, and shall have taken an oath to support the Constitution of the United States. *(margin: Voters at first election and eligibility to office.)* *(margin: At subsequent elections.)* *(margin: Proviso.)*

SEC. 6. *And be it further enacted,* That the legislative power of the Territory shall extend to all rightful subjects of legislation consistent with the Constitution of the United States and the provisions of this act; but no law shall be passed interfering with the primary disposal of the soil; no tax shall be imposed upon the property of the United States; nor shall the lands or other property of non-residents be taxed higher than the lands or other property of residents ; nor shall any law be passed impairing the rights of private property ; nor shall any discrimination be made in taxing different kinds of property; but all property subject to taxation shall be in proportion to the value of the property taxed. *(margin: Extent and limits of legislative power.)*

SEC. 7. *And be it further enacted,* That all township, district, and county officers, not herein otherwise provided for, shall be appointed or elected, as the case may be, in such manner as shall be provided by the governor and legislative assembly of the Territory. The governor shall nominate and, by and with the advice and consent of the legislative council, appoint all officers not herein otherwise provided for; and, in the first instance, the governor alone may appoint all said officers, who shall hold their offices until the end of the first session of the legislative assembly, and shall lay off the necessary districts for members of the council and house of representatives, and all other officers. *(margin: Township, district, and county officers.)*

SEC. 8. *And be it further enacted,* That no member of the legislative assembly shall hold or be appointed to any office which shall have been created, or the salary or emoluments of which shall have been increased while he was a member, during the term for which he was elected, and for one year after the expiration of such term; and no person holding a commission or appointment under the United States, except postmasters, shall be a member of the legislative assembly, or shall hold any office under the government of said Territory. *(margin: Persons disqualified to hold office.)*

SEC. 9. *And be it further enacted,* That the judicial power of said Territory shall be vested in a supreme court, district courts, probate courts, and in justices of the peace. The supreme court shall consist of a chief justice and two associate justices, any two of whom shall constitute a quorum, and who shall hold a term at the seat of government of said Territory annually, and they shall hold their offices during the period of four years. The said Territory shall be divided into three judicial districts, and a district court shall be held in each of said districts by one of the justices of the supreme court, at such time and place as may be prescribed by law; and the said judges shall, after their appointments, respectively, reside in the districts which shall be assigned them. The jurisdiction of the several courts herein provided for, both appellate and original, and that of the probate courts and of the justices of the peace, *(margin: Judicial power.)* *(margin: Supreme court.)* *(margin: District courts.)* *(margin: Jurisdiction.)*

Of justices of the peace.

shall be as limited by law: *Provided*, That justices of the peace shall not have jurisdiction of any matter in controversy when the title or boundaries of land may be in dispute, or where the debt or sum claimed shall exceed one hundred dollars; and the said supreme and district courts, respectively, shall possess chancery as well as common-law jurisdiction, and authority for redress of all wrongs committed against the Constitution or laws of the United States, or of the Territory, affecting persons or property. Each district court, or the judge thereof, shall appoint its clerk, who shall also be the register in chancery, and shall keep his office at the place where the court may be held. Writs of error, bills of exception, and appeals, shall be allowed in all cases from the final decisions of said district courts to the supreme court, under such regulations as may be prescribed by law; but in no case removed to the supreme court shall trial by jury be allowed in said court. The supreme court, or the justices thereof, shall appoint its own clerk, and every clerk shall hold his office at the pleasure of the court for which he shall have been appointed. Writs of error and appeals from the final decisions of said supreme court shall be allowed, and may be taken to the Supreme Court of the United States, in the same manner and under the same regulations as from the circuit courts of the United States, where the value of the property, or the amount in controversy, to be ascertained by the oath or affirmation of either party, or other competent witness, shall exceed one thousand dollars; and each of the said district courts shall have and exercise the same jurisdiction, in all cases arising under the Constitution and laws of the United States as is vested in the circuit and district courts of the United States; and the said supreme and district courts of the said Territory, and the respective judges thereof, shall and may grant writs of habeas corpus in all cases in which the same are grantable by the judges of the United States in the District of Columbia; and the first six days of every term of said courts, or so much thereof as shall be necessary, shall be appropriated to the trial of causes arising under the said Constitution and laws; and writs of error and appeals in all such cases shall be made to the supreme court of said Territory the same as in other cases. The said clerk shall receive, in all such cases, the same fees which the clerks of the district courts of Nebraska Territory now receive for similar services.

Of supreme and district courts.

Clerk of district court, and register in chancery.

Writs of error, &c.

Clerk of supreme court.

Writs of error, &c.

Habeas corpus.

Fees of clerk.

Attorney, &c.

SEC. 10. *And be it further enacted*, That there shall be appointed an attorney for said Territory, who shall continue in office for four years, unless sooner removed by the President, and who shall receive the same fees and salary as the attorney of the United States for the present Territory of Nebraska. There shall also be a marshal for the Territory appointed, who shall hold his office for four years, unless sooner removed by the President, and who shall execute all processes issuing from the said courts when exercising their jurisdiction as circuit and district courts of the United States; he shall perform the duties, be subject to the same regulations and penalties, and be entitled to the same fees as the marshal of the district court of the United States for the present Territory of Nebraska, and shall, in addition, be paid two hundred dollars annually as a compensation for extra services.

Marshal, &c.

Appointment of governor, &c.

SEC. 11. *And be it further enacted*, That the governor, secretary, chief justice and associate justices, attorney, and marshal, shall be nominated and, by and with the advice and consent of the Senate, appointed by the President of the United States. The governor and secretary to be appointed as aforesaid shall, before they act as such, respectively take an oath or affirmation before the district judge, or some justice of the peace in the limits of said Territory duly authorized to administer oaths and affirmations by the laws now in force therein, or before the chief justice or some associate justice of the Supreme Court of the United States, to support the Constitution of the United States and faithfully to

How qualified.

discharge the duties of their respective offices; which said oaths, when so taken, shall be certified by the person by whom the same shall have been taken; and such certificates shall be received and recorded by the secretary among the executive proceedings; and the chief justice and associate justices, and all other civil officers in said Territory, before they act as such, shall take a like oath or affirmation before the said governor or secretary, or some judge or justice of the peace of the Territory who may be duly commissioned and qualified, which said oath or affirmation shall be certified and transmitted by the person taking the same to the secretary, to be by him recorded as aforesaid; and afterwards the like oath or affirmation shall be taken, certified, and recorded in such man[n]er and form as may be prescribed by law. The governor shall receive an *Salaries.* annual salary of fifteen hundred dollars as governor, and one thousand dollars as superintendent of Indian affairs; the chief justice and associate justices shall each receive an annual salary of eighteen hundred dollars; the secretary shall receive an annual salary of eighteen hundred dollars. The said salaries shall be paid quarter-yearly at the Treasury of the United States. The members of the legislative assembly shall be entitled *Pay of the legislature.* to receive three dollars each per day during their attendance at the session thereof, and three dollars for every twenty miles' travel in going to and returning from the said sessions, estimated according to the nearest usually travelled route. There shall be appropriated annually the sum *Contingent expenses.* of one thousand dollars, to be expended by the governor, to defray the contingent expenses of the Territory. There shall also be appropriated annually a sufficient sum, to be expended by the secretary of the Terri- *Expenses of legislative assembly, &c.* tory, and upon an estimate to be made by the Secretary of the Treasury of the United States, to defray the expenses of the legislative assembly, the printing of the laws, and other incidental expenses; and the secretary of the Territory shall annually account to the Secretary of the Treasury of the United States for the manner in which the aforesaid sum shall have been expended.

SEC. 12. *And be it further enacted,* That the legislative assembly of *Time and place of first session of legislature.* the Territory of Dakota shall hold its first session at such time and place in said Territory as the governor thereof shall appoint and direct; and at said first session, or as soon thereafter as they shall deem expedient, the governor and legislative assembly shall proceed to locate and establish the seat of government for said Territory at such place as they may deem *Seat of government.* eligible; which place, however, shall thereafter be subject to be changed by the said governor and legislative assembly.

SEC. 13. *And be it further enacted,* That a delegate to the House of *Delegate to Congress.* Representatives of the United States, to serve during each Congress of the United States, may be elected by the voters qualified to elect members of the legislative assembly, who shall be entitled to the same rights and privileges as are exercised and enjoyed by the delegates from the several other Territories of the United States to the said House of Representatives. The first election shall be held at such time and places, *Election of, &c.* and be conducted in such manner, as the governor shall appoint and direct; and at all subsequent elections, the times, places, and manner of holding elections shall be prescribed by law. The person having the greatest number of votes shall be declared by the governor to be duly elected, and a certificate thereof shall be given accordingly.

SEC. 14. *And be it further enacted,* That when the land in said *School sections of land.* Territory shall be surveyed, under the direction of the government of the United States, preparatory to bringing the same into market, sections numbered sixteen and thirty-six in each township in said Territory shall be, and the same are hereby, reserved for the purpose of being applied to schools in the States hereafter to be erected out of the same.

SEC. 15. *And be it further enacted,* That temporarily, and until *Judicial districts.* otherwise provided by law, the governor of said Territory may define the judicial districts of said Territory and assign the judges who may be appointed for said Territory to the several districts, and also appoint the times and places for holding courts in the several counties or subdivisions in each of said judicial districts by proclamation to be issued by him; but the legislative assembly, at their first or any subsequent session, may organize, alter, or modify such judicial districts, and assign the judges, and alter the times and places of holding the courts, as to them shall seem proper and convenient.

Constitution and laws of United States made applicable.

SEC. 16. *And be it further enacted,* That the Constitution and all laws of the United States which are not locally inapplicable shall have the same force and effect within the said Territory of Dakota as elsewhere within the United States.

Surveyor-general.

SEC. 17. *And be it further enacted,* That the President of the United States, by and with the advice and consent of the Senate, shall be, and he is hereby, authorized to appoint a surveyor-general for Dakota, who shall locate his office at such place as the Secretary of the Interior shall from time to time direct, and whose duties, powers, obligations, responsibilities, compensation, and allowances for clerk hire, office rent, fuel, and incidental expenses, shall be the same as those of the surveyor-general of Nebraska and Kansas, under the direction of the Secretary of the Interior, and such instructions as he may from time to time deem it advisable to give him.

Land district.

Name and location.

SEC. 18. *And be it further enacted,* That so much of the public lands of the United States in the Territory of Dakota, west of its eastern boundary and east and north of the Niobrara, or Running Water river, be formed into a land district, to be called the Yancton district, at such time as the President may direct, the land office for which shall be located at such point as the President may direct, and shall be removed from time to time to other points within said district whenever, in his opinion, it may be expedient.

Register and receiver.

SEC. 19. *And be it further enacted,* That the President be, and he is hereby, authorized to appoint, by and with the advice and consent of the Senate, a register and receiver for said district, who shall respectively be required to reside at the site of said office, and who shall have the same powers, perform the same duties, and be entitled to the same compensation, as are or may be prescribed by law in relation to other land-offices of the United States.

Dakota River.

SEC. 20. *And be it further enacted,* That the river in said Territory heretofore known as the "River aux Jacques," or "James river," shall hereafter be called the Dakota river.

Portions of Utah and Washington added to Nebraska.

SEC. 21. *And be it further enacted,* That, until Congress shall otherwise direct, that portion of the Territories of Utah and Washington between the forty-first and forty-third degrees of north latitude, and east of the thirty-third meridian of longitude west from Washington, shall be, and is hereby, incorporated into and made a part of the Territory of Nebraska.

APPROVED, March 2, 1861.

———

[Doc. No.2]

Draft Constitution of 1883/85

PREAMBLE.

We, the people of South Dakota, south of the forty-sixth parallel of north latitude, through our Representatives in convention assembled, invoking the guaranties of the Federal constitution, and relying upon the pledged faith of Congress in extending to the inhabitants of this portion of the Territory of the United States the rights, privileges and immunities secured to the people of the territory northwest of the river Ohio by the ordinance of 1787, including the right to form for ourselves a State Constitution and government and be admitted into the Union on an equal footing with the original States, such right being further secured by the conditions of the cession from France of the province of Louisiana, having complied with all the conditions necessary to admission, manifesting profound reverence for the Supreme Ruler of the universe, in order to form a more perfect and independent Government, establish justice, insure tranquility, provide for the common defense, promote the general welfare and preserve to ourselves and to our posterity the blessings of liberty, do ordain and establish this constitution for the State of South Dakota.

ARTICLE I.

BOUNDARIES.

The boundaries and jurisdiction of the State shall be as follows, to-wit: Beginning at a point where the forty-sixth parallel of north latitude intersects the western boundary line of the State of Minnesota; thence southerly along the western boundary line of said state of Minnesota to the northern boundary line of the State of Iowa; thence west along the boundary line of the said State of Iowa, to the northwest corner of the said State of Iowa, thence down the Big Sioux river and along the western boundary line of the said State of Iowa to the point of intersection with the northerly boundary line of the State of Nebraska, thence up the Missouri

river and along the boundary line of the State of Nebraska to a
point where the forty-third parallel of north latitude intersects
the middle of the main channel of the Missouri river; thence west
along the said forty-third parallel of north latitude to the point of
its intersection with the twenty-seventh degree of longitude west
from Washington; thence north along said twenty-seventh degree
of longitude west from Washington to its intersection with the
said forty-sixth parallel of north latitude, thence east along the
said forty-sixth parallel of north latitude to the place of beginning.

ARTICLE II.

DECLARATION OF RIGHTS.

SECTION 1.   All men are born equally free and independent,
and have certain inherent and indefeasible rights, among which are
those of enjoying and defending life and liberty, of acquiring,
possessing and protecting property, and of pursuing their own
happiness.   To secure these rights, governments are instituted
among men, deriving their just powers from the consent of the
governed.

SEC. 2   The right of every person to worship Almighty God,
according to the dictates of his own conscience, shall never be infringed; nor shall any person be compelled to attend, erect or
support any place of worship; or to maintain any ministry against
his consent; nor shall any control of or interference with the rights
of conscience be permitted, or any preference be given by law to
any religious establishments or modes of worship; but the liberty
of conscience hereby secured shall not be so construed as to excuse
acts of licentiousness or justify practices inconsistent with the
peace or safety of the State.

SEC. 3.   No religious test or amount of property shall ever be
required as a qualification for any office of public trust under the
State; and no person shall be rendered incompetent to give evidence
in any court of law or equity in consequence of his opinions on the
subject of religion, nor shall any money be drawn from the treasury
for the benefit of religious societies, or theological seminaries.

SEC. 4.   The right of the people peaceably to assemble to
consult for the common good, to petition the Government or any
department thereof, or to instruct their representatives, shall never
be abridged.

SEC. 5.   Every person may freely speak, write and publish
his sentiments on all subjects, being responsible for the abuse of
that right, and no law shall be passed to restrain or abridge the
liberty of speech or of the press.   In all criminal prosecutions or
indictments for libel the truth may be given in evidence, and if it
shall appear to the jury that the matter charged as libelous be true

and was published with good motives and for justifiable ends, the party shall be acquitted and the jury shall have the right to determine the fact, and the law, under direction of the court.

SEC. 6. The right of trial by jury shall remain inviolate, and shall extend to all cases at law without regard to the amount in controversy, but a jury trial may be waived by the parties in all civil cases, and in all criminal prosecutions for offenses less than felony, in the manner prescribed by law. Nothing herein contained shall be deemed to prohibit the Legislature providing for a jury of less than twelve in any inferior court.

SEC. 7. In all criminal prosecutions, the accused shall have the right to be heard by himself and counsel, to demand the nature and cause of the accusation against him, to have a copy thereof, to be confronted with the witnesses against him, to have compulsory process for obtaining witnesses in his favor, and to a speedy and public trial by an impartial jury of the county or district in which the crime shall have been committed. All prosecutions shall be by indictment or information, and the accused shall not be compelled to give evidence against himself.

SEC. 8. All persons before conviction shall be bailable except for capital offenses where the proof is evident or the presumption great. The privilege of the writ of habeas corpus shall not be suspended, unless when in case of rebellion or invasion the public safety may require it.

SEC. 9. No person shall be held for a criminal offense unless on the presentment or indictment of a Grand Jury, or upon information of the public prosecutor, except in cases of impeachment, in cases cognizable by County courts by Justices of the Peace, and in cases arising in the army or navy or in the militia when in actual service in time of war or public danger. No person for the same offense shall be put twice in jeopardy. The Legislature may change, regulate or abolish the Grand Jury system.

SEC. 10. The Legislature may provide by law the number of persons which shall constitute a Grand Jury, and the number necessary to find an indictment or presentment.

SEC. 11. Treason against the State shall consist only in levying war against the same or in adhering to its enemies, giving them aid and comfort. No person shall be convicted of treason unless on the testimony of two witnesses to the same overt act or on confession in open court.

SEC. 12. The right of the people to be secure in their persons, houses, papers and effects against unreasonable searches and seizures shall not be violated, and no warrant shall issue but upon probable causes supported by oath or affirmation and particularly describing the places to be searched and the persons or things to be seized.

SEC. 13. No "ex-post facto" law, nor law impairing the obligation of contracts, or retrospective in its operation, or making any irrevocable grant of special privileges, franchise or immunities, shall be passed by the Legislature.

SEC. 14. Private property shall not be taken for public use without just compensation therefor.

SEC. 15. No distinction shall ever be made by law between resident aliens and citizens in reference to the possession, enjoyment or descent of property.

SEC. 16. No person shall be imprisoned for debt arising out of or founded on a contract, expressed or implied.

SEC. 17. The militia shall be in strict subordination to the civil power; no soldier in time of peace shall be quartered in any house without consent of the owner, nor in time of war except in the manner prescribed by law.

SEC. 18. No tax or duty shall be imposed without the consent of the people or their representatives in the Legislature, and all taxation shall be equal and uniform.

SEC. 19. No law shall be passed granting to any citizen or class of citizens privileges or immunities which upon the same terms shall not equally belong to all citizens.

SEC. 20. Elections shall be free and equal, and no power, civil or military, shall at any time interfere to prevent the free exercise of the right of suffrage.

SEC. 21. All courts shall be open, and every man for an injury done him in his goods, person or reputation, shall have remedy by due course of law, and right and justice administered without denial or delay.

SEC. 22. No power of suspending laws shall be exercised, unless by the Legislature or its authority.

SEC. 23. No person shall be attainted of treason or felony by the Legislature.

SEC. 24. Excessive bail shall not be required, nor excessive fines imposed, nor cruel punishment inflicted.

SEC. 25. The right of the citizens to bear arms in defense of themselves and the State shall not be questioned.

SEC. 26. The blessings of a free government can only be maintained by a firm adherence to justice, moderation, temperance, frugality and virtue, and by frequent recurrence to fundamental principles.

SEC. 27. The State of Dakota is an inseparable part of the American Union, and the constitution of the United States is the supreme law of the land.

SEC. 28. To guard against transgressions of the high powers we have delegated, we declare that everything in this article is excepted out of the general powers of government, and shall forever remain inviolate.

ARTICLE III.

ELECTIONS AND RIGHTS OF SUFFRAGE.

Section 1.   Every male person resident of this State, who shall be of the age of twenty-one years and upwards, not otherwise disqualified, belonging to either of the following classes, who shall be qualified electors under the laws of the Territory of Dakota at the date of the ratification of this constitution by the people, or who shall have resided in the United States one year, in this State six months, in the county thirty days, and in the election precinct where he offers his vote ten days next preceding any election, shall be deemed a qualified elector at such election:

First—Citizens of the United States.

Second—Persons of foreign birth who shall have declared their intention to become citizens, conformably to the laws of the United States upon the subject of naturalization.

Sec. 2.   All votes shall be by ballot.

Sec. 3.   Electors shall, in all cases except treason, felony or breach of the peace, be privileged from arrest during their attendance at elections and in going to and returning from the same. And no elector shall be obliged to do military duty on the days of election, except in time of war or public danger.

Sec. 4.   No elector shall be deemed to have lost his residence in this State by reason of his absence on business of the United States or of this State, or in the military or naval service of the United States.

Sec. 5.   No soldier, seaman or marine in the army or navy of the United States shall be deemed a resident of this State in consequence of being stationed therein.

Sec. 6.   No person under guardianship, non compos mentis or insane shall be qualified to vote at any election, nor shall any person convicted of treason or felony be qualified to vote at any election unless restored to civil rights.

Sec. 7.   Any woman having the qualifications enumerated in section one of this article, as to age, residence and citizenship, and including those now qualified by the laws of the Territory, may vote at any election held solely for school purposes, and may hold any office relating to schools in this State.

ARTICLE IV.

EXECUTIVE DEPARTMENT.

Section 1.   The executive power shall be vested in a Governor, who shall hold his office two years.   A Lieutenant Governor shall be elected at the same time and for the same term.

SEC. 2. No person shall be eligible to the office of Governor or Lieutenant Governor, except a citizen of the United States, and a qualified elector of the State, who shall have attained the age of thirty years, and who shall have resided two years next preceding his election within the State; nor shall either be eligible to any other office during the term for which he shall have been elected; nor shall either be eligible as his own immediate successor.

SEC. 3. The Governor and Lieutenant Governor shall be elected by the qualified electors of the State at the times and places of choosing members of the Legislature. The persons respectively having the highest number of votes for Governor and Lieutenant Governor shall be elected. But if two or more shall have an equal and the highest number of votes for Governor or Lieutenant Governor, the two houses of the Legislature, at its next regular session, shall forthwith, by joint ballot, choose one of such persons for said office. The returns of election for Governor and Lieutenant Governor shall be made in such manner as shall be prescribed by law.

SEC. 4. The Governor shall be Commander-in-Chief of the military and naval forces of the State (except when they shall be called into the service of the United States), and may call out the same to execute the laws, suppress insurrection, and repel invasion. He shall have power to convene the Legislature on extraordinary occasions. He shall, at the commencement of each session, communicate to the Legislature by message, information of the condition of the State, and shall recommend such measures as he may deem expedient. He shall transact all necessary business with the officers of the Government, civil and military. He shall expedite all such measures as may be resolved upon by the Legislature, and shall take care that the laws be faithfully executed.

SEC. 5. The Governor shall have power to remit fines and forfeitures, to grant reprieves, commutations and pardons, after conviction, for all offenses except treason and cases of impeachment; provided, that in all cases where the sentence of the Court is capital punishment, imprisonment for life, or for a longer term than two years, or a fine exceeding two hundred dollars, no pardon shall be granted, sentence commuted or fine remitted, except upon the recommendation in writing of a Board of Pardons consisting of the Chief Justice, Secretary of State and Attorney General, after full hearing in open session; and such recommendations, with the reasons therefor, shall be filed in the office of the Secretary of State. But the Legislature may by law, in all cases, regulate the manner in which remissions of fines, pardons, commutations and reprieves may be applied for. Upon conviction for treason he shall have power to suspend the execution of the sentence until the case shall be reported to the Legislature at its next regular session, when the Legislature shall either pardon or commute the sentence, direct the execution of the sentence or grant a further reprieve. He shall communicate to the Legislature at each regular session, each case of remission of fine, reprieve, commutation or pardon, granted by him in the cases in which he is authorized to act without the recommendation of the said Board of Pardons, stating the name of the convict, the crime of which he was convicted, the sentence and its date, and the date of the remission, commutation, pardon or reprieve, with his reasons for granting the same.

SEC. 6. In case of the death, impeachment, resignation, failure to qualify, absence from the State, removal from office, or other disability of Governor, the powers and duties of the office for the residue of the term, or until he shall be acquitted or the disability removed, shall devolve upon the Lieutenant Governor.

SEC. 7. The Lieutenant Governor shall be President of the Senate, but shall have only the casting vote therein. If during a vacancy in the office of Governor, the Lieutenant Governor shall be impeached, displaced, resign, die, or from mental or physical disease become incapable of performing the duties of his office, or be absent from the State, the Secretary of State shall act as Governor until the vacancy shall be filled or the disability removed.

SEC. 8. When any office shall, from any cause, become vacant, and no mode is provided by the constitution and laws for filling such vacancy, the Governor shall have power to fill such vacancy by granting a commission, which shall expire at the end of the next session of the Legislature, or at the next election by the people.

SEC. 9. Every bill which shall have passed the Legislature shall, before it becomes a law, be presented to the Governor. If he approve, he shall sign it; but if not, he shall return it, with his objections, to that house in which it originated, who shall enter the objections at large upon the journal and proceed to reconsider it. If, after such reconsideration, two-thirds of the members present shall agree to pass the bill, it shall be sent, together with the objections, to the other house, by which it shall likewise be reconsidered, and if it be approved by two-thirds of the members present, it shall become a law. But in all such cases, the vote of both houses shall be determined by ayes and noes, and the names of the members voting for and against the bill shall be entered upon the journal of each house respectively. If any bill shall not be returned by the Governor within three days (Sunday excepted) after it shall have been presented to him, the same shall be a law, unless the Legislature shall, by its adjournment, prevent its return; in which case it shall be filed, with his objections, in the office of the Secretary of State, within ten days after such adjournment, or become a law.

SEC. 10. The Governor shall have power to disapprove of any item or items of any bill making appropriations of money embracing distinct items, and part or parts of the bill approved shall be law, and the item or items disapproved shall be void, unless enacted in the manner following: If the Legislature being in session, he shall transmit to the house in which the bill originated, a copy of the item or items thereof disapproved, together with his objections thereto, and the items objected to shall be separately reconsidered, and each item shall then take the same course as is prescribed for the passage of bills over the executive veto.

Sec. 11.   There shall be chosen by the qualified electors of the State, at the times and places of choosing members of the Legislature, a Secretary of State, Auditor, Treasurer, Superintendent of Public Instruction and Attorney General, who shall severally hold their offices for the term of two years, and shall respectively keep their offices at the seat of government.

Sec. 12.   The powers and duties of the Secretary of State, Auditor, Treasurer, Superintendent of Public Instruction and Attorney General shall be prescribed by law.

ARTICLE V.

LEGISLATIVE DEPARTMENT.

Section 1.   The legislative power shall be vested in a Senate and House of Representatives.

Sec. 2.   The number of the House of Representatives shall never be less than fifty-five nor more than 100.   The number of members of the Senate shall never be less than twenty-five nor more than thirty-three.   The sessions of the Legislature shall be biennial, except as otherwise provided in this constitution.

Sec. 3.   No person shall be eligible to the office of Senator or member of the House of Representatives who shall not have attained the age of 25 years and resided one year within the State, and be a qualified elector in the district which he may be chosen to represent.

Sec. 4.   The Legislature shall provide by law for an enumeration of the inhabitants of the State in the year eighteen hundred and eighty-five, and every ten years thereafter; and at its first regular session after each enumeration, made by authority of the United States, but at no other time, the Legislature shall apportion the Senators and Representatives according to the number of inhabitants, excluding Indians not taxed, and soldiers and officers of the United States army and navy.

Sec. 5.   The terms of office of members of the Legislature shall be two years, and they shall each receive for their services until otherwise provided by law, the sum of three dollars for each day's attendance during the session, and ten cents for every mile they shall travel in going to and returning from the place of the meeting of the Legislature on the most usual route, but they shall not receive pay for more than forty days at any one session, except in proceedings for impeachments; and they shall receive no other pay or perquisites except their per diem and mileage.

SEC. 6. The Legislature shall meet at the seat of government on the first Tuesday after the first Monday of January, in the year next ensuing the election of members thereof, and at no other time except as provided by this constitution.

SEC. 7. Members of the Legislature and all officers thereof, shall, before they enter upon the duties of their respective offices take and subscribe an oath or affirmation to support the constitution of the United States, and the constitution of the State of Dakota, and respectfully to discharge the duties of their respective offices to the best of their ability.

SEC. 8. Each house shall be the judge of the elections, returns and qualifications of its own members, and a majority of each house shall constitute a quorum to do business, but a smaller number may adjourn from day to day, and may be authorized to compel the attendance of absent members, in such manner and under such penalties as each house may provide.

SEC. 9. Each house shall have power to determine the rules of its proceedings and punish its members or other persons for contempt or for disorderly behavior in its presence, to enforce obedience to its process, to protect its members against violence or offers of bribes or private solicitation, and, with the concurrence of two-thirds, to expel a member, but not the second time for the same cause, and shall have all other powers necessary for the Legislature of a free State. A member expelled for corruption shall not thereafter be eligible to either house, and punishment for contempt or disorderly behavior shall not bar an indictment for the same offense.

SEC. 10. Each house shall choose its own officers, and the Senate shall choose a temporary President to preside when the Lieutenant Governor shall not attend as President or shall act as Governor. The Secretary of State shall call the House of Representatives to order at the opening of each new Legislature, and preside over it until a temporary presiding officer thereof shall have been chosen, and shall have taken his seat.

SEC. 11. In all elections to be made by the Legislature, the members thereof shall vote viva voce, and their votes shall be entered in the journal.

SEC. 12. Each house shall keep a journal of its proceedings and from time to time publish the same, except such parts as require secrecy, and the yeas and nays of members on any question shall at the desire of one-sixth of those present be entered on the journal.

SEC. 13. The sessions of each house and of committees of the whole shall be open, unless when the business is such as ought to be kept secret.

SEC. 14. Neither house shall, without the consent of the other, adjourn for more than three days, nor to any other place than that in which the two houses shall be sititng.

SEC. 15. No member of the Legislature shall, during the term for which he was elected, be appointed or elected to any civil office in the State, which shall have been created, or the emoluments of which shall have been increased, during the term for which he was elected.

SEC. 16. No person holding office under the authority of the United States shall be eligible to, or have a seat in, the Legislature.

SEC. 17. Members of the Legislature in all cases except treason, felony and breach of the peace, shall be privileged from arrest during the session of the Legislature, and for fifteen days before the commencement and after the termination thereof.

SEC. 18. Every bill shall be read at length, on three different days in each house. The bill and all substitutes therefor shall be printed for the use of members before the final vote is taken thereon.

SEC. 19. The enacting clause of a law shall be: "Be it enacted by the Legislature of the State of Dakota," and no law shall be enacted except by bill. No bill shall be passed unless by assent of a majority of all the members elected to each house of the Legislature. And the question upon the final passage shall be taken upon its last reading, and the yeas and nays shall be entered upon the journal.

SEC. 20. The presiding officer of each house shall in the presence of the house over which he shall preside, sign all bills and joint resolutions passed by the Legislature, after their titles have been publicly read immediately before signing; and the fact of signing shall be entered on the journal.

SEC. 21. Any bill may originate in either house of the Legislature, and a bill passed by one house may be amended in the other.

SEC. 22. No bill, except general appropriation bills, shall be passed containing more than one subject, which shall be clearly expressed in its title; but if any subject shall be embraced in any act which shall not be expressed in the title, such act shall be void only as to so much thereof as shall not be so expressed.

SEC. 23. The General Appropriation bill shall embrace nothing but appropriations for ordinary expenses of the Executive, Legislative and Judicial Departments of the State, interest on the public debt and for public schools. All other appropriations shall be made by separate bills, each embracing but one subject.

SEC. 24. No money shall be paid out of the treasury except upon appropriations made by law and on warrant drawn by the proper officer in pursuance thereof.

SEC. 25. The Legislature shall not authorize any games of

chance, lottery, or gift enterprise, under any pretense, or for any purpose whatever.

Sec. 26. No member of the Legislature shall be liable in any civil or criminal action whatever for words spoken in debate.

Sec. 27. The Legislature shall never grant any extra compensation to any public officer, agent, servant or contractor after the services shall have been rendered or the contract entered into, nor authorize the payment of any claims or part thereof created against the State under any agreement or contract made without express authority of law, and all such unauthorized agreements or contracts shall be null and void. Nor shall the compensation of any public officer be increased or diminished during his term of office; provided, however, the Legislature may make appropriations for expenditures incurred in suppressing insurrections or repelling invasions.

Sec. 28. The Governor shall issue writs of election to fill such vacancies as may occur in either house of the Legislature.

Sec. 29. The Legislature shall direct by law in what manner and in what courts suits may be brought against the State.

Sec. 30. The Legislature shall not pass any local or special law authorizing the creation, extension, or impairing of liens; granting divorces; changing names of persons or places; laying out, opening, altering or working roads or highways; vacating town plats, streets, alleys, public grounds and roads, except State or Territorial roads; locating or changing county seats; granting corporate powers or privileges, except to cities; providing for the election of officers in townships, or incorporated towns or villages; relieving defaulting officers or their bondsmen; remitting fines, penalties or forfeitures; relating to ferries or bridges, or incorporating ferry or bridge companies, except for the erecting of bridges crossing streams which form boundaries between this State and any other State or Territory; providing for the bonding of towns, precincts, school districts or counties; providing for the management of public schools; exempting property from taxation; providing for the sale or mortgage of real estate belonging to minors or others under disability; granting to any private corporation, association or individual any special or exclusive privileges, immunity or franchise whatever.

Sec. 31. No act shall take effect until ninety days after the adjournment of the session at which it passed, unless in case of emergency (to be expressed in the preamble or body of the act) the Legislature shall by a vote of two-thirds of all the members elect to each house otherwise direct.

Sec. 32. Any member of either house of the Legislature of this State who asks, receives, or agrees to receive, any bribe upon any understanding that his official vote, opinion, judgment or action shall be influenced thereby, or shall be given in any manner or upon any particular side of any question or matter upon which he may be required to act in his official capacity, or who gives or offers or promises to give any official vote in consideration that another member of the Legislature shall give any such vote, either upon the same or any other question, shall be deemed guilty of a felony, and shall be punishable as is or as may hereafter be provided by law.

SEC. 33. Any Governor of this State who asks, receives or agrees to receive any bribe upon any understanding that his official opinion, judgment or action shall be influenced thereby, or who gives or offers or promises his official influence in consideration that any member of the Legislature shall give his official vote or influence on any particular side of any question or matter upon which he may be required to act in his official capacity, or who menaces any member by the threatened use of his veto power, or who offers or promises any member that he, the said Governor, will appoint any particular person or persons to any office created, or thereafter to be created, in consideration that any member shall give his official vote or influence on any matter pending or thereafter to be intro-duced into either house of said Legislature, or who threatens any member that he, the said Governor, will remove any person or persons from any office or position, with intent to in any manner influence the official action of said member, shall be punished in the manner now or that may hereafter be provided by law, and upon conviction therefor shall forfeit all right to hold or exercise any office of trust or honor in this State.

CONGRESSIONAL AND LEGISLATIVE APPORTIONMENT.

SEC. 34. Until otherwise provided by law, the members of the House of Representatives of the United States, apportioned to this state, shall be elected from the State at large.

SEC. 35. Until otherwise provided by law, the Senatorial and Representative districts shall be formed, and the Senators and Representatives shall be apportioned, as follows:

SENATORIAL DISTRICTS.

District No. 1 shall consist of the county of Union, and be entitled to one Senator.

District No. 2 shall consist of the county of Clay, and be entitled to one Senator.

District No. 3 shall consist of the county of Yankton, and be entitled to two Senators.

District No. 4 shall consist of the county of Bon Homme, and be entitled to one Senator.

District No. 5 shall consist of the counties of Charles Mix, Brule and Buffalo, and be entitled to one Senator.

District No. 6 shall consist of the counties of Douglas and Hutchinson, and be entitled to one Senator.

District No. 7 shall consist of the county of Turner, and be entitled to one Senator.

District No. 8 shall consist of the county of Lincoln, and be entitled to one Senator.

District No. 9 shall consist of the county of Minnehaha, and be entitled to two Senators.

District No. 10 shall consist of the county of Moody, and be entitled to one Senator.

District No. 11 shall consist of the counties of Hanson and McCook, and be entitled to one Senator.

District No. 12 shall consist of the counties of Davison and Sanborn, and be entitled to one Senator.

District No. 13 shall consist of the counties of Aurora and Jerauld, and be entitled to one Senator.

District No. 14 shall consist of the counties of Lake and Miner, and shall be entitled to one Senator.

District No. 15 shall consist of the county of Brookings, and be entitled to one Senator.

District No. 16 shall consist of the counties of Kingsbury and Clark, and be entitled to one Senator.

District No. 17 shall consist of the county of Beadle, and be entitled to one Senator.

District No. 18 shall consist of the counties of Hand and Hyde, and be entitled to one Senator.

District No. 19 shall consist of the county of Hughes, and be entitled to one Senator.

District No. 20 shall consist of the counties of Sully, Potter, Walworth and Campbell, and all that portion of territory north of said counties and south of the forty-sixth parallel of north latitude, and be entitled to one Senator.

District No. 21 shall consist of the counties of Faulk, Edmunds and McPherson, and all that portion of territory north of said counties and south of the forty-sixth parallel of north latitude, and all that portion of territory lying east of said counties, extended northerly to the forty-sixth parallel, and not included in any other county, and be entitled to one Senator.

District No. 22 shall consist of the county of Spink, and be entitled to one Senator.

District No. 23 shall consist of the county of Codington, and be entitled to one Senator.

District No. 24 shall consist of the counties of Deuel and Hamlin, and be entitled to one Senator.

District No. 25 shall consist of the counties of Grant and Roberts, and be entitled to one Senator.

District No. 26 shall consist of the county of Brown, and all that portion of territory lying between said county and the forty-sixth parallel of north latitude, and be entitled to one Senator.

District No. 27 shall consist of the county of Day and all that portion of territory north of said county and south of the forty-sixth parallel of north latitude, and be entitled to one Senator.

District No. 28 shall consist of the counties of Pennington, Custer and Fall River, and be entitled to one Senator.

District No. 29 shall consist of the counties of Lawrence, Butte and Mandan, and be entitled to two Senators.

REPRESENTATIVE DISTRICTS.

District No. 1 shall consist of the county of Union, and be entitled to two Representatives.

District No. 2 shall consist of the county of Clay, and be entitled to two Representatives.

District No. 3 shall consist of the county of Yankton, and be entitled to two Representatives.

District No. 4 shall consist of the county of Bon Homme, and be entitled to three Representatives.

District No. 5 shall consist of the counties of Charles Mix, Brule and Buffalo, and be entitled to three Representatives.

District No. 6 shall consist of the counties of Douglas and Hutchinson, and be entitled to four Representatives.

District No. 7 shall consist of the county of Turner, and be entitled to two Representatives.

District No. 8 shall consist of the county of Lincoln, and be entitled to three Representatives.

District No. 9 shall consist of the county of Minnehaha, and be entitled to four Representatives.

District No. 10 shall consist of the county of Moody, and be entitled to two Representatives.

District No. 11 shall consist of the counties of Hanson and McCook, and be entitled to three Representatives.

District No. 12 shall consist of the counties of Davison and Sanborn, and be entitled to four Representatives.

District No. 13 shall consist of the counties of Aurora and Jerauld, and be entitled to two Representatives.

District No. 14 shall consist of the counties of Lake and Miner, and be entitled to three Representatives.

District No. 15 shall consist of the county of Brookings, and be entitled to two Representatives.

District No. 16 shall consist of the counties of Kingsbury and Clark, and be entitled to three Representatives.

District No. 17 shall consist of the county of Beadle, and be entitled to three Representatives.

District No. 18 shall consist of the county of Hand, and be entitled to two Representatives.

District No. 19 shall consist of the county of Hyde, and be entitled to one Representative.

District No. 20 shall consist of the counties of Sully, Potter, Walworth and Campbell, and all of that portion of territory lying north of said counties and south of the forty-sixth parallel of north latitude, and be entitled to three Representatives.

District No. 21 shall consist of the county of Hughes, and be entitled to two Representatives.

District No. 22 shall consist of the county of Faulk, and be entitled to two Representatives.

District No. 23 shall consist of the county of Spink, and be entitled to three Representatives.

District No. 24 shall consist of the county of Codington, and be entitled to two Representatives.

District No. 25 shall consist of the county of Deuel, and be entitled to one Representative.

District No. 26 shall consist of the county of Hamlin, and be entitled to one Representative.

District No. 27 shall consist of the county of Grant, and be entitled to two Representatives.

District No. 28 shall consist of the county of Roberts, and be entitled to one Representative.

District No. 29 shall consist of the county of Brown, and all that portion of territory north of said county and south of the forty-sixth parallel of north latitude, and be entitled to three Representatives.

District No. 30 shall consist of the county of Day, and all that portion of territory north of said county and south of the forty-sixth parallel of north latitude, and be entitled to one Representative.

District No. 31 shall consist of the county of Pennington, and be entitled to two Representatives.

District No. 32 shall consist of the counties of Custer and Fall River, and be entitled to one Representative.

District No. 33 shall consist of the counties of Lawrence, Butte and Mandan, and be entitled to five Representatives.

District No. 34 shall consist of the county of Edmunds and all that portion of territory lying east of said county and west of Brown county, and be entitled to one Representative.

District No. 35 shall consist of the county of McPherson, and all that portion of territory lying north of said county and south of the forty-sixth parallel of north latitude, and also all that portion of territory which lies east of said county and west of the county of Brown extended northerly to the forty-sixth parallel of north latitude, and be entitled to one Representative.

ARTICLE VI.

JUDICIAL DEPARTMENT.

SECTION 1   The judicial powers of the State, except as in this constitution otherwise provided, shall be vested in a Supreme Court, Circuit Courts, County Courts and Justices of the Peace, and such other courts as may be created by law for cities and incorporated towns.

SUPREME COURT.

SEC. 2.   The Supreme court, except as otherwise provided in this constitution, shall have appellate jurisdiction only, which shall be co-extensive with the State, and shall have a general superintending control over all inferior courts under such regulations and limitations as may be prescribed by law.

SEC. 3.   It shall have power to issue writs of habeas corpus. It shall also have power to issue writs of mandamus, quo warranto, certiorari, injunction and other original and remedial writs, with authority to hear and determine the same in such cases and under such regulations as may be provided by law; provided, however, that no jury trials shall be allowed in said Supreme court, but in proper cases questions of fact may be sent by said court to a Circuit court for trial before a jury.

SEC. 4.   At least two terms of the Supreme court shall be held each year at the seat of government.

SEC. 5.   The Supreme court shall consist of three Judges, to be chosen from districts by the qualified electors of the State at large, as hereinafter provided.

SEC. 6.   The number of said Judges and districts may, after five years from the taking effect of this constitution, be increased by law to not exceeding five.

SEC. 7.   A majority of the Judges of the Supreme court shall be necessary to form a quorum or pronounce a decision, but one or more of said Judges may adjourn the court from day to day, or to a day certain.

SEC. 8.   The Judges of the Supreme court shall immediately after the first election under this constitution, and their taking office, be classified by lot so that one shall hold his office for the term of two years, one for the term of three years, and one for the term of four years, from and after the first Monday of January succeeding their election. The lot shall be drawn by the Judges, who shall for that purpose assemble at the seat of government, and they shall cause the result thereof to be certified to the Secretary of State and filed in his office.

SEC. 9.   The Judge having the shortest term to serve, not holding his office by appointment or election to fill a vacancy, shall be the Chief Justice, and shall preside at all terms of the Supreme court; and, in case of his absence, the Judge having, in like manner, the next shortest to serve, shall preside in his stead.

Sec. 10. The terms of office of all Judges of the Supreme court, elected after the said first election, shall be four years, except as herein provided. In case of the re-election of a Judge then holding such office, the second term of such Judge shall be eight years. And if any such Judge shall have served two full terms, and shall be re-elected for the third term while still in such office, his third term shall be twelve years.

Sec. 11. Provision may be made by law for the voluntary retirement of any of said Judges at any time after they shall have arrived at the age of seventy years; provided, that the Judge so retired shall have been in the actual discharge of his duties as such Judge for at least sixteen years immediately preceding such retirement.

Sec. 12. No person shall be eligible to the office of Judge of the Supreme court unless he be learned in the law, be at least thirty years of age, and a citizen of the United States, nor unless he shall have resided in this State or the Territory at least two years next preceding his election, and at the time of his election be a resident of the district for which he is elected; but for the purpose of a re-election no such Judge shall be deemed to have lost his residence in the district by reason of his removal to the seat of government in the discharge of his official duties.

Sec. 13. Until otherwise provided by law, the districts from which the said Judges of the Supreme court shall be elected, shall be constituted as follows:

First District—All that portion of the State lying west of the Missouri river.

Second District—All that portion of the State lying east of the Missouri river and west of the Dakota river.

Third District—All that portion of the State lying east of the Dakota river.

Sec. 14. There shall be a Clerk of the Supreme court, who shall be appointed by the Judges thereof, and shall hold his office during the pleasure of said Judges, and whose duties and emoluments shall be as prescribed by law and by the rules of the Supreme court not inconsistent with law.

CIRCUIT COURTS.

Sec. 15. The Circuit courts shall have original jurisdiction of all actions and causes, both at law and in equity, and such appellate jurisdiction as may be conferred by law and consistent with this constitution; such jurisdiction as to value and amount and grade of offense may be limited by law. They and the Judges thereof shall have jurisdiction, also, and power to issue writs of habeas corpus, mandamus, quo warranto, certiorari, injunction and other original and remedial writs, with authority to hear and determine the same.

Sec. 16.   The State shall be divided into judicial courts, in each of which there shall be elected by the electors thereof, one Judge of the Circuit court therein, whose term of office shall be four years; provided, however, that the Judges elected at the first election shall hold their office for four years from and after the first Monday of January next preceding the taking effect of this constitution; and, provided further, that the term of office for all Judges after those first elected may by law be inzeased to six years.

Sec. 17.   Until otherwise provided by law, said circuits shall be five in number, and constituted as follows, viz:

First Circuit—The counties of Union, Clay, Lincoln, Turner, Lake, Minnehaha, McCook and Miner.

Second Circuit—The counties of Yankton, Bon Homme, Charles Mix, Douglas, Hutchinson, Davison, Hanson, Sanborn, Aurora, Brule, Buffalo and Jerauld.

Third Circuit—The counties of Brookings, Moody, Kingsbury, Clark, Hamlin, Deuel, Grant, Codington, Day and Roberts, the Wahpeton and Sisseton reservations, and all that strip of territory not included between the north line of the county of Day and the forty-sixth parallel of north latitude.

Fourth Circuit—The counties of Beadle, Hand, Hyde, Hughes, Spink, Brown, Sully, Potter, Edmunds, Faulk, Walworth, Campbell, McPherson, and including all that portion of said State lying east of the Missouri river not included in any other Judicial circuit.

Fifth Circuit—All that portion of said State lying west of the Missouri river.

Sec. 18.   The Legislature may, whenever two-thirds of the members of each house shall concur therein, increase the number of Judicial circuits and the Judges thereof, and divide the said State into Judicial circuits, accordingly, taking care that they be formed of compact territory and be bounded by county lines, but such increase of number or change in the boundaries of districts shall not work the removal of any Judge from his office during the term for which he shall have been elected or appointed.

Sec. 19.   Writs of error and appeals may be allowed from decisions of said Circuit courts to the Supreme court under such regulations as may be prescribed by law.

COUNTY COURTS.

Sec. 20.   There shall be elected in each organized county a County Judge, who shall be Judge of the County court of said county, whose term of office shall be two years, until otherwise provided by law, and whose compensation shall be as may be provided by law; provided, however, that the Judge first elected under the provisions of this constitution shall hold his office for the term of two years from and after the first Monday in January next preceding the taking effect of this constitution.

SEC. 21. County courts shall be Courts of Record, and shall have original jurisdiction in all matters of probate, settlement of estates of deceased persons, appointment of guardians, conservators and administrators, and settlement of their accounts, and such other civil and criminal jurisdiction as may be conferred by law; provided, that such courts shall not have jurisdiction in any case where the debt, damage, claim or value of property involved shall exceed one thousand dollars, except in cases relating to the estates of deceased persons and the appointment of guardians. Writs of error and appeals may be allowed from County to Circuit courts, or to the Supreme court in such cases and in such manner as may be prescribed by law. No appeal shall lie to the Circuit court from any judgment given upon an appeal from a Justice of the Peace.

SEC. 22. The County courts shall not have jurisdiction in case of felony, nor shall criminal cases therein be prosecuted by indictment; but they may have such jurisdiction in criminal matters, not of the grade of felony, as the Legislature may prescribe, and the prosecutions therein may be by information or otherwise as the Legislature may provide.

JUSTICES OF THE PEACE.

SEC. 23. Justices of the Peace shall have such jurisdiction as may be conferred by law, but they shall not have jurisdiction of any cause wherein the value of the property or the amount in controversy exceeds the sum of $100, or where the boundaries or title to real property shall be called in question.

POLICE MAGISTRATES.

SEC. 24. The Legislature shall have power to provide for creating such Police Magistrates for cities and towns as may be deemed from time to time necessary, who shall have jurisdiction of all cases arising under the ordinance of such cities and towns respectively, and such Police Magistrates may also be constituted ex officio Justices of the Peace for their respective counties.

STATES ATTORNEYS.

SEC. 25. The Legislature shall have power to provide for an Attorney General for the State and States Attorneys, and to pre-

scribe their duties and fix their compensation; but no person shall
be eligible to the office of Attorney General or States Attorney who
shall not at the time of his election be at least 25 years of age and
possess all the other qualifications for Judges of Circuit courts as
prescribed in this article.

MISCELLANEOUS.

Sec. 26.   No person shall be eligible to the office of Judge of
the Circuit or County courts unless he be learned in the law, be at
least 25 years of age, and a citizen of the United States, nor unless
he shall have resided in this State or Territory at least one year
next preceding his election, and at the time of his election be a
resident of the county or circuit, as the case may be, for which he
is elected.

Sec. 27.   The Judges of the Supreme court, Circuit courts
and County courts, shall be chosen at the first election held under
the provisions of this constitution, and thereafter as provided by
law, and the Legislature may provide for the election of such
officers on a' different day from that on which an election is held
for any other purpose, and may for the purpose of making such
provision extend or abridge the term of office of any such Judges
then holding, but not in any case more than six months. The
terms of office of all Judges of the Circuit courts elected in the
several Judicial circuits throughout the State shall expire on the
same day.

Sec. 28.   The time of holding courts within said judicial
circuits and counties shall be as provided by law; but at least one
term of the Circuit court shall be held annually in each organized
county, and the Legislature shall make provision for attaching
unorganized counties or territory to organized counties for judicial
purposes.

Sec. 29.   Special terms of said courts may be held under such
regulations as may be provided by law.

Sec. 30.   The Judges of the Supreme court and Circuit courts
and County courts shall each receive such salary as may be provided by law consistent with this constitution, and no such Judge
shall receive any compensation, perquisite or emoluments for or on
account of his office in any form whatever, except such salary;
provided, that County Judges may accept and receive such fees as
may be allowed under the Land laws of the United States.

Sec. 31.   No Judges of the Supreme court or Circuit courts
shall act as attorney or counsellor at law, nor shall any County
Judge act as attorney or counselor at law in any case which is or
may be brought into his court, or which shall be appealed therefrom.

Sec. 32.   There shall be a Clerk of the Circuit court in each organized county, who shall also be Clerk of the County court, and who shall be elected by the qualified electors of such counties, and shall hold his office for a term of two years, except the Clerk elected at the first election, who shall hold his office for two years from and after the first Monday of January next preceding the taking effect of this constitution. The duties and compensation of said Clerk shall be as provided by law and regulated by the rules of the court consistent with the provisions of law.

SEC. 33. Until the Legislature shall provide by law for fixing the terms of courts, the Judges of the Supreme, Circuit and County courts, respectively, shall fix the terms thereof.

SEC. 34. All laws relating to courts shall be general and of uniform operation throughout the State, and the organization, jurisdiction, power, proceedings and practice of all the courts of the same class or grade so far as regulated by law, and the force and effect of the proceedings, judgments and decrees of such courts, severally, shall be uniform.

SEC. 35. No Judge of the Supreme or Circuit courts shall be elected to any other than a judicial office, or be eligible thereto, during the term for which he was elected such Judge. All votes for either of them during such term for any elective office, except that of Judge of the Supreme court, Circuit court or County court, given by the Legislature or the people, shall be void.

SEC. 36. All officers of the Supreme, Circuit or County courts provided for in this article shall hold their offices until their successors respectively are elected or appointed and qualified.

SEC. 37. All officers provided for in this article shall respectively reside in the district, county, precinct, city or town for which they may be elected or appointed. Vacancies in elective offices shall be filled by election, but. when the unexpired term does not exceed one year, the vacancy shall be filled by appointment, as follows: All Judges of the Supreme, Circuit and County courts by the Governor; all other judicial officers by the County Board of the county where the vacancy occurs; or, in case of Police Magistrates, by the municipality.

SEC. 38. All process shall run in the name of the "State of Dakota." All prosecution shall be carried on in the name and by the authority of the "State of Dakota."

ARTICLE VII.

EDUCATION AND SCHOOL LANDS.

SECTION 1. The stability of a republican form of government depending mainly upon the intelligence of the people, it shall be the duty of the Legislature to establish an general and uniform system of public schools.

SEC. 2. All the proceeds of the sale of public lands that have already been given, or may hereafter be given by the United States for the use of public schools, all such per cent. as may be granted by Congress on the sale of public lands, the proceeds of all property that shall fall to the State by escheat, and the proceeds of gifts or donations to the State not otherwise specified, shall be and remain a perpetual fund for the maintenance of public schools in the State. This fund may be increased, but never shall be diminished. If any loss shall accrue to this fund it shall be made good by the State.

SEC. 3. The income of this fund, together with the net proceeds of all fines for violations of State laws, shall be used annually for the benefit of public schools, but the principal shall forever remain unused and must be safely invested as hereinafter provided. No part of this fund, either principal or interest, shall ever be diverted, even temporarily, or ever used for any other purpose than the maintenance of public schools.

SEC. 4. After one year from the assembling of the first State Legislature, the public school lands may be offered for sale or rental on the following conditions: The Superintendent of Public Instruction, the State Treasurer and the State Auditor shall constitute a Board of Appraisal to fix the minimum price at which lands shall be sold or rented. But in no case shall land be sold at less than $10 per acre. The total amount of school lands offered for sale within ten years from the date of the first sale, shall not exceed one-third of all the lands set apart for the use of public schools. No lands shall be sold or rented except after sixty days' previous public notice of sale or rental by publication in a newspaper of general circulation in the vicinity of the lands to be sold, and at the seat of government; and such lands shall be sold or rented to the highest bidder. The Board of Appraisal shall at least every four years make a new appraisal of the lands, and shall always offer for sale or rental the most valuable lands first. The proceeds of all sales of school lands shall be invested by the Board of Appraisal, with the advice and consent of a committee of the Legislature, in such manner as to yield the greatest revenue consistent with safety of investment.

SEC. 5. The Legislature shall make such provision by taxation or otherwise, as, with the revenue from the permanent school fund, shall secure a thorough and efficient system of common schools throughout the State.

SEC. 6. All lands or moneys that have been given or may be given by the United States, or by other parties, for the benefit and use of a university or of normal schools in the Territory of Dakota, shall belong to, and be used by, the university and the normal schools of the State in so far as they are equitably entitled to the same.

SEC. 7. No school district or township shall be entitled to

any share in the public school money of the State for the year in which a school shall not be maintained at least five months.

SEC. 8.   No teacher, State, county, township or district school officer, shall be interested in the sale, proceeds or profit of any book, apparatus or furniture used, or to be used, in any school in this State, under such penalties as shall be provided by the Legislature.

SEC. 9.   No appropriation of money or of land, or of bonds to aid any sectarian school, shall ever be made by the Legislature, or any county, or any municipality, within the State.

ARTICLE VIII.

MILITIA.

SECTION 1.   The militia of the State of Dakota shall consist of able-bodied male persons residing in the State, between the ages of eighteen and forty-five years, except such persons as now are, or hereafter may be, exempt by the laws of the United States or of this State.

SEC. 2.   The Legislature may provide by law for the enrollment of the militia, the establishment of volunteer and such other organization, and for their equipment and discipline, as may be deemed necessary for the protection of the State and the preservation of order.

SEC. 3.   The Legislature, in providing for the organization of the militia, shall conform as nearly as practicable to the regulations for the government of the armies of the United States.

SEC. 4.   All militia officers shall be commissioned by the Governor, and may hold their commissions for such time as the Legislature may provide.

SEC. 5.   The militia shall in all cases, except treason, felony or breach of the peace, be privileged from arrest during their attendance at musters and elections and in going to and returning from the same.

SEC. 6.   All military records, banners and relics of the State shall be preserved as an enduring memorial of the patriotism and valor of Dakota, and it shall be the duty of the Legislature to provide by law for the safe keeping of the same.

SEC. 7.   No person having conscientious scruples against bearing arms shall be compelled to do military duty in time of peace, but may be required to pay an equivalent for such exemption.

ARTICLE IX.

REVENUE AND TAXATION.

SECTION 1.   The Legislature shall provide such revenue as may be needful by levying a tax by valuation, so that every person and corporation shall pay a tax in proportion to the value of his, her or its property, such value to be ascertained and fixed in such manner as the Legislature shall direct, by general laws; such laws to be uniform as to the classes of property or subjects upon which they operate.

SEC. 2. The property of the State, county and municipal corporations, both real and personal, shall be exempt from taxation.

SEC. 3. The Legislature may, by general law, exempt from taxation property used exclusively for agricultural and horticultural societies, for schools, religious, cemetery and charitable purposes and personal property to an amount not exceeding in value $200 for each individual liable to taxation.

SEC. 4. To encourage the planting and cultivation of timber, the Legislature may, by general law, exempt from taxation for a term of years, not to exceed one-fourth of any quarter section of land, and the improvements thereon to the extent of $1,000 in value.

SEC. 5. All laws exempting property from taxation, other than that enumerated in sections two, three and four of this article, shall be void.

SEC. 6. No tax shall be levied except in pursuance of a law, which shall distinctly state the object of the same, to which the tax only shall be applied.

SEC. 7. All taxes levied and collected for State purposes shall be paid into the State Treasury.

SEC. 8. The Legislature may vest the corporate authority of cities, towns and villages with power to make local improvements by special assessment, or by special taxation of contiguous property or otherwise. For all other corporate purposes, all municipal corporations may be vested with authority to assess and collect taxes; but such tax shall be uniform in respect to persons and property within the jurisdiction of the body levying the same.

SEC. 9. The making of profit, directly or indirectly, out of State, county, city, town or school district money, or using the same for any purpose not authorized by law, shall be deemed a felony, and shall be punished as provided by law.

SEC. 10. An accurate statement of the receipts and expenditures of the public moneys shall be published annually in such manner as the Legislature may provide.

ARTICLE X.

PUBLIC ACCOUNTS AND EXPENDITURES.

SECTION 1. An account shall be kept by the officers of the Executive and Administrative Departments, and of all the public institutions of the State, of all moneys received or disbursed by them, severally, from all sources and for every service performed, and a semi-annual report thereof made to the Governor, under oath; and any officer who makes a false report shall be guilty of perjury and punished accordingly.

Sec. 2. The Auditor shall within sixty days after the adjournment of each session of the Legislature, prepare and publish a full statement of all moneys expended at such session, specifying the amount of each item, and to whom and for what paid.

ARTICLE XI

COMPENSATION OF PUBLIC OFFICERS.

Section 1. The salaries of the officers named in this section shall be as follows, until otherwise provided by law: The Governor shall receive an annual salary of two thousand dollars; the State Treasurer shall receive an annual salary of one thousand dollars; the State Auditor shall receive an annual salary of one thousand dollars; the Superintendent of Public Instruction shall receive an annual salary of one thousand five hundred dollars; the Secretary of State shall receive an annual salary of one thousand five hundred dollars; the Attorney General shall receive an annual salary of one thousand dollars; the compensation of Lieutenant Governor shall be double the compensation of a State Senator; the Judges of the Supreme, Circuit and County courts shall receive such salaries as may be provided by law.

ARTICLE XII.

PUBLIC INDEBTEDNESS

Section 1. The State shall not loan its credit or make donations in aid of any individual, association or corporation, nor subscribe to or become the owner of the capital stock of any association or corporation, nor engage in any work of internal improvement.

Sec. 2. For the purpose of defraying extraordinary expenses and making public improvements, or to meet casual deficits or failure in revenue, the State may contract debts never to exceed with previous debts in the aggregate five hundred thousand dollars, and no greater indebtedness shall be incurred except for the purpose of repelling invasion, suppressing insurrection or defending the State or United States in war, and provision shall be made by law for the payment of the interest annually and the principal when due by a tax levied for the purpose, or from other sources of revenue, which law providing for the payment of such interest and principal by such law, or otherwise, shall be irrepealable until such debt is paid.

Sec. 3   No city, county, town, municipality or other subdivision of the State shall ever make donations to or loan its credit in aid of or subscribe to the capital stock of any association or corporation, or become responsible for the debts of any individual, association or corporation.

Sec. 4.   The debt of any county, city, town, school district or other subdivision shall never exceed five per centum of the assessed value of the taxable property therein.   In estimating the amount of indebtedness which a municipality or subdivision may incur, the amount of indebtedness contracted prior to the adoption of this constitution shall not be included.

Sec. 5.   Any city, county, town, school district or other subdivision incurring indebtedness, shall at or before the time of so doing, provide for the collection of an annual tax sufficient to pay the interest and also the principal thereof when due, and all laws or ordinances providing for the payment of the interest or principal of any debt shall be irrepealable.

Sec. 6.   Consent is given that Congress may make such provision for the payment by this State of the existing indebtedness of the Territory of Dakota as it shall deem just and equitable, and this State shall assume and pay so much interest thereof as Congress shall provide.

ARTICLE XIII.

COUNTIES.

Section 1.   The several counties of the Territory of Dakota south of the forty-sixth parallel of north latitude as they now exist are hereby declared to be counties of the State.

Sec 2.   No new county shall be formed or established by the Legislature with a less area than five hundred square miles, nor shall any county already formed be reduced below such area.

Sec. 3.   No county shall be divided or consolidated with any other county, or have any part stricken therefrom, without first submitting the question to a vote of the people of the county or counties interested, nor unless a majority of all the legal voters of such county or counties voting on the question shall vote for the same.

Sec. 4.   There shall be no territory stricken from any organized county unless a majority of the voters living in such territory shall petition for such division; and the portion so stricken off added to another county, or formed in whole or in part into a new county shall be holden for and obliged to pay its portion of the indebtedness of the county or counties from which it has been taken.

Sec. 5. The Legislature shall provide by law for the election of such county and township officers as may be necessary, and fix the terms thereof.

Sec. 6. The Legislature shall provide by general law for township organization, under which any county may organize whenever a majority of the legal voters of such county, voting at any general election, shall so determine. And in any county that shall have adopted a township organization, the question of continuing the same may be submitted to a vote of the electors of such county, at a general election, in the manner that shall be provided by law.

ARTICLE XIV.

EXEMPTIONS.

Section 1. The Legislature shall pass liberal homestead and exemption laws.

Sec. 2. No change in the laws relating to the kind and amount of personal or real property exempt from seizure and sale for the payment of any debt shall take effect in the collection of any debt contracted prior to the taking effect of the act making such change.

ARTICLE XV.

CORPORATIONS.

Section 1. Corporations may be created under general laws, but shall not be created by special acts. except as in this constitution otherwise allowed. All general laws or special acts enacted under the provisions of this constitution relating to corporations, may be altered or repealed by the Legislature at any time after their passage.

Sec. 2. The property of corporations, except for charitable, religious and educational purposes. now existing and to be hereafter created, shall be subjected to a uniform rate of taxation with other property, which shall be levied and collected under general laws, and in such manner as the Legislature may prescribe.

Sec. 3. The State shall not become a stockholder in any corporation; and it shall not assume or pay the debt or liability of any corporation nor grant subsidies to any corporation, unless such debt or liability shall be incurred or such subsidy granted in time of war for the benefit of the State.

Sec. 4. No street, passenger railway, or telegraph or telephone line shall be constructed within the limits of any village, town or city without the consent of its local authorities.

SEC. 5. If a general banking law shall be enacted, it shall provide for the registry and countersigning by an officer of this State of all bills or paper credit designed to circulate as money, and require security to the full amount thereof to be deposited with the State Treasurer in the approved securities of this State or of the United States, to be rated at ten per cent. below their par value, and, in case of their depreciation, the deficiency shall be made good by depositing additional securities.

SEC. 6. Every bank, banking company or corporation shall be required to cease all banking operations within twenty years from the time of its organization, and promptly thereafter close its business, but shall have the corporate capacity to sue or to be sued until its business is fully closed, but the Legislature may provide by general law for the reorganization of such banks.

SEC. 7. The shareholders or stockholders of any banking corporation shall be held individually responsible and liable for all contracts, debts and engagements of such bank to the extent of the amount of their stock therein at the par value thereof in addition to the amount invested in such shares or stock.

SEC. 8 All railroad and transportation companies are declared to be common carriers and subject to legislative control and the Legislature shall have power to enact laws regulating and controlling the rates of charges for transportation, passengers and freight as such common carriers from one point to another in this State.

SEC. 9. The Legislature shall provide by law that in all elections for directors or managers of incorporated companies, every stockholder shall have the right to vote in person or by proxy the number of shares of stock owned by him for as many persons as there are directors or managers to be elected, or to cumulate said shares and give one candidate as many votes as the number of directors multiplied by the number of his shares of stock shall equal, or to distribute them on same principle among as many candidates as he shall think fit; and such directors or managers shall not be elected in any other manner.

ARTICLE XVI.

IMPEACHMENT AND REMOVAL FROM OFFICE.

SECTION 1. The House of Representatives shall have the sole power of impeachment. The concurrence of a majority of all the members elected shall be necessary to an impeachment.

SEC. 2. All impeachments shall be tried by the Senate; when sitting for that purpose the Senators shall be upon oath or affirmation to do justice according to law and evidence. No person shall be convicted without the concurrence of two-thirds of the members elected. When the Governor or Leutenant Governor is on trial, the Chief Justice of the Supreme court shall preside.

SEC. 3. The Governor and other State and Judicial officers, except County Judges, Justices of the Peace, and Police Magistrates, shall be liable to impeachment for corrupt conduct, or malfeasance, or crimes, or misdemeanors in office, but judgment in such cases shall not extend further than to removal from office and disqualification to hold any office of trust or profit under this Sate. The person accused, whether convicted or acquitted, shall nevertheless be liable to indictment, trial, judgment and punishment according to law.

SEC. 4. All officers not liable to impeachment shall be subject to removal for misconduct or malfeasance, or crimes or misdemeanors in office, in such manner as may be provided by law.

SEC. 5. No officer shall exercise the duties of his office after he shall have been impeached and before his acquittal.

SEC. 6. On the trial of an impeachment against the Governor the Lieutenant Governor shall not act as a member of the court.

SEC. 7. No person shall be tried on impeachment before he shall have been served with a copy thereof at least twenty days previous to the day set for trial.

SEC. 8. No person shall be liable to impeachment twice for the same offense.

ARTICLE XVII.

SEAT OF GOVERNMENT.

The seat of government shall be and remain at Yankton until removed by law.

FUTURE AMENDMENTS:

SECTION 1. Any amendment or amendments to this constitution may be proposed in either house of the Legislature, and if the same shall be agreed to by a majority of the members elected to each of the two houses, such proposed amendment or amendments shall be entered on their journals, with the yeas and nays taken thereon, and referred to the Legislature to be chosen at the next general election, and shall be published for thirteen weeks previous to the time of holding such election, in such manner as may be provided by law. And if, in the Legislature next chosen, such proposed amendment or amendments shall be agreed to by a majority of all the members elected in each house, then it shall be the duty of the Legislature to submit such proposed amendment or amendments to the people, in such manner and at such time as the Legislature shall prescribe; and if the people shall approve and ratify such amendment or amendments by a majority of the electors voting thereon, such amendment or amendments shall become part of the constitution; provided, that if five thousand legal voters shall petition the Legislature sitting after the admission of the State into the Union, to amend the constitution in any particular, then the Legislature shall submit such proposed amendment or amendments to the people at the next general election thereafter, or at a special election to be held not less than ninety days nor more than six months after the session of said Legislature shall be terminated, which submission shall be made in such manner as the Legislature shall prescribe, and if the people shall approve and ratify such amendment or amendments by a majority of the electors voting thereon, such amendment or amendments shall become a part of the constitution.

Sec. 2. If more than one amendment be submitted at the same time, they shall be submitted in such manner that the people may vote for or against such amendments separately.

Sec. 3. If at any time a majority of the Senate and House of Representatives shall deem it necessary to call a convention to revise or change this constitution, they shall recommend to the electors to vote for or against a convention at the next election for members of the Legislature; and if it shall appear that a majority of the electors voting thereon have voted for a convention, the Legislature shall at its next session provide for calling such convention.

ARTICLE XIX.

MISCELLANEOUS.

Section 1. The people of the State of Dakota are declared to possess the ultimate property in and to all lands within the jurisdiction of the State; and all lands the title to which shall fail from defect of heirs or otherwise, shall revert or escheat to the people.

Sec. 2. The exercise of the right of eminent domain shall never be abridged or so construed as to prevent the Legislature from taking the property and franchises of incorporated companies and subjecting them to public use, the same as property of individuals, and the exercise of the police power of the State shall never be abridged or so construed as to permit corporations to conduct their business in such manner as to infringe the equal rights of individuals or the general well-being of the State.

Sec. 3. Institutions for the benefit of the insane, blind and deaf and dumb shall always be fostered and supported by the State, and be subject to such regulations as may be prescribed by the Legislature.

Sec. 4. Whenever grants of land or other property shall have been made to the State, especially dedicated by the grant to particular works of public improvement, the State may carry on such particular works, and shall devote thereto the avails of such grants, and may pledge or appropriate the revenues derived from such works in aid of their completion.

SEC. 5. All such lands shall be appraised and sold in the same manner and by the same officers, and the minimum price shall be the same as provided by law and the constitution for the appraisement and sale of the school lands. All moneys derived from the sale of said land shall cons itute he public improvement fund of the State.

SEC. 6. The following shall be the design of the great seal of the State of Dakota: A shield, draped with the American flag, depending from the beak of an eagle. In the background of the shield, a range of hills and the chimney of a smelting furnace. In the center of the shield, a river, bearing a steamboat. On the hither bank of the river a train of cars. In the middle foreground a field of wheat and a field of corn. In the immediate right foreground, a white man at his plow; in the left foreground, an Indian and tepees. Both white man and Indian are looking at a rift in the clouds, where appears the legend: "Fear God, and Take Your Own Part." This legend to be the motto of the State of Dakota.

SEC. 7. No law shall be passed with regard to taxes, making any distinction between the land and property of proprietors not resident in, nor citizens of, the State, and the land and property of the citizens of the State resident therein.

[Doc. No. 3]
Enabling Act of February 22, 1889

February 22, 1889.

—An act to provide for the division of Dakota into two States and to enable the people of North Dakota, South Dakota, Montana, and Washington to form constitutions and State governments and to be admitted into the Union on an equal footing with the original States, and to make donations of public lands to such States.

Be it enacted by the Senate and House of Representatives of the United States of America in Congress assembled, That the inhabitants of all that part of the area of the United States now constituting the Territories of Dakota, Montana, and Washington, as at present described, may become the States of North Dakota, South Dakota, Montana, and Washington, respectively, as hereinafter provided.

Admission of new States. North Dakota, South Dakota, Montana, and Washington.

Division of Dakota.

SEC. 2. The area comprising the Territory of Dakota shall, for the purposes of this act, be divided on the line of the seventh standard parallel produced due west to the western boundary of said Territory; and the delegates elected as hereinafter provided to the constitutional convention in districts north of said parallel shall assemble in convention, at the time prescribed in this act, at the city of Bismarck; and the delegates elected in districts south of said parallel shall, at the same time, assemble in convention at the city of Sioux Falls.

Conventions to meet at Bismarck and Sioux Falls.

Delegates to conventions to be chosen.

SEC. 3. That all persons who are qualified by the laws of said Territories to vote for representatives to the legislative assemblies thereof, are hereby authorized to vote for and choose delegates to form conventions in said proposed States; and the qualifications for delegates to such conventions shall be such as by the laws of said Territories respectively persons are required to possess to be eligible to the legislative assemblies thereof; and the aforesaid delegates to form said conventions shall be apportioned within the limits of the proposed States, in such districts as may be established as herein provided, in proportion to the population in each of said counties and districts, as near as may be, to be ascertained at the time of making said apportionments by the persons hereinafter authorized to make the same, from the best information obtainable, in each of which districts three delegates shall be elected, but no elector shall vote for more than two persons for delegates to such conventions; that said apportionments shall be made by the governor, the chief-justice, and the secretary of said Territories; and the governors of said Territories shall, by proclamation, order an election of the delegates aforesaid in each of said proposed States, to be held on the Tuesday after the second Monday in May, eighteen hundred and eighty-nine, which proclamation shall be issued on the fifteenth day of April, eighteen hundred and eighty-nine; and such election shall be conducted, the returns made, the result ascertained, and the certificates to persons elected to such convention issued in the same manner as is prescribed by the laws of the said Territories regulating elections therein for Delegates to Congress; and the number of votes cast for delegates in each precinct shall also be returned. The number of delegates to said conventions respectively shall be seventy-five; and all persons resident in said proposed States, who are qualified voters of said Territories as herein provided, shall be entitled to vote upon the election of delegates, and under such rules and regulations as said conventions may prescribe, not in conflict with this act, upon the ratification or rejection of the constitutions.

Qualifications.

Apportionment.

Governors to issue proclamation for election.

Number of delegates.

Place of meeting.

SEC. 4. That the delegates to the conventions elected as provided for in this act shall meet at the seat of government of each of said Territories, except the delegates elected in South Dakota, who shall meet at the city of Sioux Falls, on the fourth day of July, eighteen hundred and eighty-nine, and, after organization, shall declare, on behalf of the people of said proposed States, that they adopt the Constitution of the United States; whereupon the said conventions shall be, and are hereby, authorized to form constitutions and States governments for said proposed States, respectively. The constitutions shall be republican in form, and make no distinction in civil or

Time.

Adoption of Constitution.

Civil rights.

political rights on account of race or color, except as to Indians not taxed, and not be repugnant to the Constitution of the United States and the principles of the Declaration of Independence. And said conventions shall provide, by ordinances irrevocable without the consent of the United States and the people of said States:

First. That perfect toleration of religious sentiment shall be secured and that no inhabitant of said States shall ever be molested in person or property on account of his or her mode of religious worship. Religious freedom.

Second. That the people inhabiting said proposed States do agree and declare that they forever disclaim all right and title to the unappropriated public lands lying within the boundaries thereof, and to all lands lying within said limits owned or held by any Indian or Indian tribes; and that until the title thereto shall have been extinguished by the United States, the same shall be and remain subject to the disposition of the United States, and said Indian lands shall remain under the absolute jurisdiction and control of the Congress of the United States; that the lands belonging to citizens of the United States residing without the said States shall never be taxed at a higher rate than the lands belonging to residents thereof; that no taxes shall be imposed by the States on lands or property therein belonging to or which may hereafter be purchased by the United States or reserved for its use. But nothing herein, or in the ordinances herein provided for, shall preclude the said States from taxing as other lands are taxed any lands owned or held by any Indian who has severed his tribal relations, and has obtained from the United States or from any person a title thereto by patent or other grant, save and except such lands as have been or may be granted to any Indian or Indians under any act of Congress containing a provision exempting the lands thus granted from taxation; but said ordinances shall provide that all such lands shall be exempt from taxation by said States so long and to such extent as such act of Congress may prescribe. Renunciation of public lands. Taxation of lands. Taxing lands of Indians.

Third. That the debts and liabilities of said Territories shall be assumed and paid by said States, respectively. Territorial debts.

Fourth. That provision shall be made for the establishment and maintenance of systems of public schools, which shall be open to all the children of said States, and free from sectarian control. Public schools.

SEC. 5. That the convention which shall assemble at Bismarck shall form a constitution and State government for a State to be known as North Dakota, and the convention which shall assemble at Sioux Falls shall form a constitution and State government for a State to be known as South Dakota: *Provided,* That at the election for delegates to the constitutional convention in South Dakota, as hereinbefore provided, each elector may have written or printed on his ballot the words " For the Sioux Falls constitution," or the words "against the Sioux Falls constitution," and the votes on this question shall be returned and canvassed in the same manner as for the election provided for in section three of this act; and if a majority of all votes cast on this question shall be " for the Sioux Falls constitution" it shall be the duty of the convention which may assemble at Sioux Falls, as herein provided, to resubmit to the people of South Dakota, for ratification or rejection at the election hereinafter provided for in this act, the constitution framed at Sioux Falls and adopted November third, eighteen hundred and eighty-five, and also the articles and propositions separately submitted at that election, including the question of locating the temporary seat of government, with such changes only as relate to the name and boundary of the proposed State, to the re-apportionment of the judicial and legislative districts, and such amendments as may be necessary in order to comply with the provisions of this act; and if a majority of the votes cast on the ratification or rejection of the constitution shall be for the constitution irrespective of the articles separately submitted, the State of South Dakota North Dakota. South Dakota. *Proviso.* Vote on " Sioux Falls constitution." To be resubmitted

Archives, etc.

shall be admitted as a State in the Union under said constitution as hereinafter provided; but the archives, records, and books of the Territory of Dakota shall remain at Bismarck, the capital of North Dakota, until an agreement in reference thereto is reached by said States.

Adoption of new constitution.

But if at the election for delegates to the constitutional convention in South Dakota a majority of all the votes cast at that election shall be "against the Sioux Falls constitution", then and in that event it shall be the duty of the convention which will assemble at the city of Sioux Falls on the fourth day of July, eighteen hundred and eighty-nine, to proceed to form a constitution and State government as provided in this act the same as if that question had not been submitted to a vote of the people of South Dakota.

Joint commission to divide property of Dakota Territory.

SEC. 6. It shall be the duty of the constitutional conventions of North Dakota and South Dakota to appoint a joint commission, to be composed of not less than three members of each convention, whose duty it shall be to assemble at Bismarck, the present seat of government of said Territory, and agree upon an equitable division of all property belonging to the Territory of Dakota, the disposition of all public records, and also adjust and agree upon the amount of the debts and liabilities of the Territory, which shall be assumed and paid by each of the proposed States of North Dakota and South Dakota; and the agreement reached respecting the Territorial debts and liabilities shall be incorporated in the respective constitutions, and each of said States shall obligate itself to pay its proportion of such debts and liabilities the same as if they had been created by such States respectively.

Territorial government to continue if constitution rejected.

SEC. 7. If the constitutions formed for both North Dakota and South Dakota shall be rejected by the people at the elections for the ratification or rejection of their respective constitutions as provided for in this act, the Territorial government of Dakota shall continue in existence the same as if this act had not been passed. But if the constitution formed for either North Dakota or South Dakota shall be rejected by the people, that part of the Territory so rejecting its proposed constitution shall continue under the Territorial government of the present Territory of Dakota, but shall, after the State adopting its constitution is admitted into the Union, be called by the name of the Territory of North Dakota or South Dakota, as the case may be: *Provided,* That if either of the proposed States provided for in this act shall reject the constitution which may be submitted for ratification or rejection at the election provided therefor, the governor of the Territory in which such proposed constitution was rejected shall issue his proclamation reconvening the delegates elected to the convention which formed such rejected constitution, fixing the time and place at which said delegates shall assemble; and when so assembled they shall proceed to form another constitution or to amend the rejected constitution, and shall submit such new constitution or amended constitution to the people of the proposed State for ratification or rejection, at such time as said convention may determine; and all the provisions of this act, so far as applicable, shall apply to such convention so reassembled and to the constitution which may be formed, its ratification or rejection, and to the admission of the proposed State.

Provisions in case of rejection by either North or South Dakota.

Proviso.

Reconvening of delegates to form new constitution.

South Dakota.
Submission of constitution for ratification.

SEC. 8. That the constitutional convention which may assemble in South Dakota shall provide by ordinance for resubmitting the Sioux Falls constitution of eighteen hundred and eighty-five, after having amended the same as provided in section five of this act, to the people of South Dakota for ratification or rejection at an election to be held therein on the first Tuesday in October, eighteen hundred and eighty-nine; but if said constitutional convention is authorized and required to form a new constitution for South Dakota it shall provide for submitting the same in like manner to the people of South Dakota for ratification or rejection at an election to be held in said proposed State on the said first Tuesday in October. And the constitutional conventions which may assemble in North Dakota, Montana, and Washington shall provide in like manner for submitting the constitutions formed by them to the people of said proposed States, respectively. for ratification or rejection at elections to be held in said proposed States on the said first Tuesday in October. At the elections provided for in this section the qualified voters of said proposed States shall vote directly for or against the proposed constitutions, and for or against any articles or propositions separately submitted. The returns of said elections shall be made to the secretary of each of said Territories, who, with the governor and chief-justice thereof, or any two of them, shall canvass the same; and if a majority of the legal votes cast shall be for the constitution the governor shall certify the result to the President of the United States, together with a statement of the votes cast thereon and upon separate articles or propositions, and a copy of said constitution, articles, propositions, and ordinances. And if the constitutions and governments of said proposed States are republican in form, and if all the provisions of this act have been complied with in the formation thereof, it shall be the duty of the President of the United States to issue his proclamation announcing the result of the election in each, and thereupon the proposed States which have adopted constitutions and formed State governments as herein provided shall be deemed admitted by Congress into the Union under and by virtue of this act on an equal footing with the original States from and after the date of said proclamation.

North Dakota, Montana, and Washington.

Vote on constitution.

Canvass of returns.

Certifying result.

Proclamation of admission by President.

SEC. 9. That until the next general census, or until otherwise provided by law, said States shall be entitled to one Representative in the House of Representatives of the United States, except South Dakota, which shall be entitled to two ; and the Representatives to the Fifty-first Congress, together with the governors and other officers provided for in said constitutions, may be elected on the same day of the election for the ratification or rejection of the constitutions; and until said State officers are elected and qualified under the provisions of each constitution and the States, respectively, are admitted into the Union, the Territorial officers shall continue to discharge the duties of their respective offices in each of said Territories.

Representation in Congress.

Election.

SEC. 10. That upon the admission of each of said States into the Union sections numbered sixteen and thirty-six in every township of said proposed States, and where such sections, or any parts thereof, have been sold or otherwise disposed of by or under the authority of any act of Congress, other lands equivalent thereto, in legal subdivisions of not less than one-quarter section, and as contiguous as may be to the section in lieu of which the same is taken, are hereby granted to said States for the support of common schools, such indemnity lands to be selected within said States in such manner as the legislature may provide, with the approval of the Secretary of the Interior: *Provided*, That the sixteenth and thirty-sixth sections embraced in permanent reservations for national purposes shall not, at any time, be subject to the grants nor to the indemnity provisions of this act, nor shall any lands embraced in Indian, military, or other reservations of any character be subject to the grants or to the indemnity provisions of this act until the reservation shall have been extinguished and such lands be restored to, and become a part of, the public domain.

School lands granted to States.

Proviso.

Lands in reservations excepted.

SEC. 11. That all lands herein granted for educational purposes shall be disposed of only at public sale, and at a price not less than ten dollars per acre, the proceeds to constitute a permanent school-fund, the interest of which only shall be expended in the support of said schools. But said lands may, under such regulations as the legislatures shall prescribe, be leased for periods of not more than five years, in quantities not exceeding one section to any one person

Sale of school lands.

Lease.

or company; and such land shall not be subject to pre-emption, homestead entry, or any other entry under the land laws of the United States, whether surveyed or unsurveyed, but shall be reserved for school purposes only.

Lands for public buildings.

SEC. 12. That upon the admission of each of said States into the Union, in accordance with the provisions of this act, fifty sections of the unappropriated public lands within said States, to be selected and located in legal subdivisions as provided in section ten of this act, shall be, and are hereby, granted to said States for the purpose of erecting public buildings at the capital of said States for legislative, executive, and judicial purposes.

Five per cent. of proceeds of public lands to be paid to States.

SEC. 13. That five per centum of the proceeds of the sales of public lands lying within said States which shall be sold by the United States subsequent to the admission of said States into the Union, after deducting all the expenses incident to the same, shall be paid to the said States, to be used as a permanent fund, the interest of which only shall be expended for the support of common schools within said States, respectively.

University lands to vest in States.
Vol. 21, p. 326.

SEC. 14. That the lands granted to the Territories of Dakota and Montana by the act of February eighteenth, eighteen hundred and eighty-one, entitled "An act to grant lands to Dakota, Montana, Arizona, Idaho, and Wyoming for university purposes," are hereby vested in the States of South Dakota, North Dakota, and Montana, respectively, if such States are admitted into the Union, as provided in this act, to the extent of the full quantity of seventy-two sections to each of said States, and any portion of said lands that may not have been selected by either of said Territories of Dakota or Montana may be selected by the respective States aforesaid; but said act of February eighteenth, eighteen hundred and eighty-one, shall be so amended as to provide that none of said lands shall be sold for

Minimum price for lands.

less than ten dollars per acre, and the proceeds shall constitute a permanent fund to be safely invested and held by said States severally, and the income thereof be used exclusively for university

University lands to Washington.
Vol. 10, p. 305.

purposes. And such quantity of the lands authorized by the fourth section of the act of July seventeenth, eighteen hundred and fifty-four, to be reserved for university purposes in the Territory of Washington, as, together with the lands confirmed to the vendees of the

Vol. 13, p. 28.

Territory by the act of March fourteenth, eighteen hundred and sixty-four, will make the full quantity of seventy-two entire sections, are hereby granted in like manner to the State of Washington for the purposes of a university in said State. None of the lands granted in this section shall be sold at less than ten dollars per acre; but said lands may be leased in the same manner as provided

To be under exclusive State control.

in section eleven of this act. The schools, colleges, and universities provided for in this act shall forever remain under the exclusive control of the said States, respectively, and no part of the proceeds arising from the sale or disposal of any lands herein granted for educational purposes shall be used for the support of any sectarian or denominational school, college, or university. The section of land granted by the act of June sixteenth, eighteen hundred and eighty,

Insane asylum, South Dakota.
Vol. 21, p. 290.

to the Territory of Dakota, for an asylum for the insane shall, upon the admission of said State of South Dakota into the Union, become the property of said State.

Penitentiaries. South Dakota.

SEC. 15. That so much of the lands belonging to the United States as have been acquired and set apart for the purpose mentioned in

Vol. 21, p. 378.

"An act appropriating money for the erection of a penitentiary in the Territory of Dakota," approved March second, eighteen hundred and eighty-one, together with the buildings thereon, be, and the same is hereby, granted, together with any unexpended balances of the moneys appropriated therefor by said act, to said State of South

North Dakota and Washington.

Dakota, for the purposes therein designated; and the States of North Dakota and Washington shall, respectively, have like grants for the same purpose, and subject to like terms and conditions as provided in said act of March second, eighteen hundred and eighty-one, for the Territory of Dakota. The penitentiary at Deer Lodge City, Montana, and all lands connected therewith and set apart and reserved therefor, are hereby granted to the State of Montana. **Montana.**

SEC. 16. That ninety thousand acres of land, to be selected and located as provided in sectio i ten of this act, are hereby granted to each of said States, except to the State of South Dakota, to which one hundred and twenty thousand acres are granted, for the use and support of agricultural colleges in said States, as provided in the acts of Congress making donations of lands for such purpose. **Lands for agricultural colleges. Vol. 12, p. 503.**

SEC. 17. That in lieu of the grant of land for purposes of internal improvement made to new States by the eighth section of the act of September fourth, eighteen hundred and forty-one, which act is hereby repealed as to the States provided for by this act, and in lieu of any claim or demand by the said States, or either of them, under the act of September twenty-eighth, eighteen hundred and fifty, and section twenty four hundred and seventy-nine of the Revised Statutes, making a grant of swamp and overflowed lands to certain States, which grant it is hereby declared is not extended to the States provided for in this act, and in lieu of any grant of saline lands to said States, the following grants of land are hereby made, to wit : **Lands for internal improvements. Vol. 5, p. 455. Vol. 9, p. 520. R. S,, sec. 2479, p. 453**

To the State of South Dakota: For the school of mines, forty thousand acres; for the reform school, forty thousand acres; for the deaf and dumb asylum, forty thousand acres ; for the agricultural college, forty thousand acres; for the university, forty thousand acres; for State normal schools, eighty thousand acres; for public buildings at the capital of said State, fifty thousand acres, and for such other educational and charitable purposes as the legislature of said State may determine, one hundred and seventy thousand acres; in all five hundred thousand acres. **South Dakota.**

To the State of North Dakota a like quantity of land as is in this section granted to the State of South Dakota, and to be for like purposes, and in like proportion as far as practicable. **North Dakota.**

To the State of Montana: For the establishment and maintenance of a school of mines, one hundred thousand acres; for State normal schools, one hundred thousand acres; for agricultural colleges, in addition to the grant hereinbefore made for that purpose, fifty thousand acres; for the establishment of a State reform school, fifty thousand acres; for the establishment of a deaf and dumb asylum, fifty thousand acres; for public buildings at the capital of the State, in addition to the grant hereinbefore made for that purpose, one hundred and fifty thousand acres. **Montana.**

To the State of Washington: For the establishment and maintenance of a scientific school, one hundred thousand acres; for State normal schools, one hundred thousand acres; for public buildings at the State capital, in addition to the grant hereinbefore made for that purpose, one hundred thousand acres; for State charitable, educational, penal, and reformatory institutions, two hundred thousand acres. **Washington.**

That the States provided for in this act shall not be entitled to any further or other grants of land for any purpose than as expressly provided in this act. And the lands granted by this section shall be held, appropriated, and disposed of exclusively for the purposes herein mentioned, in such manner as the legislatures of the respective States may severally provide. **No further grants. To be for specified uses only.**

SEC. 18. That all mineral lands shall be exempted from the grants made by this act. But if sections sixteen and thirty-six, or any subdivision or portion of any smallest subdivision thereof in any township shall be found by the Department of the Interior to be mineral lands, said States are hereby authorized and empowered to select, in legal subdivisions, an equal quantity of other unappropriated lands **Mineral lands exempt. Lands in lieu.**

in said States, in lieu thereof, for the use and the benefit of the common schools of said States.

Selections to be under direction of Secretary of the Interior. SEC. 19. That all lands granted in quantity or as indemnity by this act shall be selected, under the direction of the Secretary of the Interior, from the surveyed, unreserved, and unappropriated public lands of the United States within the limits of the respective States entitled thereto. And there shall be deducted from the number of acres of land donated by this act for specific objects to said States the number of acres in each heretofore donated by Congress to said Territories for similar objects.

Appropriation for convention expenses. SEC. 20. That the sum of twenty thousand dollars, or so much thereof as may be necessary, is hereby appropriated, out of any money in the Treasury not otherwise appropriated, to each of said Territories for defraying the expenses of the said conventions, except to Dakota, for which the sum of forty thousand dollars is so appropriated, twenty thousand dollars each for South Dakota and North Dakota, and for the payment of the members thereof, under the same rules and regulations and at the same rates as are now provided by law for the payment of the Territorial legislatures. Any money hereby appropriated not necessary for such purpose shall be covered into the Treasury of the United States.

Circuit and district courts established. SEC. 21. That each of said States, when admitted as aforesaid, shall constitute one judicial district, the names thereof to be the same as the names of the States, respectively; and the circuit and district courts therefor shall be held at the capital of such State for the time being, and each of said districts shall, for judicial purposes, until otherwise provided, be attached to the eighth judicial circuit, except Washington and Montana, which shall be attached to the ninth judicial circuit. There shall be appointed for each of said districts one **Judge, attorney, marshal.** district judge, one United States attorney, and one United States marshal. The judge of each of said districts shall receive a yearly salary of three thousand five hundred dollars, payable in four equal installments, on the first days of January, April, July, and October of each year, and shall reside in the district. There shall be ap-**Clerks.** pointed clerks of said courts in each district, who shall keep their offices at the capital of said State. The regular terms of said courts **Terms.** shall be held in each district, at the place aforesaid, on the first Monday in April and the first Monday in November of each year, and only one grand jury and one petit jury shall be summoned in both said circuit and district courts. The circuit and district courts for each of said districts, and the judges thereof, respectively, shall pos-**Jurisdiction, etc.** sess the same powers and jurisdiction, and perform the same duties required to be performed by the other circuit and district courts and judges of the United States, and shall be governed by the same laws **Powers of officers.** and regulations. The Marshal, district attorney, and clerks of the circuit and district courts of each of said districts, and all other officers and persons performing duties in the administration of justice therein, shall severally possess the powers and perform the duties lawfully possessed and required to be performed by similar officers in other districts of the United States; and shall, for the services **Fees.** they may perform, receive the fees and compensation allowed by law to other similar officers and persons performing similar duties in the State of Nebraska.

Cases pending in Supreme Court. SEC. 22. That all cases of appeal or writ of error heretofore prosecuted and now pending in the Supreme Court of the United States upon any record from the supreme court of either of the Territories mentioned in this act, or that may hereafter lawfully be prosecuted upon any record from either of said courts may be heard and deter-**Final proceedings.** mined by said Supreme Court of the United States. And the mandate of execution or of further proceedings shall be directed by the Supreme Court of the United States to the circuit or district court hereby established within the State succeeding the Territory from which such record is or may be pending, or to the supreme court of such State, as the nature of the case may require : *Proviso*, That the mandate of execution or of further proceedings shall, in cases arising in the Territory of Dakota, be directed by the Supreme Court of the United States to the circuit or district court of the district of South Dakota, or to the supreme court of the State of South Dakota, or to the circuit or district court of the district of North Dakota, or to the supreme court of the State of North Dakota, or to the supreme court of the Territory of North Dakota, as the nature of the case may require. And each of the circuit, district, and State courts, herein named, shall, respectively, be the successor of the supreme court of the Territory, as to all such cases arising within the limits embraced within the jurisdiction of such courts respectively with full power to proceed with the same, and award mesne or final process therein; and that from all judgments and decrees of the supreme court of either of the Territories mentioned in this act, in any case arising within the limits of any of the proposed States prior to admission, the parties to such judgment shall have the same right to prosecute appeals and writs of error to the Supreme Court of the United States as they shall have had by law prior to the admission of said State into the Union.

Proviso.

Dakota causes.

Supreme Territorial courts to be succeeded by circuit, district, and State courts.

Judgments prior to admission.

SEC. 23. That in respect to all cases, proceedings, and matters now pending in the supreme or district courts of either of the Territories mentioned in this act at the time of the admission into the Union of either of the States mentioned in this act, and arising within the limits of any such State, whereof the circuit or district courts by this act established might have had jurisdiction under the laws of the United States had such courts existed at the time of the commencement of such cases, the said circuit and district courts, respectively, shall be the successors of said supreme and district courts of said Territory; and in respect to all other cases, proceedings and matters pending in the supreme or district courts of any of the Territories mentioned in this act at the time of the admission of such Territory into the Union, arising within the limits of said proposed State, the courts established by such state shall, respectively, be the successors of said supreme and district Territorial courts; and all the files, records, indictments, and proceedings relating to any such cases, shall be transferred to such circuit, district, and State courts, respectively, and the same shall be proceeded with therein in due course of law; but no writ, action, indictment, cause or proceeding now pending, or that prior to the admission of any of the States mentioned in this act, shall be pending in any Territorial court in any of the Territories mentioned in this act, shall abate by the admission of any such State into the Union, but the same shall be transferred and proceeded with in the proper United States circuit, district or State court, as the case may be: *Provided, however*, That in all civil actions, causes, and proceedings, in which the United States is not a party, transfers shall not be made to the circuit and district courts of the United States, except upon written request of one of the parties to such action or proceeding filed in the proper court; and in the absence of such request such cases shall be proceeded with in the proper State courts.

Transfer of pending actions.

Circuit and district courts.

State courts.

Transfer of files, records, etc.

Writs, etc., not to abate.

Proviso. Request for trial in federal courts.

SEC. 24. That the constitutional conventions may, by ordinance, provide for the election of officers for full State governments, including members of the legislatures and Representatives in the Fifty-first Congress; but said State governments shall remain in abeyance until the States shall be admitted into the Union, respectively, as provided in this act. In case the constitution of any of said proposed States shall be ratified by the people, but not otherwise, the legislature thereof may assemble, organize, and elect two Senators of the United States; and the governor and secretary of state of such proposed State shall certify the election of the Senators and Representatives in the manner required by law; and when such State is admitted

Election for full State governments.

Election of Senators.

into the Union, the Senators and Representatives shall be entitled to be admitted to seats in Congress, and to all the rights and privileges of Senators and Representatives of other States in the Congress of the United States; and the officers of the State governments formed in pursuance of said constitutions, as provided by the constitutional conventions, shall proceed to exercise all the functions of such State officers; and all laws in force made by said Territories, at the time of their admission into the Union, shall be in force in said States, except as modified or changed by this act or by the constitutions of the States, respectively.

Existing laws.

Repeal provision.

SEC. 25. That all acts or parts of acts in conflict with the provisions of this act, whether passed by the legislatures of said Territories or by Congress, are hereby repealed.

Approved, February 22, 1889.

[Doc. No. 4]

Constitution of 1889

CONSTITUTION OF SOUTH DAKOTA—1889 * ᵃ

PREAMBLE

We, the people of South Dakota, grateful to Almighty God for our civil and religious liberties, in order to form a more perfect and independent government, establish justice, insure tranquility, provide for the common defense, promote the general welfare and preserve to ourselves and to our posterity the blessings of liberty, do ordain and establish this constitution for the State of South Dakota.

---

* Verified from " The Enabling Act and Constitution of South Dakota. . Constitution Adopted October 1, 1889. Free Press Company, Legal Blank and Law Publishers, Pierre, S. D." LXXIX pp.

Also the Revised Codes of South Dakota, 1903, pp. 1–26; also, Laws Passed at the Ninth Session of the Legislature of South Dakota. Aberdeen, S. D.: 1905. (Constitution as amended.)

See also the Constitution of the United States, Constitution of South Dakota, and Enabling Act admitting South Dakota. Hipple Printing Co. 1904. 31 pp.

ᵃ Adopted by popular vote October 1, 1889. Yeas, 70,131; nays, 3,267.

Article I

NAME AND BOUNDARY

§ 1. The name of the State shall be South Dakota.

§ 2. The boundaries of the State of South Dakota shall be as follows: Beginning at the point of intersection of the western boundary line of the State of Minnesota with the northern boundary line of the State of Iowa, and running thence northerly along the western boundary line of the State of Minnesota to its intersection with the 7th standard parallel; thence west on the line of the 7th standard parallel produced due west to its intersection with the 27th meridian of longitude west from Washington; thence south on the 27th meridian of longitude west from Washington to its intersection with the northern boundary line of the State of Nebraska; thence easterly along the northern boundary line of the State of Nebraska to its intersection with the western boundary line of the State of Iowa; thence northerly along the western boundary line of the State of Iowa to its intersection with the northern boundary line of the State of Iowa; thence east along the northern boundary line of the State of Iowa to the place of beginning.

Article II

DIVISION OF THE POWERS OF GOVERNMENT

The powers of the government of the state are divided into three distinct departments—the legislative, executive and judicial; and the powers and duties of each are prescribed by this constitution.

Article III

LEGISLATIVE DEPARTMENT

ᵃ§ 1. The legislative power shall be vested in a legislature, which shall consist of a senate and house of representatives.

§ 2. The number of members of the house of representatives shall not be less than seventy-five nor more than one hundred and thirty-five. The number of members of the senate shall not be less than twenty-five nor more than forty-five.

The sessions of the legislature shall be biennial except as otherwise provided in this constitution.

§ 3. No person shall be eligible to the office of senator who is not a qualified elector in the district from which he may be chosen, and a citizen of the United States, and who shall not have attained the age of twenty-five years, and who shall not have been a resident of the state or territory for two years next preceding his election.

No person shall be eligible to the office of representative who is not a qualified elector in the district from which he may be chosen, and a citizen of the United States, and who shall not have been a resident of the state or territory for two years next preceding his election, and who shall not have attained the age of twenty-five years.

ᵃ See amendment, 1898.

No judge or clerk of any court, secretary of state, attorney general, state's attorney, recorder, sheriff or collector of public moneys, member of either house of congress, or person holding any lucrative office under the United States or this state, or any foreign government, shall be a member of the legislature; *Provided*, that appointments in the militia, the offices of notary public and justice of the peace shall not be considered lucrative; nor shall any person holding any office of honor or profit under any foreign government or under the government of the United States, except postmasters whose annual compensation does not exceed the sum of three hundred dollars, hold any office in either branch of the legislature or become a member thereof.

§ 4. No person who has been, or hereafter shall be, convicted of bribery, perjury or other infamous crime, nor any person who has been, or may be collector or holder of public moneys who shall not have accounted for and paid over, according to law, all such moneys due from him, shall be eligible to the legislature or to any office in either branch thereof.

§ 5. The legislature shall provide by law for the enumeration of the inhabitants of the state in the year one thousand eight hundred and ninety-five and every ten years thereafter, and at its first regular session after each enumeration, and also after each enumeration made by authority of the United States, but at no other time, the legislature shall apportion the senators and representatives according to the number of inhabitants, excluding Indians not taxed and soldiers and officers of the United States army and navy; *Provided*, that the legislature may make an apportionment at its first session after the admission of South Dakota as a State.

§ 6. The terms of the office of the members of the legislature shall be two years; they shall receive for their services the sum of five dollars for each day's attendance during the session of the legislature, and five [a] cents for every mile of necessary travel in going to and returning from the place of meeting of the legislature on the most usual route.

Each regular session of the legislature shall not exceed sixty days, except in cases of impeachment, and members of the legislature shall receive no other pay or perquisites except per diem and mileage.

§ 7. The legislature shall meet at the seat of government on the first Tuesday after the first Monday of January at 12 o'clock m., in the year next ensuing the election of members thereof, and at no other time except as provided by this constitution.

§ 8. Members of the legislature and officers thereof, before they enter upon their official duties, shall take and subscribe the following oath or affirmation: I do solemnly swear (or affirm) that I will support the constitution of the United States and the constitution of the State of South Dakota, and will faithfully discharge the duties of (senator, representative or officer) according to the best of my abilities, and that I have not knowingly or intentionally paid or contributed anything, or made any promise in the nature of a bribe, to directly or indirectly influence any vote at the election at which I

---

[a] The mileage of members of the legislature was amended by reducing from "ten" to "five" cents per mile, by popular vote of 39,364 for and 11,236 against, at the general election of 1892.

was chosen to fill said office, and have not accepted, nor will I accept or receive, directly or indirectly, any money, pass, or any other valuable thing, from any corporation, company or person, for any vote or influence I may give or withhold on any bill or resolution, or appropriation, or for any other official act.

This oath shall be administered by a judge of the supreme or circuit court, or the presiding officer of either house, in the hall of the house to which the member or officer is elected, and the secretary of state shall record and file the oath subscribed by each member and officer.

Any member or officer of the legislature who shall refuse to take the oath herein prescribed shall forfeit his office.

Any member or officer of the legislature who shall be convicted of having sworn falsely to or violated his said oath, shall forfeit his office and be disqualified thereafter from holding the office of senator or member of the house of representatives or any office within the gift of the legislature.

§ 9. Each house shall be the judge of the election returns and qualifications of its own members.

A majority of the members of each house shall constitute a quorum, but a smaller number may adjourn from day to day, and may compel the attendance of absent members in such a manner and under such penalty as each house may provide.

Each house shall determine the rules of its proceedings, shall choose its own officers and employes and fix the pay thereof, except as otherwise provided in this constitution.

§ 10. The governor shall issue writs of election to fill such vacancies as may occur in either house of the legislature.

§ 11. Senators and representatives shall, in all cases except treason, felony or breach of the peace, be privileged from arrest during the session of the legislature, and in going to and returning from the same; and for words used in any speech or debate in either house, they shall not be questioned in any other place.

§ 12. No member of the legislature shall, during the term for which he was elected, be appointed or elected to any civil office in the State which shall have been created, or the emoluments of which shall have been increased during the term for which he was elected, nor shall any member receive any civil appointment from the governor, the governor and senate, or from the legislature during the term for which he shall have been elected, and all such appointments and all votes given for any such members for any such office or appointment shall be void; nor shall any member of the legislature during the term for which he shall have been elected, or within one year thereafter, be interested, directly or indirectly, in any contract with the State or any county thereof, authorized by any law passed during the term for which he shall have been elected.

§ 13. Each house shall keep a journal of its proceedings and publish the same from time to time, except such parts as require secrecy, and the yeas and nays of members on any question shall be taken at the desire of one-sixth of those present and entered upon the journal.

§ 14. In all elections to be made by the legislature the members thereof shall vote *viva voce* and their votes shall be entered in the journal.

§ 15. The sessions of each house and of the committee of the whole shall be open, unless when the business is such as ought to be kept secret.

§ 16. Neither house shall, without the consent of the other, adjourn for more than three days, nor to any other place than that in which the two houses shall be sitting.

§ 17. Every bill shall be read three several times, but the first and second reading may be on the same day, and the second reading may be by the title of the bill, unless the reading at length be demanded. The first and third readings shall be at length.

§ 18. The enacting clause of a law shall be: " Be it enacted by the Legislature of the State of South Dakota," and no law shall be passed unless by assent of a majority of all the members elected to each house of the legislature. And the question upon the final passage shall be taken upon its last reading, and the yeas and nays shall be entered upon the journal.

§ 19. The presiding officer of each house shall, in the presence of the house over which he presides, sign all bills and joint resolutions passed by the legislature, after their titles have been publicly read immediately before signing, and the fact of signing shall be entered upon the journal.

§ 20. Any bill may originate in either house of the legislature, and a bill passed by one house may be amended in the other.

§ 21. No law shall embrace more than one subject, which shall be expressed in its title.

§ 22. No act shall take effect until ninety days after the adjournment of the session at which it passed, unless in case of emergency (to be expressed in the preamble or body of the act) the legislature shall, by a vote of two-thirds of all the members elected of each house, otherwise direct.

§ 23. The legislature is prohibited from enacting any private or special laws in the following cases:

1. Granting divorces.

2. Changing the names of persons or places, or constituting one person the heir-at-law of another.

3. Locating or changing county-seats.

4. Regulating county and township affairs.

5. Incorporating cities, towns and villages or changing or amending the charter of any town, city or village, or laying out, opening, vacating or altering town plats, streets, wards, alleys and public grounds.

6. Providing for sale or mortgage of real estate belonging to minors or others under disability.

7. Authorizing persons to keep ferries across streams wholly within the State.

8. Remitting fines, penalties or forfeitures.

9. Granting to an individual, association or corporation any special or exclusive privilege, immunity or franchise whatever.

10. Providing for the management of common schools.

11. Creating, increasing or decreasing fees, percentages or allowances of public officers during the term for which said officers are elected or appointed.

But the legislature may repeal any existing special law relating to the foregoing subdivisions.

In all other cases where a general law can be applicable, no special law shall be enacted.

§ 24. The legislature shall have no power to release or extinguish, in whole or in part, the indebtedness, liability or obligation of any corporation or individual to this State or to any municipal corporation therein.

§ 25. The legislature shall not authorize any game of chance, lottery or gift enterprise, under any pretense, or for any purpose whatever.

§ 26. The legislature shall not delegate to any special commission, private corporation or association any power to make, supervise or interfere with any municipal improvement, money, property, effects, whether held in trust or otherwise, or levy taxes or to select a capital site or to perform any municipal functions whatever.

§ 27. The legislature shall direct by law in what manner and in what court suits may be brought against the State.

§ 28. Any person who shall give, demand, offer, directly or indirectly, any money, testimonial, privilege or personal advantage, anything of value to an executive or judicial officer or member of the legislature, to influence him in the performance of any of his official or public duties shall be guilty of bribery and shall be punished in such manner as shall be provided by law.

The offense of corrupt solicitation of members of the legislature, or of public officers of the State, or any municipal division thereof, and any effort toward solicitation of said members of the legislature or officers to influence their official action shall be defined by law, and shall be punishable by fine and imprisonment.

Any person may be compelled to testify in investigation or judicial proceedings against any person charged with having committed any offense of bribery or corrupt solicitation, and shall not be permitted to withhold his testimony upon the ground that it may criminate himself, but said testimony shall not afterward be used against him in any judicial proceeding except for bribery in giving such testimony, and any person convicted of either of the offenses aforesaid shall be disqualified from holding any office or position or office of trust or profit in this State.

ARTICLE IV

EXECUTIVE DEPARTMENT

§ 1. The executive power shall be vested in a governor who shall hold his office for two years. A lieutenant governor shall be elected at the same time and for the same term.

§ 2. No person shall be eligible to the office of governor or lieutenant governor except a citizen of the United States and a qualified elector of the State, who shall have attained the age of 30 years, and who shall have resided two years next preceding the election within the State or territory; nor shall he be eligible to any other office during the term for which he shall have been elected.

§ 3. The governor and lieutenant governor shall be elected by the qualified electors of the State at the time and places of choosing members of the legislature. The persons respectively having the highest number of votes for governor and lieutenant governor shall be elected; but if two or more shall have an equal and highest number of votes for governor or lieutenant governor, the two houses of the legislature at its next regular session shall forthwith, by joint ballot, choose one of such persons for said office. The returns of the election for governor and lieutenant governor shall be made in such manner as shall be prescribed by law.

§ 4. The governor shall be commander-in-chief of the military and naval forces of the State, except when they shall be called into the service of the United States, and may call out the same to execute laws, suppress insurrection and repel invasion. He shall have power to convene the legislature on extraordinary occasions. He shall, at the commencement of each session, communicate to the legislature by message, information of the condition of the State, and shall recommend such measures as he shall deem expedient. He shall transact all necessary business with the officers of the government, civil and military. He shall expedite all such measures as may be resolved upon by the legislature and shall take care that the laws be faithfully executed.

§ 5. The governor shall have power to remit fines and forfeitures, to grant reprieves, commutations and pardons after conviction for all offences except treason and cases of impeachment; provided, that in all cases where the sentence of the court is capital punishment, imprisonment for life or a longer term than two years, or a fine exceeding $200, no pardon shall be granted, sentence commuted or fine remitted except upon the recommendation in writing of a board of pardons, consisting of the presiding judge, secretary of state and attorney general, after full hearing in open session, and such recommendation, with the reasons therefor, shall be filed in the office of the secretary of state; but the legislature may by law in all cases regulate the manner in which the remission of fines, pardons, commutations and reprieves may be applied for. Upon conviction for treason he shall have the power to suspend the execution of the sentence until the case shall be reported to the legislature at its next regular session, when the legislature shall either pardon or commute the sentence, direct the execution of the sentence or grant a further reprieve. He shall communicate to the legislature at each regular session, each case of remission of fine, reprieve, commutation or pardon granted by him in the cases in which he is authorized to act without the recommendation of the said board of pardons, stating the name of the convict, the crime of which he is convicted, the sentence and its date, and the date of the remission, commutation, pardon or reprieve, with his reasons for granting the same.

§ 6. In case of death, impeachment, resignation, failure to qualify, absence from the State, removal from office, or other disability of the governor, the powers and duties of the office for the residue of the term, or until he shall be acquitted, or the disability removed, shall devolve upon the lieutenant governor.

§ 7. The lieutenant governor shall be president of the senate, but shall have only a casting vote therein. If during a vacancy of the office of governor the lieutenant governor shall be impeached, displaced, resign or die, or from mental or physical disease or otherwise become incapable of performing the duties of his office the secretary of state shall act as governor until the vacancy shall be filled or the disability removed.

§ 8. When any office shall from any cause become vacant and no mode is provided by the constitution or law for filling such vacancy, the governor shall have the power to fill such vacancy by appointment.

§ 9. Every bill which shall have passed the legislature shall, before it becomes a law, be presented to the governor. If he approve, he shall sign it; but if not, he shall return it with his objection to the house in which it originated, which shall enter the objection at large upon the journal and proceed to reconsider it. If after such reconsideration, two-thirds of the members present shall agree to pass the bill, it shall be sent together with the objection, to the other house, by which it shall likewise be reconsidered, and if it be approved by two-thirds of the members present, it shall become a law; but in all such cases the vote of both houses shall be determined by the yeas and nays, and the names of the members voting for and against the bill shall be entered upon the journal of each house respectively. If any bill shall [not] be returned by the governor within three days (Sundays excepted) after it shall have been presented to him, the same shall be a law, unless the legislature shall by its adjournment prevent its return, in which case it shall be filed, with his objection, in the office of the secretary of state within ten days after such adjournment, or become a law.

§ 10. The governor shall have power to disapprove of any item or items of any bill making appropriations of money embracing distinct items, and the part or parts of the bill approved shall be law, and the item or items disapproved shall be void, unless enacted in the following manner: If the legislature be in session he shall transmit to the house in which the bill originated, a copy of the item or items thereof disapproved, together with his objections thereto, and the items objected to shall be separately reconsidered, and each item shall then take the same course as is prescribed for the passage of bills over the executive veto.

§ 11. Any governor of this State who asks, receives, or agrees to receive any bribe upon any understanding that his official opinion, judgment or action shall be influenced thereby, or who gives or offers, or promises his official influence in consideration that any member of the legislature shall give his official vote or influence on any particular side of any question or matter upon which he may be required to act in his official capacity, or who menaces any member by the threatened use of his veto power or who offers or promises any member that he, the said governor, will appoint any particular person or persons to any office created or thereafter to be created in consideration that any member shall give his official vote or influence on any matter pending or thereafter to be introduced into either house of said legislature or who threatenes any member that he, the said governor, will remove any person or persons from any office or position with intent to in any manner influence the official action of said member, shall be punished in the manner now, or that may hereafter be, provided by law, and upon conviction thereon shall forfeit all right to hold or exercise any office of trust or honor in this State.

§ 12. There shall be chosen by the qualified electors of the State at the times and places of choosing members of the legislature, a secretary of state, auditor, treasurer, superintendent of public instruction, commissioner of school and public lands, and attorney general, who shall severally hold their offices for the term of two years, but no person shall be eligible to the office of treasurer for more than two terms consectively. They shall respectively keep their offices at the seat of government.

§ 13. The powers and duties of the secretary of state, auditor, treasurer, superintendent of public instruction, commissioner of school and public lands and attorney general shall be as prescribed by law.

ARTICLE V

JUDICIAL DEPARTMENT

§ 1. The judicial powers of the State, except as in this constitution otherwise provided, shall be vested in a supreme court, circuit courts, county courts and justices of the peace, and such other courts as may be created by law for cities and incorporated towns.

SUPREME COURT

§ 2. The supreme court, except as otherwise provided in this constitution, shall have appellate jurisdiction only, which shall be co-extensive with the State, and shall have a general superintending control over all inferior courts, under such regulations and limitations as may be prescribed by law.

§ 3. The supreme court and the judges thereof shall have power to issue writs of habeas corpus. The supreme court shall have power to issue writs of mandamus, quo warranto, certiorari, injunction and other original and remedial writs, with authority to hear and determine the same in such cases and under such regulations as may be prescribed by law, provided, however, that no jury trials shall be allowed in said supreme court, but, in proper cases, questions of fact may be sent by said court to a circuit court for a trial before a jury.

§ 4. At least two terms of the supreme court shall be held each year at the seat of government.

§ 5. The supreme court shall consist of three judges, to be chosen from districts by qualified electors of the State at large, as hereinafter provided.

§ 6. The number of said judges and districts may, after five years from the admission of this State under this constitution, be increased by law to not exceeding five.

§ 7. A majority of the judges of the supreme court shall be necessary to form a quorum or to pronounce a decision, but one or more of said judges may adjourn the court from day to day or to a day certain.

§ 8. The term of the judges of the supreme court who shall be elected at the first election under this constitution shall be four years. At all subsequent elections the term of said judges shall be six years.

§ 9. The judges of the supreme court shall by rules select from their number a presiding judge, who shall act as such for the term prescribed by such rule.

§ 10. No person shall be eligible to the office of judge of the supreme court unless he be learned in the law, be at least thirty years of age, a citizen of the United States, nor unless he shall have resided in this State or territory at least two years next preceding his election and at the time of his election be a resident of the district from which he is elected; but for the purpose of re-election, no such judge shall be deemed to have lost his residence in the district by reason of his removal to the seat of government in the discharge of his official duties.

§ 11. Until otherwise provided by law, the districts from which the said judges of the supreme court shall be elected shall be constituted as follows:

First District—All that portion of the State lying west of the Missouri river.

Second District—All that portion of the State lying east of the Missouri river and south of the second standard parallel.

Third District—All that portion of the State lying east of the Missouri river and north of the second standard parallel.

§ 12. There shall be a clerk and also a reporter of the supreme court, who shall be appointed by the judges thereof and who shall hold office during the pleasure of said judges, and whose duties and emoluments shall be prescribed by law, and by the rules of the supreme court not inconsistent with law. The legislature shall make provisions for the publication and distribution of the decisions of the supreme court, and for the sale of the published volumes thereof. No private person or corporation shall be allowed to secure any copyright to such decisions, but if any copyrights are secured they shall inure wholly to the benefit of the State.

§ 13. The governor shall have authority to require the opinions of the judges of the supreme court upon important questions of law involved in the exercise of his executive powers and upon solemn occasions.

CIRCUIT COURTS

§ 14. The circuit courts shall have original jurisdiction of all actions and causes, both at law and in equity, and such appellate jurisdiction as may be conferred by law and consistent with this constitution; such jurisdiction as to value and amount and grade of offense, may be limited by law. They and the judges thereof shall also have jurisdiction and power to issue writs of habeas corpus, mandamus, quo warranto, certiorari, injunction and other original and remedial writs, with authority to hear and determine the same.

§ 15. The state shall be divided into judicial circuits in each of which there shall be elected by the electors thereof one judge of the circuit court therein, whose term of office shall be four years.

§ 16. Until otherwise ordered by law, said circuits shall be eight in number and constituted as follows, viz.

First Circuit—The counties of Union, Clay, Yankton, Turner, Bon Homme, Hutchinson, Charles Mix, Douglas, Todd, Gregory, Tripp and Meyer.

Second Circuit—The counties of Lincoln, Minnehaha, McCook, Moody and Lake.

Third Circuit—The counties of Brookings, Kingsbury, Deuel,

Hamlin, Codington, Clark, Grant, Roberts, Day, and the Wahpeton and Sisseton reservation, except such portion of such reservation as lies in Marshall county.

Fourth Circuit—The counties of Sanborn, Davison, Aurora, Brule, Buffalo, Jerauld, Hanson, Miner, Lyman, Presho and Pratt.

Fifth Circuit—The counties of Beadle, Spink, Brown and Marshall.

Sixth Circuit—The counties of Hand, Hyde, Hughes, Sully, Stanley, Potter, Faulk, Edmunds, Walworth, Campbell and McPherson and all that portion of said state lying east of the Missouri river and not included in any other judicial circuit.

Seventh Circuit—The counties of Pennington, Custer, Fall River, Shannon, Washington, Ziebach, Sterling, Nowlin, Jackson, Washabaugh and Lugenbeel.

Eighth Circuit—The counties of Lawrence, Meade, Scobey, Butte, Delano, Pyatt, Dewey, Boreman, Schnasse, Rinehart, Martin, Choteau, Ewing and Harding and all that portion of said state west of the Missouri river and north of the Big Cheyenne river and the north fork of the Cheyenne river not included in any other judicial circuit.

§ 17. The legislature may, whenever two-thirds of the members of each house shall concur therein, increase the number of judicial circuits and the judges thereof, and divide the State into judicial circuits accordingly, taking care that they be formed of compact territory and be bounded by county lines, but such increase of number or change in the boundaries of districts shall not work the removal of any judge from his office during the term for which he shall have been elected or appointed.

§ 18. Writs of error and appeals may be allowed from the decisions of the circuit courts to the supreme court under such regulations as may be prescribed by law.

COUNTY COURTS

§ 19. There shall be elected in each organized county a county judge who shall be judge of the county court of said county, whose term of office shall be two years until otherwise provided by law.

§ 20. County courts shall be courts of record and shall have original jurisdiction in all matters of probate guardianship and settlement of estates of deceased persons, and such other civil and criminal jurisdiction as may be conferred by law; *Provided*, that such courts shall not have jurisdiction in any case where the debt, damage, claim or value of property involved shall exceed one thousand dollars except in matters of probate, guardianship and the estates of deceased persons. Writs of error and appeal may be allowed from county to circuit courts, or to the supreme court, in such cases and in such manner as may be prescribed by law; *Provided*, that no appeal or writ of error shall be allowed to the circuit court from any judgment rendered upon an appeal from a justice of the peace or police magistrate for cities or towns.

§ 21. The county court shall not have jurisdiction in cases of felony, nor shall criminal cases therein be prosecuted by indictment; but they may have such jurisdiction in criminal matters, not of the grade of felony, as the legislature may prescribe, and the prosecutions therein may be by information or otherwise as the legislature may provide.

JUSTICE OF THE PEACE

§ 22. Justices of the peace shall have such jurisdiction as may be conferred by law, but they shall not have jurisdiction of any cause wherein the value of the property or the amount in controversy exceeds the sum of one hundred dollars, or where the boundaries or title to real property shall be called in question.

POLICE MAGISTRATE

§ 23. The legislature shall have power to provide for creating such police magistrates for cities and towns as may be deemed from time to time necessary, who shall have jurisdiction of all cases arising under the ordinances of such cities and towns respectively, and such police magistrates may also be constituted ex-officio justices of the peace for their respective counties.

STATE'S ATTORNEY

§ 24. The legislature shall have power to provide for State's attorneys and to prescribe their duties and fix their compensation; but no person shall be eligible to the office of attorney general or State's attorney who shall not at the time of his election be at least 25 years of age and possess all the other qualifications for judges of circuit courts as prescribed in this article.

MISCELLANEOUS

§ 25. No person shall be eligible to the office of judge of the circuit or county courts unless he be learned in the law, be at least 25 years of age, and a citizen of the United States; nor unless he shall have resided in this state or territory at least one year next preceding his election, and at the time of his election be a resident of the county or circuit, as the case may be, for which he is elected.

§ 26. The judges of the supreme court, circuit courts and county courts shall be chosen at the first election held under the provisions of this constitution, and thereafter as provided by law, and the legislature may provide for the election of such officers on a different day from that on which an election is held for any other purpose and may, for the purpose of making such provision, extend or abridge the term of office for any such judges, then holding, but not in any case more than six months. The term of office of all judges of circuit courts, elected in the several judicial circuits throughout the state, shall expire on the same day.

§ 27. The time of holding courts within said judicial circuits and counties shall be as provided by law; but at least one term of the circuit court shall be held annually in each organized county, and the legislature shall make provision for attaching unorganized counties or territory to original counties for judicial purposes.

§ 28. Special terms of said courts may be held under such regulations as may be provided by law.

§ 29. The judges of the circuit courts may hold courts in other circuits than their own under such regulations as may be prescribed by law.

§ 30. The judges of the supreme court, circuit courts and county courts shall each receive such salary as may be provided by law, consistent with this constitution, and no such judge shall receive any compensation, perquisite or emoluments for or on account of his office in any form whatever except such salary; provided that county judges may accept and receive such fees as may be allowed under the land laws of the United States.

§ 31. No judge of the supreme court or circuit court shall act as attorney or counselor at law, nor shall any county judge act as an attorney or counselor at law in any case which is or may be brought into his court, or which may be appealed therefrom.

§ 32. There shall be a clerk of the circuit court in each organized county who shall also be clerk of the county court, and who shall be elected by the qualified electors of such county. The duties and compensation of said clerk shall be as provided by law and regulated by the rules of the court consistent with the provisions of law.

§ 33. Until the legislature shall provide by law for fixing the terms of courts, the judges of the supreme, circuit and county courts respectively shall fix the terms thereof.

§ 34. All laws relating to courts shall be general and of uniform operation throughout the state, and the organization, jurisdiction, power, proceedings and practice of all the courts of the same class or grade, so far as regulated by law, and the force and effect of the proceedings, judgments and decrees of such courts severally shall be uniform; *Provided, however,* that the legislature may classify the county courts according to the population of the respective counties and fix the jurisdiction and salary of the judges thereof, accordingly.

§ 35. No judge of the supreme or circuit courts shall be elected to any other than a judicial office or be eligible thereto, during the term for which he was elected such judge. All votes for either of them during such term for any elective office, except that of judge of the supreme court, circuit court or county court, given by the legislature or the people, shall be void.

§ 36. All judges or other officers of the supreme, circuit or county courts provided for in this article shall hold their offices until their successors respectively are elected or appointed and qualified.

§ 37. All officers provided for in this article shall respectively reside in the district, county, precinct, city or town for which they may be elected or appointed. Vacancies in the elective offices provided for in this article shall be filled by appointment until the next general election as follows: All judges of the supreme, circuit and county courts by the governor. All other judicial and other officers by the county board of the counties where the vacancy occurs; in cases of police magistrates, by the municipality.

§ 38. All process shall run in the name of the "State of South Dakota." All prosecutions shall be carried on in the name of and by authority of the "State of South Dakota."

Article VI

BILL OF RIGHTS

§ 1. All men are born equally free and independent, and have certain inherent rights, among which are those of enjoying and defending life and liberty, of acquiring and protecting property and the pursuit of happiness. To secure these rights governments are instituted among men, deriving their just powers from the consent of the governed.

§ 2. No person shall be deprived of life, liberty or property without due process of law.

§ 3. The right to worship God according to the dictates of conscience shall never be infringed. No person shall be denied any civil or political right, privilege or position on account of his religious opinions; but the liberty of conscience hereby secured shall not be so construed as to excuse licentiousness, the invasion of the rights of others, or justify practices inconsistent with the peace or safety of the State. No person shall be compelled to attend or support any ministry or place of worship against his consent, nor shall any preference be given by law to any religious establishment or mode of worship. No money or property of the state shall be given or appropriated for the benefit of any sectarian or religious society or institution.

§ 4. The right of petition, and of the people peaceably to assemble to consult for the common good and make known their opinions, shall never be abridged.

§ 5. Every person may freely speak, write and publish on all subjects, being responsible for the abuse of that right. In all trials for libel, both civil and criminal, the truth, when published, with good motives and for justifiable ends, shall be a sufficient defense. The jury shall have the right to determine the facts and the law under the direction of the court.

§ 6. The right of trial by jury shall remain inviolate, and shall extend to all cases at law without regard to the amount in controversy, but the legislature may provide for a jury of less than twelve in any court not a court of record, and for the decision of civil cases by three-fourths of the jury in any court.

§ 7. In all criminal prosecutions the accused shall have the right to defend in person and by counsel; to demand the nature and cause of the accusation against him; to have a copy thereof; to meet the witnesses against him face to face; to have compulsory process served for obtaining witnesses in his behalf, and to a speedy public trial by an impartial jury of the county or district in which the offense is alleged to have been committed.

§ 8. All persons shall be bailable by sufficient sureties, except for capital offenses when proof is evident or presumption great. The privilege of the writ of habeas corpus shall not be suspended, unless when in case of rebellion or invasion the public safety may require it.

§ 9. No person shall be compelled in any criminal case to give evidence against himself or be twice put in jeopardy for the same offense.

§ 10. No person shall be held for a criminal offense unless on the presentment or indictment of the grand jury, or information of the public prosecutor, except in cases of impeachment, in cases cognizable by county courts, by justices of the peace, and in cases arising in the army and navy, or in the militia when in actual service in time of war or public danger. *Provided*, that the grand jury may be modified or abolished by law.

§ 11. The right of the people to be secure in their persons, houses, papers and effects, against unreasonable searches and seizures, shall not be violated, and no warrant shall issued but upon probable cause supported by affidavit, particularly describing the place to be searched and the person or thing to be seized.

§ 12. No *ex post facto* law, or law imparing the obligation of contracts or making any irrevocable grant or privilege, franchise or immunity shall be passed.

§ 13. Private property shall not be taken for public use, or damaged, without just compensation as determined by a jury, which shall be paid as soon as it can be ascertained and before possession is taken. No benefit which may accrue to the owner as a result of an improvement made by any private corporation shall be considered in fixing the compensation for property taken or damaged. The fee of land taken for railroad tracks or other highways shall remain in such owners, subject to the use for which it is taken.

§ 14. No distinction shall ever be made by law between resident aliens and citizens in reference to the possession, enjoyment or descent of property.

§ 15. No person shall be imprisoned for debt arising out of or founded upon a contract.

§ 16. The military shall be in strict subordination to the civil power. No soldier in time of peace shall be quartered in any house without consent of the owner, nor in time of war except in the manner prescribed by law.

§ 17. No tax or duty shall be imposed without the consent of the people or their respresentatives in the legislature, and all taxation shall be equal and uniform.

§ 18. No law shall be passed granting to any citizen, class of citizens or corporation, privileges or immunities which upon the same terms shall not equally belong to all citizens or corporations.

§ 19. Elections shall be free and equal, and no power, civil or military, shall at any time interfere to prevent the free exercise of the right of suffrage. Soldiers in time of war may vote at their post of duty in or out of the state, under regulations to be prescribed by the legislature.

§ 20. All courts shall be open, and every man for an injury done him in his property, person or reputation, shall have remedy by due course of law, and right and justice administered without denial or delay.

§ 21. No power of suspending law shall be exercised, unless by the legislature or its authority.

§ 22. No person shall be attainted of treason or felony by the legislature.

§ 23. Excessive bail shall not be required, excessive fines imposed, nor cruel punishments inflicted.

§ 24. The right of the citizens to bear arms in defense of themselves and the state shall not be denied.

§ 25. Treason against the state shall consist only in levying war against it, or in adhering to its enemies, or in giving them aid and comfort. No person shall be convicted of treason unless on the testimony of two witnesses to the same overt act or confession in open court.

§ 26. All political power is inherent in the people and all free government is founded on their authority, and is instituted for their equal protection and benefit, and they have the right in lawful and constituted methods to alter or reform their forms of government in such manner as they may think proper. And the state of South Dakota is an inseparable part of the American Union, and the constitution of the United States is the supreme law of the land.

§ 27. The blessings of a free government can only be maintained by a firm adherence to justice, moderation, temperance, frugality and virtue, and by frequent recurrence to fundamental principles.

ARTICLE VII

ELECTIONS AND RIGHT OF SUFFRAGE

§ 1. Every male person resident of this State who shall be of the age of 21 years and upwards, not otherwise disqualified, belonging to either of the following classes, who shall be a qualified elector under the laws of the territory of Dakota at the date of the ratification of this constitution by the people, or who shall have resided in the United States one year, in this state six months, in the county thirty days and in the election precinct where he offers his vote ten days next preceding any election. shall be deemed a qualified elector at such election.

First. Citizens of the United States.

Second. Persons of foreign birth who shall have declared their intention to become citizens conformably to the laws of the United States upon the subject of naturalization.

§ 2. The legislature shall at its first session after the admission of the state into the Union, submit to a vote of the electors of the state the following question to be voted upon at the next general election held thereafter, namely: " Shall the word ' male ' be stricken from the article of the constitution relating to elections and the right of suffrage." If a majority of the votes cast upon that question are in favor of striking out said word " male " it shall be stricken out and there shall thereafter be no distinction between males and females in the exercise of the right of suffrage at any election in this state.

§ 3. All votes shall be by ballot, but the legislature may provide for numbering ballots for the purpose of preventing and detecting fraud.

§ 4. All general elections shall be biennial.

§ 5. Electors shall in all cases except treason, felony or breach of the peace, be privileged from arrest during their attendance at elections and in going to and returning from the same. And no elector shall be obliged to do military duty on the days of election except in time of war or public danger.

§ 6. No elector shall be deemed to have lost his residence in this state by reason of his absence on business of the United States or of this state, or in the military or naval service of the United States.

§ 7. No soldier, seaman or marine in the army or navy of the United States shall be deemed a resident of this state in consequence of being stationed therein.

§ 8. No person under guardianship, *non compos mentis* or insane, shall be qualified to vote at any election, nor shall any person convicted of treason or felony be qualified to vote at any election unless restored to civil rights.

§ 9. Any woman having the qualifications enumerated in Section 1, of this article, as to age, residence and citizenship, and including those now qualified by the laws of the territory, may vote at any election held solely for school purposes, and may hold any office in this state except as otherwise provided in this constitution.

Article VIII

EDUCATION AND SCHOOL LANDS

§ 1. The stability of a republican form of government depending on the morality and intelligence of the people, it shall be the duty of the legislature to establish and maintain a general and uniform system of public schools wherein tuition shall be without charge, and equally open to all; and to adopt all suitable means to secure to the people the advantages and opportunities of education.

§ 2. All proceeds of the sale of public lands that have heretofore been or may hereafter be given by the United States for the use of public schools in the State; all such per centum as may be granted by the United States on the sales of public lands; the proceeds of all property that shall fall to the State by escheat; the proceeds of all gifts or donations to the State for public schools or not otherwise appropriated by the terms of the gift; and all property otherwise acquired for public schools, shall be and remain a perpetual fund for the maintenance of public schools in the State. It shall be deemed a trust fund held by the State. The principal shall forever remain inviolate, and may be increased, but shall never be diminished, and the State shall make good all losses thereof which may in any manner occur.

§ 3. The interest and income of this fund, together with the net proceeds of all fines for violation of State laws and all other sums which may be added thereto by law, shall be faithfully used and applied each year for the benefit of the public schools of the State. and shall be for this purpose apportioned among and between all the several public-school corporations of the State in proportion to the number of children in each of school age, as may be fixed by law; and no part of the fund, either principal or interest, shall ever be diverted, even temporarily, from this purpose or used for any other purpose whatever than the maintenance of public schools for the equal benefit of all the people of the State.

§ 4. After one year from the assembling of the first legislature, the lands granted to the State by the United States for the use of public schools may be sold upon the following conditions and no other: Not more than one-third of all such lands shall be sold within the first five years, and no more than two-thirds within the first fifteen years after the title thereto is vested in the State and the legislature shall, subject to the provisions of this article, provide for the sale of the same.

The commissioner of school and public lands, the State auditor and the county superintendent of schools of the counties severally, shall constitute boards of appraisal and shall appraise all school lands within the several counties which they may from time to time select and designate for sale, at their actual value under the terms of sale. They shall take care to first select and designate for sale the most valuable lands; and they shall ascertain all such lands as may be of special and peculiar value, other than agricultural, and cause the proper sub-division of the same in order that the largest price may be obtained therefor.

§ 5. No land shall be sold for less than the appraised value, and in no case for less than ten dollars an acre. The purchaser shall pay one-fourth of the price in cash, and the remaining three-fourths as follows: One-fourth in five years, one-fourth in ten years, and one-fourth in fifteen years; with interest thereon at the rate of not less than six per centum per annum, payable annually in advance, but all such subdivided lands may be sold for cash, provided that upon payment of the interest for one full year in advance, the balance of the purchase price may be paid at any time. All sales shall be at public auction to the highest bidder, after sixty day's advertisement of the same in a newspaper of general circulation in the vicinity of the lands to be sold, and one at the seat of government. Such lands as shall not have been specially subdivided shall be offered in tracts of not more than eighty acres, and those so subdivided in the smallest subdivisions. All lands designated for sale and not sold within four years after appraisal, shall be reappraised by the board of appraisal as hereinbefore provided before they are sold.

§ 6. All sales shall be conducted through the office of the commissioner of school and public lands as may be prescribed by law, and returns of all appraisals and sales shall be made to said office. No sale shall operate to convey any right or title to any lands for sixty days after the date thereof, nor until the same shall have received the approval of the governor in such form as may be provided by law. No grant or patent for any such lands shall issue until final payment be made.

§ 7. All lands, money or other property donated, granted, or received from the United States or any other source for a university, agricultural college, normal schools or other educational or charitable institution or purpose, and the proceeds of all such lands and other property so received from any source, shall be and remain perpetual funds, the interest and income of which, together with the rents of all such lands as may remain unsold, shall be inviolably appropriated and applied to the specific objects of the original grants or gifts. The principal of every such fund may be increased, but shall never be diminished, and the interest and income only shall be used. Every such fund shall be deemed a trust fund held by the state, and the state shall make good all losses therefrom that shall in any manner occur.

§ 8. All lands mentioned in the preceding section shall be appraised and sold in the same manner and by the same officers and boards under the same limitations and subject to all the conditions as to price, sale and approval provided above for the appraisal and sale of lands for the benefit of public schools, but a distinct and separate account shall be kept by the proper officers of each of such funds.

§ 9. No lands mentioned in this article shall be leased except for pasturage and meadow purposes and at public auction after notice as hereinbefore provided in case of sale and shall be offered in tracts not greater than one section. All rents shall be payable annually in advance, and no term of lease shall exceed five years, nor shall any lease be valid until it receives the approval of the governor.

§ 10. No claim to any public lands by any tresspasser thereon by reason of occupancy, cultivation or improvement thereof, shall ever be recognized; nor shall compensation ever be made on account of any improvements made by such trespasser.

[a] § 11. The moneys of the permanent school and other educational funds shall be invested only in first mortgages upon good improved farm lands within this State as hereinafter provided, or in bonds of school corporations within the State, or in bonds of the United States, or of the State of South Dakota. The legislature shall provide by law the method of determining the amounts of said funds which shall be invested from time to time in such classes of securities respectively, taking care to secure continuous investments as far as possible.

All moneys of said funds which may from time to time be designated for investment in farm mortgages and in the bonds of school corporations shall for such purpose be divided among the organized counties of the State in proportion to population as nearly as provisions by law to secure continuous investments may permit. The several counties shall hold and manage the same as trust funds, and they shall be and remain responsible and accountable for the principal and interest of all such moneys received by them from the date of receipt until returned because not loaned; and in case of loss to any money so apportioned to any county, such county shall make the same good out of its common revenue. Counties shall invest said money in bonds of school corporations, or in first mortgages upon good improved farm lands within their limits respectively; but no farm loan shall exceed $500 to any one person, nor shall it exceed one-half the valuation of the lands as assessed for taxation, and the rate of interest shall not be less than 6 per centum per annum, and shall be such other and higher rate as the legislature may provide, and shall be payable semi-annually on the first days of January and July; provided, that whenever there are moneys of said funds in any county amounting to $1,000 that cannot be loaned according to the provisions of this section and any law pursuant thereto, the said sum may be returned to the state treasurer to be entrusted to some other county or counties, or otherwise invested under the provisions of this section.

Each county shall semi-annually, on the first day of January and July, render an account of the condition of the funds intrusted to it to the auditor of state, and at the same time pay to or account to the state treasurer for the interest due on all funds intrusted to it.

The legislature may provide by general law that counties may retain from interest collected in excess of six per centum per annum upon all said funds intrusted to them, not to exceed one per centum per annum. But no county shall be exempted from the obligation to make semi-annual payments to the state treasury of interest at the rate provided by law for such loans, except only said one per centum, and in no case shall the interest so to be paid be less than six per centum per annum.

The legislature shall provide by law for the safe investment of the permanent school and other educational funds, and for the prompt

[a] See amendment, 1902.

collection of interest and income thereof, and to carry out the objects and provisions of this section.

§ 12. The governor may disapprove any sale, lease or investment other than such as are intrusted to the counties.

§ 13. All losses to the permanent school or other educational funds of this state which shall have been occasioned by the defalcation, negligence, mismanagement or fraud of the agents or officers controlling and managing the same, shall be audited by the proper authorities of the state. The amount so audited shall be a permanent funded debt against the state in favor of the fund sustaining the loss upon which not less than six per centum of annual interest shall be paid. The amount of indebtedness so created shall not be counted as a part of the indebtedness mentioned in Article XIII, Sec. 2.

§ 14. The legislature shall provide by law for the protection of the school lands from trespass or unlawful appropriation, and for their defense against all unauthorized claims or efforts to divert them from the school fund.

§ 15. The legislature shall make such provisions by general taxation, and by authorizing the school corporations to levy such additional taxes, as with the income from the permanent school fund shall secure a thorough and efficient system of common schools throughout the state.

§ 16. No appropriation of lands, money or other property or credits to aid any sectarian school shall ever be made by the state, or any county or municipality within the state, nor shall the state or any county or municipality within the state accept any grant, conveyance, gift or bequest of lands, money or other property to be used for sectarian purposes, and no sectarian instruction shall be allowed in any school or institution aided or supported by the state.

§ 17. No teacher, State, county, township or district school officer shall be interested in the sale, proceeds or profits of any book, apparatus or furniture used or to be used in any school in this state, under such penalties as shall be provided by law.

Article IX

COUNTY AND TOWNSHIP ORGANIZATION

§ 1. The legislature shall provide by general law for organizing new counties, locating the county seats thereof and changing county lines; but no new county shall be organized so as to include an area of less than twenty-four congressional townships, as near as may be without dividing a township or fractional township, nor shall the boundaries of any organized county be changed so as to reduce the same to a less area than above specified. All changes in county boundaries in counties already organized, before taking effect, shall be submitted to the electors of the county or counties to be affected thereby, at the next general election thereafter and be adopted by a majority of the votes cast in each county at such election. Counties now organized shall remain as they are unless changed according to the above provisions.

§ 2. In counties already organized where the county seat has not been located by a majority vote, it shall be the duty of the county board to submit the location of the county seat to the electors of said county at a general election. The place receiving the majority of all votes cast at said election shall be the county seat of said county.

§ 3. Whenever a majority of the legal voters of any organized county shall petition the county board to change the location of the county seat which has once been located by a majority vote, specifying the place to which it is to be changed, said county board shall submit the same to the people of said county at the next general election, and if the proposition to change the county seat be ratified by two-thirds of the votes cast at said election, then the county seat shall be changed, otherwise not. A proposition to change the location of the county seat of any organized county shall not again be submitted before the expiration of four years.

§ 4. The legislature shall provide by general law for organizing the counties into townships, having due regard for congressional township lines and natural boundaries, and whenever the population is sufficient and the natural boundaries will permit, the civil townships shall be co-extensive with the congressional townships.

§ 5. In each organized county at the first general election held after the admission of the State of South Dakota into the Union, and every two years thereafter, there shall be elected a clerk of the court, sheriff, county auditor, register of deeds, treasurer, state's attorney, surveyor, coroner, and superintendent of schools, whose terms of office respectively shall be two years, and except the clerk of the court, no person shall be eligible for more than four years in succession to any of the above named offices.

§ 6. The legislature shall provide by general law for such county, township and district officers as may be deemed necessary, and shall prescribe the duties and compensation of all county, township and district officers.

§ 7. All county, township and district officers shall be electors in the county, township or district in which they are elected, provided that nothing in this section shall prevent the holding of school offices by any person, as provided in Section 9, Article VII.

Article X

MUNICIPAL CORPORATIONS

§ 1. The legislature shall provide by general laws for the organization and classification of municipal corporations. The number of such classes shall not exceed four, and the powers of each class shall be defined by general laws, so that no such corporations shall have any powers, or be subject to any restrictions other than those of all corporations of the same class. The legislature shall restrict the power of such corporations to levy taxes and assessments, borrow money and contract debts, so as to prevent the abuse of such power.

§ 2. Except as otherwise provided in this constitution, no tax or assessment shall be levied or collected, or debts contracted by municipal corporations, except in pursuance of law, for public purposes specified by law; nor shall money raised by taxation, loan or assessment for one purpose ever be diverted to any other.

§ 3. No street passenger railway or telegraph or telephone lines shall be constructed within the limits of any village, town or city without the consent of its local authorities.

Article XI

REVENUE AND FINANCE

§ 1. The legislature shall provide for an annual tax sufficient to defray the estimated ordinary expenses of the state, for each year, not to exceed in any one year two mills on each dollar of the assessed valuation of all taxable property in the state, to be ascertained by the last assessment made for state and county purposes.

And whenever it shall appear that such ordinary expenses shall exceed the income of the state for such year, the legislature shall provide for levying a tax for the ensuing year, sufficient with other sources of income, to pay the deficiency of the preceding year, together with the estimated expenses of such ensuing year. And for the purpose of paying the public debt, the legislature shall provide for levying a tax annually, sufficient to pay the annual interest and the principal of such debt within ten years from the final passage of the law creating the debt, provided that the annual tax for the payment of the interest and principal of the public debt shall not exceed in any one year two mills on each dollar of the assessed valuation of all taxable property in the state as ascertained by the last assessment made for the state and county purposes.

§ 2. All taxes to be raised in this state shall be uniform on all real and personal property, according to its value in money, to be ascertained by such rules of appraisement and assessment as may be prescribed by the legislature by general law, so that every person and corporation shall pay a tax in proportion to the value of his, her or its property. And the legislature shall provide by general law for the assessing and levying of taxes on all corporation property as near as may be by the same methods as are provided for assessing and levying of taxes on individual property.

§ 3. The power to tax corporations and corporate property shall not be surrendered or suspended by any contract or grant to which the state shall be a party.

§ 4. The legislature shall provide for taxing all moneys, credits, investments in bonds, stocks, joint stock companies, or otherwise; and also for taxing the notes and bills discounted or purchased, moneys loaned and all other property, effects or dues of every description, of all banks and of all bankers, so that all property employed in banking shall always be subject to a taxation equal to that imposed on the property of individuals.

§ 5. The property of the United States and of the state, county, and municpal corporations, both real and personal, shall be exempt from taxation.

§ 6. The legislature shall, by general law, exempt from taxation, property used exclusively for agricultural and horticultural societies, for school, religious, cemetery and charitable purposes, and personal property to any amount not exceeding in value two hundred dollars, for each individual liable to taxation.

§ 7. All laws exempting property from taxation, other than that enumerated in Sections 5 and 6 of this article, shall be void.

§ 8. No tax shall be levied except in pursuance of a law, which shall distinctly state the object of the same, to which the tax only shall be applied.

§ 9. All taxes levied and collected for state purposes shall be paid into the state treasury. No indebtedness shall be incurred or money expended by the state, and no warrant shall be drawn upon the state treasurer except in pursuance of an appropriation for the specific purpose first made. The legislature shall provide by suitable enactment for carrying this section into effect.

§ 10. The legislature may vest the corporate authority of cities, towns and villages with power to make local improvements by special taxation of contiguous property or otherwise. For all corporate purposes, all municipal corporations may be vested with authority to assess and collect taxes; but such tax shall be uniform in respect to persons and property within the jurisdiction of the body levying the same.

§ 11. The making of profit, directly or indirectly, out of state, county, city, town or school district money, or using the same for any purpose not authorized by law, shall be deemed a felony and shall be punished as provided by law.

§ 12. An accurate statement of the receipts and expenditures of the public moneys shall be published annually in such manner as the legislature may provide.

ARTICLE XII

PUBLIC ACCOUNTS AND EXPENDITURES

§ 1. No money shall be paid out of the treasury except upon appropriation by law and on warrant drawn by the proper officer.

§ 2. The general appropriation bill shall embrace nothing but appropriations for ordinary expenses of the executive, legislative and judicial departments of the state, the current expenses of state institutions, interest on the public debt, and for common schools. All other appropriations shall be made by separate bills, each embracing but one object, and shall require a two-thirds vote of all the members of each branch of the legislature.

§ 3. The legislature shall never grant any extra compensation to any public officer, employe, agent or contractor after the services shall have been rendered or the contract entered into, nor authorize the payment of any claims or part thereof created against the state, under any agreement or contract made without express authority of law, and all such unauthorized agreements or contracts shall be null and void; nor shall the compensation of any public officer be increased or diminished during his term of office; *Provided, however,* that the legislature may make appropriations for expenditures incurred in suppressing or repelling invasion.

§ 4. An itemized statement of all receipts and expenditures of the public moneys shall be published annually in such manner as the legislature shall provide, and such statements shall be submitted to the legislature at the beginning of each regular session by the governor with his message.

ARTICLE XIII

PUBLIC INDEBTEDNESS

§ 1. Neither the state nor any county, township or municipality shall loan or give its credit or make donations to or in aid of any individual, association or corporation except for the necessary sup-

port of the poor, nor subscribe to or become the owner of the capital
stock of any association or corporation, nor pay or become responsible
for the debt or liability of any individual, association or corporation;
Provided, that the state may assume or pay such debt or liability
when incurred in time of war for the defense of the state. Nor shall
the state engage in any work of internal improvement.

§ 2. For the purpose of defraying extraordinary expenses and making public improvements, or to meet casual deficits or failure in
revenue, the state may contract debts never to exceed, with previous
debts, in the aggregate $100,000, and no greater indebtedness shall be
incurred except for the purpose of repelling invasion, suppressing
insurrection, or defending the state or the United States in war, and
provision shall be made by law for the payment of the interest
annually, and the principal when due, by tax levied for the purpose,
or from other sources of revenue; which law providing for the payment of such interest and principal by such tax or otherwise shall be
irrepealable until such debt is paid; *Provided, however*, the State of
South Dakota shall have the power to refund the territorial debt
assumed by the State of South Dakota, by bonds of the State of
South Dakota.

§ 3. That the indebtedness of the State of South Dakota, limited
by Sec. 2 of this article shall be in addition to the debt of the Territory of Dakota assumed by and agreed to be paid by South Dakota.

§ 4. * The debt of any county, city, town, school district or other
subdivision, shall never exceed five per centum upon the assessed value
of the taxable property therein.

In estimating the amount of indebtedness which a municipality or
subdivision may incur, the amount of indebtedness contracted prior to
the adoption of this constitution shall be included.

§ 5. Any city, county, town, school district or any other subdivision
incurring indebtedness shall, at or before the time of so doing, provide for the collection of an annual tax sufficient to pay the interest
and also the principal thereof when due, and all laws or ordinances
providing for the payment of the interest or principal of any debt
shall be irrepealable until such debt be paid.

§ 6. In order that the payment of the debts and liabilities contracted or incurred by and in behalf of the Territory of Dakota may
be justly and equitably provided for and made, and in pursuance of
the requirements of an act of congress approved Feb. 22, 1889,
entitled, "An Act to provide for the division of Dakota into two states
and to enable the people of North Dakota, South Dakota, Montana
and Washington to form constitutions and state governments and to
be admitted into the Union on an equal footing with the original
states, and to make donations of public lands to such states," the
states of North Dakota and South Dakota, by proceedings of a joint
commission, duly appointed under said act, the sessions whereof were
held in Bismarck in said State of North Dakota, from July 16, 1889,
to July 31, 1889, inclusive, have agreed to the following adjustment
of the amounts of the debts and liabilities of the Territory of Dakota
which shall be assumed and paid by each of the States of North
Dakota and South Dakota respectively, towit:

---

* See amendments, 1896, 1902.

1. This agreement shall take effect and be in force from and after the admission into the Union, as one of the United States of America, of either the State of North Dakota or the State of South Dakota.

2. The words " State of North Dakota " wherever used in this agreement, shall be taken to mean the Territory of North Dakota, in case the State of South Dakota shall be admitted into the Union prior to the admission into the Union of the State of North Dakota; and the words " State of South Dakota " wherever used in this agreement, shall be taken to mean the Territory of South Dakota in case the State of North Dakota shall be admitted into the Union prior to the admission into the Union of the State of South Dakota.

3. The said State of North Dakota shall assume and pay all bonds issued by the Territory of Dakota to provide funds for the purchase, construction, repairs or maintenance of such public institutions, grounds or buildings as are located within the boundaries of North Dakota, and shall pay all warrants issued under and by virtue of that certain act of the legislative assembly of the Territory of Dakota, approved March 3, 1889, entitled, "An Act to provide for the refunding of outstanding warrants drawn on the capitol building fund."

4. The said State of South Dakota shall assume and pay all bonds issued by the Territory of Dakota to provide funds for the purchase, construction, repairs or maintenance of such public institutions, grounds or buildings as are located within the boundaries of South Dakota.

5. That is to say: The State of North Dakota shall assume and pay the following bonds and indebtedness, to-wit: Bonds issued on account of the hospital for insane at Jamestown, North Dakota, the face aggregate of which is two hundred and sixty-six thousand dollars; also, bonds issued on account of the North Dakota University at Grand Forks, North Dakota, the face aggregate of which is ninety-six thousand seven hundred dollars; also, bonds issued on account of the penitentiary at Bismarck, North Dakota, the face aggregate of which is ninety-three thousand six hundred dollars; also, refunding capitol building warrants dated April 1, 1889, eighty-three thousand five hundred and seven dollars and forty-six cents.

And the State of South Dakota shall assume and pay the following bonds and indebtedness, towit: Bonds issued on account of the Hospital for the Insane at Yankton, South Dakota, the face aggregate of which is two hundred and ten thousand dollars; also, bonds issued on account of the school for deaf mutes at Sioux Falls, South Dakota, the face aggregate of which is fifty-one thousand dollars; also, bonds issued on account of the university at Vermillion, South Dakota, the face aggregate of which is seventy-five thousand dollars; also, bonds issued on account of the penitentiary at Sioux Falls, South Dakota, the face aggregate of which is ninety-four thousand three hundred dollars; also, bonds issued on account of agricultural college at Brookings, South Dakota, the face aggregate of which is ninety-seven thousand five hundred dollars, also, bonds issued on account of the normal school at Madison, South Dakota, the face aggregate of which is forty-nine thousand four hundred dollars; also, bonds issued on account of [the] school of mines at Rapid City, South Dakota, the face aggregate of which is thirty-three thousand dollars; also, bonds issued on account of the reform school at Plankinton, South Dakota, the face aggregate of which is thirty thousand dollars; also, bonds issued on account of the normal school at Spearfish, South Dakota, the face aggregate of which is twenty-five thousand dollars; also, bonds issued on account of the soldier's home at Hot Springs, South Dakota, the face aggregate of which is forty-five thousand dollars.

6. The states of North Dakota and South Dakota shall pay one-half each of all liabilities now existing or hereafter and prior to the taking effect of this agreement incurred, except those heretofore and hereafter incurred on account of public institutions, grounds or buildings, except as otherwise herein specifically provided.

7. The State of South Dakota shall pay to the State of North Dakota forty-six thousand five hundred dollars on account of the excess of territorial appropriations for the permanent improvement of territorial institutions which under this agreement will go to South Dakota, and in full of the undivided one-half interest of North Dakota in the territorial library, and in full settlement of unbalanced accounts, and of all claims against the territory of whatever nature, legal or equitable, arising out of the alleged erroneous or unlawful taxation of the Northern Pacific railroad lands, and the payment of said amount shall discharge and exempt the State of South Dakota from all liability for or on account of the several matters hereinbefore referred to; nor shall either state be called upon to pay or answer to any portion of liability hereafter arising or accruing on account of transactions heretofore had, which liability would be a liability of the territory of Dakota had such territory remained in existence, and which liability shall grow out of matters connected with any public institution, grounds or buildings of the territory situated or located within the boundaries of the other state.

8. A final adjustment of accounts shall be made upon the following basis: North Dakota shall be charged with all sums paid on account of the public institutions, grounds or buildings located within its boundaries on account of the current appropriations since March 8, 1889; and South Dakota shall be charged with all sums paid on account of public institutions, grounds or buildings located within its boundaries on the same account and during the same time. Each state shall be charged with one-half of all other expenses of the territorial government during the same time. All moneys paid into the treasury during the period from March 8, 1889, to the time of taking effect of this agreement by any county, municipality or person within the limits of the proposed State of North Dakota, shall be credited to the State of North Dakota; and all sums paid into said treasury within the same time by any county, municipality or person within the limits of the proposed State of South Dakota shall be credited to the State of South Dakota; except that any and all taxes on gross earnings paid into said treasury by railroad corporations since the eighth day of March, 1889, based upon earnings of years prior to 1888, under and by virtue of the act of the legislative assembly of the Territory of Dakota, approved March 7, 1889, and entitled "An Act providing for the levy and collection of taxes upon property of railroad companies in this territory," being Chapter 107 of the Session Laws of 1889, (that is, the part of such sum going to the territory) shall be equally divided between the States of North Dakota and South Dakota, and all taxes heretofore or hereafter paid into the said treasury under and by virtue of the act last mentioned, based on the gross

earnings of the year 1888, shall be distributed as already provided by law, except that so much thereof as goes to the territorial treasury shall be divided as follows: North Dakota shall have so [much] thereof as shall be or has been paid by railroads within the limits of the proposed State of North Dakota and South Dakota so much thereof as shall be or has been paid by railroads within the limits of the proposed State of South Dakota. Each state shall be credited also with all balances of appropriations made by the seventeenth legislative assembly of the Territory of Dakota for the account of public institutions, grounds or buildings situated within its limits, remaining unexpended on March 8, 1889. If there be any indebtedness except the indebtedness represented by the bonds and refunding warrants hereinbefore mentioned, each state shall at the time of such final adjustments of accounts, assume its share of said indebtedness as determined by the amount paid on account of the public institutions, grounds or buildings of such state in excess of the receipts from counties, municipalities, railroad corporations or persons within the limits of said state as provided in this article; and if there should be a surplus at the time of such final adjustment, each state shall be entitled to the amounts received from counties, municipalities, railroad corporations or persons within its limits over and above the amount charged to it.

§ 7. And the State of South Dakota hereby obligates itself to pay such part of the debts and liabilities of the Territory of Dakota as is declared by the foregoing agreement to be its proportion thereof, the same as if such proportion had been originally created by said State of South Dakota as its own debt or liability.

§ 8. The territorial treasurer is hereby authorized and empowered to issue refunding bonds to the amount of $107,000, bearing interest not to exceed the rate of four per cent per annum, for the purpose of refunding the following described indebtedness of the Territory of Dakota, towit:

Seventy-seven thousand five hundred dollars 5 per cent bonds, dated May 1, 1883, issued for the construction of the west wing of the insane hospital at Yankton, and $30,000 6 per cent bonds, dated May 1, 1883, issued for permanent improvements [of the] Dakota penitentiary at Sioux Falls, such refunding bonds, if issued, to run for not more than twenty years, and shall be executed by the governor and treasurer of the territory, and shall be attested by the secretary under the great seal of the territory.

In case such bonds are issued by the territorial treasurer as hereinbefore set forth, before the first day of October, 1889, then upon the admission of South Dakota as a state it shall assume and pay said bonds in lieu of the aforesaid territorial indebtedness.

Article XIV

STATE INSTITUTIONS

§ 1. The charitable and penal institutions of the State of South Dakota shall consist of a penitentiary, insane hospital, a school for the deaf and dumb, a school for the blind and a reform school.

§ 2. The state institutions provided for in the preceding section shall be under the control of a state board of charities and corrections, under such rules and restrictions as the legislature shall provide; such board to consist of not to exceed five members, to be appointed by the governor and confirmed by the senate, and whose compensation shall be fixed by law.

* § 3. The state university, the agricultural college, the normal schools and all other educational institutions that may be sustained either wholly or in part by the state shall be under the control of a board of nine members, appointed by the governor and confirmed by the senate, to be designated the regents of education. They shall hold their office for six years, three retiring every second year.

The regents in connection with the faculty of each institution shall fix the course of study in the same.

The compensation of the regents shall be fixed by the legislature.

§ 4. The regents shall appoint a board of five members for each institution under their control, to be designated the board of trustees. They shall hold office for five years, one member retiring annually. The trustees of each institution shall appoint the faculty of the same, and shall provide for the current management of the institution, but all appointments and removals must have the approval of the regents to be valid. The trustees of the several institutions shall receive no compensation for their services, but they shall be reimbursed for all expenses incurred in the discharge of their duties, upon presenting an itemized account of the same to the proper officer. Each board of trustees at its first meeting shall decide by lot the order in which its members shall retire from office.

§ 5. The legislature shall provide that the science of mining and metallurgy be taught in at least one institution of learning under the patronage of the state.

Article XV

MILITIA

§ 1. The militia of the State of South Dakota shall consist of all able-bodied male persons residing in the state, between the ages of eighteen and forty-five years, except such persons as now are, or hereafter may be, exempted by the laws of the United States or of this state.

§ 2. The legislature shall provide by law for the enrollment, uniforming, equipment and discipline of the militia, and the establishment of volunteer and such other organizations or both, as may be deemed necessary for the protection of the state, the preservation of order and the efficiency and good of the service.

§ 3. The legislature in providing for the organization of the militia shall conform, as nearly as practicable, to the regulations for the government of the armies of the United States.

§ 4. All militia officers shall be commissioned by the governor and may hold their commissions for such period of time as the legislature may provide, subject to removal by the governor for cause, to be first ascertained by a court-martial pursuant to law.

§ 5. The militia shall in [all] cases except treason, felony or breach of the peace be privileged from arrest during their attendance at muster and elections and in going to and returning from the same.

---

* See amendment, 1896.

§ 6. All military records, banners and relics of the state, except when in lawful use, shall be preserved in the office of the adjutant general as an enduring memorial of the patriotism and valor of South Dakota; and it shall be the duty of the legislature to provide by law for the safe keeping of the same.

§ 7. No person having conscientious scruples against bearing arms shall be compelled to do military duty in time of peace.

Article XVI

IMPEACHMENT AND REMOVAL FROM OFFICE

§ 1. The house of representatives shall have the sole power of impeachment.

The concurrence of a majority of all members elected shall be necessary to an impeachment.

§ 2. All impeachments shall be tried by the senate. When sitting for that purpose the senator shall be upon oath or affirmation to do justice acording to law and evidence. No person shall be convicted without the concurrence of two-thirds of the members elected. When the governor or lieutenant governor is on trial the presiding judge of the supreme court shall preside.

§ 3. The governor and other state and judicial officers except county judges, justices of the peace and police magistrates shall be liable to impeachment for drunkenness, crimes, corrupt conduct, or malfeasance or misdemeanor in office, but judgment in such cases shall not extend further than to removal from office and disqualification to hold any office of trust or profit under the state. The person accused whether convicted or acquitted, shall nevertheless be liable to indictment, trial, judgment and punishment according to law.

§ 4. All officers not liable to impeachment shall be subject to removal for misconduct or malfeasance or crime or misdemeanor in office or for drunkenness or gross incompetency, in such manner as may be provided by law.

§ 5. No officer shall exercise the duties of his office after he shall have been impeached and before his acquittal.

§ 6. On trial of an impeachment against the governor the lieutenant governor shall not act as a member of the court.

§ 7. No person shall be tried on impeachment before he shall have been served with a copy thereof at least twenty days previous to the day set for trial.

§ 8. No person shall be liable to impeachment twice for the same offense.

Article XVII

CORPORATIONS

§ 1. No corporation shall be created or have its charter extended, changed or amended by special laws except those for charitable, educational, penal or reformatory purposes, which are to be and remain under the patronage and control of the state; but the legislature shall provide by general laws for the organization of all corporations hereafter to be created.

§ 2. All existing charters, or grants of special or exclusive privileges, under which a *bona fide* organization shall not have taken place and business been commenced in good faith at the time this constitution takes effect, shall thereafter have no validity.

§ 3. The legislature shall not remit the forfeiture of the charter of any corporation now existing nor alter or amend the same nor pass any other general or special law for the benefit of such corporation, except upon the condition that such corporation shall thereafter hold its charter subject to the provisions of this constituion.

§ 4. The exercise of the right of eminent domain shall never be abridged or so construed as to prevent the legislature from taking the property and franchises of incorporated companies and subjecting them to public use, the same as the property of individuals, and the exercise of the police power of the state shall never be abridged or so construed as to permit corporations to conduct their business in such manner as to infringe the equal rights of individuals or the general well being of the state.

§ 5. In all elections for directors or managers of a corporation each member or shareholder may cast the whole number of his votes for one candidate, or distribute them upon two or more candidates as he may prefer.

§ 6. No foreign corporation shall do any business in this state without having one or more known places of business and an authorized agent or agents in the same upon whom process may be served.

§ 7. No corporation shall engage in any business other than that expressly authorized in its charter, nor shall it take or hold any real estate except such as may be necessary and proper for its legitimate business.

§ 8. No corporation shall issue stocks or bonds except for money, labor done, or money or property actually received; and all fictitious increase of stock or indebtedness shall be void. The stock and indebtedness of corporations shall not be increased except in pursuance of general law nor without the consent of the persons holding the larger amount in value of the stock first obtained, at a meeting to be held after sixty days' notice given in pursuance of law.

§ 9. The legislature shall have the power to alter, revise or annul any charter of any corporation now existing and revokable at the taking effect of this constitution, or any that may be created, whenever in their opinion it may be injurious to the citizens of this state, in such a manner, however, that no injustice shall be done to the incorporators. No law hereafter enacted shall create, renew or extend the charter of more than one corporation.

§ 10. No law shall be passed by the legislature granting the right to construct and operate a street railroad within any city, town or incorporated village without requiring the consent of the local authorities having the control of the street or highway proposed to be occupied by said such street railroad.

§ 11. Any association or corporation organized for the purpose, or any individual, shall have the right to construct and maintain lines of telegraph in this state, and to connect the same with other lines; and the legislature shall by general law of uniform operation provide reasonable regulations to give full effect to this section. No telegraph company shall consolidate with or hold a controlling interest in the stock or bonds of any other telegraph company owning a competing line or acquire by purchase or otherwise any other competing line of telegraph.

§ 12. Every railroad corporation organized or doing business in this state under the laws or authority thereof shall have and maintain a public office or place in this state for the transaction of its business, where transfers of its stocks shall be made and in which shall be kept for public inspection books in which shall be recorded the amount of capital stock subscribed, and by whom; the names of the owners of its stock, and the amount owned by them respectively; the amount of stock paid in, and by whom; the transfers of said stock; the amount of its assets and liabilities, and the names and place of residence of its officers. The directors of every railroad corporation shall annually make a report, under oath, to the auditor of public accounts or some officer or officers to be designated by law, of all their acts and doings, which report shall include such matters relating to railroads as may be prescribed by law, and the legislature shall pass laws enforcing by suitable penalties the provisions of this section.

§ 13. The rolling stock and all other movable property belonging to any railroad company or corporation in this state shall be considered personal property, and shall be liable to execution and sale in the same manner as the personal property of individuals, and the legislature shall pass no laws exempting such property from execution and sale.

§ 14. No railroad corporation shall consolidate its stock, property or franchises with any other railroad corporation owning a parallel or competing line; and in no case shall any consolidation take place except upon public notice given out, at least sixty days to all stockholders in such manner as may be provided by law. Any attempt to evade the provisions of this section, by any railroad corporation, by lease or otherwise, shall work a forfeiture of its charter.

§ 15. Railways heretofore constructed or that may hereafter be constructed, in this state, are hereby declared public highways, and all railroads and transportation companies are declared to be common carriers and subject to legislative control; and the legislature shall have power to enact laws regulating and controlling the rates of charges for the transportation of passengers and freight as such common carrier from one point to another in this state.

§ 16. Any association or corporation organized for the purpose shall have the right to construct and operate a railroad between any points within this state, and to connect at the state line with railroads of other states. Every railroad company shall have the right with its road to intersect, connect with, or cross any other railroad, and shall receive and transport each the other's passengers, tonnage and cars, loaded or empty, without delay or discrimination.

§ 17. The legislature shall pass laws to correct abuses and prevent discrimination and extortion in the rates of freight and passenger tariffs on the different railroads in this state, and enforce such laws by adequate penalties, to the extent, if necessary for that purpose, of forfeiture of their property and franchises.

§ 18. Municipal and other corporations and individuals invested with the privilege of taking private property for public use shall make just compensation for property taken, injured or destroyed, by the construction or enlargement of their works, highways or improvements, which compensation shall be paid or secured before such taking, injury or destruction. The legislature is hereby prohibited from depriving any person of an appeal from any preliminary assessment of damages against any such corporation or individuals made by viewers or otherwise, and the amount of such damages in all cases of appeal shall, on the demand of either party, be determined by a jury as in other civil cases.

§ 19. The term "corporations" as used in this article shall be construed to include all joint stock companies or associations having any of the powers or privileges of corporations not possessed by individuals or partnerships.*

Article XVIII

BANKING AND CURRENCY

§ 1. If a general banking law shall be enacted it shall provide for the registry and countersigning by an officer of this State of all bills or paper credit designed to circulate as money, and require security to the full amount thereof, to be deposited with the state treasurer, in the approved securities of the state or of the United States, to be rated at ten per centum below their par value, and in case of their depreciation the deficiency shall be made good by depositing additional securities.

§ 2. Every bank, banking company or corporation shall be required to cease all banking operation within twenty years from the time of its organization, and promptly thereafter close its business, but shall have corporate capacity to sue or be sued until its business is fully closed, but the legislature may provide by general law for the reorganization of such banks.

§ 3. The shareholders or stockholders of any banking corporation shall be held individually responsible and liable for all contracts, debts and engagements of such corporation to the extent of the amount of their stock therein, at the par value thereof, in addition to the amount invested in such shares or stock; and such individual liabilities shall continue for one year after any transfer or sale of stock by any stockholder or stockholders.

Article XIX

CONGRESSIONAL AND LEGISLATIVE APPORTIONMENT

§ 1. Until otherwise provided by law, the members of the house of representatives of the United States, apportioned to this state, shall be elected by the state at large.

§ 2. Until otherwise provided by law, the senatorial and representative districts shall be formed, and the senators and representatives shall be apportioned, as follows:

SENATORIAL DISTRICTS

District No. 1 shall consist of the county of Union and be entitled to one senator.

District No. 2 shall consist of the county of Clay, and be entitled to one senator.

---

* For new section, 20, see amendment, 1896.

District No. 3 shall consist of the county of Yankton, and be entitled to one senator.

District No. 4 shall consist of the county of Bon Homme, and be entitled to one senator.

District No. 5 shall consist of the county of Lincoln, and be entitled to one senator.

District No. 6 shall consist of the county of Turner, and be entitled to one senator.

District No. 7 shall consist of the county of Hutchinson, and be entitled to one senator.

District No. 8 shall consist of the counties of Charles Mix and Douglas, and be entitled to one senator.

District No. 9 shall consist of the county of Minnehaha, and be entitled to two senators.

District No. 10 shall consist of the county of McCook, and be entitled to one senator.

District No. 11 shall consist of the county of Hanson, and be entitled to one senator.

District No. 12 shall consist of the county of Davison, and be entitled to one senator.

District No. 13 shall consist of the county of Aurora, and be entitled to one senator.

District No. 14 shall consist of the county of Brule, and be entitled to one senator.

District No. 15 shall consist of the county of Moody, and be entitled to one senator.

District No. 16 shall consist of the county of Lake, and be entitled to one senator.

District No. 17 shall consist of the county of Miner, and be entitled to one senator.

District No. 18 shall consist of the county of Sanborn, and be entitled to one senator.

District No. 19 shall consist of the counties of Jerauld and Buffalo, and be entitled to one senator.

District No. 20 shall consist of the county of Brookings, and be entitled to one senator.

District No. 21 shall consist of the county of Kingsbury, and be entitled to one senator.

District No. 22 shall consist of the county of Beadle, and be entitled to one senator.

District No. 23 shall consist of the county of Hand, and be entitled to one senator.

District No. 24 shall consist of the counties of Hughes and Stanley, and be entitled to one senator.

District No. 25 shall consist of the counties of Sully and Hyde, and be entitled to one senator.

District No. 26 shall consist of the county of Deuel, and be entitled to one senator.

District No. 27 shall consist of the county of Hamlin, and be entitled to one senator.

District No. 28 shall consist of the county of Codington, and be entitled to one senator.

District No. 29 shall consist of the county of Clark, and be entitled to one senator.

District No. 30 shall consist of the county of Spink, and be entitled to one senator.

District No. 31 shall consist of the county of Grant, and be entitled to one senator.

District No. 32 shall consist of the county of Day, and be entitled to one senator.

District No. 33 shall consist of the county of Brown, and be entitled to two senators.

District No. 34 shall consist of the counties of Marshall and Roberts, and be entitled to one senator.

District No. 35 shall consist of the counties of Faulk and Potter, and be entitled to one senator.

District No. 36 shall consist of the counties of Edmunds and Walworth, and be entitled to one senator.

District No. 37 shall consist of the counties of McPherson and Campbell, and be entitled to one senator.

District No. 38 shall consist of the county of Lawrence, and be entitled to one senator.

District No. 39 shall consist of the county of Pennington, and be entitled to one senator.

District No. 40 shall consist of the counties of Meade and Butte, and be entitled to one senator.

District No. 41 shall consist of the counties of Custer and Fall River, and be entitled to one Senator.

REPRESENTATIVE DISTRICTS

District No. 1 shall consist of the county of Union, and be entitled to two representatives.

District No. 2 shall consist of the county of Clay, and be entitled to two representatives.

District No. 3 shall consist of the county of Yankton, and be entitled to three representatives.

District No. 4 shall consist of the county of Lincoln and be entitled to two representatives.

District No. 5 shall consist of the county of Turner, and be entitled to three representatives.

District No. 6 shall consist of the county of Hutchinson, and be entitled to three representatives.

District No. 7 shall consist of the county of Bon Homme, and be entitled to two representatives.

District No. 8 shall consist of the county of Douglas, and be entitled to one representative.

District No. 9 shall consist of the county of Charles Mix, and be entitled to one representative.

District No. 10 shall consist of the county of Minnehaha, and be entitled to five representatives.

District No. 11 shall consist of the county of McCook, and be entitled to two representatives.

District No. 12 shall consist of the county of Hanson, and be entitled to one representative.

District No. 13 shall consist of the county of Davison, and be entitled to one representative.

District No. 14 shall consist of the county of Sanborn, and be entitled to one representative.

District No. 15 shall consist of the county of Aurora, and be entitled to one representative.

District No. 16 shall consist of the counties of Jerauld and Buffalo, and be entitled to one representative.

District No. 17 shall consist of the county of Lake, and be entitled to three representatives.

District No. 18 shall consist of the county of Miner, and be entitled to two representatives.

District No. 19 shall consist of the county of Sanborn, and be entitled to two representatives.

District No. 20 shall consist of the county of Jerauld, and be entitled to one representative.

District No. 21 shall consist of the county of Buffalo, and be entitled to one representative.

District No. 22 shall consist of the county of Brookings, and be entitled to three representatives.

District No. 23 shall consist of the county of Kingsbury, and be entitled to three representatives.

District No. 24 shall consist of the county of Beadle, and be entitled to five representatives.

District No. 25 shall consist of the county of Hand, and be entitled to three representatives.

District No. 26 shall consist of the county of Hyde, and be entitled to one representative.

District No. 27 shall consist of the county of Hughes, and be entitled to one representative.

District No. 28 shall consist of the county of Sully, and be entitled to one representative.

District No. 29 shall consist of the county of Deuel, and be entitled to two representatives.

District No. 30 shall consist of the county of Hamlin, and be entitled to two representatives.

District No. 31 shall consist of the county of Codington, and be entitled to three representatives.

District No. 32 shall consist of the county of Clark, and be entitled to three representatives.

District No. 33 shall consist of the county of Spink, and be entitled to five representatives.

District No. 34 shall consist of the county of Faulk, and be entitled to two representatives.

District No. 35 shall consist of the county of Potter, and be entitled to one representative.

District No. 36 shall consist of the county of Grant, and be entitled to two representatives.

District No. 37 shall consist of the county of Roberts, and be entitled to one representative.

District No. 38 shall consist of the county of Day, and be entitled to three representatives.

District No. 39 shall consist of the county of Marshall and be entitled to two representatives.

District No. 40 shall consist of the county of Brown, and be entitled to eight representatives.

District No. 41 shall consist of the county of Potter, and be entitled to one representative.

District No. 42 shall consist of the county of Faulk, and be entitled to one representative.

District No. 43 shall consist of the county of Custer, and be entitled to one representative.

District No. 44 shall consist of the county of Fall River, and be entitled to one representative.

District No. 45 shall consist of the county of Pennington, and be entitled to two representatives.

District No. 46 shall consist of the county of Meade, and be entitled to one representative.

District No. 47 shall consist of the county of Butte, and be entitled to one representative.

District No. 48 shall consist of the county of Lawrence, and be entitled to three representatives.

ARTICLE XX

SEAT OF GOVERNMENT

§ 1. The question of the location of the temporary seat of government shall be submitted to a vote of the electors of the proposed State of South Dakota, in the same manner and at the same election at which this constitution shall be submitted, and the place receiving the highest number of votes shall be the temporary seat of government until a permanent seat of government shall be established as hereinafter provided.

§ 2. The legislature, at its first session after the admission of this state, shall provide for the submission of the question of a place for a permanent seat of government to the qualified voters of the state at the next general election thereafter, and that place which receives a majority of all the votes cast upon that question shall be the permanent seat of government.

§ 3. Should no place voted for at said election have a majority of all votes cast upon this question, the governor shall issue his proclamation for an election to be held in the same manner at the next general election to choose between the two places having received the highest number of votes cast at the first election on this question. This election shall be conducted in the same manner as the first election for the permanent seat of government, and the place receiving a majority of all the votes cast upon this question shall be the permanent seat of government.

ARTICLE XXI

MISCELLANEOUS

§ 1. *Seal and coat of arms.*] The design of the great seal of South Dakota shall be as follows: A circle within which shall appear in the left foreground a smelting furnace and other features of mining work. In the left background a range of hills. In the right foreground a farmer at his plow. In the right background a herd of cattle and a field of corn. Between the two parts thus described shall appear a river bearing a steamboat. Properly divided between the upper and lower edges of the circle shall appear the legend

"Under God the People Rule," which shall be the motto of the State of South Dakota. Exterior to this circle and within a circumscribed circle shall appear, in the upper part, the words "State of South Dakota." In the lower part the words "Great Seal," and the date in Arabic numerals of the year in which the state shall be admitted to the Union.

COMPENSATION OF PUBLIC OFFICERS

§ 2. The governor shall receive an annual salary of two thousand five hundred dollars; the judges of the supreme court shall each receive an annual salary of two thousand five hundred dollars; the judges of the circuit courts shall each receive an annual salary of two thousand dollars; *Provided*, that the legislature may, after the year one thousand eight hundred and ninety, increase the annual salary of the governor and each of the judges of the supreme court to three thousand dollars, and the annual salary of each of the circuit court judges to two thousand five hundred dollars.

The secretary of state, state treasurer and state auditor shall each receive an annual salary of one thousand eight hundred dollars; the commissioner of school and public lands shall receive an annual salary of one thousand eight hundred dollars; the superintendent of public instruction shall receive an annual salary of one thousand eight hundred dollars; the attorney general shall receive an annual salary of one thousand dollars; the compensation of the lieutenant governor shall be double the compensation of a state senator.

They shall receive no fees or perquisites whatever for the performance of any duties connected with their offices. It shall not be competent for the legislature to increase the salaries of the officers named in this article except as herein provided.

§ 3. *Oath of office.* Every person elected or appointed to any office in this state, except such inferior offices as may be by law exempted, shall, before entering upon the duties thereof, take an oath or affirmation to support the constitution of the United States and of this state, and faithfully to discharge the duties of his office.

§ 4. *Exemptions.*] The right of the debtor to enjoy the comforts and necessaries of life shall be recognized by wholesome laws; exempting from forced sale a homestead, the value of which shall be limited and defined by law, to all heads of families, and a reasonable amount of personal property, the kind and value of which to be fixed by general law.

§ 5. *Rights of married women.*] The real and personal property of any women in this state acquired before marriage, and all property to which she may after marriage become in any manner rightfully entitled, shall be her separate property, and shall not be liable for the debts of her husband.

ARTICLE XXII

COMPACT WITH THE UNITED STATES

The following articles shall be irrevocable without the consent of the United States and the people of the State of South Dakota expressed by their legislative assembly:

First—That perfect toleration of religious sentiment shall be secured, and that no inhabitant of this state shall ever be molested in before the organization of the judicial department under this constitution issued under the authority of the Territory of Dakota, within the boundary of this state, shall be as valid as if issued in the name of the State of South Dakota.

§ 2. That all fines, penalties, forfeitures and escheats accruing to the Territory of Dakota, within the boundary of the State of South Dakota, shall accrue to the use of said state.

§ 3. That all recognizances, bonds, obligations or other undertakings, heretofore taken, or which may be taken before the organization of the judicial department under this constitution shall remain valid, and shall pass over to, and may be prosecuted in the name of the State of South Dakota; and all bonds, obligations or undertakings executed to this territory, within the boundaries of the State of South Dakota, or to any officer in his official capacity, shall pass over to the proper state authority, and to their successors in office, for the uses therein respectively expressed, and may be sued for and recovered accordingly.

All criminal prosecutions and penal actions, which have arisen, or which may arise before the organization of the judicial department under this constitution, and which shall then be pending, may be prosecuted to judgment and executed in the name of the state.

§ 4. All officers, civil and military, now holding their offices and appointments in this territory under the authority of the United States, or under the authority of the Territory of Dakota, shall continue to hold and exercise their respective offices and appointments until superseded under this constitution; *Provided*, that the provisions of the above sections shall be subject to the provisions of the act of congress providing for the admission of the State of South Dakota, approved by the president of the United States on February 22, 1889.

§ 5. This constitution shall be submitted for adoption or rejection to a vote of the electors qualified by the laws of this territory to vote at all elections, at the election to be held on Tuesday, Oct. 1, 1889.

At the said election the ballots shall be in the following form:

For the constitution: Yes. No.

For prohibition: Yes. No.

For minority representation: Yes. No.

As a heading to each of said ballots shall be printed on each ballot the following instructions to voters:

All persons desiring to vote for the constitution, or for any of the articles submitted to a separate vote, must erase the word " No."

All persons who desire to vote against the constitution, or against any article submitted separately, must erase the word " Yes."

Any person may have printed or written on his ballot only the words " For the Constitution," or "Against the Constitution," and such ballots shall be counted for, or against the constitution accordingly. The same provision shall apply to articles submitted separately.

In addition to the foregoing election for the constitution and for the article submitted by this convention for a separate vote thereon, an election shall be held at the same time and places, by the said qualified electors, for the following state officers, to be voted for on the same ballot as above provided for votes on the constitution and separate articles, towit:

A governor, lieutenant governor, secretary of state, auditor, treasurer, attorney general, superintendent of public instruction, commissioner of school and public lands, judges of the supreme, circuit and county courts, representatives in congress, state senators, and representatives in the legislature.

All the elections above provided for shall be held in the same manner and form as provided for the election for the adoption or rejection of the constitution. And the names of all the officers above specified to be voted for at such election shall be written or printed upon the same ballots as the vote for or against the constitution.

The judges of election in counting the ballots voted at such election shall count all the affirmative ballots upon the constitution as votes for the constitution; and they shall count all the negative ballots voted at said election upon the constitution as votes against the constitution; and ballots voted at said election upon which neither of said words " Yes " or " No " following the words " For the Constitution " are erased, shall not be counted upon such proposition. And they shall count all affirmative ballots so voted upon the article on prohibition, separately submitted, as votes for such article, and they shall count all negative ballots so voted upon such article, as votes against such article; and ballots upon which neither the words " Yes " or " No " following the words " For Prohibition " are erased, shall not be counted upon such proposition; and they shall count all the affirmative ballots so voted upon the article on minority representation, separately submitted, as votes for such article. And they shall count all negative ballots so voted upon such article as votes against such article; and ballots upon which neither of said words " Yes " or " No " following the words " For Minority Representation " are erased, shall not be counted upon such proposition.

If it shall appear in accordance with the returns hereinafter provided for, that a majority of the votes polled at such election, for and against the constitution, are for the constitution, then this constitution shall be the constitution of the State of South Dakota. If it shall appear, according to the returns hereinafter provided for, that a majority of all votes cast at said election for and against " Prohibition " are for prohibition, then said Article XXIV shall be and form a part of this constitution, and be in full force and effect as such from date of said election, but if a majority of said votes shall appear, according to said returns to be against prohibition, then Article XXIV shall be null and void and shall not be a part of this constitution. And if it appear, according to the returns hereinafter provided for, that a majority of all votes cast at said election for and against " Minority Representation " are for minority representation, then Article XXV shall be and form a part of said constitution, and be in full force and effect as such from the date of said election; but if a majority of said votes shall appear, according to said returns, to be against minority representation, then said Article XXV shall be null and void and shall not be a part of this constitution.

At such election the person voted for, for any one of the offices to be filled at such election, who shall receive the highest number of votes cast at said election, shall be declared elected to said office.

§ 6. At the same time and places of election there shall be held by said qualified electors an election for the place of the temporary seat of government.

On each ballot, and on the same ballot on which are the matters voted for or against, as hereinbefore provided, shall be written or printed the words "For Temporary Seat of Government," (Here insert the name of the city, town or place, to be voted for.)

And upon the canvass and return of the vote, made as hereinafter provided for, the name of the city, town or place, which shall have received the largest number of votes for said temporary seat of government, shall be declared by the governor, chief justice and secretary of the Territory of Dakota, or by any two of them, at the same time that they shall canvass the vote for or against the constitution, together with the whole number of votes cast for each city, town or place, and the officers above named, shall immediately after the result of said election shall have been ascertained, issue a proclamation directing the legislature elected at said election to assemble at said city, town or place so selected, on the day fixed by this schedule and ordinance.

§ 7. The election provided for herein shall be under the provisions of the constitution herewith submitted, and shall be conducted in all respects as elections are conducted under the general laws of the Territory of Dakota, except as herein provided. No mere technicalities or informalities in the manner or form of election, or neglect of any officer to perform his duty with regard thereto, shall be deemed to vitiate or avoid the same, it being the true intent and object of this ordinance to ascertain and give effect to the true will of the people of the State of South Dakota, as expressed by their votes at the polls.

§ 8. Immediately after the election herein provided for, the judges of election at each voting place shall make a true and complete count of all the votes duly cast at such election, and shall certify and return the result of the same, with the names of all the candidates and the number of votes cast for each candidate, and the number of votes cast for and against the constitution, and the number of votes cast for and against prohibition, and the number of votes cast for and against minority representation, and the number of votes cast for each city, town or place for the "temporary seat of government," to the county clerk, or auditor of the respective counties, together with one of the poll lists and election books used in said election.

§ 9. Within five days after said election the several boards of county canvassers provided by law for the canvassing of the results of the election, shall make and certify to the secretary of the Territory of Dakota the true and correct return of the total number of votes cast for the constitution, and against the constitution, of the number of votes cast for and against "prohibition," and the number of votes cast for and against minority representation," and the number of votes cast for each city, town or place as the "temporary seat of government," and of the number of votes cast for each person voted for at such election, except county officers and members of the legislature, and shall transmit the same to the secretary of the Territory of Dakota, by mail, and shall file with the county clerk or auditor of each of said counties a duplicate and certified copy of said return.

Said board of county canvassers shall issue certificates of election to the persons who shall have received the highest number of votes cast for the respective offices of judge of the county court and representatives in the legislature, and for state senator or senators.

§ 10. When two or more counties are connected in one senatorial or representative district, it shall be the duty of the clerks and auditors of the respective counties to attend at the office of the county clerk of the senior county in the date of organization within twenty days after the date of election, and they shall compare the votes given in the several counties comprising such senatorial and representative district and such clerks or auditors shall immediately make out a certificate of election to the person having the highest number of votes in such district for state senator or representative or both; which certificate shall be delivered to the person entitled thereto on his application to the clerk of the senior county of such district.

§ 11. The secretary of the territory shall receive all returns of election transmitted to him as above provided, and shall preserve the same, and after they have been canvassed as hereinafter provided, and after the admission of the State of South Dakota into the Union, he shall deliver said returns to the proper state officer of said State of South Dakota.

Within fifteen days after said election the secretary of the territory, with the governor and chief justice thereof, or any two of them, shall canvass such returns and certify the same to the president of the United States, as provided in the enabling act.

They shall also ascertain the total number of votes cast at such election for the constitution and against the constitution; the total number of votes cast for and against prohibition; and the total number of votes cast for and against minority representation; and the total number of votes cast for each city, town, or place as the " temporary seat of government;" and the total number of votes cast for each person voted for, for any office at said election, excepting county judges and members of the legislature, and shall declare the result of said election in conformity with such vote, and the governor of the territory shall thereupon issue a proclamation at once thereof.

They shall also make and transmit to the state legislature, immediately upon its organization, a list of all the state and judicial officers who shall thus be ascertained to be duly elected.

The various county and district canvassing boards shall make and transmit to the secretary of the territory the names of all persons declared by them to be elected members of the senate and house of representatives of the state of South Dakota; he shall make separate lists of the senators and representatives so elected, which lists shall constitute the rolls under which the senate and house of representatives shall be organized.

The governor of the territory shall make and issue certificates of election to the persons who are shown by the canvass to have received the highest number of votes for governor, lieutenant governor, secretary of state, auditor, treasurer, attorney-general, superintendent of public instruction, commissioner of schools and public lands, and judges of the supreme and circuit courts. Such certificates to be attested by the secretary of the territory.

§ 12. The apportionment made in this constitution shall govern the elections above provided for for members of the state legislature, until otherwise provided by law.

At the first election held under this ordinance for senators and representatives of the legislature, there shall be elected forty-five senators and one hundred and twenty-four representatives in the state legislature respectively.

§ 13. The legislature elected under the provisions of this ordinance and constitution shall assemble at the temporary seat of government on the third Tuesday in October, in the year A. D. 1889, at 12 o'clock noon, and on the first day of their assemblage the governor and other state officers shall take the oath of office in the presence of the legislature. The oath of office shall be administered to the members of the legislature and to the state officers by the chief justice of the territory, or by any other officer duly authorized by the laws of the territory of Dakota to administer oaths.

§ 14. Immediately after the organization of the legislature and taking the oath of office by the state officers, the legislature shall then and there proceed to the election of two senators of the United States for the State of South Dakota, in the mode and manner provided by the laws of congress for the election of United States senators. And the governor and the secretary of the State of South Dakota shall certify the election of the said senators and two representatives in congress, in the manner required by law.

§ 15. Immediately after the election of the United States senators as above provided for, said legislature shall adjourn to meet at the temporary seat of government on the first Tuesday after the first Monday of January, 1890, at 12 o'clock m.; *Provided, however*, that if the State of South Dakota has not been admitted by proclamation or otherwise at said date, then said legislature shall convene within ten days after the date of the admission of the state into the Union.

§ 16. Nothing in this constitution or schedule contained shall be construed to authorize the legislature to exercise any powers except such as are necessary to its first organization, and to elect United States senators, and to adjourn as above provided. Nor to authorize an officer of the executive, administrative or judiciary departments to exercise any duties of his office until the State of South Dakota shall have been regularly admitted into the Union, excepting such as may be authorized by the congress of the United States.

§ 17. The ordinances and schedules enacted by this convention shall be held to be valid for all the purposes thereof.

§ 18. That we, the people of the State of South Dakota, do ordain:

First—That perfect toleration of religious sentiment shall be secured, and that no inhabitant of this state shall ever be molested in person or property on account of his or her mode of religious worship.

Second—That we, the people inhabiting the State of South Dakota, do agree and declare that we forever disclaim all right and title to the unappropriated public lands lying within the boundaries of South Dakota; and to all lands lying within said limits owned or held by any Indian or Indian tribes, and that until the title thereto shall have been extinguished by the United States the same shall be and remain subject to the disposition of the United States, and said Indian lands shall remain under the absolute jurisdiction and control of the congress of the United States; that the lands belonging to citizens of the United States residing without the said state shall never be taxed at a higher rate than the lands belonging to residents of this state.

That no taxes shall be imposed by the State of South Dakota on lands or property therein belonging to or which may hereafter be purchased by the United States, or reserved for its use. But nothing herein shall preclude the State of South Dakota from taxing as other lands are taxed, any lands owned or held by any Indian who has severed his tribal relation and has obtained from the United States or from any person a title thereto by patent or other grant, save and except such lands as have been or may be granted to any Indian or Indians under any act of Congress containing a provision exempting the lands thus granted from taxation; all such lands which may have been exempted by any grant or law of the United States shall remain exempt to the extent and as prescribed by such act of Congress.

Third—That the State of South Dakota shall assume and pay that portion of the debts and liabilities of the Territory of Dakota as provided in this constitution.

Fourth—That provision shall be made for the establishment and maintenance of systems of public schools which shall be opened to all the children of this state and free from sectarian control.

Fifth—That jurisdiction is ceded to the United States over the military reservations of Fort Mead, Fort Randall and Fort Sully, heretofore declared by the president of the United States; *Provided*, legal process, civil and criminal, of this state shall extend over such reservations in all cases of which exclusive jurisdiction is not vested in the United States, or of crimes not committed within the limits of such reservations.

These ordinances shall be irrevocable without the consent of the United States, and also the people of the said State of South Dakota expressed by their legislative assembly.

§ 19. The tenure of all officers, whose election is provided for in this schedule on the first day of October, A. D. 1889, shall be as follows:

The governor, lieutenant governor, secretary of state, auditor, treasurer, attorney general, superintendent of public instruction, commissioner of school and public lands, judges of county courts, shall hold their respective offices until the first Tuesday after the first Monday in January, A. D. 1891, at twelve o'clock, M., and until their successors are elected and qualified.

The judges of the supreme court and circuit courts shall hold their offices until the first Tuesday after the first Monday in January, A. D. 1894, at twelve o'clock M., and until their successors are elected and qualified; subject to the provisions of Sec. 26 of Article V of the constitution.

The terms of office of the members of the legislature elected at the first election held under the provisions of this constitution shall expire on the first Tuesday after the first Monday in January, one thousand eight hundred and ninety-one (1891.)

§ 20. That the first general election under the provisions of this constitution shall be held on the first Tuesday after the first Monday in November, 1890, and every two years thereafter.

§ 21. The following form of ballot is adopted:

CONSTITUTIONAL TICKET.

INSTRUCTIONS TO VOTERS.

All persons desiring to vote for the constitution, or for any of the articles submitted to a separate vote, may erase the word " No."

All persons who desire to vote against the constitution, or any articles separately submitted may erase the word " Yes."

For the Constitution: Yes. No.
For Prohibition: Yes. No.
For Minority Representation: Yes. No.
For_____as the temporary seat of government.

For Governor.

For Lieutenant Governor.

For Secretary of State.

For Auditor.

For Treasurer.

For Attorney General.

For Superintendent of Public Instruction.

For Commissioner of School and Public Lands.

For Judges of the Supreme Court.

First District_____
Second District_____
Third District_____

For Judge of the Circuit Court_____Circuit.

For Representatives in Congress.

For State Senator.

For Representative in the Legislature.

For County Judge.
----

§ 22. This constitution shall be enrolled and after adoption and signing by the convention shall be delivered to Hon. A. J. Edgerton, the president of the constitutional convention, for safe keeping, and by him to be delivered to the secretary of state as soon as he assumes the duties of his office, and printed copies thereof shall be prefixed to the books containing the laws of the state, and all future editions thereof.

The president of this convention shall also supervise the making of the copy that must be sent to the president of the United States;

said copy is to be certified by the president and chief clerk of this convention.

§ 23. " The agreement made by the joint commission of the constitutional conventions of North and South Dakota concerning the records, books and archives of the Territory of Dakota is 'hereby ratified and confirmed, which agreement is in the words following: That is to say: "

The following books, records and archives of the Territory of Dakota shall be the property of North Dakota, towit:

All records, books and archives in the offices of the governor and secretary of the territory (except records of articles of incorporation of domestic corporations, returns of election of delegates to the constitutional convention of 1889, for South Dakota, returns of elections held under the so-called local option law in counties within the limits of South Dakota, bonds of notaries public appointed for counties within the limits of South Dakota, papers relating to the organization of counties situate within the limits of South Dakota, all of which records and archives are part of the records and archives of said secretary's office; excepting also census returns from counties situate within the limits of South Dakota and papers relating to requisitions issued upon the application of officers of counties situate within the limits of South Dakota, all of which are part of the records and archives of said governor's office.)

And the following records, books and archives shall also be the property of the State of North Dakota, towit:

Vouchers in the office or in the custody of the auditor of this territory relating to expenditures on account of public institutions, grounds or buildings situate within the limits of North Dakota; one warrant register in the office of the treasurer of this territory, being a record of warrants issued under and by virtue of chapter twenty-four of the laws enacted by the eighteenth legislative assembly of Dakota territory; all letters, receipts and vouchers in the same office now filed by counties and pertaining to counties within the limits of North Dakota; paid and canceled coupons in the same office representing interest on bonds which said State of North Dakota is to assume and pay; reports of gross earnings of the year 1888 in the same office, made by corporations operating lines of railroad situated wholly or mainly within the limits of North Dakota; records and papers of the office of the public examiner of the second district of the territory; records and papers of the office of the second district board of agriculture; records and papers in the office of the board of pharmacy of the district of North Dakota.

All records, books and archives of the Territory of Dakota which it is not herein agreed shall be the property of North Dakota, shall be the property of South Dakota.

The following books shall be copied and the copies shall be the property of North Dakota, and the cost of such copies shall be borne equally by the said states of North Dakota and South Dakota. That is to say:

Appropriation ledger for the years ending November, 1889 and 1890—one volume.

The current warrant auditor's register—one volume.

Insurance record for 1889—one volume.

Treasurer's cash book " D."

Assessment ledger " B."

Dakota Territory bond register—one volume.

Treasurer's current ledger—one volume.

The originals of the foregoing volumes which are to be copied, shall at any time after such copying shall have been completed, be delivered on demand to the proper authorities of the State of South Dakota.

All other records, books and archives which it is hereby agreed shall be the property of South Dakota shall remain at the capital of North Dakota until demanded by the legislature of the State of South Dakota, and until the State of North Dakota shall have had a reasonable time after such demand is made to provide copies or abstracts or such portions thereof as the said State of North Dakota may desire to have copies or abstracts of.

The State of South Dakota may also provide copies or abstracts of such records, books and archives which is agreed shall be the property of North Dakota as said State of South Dakota shall desire to have copies or abstracts of.

The expense of all copies or abstracts of records, books and archives which it is herein agreed may be made, shall be borne equally by said two states.*

ALONZO J. EDGERTON,
President of the Constitutional Convention.

Attest:
F. A. BURDICK, *Chief Clerk.*

AMENDMENTS

(November 8, 1898)*a*

ART. III. SEC. 1. The legislative power shall be vested in a legislature which shall consist of a Senate and House of Representatives. Except that the people expressly reserve to themselves the right to propose measures, which measures the legislature shall enact and submit to a vote of the electors of the state, and also the right to require that any laws which the legislature may have enacted shall be submitted to a vote of the electors of he state before going into effect (except such laws as may be necessary for the immediate preservation of the public peace, health or safety, support of state government and the existing public institutions.)

Provided, That not more than five per centum of the qualified electors of the state shall be required to invoke either the initiative or the referendum.

This section shall not be construed so as to deprive the legislature or any member thereof of the right to propose any measure. The veto power of the executive shall not be exercised as to measures referred to a vote of the people. This section shall apply to municipalities. The enacting clause of all laws approved by vote of the electors of the state shall be: " Be it enacted by the people of South Dakota." The legislature shall make suitable provisions for carrying into effect the provisions of this section.

---

* See amendment, 1900.

a This section was submitted in its present form by the legislature in 1897 as an amendment to the Constitution; (Chap. 39, Laws of 1897.) It was adopted by the people at the general election held November 8, 1898.

(November 4, 1902)

ART. VIII. SEC. 11. The rate of interest upon all investments of the permanent school or other educational funds mentioned in Sec. 11 of Art. VIII of the constitution of this state is hereby changed and reduced from six per centum per annum to five per centum per annum, wherever the said words " six per centum per annum " occur in said section. That if the foregoing amendment shall be approved and ratified by the people at said election, as provided by Article XXIII of the constitution, said Section 11 of Article VIII of the constitution shall be thereby amended by striking out the said words, " six per centum per annum " wherever they occur in said Section 11 and substituting in lieu thereof the words "five per centum per annum."

(November 8, 1904)

ART. VIII. SEC. 2. The moneys of the permanent school and other educational funds shall be invested only in first mortgages upon good improved farm lands within this state, as hereinafter provided or in bonds of school corporations within this state, or in bonds of the United States or of the State of South Dakota, or of any organized county, township or incorporated city in said state. The legislature shall provide by law the method of determining the amount of said funds, which shall be invested from time to time in such classes of securities respectively, taking care to secure continuous investments as far as possible.

All moneys of said funds which may from time to time be designated for investment in farm mortgages and in the bonds of school corporations, or in bonds or organized counties, townships or incorporated cities within this state, shall for such purpose be divided among the organized counties of the state in proportion to population as nearly as provisions by law to secure continuous investment may permit. The several counties shall hold and manage the same as trust funds, and they shall be and remain responsible and accountable for the principal and interest of all such moneys received by them from the date of receipt until returned because not loaned; and in case of loss of any money so apportioned to any county, such county shall make the same good out of its common revenue. Counties shall invest said money in bonds of school corporations, counties, townships or cities, or in first mortgages upon good improved farm lands within their limits respectively. The amount of each loan shall not exceed one-third of the actual value of the lands covered by the mortgage given to secure the same, such value to be determined by the board of county commissioners of the county in which the land is situated, and in no case shall more than five thousand dollars ($5,000) be loaned to any one person, firm or corporation, and the rate of interest shall not be less than five per cent per annum, and shall be such other and higher rate as the legislature may provide, and shall be payable semi-annually on the first day of January and July; Provided, that whenever there are moneys of said fund in any county amounting to one thousand dollars that cannot be loaned according to the provisions of this section, and any law pursuant thereto, the said sum may be returned to the state treasurer to be entrusted to some other county or counties, or otherwise invested under the provisions of this section.

Each county shall semi-annually, on the first day of January and July, render an account of the condition of the funds intrusted to it to the auditor of state, and at the same time pay to or account to the state treasurer for the interest due on all funds intrusted to it.

The legislature may provide by general law that counties may retain from interest collected in excess of five per centum per annum upon all said funds intrusted to them, not to exceed one per centum per annum. But no county shall be exempted from the obligation to make semi-annual payments to the state treasurer of interest at the rate provided by law for such loans, except only said one per centum, and in no case shall the interest, so to be paid, be less than five per centum per annum.

The legislature shall provide by law for the safe investment of the permanent school and other educational funds and for the prompt collection of interest and income thereof, and to carry out the objects and provisions of this section.

(1902)

*Art. IX. Sec. 3. Whenever a majority of the legal voters of any organized county shall petition the county board to change the location of the county seat which has once been located by a majority vote, specifying the place to which it is to be changed, said county board shall submit the same to the people of said county at the next general election, and if the proposition to change the county seat be ratified by two-thirds of the votes cast at said election, then the county seat shall be changed, otherwise not. A proposition to change the location of the county seat of any organized county shall not again be submitted before the expiration of four years.

(1896)

*Art. XIII. Sec. 4. The debt of any county, city, town, school district, civil township, or other subdivision, shall never exceed (5) five per centum upon the assessed value of the taxable property therein. In estimating the amount of indebtedness which a municipality or subdivision may incur the amount of indebtedness prior to the adoption of this constitution shall be included.

Provided, That any county, municipal corporation, civil township, district or other subdivision, may incur an additional indebtedness not exceeding ten per centum upon the assessed value of the taxable property therein for the purpose of providing water for irrigation and domestic uses: *Provided further*, That no county, municipal corporation or civil township shall be included within any such district or subdivision without a majority vote in favor thereof of the electors of the county, municipal corporation or civil township, as the case may be, which is proposed to be included therein, and no such debt

---

a Amended by popular vote of 36,486 for, to 14,612 against, at the general election held November 4, 1902.

b Submitted by the legislature in 1895, as an amendment to Section 4 of Article 13, of the Constitution, and was adopted at the general election of 1896 by a vote of 28,490 for, and 14,789 against.

That at the general election held on November 4, 1902, Section 4 of Article 13 of the Constitution was amended by a popular vote of 32,810 for to 13,599 against.

shall ever be incurred for any of the purposes in this section provided; unless authorized by a vote in favor thereof of a majority of the electors of such county, municipal corporation, civil township, district or subdivision incurring the same.

(November 4, 1902)

ART. XIII. SEC. 4. The debt of any county, city, town, school district, civil township or other subdivision, shall never exceed five (5) per centum upon the assessed valuation of the taxable property therein for the year preceding that in which said indebtedness is incurred.

In estimating the amount of the indebtedness which a municipality or subdivision may incur, the amount of indebtedness contracted prior to the adoption of this constitution shall be included.

Provided, That any county, municipal corporation, civil township, district or other subdivision may incur an additional indebtedness not exceeding ten per centum upon the assessed valuation of the taxable property therein for the year preceding that in which said indebtedness is incurred for the purpose of providing water and sewerage for irrigation, domestic uses, sewerage and other purposes; and

Provided, That in a city where the population is 8,000 or more, such city may incur an indebtedness not exceeding eight per centum upon the assessed valuation of the taxable property therein for the year next preceding that in which said indebtedness is incurred for the purpose of constructing street railways, electric lights or other lighting plants.

Provided further, That no county, municipal corporation, civil township, district or subdivision shall be included within such district or subdivision without a majority vote in favor thereof of the electors of the county, municipal corporation, civil township, district, or other subdivision as the case may be, which is purposed to be included therein, and no such debt shall ever be incurred for any of the purposes in this section provided, unless authorized by a vote in favor thereof by a majority of the electors of such county, municipal corporation, civil township, district or subdivision incurring the same.

(1896)

ART. XIV. SEC. 3.[a] The state university, the agricultural college, the normal schools and other educational institutions that may be sustained either wholly or in part by the state shall be under the control of a board of five members appointed by the governor and confirmed by the senate under such rules and restrictions as the legislature shall provide. The legislature may increase the number of members to nine.

ART. XIV. SEC. 4.[b] Stricken out, 1896, from original constitution.

---

[a] Submitted as an amendment to Constitution, Article 14, § 3, by the legislature in 1895, and at the general election in 1896, was adopted by the following vote: 31,061 for, and 11,690 against.

[b] Stricken from the Constitution, by an amendment submitted by the legislature in 1895, and adopted by the popular vote at the general election in 1896: 31,061 for, and 11,690 against.

(1896)

Art. XVII. Sec. 20.*a* Monopolies and trusts shall never be allowed in this state, and no incorporated company, co-partnership or association of persons in this state shall directly or indirectly combine or make any contract with any incorporated company, foreign or domestic, through their stockholders, or the trustees or assigns of such stockholders, or with any co-partnership or association of persons, or in any manner whatever to fix the prices, limit the production or regulate the transportation of any product or commodity so as to prevent competition in such prices, production or transportation, or to establish excessive prices therefor.

The legislature shall pass laws for the enforcement of this section by adequate penalties and in the case of incorporated companies, if necessary for that purpose, may, as a penalty, declare a forfeiture of their franchises.

Art. XXIV. (Prohibition) adopted, 1896.*b*

Art. XV. (Minority representation) rejected, 1889.*c*

Art. XXVI. Obsolete, except sections 17 and 18.*d*

Art. XXVII. (The control of, manufacture, and sale of liquor.)*e*

(1900)

Art. XXVIII.*f* Sec. 1. The several counties of the state shall invest the money of the permanent school and endowment funds in bonds of school, corporation, state, county and municipal bonds, or in first mortgages upon good improved farm lands within their limits respectively; under such regulations as the legislature may provide, but no farm loan shall exceed one thousand dollars to any one person or corporation.

---

a Submitted as an amendment to the Constitution, by the legislature in 1895, and was adopted by a popular vote of the electors of the state at the general election in 1896, by the following vote, for 36,763, against 9,136.

*b*Adopted at the time of the adoption of the Constitution, October 1st, 1889, it being voted upon separately, by the following vote: For, 40,234; against, 34,510. The legislature in 1895 submitted an amendment for the repeal of this article (24), which was adopted by a popular vote of the electors at the general election in 1896, by a vote of 31,901 for, and 24,910 against.

c Submitted to a separate vote, at the time of the adoption of the Constitution, October 1st, 1889, and was rejected by a vote of 24,161 for, and 46,200 against.

d As the provisions of this article (26), with the exception of Sections 17 and 18 thereof, have become obsolete, or fully executed, they have been omitted from this compilation.

*e*Article 27 of the constituion, providing that the manufacture and sale of liquor should be under exclusive state control, was submitted by the legislature in 1897, and adopted by a vote of the people at the general election in 1898, by a vote of 22,170 for, and 20,557 against. The legislature in 1899 submitted an amendment repealing Article 27, and at the general election held in 1900 the amendment was adopted by a vote of 48,673 for, and 33,927 against.

f Proposed by the legislature in 1899 as an amendment to the Constitution and was at the general election held in November, 1900, adopted by a popular vote of 49,989 for, and 15,653 against.

[Doc. No. 5]

Proclamation of November 2, 1889

BY THE PRESIDENT OF THE UNITED STATES OF AMERICA.

A PROCLAMATION.

Whereas the Congress of the United States did, by an act approved on the twenty-second day of February, one thousand eight hundred and eighty-nine, provide that the inhabitants of the Territory of Dakota might, upon the conditions prescribed in the said act, become the States of North Dakota and South Dakota;

And whereas it was provided by said act that the area comprising

November 2, 1889.

Preamble.
Vol. 25, p. 676.

the Territory of Dakota should, for the purposes of the act, be divided
on the line of the seventh standard parallel produced due west to
the western boundary of said Territory, and that the delegates
elected as therein provided to the Constitutional convention in districts south of said parallel should, at the time prescribed in the act,
assemble in convention at the city of Sioux Falls;

And whereas it was provided by the said act that the delegates
elected as aforesaid should, after they had met and organized, declare
on behalf of the people of South Dakota that they adopt the Constitution of the United States; whereupon the said convention should
be authorized to form a constitution and State Government for the
proposed State of South Dakota;

And whereas it was provided by said act that the constitution so
adopted should be republican in form, and make no distinction in
civil or political rights on account of race or color, except as to Indians not taxed, and not be repugnant to the Constitution of the
United States and the principles of the Declaration of Independence;
and that the convention should, by an ordinance irrevocable without
the consent of the United States and the people of said States, make
certain provisions prescribed in said act;

And whereas it was provided by said act that the constitutions of
North Dakota and South Dakota should, respectively, incorporate an
agreement to be reached in accordance with the provisions of the act,
for an equitable division of all property belonging to the Territory
of Dakota, the disposition of all public records, and also for the apportionment of the debts and liabilities of said Territory, and that each
of said States should obligate itself to pay its proportion of such
debts and liabilities the same as if they had been created by such
States respectively;

And whereas it was provided by said act that at the election for
delegates to the constitutional convention in South Dakota, as
therein provided, each elector might have written or printed on his
ballot the words "For the Sioux Falls constitution," or the words
"against the Sioux Falls constitution;" that the votes on this question should be returned and canvassed in the same manner as the
votes for the election of delegates; and, if a majority of all votes
cast on this question should be "for the Sioux Falls constitution"
it should be the duty of the convention which might assemble at
Sioux Falls, as provided in the act, to re-submit to the people of
South Dakota, for ratification or rejection, at an election provided
for in said act, the constitution framed at Sioux Falls and adopted
November third, eighteen hundred and eighty-five, and also the
articles and propositions separately submitted at that election, including the question of locating the temporary seat of government,
with such changes only as related to the name and boundary of the
proposed State, to the reapportionment of the judicial and legislative districts, and such amendments as might be necessary in order
to comply with the provisions of the act;

And whereas it was provided by said act that the constitution
formed for the people of South Dakota should, by an ordinance of
the convention forming the same, be submitted to the people of
South Dakota at an election to be held therein on the first Tuesday
in October, eighteen hundred and eighty-nine, for ratification or
rejection by the qualified voters of said proposed State, and that the
returns of said election should be made to the Secretary of the
Territory of Dakota, who, with the Governor and Chief Justice
thereof, or any two of them, should canvass the same, and if a
majority of the legal votes cast should be for the constitution the
Governor should certify the result to the President of the United
States, together with a statement of the votes cast thereon and upon
separate articles or propositions, and a copy of said constitution,
articles, propositions and ordinances;

And whereas it has been certified to me by the Governor of the Territory of Dakota that at the aforesaid election for delegates the "Sioux Falls constitution" was submitted to the people of the proposed State of South Dakota, as provided in the said act; that a majority of all the votes cast on this question was "for the Sioux Falls constitution;" and that the said constitution was, at the time prescribed in the act resubmitted to the people of South Dakota, with proper changes and amendments, and has been adopted and ratified by a majority of the qualified voters of said proposed State, in accordance with the conditions prescribed in said act;

And whereas it is also certified to me by the said Governor that at the same time that the body of said Constitution was submitted to a vote of the people, two additional articles were submitted separately to wit: an article numbered twenty-four entitled "Prohibition," which received a majority of all the votes cast for and against said article, as well as a majority of all the votes cast for and against the constitution and was adopted; and an article numbered twenty-five, entitled "Minority Representation," which did not receive a majority of the votes cast thereon or upon the constitution and was rejected;

And whereas a duly authenticated copy of said constitution, additional articles, ordinances and propositions as required by said act, has been received by me:

Now, therefore, I, Benjamin Harrison, President of the United States of America, do, in accordance with the act of Congress aforesaid, declare and proclaim the fact that the conditions imposed by Congress on the State of South Dakota to entitle that State to admission to the Union have been ratified and accepted, and that the admission of the said State into the Union is now complete.

South Dakota admitted as a State.

In testimony whereof, I have hereunto set my hand and caused the seal of the United States to be affixed.

Done at the City of Washington this second day of November in the year of our Lord one thousand eight hundred and [SEAL.] eighty-nine, and of the Independence of the United States of America the one hundred and fourteenth.

BENJ. HARRISON.

By the President:
JAMES G. BLAINE,
    Secretary of State.

SELECTED BIBLIOGRAPHY

South Dakota Constitutional Convention held at Sioux Falls, July 1889 (Huron, S.D., 2 vol., 1907)

Constitutional Debates, South Dakota, 1885, 1889, (Huron, S.D., 2 vol., 1907)

Journal of the Proceedings of the Constitutional Convention... at Sioux Falls, Dakota, September, 1885 (Sioux Falls, Dak., 1885)

Journal of the Constitutional Convention of South Dakota, July 1889 (Sioux Falls, S.D., 1889)

Askin, Thomas, ed., Parallel References, the Constitutional Debates... (Pierre, S.D. 1910)

Cape, William H., Constitutional Revision in South Dakota (Vermillion, S.D., 1957)

SOUTH DAKOTA INDEX

Tennessee

Sixteenth State

June 1, 1796

EDITORIAL NOTE

Tennessee, together with Kentucky and Ohio,
comprised the states organized out of the "western
lands" claimed in the colonial charters of some of
the original states and ceded by them to the United
States under Articles of Confederation. The Federal
Congress established under the Constitution actually
oversaw the organization of these first new states
as provided by the territorial statutes of the
outgoing Continental Congress.

TENNESSEE CONTENTS

SOURCES OF DOCUMENTS

No. 1   Williams, History of the Lost State of
         Franklin (Johnson City, Tenn., 1924),
         330-38

No. 2   1 Stat. 101

No. 3   1 Stat. 123

No. 4   2 Poore, 1667

No. 5   1 Stat. 491

No. 6   2 Poore, 1677

No. 7   14 Stat. 364

No. 8   2 Poore, 1694

TENNESSEE CONSTITUTIONS: COMPARATIVE PROVISIONS

SUBJECT MATTER BY ARTICLES

PREAMBLE AND DECLARATION OF RIGHTS	1785	1796	1870
Declaration of Rights	*1-25, 34 39	XI	I
Distribution of Powers	1-6,9,10, 11,13-16	I	II
Executive Department	17-26,33	II	III
Elections	7,8,37	III	IV
Impeachments		IV	V
Judicial Department		V	VI
State and County Officers	38	VI	VII
Militia	27	VII	VIII
Disqualifications	28,32-35	VIII	IX
Oaths, Bribery of Electors, New Counties	12,40	IX	X
Miscellaneous Provisions	41-46	X	XI
Schedule			§1-4

SUBJECT MATTER BY SECTIONS

PREAMBLE AND DECLARATION OF RIGHTS

DECLARATION OF RIGHTS		XI	I
All power inherent in the people - Government under their control		1	1
Doctrine of monresistance, condemned		2	2
Freedom of Worship		3	3
No religious or political test		4	4
Elections to be free and equal - Right of Suffrage			
Trial by jury - Qualifications of jurors		6	6
Unreasonable Searches and Seizures General Warrants		7	7
No man to be disturbed but by law		8	8
Right of the accused in criminal prosecutions		9	9
Dou b le jeopardy prohibited		10	10
No ex post facto laws		11	11
No corruption of blood or forfeiture of estates		12	12
Treatment after arrest		13	13
Prerequisites to criminal charge		14	14
Bailable offenses- Habeas Corpus		15	15
Restrictions on bail, fines, and punishment		16	16
Open courts-Redress of injuries- Suits against the State		17	17
No imprisonment for debt		18	18
Freedom of speech and press		19	19
No retrospective law		20	20
No man's services or property taken without consent or compensation		21	21
No perpetuities or monopolies		23	22

	1785	1796	1870
Right of assembly		22	23
Militia – Civil Authority		24	24
Martial law – punishment		25	25
Right to bear arms – regulations		26	26
Quartering soldiers		27	27
No one compelled to bear arms		28	28
Navigation of the Mississippi		29	29
No hereditary honors		30	30
Boundaries of the State		32	31
Prisons and prisoners			32
Slavery prohibited			33
Right of property in Man			34
Right of preemption to tract of land		31	

DISTRIBUTION OF POWERS

			II
Division of powers			1
Limitation of powers			2

LEGISLATIVE DEPARTMENT

	1785	Art. I	1870
Legislative authority – term of office		1	3
Census		2	4
Apportionment of representatives		2	5
Apportionment of Senators		3,4	6
Time of elections		5	7
Legislative Sessions – Governor's inauguration		6	8
Qualifications of representatives		7,24	9
Senators-Qualifications		7,24	10
Election of officers-Quorum-Adjournments		8	11
Each house to make its own rules		9	12
Privilege of members		10	13
Power to punish other than members		9,11	14
Vacancies		12	15
Limitation upon power of adjournment		13	16
Origin and frame of bills		14	17
Passage of bills		15	18
Rejection of a bill		16	19
Style of laws-effective date		17	20
Journal of proceedings		18	21
Open sessions and meetings-Exception		19	22
Compensation of members of General Assembly		20	23
Appropriations of public moneys		21	24
Defaulters ineligible		22	25
Ineligibility-Lucrative offices		23	26
Right of protest		25	27
Taxable property-Valuation-Rates		26	28
Counties and towns-Power to Tax-Credit			29
Articles not taxable-Inspection fees		27	30
Articles forbidden the state			31
Amendments to Constitution of United States			32
No state bonds to defaulting railroads			33

	1785	1796	1870
EXECUTIVE DEPARTMENT		II	III
Governor's executive power		1	1
Election of Governor		2	2
Governor Qualifications		3	3
Governor's term of service		4	4
Governor as commander in chief-calling out militia		5	5
Pardons and reprieves		6	6
Governor's compensation		7	7
Governor may require information		8	8
Governor may convene the legislature		9	9
Governor to execute laws		10	10
Governor to give information to the legislature		11	11
Vacancy in office of governor		12	12
Ineligibility for governorship		13	13
Governor to make temporary appointments		14	14
Seal of State		15	15
Grants and commissions to be sealed and signed by the governor		16	16
Secretary of State		17	17
Bills to be approved by the governor – Governor's veto Bills passed over Governor's veto			18
ELECTIONS		III	IV
Right to vote-Election precincts – Military duty		1	1
Right of suffrage may be excluded for crime			2
Privileges of voters		2	3
Mode of voting		3	4
IMPEACHMENTS		IV	V
Impeachment		1	1
Trial of impeachments		2	2
How prosecuted		3	3
Who may be impeached		4	4
Officers liable to indictment and removal from office			5
JUDICIAL DEPARTMENT		V	VI
Judicial power		1	1
Supreme court			2
Supreme court judges		3,4	3
Judges of inferior courts			4
Attorney-general and reporter			5
Removal of judges and attorneys			6
Compensation of judges			7

	1785	1796	1870
Jurisdiction of inferior courts			8
Judge's charge		5	9
Certiorari		6,7	10
Incompetency of judges-Special judges		8	11
Requisites of writs and process		9	12
Clerks of courts		10	13
Fines exceeding fifty dollars to be assessed by jury		11	14
District in counties Justices and constables- Number-Term-Removal from District		12	15
General Assembly Appoints Judges		2	
STATE AND COUNTY OFFICERS		VI	VII
County officers-Their Election-Terms-Removal		1	1
Vacancies-How Filled			2
Treasurer and Comptroller		2	3
Other Elections and vacancies		3	4
Civil officers-Election-Vacancies			5
MILITIA		VII	VIII
Militia officers to be elected		1-4	1
Staff officers to be appointed		5-6	2
Exemptions from attending musters		7	3
DISQUALIFICATIONS		VIII	IX
Ineligibility of ministers and priests to seats in legislature		1	1
No atheist shall hold a civil office		2	2
Duelists shall hold no office			3
OATHS, BRIBERY OF ELECTORS, NEW COUNTIES		IX	X
Oath of office		1	1
Oath of members of the general assembly		2	2
Punishment of Electors and candidates for bribery		3	3
New counties-Approach of county lines to courthouse-Limit to reduction of counties- Exceptions-Vote necessary to detach fractions for formation of new counties or to remove a county seat-Liability for existing debt		4	5
To vote with old county			5
MISCELLANEOUS PROVISIONS		X	XI

	1785	1796	1870
Existing laws not affected by this constitution		2	1
No impairment of rights			2
Amendments to the Constitution		3	3
Power to grant divorces			4
Lotteries			5
Changing names—Adoption—Legitimation			6
Interest rates			7
General laws only to be passed			8
Power over local affairs—Home rule for cities and counties-consolidation of functions			9
Internal improvements to be encouraged			10
Homestead exemption			11
Education to be cherished—Common school fund—Poll tax—Whites and Negroes			12
Game and fish			13
Intermarriage between whites and negroes			14
Religious holidays			15
Bill of rights to remain inviolate		4	16
County offices			17
Knoxville shall be seat of Government		1	
SCHEDULE		1-8	§1-4

BACKGROUND NOTE

James Needham, a ranger commissioned by Virginia trading interests early in 1673, entered the area of present Tennessee seeking out "southwestern Indians" who might offer prospective markets for goods. His death at the hands of hostile tribes discouraged further efforts by English authorities, and some Spanish and French contacts with the outer fringes of the area, east and west, left no lasting effect. Claims of the several European colonizing powers were finally settled in favor of England, and a new class of rangers ("Long Hunters") entered the area in search of good land for settlement. Between 1769 and 1771 a cluster of farms appeared on the Nolichucky River, to become known as the Watauga Settlements. In 1772 a rudimentary government called the Watauga Association was proclaimed, but its records have not been found.

The necessity for taking an initiative in organizing some system of government was dictated not only by the remoteness of the North Carolina centers to the east, but by doubt as to whether North Carolina jurisdiction in fact extended that far. The Watauga government proved effective in its own right, providing valuable military service during the Revolution by its guarding against potential Indian attacks on the American rear, and by defeating the British at the famed Battle of King's Mountain in 1780. Shortly thereafter, however, North Carolina treated the region as part of its territory to be ceded to the United States. Feeling betrayed after its wartime contributions, the settlements which had now extended from the Watauga to the Cumberland in 1784 proclaimed themselves a separate state of Franklin (Doc. No. 1) and elected John Sevier, one of the heroes of King's Mountain, as governor.

North Carolina subsequently repealed its act of cession, and asserted that Franklin was part of its reclaimed jurisdiction. The Franklin officials adopted the constitution and laws of North Carolina but continued to function as an autonomous government. A second cession was voted in April 1790 (Doc. No. 2) and the following month Congress organized the territory "southwest of the Ohio" (Doc. No. 3) with Knoxville as the territorial capital. Because of the steady flow of immigration into

the area since the Revolution, the size of population and political experience of the settlements
warranted prompt consideration for statehood. A
constitution was drawn up at a convention in January 1796 (Doc. No. 4) and Tennessee was admitted
to the Union as the sixteenth state in June (Doc.
No. 5) John Sevier, the first and only governor
of Franklin, became the first governor of the new
state.

The constitution of 1796, which Thomas Jefferson
praised as "the least imperfect and most republican"
to that time, was succeeded by a second in 1834
(Doc. No. 6). This continued to serve the state
until modifications required by the post-Civil War
act of readmission in 1886 (Doc. No. 7). It was
replaced four years later by a new constitution
which had continued, with modernizing amendments,
to the present (Doc. No. 8).

[Doc. No. 1]

Constitution of the State of Franklin

Your committee appointed to collect and adjust the reasons which impel us to declare ourselves independent of North Carolina, report as follows, to-wit:

WHEREAS, we, the freemen inhabitants of part of the country included in the limits of an Act of North Carolina ceding certain vacant territory to Congress, having declared ourselves independent of North Carolina, a decent respect to the opinions of mankind make it proper that we should manifest to the world the reasons which induced us to a declaration, which are as follows:

FIRST. That the Constitution of North Carolina declares that it shall be justifiable to erect new States whenever the consent of the Legislature shall countenance it, and this consent is implied, we conceive, in the cession act which has thrown us into such a situation that the influence of the law in common cases was almost a nullity, and in criminal jurisdiction had ceased entirely; which reduced us to the verge of anarchy.

SECOND. The Assembly of North Carolina have detained a certain quantity of goods, which was procured to satisfy the Indians for the lands we possess, which detainure we fully conceive has so exasperated them that they have actually committed hostilities upon us, and we are alone compelled to defend ourselves from these savages.

3RDLY. The resolutions of Congress held out from time to time, encouraging the erection of new States, have appeared to us ample encouragement.

4THLY. Our local situation is such that we not only apprehend we should be separated from North Carolina, but almost every sensible, disinterested traveler has declared it is incompatible with our interest to belong in union with the eastern part of the State; for we are not only far removed from the eastern parts of North Carolina, but separated from them by high and almost impassable mountains, which naturally divide us from them, which have proved to us that our interest is also in many respects distinct from the inhabitants on the other side, and much injured by union with them.

5TH AND LASTLY. We unanimously agree that our lives, liberties and property can be more secure and our happiness much better propagated by our separation; and consequently that it is our duty and inalienable right to form ourselves into a new and independent State.

A DECLARATION OF RIGHTS MADE BY THE REPRE-
SENTATIVES OF THE FREEMEN OF THE
STATE OF FRANKLIN

SECTION 1. That all political power is vested in and derived from the people.

SEC. 2. That the people of this State ought to have the sole and exclusive right of regulating the internal government and police thereof.

SEC. 3. That no man, or set of men, are entitled to exclusive or separate emoluments or privileges from the community, but in consideration of public services.

SEC. 4. That the legislative, executive and supreme judicial powers of government ought to be forever separate and distinct from each other.

SEC. 5. That all powers of suspending laws or the execution of laws, by any authority, without the consent of the representatives of the people is injurious to their rights, and ought not to be exercised.

SEC. 6. That elections of members to serve as representatives in General Assembly ought to be free.

SEC. 7. That in all criminal prosecutions every man has a right to be informed of the accusation against him, and to confront the accusers and witnesses with other testimony, and shall not be compelled to give evidence against himself.

SEC. 8. That no freeman shall be put to answer any criminal charge but by indictment, presentment or impeachment.

SEC. 9. That no freeman shall be convicted of any crime but by the unanimous verdict of a jury of good and lawful men in open court, as heretofore used.

SEC. 10. That excessive bail should not be required, nor excessive fines imposed, nor cruel and unusual punishments be inflicted.

SEC. 11. That general warrants, whereby any officer or messenger may be commanded to search suspected places, without evidence of the fact committed, or to seize any person or persons not named whose offense is not particularly described and supported by the evidence, are dangerous to liberty and ought not to be granted.

SEC. 12. That no freeman ought to be taken, imprisoned or disseized of his freehold, liberties or privileges, or outlawed or exiled, or in any manner destroyed or deprived of his life, liberty or property, but by the laws of the land.

SEC. 13. That every freeman restrained of his liberty is entitled to a remedy to inquire into the lawfulness thereof and to remove it, if unlawful; and that such remedy ought not to be denied.

SEC. 14. That in all controversies at law respecting property, the ancient mode of trial by jury is one of the best securities of the rights of the people, and ought to remain sacred and inviolable.

SEC. 15.   That the freedom of the press is one of the greatest bulwarks of liberty, and therefore ought never to be restrained.

SEC. 16.   That the people of this State ought not to be taxed, or made subject to the payment of any impost or duty without the consent of themselves or their representatives in General Assembly freely given.

SEC. 17.   That the people have a right to bear arms for the defense of the State; and as standing armies in times of peace are dangerous to liberty, they ought not to be kept up, and that the military should be kept under strict subordination to and be governed by civil power.

SEC. 18.   That the people have a right to assemble together to consult for their common good to instruct their representatives, and to apply to the legislature for redress of grievances.

SEC. 19.   That all men have a natural and inalienable right to worship God Almighty according to the dictates of their own conscience.

SEC. 20.   That for redress of grievances and for amending and strengthening the laws, elections ought to be often held.

SEC. 21.   That a frequent recurrence to fundamental principles is absolutely necessary to preserve the blessings of liberty.

SEC. 22.   That no hereditary emoluments, privileges, or honors ought to be granted or conferred in this State.

SEC. 24.   That retrospective laws punishing acts committed before the existence of such laws, and by them only declared criminal, are oppressive, unjust and incompatible with liberty; wherefore no *ex post facto* law ought to be made.

SEC. 25.   That the people have a right by their representatives to enact laws to encourage virtue and suppress vice and immorality.[1]

THE CONSTITUTION AND FORM OF GOVERNMENT

AGREED TO AND RESOLVED UPON BY THE REPRESENTATIVES OF THE FREE MEN OF THE STATE OF FRANKLIN, ELECTED AND CHOSEN FOR THAT PARTICULAR PURPOSE, IN CONVENTION ASSEMBLED, AT JONESBOROUGH, THE 17TH DECEMBER, ANNO. DOM. 1784.[2]

SECTION 1.   That the legislative authority shall be vested in two distinct branches, both dependent on the people, to-wit: a Senate and a House of Commons.

SEC. 2.   That the Senate shall be composed of three representa-

---

[1] Section 25 of the North Carolina Bill of Rights relates to the boundaries of the State. It was omitted and another inserted in its place.

[2] In the North Carolina Constitution of 1776, this caption is followed by a preamble which recited the change of allegiance due to the prosecution of a war against the people of the Colonies by King George the Third; and the necessity for the establishment of a government to prevent anarchy and

tives annually chosen by ballot from each County [3] until there be ten Counties in the State, after that period, one from each County.

SEC. 3.   That the House of Commons shall be composed of representatives chosen by ballot, four [4] for each County, until there be ten Counties within the State, and after that period, two for each County.

SEC. 4.   That the Senate and House of Commons assembled for the purpose of legislation shall be denominated the General Assembly.

SEC. 5.   That each member of the Senate shall have usually resided in the County in which he is chosen for one year immediately preceding his election, and for the same time shall have possessed and continued to possess in the County which he represents not less than one hundred acres [5] of land in fee.

SEC. 6.   That each member of the House of Commons shall have usually resided in the county in which he is chosen for one year immediately preceding his election.[6]

SEC. 7.   That all freemen of the age of twenty-one years who have been inhabitants of any one County within the State twelve months immediately preceding the day of any election, and possessed of a freehold within the same County of fifty acres of land for six months next before and at the day of election shall be entitled to vote for a member of the Senate.

SEC. 8.   That all freemen of the age of twenty-one years who have been inhabitants of any County in this State twelve months immediately preceding the day of any election, and shall have paid public taxes, shall be entitled to vote for members of the House of Commons for the County in which he resides.

SEC. 9.   That all persons possessed of a freehold in any town in this State having a right of representation, and also all freemen who have been inhabitants of any such town twelve months next before and at the day of election, and shall have paid public taxes, shall be entitled to vote for a member to represent such town in the House of Commons; provided always, that this section shall not entitle any inhabitant of such town to vote for members of the House of Commons for the County in which he may reside, nor any freeholder in such County who resided without or beyond the limits of town to vote for a member of said town.

---

confusion. The Declaration of Independence of the people of Franklin, serving much the same purpose, precedes the Bill of Rights.

[3] The words of this section that follow, added to section 2 of the North Carolina Constitution.

[4] North Carolina Constitution "two" and without the words beginning with "until."

[5] North Carolina Constitution stipulated five hundred acres.

[6] The property qualification of one hundred acres was not brought forward. The purpose was to make the lower house representative of all the people.

SEC. 10. That the Senate and House of Commons, when met, shall each have power to choose a speaker and other officers, and shall be judges of the qualifications and election of their members, sit upon their own adjournment from day to day, and prepare bills to be passed into laws. The two houses shall direct writs of election for supplying intermediate vacancies and shall also jointly by ballot adjourn themselves to any future day.

SEC. 11. That all bills shall be read three times in each house before they pass into laws, and be signed by the speakers of both houses.[7] On motion and second, the yeas and nays shall be taken on the passing of any act, and printed with the same.

SEC. 12. That every person who shall be chosen a member of the Senate or House of Commons, or appointed to any office or place of trust, before taking his seat or entering upon the execution of his office, shall take an oath to the State, and all officers also shall take an oath of office.

SEC. 13. That the General Assembly by joint ballot of both houses shall appoint Judges of the Supreme Courts of Law and Equity and Attorney General, who shall be commissioned by the Governor and hold their offices during good behavior.[8]

SEC. 14. That the Senate and House of Commons shall have power to appoint the general [9] and field officers of the militia and all officers of the regular army of the State.

SEC. 15. That the Senate and House of Commons jointly at their first meeting after each annual election shall by ballot, elect a Governor for one year, who shall not be eligible to that office longer than three years in six successive years; that no person under thirty years of age and who has not been a resident in this State above one year and shall not have in the State a freehold in land and tenements above the value of two hundred and fifty pounds, shall be eligible as Governor.[10]

SEC. 16. That the Senate and House of Commons jointly at their first meeting after each annual election shall by ballot elect five persons to be a Council of State for one year, who shall advise the Governor in the execution of his office, and that three members shall be a quorum. Their advice and proceedings shall be entered in a journal to be kept for that purpose only, and signed by the members present, to any part of which any member present may enter his dissent; and such journals shall be laid before the General Assembly, when called for by them.[11]

---

[7] The words that follow are not in the Carolina Constitution.

[8] Judges of admiralty courts were provided for in the North Carolina Constitution.

[9] Plural in the North Carolina Constitution.

[10] Five years residence and the ownership of one thousand pounds of real estate in the N. C. Constitution.

[11] The North Carolina Council of State composed of seven members, four to constitute a quorum.

Sec. 17.   There shall be a seal of this State, which shall be kept by the Governor and used by him as occasion may require, and shall be called the great seal of the State of Franklin, and be affixed to all grants and commissions.

Sec. 18.   The Governor for the time being shall be Captain General and Commander in Chief of the Militia and in the recess of the General Assembly shall have power by and with the advice of the Council of State, to embody the Militia for public safety.

Sec. 19.   That the Governor for the time being shall have power to draw for and apply such sums of money as shall be voted by the General Assembly for the contingencies of government, and be accountable to them for the same; and he also may, by and with the advice of the Council of State, lay embargoes or prohibit the exportation of any commodities for any term not exceeding thirty days at any one time in the recess of the General Assembly; and shall have the power of granting pardons and reprieves, except where the prosecutions shall be carried on in the General Assembly or the law shall otherwise direct.   In such case, he may in the recess grant a reprieve until the next sitting of the General Assembly; and may exercise all other executive powers of government, limited and restrained as by the State; and on his death, inability or absence from the State, the Speaker of the Senate, for the time being, and in case of his death, inability or absence from the State, the Speaker of the House of Commons, shall exercise the powers of government, after such death or during such absence or inability of the Governor or Speaker of the Senate or until a new nomination is made by the General Assembly.

Sec. 20.   That in every case where any officer, the right of whose appointment is made by this Constitution vested in the General Assembly, shall during their recess die, or his office by other means become vacant, the Governor shall have power, with the advice of the Council of State, to fill up such vacancy by granting a temporary commission, which shall expire at the end of the next session of the General Assembly.

Sec. 21.   That the Governor, Judges of Supreme Courts of Law and Equity and Attorney General, shall have adequate salaries during their continuance in office.

Sec. 22.   That the General Assembly shall by joint ballot of both houses annually appoint a Treasurer or Treasurers for this State.

Sec. 23.   That the Governor or other officers offending against the State by violating any part of this Constitution, maladministration or corruption, may be prosecuted on the impeachment of the General Assembly, or presentment of the grand jury of any court or supreme jurisdiction of this State.

Sec. 24.   That the General Assembly shall by joint ballot of both houses, triennially appoint a Secretary for this State.

Sec. 25.   That no persons, who heretofore have been or hereafter may be receivers of public monies, shall have a seat in either house of General Assembly, or be eligible to any office in this State, until such persons shall have fully accounted for and paid into the treasury all sums for which they may be accountable and liable [12] if legally called upon.

SEC. 26. That no Treasurer shall have a seat in either Senate, House of Commons or Council of State during his continuance in that office, or before he shall have finally settled his accounts with the public for all monies which may be in his hands at the expiration of his office belonging to the State and have paid the same into the hands of the succeeding Treasurer.

SEC. 27. That no officer in the regular army or navy in the service and pay of the United States, of this or any other State, nor any contractor or agent for supplying such army or navy with clothing or provisions, shall have a seat either in the Senate, the House of Commons, or the Council of State, or be eligible thereto; any member of the Senate, House of Commons or Council of State being appointed to and accepting of such office shall thereby vacate his seat.

SEC. 28. That no member of the Council of State shall have a seat either in the Senate or the House of Commons; [13] provided, nevertheless, that the Governor and Council shall attend the General Assembly during the sitting of the same, and that it shall be a part of their official duty to revise all bills before they can be passed and recommend such amendments as they may think proper.

SEC. 29. That no Judge of the Supreme Court of Law or Equity shall have a seat in Senate, House of Commons or Council of State.

SEC. 30. That no Secretary of this State, Attorney General or clerk of any court of record shall have a seat in the Senate, House of Commons or Council of State.

SEC. 31. That no clergyman or preacher of the gospel of any denomination shall be capable of being a member of either the Senate or House of Commons while he continues in the service of the pastoral function.

SEC. 32. That no person shall deny the being of a God or the truth of the Protestant religion or the divine authority either of the Old or New Testament, or who shall hold religious principles incompatible with the freedom and safety of the State, shall be capable of holding any office or place of trust or profit in the civil department within this State.

SEC. 33. That the Justices of the Peace within their respective Counties in this State shall in the future be recommended to the Governor for the time being by the representatives in General Assembly, and the Governor shall commission them accordingly, and the Justices commissioned shall hold their office during good behavior, and shall be not be removed from office by the General Assembly unless for misbehavior, absence or inability.

[12] The clause that follows was an added condition.
[13] The following proviso inserted.

SEC. 34. That there shall be no establishment of any religious church or denomination in this State in preference to any other, neither shall any person on any pretense whatever be compelled to attend any place of worship contrary to his own faith or judgment, nor be obliged to pay for the purchase of any glebe or the building of any house of worship or for the maintenance of any minister or ministry contrary to what he believes right, or has voluntarily and personally engaged to perform; but all persons shall be at liberty to exercise their own mode of worship; provided that nothing therein contained shall be construed to except preachers of treasonable or seditious doctrines from legal trial or punishment.

SEC. 35. That no person in the State shall hold more than one lucrative office at any one time; provided that no appointment in the militia of the office of a Justice of the Peace shall be considered as a lucrative office.

SEC. 36. That all commissions and grants shall run in the name of the State of Franklin and bear test and be signed by the Governor; all writs shall run in the same manner and bear test and be signed by the clerks of the respective courts. Indictments shall conclude against the peace and dignity of the State.

SEC. 37. That the delegate for this State to the Constitutional Congress, while necessary, shall be chosen annually by the General Assembly, by ballot, but may be superseded in the meantime in the same manner; and no person shall be elected to serve in that capacity for more than three years successively.

SEC. 38. That there shall be a sheriff, coroner or coroners and constables in each County within the State.

SEC. 39. That the person of a debtor, where there is not a strong presumption of fraud, shall not be continued in prison after delivering up *bona fide* all his estate, real and personal, for the use of his creditors, in such manner as shall be hereafter regulated by law. All prisoners shall be bailable by sufficient sureties, unless for any capital offenses, when the proof is evident or presumption great.

SEC. 40. That any foreigner who comes to settle in this State, having first taken an oath of allegiance to the same, may purchase or by other means acquire, hold and transfer land or other real estate; and after one year's residence shall be deemed a free citizen.

SEC. 41. That a school or schools shall be established by the legislature for the convenient instruction of youth, with such salaries to the masters, paid by the public, as may enable them to instruct at low prices; and all useful learning shall be duly encouraged and promoted in one or more universities.[14]

---

[14] Some writers express the opinion that the provision for a university was inserted at the instance of Samuel Doak, who was a member of the Convention and the head of the only classical school in Franklin; but the provision was borrowed from the North Carolina Constitution of 1776.

SEC. 42. That no purchase of lands shall be made of Indian natives, but on behalf of the public, by authority of the General Assembly.

SEC. 43. That the future Legislatures of this State shall regulate entails in such manner as to prevent perpetuities.

SEC. 44. That the Declaration of Rights is hereby declared to be a part of the Constitution of this State, and ought never to be violated on any pretense whatsoever.

SEC. 45. That any member of either house of the General Assembly shall have liberty to dissent from and protest against any act or resolves which he may think injurious to public, or any individual, and have the reasons of his dissent entered on the journals.

SEC. 46. That neither house of the General Assembly shall proceed upon public business unless a majority of all the members of such house are actually present; and that upon motion made and seconded, the yeas and nays upon any question shall be taken and entered on the journals and that the journals of the proceedings of both houses of the General Assembly shall be printed and made public immediately after adjournment.

This Constitution is not intended to preclude the present Convention from making a temporary provision for the well ordering of this State until the General Assembly shall establish government agreeable to the mode herein described.

Resolved, That this Convention recommend this Constitution for the serious consideration of the people during six ensuing months, after which time and before the expiration of the year, they shall choose a Convention for the express purpose of adopting it in the name of the people, if agreed to by them, or altering it as instructed by them.[15]

A true Copy, test:

THOMAS TALBOT, Clk.

---

[15] This paragraph does not, of course, appear in the North Carolina instrument.

[Doc. No. 2]

Cession of April 2, 1790

STATUTE II.

April 2, 1790.

Recital of the deed of cession, by the senators of N. Carolina, to the United States ; and

CHAP. VI.—*An Act to accept a cession of the claims of the state of North Carolina to a certain district of Western territory.*

A deed of cession having been executed, and in the Senate offered for acceptance to the United States, of the claims of the state of North Carolina, to a district of territory therein described; which deed is in the words following, viz.

To all who shall see these Presents ·

We the underwritten Samuel Johnston and Benjamin Hawkins, Senators in the Congress of the United States of America, duly and constitutionally chosen by the legislature of the State of North Carolina, send greeting.

Whereas the General Assembly of the State of North Carolina, on the   day of December, in the year of our Lord one thousand seven hundred and eighty-nine, passed an act, entituled "An act for the purpose of ceding to the United States of America, certain western lands therein described," in the words following, to wit:

of the act of the legislature of that state, by which the execution of the said deed is authorized.

Whereas the United States in Congress assembled, have repeatedly and earnestly recommended to the respective states in the Union, claiming or owning vacant western territory, to make cessions of part of the same, as a further means, as well of hastening the extinguishment of the debts, as of establishing the harmony of the United States; and the inhabitants of the said western territory being also desirous that such cession should be made, in order to obtain a more ample protection than they have heretofore received: now this state, being ever desirous of doing ample justice to the public creditors, as well as the establishing the harmony of. the United States, and complying with the reasonable desires of her citizens; *Be it enacted by the General Assembly of the State of North Carolina, and it is hereby enacted by the authority of the same,* That the Senators of this state, in the Congress of the United States, or one of the Senators and any two of the Representatives of this state in the Congress of the United States, are hereby authorized, empowered and required to execute a deed or deeds on the part and behalf of this state, conveying to the United States of America, all right, title and claim which this state has to the sovereignty and territory of the lands situated within the chartered limits of this state, west of a line beginning on the extreme height of the Stone Mountain, at the place where the Virginia line intersects it; running thence along the extreme height of the said mountain, to the place where Watauga river breaks through it; thence a direct course to the top of the Yellow Mountain, where Bright's road crosses the same; thence along the ridge of said mountain, between the waters of Doe river and the waters of Rock Creek, to the place where the road crosses the Iron Mountain; from thence along the extreme height of said mountain, to where Nolichucky river runs through the same; thence to the top of the Bald Mountain; thence along the extreme height of the said mountain, to the Painted Rock, on French Broad river; thence along the highest ridge of the said mountain, to the place where it is called the Great Iron or Smoaky Mountain: thence along the extreme height of the said mountain, to the place where it is called Unicoy or Unaka Mountain, between the Indian towns of Cowee and Old Chota; thence along the main ridge of the said mountain, to the southern boundary of this state, upon the following express conditions, and subject thereto—that is to say: *First*, That neither the lands nor inhabitants westward of the said mountain shall be estimated after the cession made by virtue of this act shall be accepted, in the ascertaining the proportion of this state with the United States, in the common expense occasioned by the late war. *Secondly*, That the lands laid off, or directed to be laid off by any act or acts of the General Assembly of this state, for the officers and soldiers thereof, their heirs and assigns respectively, shall be and enure to the use and benefit of the said officers, their heirs and assigns respectively; and if the bounds of the said lands already prescribed for the officers and soldiers of the continental line of this state, shall not contain a sufficient quantity of lands fit for cultivation, to make good the several provisions intended by law, that such officer or soldier, or his assignee, who shall fall short of his allotment or proportion, after all the lands fit for cultivation within the said bounds are appropriated, be permitted to take his quota, or such part thereof as may be deficient, in any other part of the said territory intended to be ceded by virtue of this act, not already appropriated. And where entries have been made agreeable to law, and titles under them not perfected by grant or otherwise, then, and in that case, the governor for the time being shall, and he is hereby required to perfect, from time to time, such titles, in such manner as if this act had never been passed. And that all entries made by, or grants made to all and every person or persons whatsoever, agreeable to law, and within the limits hereby intended to be ceded to the United States, shall have the same force and effect as if such cession had not been made; and that all and every right of occupancy and pre-emption, and every other right reserved by any act or acts to persons settled on, and occupying lands within the limits of the lands hereby intended to be ceded as aforesaid, shall continue to be in full force, in the same manner as if the cession had not been made, and as conditions upon which the said lands are ceded to the United States. And further, it shall be understood, that if any person or persons shall have, by virtue of the act, entituled "An act for opening the land-office for the redemption of specie and other certificates, and discharging the arrears due to the army," passed in the year one thousand seven hundred and eighty-three, made his or their entry in the office usually called John Armstrong's office, and located the same to any spot or piece of ground, on which any other person or persons shall have previously located any entry or entries, that then, and in that case, the person or persons having made such entry or entries, or their assignee or assignees, shall have leave, and be at full liberty to remove the location of such entry or entries, to any lands on which no entry has been specially located, or on

Boundaries and conditions of the cession.

Boundaries and conditions of the cession.

any vacant lands included within the limits of the lands hereby intended to be ceded: *Provided,* That nothing herein contained shall extend or be construed to extend to the making good any entry or entries, or any grant or grants heretofore declared void, by any act or acts of the General Assembly of this state. *Thirdly,* That all the lands intended to be ceded by virtue of this act to the United States of America, and not appropriated as before mentioned, shall be considered as a common fund for the use and benefit of the United States of America, North Carolina inclusive, according to their respective and usual proportion in the general charge and expenditure, and shall be faithfully disposed of for that purpose, and for no other use or purpose whatever. *Fourthly,* That the territory so ceded, shall be laid out and formed into a state or states, containing a suitable extent of territory, the inhabitants of which shall enjoy all the privileges, benefits and advantages set forth in the ordinance of the late Congress, for the government of the western territory of the United States, that is to say; whenever the Congress of the United States shall cause to be officially transmitted to the executive authority of this state, an authenticated copy of the act to be passed by the Congress of the United States, accepting the cession of territory made by virtue of this act, under the express conditions hereby specified; the said Congress shall at the same time assume the government of the said ceded territory, which they shall execute in a manner similar to that which they support in the territory west of the Ohio; shall protect the inhabitants against enemies, and shall never bar or deprive them of any privileges which the people in the territory west of the Ohio enjoy: *Provided always,* That no regulations made or to be made by Congress, shall tend to emancipate slaves. *Fifthly,* That the inhabitants of the said ceded territory shall be liable to pay such sums of money, as may, from taking their census, be their just proportion of the debt of the United States, and the arrears of the requisitions of Congress on this state. *Sixthly,* That all persons indebted to this state, residing in the territory intended to be ceded by virtue of this act, shall be held and deemed liable to pay such debt or debts in the same manner, and under the same penalty or penalties as if this act had never been passed. *Seventhly,* That if the Congress of the United States do not accept the cession hereby intended to be made, in due form, and give official notice thereof to the executive of this state, within eighteen months from the passing of this act, then this act shall be of no force or effect whatsoever. *Eighthly,* That the laws in force and use in the State of North Carolina, at the time of passing this act, shall be, and continue in full force within the territory hereby ceded, until the same shall be repealed, or otherwise altered by the legislative authority of the said territory. *Ninthly,* That the lands of non-resident proprietors within the said ceded territory, shall not be taxed higher than the lands of residents. *Tenthly,* That this act shall not prevent the people now residing south of French Broad, between the rivers Tennessee and Big Pigeon, from entering their pre-emptions in that tract, should an office be opened for that purpose, under an act of the present General Assembly. *And be it further enacted by the authority aforesaid,* That the sovereignty and jurisdiction of this state, in and over the territory aforesaid, and all and every the inhabitants thereof, shall be and remain the same in all respects, until the Congress of the United States shall accept the cession to be made by virtue of this act, as if this act had never passed.

Read three times, and ratified in General Assembly, the day of December, A. D. 1789.

CHAS. JOHNSON, *Sp. Sen.*
S. CABARRUS, *Sp. H. C.*"

Now therefore know ye, That we, Samuel Johnston and Benjamin Hawkins, senators aforesaid, by virtue of the power and authority committed to us by the said act, and in the name, and for and on behalf of the said state, do, by these presents, convey, assign, transfer, and set over unto the United States of America, for the benefit of the said states, North Carolina inclusive, all right, title, and claim which the said state hath to the sovereignty and territory of the lands situated within the chartered limits of the said state, as bounded and described in the above recited act of the General Assembly, to and for the uses and purposes, and on the conditions mentioned in the said act.

Boundaries and conditions of the cession.

 In witness whereof, we have hereunto subscribed our names, and affixed our seals, in the senate-chamber, at New York, this twenty-fifth day of February, in the year of our Lord, one thousand seven hundred and ninety, and in the fourteenth year of the independence of the United States of America.

SAM. JOHNSTON. (L.S.)
BENJAMIN HAWKINS. (L.S.)

Signed, sealed, and delivered
 in the presence of
 SAM. A. OTIS.

Be it enacted by the Senate and House of Representatives of the United States of America in Congress assembled, That the said deed be, and the same is hereby accepted.

Accepted.

APPROVED, April 2, 1790.

[Doc. No.3]

Act of May 26, 1790

STATUTE II.

CHAP. XIV.—*An Act for the Government of the Territory of the United States, south of the river Ohio.*(b)

May 26, 1790.

SECTION 1. *Be it enacted by the Senate and House of Representatives of the United States of America in Congress assembled,* That the territory of the United States south of the river Ohio, for the purposes of temporary government, shall be one district; the inhabitants of which shall enjoy all the privileges, benefits and advantages set forth in the ordinance of the late Congress, for the government of the territory of the United States northwest of the river Ohio. And the government of the said territory south of the Ohio, shall be similar to that which is now exercised in the territory northwest of the Ohio; except so far as is otherwise provided in the conditions expressed in an act of Congress of the present session, entitled "An act to accept a cession of the claims of the State of North Carolina, to a certain district of western territory."

Act of June 1, 1796, ch. 46.
Act of April 7, 1798, ch. 26.
Territory south of the Ohio, to be one district; its privileges and government:
Act of August 7, 1789, ch. 8.
Exceptions.

SEC. 2. *And be it further enacted,* That the salaries of the officers, which the President of the United States shall nominate, and with the advice and consent of the Senate appoint, by virtue of this act, shall be the same as those, by law established, of similar officers in the government northwest of the river Ohio. And the powers, duties and emoluments of a superintendent of Indian affairs for the southern department, shall be united with those of the governor.

Act of April 2, 1790, ch. 6.
Salaries of the officers therein.

APPROVED, May 26, 1790.

(b) Ordinance for the government of the territory of the United States, northwest of the river Ohio, in note to page 51.

[Doc. No. 4]

Constitution of 1796 *

We, the people of the territory of the United States south of the river Ohio, having the right of admission into the General Government as a member State thereof, consistent with the Constitution of the United States and the act of cession of the State of North Carolina, recognizing the ordinance for the government of the territory of the United States northwest of the river Ohio, do ordain and establish the following constitution or form of government, and do mutually agree with each other to form ourselves into a free and independent State by the name of the State of Tennessee.

ARTICLE I.

SECTION 1. The legislative authority of this State shall be vested in a general assembly, which shall consist of a senate and house of representatives, both dependent on the people.

---

* This constitution was framed by a convention which assembled at Knoxville January 11, 1796, and completed its labors February 6, 1796.   It was not submitted to the people for ratification.

SEC. 2. Within three years after the first meeting of the general assembly, and within every subsequent term of seven years, an enumeration of the taxable inhabitants shall be made in such manner as shall be directed by law; the number of representatives shall, at the several periods of making such enumeration, be fixed by the legislature, and apportioned among the several counties according to the number of taxable inhabitants in each, and shall never be less than twenty-two nor greater than twenty-six until the number of taxable inhabitants shall be forty thousand, and after that event at such ratio that the whole number of representatives shall never exceed forty.

SEC. 3. The number of senators shall, at the several periods of making the enumeration before mentioned, be fixed by the legislature and apportioned among the districts formed as hereinafter directed, according to the number of taxable inhabitants in each, and shall never be less than one-third nor more than one-half of the number of representatives.

SEC. 4. The senators shall be chosen by districts, to be formed by the legislature, each district containing such a number of taxable inhabitants as shall be entitled to elect not more than three senators. When a district shall be composed of two or more counties they shall be adjoining, and no county shall be divided in forming a district.

SEC. 5. The first election for senators and representatives shall commence on the second Thursday of March next, and shall continue for that and the succeeding day, and the next election shall commence on the first Thursday of August, one thousand seven hundred and ninety-seven, and shall continue on that and the succeeding day; and forever after elections shall be held once in two years, commencing on the first Thursday in August and terminating the succeeding day.

SEC. 6. The first session of the general assembly shall commence on the last Monday of March next; the second on the third Monday of September, one thousand seven hundred and ninety-seven; and forever after the general assembly shall meet on the third Monday of September next ensuing the then election, and at no other period, unless as provided for by this constitution.

SEC. 7. That no person shall be eligible to a seat in the general assembly unless he shall have resided three years in the State and one year in the county immediately preceding the election, and shall possess in his own right in the county which he represents not less than two hundred acres of land, and shall have attained to the age of twenty-one years.

SEC. 8. The senate and house of representatives, when assembled, shall each choose a speaker and its other officers, be judges of the qualifications and elections of its members, and sit upon its own adjournments from day to day. Two-thirds of each house shall constitute a quorum to do business, but a smaller number may adjourn from day to day, and may be authorized by law to compel the attendance of absent members.

SEC. 9. Each house may determine the rules of its proceedings, punish its members for disorderly behavior, and, with the concurrence of two-thirds expel a member, but not a second time for the same offence, and shall have all other powers necessary for the legislature of a free State.

SEC. 10. Senators and representatives shall, in all cases, except treason, felony, or breach of the peace, be privileged from arrest during the session of the general assembly, and in going to and returning from the same; and for any speech or debate in either house, they shall not be questioned in any other place.

SEC. 11. Each house may punish, by imprisonment, during their session, any person, not a member, who shall be guilty of disrespect to the house, by any disorderly or contemptuous behavior in their presence.

SEC. 12. When vacancies happen in either house, the governor, for the time being, shall issue writs of election to fill such vacancies.

SEC. 13. Neither house shall, during their session, adjourn without consent of the other, for more than three days, nor to any other place than that in which the two houses shall be sitting.

SEC. 14. Bills may originate in either house, but may be amended, altered, or rejected by the other.

Sec. 15. Every bill shall be read three times, on three different days, in each house, and be signed by the respective speakers, before it becomes a law.

Sec. 16. After a bill has been rejected, no bill containing the same substance shall be passed into a law during the same session.

Sec. 17. The style of the laws of this State shall be, "*Be it enacted by the general assembly of the State of Tennessee.*"

Sec. 18. Each house shall keep a journal of its proceedings, and publish them, except such parts as the welfare of the State may require to be kept secret. And the yeas and nays of the members on any question shall, at the request of any two of them, be entered on the journals.

Sec. 19. The doors of each house, and committees of the whole, shall be kept open, unless when the business shall be such as ought to be kept secret.

Sec. 20. The legislature of this State shall not allow the following officers of government greater annual salaries than as follows, until the year one thousand eight hundred and four, to wit:

The governor not more than seven hundred and fifty dollars.

The judges of the superior courts not more than six hundred dollars each.

The secretary not more than four hundred dollars.

The treasurer or treasurers not more than 4 per cent. for receiving and paying out all moneys.

The attorney or attorneys for the State shall receive a compensation for their services, not exceeding fifty dollars for each superior court which he shall attend.

No member of the legislature shall receive more than one dollar and seventy-five cents per day, nor more for every twenty-five miles he shall travel in going to and returning from the general assembly.

Sec. 21. No money shall be drawn from the treasury but in consequence of appropriations made by law.

Sec. 22. No person who heretofore hath been, or hereafter may be, a collector or holder of public moneys shall have a seat in either house of the general assembly, until such person shall have accounted for, and paid into the treasury, all sums for which he may be accountable or liable.

Sec. 23. No judge of any court of law or equity, secretary of state, attorney-general, register, clerk of any court of record, or person holding any office under the authority of the United States shall have a seat in the general assembly; nor shall any person in this State hold more than one lucrative office at one and the same time: *Provided*, That no appointment in the militia, or to the office of a justice of the peace, shall be considered a lucrative office.

Sec. 24. No member of the general assembly shall be eligible to any office or place of trust, except to the office of a justice of the peace, or trustee of any literary institution, where the power of appointment to such office or place of trust is vested in their own body.

Sec. 25. Any member of either house of the general assembly shall have liberty to dissent from and protest against any act or resolve which he may think injurious to the public, or any individual, and have the reasons of his dissent entered on the journals.

Sec. 26. All lands liable to taxation in this State, held by deed, grant, or entry, shall be taxed equal and uniform, in such manner that no one hundred acres shall be taxed higher than another, except town-lots, which shall not be taxed higher than two hundred acres of land each; no freeman shall be taxed higher than one hundred acres, and no slave higher than two hundred acres on each poll.

Sec. 27. No article manufactured of the produce of this State shall be taxed otherwise than to pay inspection fees.

ARTICLE II.

Section 1. The supreme executive power of this State shall be vested in a governor.

Sec. 2. The governor shall be chosen by the electors of the members of the general assembly, at the times and places where they shall respectively vote for the members thereof. The returns of every election for governor shall be sealed up, and transmitted to the seat of government by the returning officers, directed to the speaker of the senate, who shall open and publish them in the presence of a majority of the members of each house of the general assembly. The person having the highest number of votes shall be governor; but if two or more shall be equal and highest in votes, one of them shall be chosen governor by joint ballot of both houses of the general assembly. Contested elections for governor shall be determined by both houses of the general assembly, in such manner as shall be prescribed by law.

SEC. 3. He shall be at least twenty-five years of age, and possess a freehold estate of five hundred acres of land, and have been a citizen or inhabitant of this State four years next before his election, unless he shall have been absent on the public business of the United States or of this State.

SEC. 4. The first governor shall hold his office until the fourth Tuesday of September, one thousand seven hundred and ninety-seven, and until another governor shall be elected and qualified to office; and forever after the governor shall hold his office for the term of two years, and until another governor shall be elected and qualified; but shall not be eligible more than six years in any term of eight.

SEC. 5. He shall be commander-in-chief of the army and navy of this State, and of the militia, except when they shall be called into the service of the United States.

SEC. 6. He shall have power to grant reprieves and pardons, after conviction, except in cases of impeachment.

SEC. 7. He shall, at stated times, receive a compensation for his services, which shall not be increased or diminished during the period for which he shall have been elected.

SEC. 8. He may require information, in writing, from the officers in the executive department, upon any subject relating to the duties of their respective offices.

SEC. 9. He may, on extraordinary occasions, convene the general assembly by proclamation, and shall state to them, when assembled, the purpose for which they shall have been convened.

SEC. 10. He shall take care that the laws shall be faithfully executed.

SEC. 11. He shall, from time to time, give to the general assembly information of the state of the government, and recommend to their consideration such measures as he shall judge expedient.

SEC. 12. In case of his death, or resignation, or removal from office, the speaker of the senate shall exercise the office of governor until another governor shall be duly qualified.

SEC. 13. No member of Congress or person holding any office under the United States, or this State, shall execute the office of governor.

SEC. 14. When any officer, the right of whose appointment is by this constitution vested in the general assembly, shall, during the recess, die, or his office by other means become vacant, the governor shall have power to fill up such vacancy by granting a temporary commission, which shall expire at the end of the next session of the legislature.

SEC. 15. There shall be a seal of this State, which shall be kept by the governor, and used by him officially, and shall be called "The Great Seal of the State of Tennessee."

SEC. 16. All grants and commissions shall be in the name and by the authority of the State of Tennessee, be sealed with the State seal, and signed by the governor.

SEC. 17. A secretary of this State shall be appointed and commissioned during the term of four years. He shall keep a fair register of all the official acts and proceedings of the governor; and shall, when required, lay the same, and all papers, minutes, and vouchers relative thereto, before the general assembly, and shall perform such other duties as shall be enjoined him by law.

ARTICLE III.

SECTION 1. Every freeman of the age of twenty-one years and upwards, possessing a freehold in the county wherein he may vote, and being an inhabitant of this

State, and every freeman, being an inhabitant of any one county in the State six months immediately preceding the day of election, shall be entitled to vote for members of the general assembly, for the county in which he shall reside.

SEC. 2. Electors shall in all cases, except treason, felony, or breach of the peace, be privileged from arrest during their attendance at elections, and in going to and returning from them.

SEC. 3. All elections shall be by ballot.

ARTICLE IV.

SECTION 1. The house of representatives shall have the sole power of impeachment.

SEC. 2. All impeachments shall be tried by the senate. When sitting for that purpose, the senators shall be upon oath or affirmation.

SEC. 3. No person shall be convicted, without the concurrence of two-thirds of the members of the whole house.

SEC. 4. The governor, and all civil officers under this State, shall be liable to impeachment for any misdemeanor in office; but judgment, in such cases, shall not extend further than to removal from office, and disqualification to hold any office of honor, trust, or profit under this State. The party shall, nevertheless, in all cases be liable to indictment, trial, judgment, and punishment, according to law.

ARTICLE V.

SECTION 1. The judicial power of the State shall be vested in such superior and inferior courts of law and equity as the legislature shall, from time to time, direct and establish.

SEC. 2. The general assembly shall, by joint ballot of both houses, appoint judges of the several courts of law and equity, also an attorney or attorneys for the State, who shall hold their respective offices during good behavior.

SEC. 3. The judges of the superior court shall, at stated times, receive a compensation for their services, to be ascertained by law; but shall not be allowed any fees or perquisites of office, nor shall they hold any other office of trust or profit under this State or the United States.

SEC. 4. The judges of the superior courts shall be justices of oyer and terminer and general jail-delivery throughout the State.

SEC. 5. The judges of the superior and inferior courts shall not charge juries with respect to matters of fact, but may state the testimony and declare the law.

SEC. 6. The judges of the superior courts shall have power, in all civil cases, to issue writs of *certiorari*, to remove any cause, or a transcript thereof, from any inferior court of record into the superior, on sufficient cause, supported by oath or affirmation.

SEC. 7. The judges or justices of the inferior courts of law shall have power, in all civil cases, to issue writs of *certiorari*, to remove any cause, or a transcript thereof, from any inferior jurisdiction into their court, on sufficient cause, supported by oath or affirmation.

SEC. 8. No judge shall sit on the trial of any cause where the parties shall be connected with him by affinity or consanguinity, except by consent of parties. In case all the judges of the superior court shall be interested in the event of any cause, or related to all or either of the parties, the governor of the State shall in such case specially commission three men of law knowledge for the determination thereof.

SEC. 9. All writs and other process shall run in the name of the State of Tennessee, and bear test and be signed by the respective clerks. Indictments shall conclude, " against the peace and dignity of the State."

SEC. 10. Each court shall appoint its own clerk, who may hold his office during good behavior.

SEC. 11. No fine shall be laid on any citizen of this State that shall exceed fifty dollars, unless it shall be assessed by a jury of his peers, who shall assess the fine at the time they find the fact, if they think the fine ought to be more than fifty dollars.

Sec. 12. There shall be justices of the peace appointed for each county, not exceeding two for each captain's company, except for the company which includes the county town, which shall not exceed three, who shall hold their offices during good behavior.

ARTICLE VI.

Section 1. There shall be appointed in each county, by the county court, one sheriff, one coroner, one trustee, and a sufficient number of constables, who shall hold their offices for two years. They shall also have power to appoint one register and ranger for the county, who shall hold their offices during good behavior. The sheriff and coroner shall be commissioned by the governor.

Sec. 2. There shall be a treasurer or treasurers appointed for the State, who shall hold his or their offices for two years.

Sec. 3. The appointment of all officers, not otherwise directed by this constitution, shall be vested in the legislature.

ARTICLE VII.

Section 1. Captains, subalterns, and non-commissioned officers shall be elected by those citizens, in their respective districts, who are subject to military duty.

Sec. 2. All field-officers of the militia shall be elected by those citizens in their respective counties who are subject to military duty.

Sec. 3. Brigadiers-general shall be elected by the field-officers of their respective brigades.

Sec. 4. Majors-general shall be elected by the brigadiers and field-officers of the respective divisions.

Sec. 5. The governor shall appoint the adjutant-general; the majors-general shall appoint their aids; the brigadiers-general shall appoint their brigade-majors, and the commanding officers of regiments their adjutants and quartermasters.

Sec. 6. The captains and the subalterns of the cavalry shall be appointed by the troops enrolled in their respective companies, and the field-officers of the district shall be appointed by the said captains and subalterns : *Provided*, That, whenever any new county is laid off, that the field-officers of the said cavalry shall appoint the captain and other officers therein *pro tempore*, until the company is filled up and completed, at which time the election of the captains and subalterns shall take place as aforesaid.

Sec. 7. The legislature shall pass laws exempting citizens, belonging to any sect or denomination of religion the tenets of which are known to be opposed to the bearing of arms, from attending private and general musters.

ARTICLE VIII.

Section 1. Whereas the ministers of the gospel are, by their professions, dedicated to God and the care of souls, and ought not to be diverted from the great duties of their functions; therefore no minister of the gospel, or priest of any denomination whatever, shall be eligible to a seat in either house of the legislature.

Sec. 2. No person who denies the being of God, or a future state of rewards and punishments, shall hold any office in the civil department of this State.

ARTICLE IX.

Section 1. That every person who shall be chosen or appointed to any office of trust or profit shall, before entering on the execution thereof, take an oath to support the constitution of this State, and also an oath of office.

Sec. 2. That each member of the senate and house of representatives shall, before they proceed to business, take an oath or affirmation to support the constitution of this State, and also the following oath:

"I, A. B., do solemnly swear [or affirm] that, as a member of this general assembly,

I will in all appointments vote without favor, affection, partiality, or prejudice, and that I will not propose or assent to any bill, vote, or resolution which shall appear to me injurious to the people, or consent to any act or thing whatever that shall have a tendency to lessen or abridge their rights and privileges, as declared by the constitution of this State."

SEC. 3. Any elector who shall receive any gift or reward for his vote, in meat, drink, money, or otherwise, shall suffer such punshiment as the laws shall direct. And any person who shall directly or indirectly give, promise, or bestow any such reward to be elected, shall thereby be rendered incapable, for two years, to serve in the office for which he was elected, and be subject to such further punishment as the legislature shall direct.

SEC. 4. No new county shall be established by the general assembly which shall reduce the county or counties, or either of them, from which it shall be taken to a less content than six hundred and twenty-five square miles; nor shall any new county be laid off of less contents. All new counties, as to the right of suffrage and representation, shall be considered as a part of the county or counties from which it was taken, until entitled by numbers to the right of representation. No bill shall be passed into a law for the establishment of a new county except upon a petition to the general assembly for that purpose, signed by two hundred of the free male inhabitants within the limits or bounds of such new county prayed to be laid off.

ARTICLE X.

SECTION 1. Knoxville shall be the seat of government until the year one thousand eight hundred and two.

SEC. 2. All laws and ordinances now in force and use in this Territory, not inconsistent with this constitution, shall continue to be in force and use in this State, until they shall expire, be altered, or repealed by the legislature.

SEC. 3. That whenever two-thirds of the general assembly shall think it necessary to amend or change this constitution, they shall recommend to the electors, at the next election for members to the general assembly, to vote for or against a convention; and if it shall appear that a majority of all the citizens of the State, voting for representatives, have voted for a convention, the general assembly shall, at their next session, call a convention, to consist of as many members as there be in the general assembly, to be chosen in the same manner, at the same place, and by the same electors that chose the general assembly, who shall meet within three months after the said election, for the purpose of revising, amending, or changing the constitution.

SEC. 4. The declaration of rights hereto annexed is declared to be a part of the constitution of this State, and shall never be violated on any pretence whatever. And to guard against transgressions of the high powers which we have delegated, we declare that everything in the bill of rights contained, and every other right not hereby delegated, is excepted out of the general powers of government, and shall forever remain inviolate.

ARTICLE XI.

DECLARATION OF RIGHTS.

SECTION 1. That all power is inherent in the people, and all free governments are founded on their authority, and instituted for their peace, safety, and happiness; for the advancement of those ends, they have at all times an unalienable and indefeasible right to alter, reform, or abolish the government in such manner as they may think proper.

SEC. 2. That, government being instituted for the common benefit, the doctrine of non-resistance against arbitrary power and oppression is absurd, slavish, and destructive to the good and happiness of mankind.

SEC. 3. That all men have a natural and indefeasible right to worship Almighty God according to the dictates of their own consciences; that no man can of right be compelled to attend, erect, or support any place of worship, or to maintain any ministry against his consent; that no human authority can in any case whatever control or interfere with the rights of conscience; and that no preference shall ever be given by law to any religious establishments or modes of worship.

SEC. 4. That no religious test shall ever be required as a qualification to any office or public trust under this State.

SEC. 5. That elections shall be free and equal.

SEC. 6. That the right of trial by jury shall remain inviolate.

SEC. 7. That the people shall be secure in their persons, houses, papers, and possessions, from unreasonable searches and seizures, and that general warrants, whereby an officer may be commanded to search suspected places, without evidence of the fact committed, or to seize any person or persons not named, whose offences are not particularly described and supported by evidence, are dangerous to liberty, and ought not to be granted.

SEC. 8. That no freeman shall be taken, or imprisoned, or disseized of his freehold, liberties, or privileges, or outlawed or exiled, or in any manner destroyed or deprived of his life, liberty, or property, but by the judgment of his peers or the law of the land.

SEC. 9. That in all criminal prosecutions the accused hath a right to be heard by himself and his counsel; to demand the nature and cause of the accusation against him, and to have a copy thereof; to meet the witnesses face to face; to have compulsory process for obtaining witnesses in his favor; and in prosecutions by indictment or presentment a speedy public trial, by an impartial jury of the county or district in which the crime shall have been committed; and shall not be compelled to give evidence against himself.

SEC. 10. That no person shall, for the same offence, be twice put in jeopardy of life or limb.

SEC. 11. That laws made for the punishment of facts committed previous to the existence of such laws, and by them only declared criminal, are contrary to the principles of a free government; wherefore no *ex post facto* law shall be made.

SEC. 12. That no conviction shall work corruption of blood or forfeiture of estate. The estate of such persons as shall destroy their own lives shall descend or vest as in case of natural death. If any person be killed by casualty, there shall be no forfeiture in consequence thereof.

SEC. 13. That no person arrested, or confined in jail, shall be treated with unnecessary rigor.

SEC. 14. That no freeman shall be put to answer any criminal charge, but by presentment, indictment, or impeachment.

SEC. 15. That all prisoners shall be bailable by sufficient sureties, unless for capital offences, when the proof is evident or the presumption great. And the privilege of the writ of *habeas corpus* shall not be suspended, unless when, in case of rebellion or invasion, the public safety may require it.

SEC. 16. That excessive bail shall not be required, nor excessive fines imposed, nor cruel and unusual punishments inflicted.

SEC. 17. That all courts shall be open; and every man, for an injury done him in his lands, goods, person, or reputation, shall have remedy by due course of law, and right and justice administered without sale, denial, or delay. Suits may be brought against the State in such manner and in such courts as the legislature may by law direct: *Provided,* The right of bringing suit be limited to the citizens of this State.

SEC. 18. That the person of a debtor, where there is not strong presumption of fraud, shall not be continued in prison after delivering up his estate for the benefit of his creditor or creditors, in such manner as shall be prescribed by law.

SEC. 19. That the printing-presses shall be free to every person who undertakes to examine the proceedings of the legislature, or of any branch or officer of government; and no law shall ever be made to restrain the right thereof. The free communication of thoughts and opinions is one of the invaluable rights of man; and every citizen may freely speak, write, and print on any subject, being responsible for the abuse of that liberty. But in prosecutions for the publication of papers investigating the official conduct of officers or men in public capacity, the truth thereof may be given in evidence; and in all indictments for libels, the jury shall have a right to determine the law and the facts, under the direction of the court, as in other cases.

SEC. 20. That no retrospective law, or law impairing the obligation of contracts, shall be made.

SEC. 21. That no man's particular services shall be demanded or property taken, or applied to public use, without the consent of his representatives, or without just compensation being made therefor.

SEC. 22. That the citizens have a right, in a peaceable manner, to assemble together for their common good, to instruct their representatives, and to apply to those invested with the powers of government for redress of grievances, or other proper purposes, by address or remonstrance.

SEC. 23. That perpetuities and monopolies are contrary to the genius of a free State, and shall not be allowed.

SEC. 24. That the sure and certain defence of a free people is a well-regulated militia; and as standing armies, in time of peace, are dangerous to freedom, they ought to be avoided, as far as the circumstances and safety of the community will admit, and that in all cases the military shall be in strict subordination to the civil authority.

SEC. 25. That no citizen in this State, except such as are employed in the Army of the United States or militia in actual service, shall be subject to corporal punishment under the martial law.

SEC. 26. That the freemen of this State have a right to keep and to bear arms for their common defence.

SEC. 27. That no soldier shall in time of peace be quartered in any house without consent of the owner, nor in time of war but in a manner prescribed by law.

SEC. 28. That no citizen of this State shall be compelled to bear arms, provided he will pay an equivalent, to be ascertained by law.

SEC. 29. That an equal participation of the free navigation of the Mississippi is one of the inherent rights of the citizens of this State; it cannot, therefore, be conceded to any prince, potentate, power, person, or persons whatever.

SEC. 30. That no hereditary emoluments, privileges, or honors shall ever be granted or conferred in this State.

SEC. 31. That the people residing south of French Broad and Holston, between the rivers Tennessee and the Big Pigeon, are entitled to the right of preëmption and occupancy in that tract.

SEC. 32. That the limits and boundaries of this State be ascertained, it is declared they are as hereafter mentioned; that is to say: Beginning on the extreme height of the Stone Mountain, at the place where the line of Virginia intersects it, in latitude thirty-six degrees and thirty minutes north; running thence along the extreme height of the said mountain to the place where Watauga River breaks through it; thence a direct course to the top of the Yellow Mountain, where Bright's road crosses the same; thence along the ridge of said mountain, between the waters of Doe River and the waters of Rock Creek, to the place where the road crosses the Iron Mountain; from thence along the extreme height of said mountain to where Nolichucky River runs through the same; thence to the top of the Bald Mountain; thence along the extreme height of said mountain to the Painted Rock, on French Broad River; thence along the highest ridge of said mountain to the place where it is called the Great Iron or Smoky Mountain; thence along the extreme height of said mountain to the place where it is called Unicoi or Unaka Mountain, between the Indian towns of Cowee and Old Chota; thence along the main ridge of the said mountain to the southern boundary of this State, as described in the act of cession of North Carolina to the United States of America, and that all the territory, lands, and waters lying west of the said line, as before mentioned, and contained within the chartered limits of the State of North Carolina, are within the boundaries and limits of this State, over which the people have the right of exercising sovereignty and right of soil so far as is consistent with the Constitution of the United States, recognizing the Articles of Confederation, the Bill of Rights, and constitution of North Carolina, the cession act of the said State, and the ordinance of the late Congress for the government of the territory northwest of the Ohio; provided nothing herein contained shall extend to affect the claim or claims of individuals to any part of the soil which is recognized to them by the aforesaid cession act.

SCHEDULE.

SECTION 1. That no inconvenience may arise from a change of the temporary to a permanent State government, it is declared that all rights, actions, prosecutions, claims, and contracts, as well of individuals as of bodies-corporate, shall continue as if no change had taken place in the administration of government.

SEC. 2. All fines, penalties, and forfeitures, due and owing to the territory of the United States of America south of the river Ohio, shall inure to the use of the State. All bonds for performance, executed to the governor of the said territory, shall be and pass over to the governor of this State, and his successors in office, for the use of the State, or by him or them respectively to be assigned over to the use of those concerned, as the case may be.

SEC. 3. The governor, secretary, judges, and brigadiers-general have a right, by virtue of their appointments, under the authority of the United States, to continue in the exercise of the duties of their respective offices in their several departments until the said officers are superseded under the authority of this constitution.

SEC. 4. All officers, civil and military, who have been appointed by the governor, shall continue to exercise their respective offices until the second Monday in June, and until successors in office shall be appointed under the authority of this constitution and duly qualified.

SEC. 5. The governor shall make use of his private seal until a State seal shall be provided.

SEC. 6. Until the first enumeration shall be made, as directed in the second section of the first article of this constitution, the several counties shall be respectively entitled to elect one senator and two representatives: *Provided*, That no new county shall be entitled to separate representation previous to taking the enumeration.

SEC. 7. That the next election for representatives and other officers to be held for the county of Tennessee shall be held at the house of William Miles.

SEC. 8. Until a land-office shall be opened, so as to enable the citizens south of French Broad and Holston, between the rivers Tennessee and Big Pigeon, to obtain titles upon their claims of occupancy and preëmption, those who hold land by virtue of such claims shall be eligible to serve in all capacities where a freehold is by this constitution made a requisite qualification.

Done in convention at Knoxville, by unanimous consent, on the sixth day of February, in the year of our Lord one thousand seven hundred and ninety-six, and of the Independence of the United States of America the twentieth. In testimony whereof we have hereunto subscribed our names.

WILLIAM BLOUNT, *President.*

WILLIAM MACLIN, *Secretary.*

[Doc. No. 5]

Act of June 1, 1796

ACT ADMITTING THE STATE OF TENNESSEE—1796.

[FOURTH CONGRESS, FIRST SESSION.]

An Act for the admission of the State of Tennessee into the Union.

Whereas by the acceptance of the deed of cession of the State of North Carolina Congress are bound to lay out into one or more States the territory thereby ceded to the United States:

Be it enacted by the Senate and House of Representatives of the United States of America in Congress assembled, That the whole of the territory ceded to the United States by the State of North Carolina shall be one State, and the same is hereby declared to be one of the United States of America, on an equal footing with the original States in all respects whatever, by the name and title of the State of Tennessee. That until the next general census the said State of Tennessee shall be entitled to one Representative in the House of Representatives of the United States, and in all other respects, as far as they may be applicable, the laws of the United States shall extend to and have force in the State of Tennessee in the same manner as if that State had originally been one of the United States.

APPROVED, June 1, 1796.

[Doc. No. 6]

Constitution of 1834

CONSTITUTION OF TENNESSEE—1834.*

Whereas the people of the territory of the United States south of the river Ohio, having the right of admission into the General Government as a member State thereof, consistent with the Constitution of the United States, and the act of cession of the State of North Carolina, recognizing the ordinance for the government of the territory of the United States northwest of the river Ohio, by their delegates and representatives in convention assembled, did, on the sixth day of February, in the year of our Lord one thousand seven hundred and ninety-six, ordain and establish a constitution or form of government, and mutually agree with each other to form themselves into a free and independent State, by the name of "the State of Tennessee;" and whereas the general assembly of said State of Tennessee, pursuant to the third section of the tenth article of the constitution, by an act passed on the twenty-seventh day of November, in the year of our Lord one thousand eight hundred and thirty-three, entitled "An act to provide for the calling of a convention," did authorize and provide for the election by the people of delegates and representatives to meet at Nashville, in Davidson County, on the third Monday in May, in the year of our Lord one thousand eight hundred and thirty-four, "for the purpose of revising and amending (or changing) the constitution:"

We, therefore, the delegates and representatives of the people of the State of Tennessee, elected and in convention assembled, in pursuance of the said act of assembly, have ordained and established the following amended constitution and form of government for this State, which we recommend to the people of Tennessee for their ratification; that is to say:

ARTICLE I.

DECLARATION OF RIGHTS.

SECTION 1. That all power is inherent in the people, and all free governments are founded on their authority and instituted for their peace, safety, and happiness; for the advancement of those ends they have at all times an unalienable and indefeasible right to alter, reform, or abolish the government in such manner as they may think proper.

SEC. 2. That government being instituted for the common benefit, the doctrine of non-resistance against arbitrary power and oppression is absurd, slavish, and destructive to the good and happiness of mankind.

SEC. 3. That all men have a natural and indefeasible right to worship Almighty God according to the dictates of their own conscience; that no man can of right be compelled to attend, erect, or support any place of worship, or to maintain any minister, against his consent; that no human authority can, in any case whatever, control or interfere with the rights of conscience; and that no preference shall ever be given by law to any religious establishment or mode of worship.

SEC. 4. That no religious test shall ever be required as a qualification to any office or public trust under this State.

---

* This constitution was framed by a convention which assembled at Nashville May 19, 1834, and completed its labors August 30, 1834. It was submitted to the people March 5 and 6, 1835, and ratified by 42,666 votes against 17,691 votes.

SEC. 5. That elections shall be free and equal.

SEC. 6. That the right of trial by jury shall remain inviolate.

SEC. 7. That the people shall be secure in their persons, houses, papers, and possessions, from unreasonable searches and seizures; and that general warrants, whereby an officer may be commanded to search suspected places, without evidence of the fact committed, or to seize any person or persons not named, whose offences are not particularly described and supported by evidence, are dangerous to liberty, and ought not to be granted.

SEC. 8. That no free man shall be taken or imprisoned, or disseized of his freehold, liberties, or privileges, or outlawed, or exiled, or in any manner destroyed or deprived of his life, liberty, or property, but by the judgment of his peers, or the law of the land.

SEC. 9. That in all criminal prosecutions the accused hath a right to be heard by himself and his counsel; to demand the nature and cause of the accusation against him, and to have a copy thereof; to meet the witnesses face to face; to have compulsory process for obtaining witnesses in his favor; and in prosecutions by indictment or presentment, a speedy public trial, by an impartial jury of the county or district in which the crime shall have been committed; and shall not be compelled to give evidence against himself.

SEC. 10. That no person shall, for the same offence, be twice put in jeopardy of life or limb.

SEC. 11. That laws made for the punishment of facts committed previous to the existence of such laws, and by them only declared criminal, are contrary to the principles of a free government; wherefore, no *ex post facto* law shall be made.

SEC. 12. That no conviction shall work corruption of blood or forfeiture of estate. The estate of such persons as shall destroy their own lives shall descend or vest as in case of natural death. If any person be killed by casualty, there shall be no forfeiture in consequence thereof.

SEC. 13. That no person arrested or confined in jail shall be treated with unnecessary rigor.

SEC. 14. That no freeman shall be put to answer any criminal charge but by presentment, indictment, or impeachment.

SEC. 15. That all prisoners shall be bailable by sufficient sureties, unless for capital offences when the proof is evident or the presumption great. And the privilege of the writ of *habeas corpus* shall not be suspended, unless when, in case of rebellion or invasion, the public safety may require it.

SEC. 16. That excessive bail shall not be required, nor excessive fines imposed, nor cruel and unusual punishments inflicted.

SEC. 17. That all courts shall be open; and every man, for an injury done him in his lands, goods, person, or reputation, shall have remedy by due course of law, and right and justice administered without sale, denial, or delay. Suits may be brought against the State in such manner, and in such courts, as the legislature may by law direct.

SEC. 18. That the person of a debtor, where there is not strong presumption of fraud, shall not be continued in prison after delivering up his estate for the benefit of his creditors, in such manner as shall be prescribed by law.

SEC. 19. That the printing-presses shall be free to every person who undertakes to examine the proceedings of the legislature, or of any branch of office of government; and no law shall ever be made to restrain the right thereof. The free communication of thoughts and opinions is one of the invaluable rights of man, and every citizen may freely speak, write, and print on any subject, being responsible for the abuse of that liberty. But in prosecutions for the publication of papers investigating the official conduct of officers or men in public capacity, the truth thereof may be given in evidence; and in all indictments for libels, the jury shall have a right to determine the law and the facts, under the direction of the court, as in other criminal cases.

SEC. 20. That no retrospective law, or law impairing the obligation of contracts, shall be made.

SEC. 21. That no man's particular services shall be demanded, or property taken, or applied to public use, without the consent of his representatives, or without just compensation being made therefor.

SEC. 22. That perpetuities and monopolies are contrary to the genius of free State, and shall not be allowed.

SEC. 23. That the citizens have a right, in a peaceable manner, to assemble together for their common good, to instruct their representatives, and to apply to those invested with the powers of government for redress of grievances or other proper purposes, by address or remonstrance.

SEC. 24. That the sure and certain defence of a free people is a well-regulated militia; and, as standing armies in time of peace are dangerous to freedom, they ought to be avoided, as far as the circumstances and safety of the community will admit; and that in all cases the military shall be kept in strict subordination to the civil authority.

SEC. 25. That no citizen of this State, except such as are employed in the Army of the United States, or militia in actual service, shall be subjected to corporeal punishment under the martial law.

SEC. 26. That the free white men of this State have a right to keep and to bear arms for their common defence.

SEC. 27. That no soldier shall, in time of peace, be quartered in any house without the consent of the owner; nor in time of war, but in a manner prescribed by law.

SEC. 28. That no citizen of this State shall be compelled to bear arms, provided he will pay an equivalent, to be ascertained by law.

SEC. 29. That an equal participation of the free navigation of the Mississippi is one of the inherent rights of the citizens of this State; it cannot, therefore, be conceded to any prince, potentate, power, person or persons whatever.

SEC. 30. That no hereditary emoluments, privileges, or honors shall ever be granted or conferred in this State.

SEC. 31. That the limits and boundaries of this State be ascertained, it is declared they are as hereafter mentioned, that is to say: Beginning on the extreme height of the Stone Mountain, at the place where the line of Virginia intersects it, in latitude thirty-six degrees and thirty minutes north; running thence along the extreme height of the said mountain to the place where Watauga River breaks through it; thence a direct course to the top of the Yellow Mountain, where Bright's road crosses the same; thence along the ridge of said mountain, between the waters of Doe River and the waters of Rock Creek, to the place where the road crosses the Iron Mountain; from thence along the extreme height of said mountain to the place where Nolichucky River runs through the same; thence to the top of the Bald Mountain; thence along the extreme height of said mountain to the Painted Rock, on French Broad River; thence along the highest ridge of said mountain to the place where it is called the Great Iron on Smoky Mountain; thence along the extreme height of said mountain to the place where it is called Unicoi or Unaka Mountain, between the Indian towns of Cowee and Old Chota; thence along the main ridge of the said mountain to the southern boundary of this State, as described in the act of cession of North Carolina to the United States of America; and that all the territory, lands, and waters lying west of the said line, as before mentioned, and contained within the chartered limits of the State of North Carolina, are within the boundaries and limits of this State, over which the people have the right of exercising sovereignty and the right of soil, so far as is consistent with the Constitution of the United States, recognizing the Articles of Confederation, the Bill of Rights, and constitution of North Carolina, the cession act of the said State, and the ordinance of Congress for the government of the territory northwest of the Ohio: *Provided*, Nothing herein contained shall extend to affect the claim or claims of individuals to any part of the soil which is recognized to them by the aforesaid cession act: *And provided also*, That the limits and jurisdiction of this State shall extend to any other land and territory now acquired, or that may hereafter be acquired by compact or agreement with other States or otherwise, although such land and territory are not included within the boundaries hereinbefore designated.

SEC. 32. The people residing south of French Broad and Holston, between the rivers Tennessee and Big Pigeon, are entitled to the right of pre-emption and occupancy in that tract.

ARTICLE II.

SECTION 1. The powers of the government shall be divided into three distinct departments, the legislative, executive, and judicial.

SEC. 2. No person or persons belonging to one of these departments shall exercise any of the powers properly belonging to either of the others, except in the cases herein directed or permitted.

SEC. 3. The legislative authority of this State shall be vested in a general assembly, which shall consist of a senate and house of representatives, both dependent on the people.

SEC. 4. An enumeration of the qualified voters and an apportionment of the representatives in the general assembly shall be made in the year one thousand eight hundred and forty-one, and within every subsequent term of ten years.

SEC. 5. The number of representatives shall, at the several periods of making the enumeration, be apportioned among the several counties or districts according to the number of qualified voters in each; and shall not exceed seventy-five, until the population of the State shall be one million and a half; and shall never thereafter exceed ninety-nine: *Provided,* That any county having two-thirds of the ratio shall be entitled to one member.

SEC. 6. The number of senators shall, at the several periods of making the enumeration, be apportioned among the several counties or districts, according to the number of qualified electors in each, and shall not exceed one-third the number of representatives. In apportioning the senators among the different counties, the fraction that may be lost by any county or counties, in the apportionment of members to the house of representatives, shall be made up to such county or counties in the senate as near as may be practicable. When a district is composed of two or more counties, they shall be adjoining; and no county shall be divided in forming a district.

SEC. 7. The first election for senators and representatives shall be held on the first Thursday in August, one thousand eight hundred and thirty-five; and forever thereafter elections for members of the general assembly shall be held once in two years, on the first Thursday in August; said elections shall terminate the same day.

SEC. 8. The first session of the general assembly shall commence on the first Monday in October, one thousand eight hundred and thirty-five; and forever thereafter the general assembly shall meet on the first Monday in October next ensuing the election.

SEC. 9. No person shall be a representative, unless he shall be a citizen of the United States of the age of twenty-one years, and shall have been a citizen of this State for three years, and a resident in the county he represents one year immediately preceding the election.

SEC. 10. No person shall be a senator unless he shall be a citizen of the United States, of the age of thirty years, and shall have resided three years in this State, and one year in the county or district, immediately preceding the election. No senator or representative shall, during the time for which he was elected, be eligible to any office or place of trust, the appointment to which is vested in the executive or the general assembly, except to the office of trustee of a literary institution.

SEC. 11. The senate and house of representatives, when assembled, shall each choose a speaker and its other officers, be judges of the qualifications and election of its members, and sit upon its own adjournments from day to day. Two-thirds of each house shall constitute a quorum to do business; but a smaller number may adjourn from day to day, and may be authorized by law to compel the attendance of absent members.

SEC. 12. Each house may determine the rules of its proceedings, punish its members for disorderly behavior, and, with the concurrence of two-thirds, expel a member, but not a second time for the same offence; and shall have all other powers necessary for a branch of the legislature of a free State.

SEC. 13. Senators and representatives shall in all cases, except treason, felony, or breach of the peace, be privileged from arrest during the session of the general assembly, and in going to and returning from the same; and, for any speech or debate in either house, they shall not be questioned in any other place.

SEC. 14. Each house may punish by imprisonment during its session any person, not a member, who shall be guilty of disrespect to the house, by any disorderly or contemptuous behavior in its presence.

SEC. 15. When vacancies happen in either house, the governor for the time being shall issue writs of election to fill such vacancies.

SEC. 16. Neither house shall, during its session, adjourn without consent of the other for more than three days, nor to any other place than that in which the two houses shall be sitting.

SEC. 17. Bills may originate in either house, but may be amended, altered, or rejected by the other.

SEC. 18. Every bill shall be read once on three different days, and be passed each time in the house where it originated, before transmission to the other. No bill shall become a law until it shall be read and passed on three different days in each house, and be signed by the respective speakers.

SEC. 19. After a bill has been rejected, no bill containing the same substance shall be passed into a law during the same session.

SEC. 20. The style of the laws of this State shall be, *"Be it enacted by the general assembly of the State of Tennessee."*

SEC. 21. Each house shall keep a journal of its proceedings, and publish it, except such parts as the welfare of the State may require to be kept secret; the ayes and nays shall be taken in each house upon the final passage of every bill of a general character, and bills making appropriations of public moneys; and the ayes and noes of the members on any question shall, at the request of any two of them, be entered on the journal.

SEC. 22. The doors of each house and of committees of the whole shall be kept open, unless when the business shall be such as ought to be kept secret.

SEC. 23. The sum of four dollars per day, and four dollars for every twenty-five miles travelling to and from the seat of government, shall be allowed to the members of the first general assembly, as a compensation for their services. The compensation of the members of the succeeding legislatures shall be ascertained by law; but no law increasing the compensation of the members shall take effect until the commencement of the next regular session after such law shall have been enacted.

SEC. 24. No money shall be drawn from the treasury but in consequence of appropriations made by law; and an accurate statement of the receipts and expenditures of the public money shall be attached to and published with the laws at the rise of each stated session of the general assembly.

SEC. 25. No person who heretofore hath been, or may hereafter be, a collector or holder of public moneys, shall have a seat in either house of the general assembly until such person shall have accounted for and paid into the treasury all sums for which he may be accountable or liable.

SEC. 26. No judge of any court of law or equity, secretary of state, attorney-general, register, clerk of any court of record, or person holding any office under the authority of the United States, shall have a seat in the general assembly; nor shall any person in this State hold more than one lucrative office at the same time: *Provided,* That no appointment in the militia, or to the office of justice of the peace, shall be considered a lucrative office, or operate as a disqualification to a seat in either house of the general assembly.

SEC. 27. Any member of either house of the general assembly shall have liberty to dissent from, and protest against, any act or resolve which he may think injurious to the public or to any individual, and to have the reasons for his dissent entered on the journals.

SEC. 28. All lands liable to taxation, held by deed, grant, or entry, town-lots, bank-stock, slaves between the ages of twelve and fifty years, and such other property as the legislature may from time to time deem expedient, shall be taxable. All property shall be taxed according to its value; that value to be ascertained in such manner as the legislature shall direct, so that the same shall be equal and uniform throughout the State. No one species of property from which a tax may be collected shall be taxed higher than any other species of property of equal value. But the legislature shall have power to tax merchants, pedlers, and privileges, in such manner as thcy may, from time to time, direct. A tax on white polls shall be laid, in such manner and of such an amount as may be prescribed by law.

SEC. 29. The general assembly shall have power to authorize tne several counties and incorporated towns in this State to impose taxes for county and corporation purposes respectively, in such manner as shall be prescribed by law; and all property shall be taxed according to its value, upon the principles established in regard to State taxation.

SEC. 30. No article manufactured of the produce of this State shall be taxed otherwise than to pay inspection fees.

SEC. 31. The general assembly shall have no power to pass laws for the emancipation of slaves, without the consent of their owner or owners.

ARTICLE III.

SECTION 1. The supreme executive power of this State shall be vested in a governor.

SEC. 2. The governor shall be chosen by the electors of the members of the general assembly, at the times and places where they shall respectively vote for the members thereof. The returns of every election for governor shall be sealed up, and transmitted to the seat of government, by the returning officers, directed to the speaker of the senate, who shall open and publish them in the presence of a majority of the members of each house of the general assembly. The person having the highest number of votes shall be governor; but if two or more shall be equal and highest in votes, one of them shall be chosen governor by joint vote of both houses of the general assembly. Contested elections for governor shall be determined by both houses of the general assembly, in such manner as shall be prescribed by law.

SEC. 3. He shall be at least thirty years of age, shall be a citizen of the United States, and shall have been a citizen of this State seven years next before his election.

SEC. 4. The governor shall hold his office for two years, and until his successor shall be elected and qualified. He shall not be eligible more than six years in any term of eight.

SEC. 5. He shall be commander-in-chief of the army and navy of this State, and of the militia, except when they shall be called into the service of the United States.

SEC. 6. He shall have power to grant reprieves and pardons, after conviction, except in cases of impeachment.

SEC. 7. He shall, at stated times, receive a compensation for his services, which shall not be increased or diminished during the period for which he shall have been elected.

SEC. 8. He may require information, in writing, from the officers in the executive department, upon any subject relating to the duties of their respective offices.

SEC. 9. He may, on extraordinary occasions, convene the general assembly, by proclamation; and shall state to them, when assembled, the purposes for which they shall have been convened; but they shall enter on no legislative business except that for which they were specially called together.

SEC. 10. He shall take care that the laws be faithfully executed.

SEC. 11. He shall, from time to time, give to the general assembly information of the state of the government, and recommend to their consideration such measures as he shall judge expedient.

SEC. 12. In case of the removal of the governor from office, or of his death or resignation, the powers and duties of the office shall devolve on the speaker of the senate; and in case of the death, removal from office, or resignation of the speaker of the senate, the powers and duties of the office shall devolve on the speaker of the house of representatives.

SEC. 13. No member of Congress, or person holding any office under the United States or this State, shall execute the office of governor.

SEC. 14. When any officer, the right of whose appointment is by this constitution vested in the general assembly, shall, during the recess, die, or the office, by the expiration of the term, or by other means, become vacant, the governor shall have the power to fill such vacancy, by granting a temporary commission, which shall expire at the end of the next session of the legislature.

SEC. 15. There shall be a seal of this State, which shall be kept by the governor, and used by him officially, and shall be called "The Great Seal of the State of Tennessee."

SEC. 16. All grants and commissions shall be in the name and by the authority of the State of Tennessee, be sealed with the State seal, and signed by the governor.

SEC. 17. A secretary of state shall be appointed by joint vote of the general assembly, and commissioned during the term of four years; he shall keep a fair register of all the official acts and proceedings of the governor, and shall, when required, lay the same, and all papers, minutes, and vouchers relative thereto, before the general assembly, and shall perform such other duties as shall be enjoined by law.

ARTICLE IV.

SECTION 1. Every free white man of the age of twenty-one years, being a citizen of the United States, and a citizen of the county wherein he may offer his vote six months next preceding the day of election, shall be entitled to vote for members of the general assembly, and other civil officers for the county or district in which he resides: *Provided*, That no person shall be disqualified from voting in any election on account of color, who is now, by the laws of this State, a competent witness in a court of justice against a white man. All free men of color shall be exempt from military duty in time of peace, and also from paying a free poll-tax.

SEC. 2. Laws may be passed excluding from the right of suffrage persons who may be convicted of infamous crimes.

SEC. 3. Electors shall in all cases, except treason, felony, or breach of the peace, be privileged from arrest or summons during their attendance at elections, and in going to and returning from them.

SEC. 4. In all elections to be made by the general assembly, the members thereof shall vote *viva voce;* and their votes shall be entered on the journal. All other elections shall be by ballot.

ARTICLE V.

SECTION 1. The house of representatives shall have the sole power of impeachment.

SEC. 2. All impeachments shall be tried by the senate; when sitting for that purpose, the senators shall be upon oath or affirmation. No person shall be convicted without the concurrence of two-thirds of the senators sworn to try the officer impeached.

SEC. 3. The house of representatives shall elect, from their own body, three members, whose duty it shall be to prosecute impeachments. No impeachment shall be tried until the legislature shall have adjourned *sine die*, when the senate shall proceed to try such impeachment.

SEC. 4. The governor, judges of the supreme court, judges of inferior courts, chancellors, attorneys for the State, and secretary of state, shall be liable to impeachment, whenever they may, in the opinion of the house of representatives, commit any crime in their official capacity which may require disqualification; but judgment shall only extend to removal from office, and disqualification to fill any office thereafter. The party shall, nevertheless, be liable to indictment, trial, judgment, and punishment, according to law.

SEC. 5. Justices of the peace and other civil officers not hereinbefore mentioned, for crimes or misdemeanors in office, shall be liable to indictment in such courts as the legislature may direct; and upon conviction, shall be removed from office, by said court, as if found guilty on impeachment; and shall be subject to such other punishment as may be prescribed by law.

ARTICLE VI.

SECTION 1. The judicial power of this State shall be vested in one supreme court, in such inferior courts as the legislature shall from time to time ordain and establish, and the judges thereof, and in justices of the peace. The legislature may also vest such jurisdiction as may be deemed necessary in corporation courts.

SEC. 2. The supreme court shall be composed of three judges, one of whom shall reside in each of the grand divisions of the State; the concurrence of two of said judges shall in every case be necessary to a decision. The jurisdiction of this court shall be appellate only, under such restrictions and regulations as may from time to time be prescribed by law; but it may possess such other jurisdiction as is now conferred by law on the present supreme court. Said courts shall be held at one place. and at one place only, in each of the three grand divisions in the State.

SEC. 3. The general assembly shall, by joint vote of both houses, appoint judges of the several courts of law and equity; but courts may be established to be holden by justices of the peace. Judges of the supreme court shall be thirty-five years of age, and shall be elected for the term of twelve years.

SEC. 4. The judges of such inferior courts as the legislature may establish shall be thirty years of age, and shall be elected for the term of eight years.

SEC. 5. The legislature shall elect attorneys for the State, by joint vote of both nouses of the general assembly, who shall hold their offices for the term of six years. In all cases where an attorney for any district fails or refuses to attend and prosecute according to law, the court shall have power to appoint an attorney *pro tempore*.

SEC. 6. Judges and attorneys for the State may be removed from office by a concurrent vote of both houses of the general assembly, each house voting separately; but two-thirds of all the members elected to each house must concur in such vote. The vote shall be determined by ayes and noes, and the names of the members voting for or against the judge or attorney for the State, together with the cause or causes of removal, shall be entered on the journals of each house respectively. The judge or attorney for the State, against whom the legislature may be about to proceed, shall receive notice thereof, accompanied with a copy of the causes alleged for his removal, at least ten days before the day on which either house of the general assembly shall act thereupon.

SEC. 7. The judges of the supreme and inferior courts shall, at stated times, receive a compensation for their services, to be ascertained by law, which shall not be increased or diminished during the time for which they are elected. They shall not be allowed any fees or perquisites of office, nor hold any other office of trust or profit under this State or the United States.

SEC. 8. The jurisdiction of such inferior courts as the legislature may from time to time establish shall be regulated by law.

SEC. 9. Judges shall not charge juries with respect to matters of fact, but may state the testimony and declare the law.

SEC. 10. The judges or justices of such inferior courts of law as the legislature may establish shall have power, in all civil cases, to issue writs of *certiorari* to remove any cause, or transcript thereof, from any inferior jurisdiction into said court, on sufficient cause, supported by oath or affirmation.

SEC. 11. No judge of the supreme or inferior courts shall preside on the trial of any cause in the event of which he may be interested, or where either of the parties shall be connected with him by affinity or consanguinity, within such degrees as may be prescribed by law, or in which he may have been of counsel, or in which he may have presided in any inferior court, except by consent of all the parties. In case all or any of the judges of the supreme court shall be thus disqualified from presiding on the trial of any cause or causes, the court, or the judges thereof, shall certify the same to the governor of the State, and he shall forthwith specially commission the requisite number of men of law knowledge for the trial and determination thereof. In case of sickness of any of the judges of the supreme or inferior courts, so that they or any of them are unable to attend, the legislature shall be authorized to make provision by the general laws that special judges may be appointed to attend said courts.

SEC. 12. All writs and other process shall run in the name of the State of Tennessee, and bear test and be signed by the respective clerks. Indictments shall conclude "against the peace and dignity of the State."

Sec. 13. Judges of the supreme court shall appoint their clerks, who shall hold their offices for the period of six years. Chancellors (if courts of chancery shall be established) shall appoint their clerks and masters, who shall hold their offices for the period of six years. Clerks of such inferior courts as may be hereafter established, which shall be required to be holden in the respective counties of this State, shall be elected by the qualified voters thereof, for the term of four years; they shall be removed from office for malfeasance, incompetency, or neglect of duty, in such manner as may be prescribed by law.

Sec. 14. No fine shall be laid on any citizen of this State that shall exceed fifty dollars, unless it shall be assessed by a jury of his peers, who shall assess the fine at the time they find the fact, if they think the fine should be more than fifty dollars.

Sec. 15. The different counties in this State shall be laid off, as the general assembly may direct, into districts of convenient size, so that the whole number in each county shall not be more than twenty-five, or four for every one hundred square miles. There shall be two justices of the peace and one constable elected in each district, by the qualified voters therein, except districts including county towns, which shall elect three justices and two constables. The jurisdiction of said officers shall be coextensive with the county. Justices of the peace shall be elected for the term of six, and constables for the term of two years. Upon the removal of either of said officers from the district in which he was elected, his office shall become vacant from the time of such removal. Justices of the peace shall be commissioned by the governor. The legislature shall have power to provide for the appointment of an additional number of justices of the peace in incorporated towns.

ARTICLE VII.

Section 1. There shall be elected in each county, by the qualified voters therein, one sheriff, one trustee, and one register; the sheriff and trustee for two years, and the register for four years: *Provided*, That no person shall be eligible to the office of sheriff more than six years in any term of eight years. There shall be elected for each county, by the justices of the peace, one coroner and one ranger, who shall hold their offices for two years. Said officers shall be removed for malfeasance, or neglect of duty, in such manner as may be prescribed by law.

Sec. 2. Should a vacancy occur, subsequent to an election, in the office of sheriff, trustee, or register, it shall be filled by the justices; if in that of the clerks to be elected by the people, it shall be filled by the courts; and the person so appointed shall continue in office until his successor shall be elected and qualified; and such office shall be filled by the qualified voters at the first election for any of the county officers.

Sec. 3. There shall be a treasurer or treasurers appointed for the State, by the joint vote of both houses of the general assembly, who shall hold his or their offices for two years.

Sec. 4. The election of all officers, and the filling of all vacancies that may happen, by death, resignation, or removal, not otherwise directed or provided for by this constitution, shall be made in such manner as the legislature shall direct.

Sec. 5. The legislature shall provide that the election of the county and other officers by the people shall not take place at the same time that the general elections are held for members of Congress, members of the legislature, and governor. The elections shall commence and terminate on the same day.

ARTICLE VIII.

Section 1. All militia officers shall be elected by persons subject to military duty, within the bounds of their several companies, battalions, regiments, brigades, and divisions, under such rules and regulations as the legislature may, from time to time, direct and establish.

Sec. 2. The governor shall appoint the adjutant-general and his other staff-officers; the majors-general, brigadiers-general, and commanding officers of regiments shall, respectively, appoint their staff-officers.

SEC. 3. The legislature shall pass laws exempting citizens belonging to any sect or denomination of religion, the tenets of which are known to be opposed to the bearing of arms, from attending private and general musters.

ARTICLE IX.

SECTION 1. Whereas ministers of the gospel are, by their profession, dedicated to God and the care of souls, and ought not to be diverted from the great duties of their functions; therefore, no minister of the gospel, or priest of any denomination whatever, shall be eligible to a seat in either house of the legislature.

SEC. 2. No person who denies the being of a God, or a future state of rewards and punishments, shall hold any office in the civil department of this State.

SEC. 3. Any person who shall, after the adoption of this constitution, fight a duel, or knowingly be the bearer of a challenge to fight a duel, or send or accept a challenge for that purpose, or be an aider or abettor in fighting a duel, shall be deprived of the right to hold any office of honor or profit in this State, and shall be punished otherwise in such manner as the legislature may prescribe.

ARTICLE X.

SECTION 1. Every person who shall be chosen or appointed to any office of trust or profit under this constitution, or any law made in pursuance thereof, shall, before entering on the duties thereof, take an oath to support the constitution of this State and of the United States, and an oath of office.

SEC. 2. Each member of the senate and house of representatives shall, before they proceed to business, take an oath or affirmation to support the constitution of this State, and of the United States, and also the following oath: " I,————, do solemnly swear [or affirm] that, as a member of this general assembly, I will, in all appointments, vote without favor, affection, partiality, or prejudice; and that I will not propose or assent to any bill, vote, or resolution which shall appear to me injurious to the people, or consent to any act or thing whatever that shall have a tendency to lessen or abridge their rights and privileges as declared by the constitution of this State."

SEC. 3. Any elector who shall receive any gift or reward for his vote, in meat, drink, money, or otherwise, shall suffer such punishment as the laws shall direct. And any person who shall directly or indirectly give, promise, or bestow any such reward to be elected, shall thereby be rendered incapable, for six years, to serve in the office for which he was elected, and be subject to such further punishment as the legislature shall direct.

SEC. 4. New counties may be established by the legislature, to consist of not less than three hundred and fifty square miles, and which shall contain a population of four hundred and fifty qualified voters. No line of such county shall approach the court-house of any old county from which it may be taken nearer than twelve miles. No part of a county shall be taken to form a new county, or a part thereof, without the consent of a majority of the qualified voters in such part taken off. And in all cases where an old county may be reduced for the purpose of forming a new one, the seat of justice in said old county shall not be removed without the concurrence of two-thirds of both branches of the legislature, nor shall said old county be reduced to less than six hundred and twenty-five square miles: *Provided, however,* That the county of Bedford may be reduced to four hundred and seventy-five square miles; and there shall not be laid off more than one new county on the west, and one on the east, adjoining the county of the dividing line, a majority of the qualified voters of said county voting in favor of said division; the counties of Carter, Rhea, and Humphreys shall not be divided into more than two counties each; nor shall more than one new county be taken out of the territory now composing the counties of Tipton and Dyer; nor shall the seats of justice in the counties of Rhea, Carter, Tipton, and Dyer be removed, without the concurrence of two-thirds of both branches of the legislature. The county of Sullivan may be reduced below the contents of six hundred and twenty-five square miles, but the line of any new county which may hereafter be laid off shall not approach the county-seat of said county nearer than ten miles. The counties of Marion and Bledsoe shall not be reduced below one thousand qualified voters each in forming a new county or counties.

SEC. 5. The citizens who may be included in any new county shall vote with the county or counties from which they may have been stricken off, for members of Congress, for governor, and for members of the general assembly, until the next apportionment of members to the general assembly after the establishment of such new county.

ARTICLE XI.

SECTION 1. All laws and ordinances now in force and use in this State, not inconsistent with this constitution, shall continue in force and use until they shall expire, be altered, or repealed by the legislature.

SEC. 2. Nothing contained in this constitution shall impair the validity of any debts or contracts, or affect any rights of property, or any suits, actions, rights of action, or other proceedings in courts of justice.

SEC. 3. Any amendment or amendments to this constitution may be proposed in the senate or house of representatives; and if the same shall be agreed to by a majority of all the members elected to each of the two houses, such proposed amendment or amendments shall be entered on their journals, with the yeas and nays thereon, and referred to the general assembly then next to be chosen; and shall be published for six months previous to the time of making such choice. And if in the general assembly next chosen as aforesaid such proposed amendment or amendments shall be agreed to by two-thirds of all the members elected to each house, then it shall be the duty of the general assembly to submit such proposed amendment or amendments to the people, in such manner and at such time as the general assembly shall prescribe. And if the people shall approve and ratify such amendment or amendments, by a majority of all the citizens of the State voting for representatives, voting in their favor, such amendment or amendments shall become part of this constitution. When any amendment or amendments to the constitution shall be proposed in pursuance of the foregoing provisions, the same shall at each of the said sessions be read three times on three several days in each house. The legislature shall not propose amendments to the constitution oftener than once in six years.

SEC. 4. The legislature shall have no power to grant divorces, but may authorize the courts of justice to grant them for such causes as may be specified by law: *Provided*, That such laws be general and uniform in their operation throughout the State.

SEC. 5. The legislature shall have no power to authorize lotteries for any purpose, and shall pass laws to prohibit the sale of lottery-tickets in this State.

SEC. 6. The legislature shall fix the rate of interest; and the rate so established shall be equal and uniform throughout the State.

SEC. 7. The legislature shall have no power to suspend any general law for the benefit of any particular individual, nor to pass any law for the benefit of individuals inconsistent with the general laws of the land; nor to pass any law granting to any individual or individuals rights, privileges, immunities, or exemptions other than such as may be by the same law extended to any member of the community who may be able to bring himself within the provisions of such law: *Provided always*, The legislature shall have power to grant such charters of corporation as they may deem expedient for the public good.

SEC. 8. The legislature shall have the right to vest such powers in the courts of justice, with regard to private and local affairs, as may be deemed expedient.

SEC. 9. A well-regulated system of internal improvement is calculated to develop the resources of the State, and promote the happiness and prosperity of her citizens; therefore, it ought to be encouraged by the general assembly.

SEC. 10. Knowledge, learning, and virtue being essential to the preservation of republican institutions, and the diffusion of the opportunities and advantages of education throughout the different portions of the State being highly conducive to the promotion of this end, it shall be the duty of the general assembly, in all future periods of this government, to cherish literature and science. And the fund called the "common-school fund," and all the lands and proceeds thereof, dividends, stocks, and other property of every description whatever, heretofore by law appropriated by the general assembly of this State for the use of common schools, and all such as shall hereafter be appropriated, shall remain a perpetual fund, the principal of which shall never be diminished by legislative appropriation, and the interest thereof shall be inviolably appropriated to the support and encouragement of common schools throughout the State, and for the equal benefit of all the people thereof; and no law shall be made authorizing said fund, or any part thereof, to be diverted to any other use than the support and encouragement of common schools; and it shall be the duty of the general assembly to appoint a board of commissioners, for such term of time as they may think proper, who shall have the general superintendence of said fund, and who shall make a report of the condition of the same, from time to time, under such rules, regulations, and restrictions as may be required by law: *Provided*, That if at any time hereafter a division of the public lands of the United States, or of the money arising from the sales of such lands, shall be made among the individual States, the part of such lands or money coming to this State shall be devoted to the purposes of education and internal improvement and shall never be applied to any other purpose.

SEC. 11. The above provisions shall not be construed to prevent the legislature from carrying into effect any laws that have been passed in favor of the colleges, universities, or academies, or from authorizing heirs or distributees to receive and enjoy escheated property, under such rules and regulations as from time to time may be prescribed by law.

SEC. 12. The declaration of rights hereto prefixed is declared to be a part of the constitution of this State, and shall never be violated on any pretence whatever. And to guard against transgression of the high powers we have delegated, we declare that everything in the bill of rights contained is excepted out of the general powers of government, and shall forever remain inviolate.

SCHEDULE.

SECTION 1. That no inconvenience may arise from a change of the constitution, it is declared that all officers, civil and military, shall continue to hold their offices; and all the functions appertaining to the same shall be exercised and performed according to the existing laws and constitution, until the end of the first session of the general assembly which shall sit under this constitution, and until the government can be reorganized and put into operation under this constitution, in such manner as the first general assembly aforesaid shall prescribe, and no longer.

SEC. 2. The general assembly which shall sit after the first apportionment of representation under the new constitution, to wit, in the year one thousand eight hundred and forty-three, shall, within the first week after the commencement of the session, designate and fix the seat of government; and when so fixed, it shall not be removed, except by the consent of two-thirds of the members of both houses of the general assembly. The first and second sessions of the general assembly under this constitution shall be held in Nashville.

SEC. 3. Until a land-office shall be opened, so as to enable the citizens south and west of the congressional reservation-line to obtain titles upon their claims of occupancy, those who hold lands by virtue of such claims shall be eligible to serve in all capacities where a freehold is, by the laws of the State, made a requisite qualification.

Done in convention, at Nashville, this thirtieth day of August, one thousand eight hundred and thirty-four, and of the Independence of the United States of America the fifty-ninth.

WILLIAM B. CARTER, *President*.

WILLIAM K. HILL, *Secretary*.

ORDINANCE.

I. *Ordered,* That it shall be the duty of the several officers of this State, authorized by law to hold elections for members of the general assembly, to open and hold an election, at the places of holding elections for members to the general assembly, in their respective counties, on the first Thursday and Friday in March next, for the purpose of receiving the votes of such qualified voters as may desire to vote for the adoption or rejection of this amended constitution : *Provided,* That no person shall be deemed a qualified voter in said election except such as are included within the provisions of the first section of the fourth article of this amended constitution.

II. *Ordered,* That it shall be the duty of said returning officers in each county in this State to prepare poll-books, which shall be opened on said days of election, and in which shall be enrolled the name of each voter by the assistance of clerks, who shall be appointed and sworn as clerks in other elections. Said officers shall prepare a ballot-box, in which shall be placed the ticket of each voter. Each ticket shall have written thereon the words "I ratify the amended constitution ;" or, if the voter is opposed to it, "I reject the amended constitution ;" or the words "Ratification" or "Rejection," or some such words as will distinctly convey the intention of the voter. The justices of the several county courts in this State, at some time previous to the day of said election, shall appoint three inspectors for each precinct, and in case of failure of the courts to appoint inspectors, then said returning officers shall appoint them. It shall be the duty of said returning officers, in presence of the said inspectors, to count the votes given for the ratification and rejection of the constitution, of which they shall keep a true and correct estimate in said poll-book. Said returning officer shall deposit the original poll-books of said election with the clerk of the county court in their respective counties, and shall, within five days after said election, make out duplicate statements of the number of votes in their respective counties for ratifying and rejecting the constitution, and shall forward by mail one of said certificates to the governor, one to the secretary of state, and shall likewise deposit one with the clerk of the county court. It shall be the duty of said several clerks carefully to examine the said poll-books, and forthwith to certify to the secretary of state a full, true, and perfect statement of the number of votes taken for and against the constitution, as appears from the poll-books filed in their office. Should said returning officers, or any of them, fail to make returns in due time, as above directed, the secretary of state shall then be authorized to despatch a special messenger for the purpose of obtaining a certified copy of the result of said elections.

III. *Ordered,* That upon the receipt of the said returns it shall be the duty of the governor, secretary of state, and any one of the judges of the supreme court, or any two of the said named officers, to compare the votes given in said election for the ratification and rejection of the amended constitution ; and if it shall appear from said returns that a majority of all the votes given in said election is for ratifying the amended constitution, then it shall be the duty of the governor forthwith to make proclamation of that fact, and thenceforth this amended constitution shall be ordained and established as the constitution of the State of Tennessee. It shall moreover be the duty of the governor, in and by said proclamation, to command the sheriffs and other officers directed by law to hold and superintend elections, to open the polls of elections at the places of holding elections for members of the general assembly in their respective counties, on the first Thursday in August, one thousand eight hundred and thirty-five, for the purpose of electing a governor and for the election of senators and representatives to the general assembly of this State from the several districts and counties, as mentioned and described in this ordinance, at which time and places elections shall also be held for members of Congress, and said officers shall make returns of said elections under the same rules and regulations as are now required by the existing laws; and it shall be the duty of the secretary of state to record the returns made from each county or district, and the result of said election, in a bound book to be preserved in his office.

IV. *Be it further ordered,* That if any sheriff or other acting officer shall fail, within the time prescribed by this ordinance, to discharge any of the duties hereby required, such sheriff or other returning officer so failing as aforesaid shall forfeit and pay the sum of five thousand dollars, to be recovered by action of debt in any of the courts of record in this State, to be sued for in the name of the governor for the use and benefit of common schools.

V. *Be it further ordered*, That until the first enumeration and apportionment of representation, in one thousand eight hundred and forty-one, as directed by the amended constitution, the following districts shall be formed, each of which shall elect one senator, and the polls of election shall be compared at the several places herein mentioned on the first Monday succeeding the day of election, to wit:

The counties of Carter, Sullivan, and Washington shall form one district; and the polls shall be compared in the town of Jonesborough.

The counties of Greene and Hawkins shall compose one district; and the polls shall be compared in the town of Greenville.

The counties of Cocke, Sevier, Jefferson, and Blount shall form one district; and the polls shall be compared in the town of Sevierville.

The counties of Grainger, Claiborne, Campbell, Anderson, and Morgan shall compose one district; and the polls shall be compared at the house of Robert Glenn, esq., in Campbell County.

The counties of Knox and Roane shall form one district; and the polls shall be compared at Campbell's Station.

The counties of Munroe and McMinn shall compose one district; and the polls shall be compared in the town of Athens.

The counties of Rhea, Bledsoe, Marion, and Hamilton shall compose one district; and the polls shall be compared at the town of Dallas.

The counties of Warren and Franklin shall compose one district; and the polls shall be compared at Hillsborough.

The counties of Overton, Jackson, Fentress, and White shall compose one district; and the polls shall be compared at Livingston.

The counties of Lincoln and Giles shall compose one district; and the polls shall be compared at the house of John Kennedy.

The counties of Smith and Sumner shall compose one district; and the polls shall be compared at Hartsville.

The county of Bedford shall compose one district; and the polls shall be compared at Shelbyville.

The county of Maury shall compose one district; and the polls shall be compared in Columbia.

The county of Rutherford shall compose one district; and the polls shall be compared in Murfreesborough.

The county of Davidson shall compose one district; and the polls shall be compared in the city of Nashville.

The county of Williamson shall compose one district; and the polls shall be compared in the town of Franklin.

The counties of Lawrence, Wayne, and Hickman shall compose one district; and the polls shall be compared at Catron and Napier's Furnace.

The counties of Dickson, Stewart, and Humphreys shall compose one district; and the polls shall be compared at Simmons's old place on Yellow Creek.

The counties of Robertson and Montgomery shall compose one district; and the polls shall be compared at Port Royal.

The county of Wilson shall compose one district; and the polls shall be compared in Lebanon.

The counties of Hardeman, Fayette, and Shelby shall compose one district; and the polls shall be compared in Sommerville.

The counties of Madison, Haywood, and Tipton shall compose one district; and the polls shall be compared in Brownsville.

The counties of Carroll, Gibson, and Dyer shall compose one district; and the polls shall be compared in Trenton.

The counties of Henry, Weakley, and Obion shall compose one district; and the polls shall be compared in Dresden.

The counties of Henderson, Perry, McNairy, and Hardin shall compose one district; and the polls shall be compared at the house of James Wright, in Hardin County.

And until said enumeration and apportionment of one thousand eight hundred and forty-one, the counties of Carter, Sullivan, Washington, Greene, Hawkins, Cocke, Sevier, Jefferson, Blount, Grainger, Claiborne, Knox, Roane, Monroe, McMinn, Rhea, and Bledsoe shall each elect one representative; and the polls shall be compared at their respective court-houses.

The counties of Sullivan and Hawkins shall jointly elect one representative; and shall compare the polls at Kingsport.

The counties of Greene and Washington shall jointly elect one representative; and the polls shall be compared at the house of Joshua Royston, esq.

The counties of Knox and Roane shall jointly elect one representative; and the polls shall be compared at Campbell's Station.

The counties of Monroe and McMinn shall jointly elect one representative; and the polls shall be compared at Athens.

The counties of Campbell, Anderson and Morgan shall jointly elect two representatives; and the polls shall be compared at the house of James Ross, esq., in Anderson County.

The counties of Marion and Hamilton shall jointly elect one representative; and the polls shall be compared at Dallas.

The counties of Warren, Franklin, Bedford, Lincoln, Giles, Maury, Rutherford, Williamson, Davidson, Wilson, Smith, and Sumner shall each elect two representatives; and the polls shall be compared at their respective court-houses.

The counties of Lawrence, Wayne, Hickman, Dickson, Humphreys, Montgomery, Stewart, Robertson, Overton, Jackson, Fentress, White, Hardin, McNairy, Hardeman, Fayette, Shelby, Perry, Henderson, Madison, Haywood, Tipton, Carroll, Gibson, Henry, and Weakley shall each elect one representative; and the polls shall be compared at their respective court-houses.

The counties of Obion and Dyer shall jointly elect one representative; and the polls shall be compared at the house of William Terrel, esq., in Dyer County.

The returns of the elections for representatives shall be made at the several places herein pointed out, on the first Saturday succeeding the day of election.

WILLIAM B. CARTER, *President.*

WILLIAM K. HILL, *Secretary.*

AMENDMENTS TO THE CONSTITUTION OF 1834.

RATIFIED 1853.

ART. VI. SEC. 3. The judges of the supreme court shall be elected by the qualified voters of the State at large, and the judges of such inferior courts as the legislature may establish shall be elected by the qualified voters residing within the bounds of any district or circuit to which such inferior judge or judges, either of law or equity, may be assigned by ballot, in the same manner that members of the general assembly are elected.   Courts may be established to be holden by justices of the peace.   Judges of the supreme court shall be thirty-five years of age, and shall be elected for the term of eight years.

SEC. 4. The judges of such inferior courts as the legislature may establish shall be thirty years of age, and shall be elected for the term of eight years.

SEC. 5. An attorney-general for the State shall be elected by the qualified voters of the State at large, and the attorney for the State for any circuit or district to which a judge of an inferior court may be assigned shall be elected by the qualified voters within the bounds of such district or circuit, in the same manner that members of the general assembly are elected; all said attorneys, both for the State and circuit or district, shall hold their offices for the term of six years.   In all cases where the attorney for any district fails or refuses to attend and prosecute according to law, the court shall have power to appoint an attorney *pro tempore.*

RATIFIED 1853.

The legislature shall appoint a day for holding the election of judges and attorneys-general, separate and apart from the days already prescribed or hereafter to be prescribed by the legislature for holding the elections for State and county officers.

RATIFIED 1866.*

ARTICLE I. SECTION 1. That slavery and involuntary servitude, except as a punishment for crime, whereof the party shall have been duly convicted, are hereby forever abolished and prohibited throughout the State.

SEC. 2. The legislature shall make no law recognizing the right of property in man.

SCHEDULE.

SECTION 1. Section thirty-one of the second article of the constitution, which is as follows: "The general assembly shall have no power to pass laws for the emancipation of slaves, without the consent of their owner or owners," is hereby abrogated.

SEC. 2. "The declaration of independence and ordinance dissolving the federal relations between the State of Tennessee and the United States of America," passed and promulgated by the legislature of Tennessee on the 6th day of May, 1861, by which the State was declared separated from the Federal Union, and all laws and ordinances by which Tennessee became a member of the Federal Union, annulled and abrogated, was in like manner an act of treason and usurpation, unconstitutional, null, and void.

SEC. 3. The convention, agreement, and military leagues entered into by the commissioners of the State of Tennessee and the commissioners of the so-called Confederate States of America, made May 7, 1861, and on the same day ratified and confirmed by the legislature, was an act of treason and usurpation, unconstitutional, null, and void.

SEC. 4. No statute of limitations shall be held to operate from and after the 6th day of May, 1861, until such time hereafter as the legislature may prescribe, nor shall any writ of error be refused, or abated in any cause, or suit decided since the 6th day of May, 1861, and prior to this time, by reason of any lapse of time. And in all actions for torts brought, or which may hereafter be brought in the courts of this State by attachment levied upon the property of the defendant, the court shall have power to proceed to judgment and collection of the same, as upon contracts, without personal service of process upon the defendant, until the legislature may see fit to change the law in such cases.

SEC. 5. All laws, ordinances, and resolutions, as well as all acts done in pursuance thereof, under the authority of the usurped State government after the declared independence of the State of Tennessee, on or after the 6th day of May, 1861, were unconstitutional, null, and void from the beginning: *Provided*, That this section shall not be construed as to effect any judicial decisions made by the State courts held at times differing from those provided by law prior to May 6, 1861; said judicial decisions being made pursuant to the laws of the State of Tennessee enacted previous to said date, and between parties present in courts and litigating their rights.

SEC. 6. All laws, ordinances, and resolutions of the usurped State governments, passed on or after the 6th day of May, 1861, providing for the issuance of State bonds, also all notes of the Bank of Tennessee, or any of its branches, issued on or after the 6th day of May, 1861, and all debts created or contracted in the name of the State by said authority, are unconstitutional, null, and void; and no legislature shall hereafter have power to pass any act authorizing the payment of said bonds or debts, or providing for the redemption of said notes.

SEC. 7. All civil and military officers which have been or may hereafter be appointed by the acting governor of the State, are hereby ratified and affirmed, and they shall continue to hold and exercise the functions of their respective offices until their suc-

---

* These amendments were framed by a convention which assembled at Nashville January 9, 1865, and completed its labors January 26, 1865. They were submitted to the people February 22, 1865, and ratified by 21,104 votes against 40 votes.

cessors shall be elected or appointed and qualified as prescribed by the laws and constitution of the State and United States.

SEC. 8. That the proposed amendments to the constitution, and the schedule thereto, be submitted to the people at the ballot-box, on the 22d day of February next, and that upon the adoption thereof, by the people, an election shall be held on the 4th day of March next for governor and members of the legislature, the latter to be voted for by general ticket, upon the basis prescribed in the act apportioning representation in the State, passed on the 19th day of February, 1852, to assemble at the capitol on the first Monday in April next, said officers to continue in office until their successors shall be elected and qualified, under the regular biennial election of 1867 : Provided, That said apportionment be so modified as to give to the counties of Johnson, Carter, Campbell, Anderson, Union, Sevier, Macon, and Hancock each one member; and the district composed of the counties of Fentress, Morgan, Scott, and Cumberland one additional member in the house of representatives.

SEC. 9. The qualifications of voters and the limitation of the elective franchise may be determined by the general assembly which shall first assemble under the amended constitution.

RESOLUTIONS.

Resolved, That at the election in February, those in favor of the foregoing amendments and schedule shall deposit a ballot, on which shall be written " Ratification;" and those who are opposed shall deposit a ballot, on which shall be written " Rejection."

Resolved, That when the above amendments of the constitution of the State of Tennessee shall be submitted to the people of the State for their ratification or rejection, and at the first election held under said constitution as amended, if ratified by the people, no person shall be permitted to vote unless he first take the following oath at the polls. And the name of each voter shall be written upon the back of his ticket, and it shall be the duty of the judges and clerks of said election to preserve said tickets and file them with the clerks of the county courts of their respective counties for future reference: Provided, That this oath shall not be required of the citizens who are well known to the judges of the election to have been unconditional Union men: Provided also, That voters otherwise qualified may vote within any county of the State, and, if in the military service, wherever they may be on the day of election; and that the commanding officer of each regiment, battalion, detachment, battery, or hospital is empowered to hold such election.

OATH.

I solemnly swear that I will henceforth support the Constitution of the United States, and defend it against the assaults of all its enemies; that I am an active friend of the Government of the United States, and the enemy of the so-called Confederate States ; that I ardently desire the suppression of the present rebellion against the Government of the United States; that I sincerely rejoice in the triumph of the armies and navies of the United States, and in the defeat and overthrow of the armies, navies, and of all armed combinations in the so-called Confederate States; that I will cordially oppose all armistices or negotiations for peace with rebels in arms, until the Constitution of the United States, and all laws and proclamations made in pursuance thereof, shall be established over all the people of every State and Territory embraced within the national Union; and that I will heartily aid and assist the loyal people in whatever measures may be adopted for the attainment of those ends; and further, that I take this oath freely and voluntarily and without mental reservation: So help me God.

Resolved, That the returns of this election shall be made to the secretary of state, and the result be declared by the proclamation of the acting governor.

Resolved, That the convention do nominate and offer to the people a candidate for governor, and that the delegates from the several senatorial and representative districts be requested to nominate and present to the convention candidates for their respective districts, to be placed upon the general legislative ticket: *Provided*, If the Union people of any district shall desire to make another selection, that they have opportunity to do so.

Resolved, That it shall be the duty of the executive committee to fill all vacancies that may occur in the list of candidates and officers for holding elections solicited by the convention.

Resolved, That the names of such as may be selected shall be forwarded to the chairman at Nashville, on or before the 10th day of February next, when the chairman shall publish the complete list in the papers of the State.

[Doc. No. 7]

Act of July 24, 1866

RESTORATION OF TENNESSEE TO THE UNION—1866.

[THIRTY-NINTH CONGRESS, FIRST SESSION.]

Joint Resolution restoring Tennessee to her relations to the Union.

Whereas in the year eighteen hundred and sixty-one the government of the State of Tennessee was seized upon and taken possession of by persons in hostility to the United States, and the inhabitants of said State, in pursuance of an act of Congress, were declared to be in a state of insurrection against the United States; and whereas said State government can only be restored to its former political relations in the Union by the consent of the law-making power of the United States; and whereas the people of said State did on the twenty-second day of February, eighteen hundred and sixty-five, by a large popular vote, adopt and ratify a constitution of government whereby slavery was abolished, and all ordinances and laws of secession and debts contracted under the same were declared void; and whereas a State government has been organized under said constitution which has ratified the amendment to the Constitution of the United States abolishing slavery, also the amendment proposed by the Thirty-ninth Congress, and has done other acts proclaiming and denoting loyalty : Therefore,

Be it resolved by the Senate and House of Representatives of the United States of America in Congress assembled, That the State of Tennessee is hereby restored to her former proper, practical relations to the Union, and is again entitled to be represented by Senators and Representatives in Congress.

APPROVED, July 24, 1866.

————————

[Doc. No.8]

Constitution of 1870

CONSTITUTION OF TENNESSEE—1870.*

Whereas the people of the territory of the United States south of the river Ohio, having the right of admission into the General Government as a member State thereof, consistent with the Constitution of the United States, and the act of cession of the State of North Carolina, recognizing the ordinance for the government of the territory of the United States northwest of the Ohio River, by their delegates and representatives in convention assembled, did, on the sixth day of February, in the year of our Lord one thousand seven hundred and ninety-six, ordain and establish a constitution, or form of government, and mutually agreed with each other to form themselves into a free and independent State, by the name of the State of Tennessee; and whereas the general assembly of said State of Tennessee, (pursuant to the third section of the tenth article of the constitution,) by an act passed on the twenty-seventh day of November, in the year of our Lord one thousand eight hundred and thirty-three, entitled "An act to provide for the calling of a convention," passed in

* This constitution was framed by a convention which assembled at Nashville January 10, 1870, and completed its labors February 22, 1870. It was submitted to the people March 26, 1870, and was ratified by 98,128 votes against 33,872 votes.

obedience to the declared will of the voters of the State, as expressed at the general election of August, in the year of our Lord one thousand eight hundred and thirty-three, did authorize and provide for the election by the people of delegates and representatives, to meet at Nashville, in Davidson County, on the third Monday in May, in the year of our Lord one thousand eight hundred and thirty-four, for the purpose of revising and amending or changing the constitution; and said convention did accordingly meet and form a constitution, which was submitted to the people, and was ratified by them on the first Friday in March, in the year of our Lord one thousand eight hundred and thirty-five; and whereas the general assembly of said State of Tennessee, under and in virtue of the first section of the first article of the declaration of rights, contained in and forming a part of the existing constitution of the State, by an act passed on the fifteenth day of November, in the year of our Lord one thousand eight hundred and sixty-nine, did provide for the calling of a convention by the people of the State, to meet at Nashville on the second Monday in January, in the year of our Lord one thousand eight hundred and seventy, and for the election of delegates for the purpose of amending or revising the present constitution, or of forming and making a new constitution; and whereas the people of the State, in the mode provided by said act, have called said convention, and elected delegates to represent them therein: Now, therefore,

We, the delegates and representatives of the people of the State of Tennessee, duly elected and in convention assembled, in pursuance of said act of assembly, have ordained and established the following constitution and form of government for this State, which we recommend to the people of Tennessee for their ratification, that is to say:

ARTICLE I.

DECLARATION OF RIGHTS.

SECTION 1. That all power is inherent in the people, and all free governments are founded on their authority, and instituted for their peace, safety, and happiness; for the advancement of those ends they have, at all times, an unalienable and indefeasible right to alter, reform, or abolish the government in such manner as they may think proper.

SEC. 2. That government being instituted for the common benefit, the doctrine of non-resistance against arbitrary power and oppression is absurd, slavish, and destructive of the good and happiness of mankind.

SEC. 3. That all men have a natural and indefeasible right to worship Almighty God according to the dictates of their own conscience; that no man can, of right, be compelled to attend, erect, or support any place of worship, or to maintain any minister against his consent; that no human authority can, in any case whatever, control or interfere with the rights of conscience; and that no preference shall ever be given by law to any religious establishment or mode of worship.

SEC. 4. That no political or religious test, other than an oath to support the Constitution of the United States and of this State, shall ever be required as a qualification to any office or public trust under this State.

SEC. 5. That elections shall be free and equal, and the right of suffrage, as hereinafter declared, shall never be denied to any person entitled thereto, except upon a conviction by a jury of some infamous crime, previously ascertained and declared by law, and judgment thereon by court of competent jurisdiction.

SEC. 6. That the right of trial by jury shall remain inviolate, and no religious or political test shall ever be required as a qualification for jurors.

SEC. 7. That the people shall be secure in their persons, houses, papers, and possessions from unreasonable searches and seizures; and that general warrants, whereby an officer may be commanded to search suspected places, without evidence of the fact committed, or to seize any person or persons not named, whose offences are not particularly described and supported by evidence, are dangerous to liberty, and ought not to be granted.

SEC. 8. That no man shall be taken or imprisoned, or disseized of his freehold, liberties, or privileges, or outlawed or exiled, or in any manner destroyed, or deprived of his life, liberty, or property, but by the judgment of his peers, or the law of the land.

SEC. 9. That in all criminal prosecutions the accused hath the right to be heard by himself and his counsel; to demand the nature and cause of the accusation against him, and to have a copy thereof; to meet the witnesses face to face; to have compulsory process for obtaining witnesses in his favor; and in prosecutions by indictment or presentment, a speedy public trial, by an impartial jury of the county in which the crime shall have been committed; and shall not be compelled to give evidence against himself.

SEC. 10. That no person shall, for the same offence, be twice put in jeopardy of life or limb.

SEC. 11. That laws made for the punishment of acts committed previous to the existence of such laws and by them only declared criminal, are contrary to the principles of a free government; wherefore no *ex post facto* law shall be made.

SEC. 12. That no conviction shall work corruption of blood or forfeiture of estate. The estate of such persons as shall destroy their own lives shall descend or vest as in case of natural death. If any person shall be killed by casualty, there shall be no forfeiture in consequence thereof.

SEC. 13. That no person arrested and confined in jail shall be treated with unnecessary rigor.

SEC. 14. That no person shall be put to answer any criminal charge but by presentment, indictment, or impeachment.

SEC. 15. That all prisoners shall be bailable by sufficient sureties, unless for capital offences, when the proof is evident or the presumption great. And the privilege of the writ of *habeas corpus* shall not be suspended, unless when, in case of rebellion or invasion, the general assembly shall declare the public safety requires it.

SEC. 16. That excessive bail shall not be required, nor excessive fines imposed, nor cruel and unusual punishments inflicted.

SEC. 17. That all courts shall be open; and every man, for an injury done him in his lands, goods, person, or reputation, shall have remedy by due course of law, and right and justice administered without sale, denial, or delay. Suits may be brought against the State in such manner and in such courts as the legislature may, by law, direct.

SEC. 18. The legislature shall pass no law authorizing imprisonment for debt in civil cases.

SEC. 19. That the printing-presses shall be free to every person to examine the proceedings of the legislature, or of any branch or officer of the government; and no law shall ever be made to restrain the right thereof.

The free communication of thoughts and opinions is one of the invaluable rights of men, and every citizen may freely speak, write, and print on any subject, being responsible for the abuse of that liberty. But in prosecutions for the publication of papers investigating the official conduct of officers or men in public capacity, the truth thereof may be given in evidence; and in all indictments for libel, the jury shall have a right to determine the law and the facts, under the direction of the court, as in other criminal cases.

SEC. 20. That no retrospective law, or law impairing the obligation of contracts, shall be made.

SEC. 21. That no man's particular services shall be demanded, or property taken, or applied to public use, without the consent of his representatives, or without just compensation being made therefor.

SEC. 22. That perpetuities and monopolies are contrary to the genius of a free State, and shall not be allowed.

SEC. 23. That the citizens have a right in a peaceable manner to assemble together for their common good, to instruct their representatives, and to apply to those invested with the powers of government for redress of grievances, or other proper purposes, by address or remonstrance.

SEC. 24. That the sure and certain defence of a free people is a well-regulated militia; and as standing armies in time of peace are dangerous to freedom, they ought to be avoided as far as the circumstances and safety of the community will admit; and that in all cases the military shall be kept in strict subordination to the civil authority.

SEC. 25. That no citizen of this State, except such as are employed in the Army of the United States, or militia in active service, shall be subjected to punishment under the martial or military law.

That martial law, in the sense of the unrestricted power of military officers or others to dispose of the persons, liberties, or property of the citizen, is inconsistent with the principles of free government, and is not confided to any department of the government of this State.

SEC. 26. That the citizens of this State have a right to keep and to bear arms for their common defence. But the legislature shall have power, by law, to regulate the wearing of arms with a view to prevent crime.

SEC. 27. That no soldier shall, in time of peace, be quartered in any house without the consent of the owner; nor in time of war but in a manner prescribed by law.

SEC. 28. That no citizen of this State shall be compelled to bear arms, provided he will pay an equivalent, to be ascertained by law.

SEC. 29. That an equal participation in the free navigation of the Mississippi is one of the inherent rights of the citizens of this State; it cannot, therefore, be conceded to any prince, potentate, power, person, or persons whatever.

SEC. 30. That no hereditary emoluments, privileges, or honors shall ever be granted or conferred in this State.

SEC. 31. That the limits and boundaries of this State being ascertained, it is declared they are as hereafter mentioned, that is to say: Beginning on the extreme height of the Stone Mountain, at the place where the line of Virginia intersects it, in latitude thirty-six degrees and thirty minutes north; running thence along the extreme height of the said mountain, to the place where Watauga River breaks through it; thence a direct course to the top of the Yellow Mountain, where Bright's road crosses the same; thence along the ridge of said mountain, between the waters of Doe River and the waters of Rock Creek, to the place where the road crosses the Iron Mountain; from thence, along the extreme height of said mountain, to the place where Nolichucky River runs through the same; thence to the top of Bald Mountain; thence along the extreme height of said mountain to the Painted Rock, on French Broad River; thence along the highest ridge of said mountain, to the place where it is called the Great Iron or Smoky Mountain; thence along the extreme height of said mountain to the place where it is called Unicoi or Unaka Mountain, between the Indian towns of Cowee and Old Chota; thence along the main ridge of the said mountain, to the southern boundary of this State, as described in the act of cession of North Carolina to the United States of America; and that all the territory, lands, and waters lying west of the said line, as before mentioned, and contained within the chartered limits of the State of North Carolina, are within the boundaries and limits of this State over which the people have the right of exercising sovereignty, and the right of soil, so far as is consistent with the Constitution of the United States, recognizing the Articles of Confederation, the Bill of Rights, and constitution of North Carolina, the cession act of the said State, and the ordinance of Congress for the government of the territory northwest of the Ohio: *Provided*, Nothing herein contained shall extend to affect the claim or claims of individuals to any part of the soil which is recognized to them by the aforesaid cession act: *And provided also*, That the limits and jurisdiction of this State shall extend to any other land and territory now acquired, or that may hereafter be acquired, by compact or agreement with other States or otherwise, although such land and territory are not included within the boundaries hereinbefore designated.

SEC. 32. That the erection of safe and comfortable prisons, the inspection of prisons, and the humane treatment of prisoners, shall be provided for.

SEC. 33. That slavery and involuntary servitude, except as a punishment for crime, whereof the party shall have been duly convicted, are forever prohibited in this State.

SEC. 34. The general assembly shall make no law recognizing the right of property in man.

ARTICLE II.

DISTRIBUTION OF POWERS.

SECTION 1. The powers of the government shall be divided into three distinct departments: the legislative, executive, and judicial.

SEC. 2. No person or persons belonging to one of these departments shall exercise any of the powers properly belonging to either of the others, except in the cases herein directed or permitted.

LEGISLATIVE DEPARTMENT.

SEC. 3. The legislative authority of this State shall be vested in a general assembly, which shall consist of a senate and house of representatives, both dependent on the people, who shall hold their offices for two years from the day of the general election.

SEC. 4. An enumeration of the qualified voters, and an apportionment of the representatives in the general assembly, shall be made in the year one thousand eight hundred and seventy-one, and within every subsequent term of ten years.

SEC. 5. The number of representatives shall, at the several periods of making the enumeration, be apportioned among the several counties or districts according to the number of qualified voters in each; and shall not exceed seventy-five, until the population of the State shall be one million and a half; and shall never exceed ninety-nine: *Provided*, That any county having two-thirds of the ratio shall be entitled to one member.

SEC. 6. The number of senators shall, at the several periods of making the enumeration, be apportioned among the several counties or districts, according to the number of qualified electors in each, and shall not exceed one-third the number of representatives. In apportioning the number of senators among the different counties, the fraction that may be lost by any county or counties in the apportionment of members to the house of representatives shall be made up to such county or counties in the senate as near as may be practicable. When a district is composed of two or more counties, they shall be adjoining; and no county shall be divided in forming a district.

SEC. 7. The first election for senators and representatives shall be held on the second Tuesday in November, one thousand eight hundred and seventy; and forever thereafter elections for members of the general assembly shall be held once in two years, on the first Tuesday after the first Monday in November. Said election shall terminate the same day.

SEC. 8. The first session of the general assembly shall commence on the first Monday in October, one thousand eight hundred and seventy-one, at which time the term of service of the members shall commence, and expire on the first Tuesday of November, 1872; at which session the governor elected on the second Tuesday in November, 1870, shall be inaugurated; and forever thereafter the general assembly shall meet on the first Monday in January next ensuing the election, at which session thereof the governor shall be inaugurated.

SEC. 9. No person shall be a representative unless he shall be a citizen of the United States, of the age of twenty-one years, and shall have been a citizen of this State for three years, and a resident in the county he represents one year immediately preceding the election.

SEC. 10. No person shall be a senator unless he shall be a citizen of the United States, of the age of thirty years, and shall have resided three years in this State, and one year in the county or district immediately preceding the election. No senator or representative shall, during the time for which he was elected, be eligible to any office or place of trust, the appointment to which is vested in the executive or the general assembly, except to the office of trustee of a literary institution.

SEC. 11. The senate and house of representatives, when assembled, shall each choose a speaker and its other officers; be judges of the qualifications and elections of its members, and sit upon its own adjournments from day to day. Not less than two-thirds of all the members to which each house shall be entitled shall constitute a

quorum to do business; but a smaller number may adjourn from day to day, and may
be authorized by law to compel the attendance of absent members.

SEC. 12. Each house may determine the rules of its proceedings, punish its members for disorderly behavior, and, with the concurrence of two-thirds, expel a member,
but not a second time for the same offence; and shall have all other powers necessary
for a branch of the legislature of a free State.

SEC. 13. Senators and representatives shall in all cases, except treason, felony, or
breach of the peace, be privileged from arrest during the session of the general assembly, and in going to or returning from the same; and for any speech or debate in
either house, they shall not be questioned in any other place.

SEC. 14. Each house may punish by imprisonment, during its session, any person
not a member, who shall be guilty of disrespect to the house, by any disorderly or
any contemptuous behavior in its presence.

SEC. 15. When vacancies happen in either house, the governor for the time being
shall issue writs of election to fill such vacancies.

SEC. 16. Neither house shall, during its session, adjourn without the consent of the
other for more than three days, nor to any other place than that in which the two
houses shall be sitting.

SEC. 17. Bills may originate in either house, but may be amended, altered, or rejected by the other. No bill shall become a law which embraces more than one
subject; that subject to be expressed in the title. All acts which repeal, revive, or
amend former laws shall recite, in their caption or otherwise, the title or substance of
the law repealed, revived, or amended.

SEC. 18. Every bill shall be read once on three different days, and be passed each
time in the house where it originated before transmission to the other. No bill
shall become a law until it shall have been read and passed on three different days
in each house, and shall have received on its final passage in each house the assent
of a majority of all the members to which that house shall be entitled under this constitution, and shall have been signed by the respective speakers in open session—the
fact of such signing to be noted on the journal; and shall have received the approval
of the governor, or shall have been otherwise passed under the provisions of this
constitution.

SEC. 19. After a bill has been rejected, no bill containing the same substance shall
be passed into a law during the same session.

SEC. 20. The style of the laws of this State shall be, *"Be it enacted by the general
assembly of the State of Tennessee."* No law of a general nature shall take effect
until forty days after its passage, unless the same, or the caption, shall state that the
public welfare requires that it should take effect sooner.

SEC. 21. Each house shall keep a journal of its proceedings, and publish it, except
such parts as the welfare of the State may require to be kept secret; the ayes and
noes shall be taken in each house upon the final passage of every bill of a general
character, and bills making appropriations of public moneys; and the ayes and noes
of the members on any question shall, at the request of any five of them, be entered
on the journal.

SEC. 22. The doors of each house and of committees of the whole shall be kept
open, unless when the business shall be such as ought to be kept secret.

SEC. 23. The sum of four dollars per day, and four dollars for every twenty-five
miles travelling to and from the seat of government shall be allowed to the members
of each general assembly elected after the ratification of this constitution, as a compensation for their services. But no member shall be paid for more than seventy-five
days of a regular session, or for more than twenty days of any extra or called session;
or for any day when absent from his seat in the legislature, unless physically unable
to attend. The senators, when sitting as a court of impeachment, shall each receive
four dollars per day of actual attendance.

SEC. 24. No money shall be drawn from the treasury but in consequence of appropriations made by law; and an accurate statement of the receipts and expenditures
of the public money shall be attached to and published with the laws at the rise of
each stated session of the general assembly.

SEC. 25. No person who heretofore hath been, or may hereafter be, a collector or holder of public moneys shall have a seat in either house of the general assembly, or hold any other office under the State government, until such person shall have accounted for, and paid into the treasury, all sums for which he may be accountable or liable.

SEC. 26. No judge of any court of law or equity, secretary of state, attorney-general, register, clerk of any court of record, or person holding any office under the authority of the United States, shall have a seat in the general assembly; nor shall any person in this State hold more than one lucrative office at the same time: *Provided*, That no appointment in the militia or to the office of justice of the peace shall be considered a lucrative office, or operate as a disqualification to a seat in either house of the general assembly.

SEC. 27. Any member of either house of the general assembly shall have liberty to dissent from, and protest against, any act or resolve which he may think injurious to the public or to any individual, and to have the reasons for his dissent entered on the journals.

SEC. 28. All property, real, personal, or mixed, shall be taxed; but the legislature may except such as may be held by the State, by counties, cities or towns, and used exclusively for public or corporation purposes, and such as may be held and used for purposes purely religious, charitable, scientific, literary, or educational; and shall except one thousand dollars' worth of personal property in the hands of each tax-payer, and the direct products of the soil in the hands of the producer and his immediate vendee. All property shall be taxed according to its value, that value to be ascertained in such manner as the legislature shall direct, so that taxes shall be equal and uniform throughout the State. No one species of property from which a tax may be collected shall be taxed higher than any other species of property of the same value. But the legislature shall have power to tax merchants, pedlers, and privileges, in such manner as they may from time to time direct.

The portion of a merchant's capital used in the purchase of merchandise sold by him to non-residents and sent beyond the State shall not be taxed at a rate higher than the *ad-valorem* tax on property.

The legislature shall have the power to levy a tax upon incomes derived from stocks and bonds, that are not taxed *ad valorem*.

All male citizens of this State over the age of twenty-one years, except such persons as may be exempted by law on account of age or other infirmity, shall be liable to a poll-tax of not less than fifty cents nor more than one dollar per annum. Nor shall any county or corporation levy a poll-tax exceeding the amount levied by the State.

SEC. 29. The general assembly shall have power to authorize the several counties and incorporated towns in this State to impose taxes for county and corporation purposes respectively, in such manner as shall be prescribed by law; and all property shall be taxed according to its value, upon the principles established in regard to State taxation.

But the credit of no county, city, or town shall be given or loaned to or in aid of any person, company, association, or corporation, except upon an election to be first held by the qualified voters of such county, city, or town, and the assent of three-fourths of the votes cast at said election. Nor shall any county, city, or town become a stockholder with others in any company, association, or corporation, except upon a like election and the assent of a like majority. But the counties of Grainger, Hawkins, Hancock, Union, Campbell, Scott, Morgan, Grundy, Sumner, Smith, Fentress, Van Buren, White, Putnam, Overton, Jackson, Cumberland, Anderson, Henderson, Wayne, Marshall, Cocke, Coffee, Macon, and the new county herein authorized to be established out of fractions of Sumner, Macon, and Smith Counties, and Roane, shall be excepted out of the provisions of this section, so far that the assent of a majority of the qualified voters of either of said counties voting on the question shall be sufficient, when the credit of such county is given or loaned to any person, association, or corporation: *Provided*, That the exception of the counties above named shall not be in force beyond the year one thousand eight hundred and eighty, and after that period they shall be subject to the three-fourths majority applicable to the other counties of the State.

SEC. 30. No article manufactured of the produce of this State shall be taxed otherwise than to pay inspection-fees.

SEC. 31. The credit of this State shall not be hereafter loaned or given to or in aid of any person, association, company, corporation, or municipality, nor shall the State become the owner, in whole or in part, of any bank, or a stockholder with others in any association, company, corporation, or municipality.

SEC. 32. No convention or general assembly of this State shall act upon any amendment of the Constitution of the United States proposed by Congress to the several States, unless such convention or general assembly shall have been elected after such amendment is submitted.

SEC. 33. No bonds of the State shall be issued to any railroad company which at the time of its application for the same shall be in default in paying the interest upon the State bonds previously loaned to it, or that shall hereafter and before such application sell or absolutely dispose of any State bonds loaned to it for less than par.

ARTICLE III.

EXECUTIVE DEPARTMENT.

SECTION 1. The supreme executive power of this State shall be vested in a governor.

SEC. 2. The governor shall be chosen by the electors of the members of the general assembly, at the time and places where they shall respectively vote for the members thereof. The returns of every election for governor shall be sealed up, and transmitted to the seat of government, by the returning officers, directed to the speaker of the senate, who shall open and publish them in the presence of a majority of the members of each house of the general assembly. The person having the highest number of votes shall be governor; but if two or more shall be equal and highest in votes, one of them shall be chosen governor by joint vote of both houses of the general assembly. Contested elections for governor shall be determined by both houses of the general assembly, in such manner as shall be prescribed by law.

SEC. 3. He shall be at least thirty years of age, shall be a citizen of the United States, and shall have been a citizen of this State seven years next before his election.

SEC. 4. The governor shall hold his office for two years, and until his successor shall be elected and qualified. He shall not be eligible more than six years in any term of eight.

SEC. 5. He shall be commander-in-chief of the army and navy of this State, and of the militia, except when they shall be called into the service of the United States; but the militia shall not be called into service except in case of rebellion or invasion, and then only when the general assembly shall declare by law that the public safety requires it.

SEC. 6. He shall have power to grant reprieves and pardons, after conviction, except in cases of impeachment.

SEC. 7. He shall, at stated times, receive a compensation for his services, which shall not be increased or diminished during the period for which he shall have been elected.

SEC. 8. He may require information, in writing, from the officers in the executive department, upon any subject relating to the duties of their respective offices.

SEC. 9. He may, on extraordinary occasions, convene the general assembly by proclamation, in which he shall state specifically the purposes for which they are to convene; but they shall enter on no legislative business except that for which they were specifically called together.

SEC. 10. He shall take care that the laws be faithfully executed.

SEC. 11. He shall, from time to time, give to the general assembly information of the state of the government, and recommend for their consideration such measures as he shall judge expedient.

SEC. 12. In case of removal of the governor from office, or of his death or resignation, the powers and duties of the office shall devolve on the speaker of the senate; and in case of the death, removal from office, or resignation of the speaker of the senate, the powers and duties of the office shall devolve on the speaker of the house of representatives.

Sec. 13. No member of Congress, or person holding any office under the United States, or this State, shall execute the office of governor.

Sec. 14. When any officer, the right of whose appointment is by this constitution vested in the general assembly, shall, during the recess, die, or the office, by the expiration of the term, or by other means, become vacant, the governor shall have power to fill such vacancy by granting a temporary commission, which shall expire at the end of the next session of the legislature.

Sec. 15. There shall be a seal of this State, which shall be kept by the governor, and used by him officially, and shall be called "The Great Seal of the State of Tennessee."

Sec. 16. All grants and commissions shall be in the name and by the authority of the State of Tennessee, be sealed with the State seal, and signed by the governor.

Sec. 17. A secretary of state shall be appointed by joint vote of the general assembly, and commissioned during the term of four years; he shall keep a fair register of all the official acts and proceedings of the governor; and shall, when required, lay the same, and all papers, minutes, and vouchers relative thereto, before the general assembly; and shall perform such other duties as shall be enjoined by law.

Sec. 18. Every bill which may pass both houses of the general assembly shall, before it becomes a law, be presented to the governor for his signature. If he approve, he shall sign it, and the same shall become a law; but if he refuse to sign it, he shall return it, with his objections thereto in writing, to the house in which it originated; and said house shall cause said objections to be entered at large upon its journal, and proceed to reconsider the bill. If, after such reconsideration, a majority of all the members elected to that house shall agree to pass the bill, notwithstanding the objections of the executive, it shall be sent, with said objections, to the other house, by which it shall be likewise reconsidered. If approved by a majority of the whole number elected to that house, it shall become a law. The votes of both houses shall be determined by yeas and nays, and the names of all the members voting for or against the bill shall be entered upon the journals of their respective houses. If the governor shall fail to return any bill, with his objections, within five days (Sundays excepted) after it shall have been presented to him, the same shall become a law without his signature, unless the general assembly, by its adjournment, prevents its return, in which case it shall not become a law. Every joint resolution or order (except on questions of adjournment) shall likewise be presented to the governor for his signature, and before it shall take effect shall receive his signature; and, on being disapproved by him, shall, in like manner, be returned with his objections, and the same, before it shall take effect, shall be repassed by a majority of all the members elected to both houses, in the manner and according to the rules prescribed in case of a bill.

ARTICLE IV.

ELECTIONS.

Section 1. Every male person of the age of twenty-one years, being a citizen of the United States, and a resident of this State for twelve months, and of the county wherein he may offer his vote for six months next preceding the day of election, shall be entitled to vote for members of the general assembly, and other civil officers for the county or district in which he resides; and there shall be no qualification attached to the right of suffrage, except that each voter shall give to the judges of election, where he offers to vote, satisfactory evidence that he has paid the poll-taxes assessed against him for such preceding period as the legislature shall prescribe, and at such time as may be prescribed by law; without which his vote cannot be received. And all male citizens of the State shall be subject to the payment of poll-taxes and the performance of military duty within such ages as may be prescribed by law. The general assembly shall have power to enact laws requiring voters to vote in the election precincts in which they may reside, and laws to secure the freedom of elections and the purity of the ballot-box.

Sec. 2. Laws may be passed excluding from the right of suffrage persons who may be convicted of infamous crimes.

Sec. 3. Electors shall, in all cases, except treason, felony, or breach of the peace, be privileged from arrest or summons, during their attendance at elections, and in going to and returning from them.

Sec. 4. In all elections to be made by the general assembly, the members thereof shall vote *viva voce*, and their votes shall be entered on the journal. All other elections shall be by ballot.

ARTICLE V.

IMPEACHMENTS.

Section 1. The house of representatives shall have the sole power of impeachment.

Sec. 2. All impeachments shall be tried by the senate. When sitting for that purpose, the senators shall be upon oath or affirmation, and the chief justice of the supreme court, or if he be on trial, the senior associate judge, shall preside over them. No person shall be convicted without the concurrence of two-thirds of the senators sworn to try the officer impeached.

Sec. 3. The house of representatives shall elect, from their own body, three members, whose duty it shall be to prosecute impeachments. No impeachment shall be tried until the legislature shall have adjourned *sine die*, when the senate shall proceed to try such impeachment.

Sec. 4. The governor, judges of the supreme court, judges of the inferior courts, chancellors, attorneys for the State, treasurer, comptroller, and secretary of state, shall be liable to impeachment whenever they may, in the opinion of the house of representatives, commit any crime in their official capacity which may require disqualification; but judgment shall only extend to removal from office, and disqualification to fill any office thereafter. The party shall, nevertheless, be liable to indictment, trial, judgment, and punishment according to law. The legislature now has, and shall continue to have, power to relieve from the penalties imposed any person disqualified from holding office by the judgment of a court of impeachment.

Sec. 5. Justices of the peace, and other civil officers not hereinbefore mentioned, for crimes or misdemeanors in office, shall be liable to indictment in such courts as the legislature may direct; and, upon conviction, shall be removed from office by said court, as if found guilty on impeachment; and shall be subject to such other punishment as be prescribed by law.

ARTICLE VI.

JUDICIAL DEPARTMENT.

Section 1. The judicial power of this State shall be vested in one supreme court, and in such circuit, chancery, and other inferior courts as the legislature shall, from time to time, ordain and establish, in the judges thereof, and in justices of the peace. The legislature may also vest such jurisdiction in corporation courts as may be deemed necessary; courts to be holden by justices of the peace may also be established.

Sec. 2. The supreme court shall consist of five judges, of whom not more than two shall reside in any one of the grand divisions of the State. The judges shall designate one of their own number who shall preside as chief justice. The concurrence of three of the judges shall, in every case, be necessary to a decision. The jurisdiction of this court shall be appellate only, under such restrictions and regulations as may, from time to time, be prescribed by law; but it may possess such other jurisdiction as is now conferred by law on the present supreme court; said court shall be held at Knoxville, Nashville, and Jackson.

Sec. 3. The judges of the supreme court shall be elected by the qualified voters of the State. The legislature shall have power to prescribe such rules as may be necessary to carry out the provisions of section two of this article. Every judge of the supreme court shall be thirty-five years of age, and shall, before his election, have been a resident of the State for five years. His term of service shall be eight years.

SEC. 4. The judges of the circuit and chancery courts, and of other inferior courts, shall be elected by the qualified voters of the district or circuit to which they are to be assigned. Every judge of such courts shall be thirty years of age, and shall, before his election, have been a resident of the State for five years, and of the circuit or district one year. His term of service shall be eight years.

SEC. 5. An attorney-general and reporter for the State shall be appointed by the judges of the supreme court, and shall hold his office for a term of eight years. An attorney for the State for any circuit or district for which a judge having criminal jurisdiction shall be provided by law shall be elected by the qualified voters of such circuit or district, and shall hold his office for a term of eight years, and shall have been a resident of the State five years, and of the circuit or district one year. In all cases where the attorney for any district fails or refuses to attend and prosecute according to law, the court shall have power to appoint an attorney *pro tempore*.

SEC. 6. Judges and attorneys for the State may be removed from office by a concurrent vote of both houses of the general assembly, each house voting separately; but two-thirds of the members to which each house may be entitled must concur in such vote; the vote shall be determined by ayes and noes, and the names of the members voting for or against the judge or attorney for the State, together with the cause or causes of removal, shall be entered on the journal of each house respectively. The judge or attorney for the State, against whom the legislature may be about to proceed, shall receive notice thereof, accompanied with a copy of the causes alleged for his removal, at least ten days before the day on which either house of the general assembly shall act thereupon.

SEC. 7. The judges of the supreme or inferior courts shall, at stated times, receive a compensation for their services, to be ascertained by law, which shall not be increased or diminished during the time for which they are elected. They shall not be allowed any fees or perquisites of office, nor hold any office of trust or profit under this State or the United States.

SEC. 8. The jurisdiction of the circuit, chancery, and other inferior courts shall be as now established by law, until changed by the legislature.

SEC. 9. Judges shall not charge juries with respect to matters of fact, but may state the testimony and declare the law.

SEC. 10. The judges or justices of inferior courts of law and equity shall have power in civil cases to issue writs of *certiorari*, to remove any cause, or the transcript of the record thereof, from any inferior jurisdiction into such court of law, on sufficient cause, supported by oath or affirmation.

SEC. 11. No judge of the supreme or inferior courts shall preside on the trial of any cause in the event of which he may be interested, or where either of the parties shall be connected with him by affinity or consanguinity, within such degrees as may be prescribed by law, or in which he may have been of counsel, or in which he may have presided in any inferior court, except by consent of all the parties. In case all or any of the judges of the supreme court shall be thus disqualified from presiding on the trial of any cause or causes, the court, or the judges thereof, shall certify the same to the governor of the State, and he shall forthwith specially commission the requisite number of men, of law knowledge, for the trial and determination thereof. The legislature may, by general laws, make provision that special judges may be appointed to hold any court, the judge of which shall be unable or fail to attend or sit, or to hear any cause in which the judge may be incompetent.

SEC 12. All writs and other process shall run in the name of the State of Tennessee, and bear test and be signed by the respective clerks. Indictments shall conclude, "against the peace and dignity of the State."

SEC. 13. Judges of the supreme court shall appoint their clerks, who shall hold their offices for six years. Chancellors shall appoint their clerks and masters, who shall hold their offices for six years. Clerks of the inferior courts, holden in the respective counties or districts, shall be elected by the qualified voters thereof for the term of four years. Any clerk may be removed from office for malfeasance, incompetency, or neglect of duty, in such manner as may be prescribed by law.

SEC. 14. No fine shall be laid on any citizen of this State that shall exceed fifty dollars, unless it shall be assessed by a jury of his peers, who shall assess the fine at the time they find the fact, if they think the fine should be more than fifty dollars.

SEC. 15. The different counties of this State shall be laid off, as the general assembly may direct, into districts of convenient size, so that the whole number in each county shall not be more than twenty-five, or four for every one hundred square miles. There shall be two justices of the peace and one constable elected in each district, by the qualified voters therein, except districts including county towns, which shall elect three justices and two constables. The jurisdiction of said officers shall be coextensive with the county. Justices of the peace shall be elected for the term of six, and constables for the term of two years. Upon removal of either of said officers from the district in which he was elected, his office shall become vacant from the time of such removal. Justices of the peace shall be commissioned by the governor. The legislature shall have power to provide for the appointment of an additional number of justices of the peace in incorporated towns.

ARTICLE VII.

STATE AND COUNTY OFFICERS.

SECTION 1. There shall be elected in each county, by the qualified voters therein, one sheriff, one trustee, and one register; the sheriff and trustee for two years, and the register for four years; but no person shall be eligible to the office of sheriff more than six years in any term of eight years. There shall be elected for each county, by the justices of the peace, one coroner and one ranger, who shall hold their offices for two years. Said officers shall be removed for malfeasance or neglect of duty in such manner as may be prescribed by law.

SEC. 2. Should a vacancy occur, subsequent to an election, in the office of sheriff, trustee, or register, it shall be filled by the justices; if in that of the clerk to be elected by the people, it shall be filled by the courts; and the person so appointed shall continue in office until his successor shall be elected and qualified; and such office shall be filled by the qualified voters at the first election for any of the county officers.

SEC. 3. There shall be a treasurer, or treasurers, and a comptroller of the treasury appointed for the State by the vote of both houses of the general assembly, who shall hold their offices for two years.

SEC. 4. The election of all officers and the filling of all vacancies not otherwise directed or provided by this constitution shall be made in such manner as the legislature shall direct.

SEC. 5. Elections for judicial and other civil officers shall be held on the first Thursday in August, one thousand eight hundred and seventy, and forever thereafter on the first Thursday in August next preceding the expiration of their respective terms of service.

The term of each officer so elected shall be computed from the first day of September next succeeding his election. The term of office of the governor and other executive officers shall be computed from the fifteenth of January next after the election of the governor. No appointment or election to fill a vacancy shall be made for a period extending beyond the unexpired term. Every officer shall hold his office until his successor is elected or appointed and qualified. No special election shall be held to fill a vacancy in the office of judge or district attorney, but at the time herein fixed for the biennial election of civil officers. And such vacancy shall be filled at the next biennial election occurring more than thirty days after the vacancy occurs.

ARTICLE VIII.

MILITIA.

SECTION 1. All militia officers shall be elected by persons subject to military duty, within the bounds of their several companies, battalions, regiments, brigades, and divisions, under such rules and regulations as the legislature may, from time to time, direct and establish.

SEC. 2. The governor shall appoint the adjutant-general and his other staff-officers; the major-generals, brigadier-generals, and commanding officers of regiments shall respectively appoint their staff-officers.

SEC. 3. The legislature shall pass laws exempting citizens belonging to any sect or denomination of religion, the tenets of which are known to be opposed to bearing arms, from attending private and general musters.

ARTICLE IX.

DISQUALIFICATIONS.

SECTION 1. Whereas ministers of the gospel are, by their profession, dedicated to God and the care of souls, and ought not to be diverted from the great duties of their functions; therefore, no minister of the gospel, or priest of any denomination whatever, shall be eligible to a seat in either house of the legislature.

SEC. 2. No person who denies the being of God, or a future state of rewards and punishments, shall hold any office in the civil department of this State.

SEC. 3. Any person who shall, after the adoption of this constitution, fight a duel, or knowingly be the bearer of a challenge to fight a duel, or send or accept a challenge for that purpose, or be an aider or abetter in fighting a duel, shall be deprived of the right to hold any office of honor or profit in this State, and shall be punished otherwise, in such manner as the legislature may prescribe.

ARTICLE X.

OATHS, BRIBERY OF ELECTORS, NEW COUNTIES.

SECTION 1. Every person who shall be chosen or appointed to any office of trust or profit under this constitution, or any law made in pursuance thereof, shall, before entering upon the duties thereof, take an oath to support the constitution of this State and of the United States, and an oath of office.

SEC. 2. Each member of the senate and house of representatives shall, before they proceed to business, take an oath or affirmation to support the constitution of this State and of the United States, and also the following oath: " I, ——— ———, do solemnly swear [or affirm] that, as a member of this general assembly, I will, in all appointments, vote without favor, affection, partiality, or prejudice; and that I will not propose or assent to any bill, vote, or resolution which shall appear to me injurious to the people, or consent to any act or thing whatever that shall have a tendency to lessen or abridge their rights and privileges, as declared by the constitution of this State."

SEC. 3. Any elector who shall receive any gift or reward for his vote, in meat, drink, money, or otherwise, shall suffer such punishment as the laws shall direct. And any person who shall directly or indirectly give, promise, or bestow any such reward to be elected shall thereby be rendered incapable, for six years, to serve in the office for which he was elected, and be subject to such further punishment as the legislature shall direct.

SEC. 4. New counties may be established by the legislature, to consist of not less than two hundred and seventy-five square miles, and which shall contain a population of seven hundred qualified voters. No line of such county shall approach the court-house of any old county, from which it may be taken, nearer than eleven miles, nor shall said old county be reduced to less than five hundred square miles. But the following exceptions are made to the foregoing provisions, viz: New counties may be established by the present or any succeeding legislature out of the following territory, to wit: Out of that portion of Obion County which lies west of low-water mark of Reel Foot Lake; out of fractions of Sumner, Macon, and Smith Counties; but no line of such new county shall approach the court-house of Sumner or Smith Counties nearer than ten miles, nor include any part of Macon County lying within nine and a half miles of the court-house of said county; nor shall more than twenty square miles of Macon County, nor any part of Sumner County lying due west of the western boundary of Macon County, be taken in the formation of said new county; out of fractions of Grainger and Jefferson Counties; but no line of such new county shall include any part of Grainger County north of Holston River, nor shall any line thereof approach the court-house of Jefferson County nearer than eleven miles; such new county may include any other territory which is not excluded by any general provisions of this constitution; out of fractions of Jackson and Overton Counties; but no line of such new county shall approach the court-house of Jackson or Overton Counties nearer than ten miles, nor shall such county contain less than four hundred qualified voters, nor shall the area of either of the old counties be reduced below four hundred and fifty square miles; out of fractions of Roane, Monroe, and Blount Counties, around the town of Loudon; but no line of such new county shall ever approach the towns of Maryville, Kingston, or Madisonville nearer than eleven miles, except that on the south side of Tennessee River said lines may approach as near as ten miles to the court-house of Roane County.

The counties of Lewis, Cheatham, and Sequatchie, as now established by legislative enactments, are hereby declared to be constitutional counties. No part of Bledsoe County shall be taken to form a new county, or a part thereof, or be attached to any adjoining county.

That portion of Marion County included within the following boundaries: Beginning on the Grundy and Marion County line, at the Nick-a-jack Trace, and running about six hundred yards west of Ben Posey's, to where the Tennessee Coal Railroad crosses the line; running thence southeast, through the Pocket, near William Summers's, crossing the Battle Creek Gulf, at the corner of Thomas Wooten's field; thence running across the Little Gizzard Gulf to Raven Point; thence in a direct line to the bridge crossing the Big Fiery Gizzard; thence in a direct line to the mouth of Holy Water Creek; thence up said creek to the Grundy County line; and thence with said line to the beginning, is hereby detached from Marion County, and attached to the county of Grundy.

No part of a county shall be taken off to form a new county, or a part thereof, without the consent of two-thirds of the qualified voters in such part taken off. And, where an old county is reduced for the purpose of forming a new one, the seat of justice in said old county shall not be removed without the concurrence of two-thirds of both branches of the legislature, nor shall the seat of justice of any county be removed without the concurrence of two-thirds of the qualified voters of the county. But the foregoing provision requiring a two-thirds majority of the voters of a county to remove its county-seat shall not apply to the counties of Obion and Cocke.

The fractions taken from old counties to form new counties, or taken from one county and added to another, shall continue liable for their *pro rata* of all debts contracted by their respective counties prior to the separation, and be entitled to their proportion of any stocks or credits belonging to such old counties.

SEC. 5. The citizens who may be included in any new county shall vote with the county or counties, from which they may have been stricken off, for members of Congress, for governor, and for members of the general assembly, until the next apportionment of members to the general assembly after the establishment of such new county.

ARTICLE XI.

MISCELLANEOUS PROVISIONS.

SECTION 1. All laws and ordinances now in force and in use in this State, not inconsistent with this constitution, shall continue in force and use until they shall expire, or be altered or repealed by the legislature. But ordinances contained in any former constitution, or schedule thereto, are hereby abrogated.

SEC. 2. Nothing contained in this constitution shall impair the validity of any debts or contracts, or affect any rights of property, or any suits, actions, rights of action, or other proceedings in courts of justice.

SEC. 3. Any amendment or amendments to this constitution may be proposed in the senate or house of representatives; and, if the same shall be agreed to by a majority of all the members elected to each of the two houses, such proposed amendment or amendments shall be entered on their journals, with the yeas and nays thereon, and referred to the general assembly then next to be chosen, and shall be published six months previous to the time of making such choice, and if in the general assembly then next chosen as aforesaid such proposed amendment or amendments shall be agreed to by two-thirds of all the members elected to each house, then it shall be the duty of the general assembly to submit such proposed amendment or amendments to the people, in such manner and at such times as the general assembly shall prescribe. And if the people shall approve and ratify such amendment or amendments, by a majority of all the citizens of the State, voting for representatives, voting in their favor, such amendment or amendments shall become a part of this constitution. When any amendment or amendments to the constitution shall be proposed in pursuance of the foregoing provisions, the same shall, at each of said sessions, be read three times on three several days in each house. The legislature shall not propose amendments to the constitution oftener than once in six years. The legislature shall have the right, at any time, by law, to submit to the people the question of calling a convention to alter, reform, or abolish this constitution, and when, upon such submission, a majority of all the votes cast shall be in favor of said proposition, then delegates shall be chosen, and the convention shall assemble in such mode and manner as shall be prescribed.

SEC. 4. The legislature shall have no power to grant divorces, but may authorize the courts of justice to grant them for such causes as may be specified by law; but such laws shall be general and uniform in their operation throughout the State.

SEC. 5. The legislature shall have no power to authorize lotteries for any purpose, and shall pass laws to prohibit the sale of lottery-tickets in this State.

SEC. 6. The legislature shall have no power to change the names of persons, or to pass acts adopting or legitimating persons, but shall, by general laws, confer this power on the courts.

SEC. 7. The legislature shall fix the rate of interest, and the rate so established shall be equal and uniform throughout the State; but the legislature may provide for a conventional rate of interest, not to exceed 10 per cent. per annum.

SEC. 8. The legislature shall have no power to suspend any general law for the benefit of any particular individual, nor to pass any law for the benefit of individuals inconsistent with the general laws of the land; nor to pass any law granting to any individual or individuals rights, privileges, immunities or exemptions other than such as may be, by the same law, extended to any member of the community who may be able to bring himself within the provisions of such law. No corporation shall be created, or its powers increased or diminished, by special laws; but the general assembly shall provide by general laws for the organization of all corporations hereafter created, which laws may, at any time, be altered or repealed; and no such alteration or repeal shall interfere with or divest rights which have become vested.

SEC. 9. The legislature shall have the right to vest such powers in the courts of justice, with regard to private and local affairs, as may be deemed expedient.

SEC. 10. A well-regulated system of internal improvement is calculated to develop the resources of the State and promote the happiness and prosperity of her citizens; therefore it ought to be encouraged by the general assembly.

SEC. 11. A homestead, in the possession of each head of a family, and the improvements thereon, to the value, of, in all, one thousand dollars, shall be exempt from sale under legal process during the life of such head of a family, to inure to the benefit of the widow, and shall be exempt during the minority of their children occupying the same. Nor shall said property be alienated without the joint consent of husband and wife when that relation exists. This exemption shall not operate against public taxes, nor debts contracted for the purchase-money of such homestead, or improvements thereon.

SEC. 12. Knowledge, learning, and virtue being essential to the preservation of republican institutions, and the diffusion of the opportunities and advantages of education throughout the different portions of the State being highly conducive to the promotion of this end, it shall be the duty of the general assembly, in all future periods of this government, to cherish literature and science. And the fund called the common-school fund, and all the lands and proceeds thereof, dividends, stocks, and other property of every description whatever, heretofore by law appropriated by the general assembly of this State for the use of common schools, and all such as shall hereafter be appropriated, shall remain a perpetual fund, the principal of which shall never be diminished by legislative appropriation ; and the interest thereof shall be inviolably appropriated to the support and encouragement of common schools throughout the State, and for the equal benefit of all the people thereof; and no law shall be made authorizing said fund, or any part thereof, to be diverted to any other use than the support and encouragement of common schools. The State taxes derived hereafter from polls shall be appropriated to educational purposes, in such manner as the general assembly shall, from time to time, direct by law. No school established or aided under this section shall allow white and negro children to be received as scholars together in the same school. The above provision shall not prevent the legislature from carrying into effect any laws that have been passed in favor of the colleges, universities, or academies, or from authorizing heirs' or distributees to receive and enjoy escheated property under such laws as may be passed from time to time.

SEC. 13. The general assembly shall have power to enact laws for the protection and preservation of game and fish within the State, and such laws may be enacted for and applied and enforced in particular counties or geographical districts designated by the general assembly.

SEC. 14. The intermarriage of white persons with negroes, mulattoes, or persons of mixed blood, descended from a negro to the third generation, inclusive, or their living together as man and wife, in this State, is prohibited. The legislature shall enforce this section by appropriate legislation.

SEC. 15. No person shall in time of peace be required to perform any service to the public on any day set apart by his religion as a day of rest.

SEC. 16. The declaration of rights hereto prefixed is declared to be a part of the constitution of this State, and shall never be violated on any pretence whatever. And to guard against transgression of the high powers we have delegated, we declare that everything in the bill of rights contained is excepted out of the general powers of the government, and shall forever remain inviolate.

SEC. 17. No county office created by the legislature shall be filled otherwise than by the people, or the county court.

SCHEDULE.

SECTION 1. That no inconvenience may arise from a change of the constitution, it is declared that the governor of the State, the members of the general assembly, and all officers elected at or after the general election of March, 1870, shall hold their offices for the terms prescribed in this constitution.

Officers appointed by the courts shall be filled by appointment, to be made and to take effect during the first term of the court held by judges elected under this constitution.

All other officers shall vacate their places thirty days after the day fixed for the election of their successors under this constitution.

The secretary of state, comptroller, and treasurer shall hold their offices until the first session of the present general assembly occurring after the ratification of this constitution, and until their successors are elected and qualified.

The officers then elected shall hold their offices until the fifteenth day of January, 1873.

SEC. 2. At the first election of judges under this constitution, there shall be elected six judges of the supreme court, two from each grand division of the State, who shall hold their offices for the term herein prescribed.

In the event any vacancy shall occur in the office of either of said judges at any time after the first day of January, 1873, it shall remain unfilled, and the court shall from that time be constituted of five judges.

While the court shall consist of six judges they may sit in two sections, and may hear and determine causes in each at the same time, but not in different grand divisions at the same time.

When so sitting, the concurrence of two judges shall be necessary to a decision.

The attorney-general and reporter for the State shall be appointed after the election and qualification of the judges of the supreme court herein provided for.

SEC. 3. Every judge and every officer of the executive department of this State, and every sheriff holding over under this constitution, shall, within twenty days after the ratification of this constitution is proclaimed, take an oath to support the same; and the failure of any officer to take such oath shall vacate his office.

SEC. 4. The time which has elapsed since the 6th day of May, 1861, until the 1st day of January, 1867, shall not be computed in any cases affected by the statutes of limitation, nor shall any writ of error be affected by such lapse of time.

Done in convention, at Nashville, the twenty-third day of February, in the year of our Lord one thousand eight hundred and seventy, and of the Independence of the United States the ninety-fourth. In testimony whereof we have hereunto set our names.

JOHN C. BROWN, *President*.

Attest:

T. E. S. RUSSWURM, *Secretary*.
THOS. W. JONES, *Assistant Secretary*.
W. S. KYLE, *Second Assistant Secretary*.

———

ORDINANCE.

SECTION 1. *Be it ordained by the convention,* That it shall be the duty of the several officers of the State, authorized by law to hold elections for members of the general assembly and other officers, to open and hold an election at the place of holding said elections in their respective counties, on the fourth Saturday in March, 1870, for the purpose of receiving the votes of such qualified voters as may desire to vote for the ratification or rejection of the constitution recommended by this convention. And the qualification of voters in said election be the same as that required in the election of delegates to this convention.

SEC. 2. It shall be the duty of said returning officers, in each county in this State, to enroll the name of each voter on the poll-books prepared for said election, and shall deposit each ballot in the ballot-boxes respectively. Each voter who wishes to ratify the new constitution shall have written or printed on his ticket the words " New constitution," or words of like import; and each voter who wishes to vote against the ratification of the new constitution shall have written or printed on his ticket the words " Old constitution," or words of like import.

SEC. 3. The election shall be held, and the judges and clerks shall be appointed, as in the case of the election of the members of the general assembly; and the returning officers, in presence of the judges or inspectors, shall count the votes given for the " New constitution," and of those given for the " Old constitution," of which they shall keep a correct estimate in said poll-books. They shall deposit the original poll-books of said election with the clerks of the county courts in the respective counties, and shall, within five days after the election, make out accurate statements of the number of votes in their respective counties, for or against the " New constitution," and immediately forward, by mail, one copy of said certificates to the governor, and one to the speaker of the senate. So soon as the poll-books are deposited with the county-court clerks, they shall certify to the president of the convention an accurate statement of the number of votes cast for or against the " New constitution," as appears on said poll-books. And, if any of said returning officers shall fail to make the returns herein provided for, within the time required, the governor shall be authorized to send special messengers for the result of the vote in those counties whose officers have so failed to make returns.

SEC. 4. Upon the receipt of said returns, it shall be the duty of the governor, speaker of the senate, and the president of this convention, or any two of them, to compare the votes cast in said election; and if it shall appear that a majority of all the votes cast for and against the new constitution were for " New constitution," it shall be the duty of the governor, speaker of the senate, and president of this convention, or any two of them, to append to this constitution a certificate of the result of the votes, from which time the constitution shall be established as the constitution of Tennessee, and the governor shall make proclamation of the result.

SEC. 5. The governor of the State is requested to issue his proclamation as to the election on the fourth Saturday in March, 1870, hereto provided for.

JOHN C. BROWN, *President.*

Attest:

T. E. S. RUSSWURM, *Secretary.*

SELECTED BIBLIOGRAPHY

Journal of the Proceedings of a Convention, Begun
and Held in Knoxville, on the Eleventh of January, one thousand seven hundred and ninety-six
(Knoxville, 1796)

The Constitution of the State of Tennessee (Knoxville, 1796)

Journal of the Convention of the State of Tennessee
(Nashville, 1834)

The Constitution of the State of Tennessee (Nashville, 1834)

Journal of the Proceedings of the Convention of
Delegates ... To Amend, Revise, or Form and
Make a New Constitution for the State (Nash-
ville, 1870)

The New Constitution of the State of Tennessee ...
1870 (Nashville, 1870)

Constitution Revision Commission Report (Nashville,
1946)

Limited Constitutional Convention Journal and Debates (Nashville, 1954)

W.P. Armstrong, Jr., "Constitutional Limits on
Income Taxes in Tennessee," 27 Vand. L. Rev.
475 (April 1974)

Caldwell, Joshua William, Jr., Studies in the Constitutional History of Tennessee (Cincinnati,
2d ed., 1907)

Combs, William H., An Unamended State Constitution:
The Tennessee Constitution of 1870 (Knoxville,
1938)

McClure, Wallace M., State Constitution-Making,
With Especial Reference to Tennessee (Nashville,
1916)

Milton, George Fort, Constitution of Tennessee
Considered With Reference to the Constitutions
of Other States (Knoxville, 1897)

Smith, Daniel, A Short Description of the State
    of Tennessee, Lately Called the Territory of
    the United States South of the River Ohio (New
    York, 1797)

Tennessee, University of, Papers on Constitutional
    Revision Knoxville, 2 vol., 1947

TENNESSEE INDEX

Texas

Twenty-Eighth State

December 29, 1845

EDITORIAL NOTE

Texas, like Hawaii (cf, Volume III), was nominally a republic annexed to the United States by Congressional resolution. As in the case of Hawaii, a certain amount of domestic political maneuvering was involved in effectuating statehood. Some of the documents relevant to this method of admission will appear in a companion collection of constitutional documents on national development.

TEXAS CONTENTS

SOURCES OF DOCUMENTS

No. 1   2 Poore, 1727

No. 2   6 Thorpe, 3520

No. 3   2 Poore, 1752

No. 4   2 Poore, 1753

No. 5   2 Poore, 1754

No. 6   5 Stat.,   797

No. 7   2 Poore, 1765

No. 8   9 Poore,   108

No. 9   2 Poore, 1784

No. 10   2 Poore, 1801

No. 11   2 Poore, 1824

TEXAS: COMPARATIVE PROVISIONS

Subject:	1827	1835	1836	1845	1870
Subject Matter By Articles					
Bill of Rights			Declaration of Rights	I	I
The Powers of Government		I	I	II	II
Legislative Department	Title 1	III	I,II	III	III
Executive Department		II	III	V	IV
Judicial Department		V	IV	IV	I
Suffrage					VI
Education - The Public Free Schools				X	VII
Taxation and Revenue					VIII
Counties					IX
Railroads					X
Municipal Corporations					XI
Private Corporations					XII
Spanish and Mexican Land Titles					XIII
Public Lands and Land Office					XIV
Impeachment				IX	XV
General Provisions				VII	XVI
Mode of Amending the Constitution of this State					XVII
Subject Matter By Sections					
Militia				VI	
Slaves				VIII	
Headright claims				XI	
Land-office				XII	
PREAMBLE					
BILL OR RIGHTS			D.R.	I	I
Texas Free and Independent					1
All Political Power Is Inherent in the People			D.R.2	1	2
All Free Men Slave Equal Rights	11		D.R.1	2	3
Untitled					3-a
There shall be no Religious Test For Office				3	4
How Oaths Shall Be					5

	1827	1835	1836	1845	1870
Administered					
Freedom in Religious Workship Guaranteed			D.R.3	4	6
No appropriation for Sectarian Purposes					7
Liberty of Speech and Press Guaranteed; Libel	12,97		D.R.4	5,6	8
No Unreasonable Seizures and Searches Allowed	191		D.R.5	7	9
Rights of Accused Persons in Criminal. Prosecutions			D.R.6	8	10
Bail			D.R.10	9	11
Untitled					11-a
The Writ of Habeas Corpus		VI	D.R.10	9,10	12
Excessive Bail and Fine and Unusual Punishment Prohibited; Courts Open			D.R.11	11	13
No person Shall Be Put Twice in jeopardy			D.R.9	12	14
Right of Trial by Jury	192		D.R.6,9	12	15
Untitled					15-a
There Shall Be No Bill of Attainder or Ex Post Facto Laws	170			14	16
Privileges and Franchises, Eminent Domain					17
No Imprisonment for Debt			D.R.12	15	18
Due Course of Law			D.R.7	16	19
No Outlawry or Deportations					20
Corruption of Blood, Forfeiture, Suicide					21
Treason			G.P.8	VII-2	22
Right to Bear Arms			D.R.14, 16	13	23
Military Subordinate to Civil Authority				17	24
Quartering Soldiers				VII-35	25
Perpetuities, Monopolies; Primogeniture; Entailments			D.R.17	18	26
Right of Petition Guaranteed				19	27
Power to Suspend Laws	172			20	28
"Bill of Rights" Inviolate				21	29
No title of nobility	28		D.R.8		
THE POWERS OF GOVERNMENT		I	I	II	II
Departments of Government to Be Kept Distinct	29	I	1		1
Provisional Government		XVI XXI			

Subject:	1827	1835	1836	1845	1870
LEGISLATIVE DEPARTMENT	(Title 1)		I	III	III
The Legislature; House and Senate	30		I-2	4	1
Number of Members Limited	33		I-5	9	2
Election of Senators; New Apportionment	34,35,46		I-7,9	8,28	3
Election of Representatives; Term of Office	46,96		I-3	5,28	4
Time of Meeting; Method of Procedure	84,87,95, 99	XII		29,33	5
Qualifications of Senators	36,42		I-8	11	6
Qualifications of Representatives	36		I-4	6	7
Each House to Judge Qualifications of Its own Members			I-13	12	8
President Pro Term of the Speaker of the House; Officers	80,82,83		I-6,10,11	12,24	9
Quorum	101	III	I-13	12	10
Rules; Power to Punish and Expel			I-14	13	11
Journal; Yeas and Nays			I-17 VI-13	14	12
Vacancies, How Filled			I-19	15	13
Members of Legislature, Privileged From Arrest			I-15	16	14
Each House May Punish Disorderly Conduct			I-16	17	15
Sessions to Be Open	86			18	16
Adjournments			I-13,18	19	17
Ineligibility of Members to Certain Offices; Not to Be Interested in Contracts	45		I-23	24	18
What Officers Ineligible to Membership in Legislature	39		I-23	25	19
Receives or Disbursers of Public Funds Not Eligible to Membership in the Legislature Until Discharge Received			I-24	26	20
Freedom in Debate	44		I-15		21
Personal Interest in Measure or Bill					22
Removal Vacates Office					23
John Tarleton Contract Validated					23-a
Mileage and Per Diem	43		I-15	23,34	24
Senatorial Districts, How Apportioned				10,32	25
Representative Districts, How Apportioned				30	26

Subject	1827	1835	1836	1845	1870
Redistricting According to Population				31	26-a
Election of Members					27
Reapportionment After Each Census					28
Ministers not eligible to the legislature Proceedings				27	
Enacting Clause					29
Laws to Be Passed By Bill; amendments					30
Bills May Originate in Either House and May Be Amended or Rejected by the Other House				20	31
Bills to Be Read on Three Several Days: Suspension of Rule			I-20	20	32
Bills for Raising Revenue				21	33
Bill or Resolution Defeated, Not to Be Considered Again	100		I-21	22	34
Bills to Contain but One Subject; Which Must Be Expressed in Title				VII-24	35
Reviving or Amending Laws				VII-25	36
Reference to Committees					37
Signing Bills	102-104		I-26,27	20	38
When Laws Lake Effect					39
Business and Duration of Special Sessions	89-93				40
Elections: Votes, How Taken					41
Style of Laws Requirements & Limitations	114		I-22		
Repealed					42
Revision and Publication of Laws			G.P.7	VII-16	43
Compensation of Officers: Payment of Claims	97			VII-7	44
Change of Venue				VII-14	45
Repealed					46
Lotteries to Be Prohibited				VII-17	47
Repealed					48
Teacher's Retirement Fund					48-a
Teacher Retirement System					48-b
Rural Fire Prevention Districts					48-d
Purpose for Which Debts May Be Created				VII-33	49
Limiting Appropriations to Anticipated Revenue; Comptroller's Certification Required			I-25	VII-8	49-a

Subject:	1827	1835	1836	1845	1870
Veterans'Land Board; Bonds Authorized for Creation of Veterans' Land Fund; Purchase of Land By State and Sales to Veterans					49-b
Texas Water Development Board Fund; Purpose					49-C
Development and Conservation of Public Waters					49-d
Water Development Bonds					49-d-1
Texas Park Development Bonds					49-e
Credit of State Not to Be Pledged					50
State Medical Education Board, Fund, Purpose					50-a
Student Loans					50-b
Untitled					50-b-1
Tax Lewy Authorized for Confederate Soldiers and					51
Sailors and Their Widows					51
Assistance and Medical Care to Needy Aged, Needy Blind, Needy Children and Totally Disabled; Limitation on Expenditures for Same					51-a
State Building Commission Created					51-b
False Imprisonment					51-c
Assistance to Survivors of Law Ebforcement Officers Killed on Duty					51-d
City and Town Pension) ȳstem					51-e
Local Pension Plans					51-f
Social Security Coverage for Municipal Employees					51-9
Counties, Cities, Etc., Not Authorized to Grant Money or Become Stockholders; Exceptions					52
Legislature Prohibited to Lend Credit of State in Building or Maintaining Toll Roads and Turnpikes					52-b
HarrisCounty Road Districts					52-d
Dallas County woad Bonds					52-e
Payment of Medical Expenses for County and Precinct Officials					52-e
Extra Compensation by Municipal Corporations					53
Liens on Railroads					54
Power of Legislature to Release Debt					55

Subject:	1827	1835	1836	1845	1870
Special Laws; Limitations					56
Notice of Local or Special Laws					57
Sessions to Be Held at Austin, Seat of Government	78			35	58
Workmen's Compensation for State Employees					59
Workmen's Compensation Insurance for County Employees					60
Untitled					61
Salary of Governor, Attorney General, Comptroller of Public Accounts, Treasurer, Commissioner of General Land Office and Secretary of State				VII-36	61-a
Continuity of State and Local Governmental Operations					62
Consolidation of Governmental Functions in Counties of 1,200,000 or More In habitants					63
Consolidation of Governmental Offices and Functions in Counties					64
Interest Rate on State Bonds					65
Congress to regulate commerce		III	II-2		
Congress to establish post offices		III	II-3		
Congress to make necessary laws	5,97	III	II-7		
Congress to introduce common law of England		VII	IV-13		
EXECUTIVE DEPARTMENT		VII	III	V	IV
Officers of Executive Department					1
Election of Executive Officers	129-138			2	2
Election Results; Ties; Contest			3	3	3
Governor, When Installed; Term; Qualifications	31,110 111,112		1,2,VI-1, 2	1,4	4
Governor's Salary and Mansion			VI-3	5;VII-36	5
Governor to Hold No Other Office, Etc.				22	6
Commander in Chief; May Call Out Militia	113	III,IV	VI-4	6	7
Governor May Convene Legislature	113		VI-7	8	8
Governor's Message; to Accounts for Moneys; Present Estimate, Etc.	85		VI-7	9	9

Subject:	1827	1835	1836	1845	1870
Governor Shall Cause the Laws to Be Executed; Intercourse With Other States	113		VI-7	10	10
Board of Pardons and Paroles; Advisory Authority to Governor in Granting Reprieves, Paroles, Pardons, Etc.	113	III	VI-4	11	11
Suspension of Sentences; Probation					11-a
Governor to Fill Vacancies in State and District Offices	113		VI-6	20	12
Where Governor Shall Reside				21	13
Approval of Bills; Veto Bill Not Returned to Become a Law	102-104			17	14
What to Be Presented for Approval	102-104			18	15
Lieutenant Governor; Election; Term; Powers and Duties	115-116		VI-14	12	16
Vacancy in Office; Compensation	119			13	17
Succession to Governorship	117-118	II	VI-15	12	18
Seal of State; Secretary of State to Keep, Etc.			VI-8 G.P.4	14	19
Commissions to Be Signed and Sealed		VIII,IX	VI-9	15	20
Secretary of State; Term; Duties; Compensation	139-144	III	VI-10 G.P.2	16	21
Attorney General; Term; Duties; Residence; Salary	201			IV-12	22
Comptroller; Treasurer, and Commissioner of the General Land Office; Terms; Salaries; Residence; Fees	207	XIII		23	23
Governor May dismiss officer		XI			
"President to make treaties			VI-5		
Dueling - deprived of holding office				VII5	
Officers to Account to the Governor; Duty of Governor; False Reports				7	24
Laws for Investigation of Breaches of Trust					25
Notaries Public		VI		19	26
No Minister eligible for office			V-1		
JUDICIAL DEPARTMENT		V	IV	IV	V
The Several Courts; Criminal Courts	32,168	VI		1	1
Retirement and Compensation of Judges	201			7-36	1-a

Subject:	1827	1835	1836	1845	1870
Supreme Court, Quorum; Qualifications; Election; Salary; Vacancy			1,7,9	2,5	2
Jurisdiction; Terms of Court			8	3	3
Time of Sitting				3	3-a
Direct Appeal	174				3-b
Court of Criminal Appeals					4
Jurisdiction; Powers; Term; Clerk, Etc					5
Supreme Judicial Districts; Courts of Civil Appeals; Jurisdiction; Term; Justices; Election; Salary; Clerk					6
Judicial Districts; Judges, Their Qualifications; Residence; Term of Office; Salary; Terms of Court			2,9	5,6	7
Jurisdiction and Powers of the District Courts			3	10,15	8
Clerk of the District Court; Term of Office; How Removed; How Vacancy is Filled			6	11	9
Jury Trial	192	VII		10,16,	10
Disqualification of Judges; Special Judges; Exchange of Districts; Vacancies	175			18,19	11
Judges Conservators of Peace; Style of Writs: Prosecution by State		VI	4	8	12
Jurors; Grand and Petit; Number Required to Return Verdict					13
Districts Fixed By ordinance					14
County Court; Election; Term of Office of County Judges; Fees			10		15
Jurisdiction of County Court; Appeals; Probate jurisdiction; May Issue Writs; judge Disqualified, When					16
Terms of County Court for Criminal Business; Prosecutions Commenced by Information; Grand Jury to Inquire Into Misdemeanors, Quashing of Grand Jury Indictments; Jury					17
Terms of Justices of the Peace; County Commissioners and Commissioners Court			12	13	18
Criminal Jurisdiction of Justices of the Peace;				17	19

Subject:	1827	1835	1836	1845	1870
Appeals; Justices of the Peace ex Officio Notaries					
County Clerk; Election; Term; Duties; Vacancies					20
County and District Attorneys; Duties; Vacancies; Fees			5	12	21
Jurisdiction of Courts May Be Changed By Legislature					22
Sheriff; Term of Office; Vacancy		VI	12	13	23
Certain Officers Removed by District Courts for Drunkeness, Incompentency, Official Misconduct, Etc.				8	24
Supreme Court to Regulate Practice					25
No Appeal in Criminal Cases by the State					26
Transfer of Cases by the Legislature					27
Vacancies in Offices of Judges of Superior Courts to be Filled by the Governor					28
Terms of County Courts; Probate Business; Prosecution					29
County Judges and Criminal District Attorneys; Terms			5		30
Clerks for Supreme Court				4	
No interested judges				14	
Arbitration	178			VII-15	
SUFFRAGE					VI
Persons Who Cannot Vote			G.P.1	III-1,2 VII-4	1
Annual Registration; Absentee Voting					2
Vote for Electors for President and Vice-President and Statewide Offices					2-a
Electors in Towns and Cities; Only Property Taxpayers to Vote in Certain Instances				III-7	3
Voter Registration	52				4
Voters Privileged From Arrest				III-3	5
Elections by Ballott			VI-12	VII-6	
Qualifications of voters	53		VI-11		

Subject:	1827	1835	1836	1845	1870
EDUCATION-THE PUBLIC FREE SCHOOLS				X	VII
Public Schools to Be Established	215-7		GP.5	1	1
Provisions Governing the Levy and Collection of Taxes for the Public Free Schools				2	2
School Taxes					3
Repealed					3-a
County School Districts					3-b
Sale of School Lands; No Release to Purchasers; the Investment of Proceeds				3	4
Permanent School Fund; Interest; Alienation; Sectarian Schools					5
County School Lands; Limitations; Settlers; Proceeds				4	6
Taxation of County School Lands					6-a
Untitled					6-b
Repealed					7
Board of Education; Terms and Duties					8
Asylums					
Lands of Asylums; Sale					9
University					
University Lands and Funds					10
University Funds; How Invested					11
Untitled					11-a
Lands to BeSold; No Relief of Purchasers					12
Agricultural and Mechanical College; Appropriations					13
Branch University for Colored					14
Land Appropriated for University How Sold					15
Terms of Office in School Systems					16
Taxation of University Lands					16(a)
Confederate Pension Fund Tax; College Building Fund Tax					17
Building Bonds Authorized for the University of Texas and Texas A&M University; Retired From Income From the Permanent University Fund, etc.					18
TAXATION AND REVENUE					VIII
Taxation to Be Equal and Uniform; Occupation and Income Taxes; Exemptions; Limitations Upon	(14)203 204			VII-27,28	1

Subject:	1827	1835	1836	1845	1870
Counties; Cities, Etc.					
Abolishing Ad Valorem Tax for State's General Fund Purposes; Providing Local Tax Rate; Etc.					1-a
Homestead Exemption Under State Tax				VII-22	1-b
Optional Provisions Relating to Sec. 1-a and Sec. 1-b					1-c
Taxation of Agricultural Land					1-d
Gradual Abolition of Ad Valorem Tax					1-e
Occupation Taxes Equal and Uniform; Exemptions Therefrom					2
Taxes to Be Collected for Public Purposes Only	97,205				3
Power to Tax Corporations Not to Be Surrendered					4
Railroad Taxes Due to Cities and Towns					5
Appropriations; How Made and for What Period	97,208				6
Special Funds Not to Be Borrowed or Diverted					7
Net Motor License Fees and Motor Fuel Tax Revenues Restricted Except One-Fourth of Fuel Taxes to Schools, to Highway Improvement, Policing and Administration					7-a
Railroad Property; How Assessed					8
Rate of State and Municipal Taxation					9
Taxes Not to Be Released Except by Two-Thirds Vote of Each House					10
Where Property Is to Be Assessed					11
Repealed					12
Tax Sales; Tax Deeds; Redemptions					13
County Tax Assessor and Collector				VII-29	14
Tax Liens and Sales					15
Sheriff to Be County Tax Assessor-Collector in Some Counties					16
Assessor-Collector of Taxes in Counties of Less than Ten Thousand					16-a
Power of Legislature as to Taxes	97	III XX	II-1		17
Equalization of Taxes					18
Farm Products in the Hands of the Producer Exempt From All Taxation					19
Limiting Ad Valorem Tax Assessment; Discount for Prompt Payment of Taxes					20

Subject:	1827	1835	1836	1845	1870
Present taxes continue until congress alters them	206				
Special regulation to govern offices of Revenue	209				
Three examiners of Treasury	210				
COUNTIES					IX
Creation and Organization of Counties; Changing of County Lines			IV-11	VII-33	1 1
Regulation of Travel of Gulf Coast Beaches					1-a
How County Seats are Created and Changed					2
Repealed					3
County-Wide Hospital District					4
Untitled					5
Lamar County Hospital District; Creation, Tax Rate					6
Hidalgo County Hospital District; Creation; Tax Rate					8
Untitled					9
Untitled					11
Establishment of Airport Authorities					12
Mental Health Services					13
RAILROADS					X
Repealed					1
Public Highways; Common Carriers; Duty of Legislature; Fixing Rate					2
MUNICIPAL CORPORATIONS					XI
Counties Are Legal Subdivisions of the State					1
Public Buildings and Roads					2
No County or Municipal Corporation Shall Become a Subscriber to the Capital Stock of Any Donation to the Same					3
Cities and Towns Having a Population of 5,000 or Less Inhabitants to Be Chartered by General Laws; Dues to Be Collected in Current Money					4

Subject:	1827	1835	1836	1845	1870
Cities of More Than 5,000 Inhabitants May By a Majority Vote of the Qualified Voters Adopt Their Own Charter; Limitation as to Taxation and Debt					5
Municipal Taxation					6
Taxation of Seawalls, Etc; Restrictions and Limitations; Eminent Domain					7
State Aid for Seawalls, Etc.					8
Public Buildings, Etc.					9
Repealed					10
Terms of Office for City Officials					11
PRIVATE CORPORATIONS					XII
Corporations Created by General Laws				VII-31	1
General Laws to Be Enacted					2
Repealed					3-5
The Issuance of Stocks and Bonds by Corporations Prohibited Except for Money Paid and Labor Done, Etc.					6
Repealed					7
SPANISH AND MEXICAN LAND TITLES					XIII
Repealed					1-7
PUBLIC LANDS AND LAND OFFICE		XIV			XIV
General Land Office; Grants to Be Registered in, Land Office to Be Self-Sustaining					1
Repealed					2-8
IMPEACHMENT				IX	XV
Power of Impeachment Vested in The House of Representatives	97,120			1 2	1
Trial by Senate			I-II		2
Oath of Senators					3
Judgment; Party Convicted Subject to Indictment Under the Criminal Law			I-12	4,6,	4

Subject:	1827	1835	1836	1845	1870
Officers Suspended During Pending Proceedings				5	5
Removal of District Judges					6
Trial and Removal of Other Officers					7
Grounds for impeachment Address			* VI-16		
Removal of Judges of Supreme Court and Courts of Appeals and of District Courts	176,202			3	8
GENERAL PROVISIONS			G.P.	VII	XVI
Official Oaths	81,220	X	V-2,3	1	1
Right of Suffrage to Be Protected; Criminals Disfranchised				VII-4	2
Repealed					3-4
Bribery in Elections Disqualifi cation for Holding Office	57,70		G.P.1	VII-3	5
Appropriations for Private Purposes Prohibited; Expenditures to Be Published			D.R.13		6
Repealed					7
Counties May Provide Workhouses, Poorhouses and Farms					8
Absence on Business of the State or United States Shall not Forfeit a Residence Once Obtained				VII-11	9
Deductions From Salaries to Be Provided For					10
Usurious Interest Prohibited					11
Officers Not Eligible				VII-13	12
Repealed					13
Residence of Officers			G.P.3	VII-9	14
Community Property of Husband and Wife; Partition Thereof				VII-11	15
Banking Corporations					16
Officers to Perform Duties Until Successor Qualified				VII-23	17
Vested Rights				VII-20	18
Qualifications of Jurors			G.P.1		19
Manufacture and Sale of Intoxicants					20
Stationery; Public Printing					21
Fence Laws					22
Stock Laws					23
Roads; Convict Labor					24
Drawbacks and Rebates in Freight Insurance, Transportation, Storage, Etc., Prohibited					25

Subject	1827	1835	1836	1845	1870
Homocide; Civil Action For					26
Vacancies in Offices Filled for Unexpired Term Only					27
Wages Exempt from Garnishment					28
Repealed					29
Duration of Offices; Term of Railroad Commissioner				VII-10	30
Board of Regents, Trustees, Managers, Etc.; Term of Office					30-a
Tenure Under Municipal Civil Service					30-b
Qualifications of Phisicians to Be Prescribed					31
Repealed					32
Condition Under Which a Person Can Not Receive Compensation From the State					33
Repealed					34-36
Merchanics Liens To Be Enforced					37
Repealed					38
Memorials of Texas History					39
Provision Against Holding More Than One Office; Exceptions				VII-26	40
Bribery of Certain Officials to Be Prohibited					41
Repealed					42
Exemption From Public Service					43
County Treasurer and Surveyor					44
Repealed					45-46
Scriples Against Bearing Arms				VI-2	47
Laws to Remain in Force					48
Exemptions From Forced Sales					49
Homestead Exemptions				VII-22	50
Homestead Defined				VII-22	51
Descent of Homestead					52
Declaration Validating Process and Writs					53
Repealed					54-55
Advertising Texas' Resources					56
Repealed					57-58
Conservation and Development of Natural Resources					59a
Repealed					60
Compensation of District and County Officials					61
Retirement; Disability and Death Compensation Funds					62
Teacher and State Employee Retirement System					63
Inspector of Hides and Animals; Elective District; County and Precinct Offices; Terms of Office					64

Subject:	1827	1835	1836	1845	1870
District and County Officials; Terms of Office					65
Pensions for Texas Rangers					66
Titles to Land Null and Void		XVIII		VII-21	
Prohibiting bills, checks				VII-32	
Who entitled to citizenship			G.P.6,10		
Citizens entitled to land		XV			
Forfeiture of land		XIX			
MODE OF AMENDING THE CONSTITUTION OF THIS STATE			G.P.11	VII	XVII
How the Constitution Is To Be Amended	212-215		G.P.11	37	1
Rewriting State Constitution					2
Convention to Adjourn		XVII			
MILITIA		IV		VI	
Organizing Militia	97,212-213	III,IV	II-5 DR.15	1	
Scruples to bear arms				2	
Ministers Not to perform Military				3	
Governor to call forth Militia		IV	II-6	4	
Congress to declare war			II-4		
Corps of civic militia	212				
No one excused from duty	214				
OF THE MILITARY (M)					
Regular Army for Texas		MI			
Consist of One Major-General		MII			
Commander-in-Chief appointed		MIII			
Subject borders of Governor and Council		MIV			
Staff		MV			
Men Enlisted and volunteers		MVI			
Governed by rules of U.S. army		MVII			
Consist of 1,120 men		MVIII			
Corps of Rangers		MIX			
Those Subject to Militia duty		MX			
Election of captain, first and second lieuenants		MXI			
Commissions		MXII			
SLAVES	13		G.P.9	VIII	
HEAD-RIGHT CLAIMS				XI	

Subject:	1827	1835	1836	1845	1870
LAND–OFFICE		XIV	G.P.10	XII	
SCHEDULE			§1=8	XIII	

ADDITIONAL PROVISIONS OF 1827 CONST. NOT COMPARABLE TO ANY OTHER CONST.

1.	State of Coahuila and Texas is union of its in habitants
2.	Independent of every foreign power
3.	Acts of sovereignty
4.	General Congress of Mexican Federation
6.	The territory of the State of Coahuila and Texas
7.	Territory divided into three departments
8.	Power to modify division
9.	Apostolic Catholic Religion's State Religion
10.	State to defray expenses of worship
15.	Vacant goods
16.	Two classes of persons
17.	Inhabitants of Coahuila and Texas
18.	Citizens of Coahuila and Texas
19.	Those not entitled tocitizenship
20.	Loss of rights of citizen ship
21.	Restoring rights of citizenship
22.	Exercise of rights of citizenship suspended
23.	How nights destroyed or suspended
24.	Employment
25.	Professional employments
26.	Object of government is happiness
27.	Officers of government are agents of State
47–66.	Of the Electoral Municipal Assemblies
67–77.	Of the Electoral Assemblies of the District
79.	Deputies to present their credentials in Congress
80.	Appointment of body of permanent deputation
94.	Congress changing its residence
98.	The attributes of the permanent deputation.
105.	Laws are annulled
106–109.	Of the Election of Deputies for the General Congress of the federation (Appendix)
121–128.	Governor shall have a council- Council of the Government
145–154.	Of the Chiefs of Police of Departments, and the Subaltern or Chiefs of Districts
154–167.	Of the Ayuntamientos
169.	Neither bongress nor Governor can interfere in pending cases
171.	Uniformity of laws
173.	Military and ecclesiastics subject to their respective authorities

BACKGROUND NOTE

The Spanish element in Texas history dates from 1519 when Alonso Alvarez de Pineda, searching for passages to the Pacific, entered the mouth of the Rio de las Palmas (Rio Grande) and made an early map of the Gulf Coast. It was the first of dozens of expeditions which covered the land north of the river in the course of the conquest and settling of Mexico. But gold was the primary concern of most of the explorations, and by 1730 there were only a dozen or so missions, and three small communities--San Antonio de Bexar, the presidio of Nuestra Senora de Loreto de Bahia del Espiritu Santo (Goliad), and Nacogdoches. By the last decade of the eighteenth century, the situation was little changed.

American adventurers ("filibusterers"), attracted by reports of good lands and growing wealth in the Spanish provinces, began entering the region in the early 1800s. The Louisiana Purchase of 1803 was followed by a tentative agreement between the United States and Spain, purporting to set up a "Neutral Ground" along the vaguely defined border; but with the Sabine River as an easily traversed barrier, the incursions continued. In 1819 a definitive treaty with Spain was signed (see Volume II, page 302) renouncing any American interest in Texas. Two years later Mexico won its independence and in 1827 drafted a constitution for the local province of Coahuila y Tejas (Doc. No. 1).

However, Mexico compounded its own difficulties by encouraging systematic American colonization of the area. Already one colony centered around San Felipe de Austin had grown up under an 1820 grant from Spain which the new government left undisturbed. Americans began arriving in increasing numbers under new colonization contracts. A fundamental problem which resulted arose in the democratic assumptions of the common law, generally familiar to the newcomer, and the more formal and rigid rules of the Spanish law, dating back in many cases to Roman legal principles. These dissatisfactions led on Hayden Edwards in 1826 to attempt to create an autonomous republic to be called Fredonia. Alarmed at such a trend, Mexico cancelled Edward's colonization contract.

Belatedly, Mexico now sought to reverse the situation by a decree in 1830 halting further American immigration into Texas. But there were already too many settlers -- thousands who had no desire or intention of becoming subject to the government in Mexico City. A meeting at San Felipe in 1833 drew up a proposed regional constitution and Stephen Austin, the first colonizer under the 1820 Spanish grant, took it to the capital to seek its approval. Instead, he was arrested and imprisoned for nearly two years. This was all that was needed to spark an uprising and attract fire-eaters to lead the way. There came Sam Houston, former governor of Tennessee, Colonel William B. Travis of South Carolina, and the brawling frontiersman with the famous knife, Jim Bowie.

A provisional constitution for an autonomous state of Texas was drafted in November 1835 (Doc. No. 2). Already, since the previous June, desultory fighting had been spreading as the new dictator, Antonio Lopez de Santa Ana, had mounted a military force to restore Mexican control. Early engagements had been won by the Texans, and open recruiting of "Volunteers for Texas" was going on from New Orleans to Cincinnati. On December 9, 1835 a group of armed frontiersmen attacked the Mexican garrison at San Antonio and captured the city. Then the main Mexican army came up and forced the recent victors to take refuge in the Alamo.

On March 2, 1836 a Declaration of Independence was adopted by a convention at Washington on the Brazos (Doc. No. 3), with an ordinance putting it into effect (Doc. No. 4). Two weeks later a constitution for the new Republic was promulaged (Doc. No. 5). In the meantime, the Mexicans had overrun the Alamo and annihilated the garrison, following this with the massacre of two other armed units. Unable to assemble a force strong enough to challenge Santa Ana's army, Houston threw up a rear guard to cover an exodus of Americans now fleeing toward the United States borders. But suddenly the Mexican army placed itself within the juncture of the San Jacinto River and Buffalo Bayou; Houston turned to give battle on April 20, and the next day the Texans suddenly charged the enemy and in the surprise destroyed the entire army. The independence of Texas thus became a reality; the settlers halted their flight, and in October Houston was elected the first president of the Texas Republic.

Formal recognition by the United States, England, France and Holland in a short time assured Texan independence; but from the beginning it had been assumed that ultimate annexation by the United States was desired. Within the decade following independence the Republic's population grew to more than 100,000, but the chronic deadlock in Congress over free and slave state balance held up the annexation plan for several terms. On March 1, 1845, however, a joint resolution of Congress offered terms of annexation (Doc. No. 6). The Republic accepted the terms on July 4 and drafted a state constitution of October 13 (Doc. No. 7). Another joint resolution of December 29 formally admitted Texas to the Union (Doc. No. 8).

Because Mexico had warned that annexation would be regarded as a hostile act, an American army under General Zachary Taylor advanced to the Rio Grande in March 1846, and after eighteen months of fighting, with several successful invasions of Mexico itself, the treaty of Guadalupe Hidalgo was signed on February 2, 1848, adding a vast new territory to American possessions from El Paso westward to the Pacific.

In 1861 Texas seceded from the Union upon outbreak of the Civil War, but its geographic remoteness from the main theaters minimized its strategic effectiveness. After failure to win acceptance of new constitutions in 1866 (Doc. No. 9) and 1868 (Doc. No. 10), the state rejoined the Union under a third constitution in 1870 (Doc. No. 11) which remains in force, as amended, today.

[Doc. No. 1]

Constitution of Coahuila y Tejas

CONSTITUTION OF COAHUILA AND TEXAS—1827.*

The Governor of the Free State of Coahuila and Texas, to all its inhabitants—*Know*, that the Constituent Congress of the same State, has *Decreed* and sanctioned the following political Constitution of the free State of Coahuila and Texas.

In the name of GOD, omnipotent, author, and supreme legislator of the Universe, the Constituent Congress of the State of Coahuila and Texas, desirous to comply with the will of the people, and in order completely to fill the great and magnificent object of promoting the glory and prosperity of the same State, *Decrees* for its administration and government the Constitution which follows:—

PRELIMINARY DISPOSITIONS.

ARTICLE 1. The State of Coahuila and Texas consists in the union of all its inhabitants.

2. It is free and independent of the other United Mexican States, and of every other foreign power and dominion.

3. The sovereignty of the State resides originally and essentially in the general

---

* The two northeastern provinces of Mexico, not having sufficient population to entitle them to enter the Mexican Union as separate states, were united as "the state of Coahuila and Texas." The state congress which met at Saltillo framed this constitution, which was proclaimed March 11, 1827.

mass of the individuals who compose it; but these do not of themselves excuse any other acts of sovereignty than those designated in this Constitution, and in the form which it prescribes.

4. In all matters relating to the Mexican Federation, the State delegates its faculties and powers to the General Congress of the same, but in all that properly relates to the administration and entire Government of the State, it retains its liberty, independence, and sovereignty.

5. THEREFORE, Belongs exclusively to the same State, the right to establish by means of its representatives, its fundamental laws, conformable to the basis sanctioned in the Constitutional Act and the General Constitution.

6. The Territory of the State is the same which comprehends the Provinces heretofore known by the name of Coahuila and Texas. A constitutional law shall fix their limits with respect to the other adjoining States of the Mexican Federation.

7. The Territory of the State is divided for the present, for its better administration, into three departments, which shall be—BEXAR—which district is extended to the whole of the Territory, which corresponds to that called the Province of TEXAS, which alone is a district. MONCLOVA, which comprehends the district of this name and that of RIO GRANDE SALTILLO, which embraces the district of this name, and that of PARRAS.

8. Congress hereafter shall have power to alter, vary, and modify this division of the Territory of the State, in the manner it may esteem most conducive to the felicity of the people.

9. The Apostolic Catholic Religion is that of the State; this it protects by wise and just laws, and prohibits the exercise of any other.

10. The State shall regulate and defray the expenses which may be necessary for the preservation of worship, in conformity with the regulation of the Concordats, which the nation shall celebrate with the Holy See, and by the laws it shall dictate relative to the exercise of patronage in the whole Federation.

11. Every man who inhabits the Territory of the State, although he be in transit, shall enjoy the imprescriptible rights of liberty, security, property, and equality; and it is the duty of the same State to conserve, and protect by laws, wise and equitable, those general rights of mankind.

12. It is also an obligation on the State to protect all its inhabitants in the right which they have to write, print, and publish freely their thoughts, and political opinions, without the necessity of examination, revision or censure, anterior to the publication, under the restrictions, and responsibilities established, or which hereafter may be established, by general laws on the subject.

13. In this State no person shall be born a slave, after this Constitution is published in the capital of each District, and six months thereafter neither will the introduction of slaves be permitted under any pretext.

14. It is the duty of every man who inhabits the State, to obey its laws, respect its constituted authorities, and contribute to the support of the same State, in the mode which it asks.

15. To the State belongs every species of vacant goods in its Territories, and those of its intestate inhabitants who have no legitimate successor in the manner laid down by the laws.

16. The State is composed only of two classes of persons, to wit: *inhabitants* of Coahuila and Texas, (Coahuittejanos) and *citizens* of Coahuila and Texas.

17. Those are inhabitants of Coahuila and Texas (Coahuittejanos.) First, All men born and domesticated in the Territory of the State and their descendants. Secondly, those born in any other part of the Territory of the Federation, or those who fix their domicile in this State. Thirdly, those foreigners who are legitimately established in the State, be they of what nation they may. Fourthly, those foreigners who obtain from Congress letters of naturalization, or have a domicile in the State obtained according to law, which shall be passed as soon as the Congress of the Union fixes the general rule of naturalization, which it ought to establish conformable to the 26th clause of the faculties which the Federal Constitution designates.

18. Those are citizens of Coahuila and Texas (Coahuittajenos.) First, all men born

in the State, and who are domiciliated in any part of its Territory. Secondly, all citizens of the other States and Territories of the Federation, as soon as they become domiciliated in the State. Thirdly, all the children of Mexican citizens, who have been born out of the Territory of the Federation, and who fix their domicile in the State. Fourthly, the foreigners who are actually and legally domiciliated in the State, whatever may have been the country of their nativity. Fifthly, foreigners who enjoy the rights of inhabitants of Coahuila and Texas, have obtained from Congress special letters of citizenship—the laws will prescribe the merits and circumstances requisite for the concession of such.

19. Those born in the Territory of the Federation, and those foreigners resident in it, (with the exception of their children,) who, at the time of the proclamation of the political emancipation of the nation, was unfaithful to the cause of independence, and emigrated to a foreign country, or that dependent on the Spanish government, are neither entitled to the rights of domiciliation nor citizenship, in the State.

20. The rights of citizenship are lost. First, by acquiring naturalization in a foreign country. Secondly, by acquiring a station of profit, or honor, under a foreign government, without permission of Congress. Thirdly, by sentence legally obtained, which imposes penal or infamous punishments. Fourthly, by selling his vote, or buying that of another, for himself or for a third person, whether in popular assemblies, or in any other whatever—and of trust in the same assemblies, either as presidents, tellers, or secretaries, or in the exercise of any other public functions. Fifthly, for having resided five consecutive years out of the limits of the Territory of the Federation, without commission of the general government, or particular one of the State, or without its leave.

21. He that has lost the rights of citizenship cannot regain them without the express act of restoration of Congress.

22. The exercise of the same rights are suspended. First, for physical or moral incapacity, previously ascertained by judicial decision. Secondly, for not being twenty-one years complete, except those who are married, who can enter upon the exercise of these rights from the time they contract matrimony, of whatever age they may be. Thirdly, for being a debtor to the public funds, the time of payment elapsed, legal requisition therefore made, and not complied with. Fourthly, for having been prosecuted criminally, unless the defendant is absolved of the matter, or condemned to punishment not painful or infamous. Fifthly, for not having an employment, trade, or any known method of obtaining a livelihood. Sixthly, for not knowing how to read and write; but this shall not take effect until the year 1850, with regard to those who hereafter enter into the rights of citizenship.

23. The rights of citizenship can only be destroyed or suspended for the causes stated in articles 20 and 22.

24. None but citizens who are in the exercise of their rights can vote for popular employments in the State in those instances stated in the law; and these only can obtain the said employments, or any others in the same State.

25. Professional employments form an exception to the second part of the anterior article, which employments can also be conferred on foreigners.

FORM OF THE STATE GOVERNMENT.

26. The object of the State government is the happiness of the individuals which compose it, for the end of all political society is no other than the welfare of the associated.

27. The officers of the government, invested with whatever kind of authority, are no more than mere agents or commissioners of the State, responsible to it for their public conduct.

28. The government of the State is popular representative federal; in consequence, it shall not have in it any hereditary office or privilege.

29. The supreme power of the State is divided for its exercise, into Legislative, Executive, and Judicial, and never can these three powers, nor two of them, be united in one corporation or person, nor the Legislative power deposited in one individual.

30. The exercise of the Legislative power shall reside in a Congress, composed of deputies popularly elected.

31. The exercise of the Executive power shall reside in a citizen, who shall be denominated Governor of the State, and who also shall be chosen popularly.

32. The exercise of the Judicial power shall reside in the Tribunals and Courts which the Constitution establishes.

TITLE 1st.—*Of the Legislative power of the State.* SECTION 1st.—*Of the Deputies of Congress.*

33. The Congress consists of the deputies which represent the State, chosen conformably to this Constitution; its number shall be that of twelve members proprietary, and six supernumerary members, until the year 1832.*

34. The Congress in that year, and in the last of every ten years which follow, shall have power to augment the number of deputies under the standard of one for every 7000 souls.

35. The election of proprietary deputies and supernumeraries shall be held in all and every one of the districts of the State. A law shall fix the number of deputies of one and the other class which each district ought to appoint.

36. To be a deputy, proprietary, or supernumerary, it is required to have, at the time of the election, the following qualities:—First, to be a citizen in the exercise of his rights. Secondly, to be of the full age of twenty-five years. Thirdly, to be an inhabitant of the State, with residence in it for two years immediately before the election. To natives of the State it is sufficient to possess the two first requisites.

37. It is necessary for those not born in the Territory of the Federation, in order to be deputies, proprietaries, or supernumeraries, to have had eight years' residence in it, and to be worth $8000 in property, or to have an income of some business of $1000 annually, and the qualifications provided in the foregoing article.

38. There is excepted from the foregoing, those born in any other part of the Territory of America, which in the year 1810, depended on Spain, and which may not have united itself to any other nation, nor remained in dependence on Spain; to those it is sufficient that they have been three years, complete, in the Mexican Republic, and possess the requisites prescribed in article 36.

39. Those cannot be deputies, proprietaries, or supernumeraries; First, The Governor, or Vice-Governor of the State; the member of the Council of Government; those employed in the Federation; the Civil Functionaries of the State Government; the Ecclesiastics who exercise any species of Jurisdiction or authority in some part of the district where the election may be held; foreigners, at the time when war may exist between the country of their nativity and Mexico.

40. In order that those public functionaries of the Federation, or of the State, comprehended in the anterior article, may be elected deputies, they ought absolutely to have ceased the exercise of their functions four months before the election.

41. If the same individual shall be named deputy proprietary for two or more districts, the election of that district in which he actually resides shall have preference. If he does not reside in either, the election of the district of his origin shall have preference. If he was neither a resident nor a native of some one of the said districts, that shall stand which the same elected deputy shall designate. In either of these cases, or of the death or inability of the deputies proprietary to discharge their functions according to the judgment of Congress, their duties shall devolve upon the respective deputies supernumerary.

42. If it shall happen that the same citizen is elected deputy supernumerary for two or more districts, in this case the same order of preference provided for in the three first parts of the anterior article prevails. And in the district which remains without a deputy supernumerary, the vacancy shall be filled up by the person who, in the respective electoral assembly, had the next greatest number of votes. In case of a tie it shall be decided by lot, (suerte.)

---

* The supernumerary deputies, are intended to supply vacancies, occasioned by death or other evil.

43. The deputies, during the discharge of their commissions, shall obtain from the public Treasury of the State, the compensation which the anterior Congress shall assign; and they shall also receive what may appear necessary for their expenses in going to the place of session, and in returning from thence to their houses on the close of the session.

44. The deputies at no time, and in no case, nor before any authority, can be responsible for the opinions which they manifest in the discharge of their duties. In criminal cases, instituted against them, they shall be judged by the Tribunals which will be hereafter mentioned; and from the day of their appointment until they have completed the two years of their deputation, they cannot be accused unless before Congress, which is constituted a Grand Jury to declare if there is, or is not, cause for an accusation. In the mean time, during the session, the deputies cannot be sued in civil suits, nor arrested for debts.

45. During the time of their deputation, counting for this purpose, from the day of their appointment, they cannot obtain for themselves any employment from the government, nor shall they solicit it for others, nor even for their promotion, except it be in the regular order of office.

SECTION 2d.—*Of the Nomination of the Deputies.*

46. For the election of the deputies, there shall be held electoral municipal assemblies, and electoral district assemblies.

PARAGRAPH 1st—*Of the Electoral municipal Assemblies.*

47. The electoral municipal assemblies shall be composed of the citizens who are in the exercise of their rights, and who may be inhabitants and residents within the limits of their respective Ayuntamientos, and no person of this can be excused from attending.

48. These assemblies shall be celebrated the first Sunday and the following day of the month of August, of the year anterior to the renovation of Congress, in order to nominate the electors of the district who are to choose the deputies, and eight days previously, the president of every Ayuntamiento, without the necessity of other order, shall call together the citizens of his district, by a proper notice, or as may be the custom, that they shall convene to make the elections at the time and in the form which this Constitution requires, giving prompt notification to the villages of the same district for the information of the inhabitants.

49. In order that the citizens can assist with the greater convenience, every Ayuntamiento according to its locality and the population of its territory, shall determine the number of municipal assemblies which it ought to form in its limits, and the public places in which they have to be held, designating the limits of each.

50. They shall be presided, one by the Political Chief or Alcalde, and the remainder by other individuals of the Ayuntamiento to whom it falls by lot, and in default of these, that corporation shall appoint as President of the respective municipal assembly an inhabitant of its own district, who shall know how to read and write.

51. On the aforesaid Sunday in August, at the hour of meeting the citizens who have convened in the place designated for it, shall open the said assembly by appointment from amongst themselves, by a plurality of votes, one Secretary and two Tellers, who shall know how to read and write.

52. The elections shall be opened on the two days mentioned in Article 48, for the space of four hours each day, divided between the morning and the evening, and in every one of these assemblies there shall be a Register, in which shall be written the votes of the citizens who come together to name the electors of the district, setting down in alphabetical order the names of the voters and those voted for.

53. To be an elector of a district, it is necessary to be a citizen in the exercise of his rights, of the age of 25 years complete, to know how to read write, and to be an inhabitant and resident in some part of the same district, the year immediately anterior to the election.

54. Every citizen shall choose by voice or writing, the respective electors of the district, whose names (the election being had according to the former mode) the

voter shall designate in a loud voice, and it shall be entered in a list and then read by the Secretary; and it is indispensable that it should be written in the Register in presence of the voter. No person shall vote for himself in this or any other instance of the election, under the penalty of losing the right to vote.

55. In those districts in which there is to be chosen only one deputy, there shall be appointed 11 electors, and in that which can choose two or more, there shall be appointed 21 electors.

56. The doubts or controversies that may arise, whether any person or persons present, possess the qualification of votes, shall be decided verbally by the assembly, and its decisions shall be executed without appeal, for this time and object only; *Provided*, that such doubt shall not turn upon the construction of this Constitution or other law. If the said resolution shall result in a tie, the doubt shall be considered removed.

57. Should complaints arise that bribery, corruption, or force had been used to determine the election in favor of particular persons, a public and verbal investigation shall be made thereof, and should it appear that the accusation is true, those who have committed the crime shall be deprived of all voice in the election, and the calumniator shall suffer the same penalty; and from this judgment there shall be no appeal. Doubts which arise as to the quality of proof, shall be decided by the assembly, in the manner prescribed in the preceding article.

58. Municipal assemblies shall be held with open doors and without any guard whatever; and no individual, whatever his class may be, shall present himself in them armed.

59. On completion of the two days for which the election is to be kept open, the President, Tellers, and Secretary of each assembly shall proceed to sum up the votes which each citizen has received, in the Register, which shall be signed by the said officers; and by this operation the assembly shall be dissolved, and any other act which may be done, shall not only be considered null, but as an attempt against the public security. The said Register shall be delivered sealed to the Secretary of the respective Ayuntamiento.

60. On the second Sunday of the said month of August, each Ayuntamiento shall convene in their respective halls in public session. In their presence, and also with the assistance of the President, Tellers, and Secretary of the municipal assemblies, the Registers shall be opened, and after examining the whole of them, a general list shall be formed in alphabetical order, in which shall be comprehended all the individuals voted for, and the number of votes they have received.

61. This list and the certificate which shall be extended on the subject, shall be signed by the President of the Ayuntamiento, the Secretary of it, and the Secretaries of the assemblies; after which, two copies of the said list shall be drawn off, certified by the same persons, one of which shall be immediately posted up in the next public place, and the other shall be delivered with accompanying official letter, signed by the President of the Ayuntamiento, to two individuals appointed by that body to proceed to the capital of the district, there to form a general classification of votes in union with the commissioners of the other Ayuntamientos.

62. On the fourth Sunday in August, the commissioners of the Ayuntamientos shall present themselves with their credentials of election to the political chief, or in his absence to the first alcalde, of the capital of the district, and presided by the first or by the second, as the case be thus, shall assemble in public session in the town hall, and after examining all the lists, they shall form a general list of all the individuals voted for as electors of the district by the citizens of each municipal district respectively, expressing the number of votes they have had and the place of their residence.

63. In order to make this general regulation of votes, the concurrence of not less than four of the commissioners is requisite. In those districts in which there is not that number, the Ayuntamiento of the capital shall name, from amongst the individuals of its own body, the number deficient.

64. The citizens, who upon the result of this general scrutiny, have the greatest number of votes on the list, shall be considered constitutionally appointed for electors. In case of a tie amongst two or more individuals, it shall be decided by lot.

65. The aforesaid list, and all acts relative to the business, shall be attested by the President, the Commissioners, and the Secretary of the Ayuntamientos of the capital of the district. There shall be extracted copies of one, and the other certified by the same; and they shall be remitted by the President to the permanent deputation of Congress, the Governor of the State, and the different municipalities of the district.

66. The same President shall pass without any delay, the corresponding certificate to the electors appointed, that they may go to the capital of the department on the day named by the Constitution, in order to celebrate the electoral assembly of the same.

PARAGRAPH 2d.—*Of the Electoral Assemblies of the District.*

67. The electoral assemblies of the district shall be composed of the electors named by the citizens in the municipal assemblies, who shall assemble in the capital of the respective district with a view to name the deputy or deputies, required to assist at the Congress as representatives of the State.

68. These assemblies shall be held 15 days after the general regulation of votes, spoken of in article 62; the electors meeting in the municipal hall, or in the building which is supposed to be more fitting for so solemn an act, with open doors, and without guards, and in the said assemblies, no person, of whatever class he may be, shall be present with arms.

69. They shall be presided by the Political Chief, or in his default, by the first Alcalde of the capital of the district, and shall commence their sessions by appointing, by plurality of votes, one Secretary and two Tellers, from amongst their own body, and in continuation, the President shall read the credentials of the electors, which are to be the certificates in which is set forth their appointment.

70. In continuation, the President shall inquire if any number is legally disqualified, and if it is proved that there is, the elector shall use his right to vote. Afterwards, the President shall also inquire if there has been bribery, corruption, or force whereby the election has been determined in favor of any particular person, and if it is proved that there has been, the delinquents shall be deprived of any voice in the election, and the calumniators shall suffer an equal punishment. The doubts which shall occur in one or the other case, the assembly shall resolve in the manner which is spoken of in Article 56.

71. Immediately after—the electors present shall proceed to name the deputy or deputies that correspond to the district, and they shall be chosen one by one by secret ballot, by means of tickets which each elector shall throw into an urn to be placed upon a table at the foot of the crucifix, after having taken an oath before the President to vote for those citizens for deputies to the Congress of the State, who, in his opinion, possess the qualifications of information, judgment, probity, and a known adherence to the independence of the nation.

72. The voting being concluded, the President, Tellers, and Secretary shall regulate the votes, and declare constitutionally elected for deputy, the citizen who has obtained more than half the votes—the President publishing each election. If no one has had an absolute plurality of votes, they shall proceed to a second ballot, for the two who may have obtained the greatest number of votes. If there are more than two who have an equal number of votes, the second ballot shall be made amongst the whole of them, doing the same when no one has obtained this majority, but all of those having an equal number of votes. In all these cases he shall be elected who has a plurality of votes, and in case of a tie, the voting shall be repeated once only, and if it again result in a tie, it shall be decided by lot.

73. If only one individual has a respective majority, (the highest number of votes) and two or more an equal number of votes, but greater than all the others, in order to decide which of them shall enter into the second ballot with the first, there shall be a second voting relative to these, and he that obtains the most votes shall enter into competition with him that had the respective majority; in case of a tie, the voting shall be repeated, and if it happens a second time, it shall be decided by lot. In the second ballot, which is had between him who had obtained the respective majority

over the whole, and his competitor, that which is established in the last part of the anterior article, shall be observed.

74. When one alone has the respective majority, and all the others have an equal number of votes, in order to know which shall enter into competition in the second ballot with him, will be carried into effect by the provisions of the foregoing articles—for this end, in respect of those who have been tied, and in order to know at the same time which of these competitors ought to be the deputy, the method established in the last part of the same article shall be observed.

75. The election of deputies proprietaries concluded—There shall follow that of the supernumeraries in the same method and form, which being finished, there shall be immediately posted up in the most public place, a list, which shall contain the names of all the deputies elected, attested by the Secretary of the respective assembly. The Act of the election shall be attested by the President and all the electors. And the President, the Secretary, and the Tellers, shall remit authenticated copies of the same to the permanent deputation of Congress, the Governor of the State, and all the Ayuntamientos of the district. These assemblies shall immediately dissolve when they have executed the acts which this Constitution prescribes, and every other act with which they intermeddle shall be null, and shall be considered an attempt against the public security.

76. The President, without delay, shall deliver to the deputies and supernumeraries, an official letter accompanied with a certificate of their election, which shall serve as their credentials.

77. No citizen can be excused upon any motive or pretext, from the discharge of the duties which are spoken of in the present section.

SECTION 3d.—*Of the Celebration of Congress.*

78. The Congress shall assemble each year, to hold its sessions in the place which shall be designated by a law and in the building which is destined for this object. Whenever it may be deemed convenient to change it to another place, it can be done with the accordance of two-thirds of the whole number of the deputies.

79. The deputies shall present their credentials to the permanent deputation of Congress, in order that they may examine them, by comparing them with the testimonies of the elections of the electoral assemblies of the district.

80. On the 28th day of the month of December, of the year anterior to the renovation of Congress, the newly elected deputies and the members of the permanent deputation shall meet in public session, and shall choose their President and Secretary from the said deputation. This meeting shall report as to the legitimacy of the credentials and qualifications of the deputies, and any doubts which may arise on these points shall be definitely determined by a plurality of votes by this assembly; but the individuals of the permanent deputation, who have not been re-elected shall not have a vote.

81. In continuation, the deputies shall take before the President an oath, that they will observe, and caused to be observed, the Constitutional Act, and the Federal Constitution of the United States of Mexico, and the Constitution of this State, and that they will completely discharge their duties.

82. In continuation, the deputies shall proceed to choose from amongst themselves by secret ballot, and by an absolute plurality of votes, a President and Vice President and two Secretaries, upon which the permanent deputation shall cease in all its functions, and those of its members not re-elected having retired, the President of Congress shall declare that it is solemnly and legitimately constituted.

83. For the celebration of the ordinary and extraordinary sessions of Congress, the deputies shall meet four days previous to its organization, in the manner prescribed in the first part of Article 80, in order to resolve in the manner expressed in the second part of the same Article upon the legitimacy of the credentials and qualifications of the new deputies who present themselves, and having approved of them, the deputies shall immediately take the oath prescribed by Article 81, and in continuation shall

proceed to make nomination of the President, Vice President, and Secretaries, in the same manner which is provided in Article 82.

84. The Congress shall open its ordinary sessions the first day of January in every year, and the first day of September in each year following the renovation of the same Congress. The Governor of the State being obliged to assist upon so important an occasion, when he shall pronounce a suitable discourse, which the President of Congress shall answer in general terms.

85. On the day after the opening of the ordinary session, the Governor shall present in person to Congress, a written account of the state of the public Administration, proposing such amendments or reforms, as may be required in its different branches.

86. The sessions of Congress shall be held daily, without other interruption than those of solemn festivals. All the proceedings shall be public, with the exception of those which treat of reserved business, which may be secret.

87. The ordinary sessions of Congress, which commence the first day of January, shall last that month and the three following, February, March, and April; and cannot be prorogued to any other month, except in the two following instances: First, by petition of the Governor; and secondly, if the same Congress deem it necessary— for this, there must be the concurrence, in both cases, of the vote of two-thirds of the deputies. The ordinary sessions, which commence on the first of September, shall last 30 days of the said month without any power to prorogue on any motive or pretext whatever. Both sessions shall be closed with the same formalities which are prescribed for their opening.

88. Before the conclusion of the ordinary session of Congress, there shall be appointed of that body a permanent deputation, composed of three individuals proprietary, and one supernumerary, which shall continue all the intervening time between one ordinary session and the other; and its President shall be its first appointed individual, and its Secretary the last individual proprietary.

89. When in the intervening time between one ordinary session and another, circumstances or business shall occur requiring the meeting of Congress, it can be convoked for extraordinary sessions, provided it is sanctioned by the unanimous vote of two-thirds of the members of the permanent deputation, and of the council of government, which shall meet for that purpose.

90. If the circumstances or business which cause the extraordinary convocation of Congress, should be very weighty and urgent, the permanent deputation, united with the council of government and the other deputies which are in the capital, shall immediately take such necessary measures as the exigency shall require, and shall give an account thereof to Congress as soon as it may meet

91. When Congress meet in extraordinary sessions, there shall be called to the same, the deputies who ought to assist at the ordinary sessions of that year, and they shall be exclusively occupied upon the business or businesses for which they have been convoked, but if they have not concluded against the day on which they ought to meet in ordinary sessions, they shall postpone those and continue the business for which the extraordinary session had been convoked.

92. The holding of the extraordinary sessions shall not impede the election of the new deputies at the time prescribed in this constitution.

93. The extraordinary sessions shall be opened and closed with the same solemnities as the ordinary sessions.

94. The resolutions which Congress may take upon the change of its residence, or the prorogation of its sessions, shall be executed by the Governor without any observations upon them.

95. The Congress, in all that belongs to its government and interior order, shall observe the regulations formed by the present, having power to make the reforms it may deem necessary.

96. The deputies shall be renewed totally every two years. Those of the anterior Congress can be re-chosen, but they cannot be compelled to accept this trust unless there should be a vacancy of one-half of the deputation. There shall be excepted in this Article, the deputies of the present Congress, who cannot be re-elected for the next Constitutional Congress.

SECTION 4th.—*Of the Attributes of Congress, and of the Permanent Deputation.*

97. The exclusive attributes of Congress are first to decree, interpret, reform, or abolish, the laws relative to the Administration, and interior government of the State in all its branches. Secondly, to regulate the votes which the citizens may have obtained in the electoral assemblies for Governor, Vice-Governor, and for members of the council of government, and to appoint those officers whenever it shall devolve upon them to do so. Thirdly, to decide by secret ballot, the ties which may happen between two or more individuals, in the election of the fore-mentioned officers. Fourthly, to resolve the doubts which may arise upon these elections and upon the qualifications of the elected. Fifthly, to examine the excuses which the elected may allege for not accepting these stations and to determine them. Sixthly, to form themselves into a Grand Jury, and to declare whether there are or are not grounds of accusation for neglect of official duty, as well as for ordinary crimes against the deputies of Congress. The Governor, the Vice-Governor, the members of the Council, the Secretary of State, and the individuals of the Supreme Court of Justice of the State. Seventhly, to render effective the responsibility of these public functionaries, and to do in this case that which is so necessary with respect to all others employed. Eighthly, to fix every year the public expenses of the State, having in view the reports on the subject which shall be presented by the Governor. Ninthly, to establish or confirm the taxes or contributions necessary to cover these expenses, under the regulations of this Constitution, and the general one of the Federation—to regulate their collection, determine their application, and approve of their distribution. Tenthly, to examine and approve the accounts of the application of all the public funds of the State. Eleventh, to contract debts in case of necessity upon the credit of the State, and to designate the guarantees for their liquidation. Twelfth, to decree whatever may be necessary for the administration, conservation, or altercation of the goods of the State. Thirteenth, to create, suspend, or suppress the public officers of the State; and to fix, diminish, or augment their salaries or pensions. Fourteenth, to grant premiums or recompenses to corporations or persons, who have rendered distinguished services to the State, and to decree posthumous public honors to the memory of great men. Fifteenth, to regulate the manner of recruiting the men which may be necessary for the service, or to fill up the permanent presidial militia companies of cavalry, and the active militia of the same army, auxiliary to that which are destined by the institution to the defence of the State, approve of the distribution which may be made among the towns of the State of their respective quotas, to effect this object. Sixteenth, to decree that which may be necessary for the enrolling and instruction of the civic militia of the State, and the appointment of its officers conformable to the discipline prescribed, or which shall be prescribed by general laws. Seventeenth, to promote and encourage, by laws, public information, and education, and the progress of the sciences, arts, and useful establishments, removing the obstacles which may palsy objects so commendable. Eighteenth, to protect the political liberty of the press. Nineteenth, to attend to, and give or deny their consent to all those acts and cases for which this Constitution has provided.

98. The attributes of the permanent deputation, are First, to watch over the observance of the Constitutional Act, the Constitution, and general laws of the Union, and the particular ones of the State, in order to give an account to Congress of infractions thereof, which they may observe. Second, to convoke the Congress for extraordinary sessions in those cases, and in the manner prescribed by this Constitution. Third, to discharge the functions which are prescribed in Articles 79 and 80. Fourth, to give notice to the supernumeraries of the time when they shall come to the Congress in the place of the deputies proprietaries, and if the death or absolute inability of one or more of them should occur, to communicate the corresponding orders to the respective district, in order that it may proceed to a new election. Fifth, to receive the testimonies of the acts of the elections of the electoral assemblies of the district, for Governor, Vice-Governor, and members of the Council of Government, and to deliver them to Congress as soon as it may be installed.

SECTION 5th. — *Of the formation and promulgation of the Laws.*

99. The interior regulations of Congress shall prescribe the form, intervals, and method of procedure in the debates and votings for the projects of laws and decrees.

100. Every project of a law or decree, which has been rejected conformable to the regulations, shall not be again proposed until the ordinary session of the following year; but this shall not impede the passage of one or more articles of it, which may compose part of other projects not rejected.

101. The half and one more (la mitad y uno mas) of the total number of the deputies, forms a Congress to dedicate measures and procedures which do not obtain the character of a law or decree, but to discuss and decide on projects of laws or decrees, and dictate of much importance, the presence of two-thirds of all the deputies is necessary.

102. If a project of a law or decree, after it is discussed, is approved, it shall be communicated to the Governor, who, if he approves of it, shall immediately proceed to promulgate and circulate it with the corresponding solemnities. But if not, after hearing the council, he shall have power to make such observations as he thinks proper, and shall return it with his remarks to the Congress within ten lawful days, counting from his receipt of it.

103. The project of a law or decree, returned by the Governor according to the antecedent Article, shall be discussed a second time; the Speaker, whom the Governor shall designate, having power to assist at the discussion and to speak upon the subject. If on this second debate, it is approved by two-thirds of the deputies present, it shall be again communicated to the Governor, who shall, without excuse, immediately proceed to its solemn promulgation, but if not approved in this form, it cannot again be proposed until the sessions of the year following.

104. If the Governor shall not return the project of a law or decree within the time prescribed in Article 102, it shall be deemed by this act as sanctioned, and as such shall be promulgated, unless previous to that time the Congress may have closed or suspended its session, in which case the return ought to be made the first day on which Congress may meet.

105. Laws are annulled with the same formalities and by the same procedure with which they are established.

APPENDIX TO THIS TITLE. — *Of the election of Deputies for the General Congress of the Federation.*

106. The electoral district assemblies on the same day and in the same form, in which the election of deputies to the Congress of the State ought to be had, shall proceed to that of the individuals who are to choose deputies for the general Congress of the general Congress of the Union, appointing one individual for every 7000 souls, who shall possess the qualifications required in Article 53 of this Constitution. In the district in which there results an excess of population which passes 3500 souls, there shall be appointed for this fraction another elector; and in those which have not a population of 7000 souls there shall be one named. The said assemblies having concluded the election, shall remit a certified copy of the Act to the Vice-Governor of the State, and shall also pass a corresponding certificate to each one of the elected, which shall serve as his credential.

107. The electors thus appointed shall proceed to the capital of the State, where they shall present themselves to the Vice-Governor, or to him that acts in his place; and having met under the presidency of the one or the other, three days previous to the first Sunday of the month of October in public session, in the edifice deemed the most appropriate; they shall appoint amongst themselves two Tellers and one Secretary, who shall examine the credentials, and on the following day shall report whether they are legal or not. The credentials of the Tellers and Secretary shall be examined by a commission of three individuals to be appointed in the same manner.

108. On the following day they shall meet again to read the returns, and if defects appear in the qualifications of the electors or in their credentials, the meeting in per

manent session shall decide upon them, and their sentence shall be executed without appeal for this time and in this instance only, it being understood that the doubt cannot arise upon the provisions of this Constitution or the Law.

109. On the first Sunday of the said month of October, the electors having met, and more than one-half of the whole being present, they shall proceed to the appointment of the deputies, who shall go from the State to the general Congress of the Federation, in the form laid down by this Constitution, for the appointment of those to the State Congress. This being done, the assembly will do what is necessary to comply with the provisions of the 17th Article of the Federal Constitution, and shall dissolve.

TITLE 2d.—*Of the Executive power of the State.* SECTION 1st.—*Of the Governor.*

110. The Governor of the State ought to possess, at the time of his appointment, the following qualifications: First, to be a citizen in the exercise of his rights. Second, to be born in the Territory of the Republic. Third, to be of the age of thirty years, complete. Fourth, an inhabitant of this State, with residence in it for five years, and two of them immediately before his election.

111. The ecclesiastics, the military, and others employed by the Federation and in the actual service of the same cannot obtain the office of Governor.

112. The Governor of the State shall continue four years in the discharge of his office, and cannot be rechosen for the same office, until the fourth year after he has ceased from its functions.

113. The prerogatives of the Governor, the attributes, and restrictions of his faculties are the following :—

PREROGATIVES OF THE GOVERNOR.

First, the Governor can make observations upon the laws and decrees of Congress, in the manner and form prescribed in Article 102, suspending their publication until the resolution of the same Congress, unless in the cases excepted in this Constitution. Second, he has power to propose laws or reforms to Congress, which he believes may conduce to the general good of the State. Third, he can pardon delinquents under the regulation of the laws. Fourth, the Governor cannot be accused by any one for offences committed at the time of his administration nor during it, nor until one year afterwards, counting from the day on which he has ceased his functions, unless before the Congress, and that time being elapsed, not even before the Congress.

ATTRIBUTES OF THE GOVERNOR.

First, to take care for the preservation of order and public tranquillity in the interior of the State and the security of the exterior, disposing for both these objects, of the militia of the State, whereof the said Governor is commander-in-chief. Second, to cause the observance of the Constitutional Act, the general Constitution, and that of the State, and of the laws, decrees, and orders of the Federation, and of the Congress of the State; issuing their decrees and necessary orders for their execution. Third, to form upon consultation with the council, those instructions and regulations which he believes necessary for the better government of the branches of the public administration of the State, which he shall pass to the Congress for its approbation. Fourth, to fill under the regulation of the Constitution and the Laws all the offices of the State which are not electoral, and which are not otherwise provided for by those laws. Fifth, to appoint and freely dismiss the Secretary of State. Sixth, to take care that justice is administered promptly and completely by the tribunals and courts of the State, and that their sentences are executed. Seventh, to take care of the administration and collection of all the rents of the State, and to decree their application in comformity with the laws. Eighth, to suspend from their offices for three months, and even to deprive them of one-half of their salaries for the same time, after hearing the opinion of the council of the State, all those in the employment of the State, under the Executive department thereof and of its nomination and appointment when they infringe its orders and decrees, passing the proceedings upon the matter to the respective tribunal, in case he believes that there is sufficient cause for accusation. Ninth, to propose to the permanent deputation the convocation of Congress to extraordinary sessions, whenever he deems it necessary, first having the opinion of the council.

RESTRICTION OF THE FACULTIES OF THE GOVERNOR.

The Governor cannot—First, command in person the civic militia of the State, without the express consent of Congress, or in its recess of the permanent deputation. When he commands, under said circumstances, the Vice-Governor shall take charge of the Government. Second, he cannot intermeddle in the examination of pending causes, nor dispose in any manner, before judgment, of the persons of criminals. Third, he cannot deprive any person of his liberty, nor impose any punishment. But when the good and security of the State requires the arrest of any person, he has power to do so, placing the persons arrested at the disposition of the tribunal or competent judge within the term of forty-eight hours. Fourth, he cannot occupy the property of any particular person or corporation, nor embarrass him in the possession, use, or profit of it, unless it may be necessary for a known object of general utility, according to the judgment of the council of government; in which case he shall have power, with the consent of the said council, and the approbation of Congress, or in its recess of the permanent deputation, always indemnifying the interested party according to the judgment of good men, chosen by said party, and by the Government. Fifth, he cannot impede or embarrass in any manner or under any pretext, the popular elections determined by this Constitution and the Laws, nor prevent those laws from taking full effect. Sixth, he cannot go from the capital to any other part of the State for more than one month. If a longer absence is necessary, or if he is obliged to go from the Territory of the State, he shall ask leave of Congress, and its recess, of the permanent deputation.

114. In order to publish the laws and decrees of the Congress of the State, the Governor shall use the following form: "The Governor of State of Coahuila and Texas, to all its inhabitants. *Know*, that the Congress of the same State has decreed the following: (here the text of the law or decree.) THEREFORE, I command that it be printed, published, and circulated, in order that it be complied with.

SECTION 2d.—*Of the Vice-Governor.*

115. There shall likewise be in the State a Vice-Governor. His qualifications shall be the same as those required for Governor. His term shall be four years, and he cannot be re-elected for the same office, unless at the fourth year after he has ceased from its functions.

116. The Vice-Governor shall be President of the Council, but without a vote, unless in case of a tie. He shall also be a chief of the police of the department of the capital, and when exercising the functions of Governor, the office of chief of police shall be discharged by deputy, who shall be appointed *ad interim* by the Vice-Governor, with the approbation of the council.

117. The Vice-Governor shall discharge the functions of Governor in his absence, or when he shall be impeded in the exercise of his office by decision of Congress or of the permanent deputation.

118. When the Vice-Governor is also absent, the councellor appointed by Congress shall fill the office of Governor. If the Congress should be in recess the permanent deputation shall do it without delay, provisionally, until the meeting of Congress.

119. In case of the death or absolute inability of the Governor or Vice-Governor, in the two first years of the exercise of their offices, a new Governor or Vice-Governor shall be elected at the next election for deputies to Congress.

120. The Vice-Governor during the exercise of his office can be accused before Congress alone, for offences committed during the time of his administration, of whatever description they may be.

Section 3d.—*Of the Council of Government.*

121. For the better discharge of the functions of his office, the Governor shall have a council, which shall be denominated *The Council of Government;* and shall be composed of three members proprietaries and two supernumeraries, amongst the whole of whom there can be but one ecclesiastic.

122. To be a member of the Council of Government, the same qualifications are required as for a deputy. Those who are prohibited from being deputies cannot be councellors.

123. Every two years the council shall be removed; the first time, one of the members proprietaries and supernumeraries going out, who have been last appointed, and the second time those other members proprietaries and other supernumerary going out, and so successively.

124. No councellor can be re-elected, except in the fourth year after having ceased from his office.

125. When the Governor of the State assists at the council he shall preside, but without a vote, and in such case the Vice-Governor shall not assist.

126. The Secretary of the Council shall be one of its members in the manner and form which may be established by its interior regulation, which regulation the said council shall form and present to the Governor, who shall pass it to Congress for its approbation.

127. The attributes of the Council are—First, to give a fixed opinion and in writing to the Governor in all those matters in which the law imposes upon him the obligation to ask it, and in all those others in which the same Governor may think proper to consult it. Second, to watch over the observance of the Constitutional Act, the Federal Constitution, and the general laws of the Union, the Constitution and particular laws of the State, giving an account to Congress of the infractions which it may observe. Third, to promote the advancement, and aid in the prosperity of the State in all its branches. Fourth, to recommend appointments to offices, in the cases where the law requires it. Fifth, agree in union with the permanent deputation conformable to the 89th Article, upon the convocation of extraordinary sessions of Congress, and to meet with the same deputation in order to do what may be necessary in those cases mentioned in Article 90. Sixth, examine the accounts of all the public funds, and pass them to Congress for its approbation.

128. The council shall be responsible for all acts relative to the exercise of its powers.

Section 4th.—*Of the Election of Governor, Vice-Governor, and Counsellors.*

129. The day following that on which the election of deputies to Congress is made, the electoral district assemblies, all and every one of them shall vote for a Governor, Vice-Governor, and three counsellors, proprietaries, and two supernumeraries, making the said election in the mode and terms prescribed in Articles 71, 72, 73, and 74.

130. The said elections being ended, there shall be immediately posted up in the most public place, a list signed by the Secretary of the assembly, which shall comprehend the names of those elected, and for what offices they have been elected. These acts shall be attested by the president and the electors, and copies certified by the President, Secretary, and Tellers, shall be remitted to the permanent deputation.

131. On the day of the opening of the first ordinary session of Congress the President of the permanent deputation shall present the aforesaid copies, and after they have been read, the Congress shall appoint a committee of its own body, and pass them to it for its revision, of which the committee shall give the result within three days.

132. On this day the Congress shall proceed to examine the elections had by the districts, and to count the votes.

133. The individual, who has the absolute majority of votes of the electoral district assemblies, computing the whole number of members which compose them, shall be the Governor, Vice-Governor, or Counsellor, as the case may be.

134. If no one has the said majority, the Congress shall choose for those offices one of the two or more individuals who may have the greatest number of votes, and the same shall take place when no one has obtained the respective majority, unless all have an equal number of votes.

135. If only one individual obtains the respective majority, and two or more an equal number of votes, but more than all the others, the Congress shall elect from among them one individual, and he shall enter into competition for the appointment with him that has the respective majority.

136. In case of a tie, the voting shall be repeated once only, and if it results again in a tie, it shall be decided by lot.

137. The offices of Governor, Vice-Governor, and Counsellors, shall be accepted in preference to any other of the State, and this preference shall take place with respect to these offices in the order in which they stand. Those elected for said offices shall occupy them the first day of March, and cannot excuse themselves from serving, unless they are deputies to Congress at the time of the election, and those who, according to the judgment of the same Congress, are physically or morally disqualified.

138. If by any means the Governor elect does not present himself on that day to enter upon the exercise of his functions, the Vice-Governor elect shall enter upon the discharge of them, and if he also does not present himself, that vacancy shall be filled conformable to article 118.

Section 5th.—*Of the Secretary of State.*

139. The dispatch of the business of the supreme government of the State, of whatever class it may be, shall be placed in the charge of a secretary, who shall be entitled Secretary of Despatch of the State Government.

140. To be a Secretary of State, it is required to be a citizen in the exercise of his rights, twenty-five years of age, born in the Territory of the Mexican Federation, and an inhabitant of this State, with residence in it three years, one of them immediately before the election. Ecclesiastics cannot obtain this office.

141. All the laws, decrees, orders, instructions, or regulations, which are circulated to the towns, or are directed to a known corporation or person, by the Governor, as well as the copies which emanate from the Secretary's department, must be attested by the Secretary; and without this requisite, they shall not be obeyed nor entitled to credit.

142. The Secretary shall be responsible in his person and office for that which he officially authorizes contrary to the Constitutional Act, the Constitution, and general laws of the Union, the laws of the State, and the orders of the President of the Republic, which are not manifestly opposed to the same Constitutions and laws, without its being an excuse that the Governor orders it.

143. For the interior Government of the Secretary of State's department, the regulations formed by the Secretary, and approved of by Congress, shall be observed.

144. The Secretary, Governor, Vice-Governor, and Counsellors, whilst they hold those offices, shall cease to discharge the duties of others they may have heretofore held, as soon as they take possession of their new employments.

Section 6th.—*Of the Chiefs of Police of Departments, and the Subaltern or Chiefs of Districts.*

145. In the capital of each department of the State there shall be a functionary, to whom shall be entrusted the political government of the same, and he shall be denominated the Political Chief of the Department.

146. To be Chief of Department, it is necessary to be a citizen in the exercise of his rights, of the age of twenty-five years, complete, an inhabitant of the State, and a resident in it three years, and one of them immediately previous to his election.

147. The Governor, on the proposition of the Council, supported by the recommendations of the Ayuntamientos of the respective department, shall appoint the Chief of Department, with the exception of that of the capital.

148. The Chief of Department shall be immediately subject to the Governor of the State, and in no manner to each other. They shall continue four years in their offices, and may be re-appointed, the same formalities concurring as are prescribed for their first nomination.

149. In every capital in the district, except that in which the Chief of Department resides, there shall be a subaltern or district chief appointed by the Governor, on the recommendation of the Chief of Department.

150. The subaltern or district chiefs, ought to possess the same qualifications as those of department, with the difference that their domicile and residence ought to be in the bounds of their district, and shall, besides, have some honest mode of living, sufficient to maintain themselves decently.

151. The duration of the district chiefs in their offices, shall be the same as those of department; and on the proposition of these they can be continued in their offices.

152. No person can be excused from serving in these trusts, except in case of re-election for the same within four years after they have served, or for other sufficient cause in the judgment of the Governor, who shall decide, after hearing from the respective Chief of Department.

153. These chiefs, as well as those of department, are responsible for all their acts against the Constitution, and general laws of the Federation, and the laws of the State, the first to the Chief of Department to whom they are immediately subordinate, and those to the Governor.

154. The attributes of the different chiefs, and the manner in which they shall discharge their duties, shall be detailed in the regulations for the political economical government of the towns.

SECTION 7th.—*Of the Ayuntamientos.*

155. It appertains to the Ayuntamientos to watch over the police and internal government of the towns of the State; and with this view they shall exist in all which have heretofore had them.

156. In the towns which may not have them, and where it is necessary they should be, they shall be placed. The capitals of districts shall have them, whatever their population may be, and also those towns which of themselves or with their precincts, contain 1000 souls, unless they are united to another municipality; in which case, should peculiar circumstances present their separation, it shall be necessary, in order for them to obtain an Ayuntamiento, that Congress shall decree it, on the recommendation of the executive, accompanied by a memorial setting forth the territory which shall compose the new municipality.

157. The towns which have not the prescribed number of souls, but which can with advantage be united to one or more, can form municipalities, which shall be formed, and the Ayuntamiento shall be established in the place which, in the judgment of the Executive, shall be deemed most suitable. In particular circumstances, the Congress may decree, upon previous petition and recommendation of the Governor, Ayuntamientos, in those places of lesser population.

158. In those settlements which cannot have the establishment of an Ayuntamiento, and in the interior government of which, by reason of their distance from other municipalities, cannot be taken care of, the electoral assemblies of the district to which it is attached, shall appoint a commissary of police and one Syndic, (procurador,) who shall discharge the function which the regulation for the political government of the towns shall designate.

159. The Ayuntamientos shall be composed of the Alcalde or Alcaldes, Syndic or Syndics, and Alderman, whose number the said regulation shall designate.

160. To be a member of the Ayuntamiento, it is requisite to be a citizen in the exercise of his rights, more than twenty-five years of age, or being married, twenty-one years of age, to be an inhabitant of the Ayuntamiento district, with residence in it three years, one of them immediately prior to the election; to have a capital or industry upon which he can subsist, and to know how to read and write.

161. The following persons cannot be members of the Ayuntamientos—Those in public employment paid by the State; the military, and those in the actual exercise of offices under the General Government, and ecclesiastics.

162. The Alcaldes shall be renewed totally every year; the Aldermen by one half, and also the Syndics, if there are two, being only one, he shall be changed every year.

163. He that has discharged any of these trusts, cannot obtain any other municipal trust, nor can he be re-chosen for the same which he has discharged, until two years after he has ceased its functions.

164. The members of the Ayuntamientos shall be appointed by means of electoral municipal assemblies, which shall be held in the same form as the municipal assemblies for the appointment of deputies to Congress. These assemblies shall be convoked on the first Sunday in December, and shall meet and discharge their functions the second Sunday and the day following.

165. In consequence of said assemblies, they shall be considered as constitutionally elected, for Alcaldes, Aldermen, and Syndics, who have received the greatest number of votes for those offices respectively. A tie which may be between two or more individuals, the Ayuntamiento sitting at the time of election, shall decide by lot.

166. If any of the individuals of the Ayuntamiento shall die, or for any other cause vacate his trust, the citizen who on the list had the next greatest number of votes, shall proceed to the discharge of its duties.

167. The offices of the Ayuntamiento are municipal charges from which no persons can excuse themselves.

TITLE 3d. *Of the Judicial Power.* ONLY SECTION.—*Of the Administration of Justice in general.*

168. The administration of justice in civil and criminal cases, belongs exclusively to those tribunals and courts, which, by the regulation of the Constitution exercise the judicial power.

169. Neither the Congress nor the Governor can interfere in pending causes, neither can they, nor the same tribunals and courts open those finished.

170. Every inhabitant of the State must be judged by tribunals and competent judges established anterior to the act for which he is tried, and in no manner by special commission, nor by retroactive (retroactiva—*ex post facto*) law.

171. The laws shall prescribe the order and formalities to be observed in all processes; which shall be uniform in all the courts and tribunals, and cannot be dispensed with by any authority.

172. The tribunals and courts, as authorities constituted only to apply the laws, have no power to interpret them or suspend their execution. ·

173. The military and ecclesiastics, resident in the State, shall continue subject to their respective authorities.

174. No suit shall have more than three hearings and as many sentences. The laws shall prescribe which of said sentences shall be executed, and no appeal shall be admitted unless in case of error, and for other causes as the said laws may provide.

175. The judge who has passed sentence in a case in one instance, cannot hear it anew in any other, nor in an appeal for any error brought upon the same.

176. Bribery, corruption, and prevarication are grounds of popular action against the Magistrate or Judge who commits them.

177. Justice shall be administered in the name of the free State of Coahuila and Texas, in the form prescribed by the laws.

PARAGRAPH 1st.—*Of the Administration of Justice in civil cases.*

178. Every inhabitant of the State can terminate his differences, be the state of the case what it may, by medium of arbitrators or any other extra-judicial manner; the agreements in this particular shall be religiously observed, and the sentence of the arbitrators executed, if the parties who have made the compromise do not reserve the right of appeal.

179. Affairs of small amount shall be terminated by inferior courts, whose judgment shall be executed without appeal. A particular law shall fix the amount and the mode of procedure in them.

180. In other civil and criminal affairs upon inquiries, an amicable settlement shall first be attempted in the form established by law, and unless it shall appear that such attempt has been made, a suit in writing cannot be sustained, except in those cases which the law shall determine.

PARAGRAPH 2d.—*Of the Administration of Justice in Criminal Cases.*

181. Every criminal charged with light offences, that ought to be punished by correctional penalties, shall be judged by inferior courts without the formalities, and from their sentence there shall not be interposed an appeal or any other remedy. A law shall fix these penalties, and class the offences to which they correspond.

182. In weighty offences, there shall be formed a summary examination of the offence, without which requisite, and the corresponding accusation, a copy of which shall be given to the defendant and to the jailor, no person shall be imprisoned.

183. If the judges cannot immediately comply with the provisions of the anterior article, the arrested person shall not be considered a prisoner, but merely as detained; and if in forty-eight hours he shall not be notified of the cause of his detention, and the same is not communicated to the jailor, he shall be set at liberty.

184. He who gives security in cases in which the law does not expressly prohibit it, shall not be imprisoned; and should it appear in any stage of the case, that corporal punishment cannot be inflicted on the prisoner, he shall be discharged on giving bail.

185. Those who have to declare relative to their own acts in criminal cases shall do so without an oath.

186. The delinquent found in the act can be arrested by any person and carried into the presence of the judge.

187. The greatest care shall be taken, that the prisons serve only for the security of the prisoners, and not for their annoyance, (y no paraf molestarlos.)

188. Trials, in criminal cases, shall be public, in the mode and form which the laws may establish, from the time that it is determined either on the confession of the criminal or on the charges against him, to commit him for trial.

189. The penalty of confiscation of goods is forever prohibited, and they can be detained only in cases where the crime involves a pecuniary responsibility, and then solely in proportion to that responsibility.

190. No torments or compulsions shall ever be used, and the penalties which are imposed, whatever may be the crime, cannot be transferable to the family of him that suffers, but shall have effect solely upon the person convicted.

191. No authority of the State shall issue an order for the search of houses, papers, and other effects of the inhabitants, unless in those cases and in the form which the law prescribe.

192. One of the principal subjects for the attention of Congress shall be to establish in criminal cases, the trial by jury, extending it gradually, and even adopting it in civil cases, in proportion as the advantages of this precious institution may be practically developed.

PARAGRAPH 3d.—*Of the Inferior Courts and Superior Tribunals.*

193. The inferior courts shall continue in the mode and form which a law shall prescribe, until there are revenues of the State, which in the judgment of Congress, may permit the appointment of District Judges, (Ineces de letas) who ought to be appointed to each district.

194. In the capital of the State, there shall be a Supreme Tribunal of Justice divided into three halls, each one composed of the magistrate or magistrates which the law designates, and this tribunal shall have one Attorney General, (Fiscal) who

shall despatch all the business of the three halls: the same law shall determine whether the hall shall be composed of one judge alone, or whether colleagues ought to be appointed, and the mode and form in which it ought to be done.

195. The two first halls shall take cognizance, in the first and second instance, of civil causes of the inferior courts, and also of the criminal causes, according as the laws shall determine.

196. To the third hall shall appertain—First, to decide the disputes between the subaltern judges. Second, to determine the appeals of error which may be interposed against the sentences to be executed in the 1st, 2d, and 3d instances. Third, to take cognizance of all appeals for grievances which may be sent up from the tribunals and ecclesiastical authorities of the State. Fourth, to examine the lists, which must be monthly remitted, of pending causes in the first, second, and third instances, to pass copies of these to the Governor, to direct their publication by the press. Fifth, to hear points of law which may be offered to the two first halls and to the tribunals of the first instance, and to pass them to Congress by means of the Governor, with the corresponding opinion.

197. The cases for delinquencies in office against the inferior judges, and also those which may be formed for delinquencies, of an equal class against the deputies of Congress, the Governor, Vice-Governor, Counsellors, Secretary of State, and the individuals of the Tribunal of Justice, shall begin and terminate before the Supreme Tribunals. The other faculties of this and its respective halls, the law shall define.

198. In case of a prosecution against the whole of this tribunal, or any of its halls, the Congress shall appoint a special tribunal, composed of the corresponding number of halls, and also the magistrate, or magistrates, which may be deemed necessary to fill them.

199. Of the appeals for errors in causes which may be preferred before the Supreme Court of Justice, in the cases of the individuals which are spoken of in the anterior Article, and in those affairs which belong to the third hall, the special tribunal appointed for these purposes by Congress shall take cognizance.

200. To be a judge or Attorney General, it is necessary to be a citizen in the exercise of his rights, upwards of twenty-five years of age, to be born in some part of the Federation, and a lawyer of probity and learning.

201. The judges and Attorney General shall be appointed by Congress on the recommendation of the Executive. They shall enjoy a competent salary, which the law shall designate, and they cannot be removed from office unless for causes legally ascertained.

202. The individuals of the Supreme Tribunal of Justice are responsible for all their proceedings in the discharge of their functions, and can be impeached before Congress by any individual of the public.

TITLE FOURTH. ONLY SECTION.—*Of the Public Revenue.*

203. The contributions of the individuals who compose the State, shall form the public Revenue of the same.

204. These contributions can be direct, indirect, general, or municipal, but of whichsoever class they may be, they must be proportioned to the expenses they have to meet, and to the means of the citizens.

205. Taxes cannot be imposed, except to pay the quota of the State, to defray that part which corresponds to the Revenue of the Federation, and to meet the expenses of the State. The taxes for this last object, shall be precisely fixed in the first sessions of every year, in conformity with the estimate which the Governor shall present, and which the Congress shall approve.

206. The present taxes shall continue until Congress shall repeal or alter them.

207. For the receipt, security, and distribution of the Revenues of the State, there shall be in the capital one Treasury General.

208. The chief of said treasury shall not receive credit for any payment which has not been made, to defray the charges approved of by Congress, and by special order of the Governor.

209. A special regulation shall govern the offices relative to the public Revenue of the State.

210. The Congress shall annually appoint three individuals of their own body or out of it, in order to examine the accounts of the Treasury of the State, who shall pass them with their report to Congress, for their approbation. And the resolution of the Congress shall be published and circulated to the Ayuntamientos, with a view that they may do the same within their districts.

TITLE 5th.   ONLY SECTION.—*Of the Civic Militia of the State.*

211. In all the towns of the State, there shall be established corps of civic militia, and these shall constitute the military force of the same.

212. The formation of these corps, their organization, discipline, and internal government, shall be regulated by Congress, conformably to the general laws of Federation on the subject.

213. The Congress shall regulate the service of this militia, so as to affect the purposes of their institution, in a manner the most useful to the State and the least burthensome to the citizens.

214. No inhabitant of Coahuila and Texas can be excused from affording his service when required by law.

TITLE 6th.   ONLY SECTION.—*Of Public Instruction.*

215. In all the towns of the State, there shall be established a competent number of common schools, (primeras letras) in which there shall be taught, reading, writing, and cyphering; the catechism of the christian religion; a short and simple explanation of this Constitution, and the general one of the Republic; the rights and duties of man in society, and that which can most conduce to the better education of youth.

216. In those places in which it may be necessary, and where circumstances permit, there shall be institutions of learning, more suitable for disseminating in the State, public instruction in the useful arts and sciences, and in these shall be fully explained the aforesaid Constitutions.

217. The method of instruction shall be uniform throughout the State, and to facilitate this end, the Congress shall form a general plan for public instruction, and shall regulate by means of statutes and laws, whatever appertains to this most important object.

TITLE 7th.   ONLY SECTION.—*Of the Observance of the Constitution.*

218. The observance of the Constitution in all its parts, is one of the most sacred obligations of the inhabitants of the State of Coahuila and Texas, and no one can be absolved from it, neither the Congress nor any other authority. And every inhabitant of Coahuila and Texas can insist upon this observance, making representations for this object to the Congress, or to the Executive.

219. Any infraction of this Constitution, creates a personal responsibility. In order to render effective this responsibility, the Congress shall issue the laws and decrees, which it believes conducive to this object. And besides every year at their first session, shall take into consideration the infractions which the permanent deputation and the council of government may present, and shall do what may be necessary thereon.

220. The public functionaries of the State, of whatever class they may be, shall at the time of entering upon their offices, take the oath to observe, sustain and defend, the Constitutional Act, the general Constitution, and that of the State, and to discharge faithfully and completely the duties of their office.

221. Propositions for the reformation, alteration, or abrogation of one or more of

the Articles of this Constitution, must be made in writing, and be supported and signed by two-thirds of the deputies.

222. The Congress, in whose time any of these propositions may be made, shall not act otherwise thereon in the second year of their session, than by reading and publishing them with the grounds upon which they are supported.

223. The following Congress will either admit or reject the discussion of these propositions, and being admitted, they shall be published anew by the press, and shall be circulated by the Governor, in order that they may be read in the next electoral assemblies before they shall make the appointment of deputies to Congress.

224. In the following Congress, they shall discuss the proposed alteration, reforms, or abrogations, and if they are approved of, they shall be immediately published with the Constitutional Articles.

225. In making the reforms, alterations, or abrogations indicated, besides the rules prescribed in the anterior articles, there shall be observed all those formalities provided for the passing or repealing of the Laws with the exception of the right conceded to the Governor of making observations, which cannot take place in these cases.

GIVEN IN SALTILLO, 11th March, 1827.—Santiago del Valle, President; Juan Vicent Campos, Vice President; Rafael Ramos Valdez, Jose Maria Viesca, Francisco Antonio Guttierez, Jose Isaquim de Arce Rosalez, Mariano Varela, Jose Maria Valdez y Guajardo, Jose Cayetamo Ramos, Deputy and Secretary; Dionisio Elisondo, Deputy and Secretary.

Therefore, I command, That it be printed, published, circulated, and complied with.

Given in Saltillo, 11th, March, 1827.

JOSE IGNACIO ARISPE.

JUAN ANTONIO VADILLA, Secretary.

[Doc. No.2]

Provisional Constitution of 1835

CONSTITUTION OF THE STATE OF TEXAS—1833

[This constitution was framed by a convention which met at San Felipe, April 1, 1833, and completed it labors April 13, 1833. It provided a State organization subordinate to the Supreme Central Government of Mexico. The right of trial by jury, the writ of *habeas corpus*, the right of petition, the freedom of the press, direct and universal suffrage, with a prohibition of banking, were duly inserted, but nothing was said on the subject of religious liberty. This constitution, which may be found in Edwards's History of Texas, pages 196–205, was never recognized by the Mexican government or put into operation, but it was the first step toward the independence of Texas.]

PROVISIONAL CONSTITUTION OF TEXAS—1835 * *a*

PLAN AND POWERS OF THE PROVISIONAL GOVERNMENT OF TEXAS.

Article I

That there shall be, and there is hereby created, a Provisional Government for Texas, which shall consist of a Governor, a Lieutenant-Governor, and a General Council, to be elected from this body, one

---

* Verified from text in " Laws of Texas, 1837," pp. 1–12.

a This Declaration of Independence and Provisional Constitution was framed by a convention which assembled October 17, 1835, at San Felipe de Austin, and adjourned until the 1st day of November. The Provisional Constitution was signed November 13, 1835.

member from each Municipality, by the majority of each separate Delegation present; and the Governor and Lieutenant-Governor shall be elected by this body.

ARTICLE II

The Lieutenant-Governor shall be President of the Council, and perform the duties of Governor in case of death, absence, or from other inability of the Governor, during which time a President " pro tem." shall be appointed to perform the duties of the Lieutenant-Governor in Council.

ARTICLE III

The duties of the General Council shall be, to devise ways and means, to advise and assist the Governor in the discharge of his functions: they shall pass no laws except such as, in their opinion, the emergency of the country requires—ever keeping in view the Army in the field, and the means necessary for its comfort and support: they shall pursue the most effective and energetic measures to rid the country of her enemies, and place her in the best possible state of defence: two-thirds of the members elect of the General Council shall form a quorum to do business; and in order that no vacancy shall happen in the Council, if any member, from death or other casualty, shall be incapacitated to act, the Governor shall immediately, on information thereof, notify the member elected to fill the place; and on his default, any member who has been elected to this body from the same jurisdiction. The Governor and Council shall be authorized to contract for loans, not to exceed one million of dollars, and to hypothecate the Public Lands and pledge the faith of the Country for the security of the payment: that they have power to impose and regulate Impost and Tonnage Duties, and provide for their collection under such regulations as may be most expedient. They shall have power, and it is hereby made the duty of the Governor and Council, to treat with the several tribes of Indians concerning their Land Claims, and if possible, to secure their friendship.

They shall establish Post-Offices and Post-Roads and regulate the rates of postage, and appoint a Postmaster-General, who shall have competent power for conducting this Department of the Provisional Government, under such rules and regulations as the Governor and Council may prescribe: they shall have power to grant pardons, remit fines, and to hear and judge all cases usual in high Courts of Admiralty, agreeably to the Law of Nations.

They shall have power to appoint their own Secretary and other officers of their own body; also, that they have the power to create and fill such offices as they may deem proper: *provided, nevertheless,* that this power does not extend to officers heretofore rejected by this House.

That the Governor and Council have power to organize, reduce, or increase the regular forces, as they may deem the emergencies of the Country require.

Article IV

The Governor, for the time being, and during the existence of the Provisional Government, shall be clothed with full and ample executive powers, and shall be Commander-in-Chief of the Army and Navy, and of all the military forces of Texas, by sea and land; and he shall have full power by himself, by and with the consent of the Council, and by his proper commander or other officer or officers, from time to time, to train, instruct, exercise and govern the Militia and Navy; and for the special defence and safety of the country, to assemble in martial array, and put in warlike attitude the inhabitants thereof; and to lead and conduct them by his proper officers, and with them to encounter, repel, resist and pursue by force of arms, as well by sea and by land, within or without the limits of Texas; and, also, to destroy, if necessary, and conquer by all proper means and enterprizes whatsoever, all and every such person or persons as shall, at any time, in a hostile manner, attempt or enterprize the destruction of our liberties, or the invasion, detriment, or annoyance of the country; and by his proper officers, use and exercise over the Army and Navy, and the Militia in actual service, the Law Martial in time of war, invasion or rebellion; and to take and surprise by all honorable ways and means consistent with the Law of Nations, all and every such person or persons, with their ships, arms, ammunition and goods as shall, in a hostile manner, invade or attempt the invading or annoying our adopted country; and that the Governor be clothed with all these and all other powers which may be thought necessary by the Permanent Council, calculated to aid and protect the country from her enemies.

Article V

There shall be constituted a Provisional Judiciary in each jurisdiction represented, or which may hereafter be represented in this House, to consist of two judges, a first and second, the latter to act only in the absence or inability of the first, and be nominated by the Council and commissioned by the Governor.

Article VI

Every Judge, so nominated and commissioned, shall have jurisdiction over all crimes and misdemeanors recognized and known to the common law of England: he shall have power to grant writs of "habeas corpus" in all cases known and practised, to and under the same laws; he shall have power to grant writs of sequestration, attachment, or arrest, in all cases established by the "Civil Code" and "Code of Practice" of the State of Louisiana, to be regulated by the forms thereof; shall possess full testamentary powers in all cases; and shall also be made a Court of Records for conveyances which may be made in English, and not on stamped paper; and that the use of stamped paper be, in all cases, dispensed with; and shall be the "Notary Public" for their respective Municipalities: all office fees shall be regulated by the Governor and Council. All other civil proceedings at law shall be suspended until the Governor and General Council shall otherwise direct. Each Municipality shall continue to elect a sheriff, alcalde and other officers of Ayuntamientos.

Article VII

All trials shall be by jury, and in criminal cases the proceedings shall be regulated and conducted upon the principles of the common law of England; and the penalties prescribed by said law, in case of conviction, shall be inflicted, unless the offender shall be pardoned, or fine remitted; for which purpose a reasonable time shall be allowed to every convict to make application to the Governor and Council.

Article VIII

The officers of the Provisional Government, except such as are elected by this House, or the people, shall be appointed by the General Council, and all officers shall be commissioned by the Governor.

Article IX

All Commissions to officers shall be, " in the name of the People, free and sovereign," and signed by the Governor and Secretary; and all pardons and remissions of fines granted, shall be signed in the same manner.

Article X

Every officer and member of the Provisional Government, before entering upon the duties of his office, shall take and subscribe the following oath of office: " I, A. B., do solemnly swear, (or affirm) that I will support the republican principles of the Constitution of Mexico of 1824, and obey the Declarations and Ordinances of the Consultation of the chosen Delegates of all Texas in General Convention assembled, and the Ordinances and Decrees of the Provisional Government; and I will faithfully perform and execute the duties of my office agreeably to law, and to the best of my abilities, so help me God."

Article XI

On charges and specifications being made against any officer of the Provisional Government for malfeasance or misconduct in office, and presented to the Governor and Council, a fair and impartial trial shall be granted, to be conducted before the General Council; and if, in the opinion of two-thirds of the members, cause sufficient be shown, he shall be dismissed from office by the Governor.

Article XII

The Governor and Council shall organize and enter upon their duties immediately after the adjournment of this House, and hold their sessions at such times and places as, in their opinion, will give the most energy and effect to the objects of the people, and to the performance of the duties assigned to them.

Article XIII

The General Council shall appoint a Treasurer, whose duties shall be clearly defined by them, and who shall give approved security for their faithful performance.

Article XIV

That all Land Commissions, Empressarios, Surveyors, or persons in anywise concerned in the location of Land, be ordered, forthwith, to cease their operations during the agitated and unsettled state of the country, and continue to desist from further locations until the Land Offices can be properly systematized by the competent authorities which may be hereafter established; that fit and suitable persons be appointed to take charge of all the archives belonging to the different Land Offices, and deposit the same in safe places, secure from the ravages of fire or devastations of enemies; and that the persons so appointed be fully authorized to carry the same into effect, and be required to take and sign triplicate schedules of all the books, papers and documents found in the several Land Offices, one of which shall be given to the Governor and Council, one left in the hands of the officers of the Land Office, the other to be retained by the said persons: and they are enjoined to hold the said papers and documents in safe custody, subject only to the orders of the Provisional Government, or such competent authority as may hereafter be created. And the said persons shall be three from each Department as Commissioners to be forthwith appointed by this House, to carry this Resolution into full effect, and report thereof to the Governor and Council; that the political chiefs immediately cease their functions. The different Archives of the different primary Judges, Alcaldes and other municipal officers of the various jurisdictions shall be handed over to their successors in office, immediately after their election and appointment; and the archives of the several Political Chiefs of Nacogdoches, Brazos, and Bexar shall be transmitted forthwith to the Governor and Council, for their disposition.

Article XV

All persons, now in Texas, and performing the duties of citizens, who have not acquired their quantum of land, shall be entitled to the benefit of the Laws on Colonization under which they emigrated; and all persons who may emigrate to Texas during her conflict for Constitutional Liberty, and perform the duties of Citizens, shall also receive the benefits of the Law under which they emigrated.

Article XVI

The Governor and Council shall continue to exist as a Provisional Government until the re-assembling of this Consultation, or until other Delegates are elected by the people and another Government established.

Article XVII

This Convention, when it may think proper to adjourn, may stand adjourned, to meet at the town of Washington on the first day of March next, unless sooner called by the Executive and Council.

Article XVIII

All grants, sales and conveyances of lands, illegally or fraudulently made by the legislature of the State of Coahuila and Texas, located, or to be located, within the limits of Texas, are hereby solemnly declared null, void and of no effect.

Article XIX

All persons who leave the country in its present crisis, with a view to avoid a participation in its present struggle, without permission from the Alcalde, or Judge of their Municipality, shall forfeit all or any lands they may hold, or may have a claim to, for the benefit of this Government: *provided*, nevertheless, that widows and minors are not included in this provision.

Article XX

All monies now due or that may hereafter become due, on lands lying within the limits of Texas, and all public funds or revenues, shall be at the disposal of the Governor and General Council, and the receipt of the Treasurer shall be a sufficient voucher for any and all persons who may pay monies into the Treasury; and the Governor and Council shall have power to adopt a system of Revenue to meet the exigencies of the country.

Article XXI

Ample powers and authority shall be delegated, and are hereby given and delegated to the Governor and General Council of the Provisional Government of all Texas, to carry into full effect the provisions and resolutions adopted by " the Consultation of the chosen Delegates of all Texas in General Convention assembled," for the creation, establishment and regulation of said Provisional Government.

OF THE MILITARY

Article I

There shall be a Regular Army created for the protection of Texas during the present war.

Article II

The Regular Army of Texas shall consist of one Major-General, who shall be Commander-in-Chief of all the forces called into public service during the war.

Article III

The Commander-in-Chief of the Regular Army of Texas shall be appointed by the Convention, and commissioned by the Governor.

Article IV

He shall be subject to the orders of the Governor and Council.

Article V

His Staff shall consist of one Adjutant-General, one Inspector-General, one Quarter-Master-General, one Pay-Master-General, one Surgeon-General, and four Aids-de-Camp with their respective ranks, as in the United States Army in time of war, to be appointed by the Major-General and commissioned by the Governor.

Article VI

The regular Army of Texas shall consist of men enlisted for two years, and volunteers for and during the continuance of war.

Article VII

The regular Army of Texas, while in the service, shall be governed by the rules, regulations and discipline, in all respects applicable to the regular Army of the United States of America, in time of war, so far as applicable to our condition and circumstances.

Article VIII

The regular Army of Texas shall consist of eleven hundred and twenty men rank and file.

Article IX

There shall be a corps of Rangers under the command of a Major. to consist of one hundred and fifty men, to be divided into three or more detachments, and which shall compose a batallion, under the Commander-in-Chief when in the field.

Article X

The Militia of Texas shall be organized as follows: all able bodied men over sixteen, and under fifty years of age, shall be subject to Militia duty.

Article XI

Every inhabitant of Texas, coming within purview of the preceding article shall, on the third Monday of December next, or as soon thereafter as practicable, assemble at each precinct of their municipality and proceed to elect one captain, one first lieutenant, and one second lieutenant to every fifty-six men.

Article XII

When said election shall have taken place, the judges shall certify to the Governor, forthwith the names of the respective officers elected, who shall, as soon as practicable, make out and sign, and transmit commissions for the same; that if there shall be found to exist any municipality, more than three Companies, the captain, or commandants on giving due notice thereof shall call together the subalterns of said Companies, and proceed to elect one Major; if of four Companies, one Lieutenant Colonel; if of five or more Companies, one Colonel, for the command of said Companies, which shall constitute a regiment of said municipality; that if there shall be found to exist more than one regiment in said municipality, the whole number of field and Company officers, shall on due notice proceed to elect a Brigadier-General, out of their number who shall command the whole Militia in said municipality.

BRANCH TANNER ARCHER, *President.*

P. B. DEXTER, *Secretary.*

[Doc. No. 3]

Texas Declaration of Independence

TEXAS DECLARATION OF INDEPENDENCE—1836.*

WHEREAS, General Antonio Lopez de Santa Anna and other Military Chieftains have, by force of arms, overthrown the Federal Institutions of Mexico, and dissolved the Social Compact which existed between Texas and the other Members of the Mexican Confederacy—Now, the good People of Texas, availing themselves of their natural rights,

SOLEMNLY DECLARE—

1st. That they have taken up arms in defence of their Rights and Liberties, which were threatened by the encroachments of military despots, and in defence of the Republican Principles of the Federal Constitution of Mexico of eighteen hundred and twenty-four.

2d. That Texas is no longer, morally or civilly, bound by the compact of Union; yet, stimulated by the generosity and sympathy common to a free people, they offer their support and assistance to such of the Members of the Mexican Confederacy as will take up arms against military despotism.

3d. That they do not acknowledge, that the present authorities of the nominal Mexican Republic have the right to govern within the limits of Texas.

4th. That they will not cease to carry on war against the said authorities, whilst their troops are within the limits of Texas.

5th. That they hold it to be their right, during the disorganization of the Federal System and the reign of despotism, to withdraw from the Union, to establish an independent Government, or to adopt such measures as they may deem best calculated to protect their rights and liberties; but that they will continue faithful to the Mexican Government so long as that nation is governed by the Constitution and Laws that were formed for the government of the Political Association.

6th. That Texas is responsible for the expenses of her Armies now in the field.

7th. That the public faith of Texas is pledged for the payment of any debts contracted by her Agents.

8th. That she will reward by donations in Land, all who volunteer their services in her present struggle, and receive them as Citizens.

These DECLARATIONS we solemnly avow to the world, and call GOD to witness their truth and sincerity; and invoke defeat and disgrace upon our heads, should we prove guilty of duplicity.

RICHARD ELLIS, *President.*

A. H. S. KIMBLE, *Secretary.*

---

* This Declaration of Independence was adopted by a convention which assembled at Washington, on the Brazos River, March 1, 1836.

[Doc. No. 4]

Ordinance of 1836 *

WHEREAS, we, the people of Texas, through our delegates in General Convention assembled, for the purpose of framing a Constitution, and organizing a Government under that Constitution, free, sovereign and independent; and finding, from the extreme emergency of the case, and our critical situation, that it is a duty we owe to our fellow-citizens and ourselves, to look upon our present danger with a calmness unruffled, and a determination unsubdued; and at the same time, to pursue a prompt and energetic course for the support of our liberty and protection of our property and lives; therefore,

1st. *Resolved,* That we deem it of vital importance to forthwith, form, organize and establish a Government, "*ad interim,*" for the protection of Texas, which shall have full, ample and plenary powers to do all and every thing which is contemplated to be done by the General Congress of the people, under the powers granted to them by the constitution, saving and excepting all legislative and judicial acts.

2nd. *Resolved,* That said Government shall consist of a chief executive officer, to be styled the "President of the Republic of Texas;" a Vice-President, Secretary of State, Secretary at War, Secretary of the Navy, Secretary of the Treasury, and Attorney General, whose salaries shall be fixed and determined by the first Congress of the Republic.

3rd. *Resolved,* That all questions touching the powers hereby confided to these officers, shall be decided by a majority of said officers.

4th. *Resolved,* That the President be elected by this convention : and that the candidate or individual having a majority of the whole number of votes given in, shall be, and is hereby, declared to be duly elected.

5th. *Resolved,* That the Vice-President, the aforesaid Secretaries and Attorney General, be elected by this Convention, a majority of the whole number of votes being requisite to a choice.

6th. *Resolved,* That the members of this body vote for the above named officers "*viva voce.*".

7th. *Resolved,* That the officers so elected, be required to take the oath prescribed by the Constitution.

8th. *Resolved,* That the President, by and with the advice and consent of a majority of his cabinet, shall have the appointment of all officers, civil, military and naval, for, and during, the existence of the Government "*ad interim.*"

9th. *Resolved,* That the Government aforesaid, shall be invested, and they are hereby, invested with full powers to create a loan, not to exceed one million of dollars; and to pledge the faith and credit of the Republic, and the proceeds of the sale of the public lands, for the repayment of the same, with the interest thereon.

10th. *Resolved,* That the President and his cabinet shall have full power to appropriate the funds of Texas, to the defence of the country, by raising and supporting the army and navy, making fortifications, &c.

11th. *Resolved,* That said officers hold their offices until their successors are chosen and qualified.

12th. *Resolved,* That the President, by and with the advice and consent of his cabinet, shall have power to issue writs of election for senators and representatives, at an earlier day than that fixed by the constitution, and convene them as soon after the election, as may be convenient.

13th. *Resolved,* That said Government have ample and plenary powers to enter into negotiations and treaties with foreign powers.

14. *Resolved,* That the President and his cabinet have power to appoint commissioners to any foreign power.

The foregoing fourteen resolutions were adopted in convention of the people of Texas, assembled at the town of Washington, on the 16th day of March, in the year of our Lord one thousand eight hundred and thirty-six.

RICHARD ELLIS, *President.*

H. S. KIMBLE, *Secretary.*

---

* This ordinance was declared by a convention which assembled at Washington, on the Brazos River, March 1, 1836. The convention then proceeded to frame a constitution.

[Doc. No. 5]

Constitution of 1836

CONSTITUTION OF THE REPUBLIC OF TEXAS—1836.*

We, the people of Texas, in order to form a government, establish justice, insure domestic tranquillity, provide for the common defence and general welfare, and to secure the blessings of liberty to ourselves and our posterity, do ordain and establish this constitution.

ARTICLE I.

SECTION 1. The powers of this government shall be divided into three departments, viz: legislative, executive, and judicial, which shall remain forever separate and distinct.

SEC. 2. The legislative power shall be vested in a senate and house of representatives, to be styled the "Congress of the republic of Texas."

SEC. 3 The members of the house of representatives shall be chosen annually, on the first Monday of September each year, until congress shall otherwise provide by law, and shall hold their offices one year from the date of their election.

SEC. 4. No person shall be eligible to a seat in the house of representatives, until he shall have attained the age of twenty-five years, shall be a citizen of the republic, and shall have resided in the county or district six months next preceding his election.

SEC. 5. The house of representatives shall not consist of less than twenty-four, nor more than forty members, until the population shall amount to one hundred thousand souls, after which time the whole number of representatives shall not be less than forty, nor more than one hundred: *Provided, however,* That each county shall be entitled to at least one representative.

SEC. 6. The house of representatives shall choose their speaker and other officers, and shall have the sole power of impeachment.

SEC. 7. The senators shall be chosen by districts, as nearly equal in free population

---

* This constitution was framed by a convention which assembled at Washington, on the Brazos River, March 1, 1836; proclaimed a declaration of independence March 2; declared an ordinance establishing a government *ad interim*, and completed its labors March 17, 1836.

(free negroes and Indians excepted) as practicable; and the number of senators shall never be less than one-third nor more than one-half the number of representatives, and each district shall be entitled to one member and no more.

Sec. 8. The senators shall be chosen for the term of three years, on the first Monday in September; shall be citizens of the republic, reside in the district for which they are respectively chosen at least one year before the election, and shall have attained the age of thirty years.

Sec. 9. At the first session of congress after the adoption of this constitution, the senators shall be divided by lot into three classes, as nearly equal as practicable; the seats of the senators of the first class shall be vacated at the end of the first year; of the second class, at the end of the second year; the third class, at the end of the third year, in such a manner that one-third shall be chosen each year thereafter.

Sec. 10. The vice-president of the republic shall be president of the senate, but shall not vote on any question, unless the senate be equally divided.

Sec. 11. The senate shall choose all other officers of their body, and a president *pro tempore*, in the absence of the vice-president, or whenever he shall exercise the office of president; shall have the sole power to try impeachments, and when sitting as a court of impeachment, shall be under oath; but no conviction shall take place without the concurrence of two-thirds of all the members present.

Sec. 12. Judgment in cases of impeachment shall only extend to removal from office, and disqualification to hold any office of honor, trust, or profit under this government; but the party shall nevertheless be liable to indictment, trial, judgment, and punishment, according to law.

Sec. 13. Each house shall be the judge of the elections, qualifications, and returns of its own members. Two-thirds of each house shall constitute a quorum to do business, but a smaller number may adjourn from day to day, and may compel the attendance of absent members.

Sec. 14. Each house may determine the rules of its own proceedings, punish its members for disorderly behavior, and, with the concurrence of two-thirds, may expel a member, but not a second time for the same offense.

Sec. 15. Senators and representatives shall receive a compensation for their services to be fixed by law, but no increase of compensation, or diminution, shall take effect during the session at which such increase or diminution shall have been made. They shall, except in cases of treason, felony, or breach of the peace, be privileged from arrest during the session of congress, and in going to and returning from the same; and for any speech or debate in either house they shall not be questioned in any other place.

Sec. 16. Each house may punish, by imprisonment, during the session, any person not a member, who shall be guilty of any disrespect to the house, by any disorderly conduct in their presence.

Sec. 17. Each house shall keep a journal of its proceedings, and publish the same, except such parts as in its judgment require secrecy. When any three members shall desire the yeas and nays on any question, they shall be entered on the journals.

Sec. 18. Neither house, without the consent of the other, shall adjourn for more than three days, nor to any other place than that in which the two houses may be sitting.

Sec. 19. When vacancies happen in either house, the executive shall issue writs of election to fill such vacancies.

Sec. 20. No bill shall become a law until it shall have been read on three several days in each house and passed by the same, unless, in cases of emergency, two-thirds of the members of the house where the bill originated shall deem it expedient to dispense with the rule.

Sec. 21. After a bill shall have been rejected, no bill containing the same substance shall be passed into a law during the same session.

Sec. 22. The style of the laws of the republic shall be, "*Be it enacted by the senate and house of representatives of the republic of Texas in congress assembled.*"

Sec. 23. No person holding an office of profit under the government shall be eligible to a seat in either house of congress, nor shall any member of either house be eligible to any office which may be created or the profits of which shall be increased during his term of service.

SEC. 24. No holder of public moneys, or collector thereof, shall be eligible to a seat in either house of congress until he shall have fully acquitted himself of all responsibility, and shall produce the proper officer's receipt thereof. Members of either house may protest against any act or resolution, and may have such protest entered on the journals of their respective houses.

SEC. 25. No money shall be drawn from the public treasury but in strict accordance with appropriations made by law; and no appropriations shall be made for private or local purposes unless two-thirds of each house concur in such appropriations.

SEC. 26. Every act of congress shall be approved and signed by the president before it becomes a law; but if the president will not approve and sign such act, he shall return it to the house in which it shall have originated with his reasons for not approving the same, which shall be spread upon the journals of such house, and the bill shall then be reconsidered, and shall not become a law unless it shall then pass by a vote of two-thirds of both houses. If any act shall be disapproved by the president, the vote on the reconsideration shall be recorded by ayes and noes. If the president shall fail to return a bill within five days (Sundays excepted) after it shall have been presented for his approval and signature, the same shall become a law, unless the congress prevent its return within the time above specified by adjournment.

SEC. 27. All bills, acts, orders, or resolutions to which the concurrence of both houses may be necessary (motions or resolutions for adjournment excepted) shall be approved and signed by the president, or, being disapproved, shall be passed by two-thirds of both houses, in manner and form as specified in section twenty.

ARTICLE II.

SECTION 1. Congress shall have power to levy and collect taxes and imposts, excise and tonnage duties; to borrow money on the faith, credit, and property of the government; to pay the debts, and to provide for the common defence and general welfare of the republic.

SEC. 2. To regulate commerce, to coin money, to regulate the value thereof and of foreign coin, to fix the standard of weights and measures; but nothing but gold and silver shall be made a lawful tender.

SEC. 3. To establish post-offices and post-roads, to grant charters of incorporation, patents, and copyrights, and secure to the authors and inventors the exclusive use thereof for a limited time.

SEC. 4. To declare war, grant letters of marque and reprisal, and to regulate captures.

SEC. 5. To provide and maintain an army and navy, and to make all laws and regulations necessary for their government.

SEC. 6. To call out the militia to execute the law, to suppress insurrections, and repel invasion.

SEC. 7. To make all laws which shall be deemed necessary and proper to carry into effect the foregoing express grants of power, and all other powers vested in the government of the republic, or in any officer or department thereof.

ARTICLE III.

SECTION 1. The executive authority of this government shall be vested in a chief magistrate, who shall be styled the president of the republic of Texas.

SEC. 2. The first president elected by the people shall hold his office for the term of two years, and shall be ineligible during the next succeeding term; and all subsequent presidents shall be elected for three years, and be alike ineligible; and in the event of a tie, the house of representatives shall determine between the two highest candidates by a *viva-voce* vote.

SEC. 3. The returns of the elections for president and vice-president shall be sealed up and transmitted to the speaker of the house of representatives by the holders of elections of each county; and the speaker of the house of representatives shall open and publish the returns in presence of a majority of each house of congress.

ARTICLE IV.

SECTION 1. The judicial powers of the government shall be vested in one supreme court, and such inferior courts as the congress may, from time to time, ordain and establish. The judges of the supreme and inferior courts shall hold their offices for four years, be eligible to re-election, and shall, at stated periods, receive for their services a compensation, not to be increased or diminished during the period for which they were elected.

SEC. 2. The republic of Texas shall be divided into convenient judicial districts, not less than three nor more than eight. There shall be appointed for each district a judge, who shall reside in the same, and hold the courts at such times and places as congress may by law direct.

SEC. 3. In all admiralty and maritime cases, in all cases affecting ambassadors, public ministers, or consuls, and in all capital cases, the district courts shall have exclusive original jurisdiction, and original jurisdiction in all civil cases when the matter in controversy amounts to one hundred dollars.

SEC. 4. The judges, by virtue of their offices, shall be conservators of the peace throughout the republic. The style of all process shall be, "The Republic of Texas;" and all prosecutions shall be carried on in the name and by the authority of the same, and conclude, "against the peace and dignity of the republic."

SEC. 5. There shall be a district attorney appointed for each district, whose duties, salaries, perquisites, and term of service shall be fixed by law.

SEC. 6. The clerks of the district courts shall be elected by the qualified voters for members of congress, in the counties where the courts are established, and shall hold their offices for four years, subject to removal by presentment of a grand jury, and conviction of a petit jury.

SEC. 7. The supreme court shall consist of a chief-justice and associate judges; the district judges shall compose the associate judges, a majority of whom, with the chief-justice, shall constitute a quorum.

SEC. 8. The supreme court shall have appellate jurisdiction only, which shall be conclusive within the limits of the republic; and shall hold its sessions annually at such times and places as may be fixed by law: *Provided*, That no judge shall sit in a case in the supreme court tried by him in the court below.

SEC. 9. The judges of the supreme and district courts shall be elected by joint ballot of both houses of congress.

SEC. 10. There shall be in each county a county court, and such justices' courts as the congress may, from time to time, establish.

SEC. 11. The republic shall be divided into convenient counties, but no new county shall be established unless it be done on the petition of one hundred free male inhabitants of the territory sought to be laid off and established, and unless the said territory shall contain nine hundred square miles.

SEC. 12. There shall be appointed for each county a convenient number of justices of the peace, one sheriff, one coroner, and a sufficient number of constables, who shall hold their offices for two years, to be elected by the qualified voters of the district or county, as congress may direct. Justices of the peace and sheriff shall be commissioned by the president.

SEC. 13. The congress shall, as early as practicable, introduce, by statute, the common law of England, with such modifications as our circumstances, in their judgment, may require; and in all criminal cases the common law shall be the rule of decision.

ARTICLE V.

SECTION 1. Ministers of the gospel being, by their profession, dedicated to God and the care of souls, ought not to be diverted from the great duties of their functions;

therefore, no minister of the gospel, or priest of any denomination whatever, shall be eligible to the office of the executive of the republic, nor to a seat in either branch of the congress of the same.

SEC. 2. Each member of the senate and house of representatives shall, before they proceed to business, take an oath to support the constitution, as follows:

"I, A. B., do solemnly swear (or affirm, as the case may be) that, as a member of this general congress, I will support the constitution of the republic, and that I will not propose or assent to any bill, vote, or resolution which shall appear to me injurious to the people."

SEC. 3. Every person who shall be chosen or appointed to any office of trust or profit shall, before entering on the duties thereof, take an oath to support the constitution of the republic, and also an oath of office.

ARTICLE VI.

SECTION 1. No person shall be eligible to the office of president who shall not have attained the age of thirty-five years, shall be a citizen of the republic at the time of the adoption of this constitution, or an inhabitant of this republic at least three years immediately preceding his election.

SEC. 2. The president shall enter on the duties of his office on the second Monday in December next succeeding his election, and shall remain in office until his successor shall be duly qualified.

SEC. 3. The president shall, at stated times, receive a compensation for his services, which shall not be increased or diminished during his continuance in office; and, before entering upon the duties of his office, he shall take and subscribe the following oath or affirmation:

"I, A. B., president of the republic of Texas, do solemnly and sincerely swear (or affirm, as the case may be) that I will faithfully execute the duties of my office, and to the best of my abilities preserve, protect, and defend the constitution of the republic."

SEC. 4. He shall be commander-in-chief of the army and navy of the republic, and militia thereof, but he shall not command in person without the authority of a resolution of congress. He shall have power to remit fines and forfeitures, and to grant reprieves and pardons, except in cases of impeachment.

SEC. 5. He shall, with the advice and consent of two-thirds of the senate, make treaties; and, with the consent of the senate, appoint ministers and consuls, and all officers whose offices are established by this constitution, not herein otherwise provided for.

SEC. 6. The president shall have power to fill all vacancies that may happen during the recess of the senate; but he shall report the same to the senate within ten days after the next congress shall convene; and should the senate reject the same, the president shall not renominate the same individual to the same office.

SEC. 7. He shall, from time to time, give congress information of the state of the republic, and recommend for their consideration such measures as he may deem necessary. He may, upon extraordinary occasions, convene both houses, or either of them. In the event of a disagreement as to the time of adjournment, he may adjourn them to such time as he may think proper. He shall receive all foreign ministers. He shall see that the laws be faithfully executed, and shall commission all the officers of the republic.

SEC. 8. There shall be a seal of the republic, which shall be kept by the president, and used by him officially; it shall be called the great seal of the republic of Texas.

SEC. 9. All grants and commissions shall be in the name and by the authority of the republic of Texas, shall be sealed with the great seal, and signed by the president.

SEC. 10. The president shall have power, by and with the advice and consent of the senate, to appoint a secretary of state, and such other heads of executive department ments as may be established by law, who shall remain in office during the term of service of the president, unless sooner removed by the president, with the advice and consent of the senate.

SEC. 11. Every citizen of the republic who has attained the age of twenty-one years, and shall have resided six months within the district or county where the election is held, shall be entitled to vote for members of the general congress.

SEC. 12. All elections shall be by ballot, unless congress shall otherwise direct.

SEC. 13. All elections by joint vote of both houses of congress shall be *viva voce*, shall be entered on the journals, and a majority of the votes shall be necessary to a choice.

SEC. 14. A vice-president shall be chosen at every election for president, in the same manner, continue in office for the same time, and shall possess the same qualifications of the president. In voting for president and vice-president, the electors shall distinguish for whom they vote as president and for whom as vice-president.

SEC. 15. In cases of impeachment, removal from office, death, resignation, or absence of the president from the republic, the vice-president shall exercise the powers and discharge the duties of the president until a successor be duly qualified or until the president, who may be absent or impeached, shall return or be acquitted.

SEC. 16. The president, vice-president, and all civil officers of the republic shall be removable from office by impeachment for, and on conviction of, treason, bribery, and other high crimes and misdemeanors.

SCHEDULE.

SECTION 1. That no inconvenience may arise from the adoption of this constitution, it is declared by this convention that all laws now in force in Texas, and not inconsistent with this constitution, shall remain in full force until declared void, repealed, altered, or expire by their own limitation.

SEC. 2. All fines, penalties, forfeitures, and escheats which have accrued to Coahuila and Texas, or Texas, shall accrue to this republic.

SEC. 3. Every male citizen who is by this constitution a citizen and shall be otherwise qualified shall be entitled to hold any office or place of honor, trust, or profit under the republic, anything in this constitution to the contrary notwithstanding.

SEC. 4. The first president and vice-president that shall be appointed after the adoption of this constitution shall be chosen by this convention, and shall immediately enter on the duties of their offices, and shall hold said offices until their successors be elected and qualified, as prescribed in this constitution, and shall have the same qualifications, be invested with the same powers, and perform the same duties which are required and conferred on the executive head of the republic by this constitution.

SEC. 5. The president shall issue writs of election directed to the officers authorized to hold elections of the several counties, requiring them to cause an election to be held for president, vice-president, representatives, and senators to congress, at the time and mode prescribed by this constitution, which election shall be conducted in the manner that elections have been heretofore conducted. The president, vice-president, and members of congress, when duly elected, shall continue to discharge the duties of their respective offices for the time and manner prescribed by this constitution, until their successors be duly qualified.

SEC. 6. Until the first enumeration shall be made as directed by this constitution, the precinct of Austin shall be entitled to one representative; the precinct of Brazoria to two representatives; the precinct of Bexar two representatives; the precinct of Colorado one representative; Sabine one; Gonzales one; Goliad one; Harrisburgh one; Jasper one; Jefferson one; Liberty one; Matagorda one; Mina two; Nacogdoches two; Red River three; Victoria one; San Augustine two; Shelby two; Refugio one; San Patricio one; Washington two; Milan one; and Jackson one representative.

SEC. 7. Until the first enumeration shall be made as described by this constitution, the senatorial districts shall be composed of the following precincts: Bexar shall be entitled to one senator; San Patricio, Refugio, and Goliad one; Brazoria one; Mina and Gonzales one; Nacogdoches one; Red River one; Shelby and Sabine one; Washington one; Matagorda, Jackson, and Victoria one; Austin and Colorado one; San Augustine one; Milam one; Jasper and Jefferson one; and Liberty and Harrisburgh one senator.

SEC. 8. All judges, sheriffs, commissioners, and other civil officers shall remain in office, and in the discharge of the powers and duties of their respective offices, until there shall be others appointed or elected under the constitution.

GENERAL PROVISIONS.

SECTION 1. Laws shall be made to exclude from office, from the right of suffrage, and from serving on juries, those who shall hereafter be convicted of bribery, perjury, or other high crimes and misdemeanors.

SEC. 2. Returns of all elections for officers who are to be commissioned by the president shall be made to the secretary of state of this republic.

SEC. 3. The presidents and heads of departments shall keep their offices at the seat of government, unless removed by the permission of congress, or unless, in cases of emergency in time of war, the public interest may require their removal.

SEC. 4. The president shall make use of his private seal, until a seal of the republic shall be provided.

SEC. 5. It shall be the duty of congress, as soon as circumstances will permit, to provide by law a general system of education.

SEC. 6. All free white persons who shall emigrate to this republic, and who shall, after a residence of six months, make oath before some competent authority that he intends to reside permanently in the same, and shall swear to support this constitution, and that he will bear true allegiance to the republic of Texas, shall be entitled to all the privileges of citizenship.

SEC. 7. So soon as convenience will permit, there shall be a penal code formed on principles of reformation, and not of vindictive justice; and the civil and criminal laws shall be revised, digested, and arranged under different heads; and all laws relating to land-titles shall be translated, revised, and promulgated.

SEC. 8. All persons who shall leave the country for the purpose of evading a participation in the present struggle, or shall refuse to participate in it, or shall give aid or assistance to the present enemy, shall forfeit all rights of citizenship, and such lands as they may hold in the republic.

SEC. 9. All persons of color who were slaves for life previous to their emigration to Texas, and who are now held in bondage, shall remain in the like state of servitude: *Provided*, The said slave shall be the *bona-fide* property of the person so holding said slave as aforesaid. Congress shall pass no laws to prohibit emigrants from bringing their slaves into the republic with them, and holding them by the same tenure by which such slaves were held in the United States; nor shall congress have power to emancipate slaves; nor shall any slaveholder be allowed to emancipate his or her slave or slaves without the consent of congress, unless he or she shall send his or her slave or slaves without the limits of the republic. No free person of African descent, either in whole or in part, shall be permitted to reside permanently in the republic without the consent of congress; and the importation or admission of Africans or negroes into this republic, excepting from the United States of America, is forever prohibited, and declared to be piracy.

SEC. 10. All persons (Africans, the descendants of Africans, and Indians excepted) who were residing in Texas on the day of the declaration of independence shall be considered citizens of the republic and entitled to all the privileges of such. All citizens now living in Texas who have not received their portion of land in like manner as colonists shall be entitled to their land in the following proportion and manner: Every head of a family shall be entitled to one league and labor of land; and every single man of the age of seventeen and upwards shall be entitled to the third part of one league of land. All citizens who may have, previously to the adoption of this constitution, received their league of land as heads of families, and their quarter of a league of land as single persons, shall receive such additional quantity as will make the quantity of land received by them equal to one league and labor, and one-third of a league, unless by bargain, sale, or exchange they have transferred, or may henceforth transfer, their right to said land, or a portion thereof, to some other citizen of the republic; and in such case, the person to whom such right shall have been transferred shall be entitled to the same as fully and amply as the person making the transfer might or could have been. No alien shall hold land in Texas except by titles emanating directly from the government of this republic. But if any citizen of this republic should die intestate or otherwise his children or heirs shall inherit his estate, and aliens shall have a reasonable time to take possession of and dispose of the same, in a manner hereafter to be pointed out by law. Orphan children whose parents were entitled to land under the colonization laws of Mexico and who now reside in the republic shall be entitled to all the rights of which their parents were possessed at the time of their death. The citizens of the republic shall not be compelled to reside on the land, but shall have their lines plainly marked.

All orders of survey legally obtained by any citizen of the republic from any legally-authorized commissioner, prior to the act of the late consultation closing the land-offices, shall be valid. In all cases, the actual settler and occupant of the soil shall be entitled, in locating his land, to include his improvement, in preference to all other claims not acquired previous to his settlement, according to the law of the land and this constitution: *Provided*, That nothing herein contained shall prejudice the rights of any other citizen from whom a settler may hold land by rent or lease.

And whereas the protection of the public domain from unjust and fraudulent claims and quieting the people in the enjoyment of their lands is one of the great duties of this convention; and whereas the legislature of Coahuila and Texas having passed an act in the year 1834 in behalf of General John T. Mason, of New York, and another on the 14th day of March, 1835, under which the enormous amount of eleven hundred leagues of land has been claimed by sundry individuals, some of whom reside in foreign countries, and are not citizens of the republic—which said acts are contrary to articles fourth, twelfth, and fifteenth of the laws of 1824 of the general congress of Mexico, and one of said acts for that cause has by said general congress of Mexico been declared null and void—it is hereby declared that the said act of 1834, in favor of John T. Mason, and of the 14th of March, 1835, of the said legislature of Coahuila and Texas, and each and every grant founded thereon, is and was from the beginning null and void; and all surveys made under pretence of authority derived from said acts are hereby declared to be null and void; and all eleven-league claims, located within twenty leagues of the boundary-line between Texas and the United States of America which may have been located contrary to the laws of Mexico, are hereby declared to be null and void. And whereas many surveys and titles to lands have been made whilst most of the people of Texas were absent from home, serving in the campaign against Bexar, it is hereby declared that all the surveys and locations of land made since the act of the late consultation closing the land-offices, and all titles to land made since that time, are and shall be null and void.

And whereas the present unsettled state of the country and the general welfare of the people demand that the operations of the land-office and the whole land-system shall be suspended until persons serving in the army can have a fair and equal chance with those remaining at home to select and locate their lands, it is hereby declared that no survey or title which may hereafter be made shall be valid unless such survey or title shall be authorized by this convention, or some future congress of the republic. And with a view to the simplification of the land-system, and the protection of the people and the government from litigation and fraud, a general land-office shall be established, where all the land-titles of the republic shall be registered, and the whole territory of the republic shall be sectionized, in a manner hereafter to be prescribed by law, which shall enable the officers of the government, or any citizen, to ascertain with certainty the lands that are vacant, and those lands which may be covered with valid titles.

Sec. 11. Any amendment or amendments to this constitution may be proposed in the house of representatives or senate, and if the same shall be agreed to by a majority of the members elected to each of the two houses, such proposed amendment or amendments shall be entered on the journals, with the yeas and nays thereon, and referred to the congress then next to be chosen, and shall be published for three months previous to the election; and if the congress next chosen as aforesaid shall pass said amendment or amendments by a vote of two-thirds of all the members elected to each house, then it shall be the duty of said congress to submit said proposed amendment or amendments to the people in such manner and at such times as the congress shall prescribe; and if the people shall approve and ratify such amendment or amendments by a majority of the electors qualified to vote for members of congress voting thereon, such amendment or amendments shall become a part of this constitution: *Provided, however,* That no amendment or amendments be referred to the people oftener than once in three years.

DECLARATION OF RIGHTS.

This declaration of rights is declared to be a part of this constitution, and shall never be violated on any pretence whatever. And in order to guard against the transgression of the high powers which we have delegated, we declare that everything in this bill of rights contained, and every other right not hereby delegated, is reserved to the people.

1st. All men, when they form a social compact, have equal rights; and no men or set of men are entitled to exclusive public privileges or emoluments from the community.

2d. All political power is inherent in the people, and all free governments are founded on their authority and instituted for their benefit; and they have at all times an inalienable right to alter their government in such manner as they may think proper.

3d. No preference shall be given by law to any religious denomination or mode of worship over another, but every person shall be permitted to worship God according to the dictates of his own conscience.

4th. Every citizen shall be at liberty to speak, write, or publish his opinions on any subject, being responsible for the abuse of that privilege. No law shall ever be passed to curtail the liberty of speech or of the press; and in all prosecutions for libels the truth may be given in evidence, and the jury shall have the right to determine the law and fact, under the direction of the court.

5th. The people shall be secure in their persons, houses, papers, and possessions, from all unreasonable searches and seizures, and no warrant shall issue to search any place or seize any person or thing, without describing the place to be searched or the person or thing to be seized, without probable cause, supported by oath or affirmation.

6th. In all criminal prosecutions the accused shall have the right of being heard, by himself or counsel, or both; he shall have the right to demand the nature and cause of the accusation; shall be confronted with the witnesses against him, and have compulsory process for obtaining witnesses in his favor. And in all prosecutions by presentment or indictment, he shall have the right to a speedy and public trial, by an impartial jury; he shall not be compelled to give evidence against himself, or be deprived of life, liberty, or property, but by due course of law. And no freeman shall be holden to answer for any criminal charge but on presentment or indictment by a grand jury, except in the land and naval forces, or in the militia when in actual service in time of war or public danger, or in cases of impeachment.

7th. No citizen shall be deprived of privileges, outlawed, exiled, or in any manner disfranchised, except by due course of the law of the land.

8th. No title of nobility, hereditary privileges, or honors shall ever be granted or conferred in this republic. No person holding any office of profit or trust shall, without the consent of congress, receive from any foreign state any present, office, or emolument of any kind.

9th. No person, for the same offence, shall be twice put in jeopardy of life or limbs. And the right of trial by jury shall remain inviolate.

10th. All persons shall be bailable by sufficient security, unless for capital crimes, when the proof is evident or presumption strong; and the privilege of the writ of *habeas corpus* shall not be suspended, except in cases of rebellion or invasion the public safety may require it.

11th. Excessive bail shall not be required, nor excessive fines imposed, or cruel or unusual punishments inflicted. All courts shall be open, and every man for any injury done him in his lands, goods, person, or reputation shall have remedy by due course of law.

12th. No person shall be imprisoned for debt in consequence of inability to pay.

13th. No person's particular services shall be demanded, nor property taken or applied to public use, unless by the consent of himself or his representative, without just compensation being made therefor according to law.

14th. Every citizen shall have the right to bear arms in defence of himself and the republic. The military shall at all times and in all cases be subordinate to the civil power.

15th. The sure and certain defence of a free people is a well-regulated militia; and it shall be the duty of the legislature to enact such laws as may be necessary to the organizing of the militia of this republic.

16th. Treason against this republic shall consist only in levying war against it, or adhering to its enemies, giving them aid and support. No retrospective or *ex post facto* law, or laws impairing the obligation of contracts, shall be made.

17th. Perpetuities or monopolies are contrary to the genius of a free government, and shall not be allowed; nor shall the law of primogeniture or entailments ever be in force in this republic.

The foregoing constitution was unanimously adopted by the delegates of Texas, in convention assembled, at the town of Washington, on the 17th day of March, in the year of our Lord one thousand eight hundred and thirty-six, and of the independence of the republic the first year.

In witness whereof we have hereunto subscribed our names.

                                        RICHARD ELLIS, *President.*
Albert H. S. Kimble, *Secretary.*

[Doc. No.6]

Joint Resolution of March 1, 1845

THE ANNEXATION OF TEXAS—1845.*
[TWENTY-EIGHTH CONGRESS, SECOND SESSION.]

Joint Resolution for annexing Texas to the United States.

Resolved by the Senate and House of Representatives of the United States of America in Congress assembled, That Congress doth consent that the territory properly included within, and rightfully belonging to, the Republic of Texas may be erected into a new State, to be called the State of Texas, with a republican form of government, to be adopted by the people of said republic, by deputies in convention assembled, with the consent of the existing government, in order that the same may be admitted as one of the States of this Union.

SEC. 2. *And be it further resolved*, That the foregoing consent of Congress is given upon the following conditions, and with the following guarantees, to wit: First. Said State to be formed, subject to the adjustment of this Government of all questions of boundary that may arise with other governments, and the constitution thereof, with the proper evidence of its adoption by the people of said Republic of Texas, shall be transmitted to the President of the United States, to be laid before Congress for its final action on or before the first day of January, one thousand eight hundred and forty-six. Second. Said State, when admitted into the Union, after ceding to the United States all public edifices, fortifications, barracks, ports, and harbors, navy and navy-yards, docks, magazines, arms, armaments, and all other property and means pertaining to the public defence belonging to said Republic of Texas, shall retain all the public funds, debts, taxes, and dues of every kind which may belong to or be due and owing said republic, and shall also retain all the vacant and unappropriated lands lying within its limits, to be applied to the payment of the debts and liabilities of said Republic of Texas, and the residue of said lands, after discharging said debts and liabilities, to be disposed of as said State may direct, but in no event are said debts and liabilities to become a charge upon the Government of the United States. Third. New States, of convenient size, not exceeding four in number, in addition to said State of Texas, and having sufficient population, may hereafter, by the consent of said State, be formed out of the territory thereof, which shall be entitled to admission under the provisions of the Federal Constitution; and such States as may be formed out of that portion of said territory lying south of thirty-six degrees thirty minutes north latitude, commonly known as the Missouri compromise line, shall be admitted into the Union with or without slavery, as the people of each State asking admission may desire; and in such State or States as shall be formed out of said territory north of said Missouri compromise line, slavery or involuntary servitude (except for crime) shall be prohibited.

SEC. 3. *And be it further resolved*, That if the President of the United States shall in his judgment and discretion deem it most advisable, instead of proceeding to submit the foregoing resolution to the Republic of Texas, as an overture on the part of the United States for admission, to negotiate with that republic; then,

Be it resolved, That a State, to be formed out of the present Republic of Texas, with suitable extent and boundaries, and with two Representatives in Congress, until the next apportionment of representation, shall be admitted into the Union, by virtue of this act, on an equal footing with the existing States, as soon as the terms and conditions of such admission and the cession of the remaining Texan territory to the United States shall be agreed upon by the governments of Texas and the United States; and that the sum of one hundred thousand dollars be, and the same is hereby, appropriated to defray the expenses of missions and negotiations, to agree upon the terms of said admission and cession, either by treaty to be submitted to the Senate or by articles to be submitted to the two Houses of Congress, as the President may direct. APPROVED, March 1, 1845.

---

* This joint resolution of Congress was passed in the House of Representatives, by a vote of 120 against 98, February 25, 1845, and in the Senate, by a vote of 27 against 25, March 1, 1845, and it was approved by President Polk March 1, 1845.

[Doc. No. 7]

Constitution of 1845

CONSTITUTION OF TEXAS—1845.*

We, the people of the Republic of Texas, acknowledging with gratitude the grace and beneficence of God in permitting us to make a choice of our form of government, do, in accordance with the provisions of the joint resolution for annexing Texas to the United States, approved March 1, one thousand eight hundred and forty-five, ordain and establish this constitution.

ARTICLE I.

BILL OF RIGHTS.

That the general, great, and essential principles of liberty and free government may be recognized and established, we declare that—

SECTION 1. All political power is inherent in the people, and all free governments are founded on their authority and instituted for their benefit; and they have, at all times, the unalienable right to alter, reform, or abolish their form of government, in such manner as they may think expedient.

SEC. 2. All freemen, when they form a social compact, have equal rights; and no man, or set of men, is entitled to exclusive, separate public emoluments or privileges, but in consideration of public services.

SEC. 3. No religious test shall ever be required as a qualification to any office or public trust in this State..

SEC. 4. All men have a natural and indefeasible right to worship God according to the dictates of their own consciences; no man shall be compelled to attend, erect, or support any place of worship, or to maintain any ministry against his consent; no human authority ought, in any case whatever, to control or interfere with the rights of conscience, in matters of religion, and no preference shall ever be given by law to any religious societies or mode of worship; but it shall be the duty of the legislature to pass such laws as may be necessary to protect every religious denomination in the peaceable enjoyment of their own mode of public worship.

SEC. 5. Every citizen shall be at liberty to speak, write, or publish his opinions on any subject, being responsible for the abuse of that privilege; and no law shall ever be passed curtailing the liberty of speech or of the press.

SEC. 6. In prosecutions for the publication of papers investigating the official conduct of officers, or men in a public capacity, or when the matter published is proper for public information, the truth thereof may be given in evidence; and, in all indictments for libels, the jury shall have the right to determine the law and the facts under the direction of the court, as in other cases.

SEC. 7. The people shall be secure in their persons, houses, papers, and possessions from unreasonable seizures or searches; and no warrant to search any place, or to seize any person or thing, shall issue without describing them as near as may be; nor without probable cause, supported by oath or affirmation.

SEC. 8. In all criminal prosecutions the accused shall have a speedy public trial by an impartial jury; he shall not be compelled to give evidence against himself; he shall have the right of being heard by himself or counsel, or both; shall be confronted with the witnesses against him, and shall have compulsory process for obtaining witnesses in his favor; and no person shall be holden to answer for any criminal charge, but on indictment or information, except in cases arising in the land or naval forces, or offences against the laws regulating the militia.

SEC. 9. All prisoners shall be bailable by sufficient sureties, unless for capital offences, when the proof is evident or the presumption great; but this provision shall not be so construed as to prohibit bail after indictment found, upon an examination of

---

* This constitution was framed by a convention which met at Austin, July 4, 1845, and completed its labors August 27, 1845. It was submitted to the people October 13, 1845, and ratified by 4,174 votes against 312 votes.

the evidence by a judge of the supreme or district court, upon the return of a writ of *habeas corpus*, returnable in the county where the offence is committed.

SEC. 10. The privilege of the writ of *habeas corpus* shall not be suspended, except when, in case of rebellion or invasion, the public safety may require it.

SEC. 11. Excessive bail shall not be required nor excessive fines imposed, nor cruel and unusual punishment inflicted. All courts shall be open; and every person, for an injury done him in his lands, goods, person, or reputation, shall have remedy by due course of law.

SEC. 12. No person, for the same offence, shall be twice put in jeopardy of life or limb; nor shall a person be again put upon trial for the same offence after a verdict of not guilty; and the right of trial by jury shall remain inviolate.

SEC. 13. Every citizen shall have the right to keep and bear arms in the lawful defence of himself or the State.

SEC. 14. No bill of attainder, *ex post facto* law, retroactive law, or any law impairing the obligation of contracts shall be made, and no person's property shall be taken or applied to public use, without adequate compensation being made, unless by the consent of such person.

SEC. 15. No person shall ever be imprisoned for debt.

SEC. 16. No citizen of this State shall be deprived of life, liberty, property, or privileges, outlawed, exiled, or in any manner disfranchised, except by due course of the law of the land.

SEC. 17. The military shall at all times be subordinate to the civil authority.

SEC. 18. Perpetuities and monopolies are contrary to the genius of a free government, and shall never be allowed; nor shall the law of primogeniture or entailments ever be in force in this State.

SEC. 19. The citizens shall have the right, in a peaceable manner, to assemble together for their common good, and to apply to those invested with the powers of government for redress of grievances, or other purposes, by petition, address, or remonstrance.

SEC. 20. No power of suspending laws in this State shall be exercised, except by the legislature or its authority.

SEC. 21. To guard against transgressions of the high powers herein delegated, we declare that everything in this bill of rights is excepted out of the general powers of government, and shall forever remain inviolate; and all laws contrary thereto, or to the following provisions, shall be void.

ARTICLE II.

DIVISION OF THE POWERS OF GOVERNMENT.

The powers of the government of the State of Texas shall be divided into three distinct departments, and each of them to be confided to a separate body of magistracy, to wit: Those which are legislative, to one; those which are executive, to another; and those which are judicial, to another; and no person or collection of persons, being of one of those departments, shall exercise any power properly attached to either of the others, except in the instances herein expressly permitted.

ARTICLE III.

LEGISLATIVE DEPARTMENT.

SECTION 1. Every free male person who shall have attained the age of twenty-one years, and who shall be a citizen of the United States, or who is at the time of the adoption of this constitution by the Congress of the United States a citizen of the republic of Texas, and shall have resided in this State one year next preceding an election, and the last six months within the district, county, city, or town in which he offers to vote, (Indians not taxed, Africans and descendants of Africans excepted,) shall be deemed a qualified elector; and should such qualified elector happen to be in any other county situated in the district in which he resides at the time of an election, he shall be permitted to vote for any district officer: *Provided*, That the qualified electors shall be permitted to vote anywhere in the State for State officers: *And provided further*, That no soldier, seaman, or marine in the Army or Navy of the United States shall be entitled to vote at any election created by this constitution.

SEC. 2. All free male persons over the age of twenty-one years, (Indians not taxed, Africans and descendants of Africans excepted,) who shall have resided six months in Texas, immediately preceding the acceptance of this constitution by the Congress of the United States, shall be deemed qualified electors.

SEC. 3. Electors in all cases shall be privileged from arrest during their attendance at elections, and in going to and returning from the same, except in cases of treason, felony, or breach of the peace.

SEC. 4. The legislative powers of this State shall be vested in two distinct branches; the one to be styled the senate and the other the house of representatives, and both together the legislature of the State of Texas. The style of all laws shall be, "*Be it enacted by the legislature of the State of Texas.*"

SEC. 5. The members of the house of representatives shall be chosen by the qualified electors, and their term of office shall be two years from the day of the general election; and the sessions of the legislature shall be biennial, at such times as shall be prescribed by law.

SEC. 6. No person shall be a representative unless he be a citizen of the United States, or at the time of the adoption of this constitution a citizen of the Republic of Texas, and shall have been an inhabitant of this State two years next preceding his election, and the last year thereof a citizen of the county, city, or town for which he shall be chosen, and shall have attained the age of twenty-one years at the time of his election.

SEC. 7. All the elections by the people shall be held at such time and places, in the several counties, cities, or towns, as are now or may hereafter be designated by law.

SEC. 8. The senators shall be chosen by the qualified electors for the term of four years; and shall be divided by lot into two classes, as nearly equal as can be. The seats of senators of the first class shall be vacated at the expiration of the first two years, and of the second class at the expiration of four years; so that one-half thereof shall be chosen biennially thereafter.

SEC. 9. Such mode of classifying new additional senators shall be observed as will as nearly as possible preserve an equality of number in each class.

SEC. 10. When a senatorial district shall be composed of two or more counties, it shall not be separated by any county belonging to another district.

SEC. 11. No person shall be a senator unless he be a citizen of the United States, or at the time of the acceptance of this constitution by the Congress of the United States a citizen of the Republic of Texas, and shall have been an inhabitant of this State three years next preceding the election, and the last year thereof a resident of the district for which he shall be chosen, and have attained the age of thirty years.

SEC. 12. The house of representatives, when assembled, shall elect a speaker and its other officers, and the senate shall choose a president for the time being and its other officers. Each house shall judge of the qualifications and elections of its own members; but contested elections shall be determined in such manner as shall be directed by law. Two-thirds of each house shall constitute a quorum to do business, but a smaller number may adjourn from day to day, and compel the attendance of absent members, in such manner and under such penalties as each house may provide.

SEC. 13. Each house may determine the rules of its own proceedings, punish members for disorderly conduct, and, with the consent of two-thirds, expel a member, but not a second time for the same offence.

SEC. 14. Each house shall keep a journal of its own proceedings, and publish the same; and the yeas and nays of the members of either house on any question shall, at the desire of any three members present, be entered on the journals.

SEC. 15. When vacancies happen in either house, the governor, or the person exercising the power of the governor, shall issue writs of election to fill such vacancies.

SEC. 16. Senators and representatives shall in all cases, except in treason, felony, or breach of the peace, be privileged from arrest during the session of the legislature; and in going to and returning from the same, allowing one day for every twenty miles such member may reside from the place at which the legislature is convened.

SEC. 17. Each house may punish by imprisonment, during the session, any person not a member, for disrespectful or disorderly conduct, in its presence, or for obstructing any of its proceedings: *Provided*, Such imprisonment shall not at any one time exceed forty-eight hours.

SEC. 18. The doors of each house shall be kept open.

SEC. 19. Neither house shall, without the consent of the other, adjourn for more than three days; nor to any other place than that in which they may be sitting, without the concurrence of both houses.

SEC. 20. Bills may originate in either house, and be amended, altered, or rejected by the other; but no bill shall have the force of a law until, on three several days, it be read in each house, and free discussion be allowed thereon, unless, in case of great emergency, four-fifths of the house in which the bill shall be pending may deem it expedient to dispense with this rule; and every bill, having passed both houses, shall be signed by the speaker and president of their respective houses.

SEC. 21. All bills for raising revenue shall originate in the house of representatives, but the senate may amend or reject them as other bills.

SEC. 22. After a bill or resolution has been rejected by either branch of the legislature, no bill or resolution containing the same substance shall be passed into a law during the same session.

SEC. 23. Each member of the legislature shall receive from the public treasury a compensation for his services, which may be increased or diminished by law; but no increase of compensation shall take effect during the session at which such increase shall be made.

SEC. 24. No senator or representative shall, during the term for which he may be elected, be eligible to any civil office of profit under this State, which shall have been created, or the emoluments of which may have been increased, during such term; and no member of either house of the legislature shall, during the term for which he is elected, be eligible to any office or place the appointment to which may be made in whole or in part by either branch of the legislature; nor shall the members thereof be capable of voting for a member of their own body, for any office whatever, except it be in such cases as are herein provided. The president for the time being of the senate, and speaker of the house of representatives, shall be elected from their respective bodies.

SEC. 25. No judge of any court of law or equity, secretary of state, attorney-general, clerk of any court of record, sheriff, or collector, or any person holding a lucrative office under the United States, or this State, or any foreign government, shall be eligible to the legislature, nor shall at the same time hold or exercise any two offices, agencies, or appointments of trust or profit under this State: *Provided*, That offices of the militia, to which there is attached no annual salary, or the office of justice of the peace, shall not be deemed lucrative.

SEC. 26. No person who at any time may have been a collector of taxes, or who may have been otherwise intrusted with public money, shall be eligible to the legislature or to any office of profit or trust under the State government, until he shall have obtained a discharge for the amount of such collections, and for all public moneys with which he may have been intrusted.

SEC. 27. Ministers of the gospel, being by their profession dedicated to God and the care of souls, ought not to be diverted from the great duties of their functions; therefore, no minister of the gospel or priest of any denomination whatever, shall be eligible to the legislature.

SEC. 28. Elections for senators and representatives shall be general throughout the State, and shall be regulated by law.

SEC. 29. The legislature shall at their first meeting, and in the year one thousand eight hundred and forty-eight and fifty, and every eight years thereafter, cause an enumeration to be made of all the free inhabitants (Indians not taxed, Africans and descendants of Africans excepted) of the State, designating particularly the number of qualified electors; and the whole number of representatives shall, at the several periods of making such enumeration, be fixed by the legislature, and apportioned among the several counties, cities, or towns, according to the number of free population in each; and shall not be less than forty-five, nor more than ninety.

SEC. 30. Until the first enumeration and apportionment under this constitution, the following shall be the apportionment of representatives amongst the several counties, viz:

The county of Montgomery shall elect four representatives.

The counties of Red River, Harrison, Nacogdoches, Harris, and Washington shall elect three representatives each.

The counties of Fannin, Lamar, Bowie, Shelby, San Augustine, Rusk, Houston, Sabine, Liberty, Robertson, Galveston, Brazoria, Fayette, Colorado, Austin, Gonzales, and Bexar, two representatives each.

The counties of Jefferson, Jasper, Brazos, Milam, Bastrop, Travis, Matagorda, Jackson, Fort Bend, Victoria, Rufugio, Goliad, and San Patricio, one representative each.

SEC. 31. The whole number of senators shall, at the next session after the several periods of making the enumeration, be fixed by the legislature, and apportioned among the several districts to be established by law, according to the number of qualified electors, and shall never be less than nineteen, nor more than thirty-three.

SEC. 32. Until the first enumeration, as provided for by this constitution, the senatorial districts shall be as follows, to wit:

The counties of Fannin and Lamar shall constitute the first district, and elect one senator;

The counties of Red River and Bowie, the second district, and elect one senator;

The counties of Fannin, Lamar, Red River, and Bowie, conjointly, shall elect one senator;

The county of Harrison, the third district, shall elect one senator;

The counties of Nacogdoches, Rusk, and Houston, the fourth district, shall elect two senators;

The counties of San Augustine and Shelby, the fifth district, shall elect one senator;

The counties of Sabine and Jasper, the sixth district, shall elect one senator;

The counties of Liberty and Jefferson, the seventh district, shall elect one senator;

The counties of Robertson and Brazos, the eighth district, shall elect one senator;

The county of Montgomery, the ninth district, shall elect one senator;

The county of Harris, the tenth district, shall elect one senator;

The county of Galveston, the eleventh district, shall elect one senator;

The counties of Brazoria and Matagorda, the twelfth district, shall elect one senator;

The counties of Austin and Fort Bend, the thirteenth district, shall elect one senator;

The counties of Colorado and Fayette, the fourteenth district, shall elect one senator;

The counties of Bastrop and Travis, the fifteenth district, shall elect one senator;

The counties of Washington and Milam, the sixteenth district, shall elect one senator;

The counties of Victoria, Gonzales, and Jackson, the seventeenth district, shall elect one senator;

The county of Bexar, the eighteenth district, shall elect one senator; and

The counties of Goliad, Refugio, and San Patricio, the nineteenth district, shall elect one senator.

SEC. 33. The first session of the legislature after the adoption of this constitution by the Congress of the United States shall be held at the city of Austin, the present seat of government, and thereafter until the year one thousand eight hundred and fifty; after which period the seat of government shall be permanently located by the people.

SEC. 34. The members of the legislature shall, at their first session, receive from the treasury of the State, as their compensation, three dollars for each day they shall be in attendance on, and three dollars for every twenty-five miles travelling to and from the place of convening the legislature.

SEC. 35. In order to settle permanently the seat of government, an election shall be holden throughout the State, at the usual places of holding elections, on the first Monday in March, one thousand eight hundred and fifty, which shall be conducted according to law; at which time the people shall vote for such place as they may see proper for the seat of government. The returns of said election to be transmitted to the governor by the first Monday in June; if either place voted for shall have a majority of the whole number of votes cast, then the same shall be the permanent seat of government until the year one thousand eight hundred and seventy, unless the State shall sooner be divided. But in case neither place voted for shall have the majority of the whole number of votes given in, then the governor shall issue his proclamation for an election to be holden in the same manner, on the first Monday in October, one thousand eight hundred and fifty, between the two places having the highest number of votes at the first election. The election shall be conducted in the same manner as at the first, and the returns made to the governor, and the place having the highest number of votes shall be the seat of government for the time hereinbefore provided.

ARTICLE IV.

JUDICIAL DEPARTMENT.

SECTION 1. The judicial power of this State shall be vested in one supreme court, in district courts, and in such inferior courts as the legislature may from time to time ordain and establish, and such jurisdiction may be vested in corporation courts as may be deemed necessary, and be directed by law.

SEC. 2. The supreme court shall consist of a chief justice and two associates, any two of whom shall form a quorum.

SEC. 3. The supreme court shall have appellate jurisdiction only, which shall be coextensive with the limits of the State; but in criminal cases, and in appeals from interlocutory judgments, with such exceptions and under such regulations as the legislature shall make; and the supreme court, and judges thereof, shall have power to issue the writ of *habeas corpus*, and, under such regulations as may be prescribed by law, may issue writs of *mandamus*, and such other writs as shall be necessary to enforce its own jurisdiction; and also compel a judge of the district court to proceed to trial and judgment in a cause; and the supreme court shall hold its sessions once every year, between the months of October and June inclusive, at no more than three places in the State.

SEC. 4. The supreme court shall appoint its own clerks, who shall hold their offices for four years, and be subject to removal by the said court, for neglect of duty, misdemeanor in office, and such other causes as may be prescribed by law.

SEC. 5. The governor shall nominate, and, by and with the advice and consent of two-thirds of the senate, shall appoint the judges of the supreme and district courts, and they shall hold their offices for six years.

SEC. 6. The State shall be divided into convenient judicial districts. For each district there shall be appointed a judge, who shall reside in the same, and hold the courts at one place in each county, and at least twice in each year, in such manner as may be prescribed by law.

SEC. 7. The judges of the supreme court shall receive a salary not less than two thousand dollars annually, and the judges of the district court a salary not less than seventeen hundred and fifty dollars annually; and the salaries of the judges shall not be increased or diminished during their continuance in office.

SEC. 8. The judges of the supreme and district courts shall be removed by the governor, on the address of two-thirds of each house of the legislature, for wilful neglect of duty, or other reasonable cause, which shall not be sufficient ground for impeachment: *Provided, however,* That the cause or causes for which such removal shall be required shall be stated at length in such address, and entered on the journals of each house: *And provided further,* That the cause or causes shall be notified to the judges so intended to be removed; and he shall be admitted to a hearing in his own defence, before any vote for such address shall pass; and in all such cases the vote shall be taken by yeas and nays and entered on the journals of each house respectively.

SEC. 9. All judges of the supreme and district courts shall, by virtue of their offices, be conservators of the peace throughout the State. The style of all writs and process shall be "The State of Texas." All prosecutions shall be carried on in the name and by the authority of the State of Texas, and conclude "against the peace and dignity of the State."

SEC. 10. The district court shall have original jurisdiction of all criminal cases, of all suits in behalf of the State to recover penalties, forfeitures, and escheats, and of all cases of divorce, and of all suits, complaints, and pleas whatever, without regard to any distinction between law and equity, when the matter in controversy shall be valued at, or amount to, one hundred dollars, exclusive of interest; and the said courts, or the judges thereof, shall have power to issue all writs necessary to enforce their own jurisdiction, and give them a general superintendence and control over inferior jurisdictions. And in the trial of all criminal cases, the jury trying the same shall find and assess the amount of punishment to be inflicted, or fine imposed; except in capital cases, and where the punishment or fine imposed shall be specifically imposed by law.

SEC. 11. There shall be a clerk of the district courts for each county, who shall be elected by the qualified voters for members of the legislature, and who shall hold his office for four years, subject to removal by information, or by presentment of a grand jury and conviction of a petit jury. In case of vacancy, the judge of the district shall have the power to appoint a clerk until a regular election can be held.

SEC. 12. The governor shall nominate and, by and with the advice and consent of two-thirds of the senate, appoint an attorney-general, who shall hold his office for two years; and there shall be elected by joint vote of both houses of the legislature a district attorney for each district, who shall hold his office for two years; and the duties, salaries, and perquisites of the attorney-general and district attorneys shall be prescribed by law.

SEC. 13. There shall be appointed for each county a convenient number of justices of the peace, one sheriff, one coroner, and a sufficient number of constables, who shall hold their offices for two years, to be elected by the qualified voters of the district or county as the legislature may direct. Justices of the peace, sheriffs, and coroners shall be commissioned by the governor. The sheriff shall not be eligible more than four years in every six.

SEC. 14. No judge shall sit in any case wherein he may be interested, or where either of the parties may be connected with him by affinity or consanguinity, within such degrees as may be prescribed by law, or where he shall have been of counsel in the cause. When the supreme court, or any two of its members, shall be thus disqualified to hear and determine any cause or causes in said court, or when no judgment can be rendered in any case or cases in said court, by reason of the equal division of opinion of said judges, the same shall be certified to the governor of the State, who shall immediately commission the requisite number of persons, learned in the law, for the trial and determination of said case or cases. When the judges of the district court are thus disqualified, the parties may, by consent, appoint a proper person to try the said case; and the judges of the said courts may exchange districts, or hold courts for each other, when they may deem it expedient, and shall do so when directed by law. The disqualifications of judges of inferior tribunals shall be remedied as may hereafter be by law prescribed.

SEC. 15. Inferior tribunals shall be established in each county for appointing guardians, granting letters testamentary and of administration, for settling the accounts of executors, administrators, and guardians, and for the transaction of business appertaining to estates; and the district courts shall have original and appellate jurisdiction, and general control over the said inferior tribunals, and original jurisdiction and control over executors, administrators, guardians, and minors, under such regulations as may be prescribed by law.

SEC. 16. In the trial of all causes in equity in the district court, the plaintiff or defendant shall, upon application made in open court, have the right of trial by jury, to be governed by the rules and regulations prescribed in trials at law.

SEC. 17. Justices of the peace shall have such civil and criminal jurisdiction as shall be provided for by law.

SEC. 18. In all cases arising out of a contract, before any inferior judicial tribunal, when the amount in controversy shall exceed ten dollars, the plaintiff or defendant shall, upon application to the presiding officer, have the right of trial by jury.

SEC. 19. In all cases where justices of the peace or other judicial officers of inferior tribunals shall have jurisdiction in the trial of causes where the penalty for the violation of a law is fine or imprisonment, (except in cases of contempt,) the accused shall have the right of trial by jury.

ARTICLE .V.

EXECUTIVE DEPARTMENT.

SECTION 1. The supreme executive power of this State shall be vested in a chief magistrate, who shall be styled the governor of the State of Texas.

SEC. 2. The governor shall be elected by the qualified electors of the State, at the time and places of elections for members of the legislature.

SEC. 3. The returns of every election for governor, until otherwise provided by law, shall be made out, sealed up, and transmitted to the seat of government, and directed to the speaker of the house of representatives, who shall, during the first week of the session of the legislature thereafter, open and publish them in the presence of both houses of the legislature; the person having the highest number of votes, and being constitutionally eligible, shall be declared by the speaker, under the direction of the legislature, to be governor; but if two or more persons shall have the highest and an equal number of votes, one of them shall be immediately chosen governor by joint vote of both houses of the legislature. Contested elections for governor shall be determined by both houses of the legislature.

SEC. 4. The governor shall hold his office for the term of two years from the regular time of installation, and until his successor shall be duly qualified, but shall not be eligible for more than four years in any term of six years; he shall be at least thirty years of age, shall be a citizen of the United States, or a citizen of the State of Texas, at the time of the adoption of this constitution, and shall have resided in the same three years immediately preceding his election.

SEC. 5. He shall, at stated times, receive a compensation for his services, which shall not be increased or diminished during the term for which he shall have been elected. The first governor shall receive an annual salary of two thousand dollars, and no more.

SEC. 6. The governor shall be commander-in-chief of the army and navy of this State, and of the militia, except when they shall be called into the service of the United States.

SEC. 7. He may require information in writing from the officers of the executive department on any subject relating to the duties of their respective offices.

SEC. 8. He may, by proclamation, on extraordinary occasions, convene the legislature at the seat of government, or at a different place, if that should be in the actual possession of a public enemy; in case of disagreement between the two houses with respect to adjournment, he may adjourn them to such time as he shall think proper, not beyond the day of the next regular meeting of the legislature.

SEC. 9. He shall, from time to time, give to the legislature information in writing of the state of the government, and recommend to their consideration such measures as he may deem expedient.

SEC. 10. He shall take care that the laws be faithfully executed.

SEC. 11. In all criminal cases, except in those of treason and impeachment, he shall have power, after conviction, to grant reprieves and pardons, and, under such rules as the legislature may prescribe, he shall have power to remit fines and forfeitures. In cases of treason, he shall have power, by and with the advice and consent of the senate, to grant reprieves and pardons, and he may, in the recess of the senate, respite the sentence until the end of the next session of the legislature.

SEC. 12. There shall also be a lieutenant-governor, who shall be chosen at every election for governor, by the same persons and in the same manner, continue in office for the same time, and possess the same qualifications. In voting for governor and lieutenant-governor, the electors shall distinguish for whom they vote as governor and for whom as lieutenant-governor. The lieutenant-governor shall, by virtue of his office, be president of the senate, and have, when in committee of the whole, a right to debate and vote on all questions, and when the senate is equally divided to give the casting vote. In case of the death, resignation, removal from office, inability or refusal of the governor to serve, or of his impeachment or absence from the State, the lieutenant-governor shall exercise the powers and authority appertaining to the office of governor until another be chosen at the periodical election and be duly qualified, or until the governor impeached, absent, or disabled shall be acquitted, return, or his disability be removed.

SEC. 13. Whenever the government shall be administered by the lieutenant-governor, or he shall be unable to attend as president of the senate, the senate shall elect one of their own members as president for the time being. And if, during the vacancy of the office of governor, the lieutenant-governor shall die, resign, refuse to serve, or be removed from office, or be unable to serve, or if he shall be impeached, or absent from the State, the president of the senate for the time being shall, in like manner, administer the government until he shall be superseded by a governor or lieutenant-governor; the lieutenant-governor shall, whilst he acts as president of the senate, receive for his services the same compensation which shall be allowed to the speaker of the house of representatives, and no more, and during the time he administers the government as governor shall receive the same compensation which the governor would have received had he been employed in the duties of his office, and no more. The president for the time being of the senate shall, during the time he administers the government, receive in like manner the same compensation which the governor would have received had he been employed in the duties of his office. If the lieutenant-governor shall be required to administer the government, and shall whilst in such administration die, resign, or be absent from the State, during the recess of the legislature, it shall be the duty of the secretary of state to convene the senate for the purpose of choosing a president for the time being.

SEC. 14. There shall be a seal of the State, which shall be kept by the governor, and used by him officially. The said seal shall be a star of five points, encircled by an olive and live-oak branches, and the words "The State of Texas."

SEC. 15. All commissions shall be in the name and by the authority of the State of Texas, be sealed with the State seal, signed by the governor, and attested by the secretary of state.

SEC. 16. There shall be a secretary of state, who shall be appointed by the governor, by and with the advice and consent of the senate, and shall continue in office during the term of service of the governor-elect. He shall keep a fair register of all official acts and proceedings of the governor, and shall, when required, lay the same, and all papers, minutes, and vouchers relative thereto, before the legislature, or either house thereof, and shall perform such other duties as may be required of him by law.

SEC. 17. Every bill which shall have passed both houses of the legislature shall be presented to the governor; if he approve, he shall sign it; but if not, he shall return it with his objections to the house in which it shall have originated, who shall enter the objections at large upon the journals and proceed to reconsider it; if, after such reconsideration, two-thirds of the members present shall agree to pass the bill, it shall be sent, with the objections, to the other house, by which it shall likewise be reconsidered; if approved by two-thirds of the members present, of that house, it shall become a law; but in such cases the votes of both houses shall be determined by yeas and nays, and the names of the members voting for or against the bill shall be entered on the journals of each house respectively; if any bill shall not be returned by the governor within five days (Sundays excepted) after it shall have been presented to him, the same shall be a law, in like manner as if he had signed it. Every bill presented to the governor one day previous to the adjournment of the legislature, and not returned to the house in which it originated before its adjournment, shall become a law, and have the same force and effect as if signed by the governor.

SEC. 18. Every order, resolution, or vote, to which the concurrence of both houses of the legislature may be necessary, except on questions of adjournment, shall be presented to the governor, and, before it shall take effect, be approved by him; or being disapproved, shall be repassed by both houses according to the rules and limitations prescribed in the case of a bill.

SEC. 19. The governor, by and with the advice and consent of two-thirds of the senate, shall appoint a convenient number of notaries public, not exceeding six for each county, who, in addition to such duties as are prescribed by law, shall discharge such other duties as the legislature may, from time to time, prescribe.

SEC. 20. Nominations to fill all vacancies that may have occurred during the recess shall be made to the senate during the first ten days of its session. And should any nomination so made be rejected, the same individual shall not again be nominated during the session to fill the same office. And should the governor fail to make nominations to fill any vacancy during the session of the senate, such vacancy shall not be filled by the governor until the next meeting of the senate.

SEC. 21. The governor shall reside, during the session of the legislature, at the place where their sessions may be held, and at all other times whenever, in their opinion, the public good may require.

SEC. 22. No person holding the office of governor shall hold any other office or commission, civil or military.

SEC. 23. A State treasurer and comptroller of public accounts shall be biennially elected by the joint ballot of both houses of the legislature; and in case of vacancy in either of said offices during the recess of the legislature, such vacancy shall be filled by the governor, which appointment shall continue until the close of the next session of the legislature thereafter.

ARTICLE VI.

MILITIA.

SECTION 1. The legislature shall provide by law for organizing and disciplining the militia of this State, in such manner as they shall deem expedient, not incompatible with the Constitution and laws of the United States in relation thereto.

SEC. 2. Any person who conscientiously scruples to bear arms shall not be compelled to do so, but shall pay an equivalent for personal service.

SEC. 3. No licensed minister of the gospel shall be required to perform military duty, work on roads, or serve on juries in this State.

SEC. 4. The governor shall have power to call forth the militia to execute the laws of the State, to suppress insurrections, and to repel invasions.

ARTICLE VII.

GENERAL PROVISIONS.

SECTION 1. Members of the legislature, and all officers, before they enter upon the duties of their offices, shall take the following oath or affirmation: "I, A. B., do solemnly swear [or affirm] that I will faithfully and impartially discharge and perform all the duties incumbent on me as ———, according to the best of my skill and ability, agreeably to the Constitution and laws of the United States and of this State; and I do further solemnly swear [or affirm] that since the adoption of this constitution by the Congress of the United States I, being a citizen of this State, have not fought a duel with deadly weapons, within this State nor out of it; nor have I sent or accepted a challenge to fight a duel with deadly weapons; nor have I acted as second in carrying a challenge, or aided, advised, or assisted any person thus offending: So help me God."

SEC. 2. Treason against this State shall consist only in levying war against it, or in adhering to its enemies, giving them aid and comfort; and no person shall be convicted of treason unless on the testimony of two witnesses to the same overt act, or his own confession in open court.

SEC. 3. Every person shall be disqualified from holding any office of trust or profit in this State who shall have been convicted of having given or offered a bribe to procure his election or appointment.

SEC. 4. Laws shall be made to exclude from office, serving on juries, and from the right of suffrage those who shall hereafter be convicted of bribery, perjury, forgery, or other high crimes. The privilege of free suffrage shall be supported by laws regulating elections and prohibiting, under adequate penalties, all undue influence thereon, from power, bribery, tumult, or other improper practice.

SEC. 5. Any citizen of this State who shall, after the adoption of this constitution, fight a duel with deadly weapons, or send or accept a challenge to fight a duel with deadly weapons, either within the State or out of it, or who shall act as second, or knowingly aid and assist, in any manner, those thus offending, shall be deprived of holding any office of trust or profit under this State.

SEC. 6. In all elections by the people, the vote shall be by ballot until the legislature shall otherwise direct; and in all elections by the senate and house of representatives, jointly or separately, the vote shall be given *viva voce*, except in the election of their officers.

SEC. 7. The legislature shall provide by law for the compensation of all officers, servants, agents, and public contractors not provided for by this constitution; and shall not grant extra compensation to any officer, agent, servant, or public contractor, after such public service shall have been performed, or contract entered into for the performance of the same; nor grant, by appropriation or otherwise, any amount of money out of the treasury of the State to any individual, on a claim real or pretended, where the same shall not have been provided for by preëxisting law: *Provided*, That nothing in this section shall be so construed as to affect the claims of persons against the Republic of Texas heretofore existing.

SEC. 8. No money shall be drawn from the treasury but in pursuance of specific appropriations made by law; nor shall any appropriation of money be made for a longer term than two years, except for purposes of education; and no appropriation for private or individual purposes, or for purposes of internal improvement, shall be made without the concurrence of two-thirds of both houses of the legislature. A regular statement and account of the receipts and expenditures of all public money shall be published annually, in such manner as shall be prescribed by law. And in no case shall the legislature have the power to issue treasury warrants, treasury notes, or paper of any description intended to circulate as money.

SEC. 9. All civil officers shall reside within the State; and all district or county officers within their districts or counties, and shall keep their offices at such places therein as may be required by law.

SEC. 10. The duration of all offices not fixed by this constitution shall never exceed four years.

SEC. 11. Absence on the business of this State, or of the United States, shall not forfeit a residence once obtained so as to deprive any one of the right of suffrage, or of being elected or appointed to any office under the exceptions contained in this constitution.

SEC. 12. The legislature shall have power to provide for deductions from the salaries of public officers who may neglect the performance of any duty that may be assigned them by law.

SEC. 13. No member of Congress, nor person holding or exercising any office of profit or trust under the United States, or either of them, or under any foreign power, shall be eligible as a member of the legislature, or hold or exercise any office of profit or trust under this State.

SEC. 14. The legislature shall provide for a change of venue in civil and criminal cases; and for the erection of a penitentiary at as early a day as practicable.

SEC. 15. It shall be the duty of the legislature to pass such laws as may be necessary and proper to decide differences by arbitration, when the parties shall elect that method of trial.

SEC. 16. Within five years after the adoption of this constitution, the laws, civil and criminal, shall be revised, digested, arranged, and published in such manner as the legislature shall direct; and a like revision, digest, and publication shall be made every ten years thereafter.

SEC. 17. No lottery shall be authorized by this State; and the buying or selling of lottery-tickets within this State is prohibited.

SEC. 18. No divorce shall be granted by the legislature.

SEC. 19. All property, both real and personal, of the wife, owned or claimed by her before marriage, and that acquired afterwards by gift, devise, or descent, shall be her separate property; and laws shall be passed more clearly defining the rights of the wife, in relation as well to her separate property, as that held in common with her husband. Laws shall also be passed providing for the registration of the wife's separate property.

SEC. 20. The rights of property and of action which have been acquired under the constitution and laws of the Republic of Texas shall not be divested; nor shall any rights or actions which have been divested, barred, or declared null and void by the constitution and laws of the Republic of Texas be reinvested, revived, or reinstated by this constitution; but the same shall remain precisely in the situation in which they were before the adoption of this constitution.

SEC. 21. All claims, locations, surveys, grants, and titles to land which are declared null and void by the constitution of the Republic of Texas, are, and the same shall remain forever, null and void.

SEC. 22. The legislature shall have power to protect, by law, from forced sale a certain portion of the property of all heads of families. The homestead of a family, not to exceed two hundred acres of land, (not included in a town or city, or any town or city lot or lots,) in value not to exceed two thousand dollars, shall not be subject to forced sale for any debts hereafter contracted; nor shall the owner, if a married man, be at liberty to alienate the same, unless by the consent of the wife, in such manner as the legislature may hereafter point out.

SEC. 23. The legislature shall provide in what cases officers shall continue to perform the duties of their offices, until their successors shall be duly qualified.

SEC. 24. Every law enacted by the legislature shall embrace but one object, and that shall be expressed in the title.

SEC. 25. No law shall be revised or amended by reference to its title; but in such case the act revised, or section amended, shall be reënacted, and published at length.

SEC. 26. No person shall hold or exercise at the same time more than one civil office of emolument, except that of justice of the peace.

SEC. 27. Taxation shall be equal and uniform throughout the State. All property in this State shall be taxed in proportion to its value, to be ascertained as directed by law; except such property as two-thirds of both houses of the legislature may think proper to exempt from taxation. The legislature shall have power to lay an income-tax, and to tax all persons pursuing any occupation, trade, or profession: *Provided*, That the term "occupation" shall not be construed to apply to pursuits either agricultural or mechanical.

SEC. 28. The legislature shall have power to provide by law for exempting from taxation two hundred and fifty dollars' worth of the household-furniture or other property belonging to each family in this State.

SEC. 29. The assessor and collector of taxes shall be appointed in such manner and under such regulations as the legislature may direct.

SEC. 30. No corporate body shall hereafter be created, renewed, or extended with banking or discounting privileges.

SEC. 31. No private corporation shall be created, unless the bill creating it shall be passed by two-thirds of both houses of the legislature; and two-thirds of the legislature shall have power to revoke and repeal all private corporations, by making compensation for the franchise. And the State shall not be part owner of the stock or property belonging to any corporation.

SEC. 32. The legislature shall prohibit, by law, individuals from issuing bills, checks, promissory notes, or other paper, to circulate as money.

SEC. 33. The aggregate amount of debts hereafter contracted by the legislature shall never exceed the sum of one hundred thousand dollars, except in case of war, to repel invasions, or suppress insurrections. And in no case shall any amount be borrowed, except by a vote of two-thirds of both houses of the legislature.

SEC. 34. The legislature shall at the first session thereof, and may at any subsequent session, establish new counties for the convenience of the inhabitants of such new county or counties : *Provided*, That no new county shall be established which shall reduce the county or counties, or either of them, from which it shall be taken to a less area than nine hundred square miles, (except the county of Bowie,) unless by consent of two-thirds of the legislature; nor shall any county be laid off of less contents. Every new county, as to the right of suffrage and representation, shall be considered as part of the county or counties from which it was taken, until entitled by numbers to right of separate representation.

SEC. 35. No soldier shall, in time of peace, be quartered in the house or within the inclosure of any individual, without the consent of the owner; nor in time of war but in a manner prescribed by law.

SEC. 36. The salaries of the governor and judges of the supreme and district courts are hereby fixed at the minimum established in the constitution, and shall not be increased for ten years.

MODE OF AMENDING THE CONSTITUTION.

SEC. 37. The legislature, whenever two-thirds of each house shall deem it necessary, may propose amendments to this constitution; which proposed amendments shall be duly published in the public prints of the State, at least three months before the next general election of representatives, for the consideration of the people ; and it shall be the duty of the several returning officers at the next election which shall be thus holden to open a poll for, and make a return to the secretary of the State of, the names of all those voting for representatives who have voted on such proposed amendments; and if, thereupon, it shall appear that a majority of all the citizens of this State voting for representatives have voted in favor of such proposed amendments, and two-thirds of each house of the next legislature shall, after such election, and before another, ratify the same amendments by yeas and nays, they shall be valid, to all intents and purposes, as parts of this constitution : *Provided*, That the said proposed amendments shall, at each of the said sessions, have been read on three several days in each house.

ARTICLE VIII.

SLAVES.

SECTION 1. The legislature shall have no power to pass laws for the emancipation of slaves, without the consent of their owners ; nor without paying their owners, previous to such emancipation, a full equivalent in money for the slaves so emancipated. They shall have no power to prevent emigrants to this State from bringing with them such persons as are deemed slaves by the laws of any of the United States, so long as any person of the same age or description shall be continued in slavery by the laws of this State: *Provided*, That such slave be the *bona-fide* property of such emigrants: *Provided also*, That laws shall be passed to inhibit the introduction into this State of slaves who have committed high crimes in other States or Territories. They shall have the right to pass laws to permit the owners of slaves to emancipate them, saving the rights of creditors, and preventing them from becoming a public charge. They shall have full power to pass laws which will oblige the owners of slaves to treat them with humanity ; to provide for their necessary food and clothing; to abstain from all injuries to them extending to life or limb; and, in case of their neglect or refusal to comply with the directions of such laws, to have such slave or slaves taken from such owner and sold for the benefit of such owner or owners. They may pass laws to prevent slaves from being brought into this State as merchandise only.

SEC. 2. In the prosecution of slaves for the crimes of a higher grade than petit larceny, the legislature shall have no power to deprive them of an impartial trial by a petit jury.

SEC. 3. Any person who shall maliciously dismember or deprive a slave of life shall suffer such punishment as would be inflicted in case the like offence had been committed upon a free white person, and on the like proof, except in case of insurrection of such slave.

ARTICLE IX.

IMPEACHMENT.

SECTION 1. The power of impeachment shall be vested in the house of representatives.

SEC. 2. Impeachments of the governor, lieutenant-governor, attorney-general, secretary of state, treasurer, comptroller, and of the judges of the district courts shall be tried by the senate.

SEC. 3. Impeachments of judges of the supreme court shall be tried by the senate. When sitting as a court of impeachment the senators shall be upon oath or affirmation; and no person shall be convicted without the concurrence of two-thirds of the senators present.

SEC. 4. Judgment, in cases of impeachment, shall extend only to removal from office and disqualification from holding any office of honor, trust, or profit under this State; but the parties convicted shall, nevertheless, be subject to indictment, trial, and punishment according to law.

SEC. 5. All officers against whom articles of impeachment may be preferred shall be suspended from the exercise of the duties of their office during the pendency of such impeachment. The appointing power may make a provisional appointment to fill the vacancy occasioned by the suspension of an officer until the decision on the impeachment.

SEC. 6. The legislature shall provide for the trial, punishment, and removal from office of all other officers of the State, by indictment or otherwise.

ARTICLE X.

EDUCATION.

SECTION 1. A general diffusion of knowledge being essential to the preservation of the rights and liberties of the people, it shall be the duty of the legislature of this State to make suitable provision for the support and maintenance of public schools.

SEC. 2. The legislature shall, as early as practicable, establish free schools throughout the State, and shall furnish means for their support by taxation on property; and it shall be the duty of the legislature to set apart not less than one-tenth of the annual revenue of the State, derivable from taxation, as a perpetual fund, which fund shall be appropriated to the support of free public schools; and no law shall ever be made diverting said fund to any other use; and until such time as the legislature shall provide for the establishment of such schools in the several districts of the State, the fund thus created shall remain as a charge against the State, passed to the credit of the free common-school fund.

SEC. 3. All public lands which have been heretofore, or may hereafter be, granted for public schools to the various counties, or other political divisions in this State, shall not be alienated in fee, nor disposed of otherwise than by lease for a term not exceeding twenty years, in such manner as the legislature may direct.

SEC. 4. The several counties in this State which have not received their quantum of lands for the purposes of education shall be entitled to the same quantity heretofore appropriated by the congress of the Republic of Texas to other counties.

ARTICLE XI.

SECTION 1. All certificates for head-right claims to lands issued to fictitious persons, or which were forged, and all locations and surveys thereon, are, and the same were, null and void from the beginning.

SEC. 2. The district courts shall be opened until the first day of July, one thousand eight hundred and forty-seven, for the establishment of certificates for head-rights not recommended by the commissioners appointed under the act to detect fraudulent land certificates, and to provide for issuing patents to legal claimants; and the parties suing shall produce the like proof, and be subjected to the requisitions which were necessary, and were prescribéd by law, to sustain the original application for the said certificates; and all certificates above referred to not established or sued upon before the period limited shall be barred; and the said certificates, and all locations and surveys thereon, shall be forever null and void; and all relocations made on such surveys shall not be disturbed until the certificates are established as above directed.

ARTICLE XII.

LAND-OFFICE.

There shall be one general land-office in the State, which shall be at the seat of government, where all titles which have heretofore emanated, or may hereafter emanate, from government shall be registered; and the legislature may establish, from time to time, such subordinate offices as they may deem requisite.

ARTICLE XIII.

SCHEDULE.

SECTION 1. That no inconvenience may arise from a change of separate national government to a State government, it is declared that all process which shall be issued in the name of the Republic of Texas, prior to the organization of the State government under this constitution, shall be as valid as if issued in the name of the State of Texas.

SEC. 2. The validity of all bonds and recognizances, executed in conformity with the constitution and laws of the Republic of Texas, shall not be impaired by the change of government, but may be sued for and recovered in the name of the governor of the State of Texas; and all criminal prosecutions or penal actions which shall have arisen prior to the organization of the State government under this constitution, in any of the courts of the Republic of Texas, shall be prosecuted to judgment and execution in the name of said State. All suits at law and equity which may be depending in any of the courts of the Republic of Texas, prior to the organization of the State government under this constitution, shall be transferred to the proper court of the State which shall have jurisdiction of the subject-matter thereof.

SEC. 3. All laws or parts of laws now in force in the Republic of Texas, which are not repugnant to the Constitution of the United States, the joint resolutions for annexing Texas to the United States, or to the provisions of this constitution, shall continue and remain in force as the laws of this State until they expire by their own limitation, or shall be altered or repealed by the legislature thereof.

SEC. 4. All fines, penalties, forfeitures, and escheats which have accrued to the Republic of Texas under the constitution and laws shall accrue to the State of Texas; and the legislature shall, by law, provide a method for determining what lands may have been forfeited or escheated.

SEC. 5. Immediately after the adjournment of this convention, the President of the republic shall issue his proclamation, directing the chief justices of the several counties of this republic, and the several chief justices and their associates are hereby required, to cause polls to be opened in their respective counties, at the established precincts, on the second Monday of October next, for the purpose of taking the sense of the people of Texas in regard to the adoption or rejection of this constitution; and the votes of all persons entitled to vote under the existing laws or this constitution shall be received. Each voter shall express his opinion by declaring by a *viva-voce* vote for "the constitution accepted" or "the constitution rejected," or some words clearly expressing the intention of the voter, and at the same time the vote shall be taken in like manner for and against annexation. The election shall be conducted in conformity with the existing laws regulating elections, and the chief justices of the several counties shall carefully and promptly make duplicate returns of said polls, one of which shall be transmitted to the secretary of state of the Republic of Texas, and the other deposited in the clerk's office of the county court.

SEC. 6. Upon the receipt of the said returns, or on the second Monday of November next, if the returns be not sooner made, it shall be the duty of the President, in presence of such officers of his cabinet as may be present, and of all persons who may choose to attend, to compare the votes given for the ratification or rejection of this constitution; and if it should appear from the returns that a majority of all the votes given is for the adoption of the constitution, then it shall be the duty of the President to make proclamation of that fact; and thenceforth this constitution shall be ordained and established as the constitution of the State, to go into operation and be of force and effect from and after the organization of the State government under this constitution; and the President of this republic is authorized and required to transmit to the President of the United States duplicate copies of this constitution, properly authenticated, together with certified statements of the number of votes given for the ratification thereof and the number for rejection, one of which copies shall be transmitted by mail, and one copy by a special messenger, in sufficient time to reach the seat of government of the United States early in December next.

SEC. 7. Should this constitution be accepted by the people of Texas, it shall be the duty of the President, on or before the second Monday in November next, to issue his proclamation, directing and requiring elections to be holden in all the counties of this republic, on the third Monday in December next, for the office of governor, lieutenant-governor, and members of the senate and house of representatives of the State legislature, in accordance with the apportionment of representation directed by this constitution. The returns for members of the legislature of this State shall be made to the department of state of this republic, and those for governor and lieu-tenant-governor shall be addressed to the speaker of the house of representatives, indorsed "Election returns of ———— county for governor," and directed to the department of state; and should, from any cause whatever, the chief justices of counties fail to cause to be holden any of the polls or elections provided for by this constitution at the times and places herein directed, the people of the precincts where such failure exists are hereby authorized to choose managers, judges, and other officers to conduct said elections.

SEC. 8. Immediately on the President of this republic receiving official information of the acceptance of this constitution by the Congress of the United States, he shall issue his proclamation, convening, at an early day, the legislature of the State of Texas at the seat of government established under this constitution, and after the said legislature shall have organized, the speaker of the house of representatives shall, in presence of both branches of the legislature, open the returns of the elections for governor and lieutenant-governor, count and compare the votes, and declare the names of the persons who shall be elected to the offices of governor and lieutenant-governor, who shall forthwith be installed in their respective offices; and the legisla-ture shall proceed, as early as practicable, to elect Senators to represent this State in the Senate of the United States, and also provide for the election of Representatives to the Congress of the United States. The legislature shall also adopt such measures as may be required to cede to the United States, at the proper time, all public edifices, fortifications, barracks, ports, harbors, navy and navy-yards, docks, magazines, arms and armaments, and all other property and means pertaining to the public defence now belonging to the Republic of Texas, and to make the necessary preparations for transferring to the said United States all custom-houses and other places for the col-lection of impost duties and other foreign revenues.

SEC. 9. It shall be the duty of the President of Texas, immediately after the inau-guration of the governor, to deliver to him all records, public money, documents, archives, and public property of every description whatsoever under the control of the executive branch of the government; and the governor shall dispose of the same in such manner as the legislature may direct.

SEC. 10. That no inconvenience may result from the change of government, it is declared that the laws of this republic relative to the duties of officers, both civil and military, of the same shall remain in full force, and the duties of their several offices shall be performed in conformity with the existing laws, until the organization of the government of the State under this constitution, or until the first day of the meeting of the legislature; that then the offices of President, Vice-President, of the President's cabinet, foreign ministers, chargés and agents, and others repugnant to this constitution, shall be superseded by the same, and that all others shall be holden and exercised until they expire by their own limitation, or be superseded by the authority of this constitution, or laws made in pursuance thereof.

SEC. 11. In case of any disability on the part of the President of the Republic of Texas to act as herein required, it shall be the duty of the secretary of state of the Republic of Texas, and in case of disability on the part of the secretary of state, then it shall be the duty of the attorney-general of the Republic of Texas, to perform the duties assigned to the President.

SEC. 12. The first general election for governor, lieutenant-governor, and members of the legislature, after the organization of the government, shall take place on the first Monday in November, one thousand eight hundred and forty-seven, and shall be held biennially thereafter on the first Monday in November until otherwise provided by the legislature, and the governor and lieutenant-governor elected in December next shall hold their offices until the installation in office of the governor and lieutenant-governor to be elected in the year one thousand eight hundred and forty-seven.

SEC. 13. The ordinance passed by the convention on the fourth day of July, assenting to the overtures for the annexation of Texas to the United States, shall be attached to this constitution and form a part of the same.

Done in convention by the deputies of the people of Texas, at the city of Austin, this twenty-seventh day of August, in the year of our Lord one thousand eight hundred and forty-five.

THOMAS J. RUSK, *President.*

[Doc. No. 8]

Resolution of December 29, 1845

Dec. 29, 1845.

[No. 1.] — *Joint Resolution for the Admission of the State of Texas into the Union.*

Preamble.

WHEREAS the Congress of the United States, by a joint resolution approved March the first, eighteen hundred and forty-five, did consent that the territory properly included within, and rightfully belonging to, the Republic of Texas, might be erected into a new State, to be called *The State of Texas*, with a republican form of government, to be adopted by the people of said republic, by deputies in convention assembled, with the consent of the existing government, in order that the same might be admitted as one of the States of the Union; which consent of Congress was given upon certain conditions specified in the first and second sections of said joint resolution; and whereas the people of the said Republic of Texas, by deputies in convention assembled, with the consent of the existing government, did adopt a constitution, and erect a new State with a republican form of government, and, in the name of the people of Texas, and by their authority, did ordain and declare that they assented to and accepted the proposals, conditions, and guaranties contained in said first and second sections of said resolution: and whereas the said constitution, with the proper evidence of its adoption by the people of the Republic of Texas, has been transmitted to the President of the United States and laid before Congress, in conformity to the provisions of said joint resolution: Therefore —

Texas admitted into the Union.

Resolved by the Senate and House of Representatives of the United States of America in Congress assembled, That the State of Texas shall be one, and is hereby declared to be one, of the United States of America, and admitted into the Union on an equal footing with the original States in all respects whatever.

To be entitled to two representatives.

SEC. 2. *And be it further resolved*, That until the representatives in Congress shall be apportioned according to an actual enumeration of the inhabitants of the United States, the State of Texas shall be entitled to choose two representatives.

APPROVED, December 29, 1845.

[Doc. No. 9]

Constitution of 1866

CONSTITUTION OF TEXAS—1866.*

We, the people of Texas, acknowledging with gratitude the grace and beneficence of God in permitting us to make a choice of our form of government, do ordain and establish this constitution.

ARTICLE I.

BILL OF RIGHTS.

That the general, great, and essential principles of liberty and free government may be recognized and established, we declare that—

SECTION 1. All political power is inherent in the people, and all free governments are founded on their authority and instituted for their benefit, and they have, at all times, the unalienable right to alter, reform, or abolish their form of government, in such manner as they may think expedient.

SEC. 2. All freemen, when they form a social compact, have equal rights; and no man, or set of men, is entitled to exclusive, separate public emoluments or privileges but in consideration of public services.

SEC. 3. No religious test shall ever be required as a qualification to any office or public trust in this State.

SEC. 4. All men have a natural and indefeasible right to worship God according to the dictates of their own consciences; no man shall be compelled to attend, erect, or support any place of worship, or to maintain any ministry, against his consent; no human authority ought, in any case whatever, to control or interfere with the rights of conscience in matters of religion, and no preference shall ever be given, by law, to any religious societies or mode of worship; but it shall be the duty of the legislature to pass such laws as shall be necessary to protect every religious denomination in the peaceable enjoyment of their own mode of public worship.

---

* This constitution was framed by a convention which assembled at Austin in March, 1866, and completed its labors April 2, 1866. It was submitted to the people June 25, 1866, and ratified by 34,794 votes against 11,235 votes. The convention also adopted twenty-nine ordinances, among which the more important were the following: Declaring the ordinance of secession null and void; declaring the war debt void, and for other purposes; assuming the direct tax levied upon the State by the United States; consenting to a division of the State, and the formation of one or more new States within its limits; soliciting the Federal Government to construct certain railroads within their territory.

Sec. 5. Every citizen shall be at liberty to speak, write, or publish his opinions on any subject, being responsible for the abuse of that privilege; and no law shall ever be passed curtailing the liberty of speech or of the press.

Sec. 6. In prosecutions for the publication of papers investigating the official conduct of officers or men in a public capacity, or when the matter published is proper for public information, the truth thereof may be given in evidence; and, in all indictments for libels, the jury shall have the right to determine the law and the facts under the direction of the court, as in other cases.

Sec. 7. The people shall be secure in their persons, houses, papers, and possessions from all unreasonable seizures or searches; and no warrant to search any place, or to seize any person or thing, shall issue without describing them as near as may be; nor without probable cause, supported by oath or affirmation.

Sec. 8. In all criminal prosecutions the accused shall have a speedy public trial, by an impartial jury; he shall not be compelled to give evidence against himself; he shall have the right of being heard by himself or counsel, or both; shall be confronted with the witnesses against him, and shall have compulsory process for obtaining witnesses in his favor; and no person shall be holden to answer for any criminal charge but on indictment or information, except in cases arising in the land or naval forces, or offences against the laws regulating the militia: *Provided*, That in criminal prosecutions, the punishment whereof shall be fine not exceeding one hundred dollars and imprisonment not exceeding thirty days, or either, or any less punishment, the accused may be tried for the same by a jury, or otherwise, as the legislature may provide.

Sec. 9. All prisoners shall be bailable by sufficient sureties, unless for capital offences, when the proof is evident; but this provision shall not be so construed as to prohibit bail after indictment found, upon an examination of the evidence by a judge of the supreme or district court, upon the return of a writ of *habeas corpus*, returnable in the county where the offence is committed; or to such other counties as the same may by consent of parties be made returnable.

Sec. 10. The privilege of the writ of *habeas corpus* shall not be suspended, except when, in case of rebellion or invasion, the public safety may require it.

Sec. 11. Excessive bail shall not be required, nor excessive fines imposed, nor cruel or unusual punishment inflicted. All courts shall be open; and every person, for an injury done him in his lands, goods, person, or reputation, shall have remedy by due course of law.

Sec. 12. No person, for the same offence, shall be twice put in jeopardy of life or limb; nor shall a person be again put upon trial for the same offence, after a verdict of not guilty; and the right of trial by jury shall remain inviolate.

Sec. 13. Every citizen shall have the right to keep and bear arms in the lawful defence of himself or the State.

Sec. 14. No bill of attainder, *ex post facto* law, retroactive law, or any law impairing the obligation of contracts shall be made, and no person's property shall be taken, or applied to public use, without adequate compensation being made, unless by the consent of such person.

Sec. 15. No person shall ever be imprisoned for debt.

Sec. 16. No citizen of this State shall be deprived of life, liberty, property, or privileges, outlawed, exiled, or in any manner disfranchised, except by due course of the law of the land.

Sec. 17. The military shall, at all times, be subordinate to the civil authority.

Sec. 18. Perpetuities and monopolies are contrary to the genius of a free government, and shall never be allowed; nor shall the law of primogeniture or entailments ever be in force in this State.

Sec. 19. The citizens shall have the right, in a peaceable manner, to assemble together for their common good, and to apply to those invested with the powers of government for redress of grievances, or other purposes, by petition, address, or remonstrance.

Sec. 20. No power of suspending laws in this State shall be exercised, except by the legislature or its authority.

SEC. 21. To guard against transgressions of the high powers herein delegated, we declare that everything in this bill of rights is excepted out of the general powers of government, and shall forever remain inviolate; and all laws contrary thereto, or to the following provisions, shall be void.

ARTICLE II.
DIVISION OF THE POWERS OF GOVERNMENT.

The powers of the government of the State of Texas shall be divided into three distinct departments, and each of them to be confided to a separate body of magistracy, to wit: those which are legislative, to one; those which are executive, to another; and those which are judicial, to another; and no person, or collection of persons, being of one of those departments, shall exercise any power properly attached to either of the others, except in the instances herein expressly permitted.

ARTICLE III.
LEGISLATIVE DEPARTMENT.

SECTION 1. Every free male person who shall have attained the age of twenty-one years, and who shall be a citizen of the United States, and shall have resided in this State one year next preceding an election, and the last six months within the district, county, city, or town in which he offers to vote, (Indians not taxed, Africans and descendants of Africans excepted,) shall be deemed a qualified elector; and should such qualified elector happen to be in any other county situated in the district in which he resides at the time of an election, he shall be permitted to vote for any district officer: *Provided*, That the qualified electors shall be permitted to vote anywhere in the State for State officers: *And provided further*, That no soldier, seaman, or marine in the Army or Navy of the United States shall be entitled to vote at any election created by this constitution.

SEC. 2. Electors in all cases shall be privileged from arrest during their attendance at elections, and in going to and returning from the same, except in cases of treason, felony, or breach of the peace.

SEC. 3. The legislative powers of this State shall be vested in two distinct branches; the one to be styled the senate and the other the house of representatives, and both together the legislature of the State of Texas. The style of all laws shall be, *"Be it enacted by the legislature of the State of Texas."*

SEC. 4. The members of the house of representatives shall be chosen by the qualified electors, and their term of office shall be two years from the day of the general election; and the sessions of the legislature shall be biennial, at such times as shall be prescribed by law.

SEC. 5. No person shall be a representative unless he be a white citizen of the United States, and shall be a qualified elector at the time ot his election, and a resident of the State for five years next preceding his election, and the last year thereof a citizen of the county, city, town, or district for which he shall be chosen.

SEC. 6. All elections by the people shall be held at such time and places, in the several counties, cities, or towns, as are now, or may hereafter be, designated by law.

SEC. 7. The senators shall be chosen by the qualified electors for the term of four years; and shall be divided by lot into two classes, as nearly equal as can be. The seats of senators of the first class shall be vacated at the expiration of the first two years; and of the second class at the expiration of four years; so that one-half thereof shall be chosen biennially thereafter.

SEC. 8. Such mode of classifying new additional senators shall be observed as will as nearly as possible preserve an equality of number in each class.

SEC. 9. When a senatorial district shall be composed of two or more counties, it shall not be separated by any county belonging to another district.

SEC. 10. No person shall be a senator unless he be a white citizen of the United States, and shall have been a qualified elector of this State at the time of his election, and a resident of the State five years next preceding the election; and the last year thereof a resident of the district for which he shall be chosen, and have attained the age of thirty years.

SEC. 11. The house of representatives, when assembled, shall elect a speaker and its other officers, and the senate shall choose a president·for the time being and its other officers. Each house shall judge of the qualifications and elections of its own members, but contested elections shall be .determined in such manner as shall be directed by law; two-thirds of each house shall constitute a quorum to do business, but a smaller number may adjourn from day to day, and compel the attendance of absent members, in such manner and under such penalties as each house may provide.

SEC. 12. Each house may determine the rules of its own proceedings, punish members for disorderly conduct, and, with the consent of two-thirds, expel a member, but not a second time for the same offence.

SEC. 13. Each house shall keep a·journal of its own proceedings, and publish the same; and the yeas and nays of the members of either house on any question shall, at the desire of any three members present, be entered on the journal.

SEC. 14. When vacancies happen in either house, the governor, or the person exercising the power of the governor, shall issue writs of election to fill such vacancies; and should the governor fail to issue a writ of election to fill such vacancies, the returning officer for the district or county shall be authorized to order an election for that purpose.

SEC. 15. The senators and representatives shall in all cases, except in treason, felony, or breach of the peace, be privileged from arrest during the session of the legislature, and in going to and returning from the same, allowing one day for every twenty miles such member may reside from the place at which the legislature is convened.

SEC. 16. Each house may punish by imprisonment, during the session, any person not a member for disrespectful or disorderly conduct in its presence, or for obstructing any of its proceedings: *Provided*, Such imprisonment shall not at any one time exceed forty-eight hours.

SEC. 17. The doors of each house shall be kept open.

SEC. 18. Neither house shall, without the consent of the other, adjourn for more than three days, nor to any other place than that in which they may be sitting, without the concurrence of both houses.

SEC. 19. Bills may originate in either house, and be amended, altered, or rejected by the other; but no bill shall have the force of a law until, on three several days, it be read in each house, and free discussion be allowed thereon, unless, in case of great emergency, four-fifths of the house in which the bill shall be pending may deem it expedient to dispense with this rule; and every bill, having passed both houses, shall be signed by the speaker and president of their respective houses.

SEC. 20. All bills for raising revenue shall originate in the house of representatives, but the senate may amend or reject them as other bills.

SEC. 21. After a bill or resolution has been rejected by either branch of the legislature, no bill or resolution containing the same substance shall be passed into a law during the same session.

SEC. 22. Each member of the legislature shall receive from the public treasury a compensation for his services, which may be increased or diminished by law; but no increase of compensation shall take effect during the session at which such increase shall be made.

SEC. 23. No senator or representative shall, during the term for which he may be elected, be eligible to any office of profit under this State, which shall have been created or the emoluments of which may have been increased during such term; and no member of either house of the legislature shall, during the term for which he is elected, although he may resign his seat as such member, shall be eligible to any office or place, the appointment to which may be made, in whole or in part, by either branch of the legislature; nor shall members of either house vote for a member of their own body, though he resign his seat in the same, for Senator in the Congress of the United States; nor shall members thereof be capable of voting for a member of their own body for any office whatever, except it be for speaker of the house of representatives and president for the time being of the senate, who shall be elected from their respective bodies.

SEC. 24. No judge of any court of law or equity, secretary of state, attorney-general, clerk of any court of record, sheriff or collector, or any person holding a lucrative office under the United States, or this State, or any foreign government, shall be eligible to the legislature, nor shall at the same time hold or exercise any two offices, agencies, or appointments of trust or profit under this State: *Provided*, That offices of the militia, to which there is attached no annual salary, the office of notary public, and the office of justice of the peace shall not be deemed lucrative, and that one person may hold two or more county offices, if so provided by the legislature.

SEC. 25. No person who at any time may have been a collector of taxes, or who may have been otherwise intrusted with public money, shall be eligible to the legislature, or to any office of profit or trust under the State government, until he shall have obtained a discharge for the amount of such collections, and for all public moneys with which he may have been intrusted.

SEC. 26. Ministers of the gospel, being by their profession dedicated to God and the care of souls, ought not to be diverted from the great duties of their functions; therefore, no minister of the gospel, or priest of any denomination whatever, shall be eligible to the legislature.

SEC. 27. Elections for senators and representatives shall be general throughout the State, and shall be regulated by law.

SEC. 28. The legislature shall cause an enumeration to be made every ten years, commencing on the sixth day of February, A. D. 1875, of all the inhabitants (including Indians taxed) of the State, designating particularly the number of qualified electors and the age, sex, and color of all others, herein following the classification of the United States census, and the whole number of representatives shall, at the several periods of making such enumeration, be fixed by the legislature, and apportioned among the several counties, cities, or towns, according to the number of white population in each; and shall not be less than forty-five, nor more than ninety: *Provided*, That there shall be an enumeration and an apportionment made in the year 1870, in the manner here indicated.

SEC. 29. Until changed by law, the act of apportionment passed the 6th day of February, A. D. 1860, by the legislature of this State, shall remain in force.

SEC. 30. The whole number of senators shall, at the next session after the several periods of making the enumeration, be fixed by the legislature, and apportioned among the several districts to be established by law, according to the number of qualified electors, and shall never be less than nineteen, nor more than thirty-three.

SEC. 31. The members of the legislature shall, at their first session hereafter, receive from the treasury of the State, as their compensation, eight dollars for each day they shall be in attendance, and eight dollars for each twenty-five miles in travelling to and from the seat of government. The above rates of compensation shall remain till changed by law.

SEC. 32. The legislature shall proceed as early as practicable to elect Senators to represent this State in the Senate of the United States, and also provide for the election of Representatives to the Congress of the United States.

SEC. 33. The city of Austin is hereby declared to be the seat of government of this State until removed by an election of the people; and the title to the tract of land surveyed by virtue of the head-right certificate of Samuel Goucher, for one-third of a league, which was selected and condemned to the use of the Republic of Texas, under an act of the Republic of Texas entitled "An act for the permanent location of the seat of government," approved the 14th day of January, A. D. 1839, be, and the same is hereby, confirmed; any irregularity or failure to make proper parties, or other defects in the proceedings had under said act, to the contrary notwithstanding: *Provided, nevertheless*, That the lawful owner of said land, his heirs, assigns, or legal representatives, may, at any time within one year from the adoption of this constitution, institute proceedings and have compensation as provided by act of the legislature of the State of Texas, entitled "An act for quieting the title to real estate in the city of Austin," approved 18th December, 1857.

ARTICLE IV.

JUDICIAL DEPARTMENT.

SECTION 1. The judicial power of this State shall be vested in one supreme court, in district courts, in county courts, and in such corporation courts and other inferior courts or tribunals as the legislature may from time to time ordain and establish. The legislature may establish criminal courts, in the principal cities within this State, with such criminal jurisdiction, coextensive with the limits of the county wherein such city may be situated, and under such regulations as may be prescribed by law, and the judge therein may preside over the courts of one or more cities, as the legislature may direct.

SEC. 2. The supreme court shall consist of five justices, any three of whom shall constitute a quorum. They shall be elected by the qualified voters of the State at a general election for State or county officers, and they shall elect from their own number a presiding officer, to be styled the chief justice; they shall have arrived at the age of thirty-five years at the time of election, shall hold their offices for the term of ten years, and each of them shall receive an annual salary of at least four thousand five hundred dollars, which shall not be increased or diminished during his term of office.

SEC. 3. The supreme court shall have appellate jurisdiction only, which shall be coextensive with the limits of the State; but in criminal cases below the grade of felony, and in appeals from interlocutory judgments, with such exceptions and under such regulations as the legislature shall make; and the supreme court and the judges thereof shall have power to issue the writ of *habeas corpus*, and under such regulations as may be prescribed by law; the said court and the judges thereof may issue the writ of *mandamus*, and such other writs as may be necessary to enforce its own jurisdiction. The supreme court shall also have power upon affidavits, or otherwise, as by the court may be thought proper, to ascertain in such matters of fact as may be necessary to the proper exercise of its jurisdiction. The supreme court shall sit for the transaction of business from the first Monday of October until the last Saturday of June of every year, at the capital, and at not more than two other places in the State.

SEC. 4. The supreme court shall appoint its own clerks, who shall give bond in such manner as is now, or may hereafter be, required by law, shall hold their offices for four years, and shall be subject to removal by the said court for good cause, entered of record on the minutes of said court.

SEC. 5. The State shall be divided into convenient judicial districts. For each district there shall be elected by the qualified voters thereof, at a general election for State or county officers, a judge, who shall reside in the same, shall hold his office for the term of eight years, shall receive an annual salary of not less than three thousand five hundred dollars, which shall not be increased or diminished during his term of service, and shall hold the courts at one place in each county in the district at least twice in each year, in such manner as may be prescribed by law.

SEC. 6. The district court shall have original jurisdiction of all criminal cases; of all suits in behalf of the State to recover penalties, forfeitures, and escheats; of all cases of divorce; of all suits to recover damages for slander or defamation of character; of all suits for the trial of title to land; of all suits for the enforcement of liens; of all suits for the trial of the right of property, levied on by virtue of any writ of execution, sequestration, or attachment, when the property levied on shall be equal to or exceed in value one hundred dollars; and of all suits, complaints, or pleas whatever, without regard to any distinction between law and equity, when the matter in controversy shall be valued at, or amount to, one hundred dollars, exclusive of interest; and the said courts and the judges thereof shall have power to issue writs of injunction, *certiorari*, and all other writs necessary to enforce their own jurisdiction, and to give them a general superintendence and control over inferior tribunals. The district courts shall have appellate jurisdiction in cases originating in inferior courts, which may be final in such cases as the legislature may prescribe; and original and appellate jurisdiction and general control over the county court established in each county, for appointing guardians, granting letters testamentary and of administration; for settling the accounts of executors, administrators, and guardians, and for the transaction of business appertaining to estates, and original jurisdiction and general control over executors, administrators, guardians, and minors, under such regulations as may be prescribed by law.

SEC. 7. There shall be a clerk of the district court for each county, who shall be elected by the qualified voters for members of the legislature, and who shall hold his office for four years, subject to removal by information, or by indictment of a grand jury and conviction by a petit jury. In case of vacancy, the judge of the district court shall have the power to appoint a clerk, until a regular election can be held.

SEC. 8. In the trial of all causes in equity in the district courts, the plaintiff or defendant shall, upon application made in open court, have the right of trial by jury, to be governed by the rules and regulations prescribed in trials at law.

SEC. 9. All judges of the supreme and district courts shall, by virtue of their offices, be conservators of the peace throughout the State. The style of all writs and process shall be "The State of Texas." All prosecutions shall be carried on in the name and by the authority of the State of Texas, and conclude "against the peace and dignity of the State."

SEC. 10. In the case of a vacancy in the offices of justice of the supreme court, judges of the district court, attorney-general, and district attorneys, the governor of the State shall have power to fill the same by appointment, which shall continue in force until the office can be filled at the next general election for State or county officers, and the successor duly qualified.

SEC. 11. The judges of the supreme and district courts shall be removed by the governor, on the address of two-thirds of each house of the legislature, for wilful neglect of duty or other reasonable cause, which shall not be sufficient ground for impeachment: *Provided, however*, That the cause or causes for which such removal shall be required shall be stated at length in such address, and entered on the journals of each house: *And provided further*, That the cause or causes shall be notified to the judge so intended to be removed; and he shall be admitted to a hearing in his own defence before any vote for such address shall pass. And in all such cases the vote shall be taken by yeas and nays, and entered on the journals of each house respectively.

SEC. 12. No judge shall sit in any case wherein he may be interested, or where either of the parties may be connected with him by affinity or consanguinity, within such degrees as may be prescribed by law, or where he shall have been of counsel in the case. When the supreme court, or any three of its members, shall be thus disqualified to hear and determine any case or cases in said court, or when no judgment can be rendered in any case or cases in said court, by reason of the equal division of opinion of said judges, the same shall be certified to the governor of the State, who shall immediately commission the requisite number of persons, learned in the law, for the trial and determination of said case or cases. When a judge of the district court is thus disqualified, the parties may, by consent, appoint a proper person to try the said case; or, upon their failing to do so, a competent person shall be appointed to try the same in the county where it is pending, in such manner as may be prescribed by law. And the district judges may exchange districts, or hold courts for each other, when they may deem it expedient, and shall do so when directed by law. The disqualification of judges of inferior tribunals shall be remedied, and vacancies in their offices shall be filled, as prescribed by law.

SEC. 13. An attorney-general shall be elected by the people, who shall reside at the capital of the State during his continuance in office, whose duties shall be prescribed by law, who shall hold his office for four years, and who, in addition to perquisites, shall receive an annual salary of three thousand dollars, which shall not be increased or diminished during his term of office.

SEC. 14. There shall be a district attorney for each judicial district in the State, elected by the qualified electors of the district, who shall reside in the district for which he shall be elected, shall hold his office for four years, and, together with the perquisites prescribed by law, shall receive an annual salary of one thousand dollars, which shall not be increased or diminished during his term of office.

SEC. 15. There shall be established in each county in the State an inferior tribunal, styled the county court; and there shall be elected, by the persons in each county who are qualified to vote for members of the legislature, a judge of the county court, who shall be a conservator of the peace, who shall hold his office for four years, and who shall receive such compensation as may be prescribed by law, and who may be removed from office for neglect of duty, incompetency, or malfeasance, in such manner as may be prescribed by law.

SEC. 16. The county court shall have jurisdiction of all misdemeanors and petty offences, as the same are now, or may hereafter be, defined by law; of such civil cases, where the matter in controversy shall not exceed five hundred dollars, exclusive of interest, under such regulations, limitations, and restrictions as may be prescribed by law, without regard to any distinction between law and equity; to probate wills, to appoint guardians of minors, idiots, lunatics, and persons *non compos mentis;* to grant letters testamentary and of administration; to settle the accounts of executors, administrators, and guardians; to transact all business appertaining to the estates of deceased persons, minors, idiots, lunatics, and persons *non compos mentis*, including the settlement, partition, and distribution of such estates; and to apprentice minors under such regulations as may be prescribed by law. One term of the county court shall be held in each county at least once in every two months; and the legislature may provide for the appointment of a county attorney to represent the State and county in said court, whose term of office, duties, and compensation shall be such as may be prescribed by law.

SEC. 17. There shall be elected in each county in the State, by the persons qualified to vote for members of the legislature, four county commissioners, whose term of office shall be four years, who, with the judge of the county court, shall constitute and be styled the police court for the county, whose powers, duties, and mode of action, in regulating, promoting, and protecting the public interest relating to the county, shall be the same as that now prescribed by law for the commissioners' court of roads and revenue, until otherwise provided for and regulated by the legislature.

SEC. 18. There shall be elected for each county, by the qualified voters, a county clerk, who shall hold his office for four years, who shall be the clerk of the county and police courts, whose duties and perquisites and fees of office shall be prescribed by the legislature, and a vacancy in whose office shall be filled by the judge of the county court, until the next general election for county or State offices, who may be removed from office for such cause and in such manner as may be prescribed by law.

SEC. 19. There shall be elected a convenient number of justices of the peace, who shall have such civil and criminal jurisdiction as shall be provided by law, where the. matter in controversy shall not exceed in value one hundred dollars, exclusive of interest; also one sheriff, one coroner, and a sufficient number of constables, who shall hold their offices for four years, to be elected by the qualified voters of the district or county, as the legislature may direct. Justices of the peace, sheriffs, and coroners shall be commissioned by the governor. The sheriff shall not be eligible more than eight years in every twelve.

SEC. 20. In all cases of law or equity, where the matter in controversy shall be valued at or exceed twenty dollars, the right of trial by jury shall be preserved.

ARTICLE V.

EXECUTIVE DEPARTMENT.

SECTION 1. The supreme executive power of this State shall be vested in the chief magistrate, who shall be styled "the governor of the State of Texas."

SEC. 2. The governor shall be elected by the qualified electors of the State, at the time and places of election for members of the legislature.

SEC. 3. The returns of every election for governor, until otherwise provided by law, shall be made out, sealed up, and transmitted to the seat of government, and directed to the speaker of the house of representatives, who shall, during the first week of the session of the legislature thereafter, open and publish them in the presence of both houses of the legislature; the person having the highest number of votes, and being constitutionally eligible, shall be declared by the speaker, under the direction of the legislature, to be governor; but if two or more persons shall have the highest and an equal number of votes, one of them shall be immediately chosen governor, by joint vote of both houses of the legislature. Contested elections for governor shall be determined by both houses of the legislature.

SEC. 4. The governor shall hold his office for the term of four years from the regular time of installation, and until his successor shall be duly qualified, but shall not be eligible for more than eight years in any term of twelve years; he shall be at least thirty years of age, shall be a citizen of the United States, or a citizen of the State of Texas at the time of the adoption of this constitution, and shall have resided in the same six years immediately preceding his election, and shall be inaugurated on the first Thursday after the organization of the legislature, or as soon thereafter as practicable.

SEC. 5. He shall, at stated times, receive a compensation for his services, which shall not be increased or diminished during the term for which he may have been elected. He shall receive an annual salary of four thousand dollars, until otherwise provided by law.

SEC. 6. The governor shall be commander-in-chief of the army and navy of this State, and of the militia, except when they shall be called into the service of the United States.

SEC. 7. He may require information, in writing, from the officers of the executive department on any subject relating to the duties of their respective offices.

SEC. 8. He may, by proclamation, on extraordinary occasions, convene the legislature at the seat of government, or at a different place if that should be dangerous by reason of disease or the public enemy. In case of disagreement between the two houses with respect to adjournment, he may adjourn them to such time as he shall think proper, not beyond the day of the next regular meeting of the legislature.

SEC. 9. He shall from time to time give to the legislature information, in writing, of the state of the government, and recommend to their consideration such measures as he may deem expedient.

SEC. 10. He shall take care that the laws be faithfully executed.

SEC. 11. In all criminal cases, except in those of treason and impeachment, he shall have power, after conviction, to grant reprieves and pardons; and, under such rules as the legislature may prescribe, he shall have power to remit fines and forfeitures. In cases of treason, he shall have power, by and with the advice and consent of the senate, to grant reprieves and pardons; and he may, in the recess of the senate, respite the sentence until the end of the next session of the legislature.

SEC. 12. There shall also be a lieutenant-governor, who shall be chosen at every election for governor, by the same persons and in the same manner, continue in office for the same time, and possess the same qualifications. In voting for governor or lieutenant-governor, the electors shall distinguish for whom they vote as governor and for whom as lieutenant-governor. The lieutenant-governor shall, by virtue of his office, be president of the senate, and have, when in committee of the whole, a right to debate and vote on all questions, and when the senate is equally divided to give the casting vote. In case of death, resignation, removal from office, inability or refusal of the governor to serve, or of his impeachment or absence from the State, the lieutenant-governor shall exercise the powers and authority appertaining to the office of governor, until another be chosen at the periodical election, and be duly qualified, or until the governor impeached, absent, or disabled shall be acquitted, return, or his disability be removed.

SEC. 13. Whenever the government shall be administered by the lieutenant-governor, or he shall be unable to attend as president of the senate, the senate shall elect one of their own members as president for the time being. And if, during the vacancy of the office of governor, the lieutenant-governor shall die, resign, refuse to serve, or be removed from office, or be unable to serve, or if he shall be impeached or absent from the State, the president of the senate for the time being shall in like manner administer the government until he shall be superseded by a governor or lieutenant-governor. The lieutenant-governor shall, whilst he acts as president of the senate, receive for his services the same compensation which shall be allowed to the speaker of the house of representatives, and no more; and during the time he administers the government as governor shall receive the same compensation which the governor would have received had he been employed in the duties of his office, and no more. The president for the time being of the senate shall, during the time he administers the government, receive in like manner the same compensation which the governor would have received had he been employed in the duties of his office. If the lieutenant-governor shall be required to administer the government, and shall, whilst in such administration, die, resign, or be absent from the State during the recess of the legislature, it shall be the duty of the secretary of state to convene the senate, for the purpose of choosing a president for the time being.

SEC. 14. There shall be a seal of the State, which shall be kept by the governor. and used by him officially; the said seal shall be a star of five points encircled by an olive and live-oak branches, and the words "The State of Texas."

SEC. 15. All commissions shall be in the name and by the authority of the State of Texas, be sealed with the State seal, signed by the governor, and attested by the secretary of state.

SEC. 16. There shall be a secretary of state, who shall be appointed by the governor, by and with the advice and consent of the senate, and shall continue in office during the term of service of the governor-elect. He shall keep a fair register of all official acts and proceedings of the governor, and shall, when required, lay the same, and all papers, minutes, and vouchers relative thereto, before the legislature, or either house thereof, and shall perform such other duties as may be required of him by law.

SEC. 17. Every bill which shall have passed both houses of the legislature shall be presented to the governor; if he approve, he shall sign it; but if not, he shall return it, with his objections, to the house in which it shall have originated, who shall enter the objections at large upon the journals and proceed to reconsider it. If, after such reconsideration, two-thirds of the members present shall agree to pass the bill, it shall be sent, with the objection, to the other house, by which it shall likewise be reconsidered. If approved by two-thirds of the members present of that house, it shall become a law; but in such cases the votes of both houses shall be determined by yeas and nays, and the names of the members voting for or against the bill shall be entered on the journals of each house respectively. If any bill shall not be returned by the governor within five days, Sundays excepted, after it shall have been presented to him, the same shall be a law in like manner as if he had signed it. Every bill presented to the governor one day previous to the adjournment of the legislature, and not returned to the house in which it originated before its adjournment, shall become a law, and have the same force and effect as if signed by the governor. The governor may approve any appropriation and disapprove any other appropriation in the same bill. In such case he shall, in signing the bill, designate the appropriations disapproved, and shall return a copy of such appropriations, with his objections, to the house in which the bill shall have originated; and the same proceedings shall then be had as in the case of other bills disapproved by the governor; but if the legislature has adjourned before the bill is returned to the house, he shall return the same to the secretary of state, with his objections, and also to the next session of the legislature.

SEC. 18. Every order, resolution, or vote to which the concurrence of both houses of the legislature may be necessary, except on questions of adjournment, shall be presented to the governor, and before it shall take effect be approved by him, or, being disapproved, shall be repassed by both houses according to the rules and limitations prescribed in the case of a bill.

SEC. 19. The governor, by and with the advice and consent of two-thirds of the senate, shall appoint a convenient number of notaries public, not exceeding six for each county; who, in addition to such duties as are prescribed by law, shall discharge such other duties as the legislature may from time to time prescribe.

SEC. 20. Nominations to fill all vacancies that may have occurred during the recess shall be made to the senate during the first ten days of its session. And should any nomination so made be rejected, the same individual shall not again be nominated during the session to fill the same office; and should the governor fail to make nominations to fill any vacancy during the session of the senate, such vacancy shall not be filled by the governor until the next meeting of the senate.

SEC. 21. The governor shall reside, during the session of the legislature, at the place where the session may be held, and at all other times wherever, in their opinion, the public good may require.

SEC. 22. No person holding the office of governor shall hold any other office or commission, civil or military.

SEC. 23. There shall be elected by the qualified electors of this State, in the manner prescribed by law, a comptroller of public accounts and a State treasurer, each of whom shall hold his office for the term of four years; and in case of a vacancy in either of said offices, the governor shall have power to fill the same by appointment, which shall continue in force until the office can be filled at the next general election for State and county officers and the successor duly qualified.

ARTICLE VI.

MILITIA.

SECTION 1. The legislature shall provide by law for organizing and disciplining the militia of the State, in such manner as they shall deem expedient, not incompatible with the Constitution and laws of the United States in relation thereto.

SEC. 2. Any person who conscientiously scruples to bear arms shall not be compelled to do so, but shall pay an equivalent for personal service.

SEC. 3. No licensed minister of the gospel shall be required to perform military duty, work on roads, or serve on juries in this State.

SEC. 4. The governor shall have power to call forth the militia to execute the laws of the State, to suppress insurrections, and to repel invasion.

ARTICLE VII.

GENERAL PROVISIONS.

SECTION 1. Members of the legislature and all officers, before they enter upon the duties of their offices, shall take the following oath or affirmation: "I, A. B., do solemnly swear [or affirm] that I will faithfully and impartially discharge and perform all the duties imcumbent on me as ———, according to the best of my skill and ability, agreeable to the constitution and laws of the United States and of this State; and I do further solemnly swear [or affirm] that, since the adoption of this constitution by the Congress of the United States, I, being a citizen of this State, have not fought a duel with deadly weapons, within this State nor out of it, nor have I sent or accepted a challenge to fight a duel with deadly weapons, nor have I acted as second in carrying a challenge, or aided, advised, or assisted any person thus offending: So help me God."

SEC. 2. Treason against this State shall consist only in levying war against it, or in adhering to its enemies, giving them aid and comfort; and no person shall be convicted of treason unless on the testimony of two witnesses to the same overt act, or his own confession in open court.

SEC. 3. Every person shall be disqualified from holding any office of trust or profit in this State who shall have been convicted of having given or offered a bribe to procure his election or appointment.

SEC. 4. Laws shall be made to exclude from office, serving on juries, and from the right of suffrage those who shall hereafter be convicted of bribery, perjury, forgery, or other high crimes. The privilege of free suffrage shall be supported by laws regulating elections, and prohibiting, under adequate penalties, all undue influence thereon from power, bribery, tumult, or other improper practice.

SEC. 5. Any citizen of this State who shall, after the adoption of this constitution, fight a duel with deadly weapons, or send or accept a challenge to fight a duel with deadly weapons, either within the State or out of it, or who shall act as second, or knowingly aid and assist in any manner those thus offending, shall be deprived of holding any office of trust or profit under this State.

SEC. 6. In all elections by the people, the vote shall be by ballot, until the legisla ture shall otherwise direct; and in all elections by the senate and house of represent- atives, jointly or separately, the vote shall be given *viva voce*, except in the election of their officers.

SEC. 7. The legislature shall provide by law for the compensation of all officers, servants, agents, and public contractors, not provided for by this constitution, and shall not grant extra compensation to any officer, agent, servant, or public contractor after such public service shall have been performed, or contract entered into for the per- formance of the same; nor grant, by appropriation or otherwise, any amount of money out of the treasury of the State to any individual on a claim, real or pretended, where the same shall not have been provided for by preëxisting law: *Provided*, That nothing in this section shall be so construed as to affect the claims of persons against the Republic of Texas heretofore existing.

SEC. 8. No money shall be drawn from the treasury but in pursuance of specific appropriations made by law; nor shall any appropriation of money be made for a longer term than two years, except for purposes of education; and no appropriation for private or individual purposes, or for purposes of internal improvement, shall be made without the concurrence of two-thirds of both houses of the legislature. A regu- lar statement and account of the receipt and expenditures of all public money shall be published annually in such manner as shall be prescribed by law. And in no case shall the legislature have the power to issue treasury warrants, treasury notes, or paper of any description, intended to circulate as money.

SEC. 9. All civil officers shall reside within the State, and all district or county officers within their districts or counties, and shall keep their offices at such places therein as may be required by law.

SEC. 10. The duration of all offices, not fixed by this constitution, shall never exceed four years, (except the office of superintendent of the lunatic asylum, or other asylums that may be established by law, who shall continue in office during good behavior: *Provided*, That in all cases where the governor has the authority under this constitu- tion, or laws made in pursuance thereof, to appoint to office, he shall also have power to remove from the same for malfeasance in office, neglect of duty, or other good cause: *Provided*, That a statement of the cause shall, at the time of removal, be fur- nished the party interested, and a copy thereof shall also be recorded in the office of the secretary of state.)

SEC. 11. Absence on the business of this State, or of the United States, shall not forfeit a residence once obtained, so as to deprive any one of the right of suffrage, or of being elected or appointed to any office, under the exceptions contained in this constitution.

SEC. 12. The legislature shall have power to provide for deduction from the salaries of public officers who may neglect the performance of any duty that may be assigned them by law.

SEC. 13. No member of Congress, nor person holding or exercising any office of profit or trust under the United States, or either of them, or under any foreign power, shall be eligible as a member of the legislature, or hold or exercise any office of profit or trust under this State.

SEC. 14. The legislature shall provide for a change of venue in civil and criminal cases, and for the erection of a penitentiary at as early a day as practicable.

SEC. 15. It shall be the duty of the legislature to pass such laws as may be neces- sary and proper to decide differences by arbitration, when the parties shall elect that mode of trial.

SEC. 16. Within five years after the adoption of this constitution, the laws, civil and criminal, shall be revised, digested, arranged, and published, in such manner as the legislature shall direct; and a like revision, digest, and publication shall be made every ten years thereafter.

SEC. 17. No lottery shall be authorized by this State; and the buying or selling of lottery-tickets within this State is prohibited.

SEC. 18. No divorce shall be granted by the legislature.

SEC. 19. All property, both real and personal, of the wife, owned or claimed by her before marriage, and that acquired afterward by gift, devise, or descent, shall be her separate property; and laws shall be passed more clearly defining the rights of the wife in relation as well to her separate property as that held in common with her husband. Laws shall also be passed providing for the registration of the wife's separate property.

SEC. 20. The rights of property and of actions which have been acquired under the constitution and laws of the Republic of Texas shall not be divested; nor shall any rights or actions which have been divested, barred, or declared null and void by the constitution and laws of the Republic of Texas be reinvested, revived, or reinstated by this constitution; but the same shall remain precisely in the situation which they were before the adoption of this constitution.

SEC. 21. All claims, locations, surveys, grants, and titles to land which are declared null and void by the constitution of the Republic of Texas, are, and the same shall remain forever, null and void.

SEC. 22. The legislature shall have power to protect, by law, from forced sale a certain portion of the property of all heads of families. The homestead of a family not to exceed two hundred acres of land, (not included in a town or city,) or any town or city lot or lots, in value not to exceed two thousand dollars, shall not be subject to forced sale for any debts hereafter contracted, nor shall the owner, if a married man, be at liberty to alienate the same, unless by the consent of the wife, in such manner as the legislature may hereafter point out.

SEC. 23. The legislature shall provide in what cases officers shall continue to perform the duties of their offices until their successors shall be duly qualified.

SEC. 24. Every law enacted by the legislature shall embrace but one object, and that shall be expressed in the title.

SEC. 25. No law shall be revised or amended by reference to its title; but in such case the act revised, or section amended, shall be reënacted and published at length.

SEC. 26. No person shall hold or exercise at the same time more than one civil office of emolument, except that of justice of the peace.

SEC. 27. Taxation shall be equal and uniform throughout the State. All property in this State shall be taxed in proportion to its value, to be ascertained as directed by law, except such property as two-thirds of both houses of the legislature may think proper to exempt from taxation. The legislature shall have power to lay an income-tax, and to tax all persons pursuing any occupation, trade, or profession: *Provided*, That the term "occupation" shall not be construed to apply to pursuits either agricultural or mechanical.

SEC. 28. The legislature shall have power to provide by law for exemption from taxation, two hundred and fifty dollars' worth of household-furniture, or other property, belonging to each family in this State.

SEC. 29. The assessor and collector of taxes shall be appointed in such manner and under such regulations as the legislature may direct.

SEC. 30. No corporate body shall hereafter be created, renewed, or extended with banking or discounting privileges:

SEC. 31. No private corporation shall be created, unless the bill creating it shall be passed by two-thirds of both houses of the legislature; and two-thirds of the legislature shall have power to revoke and repeal all private corporations by making compensation for the franchise. And the State shall not be part owner of the stock or property belonging to any corporation.

SEC. 32. The legislature shall prohibit, by law, individuals from issuing bills, checks, promissory notes, or other paper to circulate as money.

SEC. 33. The aggregate amount of debts hereafter contracted by the legislature shall never exceed the sum of one hundred thousand dollars, except in case of war, to repel invasion, or suppress insurrections. And in no case shall any amount be borrowed, except by a vote of two-thirds of both houses of the legislature.

SEC. 34. The legislature may, from time to time, establish new counties for the convenience of the inhabitants of such new county or counties: *Provided*, That no new county shall be established which shall reduce the county or counties, or either of them, from which it shall be taken to a less area than nine hundred square miles, unless by consent of two-thirds of the legislature, nor shall any county be organized of less contents: *Provided further,* That all counties heretofore created are hereby declared to be legally-constituted counties. Every new county has the right of suffrage and representation, shall be considered as part of the county or counties from which it was taken until the next apportionment of representation thereafter: *Provided also,* That no new county shall be laid off when less than one hundred and twenty qualified jurors are at the time resident therein.

SEC. 35. No soldier shall, in time of peace, be quartered in the house, or within the inclosure, of any individual without the consent of the owner, nor in time of war but in a manner prescribed by law.

SEC. 36. A well-regulated system of internal improvements is calculated to develop the resources of the State and promote the happiness and prosperity of her citizens. Therefore the legislature shall have power, and it shall be its duty, to encourage the same; and the legislature shall have power to guarantee the bonds of railroad companies to any amount not exceeding in any case the sum of fifteen thousand dollars per mile: *Provided,* That in no case shall the State guarantee the payment of the bonds of any railroad company until such company shall have previously graded and prepared at least twenty-five miles of its roadway, ready to lay the iron rails thereon, and so on continuously, on each additional section of ten miles, so graded and prepared, after the preceding section has been finished and in operation, until the whole road shall be completed: *Further provided,* That the legislature shall require that the company or companies which receive aid from the State shall use the same exclusively for the purchase of iron rails, fastening and rolling-stock, and placing the same upon the road, and upon the failure to do so shall forfeit all their rights under this provision, together with their property and franchises; and it shall be declared a felony for any officer or agent of any railroad company to misappropriate any funds granted under the provisions of this section, or any other funds or property of the company. The State shall always be secured for all bonds guaranteed for any railroad company by a first lien or mortgage upon the road, rolling-stock, depots, and franchises of the corporation whose bonds may be guaranteed. The legislature shall provide, by law, that the managers of railroad companies shall make reports periodically of their acts, and the condition of the corporation affairs, which shall be officially published for public information. And in no case shall the State guarantee the bonds of railroad companies, as herein provided, except by a vote of two-thirds of both houses of the legislature: *Provided,* The legislature shall have no power, directly or indirectly, to release any railroad company from the payment, in specie, of the principal or interest of the obligations or debts due to the school-fund or to the State. An act entitled "An act supplemental and amendatory of an act to regulate railroad companies, approved February 7th, 1853," approved 21st December, 1857, be, and the same is hereby, repealed and of no further effect; and the franchise or corporate privileges of any incorporated company shall not be sold under judgments, except for the foreclosure of mortgages or liens created in the manner prescribed by law. The comptroller of the State is authorized to take possession of any railroad, in default of paying any bonds which may be guaranteed by the State, under such regulations as may be prescribed by law.

MODE OF CALLING A CONVENTION AND AMENDING THE CONSTITUTION OF THIS STATE.

SEC. 37. The legislature, by a vote of three-fourths of all the members of each house, with the approval of the governor, shall have the power to call a convention of the people, for the purpose of altering, amending, or reforming the constitution of this State; the manner of electing delegates to the convention, the time and place of assembling them, to be regulated by law.

SEC. 38. The legislature, at any biennial session, by a vote of two-thirds of all the members of each house, may propose amendments to the constitution, to be voted upon by persons legally qualified to vote for members of the house of representatives of the State; which proposed amendments shall be duly published in the public prints of this State, at least three months before the next general election for the representatives to the legislature for the consideration of the people; and it shall be the duty of the several returning officers at said general election to open a poll for, and make returns to the secretary of state of, the number of legal votes cast at said election for and against said amendment; and if more than one be proposed, then the number of legal votes cast for and against each of them; and if it shall appear, from said return, that a majority of the votes cast upon said proposed amendment or amendments have been cast in favor of the same, and two-thirds of each house of the legislature, at the next regular session thereafter, shall ratify said proposed amendment or amendments so voted upon by the people, the same shall be valid to all intents and purposes as parts of the constitution of the State of Texas: *Provided,* That the said proposed amendments shall, at each of said sessions, have been read on three several days in each house of the legislature, and the vote thereon shall have been taken by yeas and nays: *And provided further,* That the rule in the above proviso shall never be suspended by either of said houses.

SEC. 39. That the State of Texas hereby releases to the owner of the soil all mines and mineral substances that may be on the same, subject to such uniform rate of taxation as the legislature may impose. All islands along the Gulf coast of the State not now patented or appropriated by locations under valid land certificates are reserved from location or appropriated [appropriations] in any other manner by private individuals than as the legislature may direct.

ARTICLE VIII.

FREEDMEN.

SECTION 1. African slavery, as it heretofore existed, having been terminated within this State by the Government of the United States, by force of arms, and its reestablishment being prohibited by the amendment to the Constitution of the United States, it is declared that neither slavery nor involuntary servitude, except as a punishment for crime, whereof the party shall have been duly convicted, shall exist in this State; and Africans and their descendants shall be protected in their rights of person and property by appropriate legislation; they shall have the right to contract and be contracted with; to sue and be sued; to acquire, hold, and transmit property; and all criminal prosecutions against them shall be conducted in the same manner as prosecutions for like offences against the white race, and they shall be subject to like penalties.

SEC. 2. Africans and their descendants shall not be prohibited, on account of their color or race, from testifying orally, as witnesses, in any case, civil or criminal, involving the right of injury to, or crime against, any of them in person or property, under the same rules of evidence that may be applicable to the white race; the credibility of their testimony to be determined by the court or jury hearing the same; and the legislature shall have power to authorize them to testify as witnesses in all other cases, under such regulations as may be prescribed, as to facts hereafter occurring.

ARTICLE IX.

IMPEACHMENT.

SECTION 1. The power of impeachment shall be vested in the house of representatives.

SEC. 2. Impeachments of the governor, lieutenant-governor, attorney-general, secretary of state, treasurer, comptroller, and of the judges of the district court shall be tried by the senate.

SEC. 3. Impeachment of judges of the supreme court shall be tried by the senate; when sitting as a court of impeachment, the senators shall be upon oath or affirmation; and no person shall be convicted without the concurrence of two-thirds of the senators present.

SEC. 4. Judgment in cases of impeachment shall extend only to removal from office and disqualification from holding any office of honor, trust, or profit under this State;

but the parties convicted shall, nevertheless, be subject to indictment, trial, and punishment according to law.

SEC. 5. All officers against whom articles of impeachment may be preferred shall be suspended from the exercise of the duties of their office during the pendency of such impeachment. The appointing power may make a provisional appointment to fill the vacancy occasioned by the suspension of an officer until the decision on the impeachment.

SEC. 6. The legislature shall provide for the trial, punishment, and removal from office of all other officers of the State, by indictment or otherwise.

ARTICLE X.

EDUCATION.

SECTION 1. A general diffusion of knowledge being essential to the preservation of the rights and liberties of the people, it shall be the duty of the legislature of this State to make suitable provisions for the support and maintenance of public schools.

SEC. 2. The legislature shall, as early as practicable, establish a system of free schools throughout the State; and as a basis for the endowment and support of said system, all the funds, lands, and other property heretofore set apart and appropriated, or that may hereafter be set apart and appropriated, for the support and maintenance of public schools shall constitute the public-school fund; and said fund and the income derived therefrom shall be a perpetual fund exclusively for the education of all the white scholastic of this State, and no law shall ever be made appropriating said fund to any use or purpose whatever. And until such time as the legislature shall provide for the establishment of such system of public schools in the State, the fund thus created and the income derived therefrom shall remain as a charge against the State, and be passed to the credit of the free common-school fund.

SEC. 3. And all the alternate sections of land reserved by the State out of grants heretofore made, or that may hereafter be made, to railroad companies or other corporations of any nature whatever, for internal improvements, or for the development of the wealth and resources of the State, shall be set apart as a part of the perpetual school-fund of the State: *Provided*, That if at any time hereafter any portion of the public domain of this State shall be sold, and by virtue of said sale the jurisdiction over said land shall be vested in the United States Government, in such event, one-half of the proceeds derived from said sale shall become a part of the perpetual school-fund of the State, and the legislature shall hereafter appropriate one-half of the proceeds resulting from all sales of the public lands to the perpetual public-school fund.

SEC. 4. The legislature shall provide from time to time for the sale of lands belonging to the perpetual public-school fund, upon such time and terms as it may deem expedient: *Provided*, That in cases of sale the preference shall be given to actual settlers: *And provided further*, That the legislature shall have no power to grant relief to purchasers by granting further time for payment, but shall, in all cases, provide for the forfeiture of the land to the State for the benefit of a perpetual public-school fund, and that all interest accruing upon such sales shall be a part of the income belonging to the school-fund, and subject to appropriation annually for educational purposes.

SEC. 5. The legislature shall have no power to appropriate, or loan, or invest, except as follows, any part of the principal sum of the perpetual school-fund for any purpose whatever, and it shall be the duty of the legislature to appropriate annually the income which may be derived from said fund for educational purposes, under such system as it may adopt, and it shall, from time to time, cause the principal sum now on hand and arising from sales of land, or from any other source, to be invested in the bonds of the United States of America, or the bonds of the State of Texas, or such bonds as the State may guarantee.

SEC. 6. All public lands which have been heretofore, or may be hereafter, granted for public schools to the various counties or other political divisions in this State shall be under the control of the legislature, and may be sold on such terms and under such regulations as the legislature shall by law prescribe, and the proceeds of the sale of said lands shall be added to the perpetual school-fund of the State; but each county shall receive the full benefit of the interest arising from the proceeds of the sale of the lands granted to them respectively: *Provided*, That the lands already patented to the counties shall not be sold without the consent of such county or counties to which the lands may belong.

SEC. 7. The legislature may provide for the levying of a tax for educational purposes: *Provided*, The taxes levied shall be distributed from year to year, as the same may be collected: *And provided*, That all the sums arising from said tax which may be collected from Africans, or persons of African descent, shall be exclusively appropriated for the maintenance of a system of public schools for Africans and their children; and it shall be the duty of the legislature to encourage schools among these people.

SEC. 8. The moneys and lands heretofore granted to, or which may hereafter be granted for, the endowment and support of one or more universities shall constitute a special fund for the maintenance of said universities, and until the university or universities are located and commenced, the principal and the interest arising from the investment of the principal shall be invested in like manner and under the same restrictions as provided for the investment and control of the perpetual public-school fund, in section four and five in this article of the constitution, and the legislature shall have no power to appropriate the university fund for any other purpose than that of the maintenance of said universities, and the legislature shall, at an early day, make such provisions by law as will organize and put into operation the university.

SEC. 9. The four hundred thousand acres of land that have been surveyed and set apart, under the provisions of a law approved 30th August, A. D. 1856, for the benefit of a lunatic asylum, a deaf and dumb asylum, a blind asylum, and an orphan asylum, shall constitute a fund for the support of such institutions, one-fourth part for each, and the said fund shall never be diverted to any other purpose. The said lands may be sold and the funds invested under the same rules and regulations as provided for the lands belonging to the school-fund. The income of said fund only shall be applied to the support of such institutions, and until so applied shall be invested in the same manner as the principal.

SEC. 10. The governor, by and with the advice and consent of two-thirds of the senate, shall appoint an officer to be styled the superintendent of public instruction. His term of office shall be four years, and his annual salary shall not be less than two thousand dollars, payable at stated times; and the governor, comptroller, and superintendent of public education shall constitute a board to be styled a board of education, and shall have the general management and control of the perpetual school-fund and common schools, under such regulations as the legislature may hereafter prescribe.

SEC. 11. The several counties in this State which have not received their quantum of the lands for the purposes of education shall be entitled to the same quantity heretofore appropriated by the congress of the Republic of Texas (and the State) to other counties; and the counties which have not had the lands to which they are entitled for educational purposes located shall have a right to contract for the location, surveying, and procuring the patents for said lands, and of paying for the same with any portion of said lands so patented, not to exceed one-fourth of the whole amount to be so located, surveyed, and patented, to be divided according to quantity, allowing to each part a fair proportion of land, water, and timber.

ARTICLE XI.

All certificates for head-right claims to land, issued to fictitious persons, or which were forged, and all locations and surveys thereon, are, and the same were, null and void from the beginning.

ARTICLE XII.

LAND-OFFICE.

There shall be one general land-office in the State, which shall be at the seat of government, where all titles which have heretofore emanated, or may hereafter emanate, from government shall be registered, and the legislature may establish, from time to time, such subordinate officers as they may deem requisite.

Done in convention by the deputies of the people of Texas, at the city of Austin, this second day of April, in the year of our Lord one thousand eight hundred and sixty-six.   In testimony whereof we have hereunto subscribed our names.

J. W. THROCKMORTON, *President.*

D. C. DICKSON, *President pro tempore.*

WM. M. TAYLOR, *President pro tempore.*

LEIGH CHALMERS, *Secretary.*

[Doc. No. 10]

Constitution of 1868

CONSTITUTION OF TEXAS—1868.*

We, the people of Texas, acknowledging with gratitude the grace of God in permitting us to make a choice of our form of government, do hereby ordain and establish this constitution:

ARTICLE I.

BILL OF RIGHTS.

That the heresies of nullification and secession, which brought the country to grief, may be eliminated from future political discussion; that public order may be restored, private property and human life protected, and the great principles of liberty and equality secured to us and our posterity, we declare that—

SECTION 1. The Constitution of the United States, and the laws and treaties made and to be made in pursuance thereof, are acknowledged to be the supreme law; that this constitution is framed in harmony with and in subordination thereto; and that the fundamental principles embodied herein can only be changed subject to the national authority.

SEC. 2. All freemen, when they form a social compact, have equal rights; and no man or set of men is entitled to exclusive separate public emoluments or privileges.

SEC. 3. No religious test shall be required as a qualification to any office of public trust in this State.

SEC. 4. All men have a natural and indefeasible right to worship God according to the dictates of their own consciences. No man shall be compelled to attend, erect, or support any place of worship, or to maintain any ministry, against his consent. No human authority ought, in any case whatever, to control or interfere with the rights of conscience in matters of religion; and no preference shall ever be given, by law, to any religious societies or mode of worship. But it shall be the duty of the legislature to pass such laws as may be necessary to protect every religious denomination in the peaceable enjoyment of their own mode of public worship.

SEC. 5. Every citizen shall be at liberty to speak, write, or publish his opinions on any subject, being responsible for the abuse of that privilege; and no law shall ever be passed curtailing the liberty of speech or of the press.

SEC. 6. In prosecutions for the publication of papers investigating the official conduct of officers, or of men in a public capacity, or when the matter published is proper for public information, the truth thereof may be given in evidence; and in all prosecutions for libels the jury shall have the right to determine the law and the facts, under the direction of the court as in other cases.

SEC. 7. The people shall be secure in their persons, houses, papers, and possessions from all unreasonable seizures or searches; and no warrant to search any place, or to seize any person, or thing, shall issue, without describing such place, person, or thing, as near as may be, nor without probable cause, supported by oath or affirmation.

* This constitution was framed by a convention called, under the reconstruction acts of Congress, by Major-General Hancock, which met at Austin June 1, 1868, and, after two adjournments, completed its labors in December, 1868. It was submitted to the people November 30 to December 3, 1869, and ratified by 72,395 votes against 4,924 votes.

This constitution was laid before Congress March 30, 1869, and an act was passed March 30, 1870, readmitting Texas to representation upon certain fundamental conditions.

SEC. 8. In all criminal prosecutions, the accused shall have a speedy public trial, by an impartial jury. He shall not be compelled to give evidence against himself. He shall have the right of being heard by himself, or by counsel, or both; shall be confronted with the witnesses against him, and shall have compulsory process for obtaining witnesses in his favor. And no person shall be holden to answer for any criminal charge but on indictment or information, except in cases arising in the land or naval forces, or offences against the laws regulating the militia.

SEC. 9. All prisoners shall be bailable upon sufficient sureties, unless for capital offences, when the proof is evident; but this provision shall not be so construed as to prohibit bail after indictment found, upon an examination of the evidence by a judge of the supreme or district court, upon the return of the writ of *habeas corpus*, returnable in the county where the offence is committed.

SEC. 10. The privileges of the writ of *habeas corpus* shall not be suspended, except by act of the legislature, in case of rebellion or invasion, when the public safety may require it.

SEC. 11. Excessive bail shall not be required, nor excessive fines imposed, nor cruel nor unusual punishment inflicted. All courts shall be open, and every person, for an injury done him in his lands, goods, person, or reputation, shall have remedy by due course of law.

SEC. 12. No person, for the same offence, shall be twice put in jeopardy of life; nor shall a person be again put upon trial for the same offence, after a verdict of not guilty; and the right of trial by jury shall remain inviolate.

SEC. 13. Every person shall have the right to keep and bear arms, in the lawful defence of himself or the State, under such regulations as the legislature may prescribe.

SEC. 14. No bill of attainder, *ex post facto* law, retroactive law, or any law impairing the obligation of contracts, shall be made; and no person's property shall be taken or applied to public use without just compensation being made, unless by the consent of such person; nor shall any law be passed depriving a party of any remedy for the enforcement of a contract which existed when the contract was made.

SEC. 15. No person shall be imprisoned for debt.

SEC. 16. No citizen of this State shall be deprived of life, liberty, property, privileges, outlawed, exiled, or in any manner disfranchised, except by due course of the law of the land.

SEC. 17. The military shall at all times be subordinate to the civil authority.

SEC. 18. Perpetuities and monopolies are contrary to the genius of a free government, and shall never be allowed, nor shall the law of primogeniture or entailments ever be in force in this State.

SEC. 19. The people shall have the right, in a peaceable manner, to assemble together for their common good, and to apply to those invested with powers of government for redress of grievances, or other purposes, by petition, address, or remonstrance.

SEC. 20. No power of suspending laws in the State shall be exercised, except by the legislature, or its authority.

SEC. 21. The equality of all persons before the law is herein recognized, and shall ever remain inviolate; nor shall any citizen ever be deprived of any right, privilege, or immunity, nor be exempted from any burden or duty, on account of race, color, or previous condition.

SEC. 22. Importations of persons under the name of "coolies," or any other name or designation, or the adoption of any system of peonage, whereby the helpless and unfortunate may be reduced to practical bondage, shall never be authorized or tolerated by the laws of this State; and neither slavery nor involuntary servitude, except as a punishment for crime, whereof the party shall have been duly convicted, shall ever exist in this State.

SEC. 23. To guard against transgressions of the high powers herein delegated, we declare that everything in this bill of rights is excepted out of the general powers of government, and shall forever remain inviolate; and all laws contrary thereto, or the following provisions, shall be void.

ARTICLE II.

DIVISION OF THE POWERS OF GOVERNMENT.

The powers of the government of the State of Texas shall be divided into three distinct departments, and each of them be confided to a separate body of magistracy, to wit: those which are legislative to one, those which are executive to another, and those which are judicial to another; and no person, or collection of persons, being of one of those departments, shall exercise any power properly attached to either of the others, except in the instances herein expressly permitted.

ARTICLE III.

LEGISLATIVE DEPARTMENT.

SECTION 1. Every male person who shall have attained the age of twenty-one years, and who shall be (or who shall have declared his intention to become) a citizen of the United States, or who is at the time of the acceptance of this constitution by the Congress of the United States a citizen of Texas, and shall have resided in this State one year next preceding an election, and the last six months within the district or county in which he offers to vote, and is duly registered, (Indians not taxed excepted,) shall be deemed a qualified elector; and should such qualified electors happen to be in any other county, situated in the district in which he resides, at the time of an election, he shall be permited to vote for any district officer: *Provided*, That the qualified electors shall be permitted to vote anywhere in the State for State officers: *And provided further*, That no soldier, seaman, or marine in the Army or Navy of the United States shall be entitled to vote at any election created by this constitution.

SEC. 2. Electors in all cases shall be privileged from arrest during their attendance at elections, and in going to and returning from the same, except in cases of treason, felony, or breach of the peace.

SEC. 3. The legislative power of the State shall be vested in two distinct branches; the one to be styled the senate, and the other the house of representatives; and both together, the legislature of the State of Texas. The style of the laws shall be: "*Be it enacted by the legislature of the State of Texas.*"

SEC. 4. The members of the house of representatives shall be chosen by the qualified electors, and their term of office shall be two years from the day of general election; and the sessions of the legislature shall be annual, at such times as shall be prescribed by law.

SEC. 5. No person shall be a representative unless he be a citizen of the United States, and shall have been a citizen of this State two years next preceding his election, and the last year thereof a citizen of the county, city, or town from which he shall be chosen, and shall have attained the age of twenty-one years at the time of his election.

SEC. 6. All elections for State, district, and county officers shall be held at the county seats of the several counties until otherwise provided by law; and the polls shall be opened for four days, from 8 o'clock a. m. until 4 o'clock p. m. of each day.

SEC. 7. The house of representatives shall consist of ninety members, and no more.

SEC. 8. The senators shall be chosen by the qualified electors hereafter for the term of six years. Those elected at the first election shall be divided by lot into three classes, as nearly equal as can be. The seats of senators of the first class shall be vacated at the expiration of the first two years, and of the second class at the expiration of four years, and the third class at the expiration of six years; so that one-third thereof shall be chosen biennially thereafter.

SEC. 9. Such mode of classifying new additional senators shall be observed as will, as nearly as possible, preserve an equality of number in each class.

SEC. 10. The senate shall consist of thirty senators, and no more.

SEC. 11. A new apportionment for representative and senatorial districts shall be made by the first legislature in session, after the official publication of the United States census, every ten years.

SEC. 12. When a senatorial district shall be composed of two or more counties, it shall not be separated by any county belonging to another district.

SEC. 13. No person shall be a senator unless he be a citizen of the United States, and shall have been a citizen of this State three years next preceding the election, and the last year thereof a resident of the district for which he shall be chosen, and have attained the age of twenty-five years.

SEC. 14. No person shall be eligible to any office, State, county, or municipal, who is not a registered voter in the State.

SEC. 15. The house of representatives, when assembled, shall elect a speaker and its other officers; and the senate shall choose a president, for the time being, and its other officers. Each house shall adjudge of the elections and qualifications of its own members; but contested elections shall be determined in such manner as shall be directed by law. Two-thirds of each house shall constitute a quorum to do business, but a smaller number may adjourn from day to day, and compel the attendance of absent members, in such manner and under such penalties as each house may provide.

SEC. 16. Each house may determine the rules of its own proceedings, punish members for disorderly conduct, and, with the consent of two-thirds, expel a member.

SEC. 17. Each house shall keep a journal of its own proceedings, and publish the same; and the yeas and nays of the members of either house, on any question, shall, at the desire of any three members present, be entered upon the journals.

SEC. 18. Any member of either house shall have liberty to dissent from or protest against any act or resolution which he may think injurious to the public or an individual, and have the reasons for dissent entered on the journals.

SEC. 19. When vacancies happen in either house, the governor, or the person exercising the power of the governor, shall issue writs of election to fill such vacancies; and should the governor fail to issue a writ of election to fill such vacancies, the returning officer for the district or county shall be authorized to order an election for that purpose.

SEC. 20. Senators and representatives shall in all cases, except in treason, felony, or breach of the peace, be privileged from arrest during the session of the legislature and in going to and returning from the same, allowing one day for every twenty-five miles such member may reside from the place at which the legislature is convened.

SEC. 21. Each house, during the session, may punish, by imprisonment, any person, not a member, for disrespectful or disorderly conduct in its presence, or for obstructing any of its proceedings, provided such imprisonment shall not at any one time exceed forty-eight hours.

SEC. 22. The doors of each house shall be kept open, except upon a call of either house, and when there is an executive session of the senate.

SEC. 23. Neither house shall, without the consent of the other, adjourn for more than three days; nor to any other place than that in which they may be sitting, without the concurrence of both houses.

SEC. 24. Bills may originate in either house, and be amended, altered, or rejected by the other; but no bill shall have the force of a law until on three several days it be read in each house, and free discussion be allowed thereon, unless, in case of great emergency, four-fifths of the house in which the bill shall be pending may deem it expedient to dispense with this rule; and every bill having passed both houses shall be signed by the speaker and president of their respective houses: *Provided*, That the final vote on all bills or joint resolutions, appropriating money or lands for any purpose, shall be by the yeas and nays.

SEC. 25. The legislature shall not authorize, by private or special law, the sale or conveyance of any real estate belonging to any person, or vacate or alter any road laid out by legal authority, or any street in any city or village, or in any recorded town plat, but shall provide for the same by general laws.

SEC. 26. After a bill or resolution has been rejected by either branch of the legislature, no bill or resolution containing the same substance shall be passed into a law during the same session.

SEC. 27. The legislature shall not authorize any lottery, and shall prohibit the sale of lottery-tickets.

SEC. 28. Each member of the legislature shall receive from the public treasury a compensation for his services, which may be increased or diminished by law; but no increase of compensation shall take effect during the session at which such increase shall be made.

SEC. 29. No senator or representative shall, while a member of the legislature, be eligible to any civil office of profit under this State which shall have been created or the emoluments of which may have been increased during such term, except it be in such cases as are herein provided. The president, for the time being, of the senate and speaker of the house of representatives shall be elected from their respective bodies.

SEC. 30. No judge of any court of law or equity, secretary of state, attorney-general, clerk of any court of record, sheriff, or collector, or any person holding a lucrative office under the United States or this State, or any foreign government, shall be eligible to the legislature, nor shall at the same time hold or exercise any two offices, agencies, or appointments of trust or profit under this State: *Provided,* That offices of militia to which there is attached no annual salary, the office of postmaster, notary public, and the office of justice of the peace, shall not be deemed lucrative; and that one person may hold two or more county offices, if so provided by the legislature.

SEC. 31. No person who at any time may have been a collector of taxes, or who may have been otherwise intrusted with public money, shall be eligible to the legislature, or to any office of profit or trust under the State government, until he shall have obtained a discharge for the amount of such collection, and for all public moneys with which he may have been intrusted.

SEC. 32. It shall be the duty of the legislature immediataly to expel from the body any member who shall receive or offer a bribe, or suffer his vote influenced by promise of preferment or reward; and every person so offending and so expelled shall thereafter be disabled from holding any office of honor, trust, or profit in this State.

SEC. 33. Elections of senators and representatives shall be general throughout the State, and shall be regulated by law.

SEC. 34. The whole number of senators shall, at the next session after the several periods of making the enumeration, be fixed by the legislature, and apportioned among the several districts to be established by law, according to the number of qualified electors, and shall never be less than nineteen nor more than thirty.

SEC. 35. The members of the legislature shall, at their first session hereafter, receive from the treasury of the State as their compensation eight dollars for each day they shall be in attendance, and eight dollars for each twenty-five miles in travelling to and from the seat of government. The above rates of compensation shall remain till changed by law.

SEC. 36. The legislature shall proceed, as early as practicable, to elect Senators to represent this State in the Senate of the United States, and also provide for future elections of Representatives to the Congress of the United States; and on the second Tuesday after the first assembling of the legislature after the ratification of this constitution, the legislature shall proceed to ratify the thirteenth and fourteenth articles of amendment to the Constitution of the United States of America.

SEC. 37. In order to settle permanently the seat of government, an election shall be holden throughout the State at the usual places of holding elections, at the first general election after the acceptance of this constitution by the Congress of the United States, which shall be conducted according to law, at which time the people shall vote for such place as they may see proper for the seat of government; the returns of said election to be transmitted to the governor with other returns of that election.

If either place voted for shall have a majority of the whole number of votes cast, then the same shall be the permanent seat of government. But in case neither place voted for shall have the majority of the whole number of votes given in, the governor shall issue his proclamation for an election to be holden in the same manner, at the next following general election, between the two places having the highest number of votes at the first election. This election shall be conducted in the same manner as at the first and the returns made to the governor, and the place having the highest number of votes shall be the permanent seat of government.

SEC. 38. The first legislature shall pass such laws as will authorize the clerks of the district court and the justices of the peace of the several counties to issue executions, after the adjournment of each term of their respective courts, against the plaintiff or defendant, for all costs created by them in any suit or suits therein.

SEC. 39. Until otherwise provided by law, the senatorial and representative districts shall be composed of the following counties:

First district.—Counties of Chambers, Jefferson, Orange, Liberty, Hardin, Newton, Jasper, Tyler, and Polk.

Second district.—Counties of Trinity, Angelina, San Augustine, Sabine, Nacogdoches, and Shelby.

Third district.—Counties of Houston and Cherokee.

Fourth district.—Counties of Anderson, Henderson, and Van Zandt.

Fifth district.—Counties of Rusk and Panola.

Sixth district.—Counties of Smith and Upshur.

Seventh district.—County of Harrison.

Eighth district.—Counties of Marion, Davis, and Bowie.

Ninth district.—Counties of Titus and Red River.

Tenth district.—Counties of Wood, Hopkins, and Hunt.

Eleventh district.—Counties of Lamar and Fannin.

Twelfth district.—Counties of Galveston, Brazoria, and Matagorda.

Thirteenth district.—Counties of Wharton, Fort Bend, and Austin.

Fourteenth district.—Counties of Harris and Montgomery.

Fifteenth district.—Counties of Walker, Grimes, and Madison.

Sixteenth district.—County of Washington.

Seventeenth district.—Counties of Burleson, Brazos, Milam.

Eighteenth district.—Counties of Robertson, Leon, and Freestone.

Nineteenth district.—Counties of McLennan, Limestone, and Falls.

Twentieth district.—Counties of Hill, Navarro, Ellis, and Kaufman.

Twenty-first district.—Counties of Dallas, Collin, and Tarrant.

Twenty-second district.—Counties of Grayson, Cook, Denton, Wise, Montague, Jack, Clay, Young, Wichita, Throckmorton, Baylor, Wilbarger, Haskell, Knox, and Hardeman.

Twenty-third district.—Counties of Bosque, Johnson, Hood, Parker, Erath, Palo Pinto, Eastland, Stephens, Callahan, Jones, Shackelford, and Taylor.

Twenty-fourth district.—Counties of Calhoun, Jackson, Victoria, Refugio, San Patricio, Bee, Goliad, and DeWitt.

Twenty-fifth district.—Counties of Lavaca and Colorado.

Twenty-sixth district.—Counties of Fayette and Bastrop.

Twenty-seventh district.—Counties of Gonzales, Guadalupe, and Caldwell.

Twenty-eighth district.—Counties of Hays, Travis, Williamson, Bell, Coryell, Lampasas, San Saba, Hamilton, Comanche, Brown, Coleman, Concho, and McCulloch.

Twenty-ninth district.—Bexar, Wilson, Comal, Kendall, Blanco, Burnett, Llano, Mason, Gillespie, Kerr, Bandera, Edwards, Kimball, and Menard.

Thirtieth district.—Cameron, Hidalgo, Starr, Nueces, Duval, Zapata, Live Oak, McMullen, Encinal, La Salle, Webb, Dimmit, Maverick, Zavalla, Frio, Atascosa, Karnes, Kinney, Uvalde, Presidio, and El Paso.

SEC. 40. The senators and representatives shall be apportioned among the several senatorial and representative districts as follows, to wit:

First district, one senator and three representatives.

Second district, one senator and three representatives.

Third district, one senator and three representatives.

Fourth district, one senator and three representatives.

Fifth district, one senator and three representatives.

Sixth district, one senator and three representatives.

Seventh district, one senator and two representatives.

Eighth district, one senator and three representatives.

Ninth district, one senator and three representatives.

Tenth district, one senator and three representatives.

Eleventh district, one senator and three representatives.

Twelfth district, one senator and three representatives.
Thirteenth district, one senator and three representatives.
Fourteenth district, one senator and three representatives.
Fifteenth district, one senator and three representatives.
Sixteenth district, one senator and two representatives.
Seventeenth district, one senator and three representatives.
Eighteenth district, one senator and three representatives.
Nineteenth district, one senator and three representatives.
Twentieth district, one senator and three representatives.
Twenty-first district, one senator and three representatives.
Twenty-second district, one senator and three representatives.
Twenty-third district, one senator and three representatives.
Twenty-fourth district, one senator and three representatives.
Twenty-fifth district, one senator and three representatives.
Twenty-sixth district, one senator and three representatives.
Twenty-seventh district, one senator and three representatives.
Twenty-eighth district, one senator and four representatives.
Twenty-ninth district, one senator and four representatives.
Thirtieth district, one senator and three representatives.

SEC. 41. In the several senatorial and representative districts, composed of more counties than one, the chief justice of the following-named counties shall receive the returns and give certificates of election to the persons respectively receiving the highest number of votes, to wit:

First district, chief justice of Liberty County.
Second district, chief justice of Nacogdoches County.
Third district, chief justice of Cherokee County.
Fourth district, chief justice of Anderson County.
Fifth district, chief justice of Rusk County.
Sixth district, chief justice of Smith County.
Seventh district, chief justice of Harrison County.
Eighth district, chief justice of Marion County.
Ninth district, chief justice of Red River County.
Tenth district, chief justice of Hopkins County.
Eleventh district, chief justice of Lamar County.
Twelfth district, chief justice of Galveston County.
Thirteenth district, chief justice of Fort Bend County.
Fourteenth district, chief justice of Harris County.
Fifteenth district, chief justice of Grimes County.
Sixteenth district, chief justice of Washington County.
Seventeenth district, chief justice of Burleson County.
Eighteenth district, chief justice of Robertson County.
Nineteenth district, chief justice of McLennan County.
Twentieth district, chief justice of Navarro County.
Twenty-first district, chief justice of Dallas County.
Twenty-second district, chief justice of Grayson County.
Twenty-third district, chief justice of Bosque County.
Twenty-fourth district, chief justice of Victoria County.
Twenty-fifth district, chief justice of Colorado County.
Twenty-sixth district, chief justice of Fayette County.
Twenty-seventh district, chief justice of Gonzales County.
Twenty-eighth district, chief justice of Travis County.
Twenty-ninth district, chief justice of Bexar County.
Thirtieth district, chief justice of Nueces County.

ARTICLE IV.

EXECUTIVE DEPARTMENT.

SECTION 1. The executive department of the State shall consist of a chief magistrate, who shall be styled the governor, a lieutenant-governor, secretary of state, comptroller of public accounts, treasurer, commissioner of the general land-office, attorney-general, and superintendent of public instruction.

SEC. 2. The governor shall be elected by the qualified voters of the State, at the time and places at which they shall vote for representatives to the legislature.

SEC. 3. The returns for every election of governor shall be made out, sealed up, and transmitted by the returning officers to the seat of government, directed to the speaker of the house of representatives, who shall, during the first week of the session of the legislature thereafter, open and publish them, in the presence of both houses of the legislature. The person having the highest number of votes, and being constitutionally eligible, shall be declared by the speaker, under the direction of the legislature, to be governor; but if two or more persons shall have the highest and an equal number of votes, one of them shall be forthwith chosen governor, by a joint vote of both houses of the legislature. Whenever there shall be a contested election for the office of governor, or of any of the executive officers to be elected by the qualified voters of the State, it shall be determined by the joint action of both houses of the legislature.

SEC. 4. The governor shall hold his office for the term of four years from the time of his instalment, and until his successor shall be duly qualified. He shall be at least thirty years of age, a citizen of the United States, and shall have been a resident and citizen of the State of Texas for three years immediately preceding his election He shall be inaugurated on the first Thursday after the organization of the legislature, or as soon thereafter as practicable.

SEC. 5. The governor shall, at stated times, receive a compensation for his services, which shall not be increased nor diminished during the term for which he may have been elected. His annual salary shall be five thousand dollars, until otherwise provided by law, exclusive of the use and occupation of the governor's mansion, fixtures and furniture.

SEC. 6. He shall be commander-in-chief of the militia of the State except when they are called into the actual service of the United States.

SEC. 7. He may, at all times, require information in writing from all the officers of the executive department, on any subject relating to the duties of their offices. If a vacancy occurs in any of the executive offices, by death, resignation, or removal, or from any other cause, during the recess of the legislature, the governor shall have power, by appointment, to fill such vacancy; which appointment shall continue in force till the succeeding session of the legislature, when he shall communicate such appointment to the senate for confirmation or rejection. If it be confirmed by the senate, the tenure of office shall continue until the regular return of the periodic election of said office.

SEC. 8. He shall have power, by proclamation, on extraordinary occasions, to convene the legislature at the seat of government; but if the prevalence of dangerous disease, or the presence of the public enemy there, shall render it necessary, then at any other place within the State he may deem expedient.

SEC. 9. He shall, from time to time, give to the legislature information, in writing, of the condition of the State, and recommend to their consideration such measures as he may deem expedient.

SEC. 10. He shall take care that the laws be faithfully executed.

SEC. 11. In all criminal cases, except treason and impeachment, he shall have power, after conviction, to grant reprieves and pardons; and under such rules as the legislature may prescribe, he shall have power to remit fines and forfeitures. With the advice and consent of the senate, he may grant pardons in cases of treason; and to this end he may respite a sentence therefor until the close of the succeeding session of the legislature: *Provided*, That in all cases of remission of fines or forfeitures, or grants of reprieve or pardon, the governor shall file, in the office of the secretary of state, his reasons therefor.

SEC. 12. Nominations to fill vacancies occurring in the recess of the legislature shall be made by the governor during the first ten days of its session; and should any such nomination be rejected, the same person shall not again be nominated, during the session, to fill the same office.

SEC. 13. During the sessions of the legislature, the governor shall reside where its sessions are held; and at all other times at the capital, except when, in the opinion of the legislature, the public good may otherwise require.

SEC. 14. No person holding the office of governor shall hold any other office or commission, civil or military.

SEC. 15. At the time of the election of a governor, there shall also be elected by the qualified voters of the State a lieutenant-governor possessing the same qualifications as the governor, and who shall continue in office for the same period of time. He shall, by virtue of his office, be president of the senate; and shall have, when in committee of the whole, the right to debate and vote on all questions; and when the senate is equally divided, to give the casting vote. In case of the death, resignation, removal from office, inability, or refusal of the governor to serve, or of his impeachment or absence from the State, the lieutenant governor shall exercise the powers and authority appertaining to the office of governor, until another be chosen at the periodical election, and be duly qualified; or until the governor impeached, absent, or disabled shall be acquitted, returned, or his disability be removed.

SEC. 16. Whenever the lieutenant-governor shall become the acting governor, or shall be unable to preside over the senate, that body shall elect from its own members a president for the time being. If, during the vacancy in the office of the governor, the lieutenant-governor shall die, resign, refuse to serve, be removed from office, or be unable to serve, or if he be impeached, or absent from the State, the president of the senate for the time being shall, in a like manner, administer the government until he shall be superseded by a governor or lieutenant-governor. The compensation of the lieutenant-governor shall be twice the per diem or pay of a senator, and no more; and while acting governor, the same compensation as a governor would receive for a like period of service in his office, and no more. The president of the senate, for the time being, if called upon to administer the government in any of the contingencies enumerated, shall be entitled to the portion of the salary of the governor due for the time of such service. If the lieutenant-governor, while acting governor by succession, shall die, resign, or be absent from the State, during the recess of the legislature, it shall be the duty of the secretary of state to convene the senate for the purpose of choosing a president of the senate for the time being.

SEC. 17. There shall be a secretary of state appointed by the governor, by and with the advice and consent of the senate, who shall continue in office during the term of service of the governor-elect. He shall keep a fair register of all official acts and proceedings of the governor, and shall, when required, lay the same, with all papers, minutes, and vouchers relative thereto, before the legislature, or either house thereof, and shall perform such other duties as may be required of him by law.

SEC. 18. There shall be a seal of the State, which shall be kept by the governor and used by him officially. The seal shall be a star of five points, encircled by an olive and live-oak branches, and the words, "The State of Texas."

SEC. 19. All commissions shall be in the name and by the authority of the State of Texas, be sealed with the State seal, signed by the governor, and attested by the secretary of state.

SEC. 20. There shall be a comptroller of public accounts, elected by the qualified voters of the State, at the same time and in the same manner as the governor is elected, and having the same qualifications, who shall hold his office for the term of four years. He shall superintend the fiscal affairs of the State; give instructions to the assessors and collectors of the taxes; settle with them for taxes; take charge of all escheated property; keep an accurate account of all moneys paid into the treasury, and of all lands escheated to the State; publish annually a list of delinquent assessors and collectors, and demand of them an annual list of all tax-payers in their respective counties, to be filed in his office; keep all the accounts of the State; audit all the claims against the State; draw warrants upon the treasury in favor of the public creditors; and perform such other duties as may be prescribed by law.

SEC. 21. There shall be a treasurer of the State elected at the same time of the election of governor, having the same qualifications as the governor and comptroller of public accounts, who shall hold his office for the same period of time. He shall receive and take charge of all public money paid into the treasury; countersign all warrants drawn by the comptroller of public accounts; pay off the public creditors upon the warrant of the comptroller of public accounts; and perform all such other duties as may be prescribed by law.

SEC. 22. A commissioner of the general land-office shall be elected by the qualified voters of the State at the same time and in the same manner as the governor, comptroller of public accounts, and treasurer may be elected, who shall hold his office for a like period of time and shall possess the same qualifications. He shall be the custodian of the archives of the land-titles of the State, the register of all land-titles hereafter granted, and shall perform such other duties as may be required by law.

SEC. 23. There shall be an attorney-general of the State, having the same qualifications as the governor, lieutenant-governor, comptroller of public accounts, and treasurer, who shall be appointed by the governor, with the advice and consent of the senate. He shall hold his office for the term of four years. He shall reside at the capital of the State during his term of office. He shall represent the interests of the State in all suits or pleas in the supreme court, in which the State may be a party; superintend, instruct, and direct the official action of the district attorneys so as to secure all fines and forfeitures, all escheated estates, and all public moneys to be collected by suit; and he shall, when necessary, give legal advice in writing to all officers of the government, and perform such other duties as may be required by law.

SEC. 24. The secretary of state, comptroller of public accounts, treasurer, commissioner of the general land-office, and attorney-general shall each receive for his services the annual salary of three thousand dollars, and which shall neither be increased nor diminished during his continuance in office.

SEC. 25. Every bill which shall have passed both houses of the legislature shall be presented to the governor for his approval. If he approve, he shall sign it, but if he disapprove it, he shall return it, with his objections, to that house in which it originated; which house shall enter the objections at large upon the journals of the house, and proceed to reconsider it. If, after such reconsideration, two-thirds of the members present shall agree to pass the bill, it shall be sent, with the objections, to the other house, by which it shall likewise be reconsidered. If approved by two-thirds of the members present of that house, it shall become a law; but, in such case, both houses shall determine the question by yeas and nays, with the names of the members respectively entered upon the journals of each house. If a bill shall not be returned by the governor within five days (Sundays excepted) after it shall have been presented to him, it shall become a law in like manner as if he had signed it. Every bill presented to the governor one day before the final adjournment of the two houses, and not signed by him, shall become a law, and shall have the same force and effect as if signed by him. The governor may approve any appropriation and disapprove any other appropriation in the same bill, by signing the bill, and designating the appropriation disapproved, and sending a copy of such appropriation, with his objections, to the house in which it originated; and the same proceedings shall be had, on that part disapproved, as on other bills disapproved by him; but if the legislature shall have adjourned before it is returned, he shall return it, with his objections, to the secretary of state, to be submitted to both houses at the succeeding session of the legislature.

SEC. 26. Every order, resolution, or vote in which the concurrence of both houses shall be required, except the question of adjournment, shall be presented to the governor, and must be approved by him before it can take effect; or, being disapproved, shall be repassed in the manner prescribed in the case of a bill.

ARTICLE V.

JUDICIAL DEPARTMENT.

SECTION 1. The judicial power of this State shall be vested in one supreme court, in district courts, and in such inferior courts and magistrates as may be created by this constitution, or by the legislature under its authority.

The legislature may establish criminal courts in the principal cities within the State with such criminal jurisdiction, coextensive with the limits of the county wherein such city may be situated, and under such regulations as may be prescribed by law; and the judge thereof may preside over the courts of one or more cities, as the legislature may direct.

SEC. 2. The supreme court shall consist of three judges, any two of whom shall constitute a quorum. They shall be appointed by the governor, by and with the advice and consent of the senate, for a term of nine years. But the judges first appointed under this constitution shall be so classified by lot that the term of one of them shall expire at the end of every three years. The judge whose term shall soonest expire shall be the presiding judge. All vacancies shall be filled for the unexpired term. If a vacancy shall occur, or a term shall expire, when the senate is not in session, the governor shall fill the same by appointment, which shall be sent to the senate within ten days after that body shall assemble, and if not confirmed the office shall immediately become vacant.

SEC. 3. The supreme court shall have appellate jurisdiction only, which, in civil cases, shall be coextensive with the limits of the State. In criminal cases no appeal shall be allowed to the supreme court unless some judge thereof shall, upon inspecting a transcript of the record, believing that some error of law has been committed by the judge before whom the cause was tried: *Provided*, That said transcript of the record shall be presented within sixty days from the date of the trial, under such rules and regulations as shall be prescribed by the legislature. Appeals from interlocutory judgments may be allowed, with such exceptions and under such regulations as the legislature may prescribe. The supreme court, and the judges thereof, shall have power to issue the writ of *habeas corpus*, and, under such regulations as may be prescribed by law, may issue the writ of *mandamus*, and such other writs as may be necessary to enforce its own jurisdiction. The supreme court shall also have power to ascertain such matters of fact as may be necessary to the proper exercise of its jurisdiction.

SEC. 4. The supreme court shall hold its sessions annually at the capital of the State.

SEC. 5. The supreme court shall appoint its own clerk, who shall hold his office for four years, unless sooner removed by the court for good cause, entered of record on the minutes of the court. The said clerk shall give bond in such manner as is now or may be hereafter required by law.

SEC. 6. The State shall be divided into convenient judicial districts, for each of which one judge shall be appointed by the governor, by and with the advice and consent of the senate, for a term of eight years, who shall after his appointment reside within the district, and shall hold a court three times a year in each county thereof, at such time and place as may be prescribed by law: *Provided*, That at the first general election after the 4th of July, 1876, the question shall be put to the people whether the mode of election of judges of the supreme and district courts shall not be returned to.

SEC. 7. The district court shall have original jurisdiction of all criminal cases; of all causes in behalf of the State to recover penalties, forfeiture, and escheats; and of all suits and cases in which the State may be interested; of all cases of divorce; of all suits to recover damages for slander or defamation of character; of all suits for the trial of title to land; of all suits for the enforcement of liens; and of all suits, complaints, and pleas whatever, without regard to any distinction between law and equity, when the matter in controversy shall be valued at or amount to one hundred dollars, exclusive of interest; and the said courts, and the judges thereof, shall have power to issue the writ of *habeas corpus* and all other writs necessary to enforce their own jurisdiction and to give them a general superintendence and control over inferior tribunals. The district court shall also have appellate jurisdiction in cases originating in inferior courts, with such exceptions and under such regulations as the legislature may prescribe. And the district court shall also have original and exclusive jurisdiction for the probate of wills; for the appointing of guardians; for the granting of letters testamentary and of administration; for settling the accounts of executors, administrators, and guardians; and for the transaction of all business appertaining to the estates of deceased persons, minors, idiots, lunatics, and persons of unsound mind; and for the settlement, partition, and distribution of such estates, under such rules and regulations as may be prescribed by law.

SEC. 8. In the trial of all criminal cases the jury trying the same shall find and assess the amount of punishment to be inflicted, or fine to be imposed, except in cases where the punishment or fine shall be specifically imposed by law : *Provided,* That in all cases where by law it may be provided that capital punishment may be inflicted, the jury shall have the right, in their discretion, to substitute imprisonment at hard labor for life.

SEC. 9. A clerk of the district court for each county shall be elected by the qualified electors in each county, who shall hold his office for four years, subject to removal by the judge of said court for cause spread upon the minutes of the court. The said clerk shall exercise such powers and perform such duties appertaining to the estates of deceased persons, lunatics, idiots, minors, and persons of unsound mind, in vacation, as may be prescribed by law : *Provided,* That all contested issues of law or fact shall be determined by the district court; and the clerk of the district court shall be recorder for the county of all deeds, bonds, and other instruments required by law to be recorded; and also *ex-officio* clerk of the police or county court; and by virtue of his office shall have control of the records, papers, and books of the district and county or police court, and shall generally perform the duties heretofore required of county and district clerks.

SEC. 10. The judges of the supreme and district courts shall be removed by the governor on the address of two-thirds of the members elected to each house of the legislature, for incompetency, neglect of duty, or other reasonable causes, which are not sufficient ground for impeachment : *Provided, however,* That the cause or causes for which such removal shall be required shall be stated at length in such address, and entered on the journals of each house : *And provided further,* That the cause or causes shall be notified to the judge so intended to be removed, and he shall be admitted to a hearing in his own defence before any vote for such address shall pass; and in all such cases the vote shall be taken by yeas and nays and entered on the journals of each house respectively.

SEC. 11. No judge shall sit in any case wherein he may be interested, or where either of the parties may be connected with him, by affinity or consanguinity, within such degrees as may be prescribed by law, or where he shall have been of counsel in the case. When the supreme court, or a quorum thereof, shall be thus disqualified to hear and determine any case or cases in said court, by reason of the equal division of opinion of said judges, the same shall be certified to the governor of the State, who shall immediately commission the requisite number of persons, learned in the law, for the trial and determination of said case or cases. When a judge of the district court is thus disqualified, the parties may, by consent, appoint a proper person to try the case, and upon their failing to do so, the case shall be transferred for trial to the county in the adjoining district whose county-seat is nearest to that of the county where the case is pending. District judges may exchange districts or hold courts for each other when they may deem it expedient, and shall do so when directed by law; and when the district judge is disqualified to try any case or cases within his district, the governor of the State, on such facts being certified to him, may appoint some person, learned in the law, to try such case or cases, who shall receive such compensation as may be given by law. The disqualification of judges of inferior tribunals shall be remedied as prescribed by law.

SEC. 12. There shall be a district attorney elected by the qualified voters of each judicial district, who shall hold his office for four years; and the duties, salaries, and perquisites of district attorney shall be prescribed by law.

SEC. 13. The judges of the supreme court shall receive a salary of not less than four thousand five hundred dollars annually, and the judges of the district court a salary not less than three thousand five hundred dollars annually. And the salaries of the judges shall not be diminished during their continuance in office.

SEC. 14. When a vacancy shall occur in the office of judge of the district court, at a time when the senate is not in session, the governor shall fill the same by appointment, which shall be sent to the senate within ten days after that body shall assemble; and if not confirmed, the office shall immediately become vacant.

SEC. 15. The judges of the supreme and district courts shall, by virtue of their offices, be conservators of the peace throughout the State. The style of all writs and process shall be " The State of Texas." All prosecutions shall be carried on in the name and by the authority of the State of Texas, and conclude, "against the peace and dignity of the State."

SEC. 16. In all cases of law or equity, when the matter in controversy shall be valued at or exceed ten dollars, the right of trial by jury shall be preserved, unless the same shall be waived by the parties or their attorneys, except in cases where a defendant may fail to appear and answer within the time prescribed by law, and the cause of action is liquidated and proved by an instrument in writing.

SEC. 17. Every criminal offence that may by law be punished by death, or in discretion of the jury by imprisonment to hard labor for life, and every offence that may by law be punished by imprisonment in the State penitentiary, shall be deemed a felony, and shall only be tried upon an indictment found by a grand jury. But all offences of a less grade than a felony may be prosecuted upon complaint, under oath, by any peace officer or citizen, before any justice of the peace or other inferior tribunal that may be established by law ; and the party so prosecuted shall have the right of trial by a jury, to be summoned in such manner as may be prescribed by law.

SEC. 18. One sheriff for each county shall be elected by the qualified voters thereof, who shall hold his office for four years, subject to removal by the judge of the district court for said county, for cause spread upon the minutes of the court. Process against the sheriff, and all such writs as, by reason of interest in the suit, or connection with the parties, or for other cause, the sheriff is incompetent to execute, shall issue to and be executed by any constable in the county.

SEC. 19. There shall be elected in each county, by the qualified voters thereof, as may be directed by law, five justices of the peace, one of whom shall reside after his election at the county-seat; and not more than one of said justices shall be a resident of the same justice's precinct. They shall hold their offices for four years; and should a vacancy occur in either of said offices, an election shall be held for the unexpired term.

SEC. 20. Justices of the peace shall have such civil and criminal jurisdiction as shall be provided by law. And the justices of the peace in each county, or any three of them, shall constitute a court, having such jurisdiction, similar to that heretofore exercised by county commissioners and police courts, as may be prescribed by law. And, when sitting as such court, the justice who resides at the county-seat shall be the presiding justice. The times and manner of holding said courts shall be prescribed by law. Justices of the peace shall also be commissioned to act as notaries public. Justices of the peace shall also discharge all the duties of coroner, except such as by section 21 of this article are devolved upon constables.

SEC. 21. Each county shall be divided into five justices' precincts. And the justices of the peace in each county, sitting as a county court, shall appoint one constable for each justice's precinct, who shall hold his office for four years, subject to removal by said court for cause spread upon the minutes of the court. And said constables, or either of them, in addition to the ordinary duties of their office, shall discharge the duties of sheriff in all such cases as heretofore devolved those duties upon the coroner.

SEC. 22. Sheriffs and justices of the peace shall be commissioned by the governor.

SEC. 23. Sheriffs, district clerks, and justices of the peace, when acting as such, and when acting as a county court, shall receive such fees or other compensation as may be provided for by law.

SEC. 24. All county and district officers, whose removals are not otherwise provided for, may be removed, on conviction by a jury, after indictment, for malfeasance, nonfeasance, or misfeasance in office.

SEC. 25. In all cases arising out of a contract, before any inferior tribunal, when the amount in controversy shall exceed ten dollars, the plaintiff or defendant shall, upon application to the presiding officer, have the right of trial by jury.

SEC. 26. In the trial of all causes in the district court, the plaintiff or defendant shall, upon application made in open court, have the right of trial by jury, to be governed by the rules and regulations prescribed by law.

ARTICLE VI.

RIGHT OF SUFFRAGE.

Every male citizen of the United States of the age of twenty-one years and upwards, not laboring under the disabilities named in this constitution, without distinction of race, color, or former condition, who shall be a resident of this State at the time of the adoption of this constitution, or who shall thereafter reside in this State one year, and in the county in which he offers to vote sixty days next preceding any election, shall be entitled to vote for all officers that are now or hereafter may be elected by the people, and upon all questions submitted to the electors at any election : *Provided*, That no person shall be allowed to vote or hold office who is now, or hereafter may be, disqualified therefor by the Constitution of the United States, until such disqualification shall be removed by the Congress of the United States : *Provided further*, That no person while kept in any asylum, or confined in prison, or who has been convicted of a felony, or who is of unsound mind, shall be allowed to vote or hold office.

ARTICLE VII.

MILITIA.

The governor shall have power to call forth the militia to execute the laws of the State, to suppress insurrection, and repel invasions.

ARTICLE VIII.

IMPEACHMENT.

SECTION 1. The power of impeachment shall be vested in the house of representatives.

SEC. 2. Impeachment of the governor, attorney-general, secretary of state, treasurer, comptroller, and of the judges of the district courts shall be tried by the senate.

SEC. 3. Impeachment of judges of the supreme court shall be tried by the senate. When sitting as a court of impeachment, the senators shall be upon oath or affirmation; and no person shall be convicted without the concurrence of two-thirds of the senators present.

SEC. 4. Judgment, in cases of impeachment, shall extend only to removal from office and disqualification from holding any office of honor, trust, or profit under this State; but the parties convicted shall, nevertheless, be subject to indictment, trial, and punishment, according to law.

SEC. 5. All officers against whom articles of impeachment may be preferred shall be suspended from the exercise of the duties of their office during the pendency of such impeachment. The appointing power may make a provisional appointment to fill the vacancy occasioned by the suspension of an officer, until the decision on the impeachment.

SEC. 6. The legislature shall provide for the trial, punishment, and removal from office of all other officers of the State, by indictment or otherwise.

ARTICLE IX.

PUBLIC SCHOOLS.

SECTION 1. It shall be the duty of the legislature of this State to make suitable provisions for the support and maintenance of a system of public free schools, for the gratuitous instruction of all the inhabitants of this State between the ages of six and eighteen years.

SEC. 2. There shall be a superintendent of public instruction, who, after the first term of office, shall be elected by the people; the first term of office shall be filled by appointment of the governor, by and with the advice and consent of the senate. The superintendent shall hold his office for the term of four years. He shall receive an annual salary of two thousand five hundred dollars, until otherwise provided by law. In case of vacancy in the office of the superintendent, it shall be filled by appointment of the governor, until the next general election.

Sec. 3. The superintendent shall have the supervision of the public free schools of the State, and shall perform such other duties concerning public instruction as the legislature may direct. The legislature may lay off the State into convenient school districts, and provide for the formation of a board of school directors in each district. It may give the district boards such legislative powers, in regard to the schools, school-houses, and school-fund of the district, as may be deemed necessary and proper. It shall be the duty of the superintendent of public instruction to recommend to the legislature such provisions of law as may be found necessary, in the progress of time, to the establishment and perfection of a complete system of education, adapted to the circumstances and wants of the people of this State. He shall, at each session of the legislature, furnish that body with a complete report of all the free schools in the State, giving an account of the condition of the same, and the progress of education within the State. Whenever required by either house of the legislature, it shall be his duty to furnish all information called for in relation to public schools.

Sec. 4. The legislature shall establish a uniform system of public free schools throughout the State.

Sec. 5. The legislature, at its first session, (or as soon thereafter as may be possible,) shall pass such laws as will require the attendance on the public free schools of the State of all the scholastic population thereof, for the period of at least four months of each and every year: *Provided*, That when any of the scholastic inhabitants may be shown to have received regular instruction, for said period of time in each and every year, from any private teacher having a proper certificate of competency, this shall exempt them from the operation of the laws contemplated by this section.

Sec. 6. As a basis for the establishment and endowment of said public free schools, all the funds, lands, and other property heretofore set apart and appropriated, or that may hereafter be set apart and appropriated, for the support and maintenance of public schools, shall constitute the public-school fund. And all sums of money that may come to this State hereafter from the sale of any portion of the public domain of the State of Texas shall also constitute a part of the public-school fund. And the legislature shall appropriate all the proceeds resulting from sales of public lands of this State to such public-school fund. The legislature shall set apart, for the benefit of public schools, one-fourth of the annual revenue derivable from general taxation; and shall also cause to be levied and collected an annual poll-tax of one dollar, on all male persons in this State between the ages of twenty-one and sixty years, for the benefit of public schools. And said fund, and the income derived therefrom, and the taxes herein provided for school purposes, shall be a perpetual fund, to be applied, as needed, exclusively for the education of all the scholastic inhabitants of this State; and no law shall ever be made appropriating such fund for any other use or purpose whatever.

Sec. 7. The legislature shall, if necessary, in addition to the income derived from the public-school fund, and from the taxes for school purposes provided for in the foregoing section, provide for the raising of such amount by taxation, in the several school districts in the State, as will be necessary to provide the necessary school-houses in each district, and insure the education of all the scholastic inhabitants of the several districts.

Sec. 8. The public lands heretofore given to counties shall be under the control of the legislature, and may be sold under such regulations as the legislature may prescribe; and in such case the proceeds of the same shall be added to the public-school fund.

Sec. 9. The legislature shall, at its first session, (and from time to time thereafter, as may be found necessary,) provide all needful rules and regulations for the purpose of carrying into effect the provisions of this article. It is made the imperative duty of the legislature to see to it that all the children in the State, within the scholastic age, are, without delay, provided with ample means of education. The legislature shall annually appropriate for school purposes, and to be equally distributed among all the scholastic population of the State, the interest accruing on the school-fund, and the income derived from taxation for school purposes; and shall, from time to time, as may be necessary, invest the principal of the school-fund in the bonds of the United States Government, and in no other security.

ARTICLE X.

LAND-OFFICE.

SECTION 1. There shall be one general land-office in the State, which shall be at the seat of government, where all titles which have heretofore emanated or may hereafter emanate from government shall be registered; and the legislature may establish, from time to time, such subordinate officers as they may deem requisite.

SEC. 2. That the residue of the public lands may be ascertained, it is declared that all surveys of land heretofore made, and not returned to the general land-office, in accordance with the provisions of an act entitled "An act concerning surveys of land," approved 10th February, 1852, are hereby declared null and void.

SEC. 3. All certificates for land located after the 30th day of October, 1856, upon lands which were titled before such location of certificate, are hereby declared null and void: *Provided*, That in cases where the location, for the want of correct maps, or proper connection of surveys, is found to be in conflict with older surveys, whether titled or not, such certificates may be lifted and relocated.

SEC. 4. All unsatisfied genuine land certificates now in existence shall be surveyed and returned to the general land-office by the first day of January, 1875, or be forever barred.

SEC. 5. All public lands heretofore reserved for the benefit of railroads or railway companies shall hereafter be subject to location and survey by any genuine land certificates.

SEC. 6. The legislature shall not hereafter grant lands to any person or persons, nor shall any certificates for land be sold at the land-office, except to actual settlers upon the same, and in lots not exceeding one hundred and sixty acres.

SEC. 7. All lands granted to railway companies, which have not been alienated by said companies, in conformity with the terms of their charters, respectively, and the laws of the State under which the grants were made, are hereby declared forfeited to the State for the benefit of the school-fund.

SEC. 8. To every head of a family, who has not a homestead, there shall be donated one hundred and sixty acres of land, out of the public domain, upon the condition that he will select, locate, and occupy the same for three years, and pay the office fees on the same. To all single men, twenty-one years of age, there shall be donated eighty acres of land, out of the public domain, upon the same terms and conditions as are imposed upon the head of a family.

SEC. 9. The State of Texas hereby releases to the owner or owners of the soil all mines and mineral substances that may be on the same, subject to such uniform rate of taxation as the legislature may impose.

ARTICLE XI.

IMMIGRATION.

SECTION 1. There shall be a bureau, known as the "bureau of immigration," which shall have supervision and control of all matters connected with immigration. The head of this bureau shall be styled the "superintendent of immigration." He shall be appointed by the governor, by and with the advice and consent of the senate. He shall hold his office for four years, and, until otherwise fixed by law, shall receive an annual compensation of two thousand dollars. He shall have such further powers and duties, connected with immigration, as may be given by law.

SEC. 2. The legislature shall have power to appropriate part of the ordinary revenue of the State for the purpose of promoting and protecting immigration. Such appropriation shall be devoted to defraying the expenses of this bureau, to the support of agencies in foreign sea-ports, or sea-ports of the United States, and to the payment, in part or *in toto*, of the passage of immigrants from Europe to this State, and their transportation within this State.

ARTICLE XII.

GENERAL PROVISIONS.

SECTION 1. Members of the legislature, and all officers, before they enter upon the
duties of their offices, shall take the following oath or affirmation: "I, A. B., do
solemnly swear [or affirm] that I will faithfully and impartially discharge and perform all duties incumbent on me as ———— according to the best of my skill and
ability, and that I will support the Constitution and laws of the United States and of
this State. And I do further swear [or affirm] that, since the acceptance of this constitution by the Congress of the United States, I, being a citizen of this State, have
not fought a duel with deadly weapons, or committed an assault upon any person
with deadly weapons, or sent or accepted a challenge to fight a duel with deadly
weapons, or acted as second in fighting a duel, or knowingly aided or assisted any
one thus offending, either within this State or out of it; that I am not disqualified from
holding office under the fourteenth amendment to the Constitution of the United
States, [or, as the case may be, my disability to hold office under the fourteenth
amendment to the Constitution of the United States has been removed by act of Congress;] and further, that I am a qualified elector in this State."

SEC. 2. Laws shall be made to exclude from office, serving on juries, and from the
right of suffrage those who shall hereafter be convicted of bribery, perjury, forgery,
or other high crimes. The privilege of free suffrage shall be supported by laws regulating elections, and prohibiting, under adequate penalties, all undue influence thereon,
from power, bribery, tumult, or other improper practice.

SEC. 3. Any citizen of this State who shall, after the adoption of this constitution,
fight a duel with deadly weapons, or commit an assault upon any person with deadly
weapons, or send or accept a challenge to fight a duel with deadly weapons, either
within this State or out of it, or who shall act as second, or knowingly aid and assist
in any manner those thus offending, shall be deprived of the right of suffrage, or of
holding any office of trust or profit under this State.

SEC. 4. In all elections by the people, the vote shall be by ballot; and in all elections
by the senate and house of representatives, jointly or separately, the vote shall be
given *viva voce*, except in the election of their officers.

SEC. 5. The legislature shall provide, by law, for the compensation of all officers,
servants, agents, and public contractors, not provided for by this constitution; and
shall not grant extra compensation to any officer, agent, servant, or public contractor,
after such public service shall have been performed, or contract entered into for the
performance of the same; nor grant, by appropriation or otherwise, any amount of
money out of the treasury of the State to any individual, on a claim, real or pretended, where the same shall not have been provided for by preëxisting law.

SEC. 6. No money shall be drawn from the treasury but in pursuance of specific
appropriation made by law; nor shall any appropriation of money be made for a
longer term than two years, except for purposes of education; and no appropriations
for private or individual purposes, or for purposes of internal improvement, shall be
made without the concurrence of two-thirds of both houses of the legislature. A
regular statement and account of the receipts and expenditures of all public money
shall be published annually, in such manner as shall be provided by law; and in no
case shall the legislature have the power to issue treasury warrants, treasury notes,
or paper of any description intended to circulate as money.

SEC. 7. Absence on business of the State, or of the United States, shall not forfeit
a residence once obtained, so as to deprive any one of the right of suffrage, or being
elected or appointed to any office, under the exceptions contained in this constitution.

SEC. 8. The legislature shall have power to provide for deductions from the salaries
of public officers who may neglect the performance of any duty that may be assigned
them by law.

SEC. 9. No member of Congress, nor person holding or exercising any office of
profit or trust under the United States, or either of them, or under any foreign power,

shall be eligible as a member of the legislature, or hold or exercise any office of profit or trust under this State.

SEC. 10. The legislature shall provide for a change of venue in civil and criminal cases.

SEC. 11. It shall be the duty of the legislature to pass such laws as may be necessary and proper to decide differences by arbitration, when the parties shall elect that method of trial.

SEC. 12. All civil officers shall reside within the State, and all district or county officers within their district or counties; and shall keep their offices at such places therein as may be required by law.

SEC. 13. General laws regulating the adoption of children, emancipation of minors, and the granting of divorces shall be made; but no special law shall be enacted relating to particular or individual cases.

SEC. 14. The rights of married women to their separate property, real and personal, and the increase of the same, shall be protected by law; and married women, infants, and insane persons shall not be barred of their rights of property by adverse possession, or law of limitation, of less than seven years from and after the removal of each and all of their respective legal disabilities.

SEC. 15. The legislature shall have power, and it shall be their duty, to protect by law from forced sale a certain portion of the property of all heads of families. The homestead of a family, not to exceed two hundred acres of land, (not included in a city, town, or village,) or any city, town, or village lot or lots, not to exceed five thousand dollars in value, at the time of their destination as a homestead, and without reference to the value of any improvements thereon, shall not be subject to forced sale for debts, except they be for the purchase thereof, for the taxes assessed thereon, or for labor and materials expended thereon; nor shall the owner, if a married man, be at liberty to alienate the same, unless by the consent of the wife, and in such manner as may be prescribed by law.

SEC. 16. The legislature shall provide in what cases officers shall continue to perform the duties of their offices until their successors shall be duly qualified.

SEC. 17. Every law enacted by the legislature shall embrace but one object, and that shall be expressed in the title.

SEC. 18. No law shall be revised or amended by reference to its title; but in such cases the act revised or section amended shall be reënacted and published at length.

SEC. 19. Taxation shall be equal and uniform throughout the State. All property in the State shall be taxed in proportion to its value, to be ascertained as directed by law, except such property as two-thirds of both houses of the legislature may think proper to exempt from taxation. The legislature shall have power to levy an income-tax, and to tax all persons pursuing any occupation, trade, or profession: *Provided*, That the term "occupation" shall not be construed to apply to pursuits either agricultural or mechanical.

SEC. 20. The annual assessments made upon landed property shall be a lien upon the property, and interest shall run thereon upon each year's assessment.

SEC. 21. Landed property shall not be sold for the taxes due thereon, except under a decree of some court of competent jurisdiction.

SEC. 22. Provisions shall be made by the first legislature for the condemnation and sale of all lands for taxes due thereon; and, every five years thereafter, of all lands the taxes upon which have not been paid to that date.

SEC. 23. It shall be the duty of the legislature to provide by law, in all cases where State or county debt is created, adequate means for the payment of the current interest, and 2 per cent. as a sinking-fund for the redemption of the principal; and all such laws shall be irrepealable until principal and interest are fully paid.

SEC. 24. The legislature shall, at the first session thereof, and may at any subsequent session, establish new counties for the convenience of the inhabitants of such new county or counties: *Provided,* That no new county shall be established which shall reduce the county or counties, or either of them, from which it shall be taken to a less area than nine hundred square miles, unless by consent of two-thirds of the legislature; nor shall any county be laid off of less contents. Every new county, as to the right of suffrage and representation, shall be considered as part of the county or counties from which it was taken, until entitled, by numbers, to the right of separate representation. No new county shall be laid off with less than one hundred and fifty qualified jurors resident at the time therein; nor where the county (or counties) from which the new county is proposed to be taken would thereby be reduced below that number of qualified jurors; and in all cases where, from the want of qualified jurors, or other cause, the courts cannot properly be held in any county, it shall be the duty of the district judge to certify such fact to the governor; and the governor shall, by proclamation, attach such county, for judicial purposes, to that county the county-seat of which is nearest the county-seat of the county so to be attached.

SEC. 25. Annual pensions may be provided for the surviving veterans of the revolution which separated Texas from Mexico; and for those permanently disabled in the service of the United States during the late rebellion, provided they entered the service from this State.

SEC. 26. Each county in the State shall provide, in such manner as may be prescribed by law, a manual-labor poor-house, for taking care of, managing, employing, and supplying the wants of its indigent and poor inhabitants; and, under such regulations as the legislature may direct, all persons committing petty offences in the county may be committed to such manual-labor poor-house for correction and employment.

SEC. 27. All persons who, at any time heretofore, lived together as husband and wife, and both of whom, by the law of bondage, were precluded from the rites of matrimony, and continued to live together until the death of one of the parties, shall be considered as having been legally married; and the issue of such cohabitation shall be deemed legitimate. And all such persons as may be now living together in such relation shall be considered as having been legally married; and the children heretofore or hereafter born of such cohabitations shall be deemed legitimate.

SEC. 28. Justices of the peace shall assess the property in their respective precincts, under such laws as shall be provided and enacted by the legislature; and the sheriffs of the several counties of this State shall collect the taxes so assessed.

SEC. 29. Provision shall be made, under adequate penalties, for the complete registration of all births, deaths, and marriages, in every organized county of this State.

SEC. 30. Every person, corporation, or company that may commit a homicide through wilful act, or omission, shall be responsible in exemplary damages to the surviving husband, widow, heirs of his or her body, or such of them as there may be, separately and consecutively, without regard to any criminal proceeding that may or may not be had in relation to the homicide.

SEC. 31. No minister of the gospel or priest of any denomination whatever, who accepts a seat in the legislature as representative, shall, after such acceptance, be allowed to claim exemption from military service, road duty, or serving on juries, by reason of his said profession.

SEC. 32. The inferior courts of the several counties in this State shall have the power, upon a vote of two-thirds of the qualified voters of the respective counties, to assess and provide for the collection of a tax upon the taxable property, to aid in the construction of internal improvements: *Provided*, That said tax shall never exceed 2 per cent. upon the value of such property.

SEC. 33. The ordinance of the convention passed on the first day of February, A. D. 1861, commonly known as the ordinance of secession, was in contravention of the Constitution and laws of the United States, and therefore null and void from the beginning; and all laws and parts of laws founded upon said ordinance were also null and void from the date of their passage. The legislatures which sat in the State of Texas from the 18th day of March, A. D. 1861, until the 6th day of August, A. D. 1866, had no constitutional authority to make laws binding upon the people of the State of Texas: *Provided*, That this section shall not be construed to inhibit the authorities of this State from respecting and enforcing such rules and regulations as were prescribed by the said legislatures which were not in violation of the Constitution and laws of the United States, or in aid of the rebellion against the United

States, or prejudicial to the citizens of this State who were loyal to the United States, and which have been actually in force or observed in Texas during the above period of time; nor to affect, prejudicially, private rights which may have grown up under such rules and regulations; nor to invalidate official acts not in aid of the rebellion against the United States during said period of time. The legislature which assembled in the city of Austin on the 6th day of August, A. D. 1866, was provisional only, and its acts are to be respected only so far as they were not in violation of the Constitution and laws of the United States, or were not intended to reward those who participated in the late rebellion; or to discriminate between citizens on account of race or color; or to operate prejudicially to any class of citizens.

SEC. 34. All debts created by the so-called State of Texas, from and after the 28th day of January, 1861, and prior to the 5th day of August, 1865, were and are null and void; and the legislature is prohibited from making any provision for the acknowledgment or payment of such debts. All unpaid balances, whether of salary, per diem, or monthly allowance, due to employés of the State, who were in the service thereof on the said 28th day of January, 1861, civil or military, and who gave their aid, countenance, or support to the rebellion then inaugurated against the Government of the United States, or turned their arms against the said Government, thereby forfeited the sums severally due to them. All the 10 per cent. warrants issued for military services, and exchanged during the rebellion at the treasury for non-interest warrants, are hereby declared to have been fully paid and discharged: *Provided*, That any loyal person or his or her heirs or legal representative may, by proper legal proceedings, to be commenced within two years after the acceptance of this constitution by the Congress of the United States, show proof in avoidance of any contract made, or revise or annul any decree or judgment rendered since the said 28th day of January, 1861, when, through fraud practised, or threats of violence used towards such persons, no adequate consideration for the contract has been received; or when, through absence from the State of such person, or through political prejudice against such person, the decision complained of was not fair or impartial.

SEC. 35. Within five years after the acceptance of this constitution, the laws, civil and criminal, shall be revised, digested, arranged, and published in such manner as the legislature shall direct; and a like revision, digest, and publication shall be made every ten years thereafter.

SEC. 36. No lottery shall be authorized by this State, and the buying and selling of lottery-tickets within this State is prohibited.

SEC. 37. No divorce shall be granted by the legislature.

SEC. 38. The duration of all offices not fixed by this constitution shall never exceed four years.

SEC. 39. No soldier shall, in time of peace, be quartered in the house or within the inclosure of any individual, without the consent of the owner; nor in time of war, but in a manner prescribed by law.

SEC. 40. All sales of landed property, made under decrees of courts in this State, shall be offered to bidders in lots of not less than ten nor more than forty acres, except in towns or cities, including sales for taxes.

SEC. 41. All civil officers of this State shall be removable by an address of two-thirds of the members-elect to each house of the legislature, except those whose removal is otherwise provided for by this constitution.

SEC. 42. The accounting officers of this State shall neither draw nor pay a warrant upon the treasury, in favor of any person, for salary or compensation, as agent, officer, or appointee, who holds, at the same time, any other office or position of honor, trust, or profit under the State, or the United States, except as prescribed in this constitution.

SEC. 43. The statutes of limitation of civil suits were suspended by the so-called act of secession of the 28th of January, 1861, and shall be considered as suspended within this State until the acceptance of this constitution by the United States Congress.

SEC. 44. All usury laws are abolished in this State, and the legislature is forbidden from making laws limiting the parties to contracts in the amount of interest they may agree upon for loans of money or other property: *Provided*, This section is not intended to change the provisions of law fixing rate of interest in contracts, where the rate of interest is not specified.

SEC. 45. All the qualified voters of each county shall also be qualified jurors of such county.

SEC. 46. It shall be the duty of the legislature, after the adoption of this constitution, to levy a special road-tax upon the taxable property of all persons in this State, and appropriate the same to the building of bridges, and the improvement of public roads in the different counties in the State, under such rules and regulations as the legislature shall provide; and no law shall be passed requiring the personal services of any portion of the people on public roads.

SEC. 47. Mechanics and artisans of every class shall have a lien upon the articles manufactured or repaired by them, for the value of their labor done thereon, or materials furnished therefor; and the legislature shall provide by law for the speedy and efficient enforcement of said liens.

SEC. 48. The legislature may prohibit the sale of all intoxicating or spirituous liquors in the immediate vicinity of any college or seminary of learning; provided said college or seminary be located other than at a county seat or at the State capital.

SEC. 49. The legislature shall give effect to the foregoing general provisions, and all other provisions of this constitution, which require legislative action, according to their spirit and intent, by appropriate acts, bills, or joint resolutions.

SEC. 50. The legislature, whenever two-thirds of each house shall deem it necessary, may propose amendments to this constitution; which proposed amendments shall be duly published in the public prints of this State, at least three months before the next general election of representatives, for the consideration of the people; and it shall be the duty of the several returning officers, at the next general election which shall be thus holden, to open a poll for, and make a return to the secretary of state of, the names of all those voting for representatives, who have voted on such proposed amendments, and if thereupon it shall appear that a majority of those voting upon the proposed amendments have voted in favor of such proposed amendments, and two-thirds of each house of the next legislature shall, after such election, ratify the same amendments by yeas and nays, they shall be valid to all intents and purposes as parts of this constitution: *Provided*, That the said proposed amendments shall, at each of the said sessions, have been read on three several days in each house.

DECLARATION.

Be it declared by the people of Texas in convention assembled, That the territory comprised within the limits of the following-named counties shall compose the congressional districts of the State of Texas, until otherwise provided by law:

SEC. 2. The first congressional district shall be composed of the counties of Anderson, Angelina, Cherokee, Harrison, Henderson, Houston, Jasper, Jefferson, Liberty, Nacogdoches, Newton, Orange, Panola, Polk, Rusk, Sabine, San Augustine, Shelby, Smith, Trinity, Tyler, Hardin, Chambers, Van Zandt, and Wood.

SEC. 3. The second congressional district shall consist of the counties of Marion, Upshur, Davis, Bowie, Titus, Red River, Lamar, Hopkins, Kaufman, Fannin, Grayson, Hunt, Collin, Dallas, Tarrant, Cooke, Denton, Montague, Wise, Parker, Palo Pinto, Jack, Clay, Wichita, Archer, Young, Throckmorton, Wilbarger, Hardeman, Knox, Haskell, Jones, Shackleford, Stephens, Ellis, Johnson, Callahan, Eastland, Erath, Hood, and Taylor.

SEC. 4. The third congressional district shall consist of the counties of Galveston, Brazoria, Fort Bend, Harris, Austin, Montgomery, Walker, Grimes, Brazos, Washington, Burleson, Milam, Robertson, Madison, Leon, Freestone, Limestone, Falls, McLennan, Matagorda, Wharton, Bosque, Hill, and Navarro.

SEC. 5. The fourth congressional district shall consist of the counties of Colorado, Fayette, Lavaca, Jackson, Bastrop, Travis, Williamson, Bell, Hamilton, Comanche, Brown, Coleman, Runnels, Concho, McCulloch, San Saba, Lampasas, Burnet, Llano, Mason, Kendall, Edwards, Kerr, Gillespie, Blanco, Bandera, Comal, Hays, Caldwell,

Guadalupe, Bexar, Wilson, Gonzales, De Witt, Karnes, Goliad, Victoria, Calhoun, Refugio, San Patricio, Nueces, Bee, Live Oak, Atascosa, Medina, Uvalde, Dawson, Zavala, Frio, Dimmitt, La Salle, McMullin, Encinal, Duval, Cameron, Hidalgo, Starr, Zapata, Webb, Kinney, Presidio, Maverick, El Paso, and Coryell.

ELECTION DECLARATION

CONCERNING THE ELECTION FOR RATIFICATION OR REJECTION OF THE CONSTITUTION, AND FOR STATE, DISTRICT, AND COUNTY OFFICERS, AND MEMBERS OF CONGRESS.

Be it declared by the people of Texas in convention assembled, That the constitution adopted by this convention be submitted for ratification or rejection to the voters of this State, registered and qualified as provided by the acts of Congress known as the reconstruction laws, at an election commencing on the first Monday in July, 1869, and continuing for the number of days specified in the constitution adopted by this convention, for the holding of general elections. The vote on said constitution shall be "For the constitution," and "Against the constitution." The said election shall be held at the places and under the regulations to be prescribed by the commanding general of this military district, and the returns made to him as directed by law.

SEC. 2. An election shall be held at the same time and place as for the ratification or rejection of the constitution, for senators and representatives in the legislature, and for all State, district, and county officers who are to be elected by the people under this constitution.

SEC. 3. The said election for State, district, and county officers shall be conducted under the same regulations as the election for the ratification or rejection of the constitution, and by the same persons. The returns of elections shall be made to the commanding general, who shall give certificates of election to the persons chosen for the respective offices. The officers as elected shall commence the discharge of the duties of the office for which they have been chosen as soon as elected and qualified, in compliance with the provisions of the constitution herewith submitted, and shall hold their respective offices for the term of years prescribed by the constitution, beginning from the day of their election, and until their successors are elected and qualified.

SEC. 4. An election for members of the United States Congress shall be held in each congressional district as established by this convention, at the same time and place as the election for ratification or rejection of the constitution. Said election shall be conducted by the same persons and under the same regulations as before mentioned in this declaration. The returns shall be made to the commanding general, who shall give the persons chosen certificates of election.

SEC. 5. The members of the legislature, elected under this declaration, shall assemble at the capitol, in the city of Austin, on the second Monday in September, A. D. 1865.

SEC. 6. The commanding general of this military district is requested to enforce this declaration.

ED. J. DAVIS, *President.*

WM. V. TUNSTALL, *Secretary.*

AMENDMENTS TO THE CONSTITUTION OF 1868.

RATIFIED 1872.

That section six of article ten be so amended as to read:

ART. X. SEC. 6. The legislature of the State of Texas shall not hereafter grant lands except for purposes of internal improvement, to any person or persons, nor shall any certificate for land be sold at the land-office, except to actual settlers upon the same, and in lots not exceeding one hundred and sixty acres: *Provided,* That the Legislature shall not grant, out of the public domain, more than twenty sections of land for each mile of completed work, in aid of the construction of which land may be granted: *And provided further*, That nothing in the foregoing proviso shall affect any rights granted or secured by laws passed prior to the final adoption of this amendment.

RATIFIED 1873.

That section twenty of article one, bill of rights; sections two, three, and four of article five; sections twenty-eight, forty, and forty-eight of article twelve of the general provisions of the constitution be so amended as to read:

BILL OF RIGHTS: ART. I. SEC. 20. No power of suspending the laws in the State shall be exercised except by the legislature.

ART. V. SEC. 2. The supreme court shall consist of one chief-justice and four associate justices, any three of whom shall constitute a quorum; they shall be appointed by the governor, by and with the advice and consent of the senate, for a term of nine years. All vacancies shall be filled for the unexpired term. If a vacancy shall occur, or a term shall expire, when the senate is not in session, the governor shall fill the same by appointment, which shall be sent to the senate within ten days after that body shall assemble, and, if not confirmed, the office shall immediately become vacant.

SEC. 3. The supreme court shall have appellate jurisdiction only, which, in civil cases and criminal cases, shall be co-extensive with the limits of the State. Appeal from interlocutory judgments may be allowed with such exceptions and under such regulations as the legislature may prescribe. The supreme court and the judges thereof shall have power to issue the writ of *habeas corpus;* and under such regulations as may be prescribed by law may issue the writ of *mandamus* and such other writs as may be necessary to inforce its own jurisdiction. The supreme court shall also have power to ascertain such matters of fact as may be necessary to the proper exercise of its jurisdiction.

SEC. 4. The supreme court shall hold its sessions at the capital and two other places in the State.

ART. XII. SEC. 28. In each and every organized county in this State there shall be an assessor and collector of taxes elected by the people at the next ensuing general election, and every four years thereafter, who shall assess the property and collect the taxes so assessed in conformity to such laws as now exist, or may be enacted hereafter by the legislature relative to the assessment and collection of taxes.

SEC. 40. The legislature shall not pass local or special laws in any of the following enumerated cases, that is to say, for locating or changing county-seats, regulating county or town affairs, regulating the practice in courts of justice, regulating the duties and jurisdiction of justices of the peace and constables, providing for changes of venue in civil and criminal cases, incorporating cities or towns, or changing or amending the charter of any city or village, providing for the management of common schools, regulating the rate of interest on money, remitting fines, forfeitures, or penalties, changing the laws of descent. In all other cases where a general law can be made applicable, no special law shall be enacted; or in any case where a general law can be made applicable, no special law shall be enacted. The legislature shall pass general laws providing for the cases before enumerated in this section, and for all other cases which in its judgment may be provided by general laws.

[Doc. No. 11]

Constitution of 1870 *

PREAMBLE.

Humbly invoking the blessing of Almighty God, the people of the State of Texas do ordain and establish this constitution.

ARTICLE I.

BILL OF RIGHTS.

That the general, great, and essential principles of liberty and free government may be recognized and established, we declare—

SECTION 1. Texas is a free and independent State, subject only to the Constitution of the United States; and the maintenance of our free institutions and the perpetuity of the Union depend upon the preservation of the right of local self-government unimpaired to all the States.

SEC. 2. All political power is inherent in the people, and all free governments are founded on their authority, and instituted for their benefit. The faith of the people of Texas stands pledged to the preservation of a republican form of government, and, subject to this limitation only, they have at all times the inalienable right to alter, reform, or abolish their government in such manner as they may think expedient.

SEC. 3. All free men when they form a social compact have equal rights, and no man, or set of men, is entitled to exclusive separate public emoluments, or privileges, but in consideration of public services.

SEC. 4. No religious test shall ever be required as a qualification to any office, or public trust, in this State; nor shall any one be excluded from holding office on account of his religious sentiments, provided he acknowledge the existence of a Supreme Being.

SEC. 5. No person shall be disqualified to give evidence in any of the courts of this State on account of his religious opinions, or for the want of any religious belief, but all oaths or affirmations shall be administered in the mode most binding upon the conscience, and shall be taken subject to the pains and penalties of perjury.

SEC. 6. All men have a natural and indefeasible right to worship Almighty God according to the dictates of their own consciences. No man shall be compelled to attend, erect, or support any place of worship, or to maintain any ministry against his consent. No human authority ought, in any case whatever, to control or interfere with the rights of conscience in matters of religion, and no preference shall ever be given by law to any religious society or mode of worship. But it shall be the duty of the legislature to pass such laws as may be necessary to protect equally every religious denomination in the peaceable enjoyment of its own mode of public worship.

SEC. 7. No money shall be appropriated or drawn from the treasury for the benefit of any sect or religious society, theological or religious seminary; nor shall property belonging to the State be appropriated for any such purposes.

SEC. 8. Every person shall be at liberty to speak, write, or publish his opinions on any subject, being responsible for the abuse of that privilege; and no law shall ever be passed curtailing the liberty of speech or of the press. In prosecutions for the publication of papers investigating the conduct of officers or men in public capacity, or when the matter published is proper for public information, the truth thereof may be given in evidence. And in all indictments for libels the jury shall have the right to determine the law and the facts under the direction of the court, as in other cases.

SEC. 9. The people shall be secure in their persons, houses, papers, and possessions from all unreasonable seizures or searches; and no warrant to search any place, or to seize any person or thing, shall issue without describing them as near as may be, nor without probable cause, supported by oath or affirmation.

---

* This constitution was framed by a convention which assembled at Austin, September 6, 1875, and completed its labors November 24, 1875. It was submitted to the people February 17, 1876, and ratified by a large majority.

SEC. 10. In all criminal prosecutions the accused shall have a speedy public trial by an impartial jury. He shall have the right to demand the nature and cause of the accusation against him and to have a copy thereof. He shall not be compelled to give evidence against himself. He shall have the right of being heard by himself or counsel, or both; shall be confronted with the witnesses against him, and shall have compulsory process for obtaining witnesses in his favor. And no person shall be held to answer for a criminal offence, unless on indictment of a grand jury, except in cases in which the punishment is by fine, or imprisonment otherwise than in the penitentiary, in cases of impeachment, and in cases arising in the army or navy, or in the militia, when in actual service in time of war or public danger.

SEC. 11. All prisoners shall be bailable by sufficient sureties, unless for capital offences when the proof is evident; but this provision shall not be so construed as to prevent bail after indictment found, upon examination of the evidence in such manner as may be prescribed by law.

SEC. 12. The writ of *habeas corpus* is a writ of right, and shall never be suspended. The legislature shall enact laws to render the remedy speedy and effectual.

SEC. 13. Excessive bail shall not be required, nor excessive fines imposed, nor cruel or unusual punishment inflicted. All courts shall be open, and every person for an injury done him in his lands, goods, person, or reputation, shall have remedy by due course of law.

SEC. 14. No person, for the same offence, shall be twice put in jeopardy of life or liberty; nor shall a person be again put upon trial for the same offence after a verdict of not guilty in a court of competent jurisdiction.

SEC. 15. The right of trial by jury shall remain inviolate. The legislature shall pass such laws as may be needed to regulate the same, and to maintain its purity and efficiency.

SEC. 16. No bill of attainder, *ex post facto* law, retroactive law, or any law impairing the obligation of contracts, shall be made.

SEC. 17. No person's property shall be taken, damaged, or destroyed for or applied to public use without adequate compensation being made, unless by the consent of such person; and, when taken, except for the use of the State, such compensation shall be first made, or secured, by a deposit of money; and no irrevocable or uncontrollable grant of special privileges or immunities shall be made; but all privileges and franchises granted by the legislature or created under its authority shall be subject to the control thereof.

SEC. 18. No person shall ever be imprisoned for debt.

SEC. 19. No citizen of this State shall be deprived of life, liberty, property, privileges, or immunities, or in any manner disfranchised, except by the due course of the law of the land.

SEC. 20. No citizen shall be outlawed; nor shall any person be transported out of the State for any offence committed within the same.

SEC. 21. No conviction shall work corruption of blood or forfeiture of estate; and the estates of those who destroy their own lives shall descend or vest as in case of natural death.

SEC. 22. Treason against the State shall consist only in levying war against it, or adhering to its enemies, giving them aid and comfort; and no person shall be convicted of treason except on the testimony of two witnesses to the same overt act, or on confession in open court.

SEC. 23. Every citizen shall have the right to keep and bear arms in the lawful defence of himself or the State; but the legislature shall have power by law to regulate the wearing of arms with a view to prevent crime.

SEC. 24. The military shall at all times be subordinate to the civil authority.

SEC. 25. No soldier shall, in time of peace, be quartered in the house of any citizen without the consent of the owner, nor in time of war but in a manner prescribed by law.

SEC. 26. Perpetuities and monopolies are contrary to the genius of a free government, and shall never be allowed; nor shall the law of primogeniture or entailments ever be in force in this State.

SEC. 27. The citizens shall have the right, in a peaceable manner, to assemble together for their common good, and apply to those invested with the power of government for redress of grievances or other purposes, by petition, address, or remonstrance.

SEC. 28. No power of suspending laws in this State shall be exercised except by the legislature.

SEC. 29. To guard against transgressions of the high powers herein delegated, we declare that everything in this "Bill of Rights" is excepted out of the general powers of government, and shall forever remain inviolate, and all laws contrary thereto, or to the following provisions, shall be void.

ARTICLE II.

THE POWERS OF GOVERNMENT

SECTION 1. The powers of the government of the State of Texas shall be divided into three distinct departments, each of which shall be confided to a separate body of magistracy, to wit: Those which are legislative to one, those which are executive to another, and those which are judicial to another; and no person, or collection of persons, being of one of these departments, shall exercise any power properly attached to either of the others, except in the instances herein expressly permitted.

ARTICLE III.

LEGISLATIVE DEPARTMENT.

SECTION 1. The legislative power of this State shall be vested in a senate and house of representatives, which together shall be styled "The Legislature of the State of Texas."

SEC. 2. The senate shall consist of thirty-one members, and shall never be increased above this number. The house of representatives shall consist of ninety-three members until the first apportionment after the adoption of this constitution, when, or at any apportionment thereafter, the number of representatives may be increased by the legislature, upon the ratio of not more than one representative for every fifteen thousand inhabitants: *Provided*, The number of representatives shall never exceed one hundred and fifty.

SEC. 3. The Senators shall be chosen by the qualified electors for the term of four years; but a new senate shall be chosen after every apportionment, and the senators elected after each apportionment shall be divided by lot into two classes. The seats of the senators of the first class shall be vacated at the expiration of the first two years, and those of the second class at the expiration of four years, so that one-half of the senators shall be chosen biennially thereafter.

SEC. 4. The members of the house of representatives shall be chosen by the qualified electors, and their term of office shall be two years from the day of their election.

SEC. 5. The legislature shall meet every two years, at such time as may be provided by law, and at other times when convened by the governor.

SEC. 6. No person shall be a senator unless he be a citizen of the United States, and at the time of his election a qualified elector of this State, and shall have been a resident of this State five years next preceding his election, and the last year thereof a resident of the district for which he shall be chosen, and shall have attained the age of twenty-six years.

SEC. 7. No person shall be a representative unless he be a citizen of the United States and at the time of his election a qualified elector of this State, and shall have been a resident of this State two years next preceding his election, the last year thereof a resident of the district for which he shall be chosen, and shall have attained the age of twenty-one years.

SEC. 8. Each house shall be the judge of the qualifications and election of its own members; but contested elections shall be determined in such a manner as shall be provided by law.

SEC. 9. The senate shall, at the beginning and close of each session, and at such other times as may be necessary, elect one of its members president *pro tempore*, who shall perform the duties of the lieutenant-governor in any case of absence or disability of that officer, and whenever the said office of lieutenant-governor shall be vacant. The house of representatives shall, when it first assembles, organize temporarily, and thereupon proceed to the election of a speaker from its own members; and each house shall choose its other officers.

SEC. 10. Two-thirds of each house shall constitute a quorum to do business, but a smaller number may adjourn from day to day, and compel the attendance of absent members, in such manner and under such penalties as each house may provide.

SEC. 11. Each house may determine the rules of its own proceedings, punish members for disorderly conduct, and, with the consent of two-thirds, expel a member, but not a second time for the same offence.

SEC. 12. Each house shall keep a journal of its proceedings, and publish the same; and the yeas and nays of the members of either house on any question shall, at the desire of any three members present, be entered on the journals.

SEC. 13. When vacancies occur in either house, the governor, or the person exercising the power of the governor, shall issue writs of election to fill such vacancies; and should the governor fail to issue a writ of election to fill any such vacancy within twenty days after it occurs, the returning-officer of the district in which such vacancy may have happened shall be authorized to order an election for that purpose.

SEC. 14. Senators and representatives shall, except in cases of treason, felony, or breach of the peace, be privileged from arrest during the session of the legislature, and in going to and returning from the same, allowing one day for every twenty miles such member may reside from the place at which the legislature is convened.

SEC. 15. Each house may punish, by imprisonment, during its sessions, any person not a member, for disrespectful or disorderly conduct in its presence, or for obstructing any of its proceedings: *Provided*, Such imprisonment shall not, at any one time, exceed forty-eight hours.

SEC. 16. The sessions of each house shall be open, except the senate when in executive session.

SEC. 17. Neither house shall, without the consent of the other, adjourn for more than three days, nor to any other place than that where the legislature may be sitting.

SEC. 18. No senator or representative shall, during the term for which he may be elected, be eligible to any civil office of profit under this State which shall have been created or the emoluments of which may have been increased during such term; no member of either house shall, during the term for which he is elected, be eligible to any office or place, the appointment to which may be made, in whole or in part, by either branch of the legislature; and no member of either house shall vote for any other member for any office whatever which may be filled by a vote of the legislature, except in such cases as are in this constitution provided. Nor shall any member of the legislature be interested, either directly or indirectly, in any contract with the State, or any county thereof, authorized by any law passed during the term for which he shall have been elected.

SEC. 19. No judge of any court, secretary of state, attorney-general, clerk of any court of record, or any person holding a lucrative office under the United States or this State, or any foreign government, shall, during the term for which he is elected or appointed, be eligible to the legislature.

SEC. 20. No person who at any time may have been a collector of taxes, or who may have been otherwise intrusted with public money, shall be eligible to the legislature, or to any office of profit or trust under the State government, until he shall have obtained a discharge for the amount of such collections, or for all public moneys with which he may have been intrusted.

SEC. 21. No member shall be questioned in any other place for words spoken in debate in either house.

SEC. 22. A member who has a personal or private interest in any measure or bill proposed or pending before the legislature, shall disclose the fact to the house of which he is a member, and shall not vote thereon.

SEC. 23. If any senator or representative remove his residence from the district or county for which he was elected, his office shall thereby become vacant, and the vacancy shall be filled as provided in section 13 of this article.

SEC. 24. The members of the legislature shall receive from the public treasury such compensation for their services as may, from time to time, be provided by law, not exceeding five dollars per day for the first sixty days of each session, and after that not exceeding two dollars per day for the remainder of the session; except the first session held under this constitution, when they may receive not exceeding five dollars per day for the first ninety days, and after that not exceeding two dollars per day for the remainder of the session In addition to the per diem, the members of each house shall be entitled to mileage in going to and returning from the seat of government, which mileage shall not exceed five dollars for every twenty-five miles, the distance to be computed by the nearest and most direct route of travel by land, regardless of railways or water-routes; and the comptroller of the State shall prepare and preserve a table of distances to each county-seat now or hereafter to be established, and by such table the mileage of each member shall be paid; but no member shall be entitled to mileage for any extra session that may be called within one day after the adjournment of a regular or called session.

SEC. 25. The State shall be divided into senatorial districts of contiguous territory, according to the number of qualified electors, as nearly as may be, and each district shall be entitled to elect one senator; and no single county shall be entitled to more than one senator.

SEC. 26. The members of the house of representatives shall be apportioned among the several counties, according to the number of population in each, as nearly as may be, on a ratio obtained by dividing the population of the State, as ascertained by the most recent United States census, by the number of members of which the house is composed: *Provided*, That whenever a single county has sufficient population to be entitled to a representative, such county shall be formed into a separate representative district, and when two or more counties are required to make up the ratio of representation such counties shall be contiguous to each other; and when any one county has more than sufficient population to be entitled to one or more representatives, such representative or representatives shall be apportioned to such county, and for any surplus of population it may be joined in a representative district with any other contiguous county or counties.

SEC. 27. Elections for senators and representatives shall be general throughout the State, and shall be regulated by law.

SEC. 28. The legislature shall, at its first session after the publication of each United States decennial census, apportion the State into senatorial and representative districts, agreeably to the provisions of sections 25 and 26 of this article; and until the next decennial census, when the first apportionment shall be made by the legislature, the State shall be, and it is hereby, divided into senatorial and representative districts as provided by an ordinance of the convention on that subject.

PROCEEDINGS.

SEC. 29. The enacting clause of all laws shall be, "*Be it enacted by the legislature of the State of Texas.*"

SEC. 30. No law shall be passed except by bill, and no bill shall be so amended in its passage through either house as to change its original purpose.

SEC. 31. Bills may originate in either house, and when passed by such house may be amended, altered, or rejected by the other.

SEC. 32. No bill shall have the force of a law until it has been read on three several days in each house, and free discussion allowed thereon; but in cases of imperative public necessity (which necessity shall be stated in a preamble or in the body of the bill) four-fifths of the house in which the bill may be pending may suspend this rule, the yeas and nays being taken on the question of suspension, and entered upon the journals.

SEC. 33. All bills for raising revenue shall originate in the house of representatives, but the senate may amend or reject them as other bills.

SEC. 34. After a bill has been considered and defeated by either house of the legislature, no bill containing the same substance shall be passed into a law during the same session. After a resolution has been acted on and defeated, no resolution containing the same substance shall be considered at the same session,

SEC. 35. No bill (except general appropriation bills, which may embrace the various subjects and accounts for and on account of which moneys are appropriated) shall contain more than one subject, which shall be expressed in its title. But if any subject shall be embraced in an act which shall not be expressed in the title, such act shall be void only as to so much thereof as shall not be so expressed.

SEC. 36. No law shall be revived or amended by reference to its title; but in such case the act revived or the section or sections amended shall be re-enacted and published at length.

SEC. 37. No bill shall be considered unless it has been first referred to a committee and reported thereon; and no bill shall be passed which has not been presented and referred to and reported from a committee at least three days before the final adjournment of the legislature.

SEC. 38. The presiding officer of each house shall, in the presence of the house over which he presides, sign all bills and joint resolutions passed by the legislature, after their titles have been publicly read before signing; and the fact of signing shall be entered on the journals.

SEC. 39. No law passed by the legislature, except the general appropriation act, shall take effect or go into force until ninety days after the adjournment of the session at which it was enacted, unless in case of an emergency, which emergency must be expressed in a preamble or in the body of the act, the legislature shall, by a vote of two-thirds of all the members elected to each house, otherwise direct; said vote to be taken by yeas and nays, and entered upon the journals.

SEC. 40. When the legislature shall be convened in special session, there shall be no legislation upon subjects other than those designated in the proclamation of the governor calling such session, or presented to them by the governor; and no such session shall be of longer duration than thirty days.

SEC. 41. In all elections by the senate and house of representatives, jointly or separately, the vote shall be given *viva voce*, except in the election of their officers.

REQUIREMENTS AND LIMITATIONS.

SEC. 42. The legislature shall pass such laws as may be necessary to carry into effect the provisions of this constitution.

SEC. 43. The first session of the legislature under this constitution shall provide for revising, digesting, and publishing the laws, civil and criminal; and a like revision, digest, and publication may be made every ten years thereafter: *Provided*, That in the adoption of and giving effect to any such digest or revision the legislature shall not be limited by sections 35 and 36 of this article.

SEC. 44. The legislature shall provide by law for the compensation of all officers, servants, agents, and public contractors not provided for in this constitution, but shall not grant extra compensation to any officer, agent, servant, or public contractors after such public service shall have been performed or contract entered into for the performance of the same; nor grant, by appropriation or otherwise, any amount of money out of the treasury of the State, to any individual, on a claim, real or pretended, when the same shall not have been provided for by pre-existing law; nor employ any one in the name of the State unless authorized by pre-existing law.

SEC. 45. The power to change the venue in civil and criminal cases shall be vested in the courts, to be exercised in such manner as shall be provided by law; and the legislature shall pass laws for that purpose.

SEC. 46. The legislature shall, at its first session after the adoption of this constitution, enact effective vagrant laws.

SEC. 47. The legislature shall pass laws prohibiting the establishment of lotteries and gift enterprises in this State, as well as the sale of tickets in lotteries, gift enterprises, or other evasions involving the lottery principle, established or existing in other States.

Sec. 48. The legislature shall not have the right to levy taxes or impose burdens upon the people, except to raise revenue sufficient for the economical administration of the government, in which may be included the following purposes:

The payment of all interest upon the bonded debt of the State;

The erection and repairs of public buildings;

The benefit of the sinking-fund, which shall not be more than two per centum of the public debt; and for the payment of the present floating debt of the State, including matured bonds for the payment of which the sinking-fund is inadequate;

The support of public schools, in which shall be included colleges and universities established by the State; and the maintenance and support of the Agricultural and Mechanical College of Texas;

The payment of the cost of assessing and collecting the revenue; and the payment of all officers, agents, and employés of the State government, and all incidental expenses connected therewith;

The support of the blind asylum, the deaf and dumb asylum, and the insane asylum, the State cemetery, and the public grounds of the State;

The enforcement of quarantine regulations on the coast of Texas;

The protection of the frontier.

Sec. 49. No debt shall be created by or on behalf of the State, except to supply casual deficiencies of revenue, repel invasion, suppress insurrection, defend the State in war, or pay existing debt; and the debt created to supply deficiencies in the revenue shall never exceed in the aggregate at any one time two hundred thousand dollars.

Sec. 50. The legislature shall have no power to give or to lend, or to authorize the giving or lending, of the credit of the State in aid of, or to any person, association, or corporation, whether municipal or other; or to pledge the credit of the State in any manner whatsoever for the payment of the liabilities, present or prospective, of any individual, association of individuals, municipal or other corporation whatsoever.

Sec. 51. The legislature shall have no power to make any grant, or authorize the making of any grant, of public money to any individual, association of individuals, municipal or other corporation whatsoever: *Provided*, That this shall not be so construed as to prevent the grant of aid in case of public calamity.

Sec. 52. The legislature shall have no power to authorize any county, city, town, or other political corporation, or subdivision of the State, to lend its credit or to grant public money or thing of value, in aid of or to any individual, association, or corporation whatsoever; or to become a stockholder in such corporation, association, or company.

Sec. 53. The legislature shall have no power to grant, or to authorize any county or municipal authority to grant, any extra compensation, fee, or allowance to a public officer, agent, servant, or contractor after service has been rendered or a contract has been entered into and performed in whole or in part; nor pay, nor authorize the payment of, any claim created against any county or municipality of the State, under any agreement or contract, made without authority of law.

Sec. 54. The legislature shall have no power to release or alienate any lien held by the State upon any railroad, or in anywise change the tenor or meaning, or pass any act explanatory thereof; but the same shall be enforced in accordance with the original terms upon which it was acquired.

Sec. 55. The legislature shall have no power to release or extinguish, or to authorize the releasing or extinguishing, in whole or in part, the indebtedness, liability, or obligation of any incorporation or individual to this State, or to any county, or other municipal corporation therein.

Sec. 56. The legislature shall not, except as otherwise provided in this constitution, pass any local or special law, authorizing—

The creation, extension, or repairing of liens;

Regulating the affairs of counties, cities, towns, wards, or school districts;

Changing the names of persons or places; changing the venue in civil or criminal cases;

Authorizing the laying out, opening, altering or maintaining of roads, highways, streets, or alleys;

Relating to ferries or bridges, or incorporating ferry or bridge companies, except for the erection of bridges crossing streams which form boundaries between this and any other State;

Vacating roads, town-plats, streets, or alleys;

Relating to cemeteries, graveyards, or public grounds not of the State;

Authorizing the adoption or legitimation of children;

Locating or changing county-seats;

Incorporating cities, towns, or villages, or changing their charters;

For the opening and conducting of elections, or fixing or changing the places of voting;

Granting divorces;

Creating offices, or prescribing the powers and duties of officers, in counties, cities, towns, election or school districts;

Changing the law of descent or succession;

Regulating the practice or jurisdiction of or changing the rules of evidence in any judicial proceeding or inquiry before courts, justices of the peace, sheriffs, commissioners, arbitrators, or other tribunals, or providing or changing methods for the collection of debts, or the enforcing of judgments, or prescribing the effect of judicial sales of real estate;

Regulating the fees, or extending the powers and duties of aldermen, justices of the peace, magistrates, or constables;

Regulating the management of public schools, the building or repairing of school-houses, and the raising of money for such purposes;

Fixing the rate of interest;

Affecting the estates of minors or persons under disability;

Remitting fines, penalties, and forfeitures, and refunding moneys legally paid into the treasury;

Exempting property from taxation;

Regulating labor, trade, mining, and manufacturing;

Declaring any named person of age;

Extending the time for the assessment or collection of taxes, or otherwise relieving any assessor or collector of taxes from the due performance of his official duties, or his securities from liability;

Giving effect to informal or invalid wills or deeds;

Summoning or impanelling grand or petit juries;

For limitation of civil or criminal actions;

For incorporating railroads or other works of internal improvements;

And in all other cases where a general law can be made applicable, no local or special law shall be enacted: *Provided*, That nothing herein contained shall be construed to prohibit the legislature from passing special laws for the preservation of the game and fish of this State in certain localities.

SEC. 57. No local or special law shall be passed, unless notice of the intention to apply therefor shall have been published in the locality where the matter or thing to be affected may be situated, which notice shall state the substance of the contemplated law, and shall be published at least thirty days prior to the introduction into the legislature of such bill and in the manner to be provided by law. The evidence of such notice having been published shall be exhibited in the legislature before such act shall be passed.

SEC. 58. The legislature shall hold its sessions at the city of Austin, which is hereby declared to be the seat of government.

ARTICLE IV.

EXECUTIVE DEPARTMENT.

SECTION 1. The executive department of the State shall consist of a governor, who shall be the chief executive officer of the State, a lieutenant-governor, secretary of state, comptroller of public accounts, treasurer, commissioner of the general land-office, and attorney-general.

SEC. 2. All the above officers of the executive department (except secretary of state) shall be elected by the qualified voters of the State at the time and places of election for members of the legislature.

SEC. 3. The returns of every election for said executive officers, until otherwise provided by law, shall be made out, sealed up, and transmitted by the returning-officers prescribed by law, to the seat of government, directed to the secretary of state, who shall deliver the same to the speaker of the house of representatives, as soon as the speaker shall be chosen; and the said speaker shall, during the first week of the session of the legislature, open and publish them in the presence of both houses of the legislature. The person voted for at said election having the highest number of votes for each of said offices respectively, and being constitutionally eligible, shall be declared by the speaker, under sanction of the legislature, to be elected to said office. But if two or more persons shall have the highest and an equal number of votes for either of said offices one of them shall be immediately chosen to such office by joint vote of both houses of the legislature. Contested elections for either of said offices shall be determined by both houses of the legislature in joint session.

SEC. 4. The governor shall be installed on the first Tuesday after the organization of the legislature, or as soon thereafter as practicable, and shall hold his office for the term of two years, or until his successor shall be duly installed. He shall be at least thirty years of age, a citizen of the United States, and shall have resided in this State at least five years immediately preceding his election.

SEC. 5. He shall, at stated times, receive as compensation for his services an annual salary of four thousand dollars and no more, and shall have the use and occupation of the governor's mansion, fixtures, and furniture.

SEC. 6. During the time he holds the office of governor he shall not hold any other office, civil, military, or corporate; nor shall he practice any profession, and receive compensation, reward, fee, or the promise thereof for the same; nor receive any salary, reward, or compensation, or the promise thereof, from any person or corporation, for any service rendered or performed during the time he is governor, or to be thereafter rendered or performed.

SEC. 7. He shall be commander-in-chief of the military forces of the State, except when they are called into actual service of the United States. He shall have power to call forth the militia to execute the laws of the State, to suppress insurrections, repel invasions, and protect the frontier from hostile incursions by Indians or other predatory bands.

SEC. 8. The governor may, on extraordinary occasions, convene the legislature at the seat of government, or at a different place in case that should be in possession of the public enemy or in case of the prevalence of disease thereat. His proclamation therefor should state specifically the purpose for which the legislature is convened.

SEC. 9. The governor shall, at the commencement of each session of the legislature, and at the close of his term of office, give to the legislature information, by message, of the condition of the State; and he shall recommend to the legislature such measures as he may deem expedient. He shall account to the legislature for all public moneys received and paid out by him from any funds subject to his order, with vouchers; and shall accompany his message with a statement of the same. And at the commencement of each regular session he shall present estimates of the amount of money required to be raised by taxation for all purposes.

SEC. 10. He shall cause the laws to be faithfully executed; and shall conduct, in person, or in such manner as shall be prescribed by law, all intercourse and business of the State with other States and with the United States.

SEC. 11. In all criminal cases, except treason and impeachment, he shall have power, after conviction, to grant reprieves, commutations of punishment, and pardons; and under such rules as the legislature may prescribe he shall have power to remit fines and forfeitures. With the advice and consent of the senate, he may grant pardons in cases of treason, and to this end he may respite a sentence therefor until the close of the succeeding session of the legislature: *Provided*, That in all cases of remissions of fines and forfeitures, or grants of reprieve, commutation of punishment, or pardon, he shall file in the office of the secretary of state his reasons therefor.

SEC. 12. All vacancies in State or district offices, except members of the legislature, shall be filled, unless otherwise provided by law, by appointment of the governor, which appointment, if made during its session, shall be with the advice and consent of two-thirds of the senate present. If made during the recess of the senate, the said appointee, or some other person to fill such vacancy, shall be nominated to the senate during the first ten days of its session. If rejected, said office shall immediately become vacant, and the governor shall, without delay, make further nominations, until a confirmation takes place. But should there be no confirmation during the session of the senate, the governor shall not thereafter appoint any person to fill such vacancy who has been rejected by the senate; but may appoint some other person to fill the vacancy until the next session of the senate or until the regular election to said office, should it sooner occur. Appointments to vacancies in offices elective by the people shall only continue until the first general election thereafter.

SEC. 13. During the session of the legislature the governor shall reside where its sessions are held, and at all other times at the seat of government, except when by act of the legislature he may be required or authorized to reside elsewhere.

SEC. 14. Every bill which shall have passed both houses of the legislature shall be presented to the governor for his approval. If he approve he shall sign it; but if he disapprove it, he shall return it, with his objections, to the house in which it originated, which house shall enter the objections at large upon its journal, and proceed to reconsider it. If, after such reconsideration, two-thirds of the members present agree to pass the bill, it shall be sent, with the objections, to the other house, by which likewise it shall be reconsidered; and, if approved by two-thirds of the members of that house, it shall become a law; but in such cases the votes of both houses shall be determined by yeas and nays, and the names of the members voting for and against the bill shall be entered on the journal of each house respectively. If any bill shall not be returned by the governor with his objections within ten days (Sundays excepted) after it shall have been presented to him, the same shall be a law, in like manner as if he had signed it, unless the legislature, by its adjournment, prevent its return; in which case it shall be a law, unless he shall file the same, with his objections, in the office of the secretary of state, and give notice thereof by public proclamation within twenty days after such adjournment. If any bill presented to the governor contains several items of appropriation, he may object to one or more of such items, and approve the other portion of the bill. In such case he shall append to the bill, at the time of signing it, a statement of the items to which he objects, and no item so objected to shall take effect. If the legislature be in session he shall transmit to the house in which the bill originated a copy of such statement and the items objected to shall be separately considered. If, on reconsideration, one or more of such items be approved by two-thirds of the members present of each house, the same shall be part of the law, notwithstanding the objections of the governor. If any such bill, containing several items of appropriation, not having been presented to the governor ten days (Sundays excepted) prior to adjournment, be in the hands of the governor at the time of adjournment, he shall have twenty days from such adjournment within which to file objections to any items thereof and make proclamation of the same, and such item or items shall not take effect.

SEC. 15. Every order, resolution, or vote to which the concurrence of both houses of the legislature may be necessary, except on questions of adjournment, shall be presented to the governor, and, before it shall take effect, shall be approved by him; or, being disapproved, shall be repassed by both houses; and all the rules, provisions, and limitations shall apply thereto as prescribed in the last preceding section in the case of a bill.

SEC. 16. There shall also be a lieutenant-governor, who shall be chosen at every election for governor by the same electors, in the same manner, continue in office the same time, and possess the same qualifications. The electors shall distinguish for whom they vote as governor and for whom as lieutenant-governor. The lieutenant-governor shall, by virtue of his office, be president of the Senate, and shall have, when in committee of the whole, a right to debate and vote on all questions; and, when the senate is equally divided, to give the casting vote. In case of the death, resignation, removal from office, inability, or refusal of the governor to serve, or of his impeachment or absence from the State, the lieutenant-governor shall exercise the powers and authority appertaining to the office of governor until another be chosen at the periodical election, and be duly qualified, or until the governor impeached, absent, or disabled, shall be acquitted, return, or his disability be removed.

SEC. 17. If, during the vacancy in the office of governor, the lieutenant-governor should die, resign, refuse to serve, or be removed from office, or be unable to serve, or if he shall be impeached or absent from the State, the president of the senate, for the time being, shall, in like manner, administer the government until he shall be superseded by a governor or lieutenant-governor. The lieutenant-governor shall, while he acts as president of the senate, receive for his services the same compensation and mileage which shall be allowed to the members of the senate, and no more; and during the time he administers the government, as governor, he shall receive in like manner the same compensation which the governor would have received had he been employed in the duties of his office, and no more. The president, for the time being, of the senate, shall, during the time he administers the government, receive in like manner the same compensation which the governor would have received had he been employed in the duties of his office.

SEC. 18. The lieutenant-governor or president of the senate succeeding to the office of governor shall, during the entire term to which he may succeed, be under all the restrictions and inhibitions imposed in this constitution on the governor.

SEC. 19. There shall be a seal of the State, which shall be kept by the secretary of state, and used by him officially under the direction of the governor. The seal of the State shall be a star of five points, encircled by olive and live-oak branches, and the words "The State of Texas."

SEC. 20. All commissions shall be in the name and by the authority of the State of Texas, sealed with the State seal, signed by the governor, and attested by the secretary of state.

SEC. 21. There shall be a secretary of state, who shall be appointed by the governor, by and with the advice and consent of the senate, and who shall continue in office during the term of service of the governor. He shall authenticate the publication of the laws, and keep a fair register of all official acts and proceedings of the governor, and shall, when required, lay the same and all papers, minutes, and vouchers relative thereto before the legislature, or either house thereof, and shall perform such other duties as may be required of him by law. He shall receive for his services an annual salary of two thousand dollars, and no more.

SEC. 22. The attorney-general shall hold his office for two years and until his successor is duly qualified. He shall represent the State in all suits and pleas in the supreme court of the State in which the State may be a party, and shall especially inquire into the charter-rights of all private corporations, and, from time to time, in the name of the State take such action in the courts as may be proper and necessary to prevent any private corporation from exercising any power or demanding or collecting any species of taxes, tolls, freight, or wharfage not authorized by law. He shall, whenever sufficient cause exists, seek a judicial forfeiture of such charters, unless otherwise expressly directed by law, and give legal advice, in writing, to the governor and other executive officers, when requested by them, and perform such other duties as may be required by law. He shall reside at the seat of government during his continuance in office. He shall receive for his services an annual salary of two thousand dollars, and no more, besides such fees as may be prescribed by law: *Provided*, That the fees which he may receive shall not amount to more than two thousand dollars annually.

SEC. 23. The comptroller of public accounts, the treasurer, and the commissioner of the general land-office shall each hold office for the term of two years, and until his successor is qualified; receive an annual salary of two thousand and five hundred dollars, and no more; reside at the capital of the State during his continuance in office, and perform such duties as are or may be required of him by law. They and the secretary of state shall not receive to their own use any fees, costs, or perquisites of office. All fees that may be payable by law for any service performed by any officer specified in this section, or in his office, shall be paid, when received, into the State treasury.

SEC. 24. An account shall be kept by the officers of the executive department and by all officers and managers of State institutions of all moneys and choses in action received and disbursed, or otherwise disposed of by them, severally, from all sources, and for every service performed; and a semi-annual report thereof shall be made to the governor under oath. The governor may at any time require information in writing from any and all of said officers or managers upon any subject relating to the duties, condition, management, and expenses of their respective offices and institutions, which information shall be required by the governor under oath; and the governor may also inspect their books, accounts, vouchers, and public funds; and any officer or manager who at any time shall wilfully make a false report or give false information shall be guilty of perjury, and so adjudged and punished accordingly, and removed from office.

SEC. 25. The legislature shall pass efficient laws facilitating the investigation of breaches of trust and duty by all custodians of public funds, and providing for their suspension from office on reasonable cause shown, and for the appointment of temporary incumbents of their offices during such suspension.

SEC. 26. The governor, by and with the advice and consent of two-thirds of the senate, shall appoint a convenient number of notaries public for each county, who shall perform such duties as now are or may be prescribed by law.

ARTICLE V.

JUDICIAL DEPARTMENT.

SECTION 1. The judicial power of this State shall be vested in one supreme court, in a court of appeals, in district courts, in county courts, in commissioners' courts, in courts of justices of the peace, and in such other courts as may be established by law. The legislature may establish criminal district courts with such jurisdiction as it may prescribe, but no such court shall be established unless the district includes a city containing at least thirty thousand inhabitants, as ascertained by the census of the United States or other official census: *Provided*, Such town or city shall support said criminal district courts when established. The criminal district court of Galveston and Harris Counties shall continue with the district, jurisdiction, and organization now existing by law until otherwise provided by law.

SEC. 2. The supreme court shall consist of a chief-justice and two associate justices, any two of whom shall constitute a quorum, and the concurrence of two judges shall be necessary to the decision of a case. No person shall be eligible to the office of chief-justice or associate justice of the supreme court unless he be at the time of his election a citizen of the United States and of this State, and unless he shall have attained the age of thirty years, and shall have been a practising lawyer or a judge of a court in this State, or such lawyer and judge together, at least seven years. Said chief-justice and associate justices shall be elected by the qualified voters of the State at a general election, shall hold their offices for six years, and shall each receive an annual salary of not more than three thousand five hundred and fifty dollars. In case of a vacancy in the office of chief-justice or associate justice of the supreme court, the governor shall fill the vacancy until the next general election for State officers, and at such general election the vacancy for the unexpired term shall be filled by election by the qualified voters of the State.

SEC. 3. The supreme court shall have appellate jurisdiction only, which shall be co-extensive with the limits of the State, but shall only extend to civil cases, of which the district courts have original or appellate jurisdiction. Appeals may be allowed from interlocutory judgments of the district courts, in such cases and under such regulations as may be provided by law. The supreme court and the judges thereof shall have power to issue, under such regulations as may be prescribed by law, the writ of *mandamus* and all other writs necessary to enforce the jurisdiction of said court. The supreme court shall have power upon affidavit or otherwise, as by the court may be thought proper, to ascertain such matters of fact as may be necessary to the proper exercise of its jurisdiction. The supreme court shall sit for the transaction of business from the first Monday in October until the last Saturday of June of every year, at the seat of government, and at not more than two other places in the State.

SEC. 4. The supreme court shall appoint a clerk for each place at which it may sit, and each of said clerks shall give bond in such manner as is now or may hereafter be required by law; shall hold his office for four years, and shall be subject to removal by said court for good cause entered of record on the minutes of said court.

SEC. 5. The court of appeals shall consist of three judges, any two of whom shall constitute a quorum, and the concurrence of two judges shall be necessary to a decision of said court. They shall be elected by the qualified voters of the State at a general election. They shall be citizens of the United States and of this State; shall have arrived at the age of thirty years at the time of election; each shall have been a practising lawyer or a judge of a court in this State, or such lawyer and judge together, for at least seven years. Said judges shall hold their offices for a term of six years, and each of them shall receive an annual salary of three thousand five hundred and fifty dollars, which shall not be increased or diminished during their term of office.

SEC. 6. The court of appeals shall have appellate jurisdiction, co-extensive with the limits of the State, in all criminal cases, of whatever grade, and in all civil cases, unless hereafter otherwise provided by law, of which the county courts have original or appellate jurisdiction. In civil cases its opinions shall not be published unless the publication of such opinions be required by law. The court of appeals and the judges thereof shall have power to issue the writ of *habeas corpus*, and under such regulations as may be prescribed by law issue such writs as may be necessary to enforce its own jurisdiction. The court of appeals shall have power upon affidavits or otherwise, as by the court may be thought proper, to ascertain such matters of fact as may be necessary to the exercise of its jurisdiction. The court of appeals shall sit for the transaction of business from the first Monday of October until the last Saturday of June of every year, at the capital, and at not more than two other places in the State, at which the supreme court shall hold its sessions. The court shall appoint a clerk for each place at which it may sit, and each of said clerks shall give bond in such manner as is now or may hereafter be required by law, shall hold his office for four years, and shall be subject to removal by the said court for good cause, entered of record on the minutes of said court.

SEC. 7. The State shall be divided into twenty-six judicial districts, which may be increased or diminished by the legislature. For each district there shall be elected by the qualified voters thereof, at a general election for members of the legislature, a judge, who shall be at least twenty-five years of age, shall be a citizen of the United States, shall have been a practising attorney or a judge of a court in this State for the period of four years, and shall have resided in the district in which he is elected for two years next before his election; shall reside in his district during his term of office; shall hold his office for the term of four years; shall receive an annual salary of twenty-five hundred dollars, which shall not be increased or diminished during his term of service, and shall hold the regular terms of court at one place in each county in the district twice in each year, in such manner as may be prescribed by law. The legislature shall have power by general act to authorize the holding of special terms when necessary, and to provide for holding more than two terms of the court in any county for the dispatch of business, and shall provide for the holding of district courts, when the judge thereof is absent or is from any cause disabled or disqualified from presiding.

SEC. 8. The district court shall have original jurisdiction in criminal cases of the grade of felony; of all suits in behalf of the State to recover penalties, forfeitures, and escheats; of all cases of divorce; in cases of misdemeanors involving official misconduct; of all suits to recover damages for slander or defamation of character; of all suits for the trial of title to land, and for the enforcement of liens thereon; of all suits for trial of right to property levied on by virtue of any writ of execution, sequestration, or attachment, when the property levied on shall be equal to or exceed in value five hundred dollars, and of all suits, complaints, or pleas whatever, without regard to any distinction between law and equity, when the matter in controversy shall be valued at or amount to five hundred dollars, exclusive of interest; and the said courts and the judges thereof shall have power to issue writs of *habeas corpus* in felony cases, *mandamus*, injunction, *certiorari*, and all writs necessary to enforce their jurisdiction. The district courts shall have appellate jurisdiction and general control in probate matters over the county court established in each county for appointing guardians, granting letters testamentary and of administration, for settling the accounts of executors, administrators, and guardians, and for the transaction of business appertaining to estates; and original jurisdiction and general control over executors, administrators, guardians, and minors, under such regulations as may be prescribed by the legislature. All cases now pending in the supreme court, of which the court of appeals has appellate jurisdiction under the provisions of this article, shall, as soon as practicable after the establishment of said court of appeals, be certified, and the records transmitted to the court of appeals, and shall be decided by such court of appeals as if the same had been originally appealed to such court.

SEC. 9 There shall be a clerk for the district court of each county, who shall be elected by the qualified voters for the State and county officers, and who shall hold his office for two years, subject to removal by information, or by indictment of a grand jury and conviction by a petit jury. In case of vacancy the judge of the district court shall have the power to appoint a clerk, who shall hold until the office can be filled by election.

SEC. 10. In the trial of all causes in the district courts, the plaintiff or defendant shall, upon application made in open court, have the right of trial by jury; but no jury shall be impanneled in any civil case unless demanded by a party to the case, and a jury fee be paid by the party demanding a jury, for such sum and with such exceptions as may be prescribed by the legislature.

SEC. 11. No judge shall sit in any case wherein he may be interested, or where either of the parties may be connected with him by affinity or consanguinity, within such degree as may be prescribed by law, or where he shall have been counsel in the case. When the supreme court or the appellate court, or any two of the members of either, shall be thus disqualified to hear and determine any case or cases in said court, the same shall be certified to the governor of the State, who shall immediately commission the requisite number of persons learned in the law for the trial and determination of said cause or causes. When a judge of the district court is disqualified by any of the causes above stated, the parties may, by consent, appoint a proper person to try said case; or, upon their failing to do so, a competent person may be appointed to try the same in the county where it is pending, in such manner as may be prescribed by law. And the district judges may exchange districts, or hold courts for each other, when they may deem it expedient, and shall do so when directed by law. The disqualification of judges of inferior tribunals shall be remedied, and vacancies in their offices shall be filled as prescribed by law.

SEC. 12. All judges of the supreme court, court of appeals, and district courts shall, by virtue of their offices, be conservators of the peace throughout the State. The style of all writs and process shall be "The State of Texas." All prosecutions shall be carried on in the name and by the authority of "The State of Texas," and conclude "against the peace and dignity of the State."

SEC. 13. Grand and petit juries in the district courts shall be composed of twelve men; but nine members of a grand jury shall be a quorum to transact business and present bills. In trials of civil cases, and in trials of criminal cases below the grade of felony in the district courts, nine members of the jury, concurring, may render a verdict; but when the verdict shall be rendered by less than the whole number it shall be signed by every member of the jury concurring in it. When pending the trial of any case one or more jurors, not exceeding three, may die, or be disabled from sitting, the remainder of the jury shall have the power to render the verdict:

Provided, That the legislature may change or modify the rule authorizing less than the whole number of the jury to render a verdict.

SEC. 14. The judicial districts in this State and the time of holding the courts therein are fixed by ordinance forming part of this constitution, until otherwise provided by law.

SEC. 15. There shall be established in each county in this State a county court, which shall be a court of record, and there shall be elected in each county, by the qualified voters, a county judge, who shall be well informed in the law of the State, shall be a conservator of the peace, and shall hold his office for two years, and until his successor shall be elected and qualified. He shall receive as a compensation for his services such fees and perquisites as may be prescribed by law.

SEC. 16. The county court shall have original jurisdiction of all misdemeanors, of which exclusive original jurisdiction is not given to the justice's court, as the same are now or may be hereafter prescribed by law, and when the fine to be imposed shall exceed two hundred dollars; and they shall have exclusive original jurisdiction in all civil cases when the matter in controversy shall exceed in value two hundred dollars and not exceed five hundred dollars, exclusive of interest; and concurrent jurisdiction with the district courts when the matter in controversy shall exceed five hundred and not exceed one thousand dollars, exclusive of interest, but shall not have jurisdiction of suits for the recovery of land. They shall have appellate jurisdiction in cases, civil and criminal, of which justices' courts have original jurisdiction, but of such civil cases only when the judgment of the court appealed from shall exceed twenty dollars exclusive of costs, under such regulations as may be prescribed by law. In all appeals from justices' courts there shall be a trial *de novo* in the county court, and when the judgment rendered or fine imposed by the county court shall not exceed one hundred dollars such trial shall be final; but if the judgment rendered or fine imposed shall exceed one hundred dollars, as well as in all cases, civil and criminal, of which the county court has exclusive or concurrent original jurisdiction, an appeal shall lie to the court of appeals, under such regulations as may be prescribed by law. The county courts shall have the general jurisdiction of a probate court. They shall probate wills, appoint guardians of minors, idiots, lunatics, persons *non compos mentis*, and common drunkards, grant letters testamentary and of administration, settle accounts of executors, administrators, and guardians, transact all business appertaining to the estates of deceased persons, minors, idiots, lunatics, persons *non compos mentis*, and common drunkards, including the settlement, partition, and distribution of estates of deceased persons, and to apprentice minors as provided by law. And the county courts, or judges thereof, shall have power to issue writs of mandamus, injunction, and all other writs necessary to the enforcement of the jurisdiction of said courts; and to issue writs of *habeas corpus* in cases where the offense charged is within the jurisdiction of the county court, or any other court or tribunal inferior to said court. The county court shall not have criminal jurisdiction in any county where there is a criminal district court, unless expressly conferred by law; and in such counties appeals from justices' courts and other inferior courts and tribunals in criminal cases shall be to the criminal district courts, under such regulations as may be prescribed by law, and in all such cases an appeal shall lie from such district courts to the court of appeals. Any case pending in the county court, which the county judge may be disqualified to try, shall be transferred to the district court of the same county for trial; and where there exists any cause disqualifying the county judge for the trial of a cause of which the county court has jurisdiction the district court of such county shall have original jurisdiction of such cause.

SEC. 17. The county court shall hold a term for civil business at least once in every two months, and shall dispose of probate business, either in term time or vacation, as may be provided by law; and said court shall hold a term for criminal business once in every month, as may be provided by law. Prosecutions may be commenced in said court by information filed by the county attorney or by affidavit, as may be provided by law. Grand juries impanneled in the district courts shall inquire into misdemeanors, and all indictments therefor returned into the district courts shall forthwith be certified to the county courts, or other inferior courts having jurisdiction to try them, for trial; and if such indictment be quashed in the county or other inferior court the person charged shall not be discharged if there is probable cause of guilt, but may be held by such court or magistrate to answer an information or affidavit. A jury in the county court shall consist of six men; but no jury shall be impanelled to try a civil case, unless demanded by one of the parties, who shall pay such jury fee therefor in advance, as may be prescribed by law, unless he makes affidavit that he is unable to pay the same.

SEC. 18. Each organized county in the State now or hereafter existing shall be divided from time to time, for the convenience of the people, into precincts, not less than four and not more than eight. The present county courts shall make the first division. Subsequent divisions shall be made by the commissioners' court, provided for by this constitution. In each such precinct there shall be elected at each biennial election one justice of the peace and one constable, each of whom shall hold his office for two years and until his successor shall be elected and qualified: *Provided*, That in any precinct in which there may be a city of eight thousand or more inhabitants there shall be elected two justices of the peace. Each county shall in like manner be divided into four commissioners' precincts, in each of which there shall be elected by the qualified voters thereof one county commissioner, who shall hold his office for two years and until his successor shall be elected and qualified. The county commissioners so chosen, with the county judge as presiding officer, shall compose the county commissioners' court, which shall exercise such powers and jurisdiction over all county business as is conferred by this constitution and the laws of this State, or as may be hereafter prescribed.

SEC. 19. Justices of the peace shall have jurisdiction in criminal matters of all cases where the penalty or fine to be imposed by law may not be more than for two hundred dollars, and in civil matters of all cases where the amount in controversy is two hundred dollars or less, exclusive of interest, of which exclusive original jurisdiction is not given to the district or county courts; and such other jurisdiction, criminal and civil, as may be provided by law, under such regulations as may be prescribed by law; and appeals to the county courts shall be allowed in all cases decided in justices' courts where the judgment is for more than twenty dollars, exclusive of costs, and in all criminal cases, under such regulations as may be prescribed by law. And the justices of the peace shall be *ex officio* notaries public, and they shall hold their courts at such times and places as may be provided by law.

SEC. 20. There shall be elected for each county, by the qualified voters, a county clerk, who shall hold his office for two years, who shall be clerk of the county and commissioners' courts and recorder of the county, whose duties, perquisites, and fees of office shall be prescribed by the legislature, and a vacancy in whose office shall be filled by the commissioners' court until the next general election for county and State officers: *Provided*, That in counties having a population of less than eight thousand persons there may be an election of a single clerk, who shall perform the duties of district and county clerks.

SEC. 21. A county attorney, for counties in which there is not a resident criminal district attorney, shall be elected by the qualified voters of each county, who shall be commissioned by the governor, and hold his office for the term of two years. In case of vacancy the commissioners' court of the county shall have power to appoint a county attorney until the next general election. The county attorneys shall represent the State in all cases in the district and inferior courts in their respective counties; but if any county shall be included in a district in which there shall be a district attorney, the respective duties of district attorneys and county attorneys shall in such counties be regulated by the legislature. The legislature may provide for the election of district attorneys in such districts as may be deemed necessary, and make provision for the compensation of district attorneys and county attorneys: *Provided*, District attorneys shall receive an annual salary of five hundred dollars, to be paid by the State, and such fees, commissions, and perquisites as may be provided by law. County attorneys shall receive as compensation only such fees, commissions, and perquisites as may be prescribed by law.

SEC. 22. The legislature shall have power, by local or general law, to increase, diminish, or change the civil and criminal jurisdiction of county courts; and in cases of any such change of jurisdiction the legislature shall also conform the jurisdiction of the other courts to such change.

SEC. 23. There shall be elected by the qualified voters of each county a sheriff, who shall hold his office for the term of two years, whose duties and perquisites and fees of office shall be prescribed by the legislature, and vacancies in whose office shall be filled by the commissioners' court until the next general election for county or State officers.

SEC. 24. County judges, county attorneys, clerks of the district and county courts, justices of the peace, constables, and other county officers may be removed by the judges of the district courts for incompetency, official misconduct, habitual drunkenness, or other causes defined by law, upon the cause therefor being set forth in writing and the finding of its truth by a jury.

SEC. 25. The supreme court shall have power to make rules and regulations for the government of said court and the other courts of the State, to regulate proceedings, and expedite the dispatch of business therein.

SEC. 26. The State shall have no right of appeal in criminal cases.

SEC. 27. The legislature shall, at its first session, provide for the transfer of all business, civil and criminal, pending in district courts, over which jurisdiction is given by this constitution to the county courts or other inferior courts, to such county or inferior courts, and for the trial or disposition of all such causes by such county or other inferior courts.

SEC. 28. Vacancies in the office of judges in the supreme court, of the court of appeals, and district court shall be filled by the governor until the next succeeding general election; and vacancies in the office of county judge and justices of the peace shall be filled by the commissioners' court until the next general election for such offices.

ARTICLE VI.

SUFFRAGE.

SECTION 1. The following classes of persons shall not be allowed to vote in this State, to wit:

First. Persons under twenty-one years of age.

Second. Idiots and lunatics.

Third. All paupers supported by any county.

Fourth. All persons convicted of any felony, subject to such exceptions as the legislature may make.

Fifth. All soldiers, marines, and seamen employed in the service of the Army or Navy of the United States.

SEC. 2. Every male person subject to none of the foregoing disqualifications, who shall have attained the age of twenty-one years, and who shall be a citizen of the United States, and who shall have resided in this State one year next preceding an election, and the last six months within the district or county in which he offers to vote, shall be deemed a qualified elector; and every male person of foreign birth, subject to none of the foregoing disqualifications, who, at any time before an election, shall have declared his intention to become a citizen of the United States, in accordance with the Federal naturalization laws, and shall have resided in this State one year next preceding such election, and the last six months in the county in which he offers to vote, shall also be deemed a qualified elector; and all electors shall vote in the election-precinct of their residence: *Provided*, That electors living in any unorganized county may vote at any election-precinct in the county to which such county is attached for judicial purposes.

SEC. 3. All qualified electors of the State, as herein described, who shall have resided for six months immediately preceding an election within the limits of any city or corporate town shall have the right to vote for mayor and all other elective officers; but in all elections to determine expenditure of money or assumption of debt only those shall be qualified to vote who pay taxes on property in said city or incorporated town: *Provided*, That no poll-tax for the payment of debts thus incurred shall be levied upon the persons debarred from voting in relation thereto.

SEC. 4. In all elections by the people the vote shall be by ballot, and the legislature shall provide for the numbering of tickets and make such other regulations as may be necessary to detect and punish fraud and preserve the purity of the ballot-box; but no law shall ever be enacted requiring a registration of the voters of the State.

SEC. 5. Voters shall in all cases, except treason, felony, or breach of the peace, be privileged from arrest during their attendance at elections, and in going to and returning therefrom.

ARTICLE VII.

EDUCATION—THE PUBLIC FREE SCHOOLS.

SECTION 1. A general diffusion of knowledge being essential to the preservation of the liberties and rights of the people, it shall be the duty of the legislature of the State to establish and make suitable provision for the support and maintenance of an efficient system of public free schools.

SEC. 2. All funds, lands, and other property heretofore set apart and appropriated for the support of public schools; all the alternate sections of land reserved by the State out of grants heretofore made, or that may hereafter be made, to railroads or other corporations of any nature whatsoever; one-half of the public domain of the State; and all sums of money that may come to the State from the sale of any portion of the same, shall constitute a perpetual public-school fund.

SEC. 3. There shall be set apart annually not more than one-fourth of the general revenue of the State, and a poll-tax of one dollar on all male inhabitants in this State between the ages of twenty-one and sixty years, for the benefit of the public free schools.

SEC. 4. The lands herein set apart to the public free-school fund shall be sold, under such regulations, at such times, and on such terms as may be prescribed by law; and the legislature shall not have power to grant any relief to the purchasers thereof. The comptroller shall invest the proceeds of such sales, and of those heretofore made, as may be directed by the board of education herein provided for, in the bonds of this State, if the same can be obtained, otherwise in United States bonds; and the United States bonds now belonging to said fund shall likewise be invested in State bonds, if the same can be obtained on terms advantageous to the school-fund.

SEC. 5. The principal of all bonds and other funds, and the principal arising from the sale of the lands hereinbefore set apart to said school-fund, shall be the permanent school-fund; and all the interest derivable therefrom and the taxes herein authorized and levied shall be the available school-fund, which shall be applied annually to the support of the public free schools. And no law shall ever be enacted appropriating any part of the permanent or available school-fund to any other purpose whatever; nor shall the same or any part thereof ever be appropriated to or used for the support of any sectarian school; and the available school-fund herein provided shall be distributed to the several counties according to their scholastic population, and applied in manner as may be provided by law.

SEC. 6. All lands heretofore or hereafter granted to the several counties of this State for education or schools are of right the property of said counties respectively to which they were granted, and title thereto is vested in said counties, and no adverse possession or limitation shall ever be available against the title of any county. Each county may sell or dispose of its lands, in whole or in part, in manner to be provided by the commissioners' court of the county. Actual settlers residing on said lands shall be protected in the prior right of purchasing the same to the extent of their settlement, not to exceed one hundred and sixty acres, at the price fixed by said court, which price shall not include the value of existing improvements made thereon by such settlers. Said lands and the proceeds thereof, when sold, shall be held by said counties alone as a trust for the benefit of public schools therein; said proceeds to be invested in bonds of the State of Texas or of the United States, and only the interest thereon to be used and expended annually.

SEC. 7. Separate schools shall be provided for the white and colored children, and impartial provision shall be made for both.

SEC. 8. The governor, comptroller, and secretary of state shall constitute a board of education, who shall distribute said funds to the several counties and perform such other duties concerning public schools as may be prescribed by law.

ASYLUMS.

SEC. 9. All lands heretofore granted for the benefit of the lunatic, blind, deaf and dumb, and orphan asylums, together with such donations as may have been or may hereafter be made to either of them, respectively, as indicated in the several grants, are hereby set apart to provide a permanent fund for the support, maintenance, and improvement of said asylums. And the legislature may provide for the sale of the lands and the investment of the proceeds in manner as provided for the sale and investment of school lands in section 4 of this article.

UNIVERSITY.

SEC. 10. The legislature shall, as soon as practicable, establish, organize, and provide for the maintenance, support, and direction of a university of the first class, to be located by a vote of the people of this State, and styled "The University of Texas," for the promotion of literature and the arts and sciences, including an agricultural and mechanical department.

SEC. 11. In order to enable the legislature to perform the duties set forth in the foregoing section, it is hereby declared that all lands and other property heretofore set apart and appropriated for the establishment and maintenance of "The University of Texas," together with all the proceeds of sales of the same, heretofore made or hereafter so to be made, and all grants, donations, and appropriations that may hereafter be made by the State of Texas, or from any other source, shall constitute and become a permanent university fund. And the same as realized and received into the treasury of the State (together with such sums, belonging to the fund, as may now be in the treasury) shall be invested in bonds of the State of Texas, if the same can be obtained; if not, then in United States bonds, and the interest accruing thereon shall be subject to appropriation by the legislature to accomplish the purpose declared in the foregoing section : *Provided*, That one-tenth of the alternate sections of the lands granted to railroads, reserved by the State, which were set apart and appropriated to the establishment of "The University of Texas," by an act of the legislature of February 11, 1858, entitled "An act to establish 'The University of Texas,'" shall not be included in or constitute a part of the permanent university fund.

SEC. 12. The land herein set apart to the university fund shall be sold under such regulations, at such times, and on such terms, as may be provided by law; and the legislature shall provide for the prompt collection, at maturity, of all debts due on account of university lands heretofore sold, or that may hereafter be sold, and shall in neither event have the power to grant relief to the purchasers.

SEC. 13. The Agricultural and Mechanical College of Texas, established by an act of the legislature, passed April 17, 1871, located in the county of Brazos, is hereby made and constituted a branch of the University of Texas, for instruction in agriculture, the mechanic arts, and the natural sciences connected therewith. And the legislature shall, at its next session, make an appropriation, not to exceed forty thousand dollars, for the construction and completion of the buildings and improvements, and for providing the furniture necessary to put said college in immediate and successful operation.

SEC. 14. The legislature shall also, when deemed practicable, establish and provide for the maintenance of a college or branch university for the instruction of the colored youths of the State, to be located by a vote of the people : *Provided*, That no tax shall be levied and no money appropriated out of the general revenue, either for this purpose or for the establishment and erection of the buildings of the University of Texas.

SEC. 15. In addition to the lands heretofore granted to the University of Texas, there is hereby set apart and appropriated for the endowment, maintenance, and support of said university and its branches one million acres of the unappropriated public domain of the State, to be designated and surveyed as may be provided by law; and said lands shall be sold under the same regulations, and the proceeds invested in the same manner, as is provided for the sale and investment of the permanent university fund; and the legislature shall not have power to grant any relief to the purchasers of said lands.

ARTICLE VIII.

TAXATION AND REVENUE.

SECTION 1. Taxation shall be equal and uniform. All property in this State, whether owned by natural persons or corporations, other than municipal, shall be taxed in proportion to its value, which shall be ascertained as may be provided by law. The legislature may impose a poll-tax. It may also impose occupation taxes, both upon natural persons and upon corporations, other than municipal, doing any business in this State. It may also tax incomes of both natural persons and corporations, other than municipal, except that persons engaged in mechanical and agricultural pursuits shall never be required to pay an occupation tax: *Provided*, That two hundred and fifty dollars' worth of household and kitchen furniture belonging to each family in this State shall be exempt from taxation: *And provided further*, That the occupation tax levied by any county, city, or town, for any year, on persons or corporations pursuing any profession or business, shall not exceed one-half of the tax levied by the State for the same period on such profession or business.

SEC. 2. All occupation taxes shall be equal and uniform upon the same class of subjects within the limits of the authority levying the tax; but the legislature may, by general laws, exempt from taxation public property used for public purposes, actual places of religious worship, places of burial not held for private or corporate profit, all buildings used exclusively and owned by persons or associations of persons for school purposes, (and the necessary furniture of all schools,) and institutions of purely public charity; and all laws exempting property from taxation, other than the property above mentioned, shall be void.

SEC. 3. Taxes shall be levied and collected by general laws and for public purposes only.

SEC. 4. The power to tax corporations and corporate property shall not be surrendered or suspended by act of the legislature by any contract or grant to which the State shall be a party.

SEC. 5. All property of railroad companies, of whatever description, lying or being within the limits of any city or incorporated town within this State, shall bear its proportionate share of municipal taxation, and if any such property shall not have been heretofore rendered, the authorities of the city or town within which it lies shall have power to require its rendition, and collect the usual municipal tax thereon as on other property lying within said municipality.

SEC. 6. No money shall be drawn from the treasury but in pursuance of specific appropriations made by law; nor shall any appropriation of money be made for a longer term than two years, except by the first legislature to assemble under this constitution, which may make the necessary appropriations to carry on the government until the assemblage of the sixteenth legislature.

SEC. 7. The legislature shall not have power to borrow, or in any manner divert from its purpose, any special fund that may, or ought to, come into the treasury; and shall make it penal for any person or persons to borrow, withhold, or in any manner to divert from its purpose any special fund, or any part thereof.

SEC. 8. All property of railroad companies shall be assessed, and the taxes collected, in the several counties in which said property is situated, including so much of the road-bed and fixtures as shall be in each county. The rolling-stock may be assessed in gross in the county where the principal office of the company is located, and the county tax paid upon it shall be apportioned by the comptroller, in proportion to the distance such road may run through any such county, among the several counties through which the road passes, as a part of their tax assets.

SEC. 9. The State tax on property, exclusive of the tax necessary to pay the public debt, shall never exceed fifty cents on the one hundred dollars' valuation, and no county, city, or town shall levy more than one-half of said State tax, except for the payment of debts already incurred, and for the erection of public buildings, not to exceed fifty cents on the one hundred dollars in any one year, and except as in this constitution is otherwise provided.

SEC. 10. The legislature shall have no power to release the inhabitants of, or property in, any county, city, or town from the payment of taxes levied for State or county purposes, unless in case of great public calamity in any such county, city, or town, when such release may be made by a vote of two-thirds of each house of the legislature.

SEC. 11. All property, whether owned by persons or corporations, shall be assessed for taxation, and the taxes paid in the county where situated, but the legislature may, by a two-thirds vote, authorize the payment of taxes of non-residents of counties to be made at the office of the comptroller of public accounts. And all lands and other property not rendered for taxation by the owner thereof shall be assessed at its fair value by the proper officer.

SEC. 12. All property subject to taxation in and owned by residents of unorganized counties shall be assessed and the taxes thereon paid in the counties to which such unorganized counties shall be attached for judicial purposes; and lands lying in and owned by non-residents of unorganized counties, and lands lying in the territory not laid off into counties, shall be assessed and the taxes thereon collected at the office of the comptroller of the State.

SEC. 13. Provision shall be made by the first legislature for the speedy sale of a sufficient portion of all lands and other property for the taxes due thereon, and every year thereafter for the sale of all lands and other property upon which the taxes have not been paid, and the deed of conveyance to the purchaser for all lands and other property thus sold shall be held to vest a good and perfect title in the purchaser thereof, subject to be impeached only for actual fraud: *Provided*, That the former owner shall, within two years from date of purchaser's deed, have the right to redeem the land upon the payment of double the amount of money paid for the land.

SEC. 14. There shall be elected by the qualified electors of each county, at the same time and under the same law regulating the election of State and county officers, an assessor of taxes, who shall hold his office for two years and until his successor is elected and qualified.

SEC. 15. The annual assessment made upon landed property shall be a special lien thereon, and all property, both real and personal, belonging to any delinquent taxpayer, shall be liable to seizure and sale for the payment of all the taxes and penalties due by such delinquent; and such property may be sold for the payment of the taxes and penalties due by such delinquent under such regulations as the legislature may provide.

SEC. 16. The sheriff of each county, in addition to his other duties, shall be the collector of taxes therefor. But in counties having ten thousand inhabitants, to be determined by the last preceding census of the United States, a collector of taxes shall be elected to hold office for two years and until his successor shall be elected and qualified.

SEC. 17. The specification of the objects and subjects of taxation shall not deprive the legislature of the power to require other subjects or objects to be taxed in such manner as may be consistent with the principles of taxation fixed in this constitution.

SEC. 18. The legislature shall provide for equalizing, as near as may be, the valuation of all property subject to or rendered for taxation, (the county commissioners' court to constitute a board of equalization;) and may also provide for the classification of all lands, with reference to their value, in the several counties.

ARTICLE IX.

COUNTIES.

SECTION 1. The legislature shall have power to create counties for the convenience of the people, subject to the following provisions:

First. In the territory of the State exterior to all counties now existing, no new counties shall be created with a less area than nine hundred square miles, in a square form, unless prevented by pre-existing boundary-lines. Should the State-lines render this impracticable in border counties, the area may be less. The territory referred to may, at any time, in whole or in part, be divided into counties in advance of population, and attached, for judicial and land-surveying purposes, to the most convenient organized county or counties.

Second. Within the territory of any county or counties now existing, no new county shall be created with a less area than seven hundred square miles, nor shall any such county now existing be reduced to a less area than seven hundred square miles. No new counties shall be created so as to approach nearer than twelve miles of the county-seat of any county from which it may, in whole or in part, be taken. Counties of a less area than nine hundred, but of seven hundred or more square miles, within counties now existing, may be created by a two-thirds vote of each house of the legislature, taken by yeas and nays, and entered on the journals. Any county now existing may be reduced to an area of not less than seven hundred square miles by a like two-thirds vote. When any part of a county is stricken off and attached to or created into another county, the part stricken off shall be holden for and obliged to pay its proportion of all the liabilities then existing of the county from which it was taken, in such manner as may be prescribed by law.

Third. No part of any existing county shall be detached from it and attached to another existing county until the proposition for such change shall have been submitted, in such manner as may be provided by law, to a vote of the electors of both counties, and shall have received a majority of those voting on the question in each.

COUNTY-SEATS.

SEC. 2. The legislature shall pass laws regulating the manner of removing county-seats, but no county-seat situated within five miles of the geographical centre of the county shall be removed, except by a vote of two-thirds of all the electors voting on the subject. A majority of such electors, however, voting at such election, may remove a county-seat from a point more than five miles from the geographical centre of the county to a point within five miles of such centre, in either case the centre to be determined by a certificate from the commissioner of the general land-office.

ARTICLE X.

RAILROADS.

SECTION 1. Any railroad corporation or association, organized under the law for the purpose, shall have the right to construct and operate a railroad between any points within this State, and to connect at the State-line with railroads of other States. Every railroad company shall have the right, with its road, to intersect, connect with, or cross any other railroad; and shall receive and transport each the others' passengers, tonnage, and cars, loaded or empty, without delay or discrimination, under such regulations as shall be prescribed by law.

SEC. 2. Railroads heretofore constructed, or that may hereafter be constructed, in this State are hereby declared public highways, and railroad companies common carriers. The legislature shall pass laws to correct abuses and prevent unjust discrimination and extortion in the rates of freight and passenger tariffs on the different railroads in this State; and shall from time to time pass laws establishing reasonable maximum rates of charges for the transportation of passengers and freight on said railroads, and enforce all such laws by adequate penalties.

SEC. 3. Every railroad or other corporation, organized or doing business in this State under the laws or authority thereof, shall have and maintain a public office or place in this State for the transaction of its business, where transfers of stock shall be made, and where shall be kept, for inspection by the stockholders of such corporations, books, in which shall be recorded the amount of capital stock subscribed, the names of the owners of the stock, the amounts owned by them respectively, the amount of stock paid, and by whom, the transfer of said stock, with the date of the transfer, the amount of its assets and liabilities, and the names and places of residence of its officers. The directors of every railroad company shall hold one meeting annually in this State, public notice of which shall be given thirty days previously, and the president or superintendent shall report annually, under oath, to the comptroller or governor, their acts and doings, which report shall include such matters relating to railroads as may be prescribed by law. The legislature shall pass laws enforcing by suitable penalties the provisions of this section.

SEC. 4. The rolling-stock and all other movable property belonging to any railroad company or corporation in this State shall be considered personal property, and its real and personal property, or any part thereof, shall be liable to execution and sale in the same manner as the property of individuals; and the legislature shall pass no laws exempting any such property from execution and sale.

SEC. 5. No railroad or other corporation, or the lessees, purchasers, or managers of any railroad corporation, shall consolidate the stock, property, or franchises of such corporation, with, or lease or purchase the works or franchises of, or in any way control any railroad corporation owning or having under its control a parallel or competing line; nor shall any officer of such railroad corporation act as an officer of any other railroad corporation owning or having the control of a parallel or competing line.

SEC. 6. No railroad company organized under the laws of this State shall consolidate, by private or judicial sale or otherwise, with any railroad company organized under the laws of any other State or of the United States.

SEC. 7. No law shall be passed by the legislature granting the right to construct and operate a street-railroad within any city, town, or village, or upon any public highway, without first acquiring the consent of the local authorities having control of the street or highway proposed to be occupied by such street-railroad.

SEC. 8. No railroad corporation in existence at the time of the adoption of this constitution shall have the benefit of any future legislation, except on condition of complete acceptance of all the provisions of this constitution applicable to railroads.

SEC. 9. No railroad hereafter constructed in this State shall pass within a distance of three miles of any county-seat without passing through the same, and establishing and maintaining a depot therein, unless prevented by natural obstacles, such as streams, hills, or mountains: *Provided*, Such town or its citizens shall grant the right of way through its limits and sufficient ground for ordinary depot purposes.

ARTICLE XI.

MUNICIPAL CORPORATIONS.

SECTION 1. The several counties of this State are hereby recognized as legal subdivisions of the State.

SEC. 2. The construction of jails, court-houses, and bridges, and the establishment of county poor-houses and farms, and the laying out, construction, and repairing of county roads shall be provided for by general laws.

SEC. 3. No county, city, or other municipal corporation shall hereafter become a subscriber to the capital of any private corporation or association, or make any appropriation or donation to the same, or in any wise loan its credit; but this shall not be construed to in any way affect any obligation heretofore undertaken pursuant to law.

SEC. 4. Cities and towns having a population of ten thousand inhabitants or less, may be chartered alone by general law. They may levy, assess, and collect an annual tax to defray the current expenses of their local government, but such tax shall never exceed, for any one year, one-fourth of one per cent., and shall be collectible only in current money. And all license and occupation tax levied, and all fines, forfeitures, penalties, and other dues accruing to cities and towns shall be collectible only in current money.

SEC. 5. Cities having more than ten thousand inhabitants may have their charters ganted or amended by special act of the legislature, and may levy, assess, and collect such taxes as may be authorized by law, but no tax for any purpose shall ever be lawful, for any one year, which shall exceed two and one-half per cent. of the taxable property of such city; and no debt shall ever be created by any city, unless at the same time provision be made to assess and collect annually a sufficient sum to pay the interest thereon and create a sinking-fund of at least two per cent. thereon.

SEC. 6. Counties, cities, and· towns are authorized, in such mode as may now or may hereafter be provided by law, to levy, assess, and collect the taxes necessary to pay the interest and provide a sinking-fund to satisfy any indebtedness heretofore legally made and undertaken; but all such taxes shall be assessed and collected separately from that levied, assessed, and collected for current expenses of municipal government, and shall when levied specify in the act of levying the purpose therefor, and such taxes may be paid in the coupons, bonds, or other indebtedness for the payment of which such tax may have been levied.

SEC. 7. All counties and cities bordering on the coast of the Gulf of Mexico are hereby authorized, upon a vote of two-thirds of the tax-payers therein, (to be ascertained as may be provided by law,) to levy and collect such tax for construction of sea-walls, breakwaters, or sanitary purposes, as may be authorized by law, and may create a debt for such works and issue bonds in evidence thereof. But no debt for any purpose shall ever be incurred i. any manner by any city or county, unless provision is made, at the time of creating the same, for levying and collecting a sufficient tax to pay the interest thereon and provide at least two per cent. as a sinking-fund; and the condemnation of the right of way for the erection of such works shall be fully provided for.

SEC. 8. The counties and cities on the Gulf coast being subject to calamitous overflows, and a very large proportion of the general revenue being derived from those otherwise prosperous localities, the legislature is especially authorized to aid by donation of such portion of the public domain as may be deemed proper, and in such mode as may be provided by law, the construction of sea-walls or breakwaters, such aid to be proportioned to the extent and value of the works constructed, or to be constructed, in any locality.

SEC. 9. The property of counties, cities, and towns owned and held only for public purposes, such as public buildings and the sites therefor, fire-engines and the furniture thereof, and all property used or intended for extinguishing fires, public grounds and all other property devoted exclusively to the use and benefit of the public, shall be exempt from forced sale and from taxation: *Provided*, Nothing herein shall prevent the enforcement of the vendor's lien, the mechanic's or builder's lien, or other liens now existing.

SEC. 10. The legislature may constitute any city or town a separate and independent school-district. And when the citizens of any city or town have a charter, authorizing the city authorities to levy and collect a tax for the support and maintenance of a public institution of learning, such tax may hereafter be levied and collected, if, at an election held for that purpose, two-thirds of the tax-payers of such city or town shall vote for such tax.

ARTICLE XII.

PRIVATE CORPORATIONS.

SECTION 1. No private corporation shall be created except by general laws.

SEC. 2. General laws shall be enacted providing for the creation of private corporations, and shall therein provide fully for the adequate protection of the public and of the individual stockholders.

SEC. 3. The right to authorize and regulate freights, tolls, wharfage, or fares levied and collected, or proposed to be levied and collected, by individuals, companies, or corporations, for the use of highways, landings, wharves, bridges, and ferries devoted to public use, has never been and shall never be relinquished or abandoned by the State, but shall always be under legislative control and depend upon legislative authority.

SEC. 4. The first legislature assembled after the adoption of this constitution shall provide a mode of procedure by the attorney-general and district or county attorneys, in the name and behalf of the State, to prevent and punish the demanding and receiving or collection of any and all charges as freight, wharfage, fares, or tolls, for the use of property devoted to the public, unless the same shall have been specially authorized by law.

Sec. 5. All laws granting the right to demand and collect freights, fares, tolls, or wharfage shall at all times be subject to amendment, modification, or repeal by the legislature.

Sec. 6. No corporation shall issue stock or bonds except for money paid, labor done, or property actually received, and all fictitious increase of stock or indebtedness shall be void.

Sec. 7. Nothing in this article shall be construed to divest or affect rights guaranteed by any existing grant or statute of this State or of the republic of Texas.

ARTICLE XIII.

SPANISH AND MEXICAN LAND-TITLES.

Section 1. All fines, penalties, forfeitures, and escheats which have heretofore accrued to the republic and State of Texas, under their constitutions and laws, shall accrue to the State under this constitution; and the legislature shall provide a method for determining what lands have been forfeited, and for giving effect to escheats; and all such rights of forfeiture and escheat to the State shall, *ipso facto*, inure to the protection of the innocent holders of junior titles, as provided in sections 2, 3, and 4 of this article.

Sec. 2. Any claim of title or right to land in Texas, issued prior to the 13th day of November, 1835, not duly recorded in the county where the land was situated at the time of such record, or not duly archived in the general land-office, or not in the actual possession of the grantee thereof, or some person claiming under him, prior to the accruing of junior title thereto from the sovereignty of the soil, under circumstances reasonably calculated to give notice to said junior grantee, has never had, and shall not have, standing or effect against such junior title, or color of title, acquired without such or actual notice of such prior claim of title or right; and no condition annexed to such grants, not archived or recorded or occupied as aforesaid, has been, or ever *shall* be, released or waived, but actual performance of all such conditions shall be proved by the person or persons claiming under such title or claim of right in order to maintain action thereon, and the holder of such junior title, or color of title, shall have all the rights of the government which have heretofore existed, or now exist, arising from the non-performance of all such conditions.

Sec. 3. Non-payment of taxes on any claim of title to land, dated prior to the 13th day of November, 1835, not recorded or archived, as provided in section 2, by the person or persons so claiming, or those under whom he or they so claim, from that date up to the date of the adoption of this constitution, shall be held to be a presumption that the right thereto has reverted to the State, and that said claim is a stale demand, which presumption shall only be rebutted by payment of all taxes on said lands, State, county, and city or town, to be assessed on the fair value of such lands by the comptroller, and paid to him without commutation or deduction for any part of the above period.

Sec. 4. No claim of title or right to land, which issued prior to the 13th day of November, 1835, which has not been duly recorded in the county where the land was situated at the time of such record, or which has not been duly archived in the general land-office, shall ever hereafter be deposited in the general land-office, or recorded in this State, or delineated on the maps, or used as evidence in any of the courts of this State, and the same are stale claims; but this shall not affect such rights or presumptions as arise from actual possession. By the words "duly recorded," as used in sections 2 and 4 of this article, it is meant that such claim of title or right to land shall have been recorded in the proper office, and that mere errors in the certificate of registration, or informality, not affecting the fairness and good faith of the holder thereof, with which the record was made, shall not be held to vitiate such record.

Sec. 5. All claims, locations, surveys, grants, and titles of any kind, which are declared null and void by the constitution of the republic or State of Texas, are, and the same shall remain forever, null and void.

SEC. 6. The legislature shall pass stringent laws for the detection and conviction of all forgers of land-titles, and may make such appropriations of money for that purpose as may be necessary.

SEC. 7. Sections 2, 3, 4, and 5 of this article shall not be so construed as to set aside or repeal any law or laws of the republic or State of Texas, releasing the claimants of headrights of colonists of a league of land, or less, from compliance with the conditions on which their grants were made.

ARTICLE XIV.

PUBLIC LANDS AND LAND-OFFICE.

SECTION 1. There shall be one general land-office in the State, which shall be at the seat of government, where all land-titles which have emanated, or may hereafter emanate, from the State shall be registered, except those titles the registration of which may be prohibited by this constitution. It shall be the duty of the legislature, at the earliest practicable time, to make the land-office self-sustaining, and from time to time the legislature may establish such subordinate offices as may be deemed necessary.

SEC. 2. All unsatisfied genuine land-certificates barred by section 4, article 10, of the constitution of 1869, by reason of the holders or owners thereof failing to have them surveyed and returned to the land-office by the 1st day of January, 1875, are hereby revived. All unsatisfied genuine land-certificates now in existence shall be surveyed and returned to the general land-office within five years after the adoption of this constitution, or be forever barred; and all genuine land-certificates hereafter issued by the State shall be surveyed and returned to the general land-office within five years after issuance, or be forever barred: *Provided*, That all genuine land-certificates heretofore or hereafter issued shall be located, surveyed, or patented only upon vacant and unappropriated public domain, and not upon any land titled or equitably owned under color of title from the sovereignty of the State, evidence of the appropriation of which is on the county records or in the general land-office, or when the appropriation is evidenced by the occupation of the owner, or of some person holding for him.

SEC. 3. The legislature shall have no power to grant any of the lands of this State to any railway company, except upon the following restrictions and conditions:

First. That there shall never be granted to any such corporation more than sixteen sections to the mile, and no reservation of any part of the public domain for the purpose of satisfying such grant shall ever be made.

Second. That no land-certificate shall be issued to such company until they have equipped, constructed, and in running order at least ten miles of road, and on the failure of such company to comply with the terms of its charter, or to alienate its land at a period to be fixed by law, in no event to exceed twelve years from the issuance of the patent, all said land shall be forfeited to the State, and become a portion of the public domain, and liable to location and survey. The legislature shall pass general laws only, to give effect to the provisions of this section.

SEC. 4. No certificate for land shall be sold at the land-office except to actual settlers upon the same, and in lots not to exceed one hundred and sixty acres.

SEC. 5. All lands heretofore or hereafter granted to railway companies, where the charter or law of the State required, or shall hereafter require, their alienation within a certain period, on pain of forfeiture, or is silent on the subject of forfeiture, and which lands have not been or shall not hereafter be alienated, in conformity with the terms of their charters and the laws under which the grants were made, are hereby declared forfeited to the State, and subject to pre-emption, location, and survey as other vacant lands. All lands heretofore granted to said railroad companies to which no forfeiture was attached on their failure to alienate, are not included in the foregoing clause; but in all such last-named cases it shall be the duty of the attorney-general, in every instance where alienations have been or hereafter may be made, to inquire into the same, and if such alienation has been made in fraud of the rights of the State, and is colorable only, the real and beneficial interest being still in such corporation, to institute legal proceedings in the county where the seat of government is situated to forfeit such lands to the State, and if such alienation be judicially ascertained to be fraudulent and colorable as aforesaid, such lands shall be forfeited to the State, and become a part of the vacant public domain, liable to pre-emption, location, and survey.

SEC. 6. To every head of a family without a homestead there shall be donated one hundred and sixty acres of public land, upon condition that he will select and locate said land, and occupy the same three years, and pay the office-fees due thereon. To all single men of eighteen years of age and upwards shall be donated eighty acres of public land, upon the terms and conditions prescribed for heads of families.

SEC. 7. The State of Texas hereby releases to the owner or owners of the soil all mines and minerals that may be on the same, subject to taxation as other property.

SEC. 8. Persons residing between the Nueces River and the Rio Grande, and owning grants for lands which emanated from the government of Spain or that of Mexico, which grants have been recognized and validated by the State, by acts of the legislature, approved February 10, 1852, August 15, 1870, and other acts, and who have been prevented from complying with the requirements of said acts by the unsettled condition of the country, shall be allowed until the 1st day of January, 1880, to complete their surveys and the plots thereof, and to return their field-notes to the general land-office; and all claimants failing to do so shall be forever barred: *Provided*, Nothing in this section shall be so construed as to validate any titles not already valid, or to interfere with the rights of third persons.

ARTICLE XV.

IMPEACHMENT.

SECTION 1. The power of impeachment shall be vested in the house of representatives.

SEC. 2. Impeachment of the governor, lieutenant-governor, attorney-general, treasurer, commissioner of the general land-office, comptroller, and the judges of the supreme court, court of appeals, and district court shall be tried by the senate.

SEC. 3. When the senate is sitting as a court of impeachment, the senators shall be on oath, or affirmation, impartially to try the party impeached, and no person shall be convicted without the concurrence of two-thirds of the senators present.

SEC. 4. Judgment in cases of impeachment shall extend only to removal from office, and disqualification from holding any office of honor, trust, or profit under this State. A party convicted on impeachment shall also be subject to indictment, trial, and punishment, according to law.

SEC. 5. All officers against whom articles of impeachment may be preferred shall be suspended from the exercise of the duties of their office during the pendency of such impeachment. The governor may make a provisional appointment to fill the vacancy occasioned by the suspension of an officer until the decision on the impeachment.

SEC. 6. Any judge of the district courts of the State who is incompetent to discharge the duties of his office, or who shall be guilty of partiality, or oppression, or other official misconduct, or whose habits and conduct are such as to render him unfit to hold such office, or who shall negligently fail to perform his duties as judge, or who shall fail to execute in a reasonable measure the business in his courts, may be removed by the supreme court. The supreme court shall have original jurisdiction to hear and determine the causes aforesaid, when presented in writing upon the oaths taken before some judge of a court of record of not less than ten lawyers practising in the courts held by such judge and licensed to practise in the supreme court; said presentment to be founded either upon the knowledge of the persons making it or upon the written oaths as to the facts of creditable witnesses. The supreme court may issue all needful process and prescribe all needful rules to give effect to this section. Causes of this kind shall have precedence and be tried as soon as practicable.

SEC. 7. The legislature shall provide by law for the trial and removal from office of all officers of this State, the modes for which have not been provided in this constitution.

ADDRESS.

SEC. 8. The judges of the supreme court, court of appeals, and district courts, shall be removed by the governor on the address of two-thirds of each house of the legislature for willful neglect of duty, incompetency, habitual drunkenness, oppression in office, or other reasonable cause which shall not be sufficient ground for impeachment: *Provided, however,* That the cause or causes for which such removal shall be required shall be stated at length in such address and entered on the journals of each house: *And provided further,* That the cause or causes shall be notified to the judge so intended to be removed, and he shall be admitted to a hearing in his own defense before any vote for such address shall pass; and in all such cases the vote shall be taken by yeas and nays and entered on the journals of each house, respectively.

ARTICLE XVI.

GENERAL PROVISIONS.

SECTION 1. Members of the legislature, and all officers, before they enter upon the duties of their offices, shall take the following oath or affirmation: "I, ——— ———, do solemnly swear (or affirm) that I will faithfully and impartially discharge and perform all the duties incumbent upon me as ———, according to the best of my skill and ability, agreeably to the Constitution and laws of the United States and of this State; and I do further solemnly swear (or affirm) that since the adoption of the constitution of this State, I being a citizen of this State, have not fought a duel with deadly weapons, within this State nor out of it, nor have I sent or accepted a challenge to fight a duel with deadly weapons, nor have I acted as second in carrying a challenge, or aided, advised or assisted any person thus offending. And I furthermore solemnly swear (or affirm) that I have not directly nor indirectly paid, offered, or promised to pay, contributed, nor promised to contribute any money, or valuable thing, or promised any public office or employment, as a reward for the giving or withholding a vote at the election at which I was elected, (or if the office is one of appointment, to secure my appointment:) So help me God."

SEC. 2. Laws shall be made to exclude from office, serving on juries, and from the right of suffrage those who may have been or shall hereafter be convicted of bribery, perjury, forgery, or other high crimes. The privilege of free suffrage shall be protected by laws regulating elections and prohibiting under adequate penalties all undue influence therein from power, bribery, tumult, or other improper practice.

SEC. 3. The legislature shall make provision whereby persons convicted of misdemeanors and committed to the county jails in default of payment of fines and costs shall be required to discharge such fines and costs by manual labor, under such regulations as may be prescribed by law.

SEC. 4. Any citizen of this State who shall, after the adoption of this constitution, fight a duel with deadly weapons, or send or accept a challenge to fight a duel with deadly weapons, either within this State or out of it, or who shall act as second, or knowingly assist in any manner those thus offending, shall be deprived of the right of suffrage, or of holding any office of trust or profit under this State.

SEC. 5. Every person shall be disqualified from holding any office of profit or trust in this State who shall have been convicted of having given or offered a bribe to procure his election or appointment.

SEC. 6. No appropriation for private or individual purposes shall be made. A regular statement, under oath, and an account of the receipts and expenditures of all public money shall be published annually in such manner as shall be prescribed by law.

SEC. 7. The legislature shall in no case have power to issue "treasury warrants," "treasury notes," or paper of any description intended to circulate as money.

SEC. 8. Each county in the State may provide, in such manner as may be prescribed by law, a manual-labor poor-house and farm, for taking care of, managing, employing, and supplying the wants of its indigent and poor inhabitants.

SEC. 9. Absence on business of the State, or of the United States, shall not forfeit a residence once obtained, so as to deprive any one of the right of suffrage, or of being elected or appointed to any office under the exceptions contained in this constitution.

SEC. 10. The legislature shall provide for deductions from the salaries of public officers who may neglect the performance of any duty that may be assigned them by law.

SEC. 11. The legal rate of interest shall not exceed eight per cent. per annum, in the absence of any contract as to the rate of interest; and by contract parties may agree upon any rate not to exceed twelve per cent. per annum. All interest charged above this last-named rate shall be deemed usurious, and the legislature shall, at its first session, provide appropriate pains and penalties to prevent and punish usury.

SEC. 12. No member of Congress, nor person holding or exercising any office of profit or trust under the United States, or either of them, or under any foreign power, shall be eligible as a member of the legislature, or hold or exercise any office of profit or trust under this State.

SEC. 13. It shall be the duty of the legislature to pass such laws as may be necessary and proper to decide differences by arbitration, when the parties shall elect that method of trial.

SEC. 14. All civil officers shall reside within the State; and all district or county officers within their districts or counties, and shall keep their offices at such places as may be required by law; and failure to comply with this condition shall vacate the office so held.

SEC. 15. All property, both real and personal, of the wife, owned or claimed by her before marriage, and that acquired afterward by gift, devise, or descent, shall be her separate property; and laws shall be passed more clearly defining the rights of the wife in relation as well to her separate property as that held in common with her husband. Laws shall also be passed providing for the registration of the wife's separate property.

SEC. 16. No corporate body shall hereafter be created, renewed, or extended with banking or discounting privileges.

SEC. 17. All officers within this State shall continue to perform the duties of their offices until their successors shall be duly qualified.

SEC. 18. The rights of property and of action, which have been acquired under the constitution and laws of the republic and State, shall not be divested; nor shall any rights or actions which have been divested, barred, or declared null and void by the constitution of the republic and State, be reinvested, renewed, or reinstated by this constitution; but the same shall remain precisely in the situation which they were before the adoption of this constitution, unless otherwise herein provided: *And provided further,* That no cause of action heretofore barred shall be revived.

SEC. 19. The legislature shall prescribe by law the qualification of grand and petit jurors.

SEC. 20. The legislature shall, at its first session, enact a law whereby the qualified voters of any county, justice's precinct, town or city, by a majority vote, from time to time, may determine whether the sale of intoxicating liquors shall be prohibited within the prescribed limits.

SEC. 21. All stationery and printing, except proclamations and such printing as may be done at the deaf and dumb asylum, paper, and fuel used in the legislative and other departments of the government, except the judicial department, shall be furnished, and the printing and binding of the laws, journals, and department reports, and all other printing and binding, and the repairing and furnishing the halls and rooms used for the meetings of the legislature and its committees, shall be performed under contract, to be given to the lowest responsible bidder, below such maximum price, and under such regulations, as shall be prescribed by law. No member or officer of any department of the government shall be in any way interested in such contracts; and all such contracts shall be subject to the approval of the governor, secretary of state, and comptroller.

SEC. 22. The legislature shall have the power to pass such fence-laws, applicable to any subdivision of the State or counties, as may be needed to meet the wants of the people.

SEC. 23. The legislature may pass laws for the regulation of live stock and the protection of stock-raisers in the stock-raising portion of the State, and exempt from the operation of such laws other portions, sections, or counties; and shall have power to pass general and special laws for the inspection of cattle, stock, and hides, and for the regulation of brands: *Provided*, That any local law thus passed shall be submitted to the freeholders of the section to be affected thereby, and approved by them, before it shall go into effect.

SEC. 24. The legislature shall make provision for laying out and working public roads, for the building of bridges, and for utilizing fines, forfeitures, and convict labor to all these purposes.

SEC. 25. That all drawbacks and rebatement of insurance, freight, transportation, carriage, wharfage, storage, compressing, baling, repairing, or for any other kind of labor or service, of or to any cotton, grain, or any other produce or article of commerce in this State, paid, or allowed, or contracted for, to any common carrier, shipper, merchant, commission-merchant, factor, agent, or middle-man of any kind, not the true and absolute owner thereof, are forever prohibited, and it shall be the duty of the legislature to pass effective laws punishing all persons in this State who pay, receive, or contract for or respecting the same.

SEC. 26. Every person, corporation, or company, that may commit a homicide, through wilful act, or omission, or gross neglect, shall be responsible, in exemplary damages, to the surviving husband, widow, heirs of his or her body, or such of them as there may be, without regard to any criminal proceeding that may or may not be had in relation to the homicide.

SEC. 27. In all elections to fill vacancies of office in this State it shall be to fill the unexpired term only.

SEC. 28. No current wages for personal service shall ever be subject to garnishment.

SEC. 29. The legislature shall provide by law for defining and punishing barratery.

SEC. 30. The duration of all offices not fixed by this constitution shall never exceed two years.

SEC. 31. The legislature may pass laws prescribing the qualifications of practitioners of medicine in this State, and to punish persons for malpractice, but no preference shall ever be given by law to any schools of medicine.

SEC. 32. The legislature may provide by law for the establishment of a board of health and vital statistics, under such rules and regulations as it may deem proper.

SEC. 33. The accounting-officers of this State shall neither draw nor pay a warrant upon the treasury in favor of any person, for salary or compensation as agent, officer, or appointee, who holds at the same time any other office or position of honor, trust, or profit under this State or the United States, except as prescribed in this constitution.

SEC. 34. The legislature shall pass laws authorizing the governor to lease, or sell to the Government of the United States, a sufficient quantity of the public domain of the State necessary for the erection of forts, barracks, arsenals, and military stations, or camps, and for other needful military purposes; and the action of the governor therein shall be subject to the approval of the legislature.

SEC. 35. The legislature shall, at its first session, pass laws to protect laborers on public buildings, streets, roads, railroads, canals, and other similar public works against the failure of contractors and subcontractors to pay their current wages when due, and to make the corporation, company, or individual for whose benefit the work is done responsible for their ultimate payment.

SEC. 36. The legislature shall, at its first session, provide for the payment, or funding, as they may deem best, of the amounts found to be justly due to the teachers in the public schools, by the State, for service rendered prior to the 1st day of July, 1873, and for the payment by the school-districts in the State of amounts justly due teachers of public schools by such district to January, 1876.

Sec. 37. Mechanics, artisans, and material-men of every class, shall have a lien upon the buildings and articles made or repaired by them for the value of their labor done thereon or material furnished therefor; and the legislature shall provide by law for the speedy and efficient enforcement of said liens.

Sec. 38. The legislature may, at such time as the public interest may require, provide for the office of commissioner of insurance, statistics, and history, whose term of office, duties, and salary shall be prescribed by law.

Sec. 39. The legislature may, from time to time, make appropriations for preserving and perpetuating memorials of the history of Texas, by means of monuments, statues, paintings, and documents of historical value.

Sec. 40. No person shall hold or exercise, at the same time, more than one civil office of emolument, except that of justice of the peace, county commissioner, notary public, and postmaster, unless otherwise specially provided herein.

Sec. 41. Any person who shall, directly or indirectly, offer, give, or promise, any money or thing of value, testimonial, privilege, or personal advantage, to any executive or judicial officer or member of the legislature to influence him in the performance of any of his public or official duties, shall be guilty of bribery, and be punished in such manner as shall be provided by law. And any member of the legislature, or executive or judicial officer, who shall solicit, demand, or receive, or consent to receive, directly or indirectly, for himself or for another, from any company, corporation, or person, any money, appointment, employment, testimonial, reward, thing of value or employment, or of personal advantage or promise thereof, for his·vote or official influence, or for withholding the· same, or with any understanding, expressed or implied, that his vote or official action shall be in any way influenced thereby, or who shall solicit, demand, and receive any such money or other advantage, matter, or thing aforesaid for another, as the consideration of his vote or official influence, in consideration of the payment or promise of such money, advantage, matter or thing to another, shall be held guilty of bribery, within the meaning of the constitution, and shall incur the disabilities provided for said offenses, with a forfeiture of the office he may hold, and such other additional punishment as is or shall be provided by law.

Sec. 42. The legislature may establish an inebriate asylum, for the cure of drunkenness and reform of inebriates.

Sec. 43. No man or set of men shall ever be exempted, relieved, or discharged from the performance of any public duty or service imposed by general law by any special law. Exemptions from the performance of such public duty or service shall only be made by general law.

Sec. 44. The legislature shall prescribe the duties and provide for the election, by the qualified voters of each county in this State, of a county treasurer and a county surveyor, who shall have an office at the county-seat, and hold their office for two years, and until their successors are qualified; and shall have such compensation as may be provided by law.

Sec. 45. It shall be the duty of the legislature to provide for collecting, arranging, and safely keeping such records, rolls, correspondence, and other documents, civil and military, relating to the history of Texas, as may be now in the possession of parties willing to confide them to the care and preservation of the State.

Sec. 46. The legislature shall provide by law for organizing and disciplining the militia of the State in such manner as they shall deem expedient, not incompatible with the Constitution and laws of the United States.

Sec. 47. Any person who conscientiously scruples to bear arms shall not be compelled to do so, but shall pay an equivalent for personal service.

Sec. 48. All laws and parts of laws now in force in the State of Texas which are not repugnant to the constitution of the United States or to this constitution shall continue and remain in force as the laws of this State until they expire by their own limitation or shall be amended or repealed by the legislature.

Sec. 49. The legislature shall have power, and it shall be its duty, to protect by law from forced sale a certain portion of the personal property of all heads of families, and also of unmarried adults, male and female.

SEC. 50. The homestead of a family shall be, and is hereby, protected from forced sale, for the payment of all debts except for the purchase-money thereof, or a part of such purchase-money, the taxes due thereon, or for work and material used in constructing improvements thereon, and in this last case only when the work and material are contracted for in writing, with the consent of the wife given in the same manner as is required in making a sale and conveyance of the homestead; nor shall the owner, if a married man, sell the homestead without the consent of the wife, given in such manner as may be prescribed by law. No mortgage, trust-deed, or other lien on the homestead shall ever be valid, except for the purchase-money therefor, or improvements made thereon, as hereinbefore provided, whether such mortgage, or trust-deed, or other lien, shall have been created by the husband alone, or together with his wife; and all pretended sales of the homestead involving any condition of defeasance shall be void.

SEC. 51. The homestead, not in a town or city, shall consist of not more than two hundred acres of land, which may be in one or more parcels, with the improvements thereon; the homestead in a city, town, or village shall consist of lot, or lots, not to exceed in value five thousand dollars at the time of their designation as the homestead without reference to the value of any improvements thereon: *Provided*, That the same shall be used for the purposes of a home, or as a place to exercise the calling or business of the head of a family: *Provided also*, That any temporary renting of the homestead shall not change the character of the same when no other homestead has been acquired.

SEC. 52. On the death of the husband or wife, or both, the homestead shall descend and vest in like manner as other real property of the deceased, and shall be governed by the same laws of descent and distribution, but it shall not be partitioned among the heirs of the deceased during the life-time of the surviving husband or wife, or so long as the survivor may elect to use or occupy the same as a homestead, or so long as the guardian of the minor children of the deceased may be permitted, under the order of the proper court having the jurisdiction, to use and occupy the same.

SEC. 53. That no inconvenience may arise from the adoption of this constitution, it is declared that all process and writs of all kinds which have been or may be issued and not returned or executed when this constitution is adopted, shall remain valid, and shall not be in any way affected by the adoption of this constitution.

SEC. 54. It shall be the duty of the legislature to provide for the custody and maintenance of indigent lunatics, at the expense of the State, under such regulations and restrictions as the legislature may prescribe.

SEC. 55. The legislature may provide annual pensions, not to exceed one hundred and fifty dollars per annum, to surviving soldiers or volunteers in the war between Texas and Mexico, from the commencement of the revolution in 1835 until the 1st of January, 1837; and also to the surviving signers of the declaration of independence of Texas, and to the surviving widows, continuing unmarried, of such soldiers and signers: *Provided*, That no such pension be granted except to those in indigent circumstances, proof of which shall be made before the county court of the county where the applicant resides, in such manner as may be provided by law.

SEC. 56. The legislature shall have no power to appropriate any of the public money for the establishment and maintenance of a bureau of immigration, or for any purpose of bringing immigrants to this State.

SEC. 57. Three million acres of the public domain are hereby appropriated and set apart for the purpose of erecting a new State capitol and other necessary public buildings at the seat of government, said lands to be sold under the direction of the legislature; and the legislature shall pass suitable laws to carry this section into effect.

ARTICLE XVII.

MODE OF AMENDING THE CONSTITUTION OF THIS STATE.

SECTION 1. The legislature, at any biennial session, by a vote of two-thirds of all the members elected to each house, to be entered by yeas and nays on the journals, may propose amendments to the constitution, to be voted upon by the qualified electors for members of the legislature, which proposed amendments shall be duly published once a week for four weeks, commencing at least three months before an election, the time of which shall be specified by the legislature, in one weekly newspaper of each county in which such a newspaper may be published; and it shall be the duty of the several returning-officers of said election to open a poll for, and make returns to, the secretary of state of the number of legal votes cast at said election for and against said amendments; and if more than one be proposed, then the number of votes cast for and against each of them; and if it shall appear from said return that a majority of the votes cast have been cast in favor of any amendment, the said amendment so receiving a majority of the votes cast shall become a part of this constitution, and proclamation shall be made by the governor thereof.

Done by the delegates of the people of Texas, in convention assembled, in the city of Austin, on this the twenty-fourth day of November, in the year of our Lord one thousand eight hundred and seventy-five.

In testimony whereof we hereunto subscribe our names.

EDWARD B. PICKETT, *President.*

LEIGH CHALMERS, *Secretary.*

SELECTED BIBLIOGRAPHY

Constitutions of Mexico and the States of Coahuila and Texas, With Documents Relating to Land Claims in Texas (New York, 1832)

Constitution or Form of Government of the State of Texas (New Orleans, 1833)

Constitution of the Republic of Texas (Columbia, Tex., 1936)

Journals of the Convention Assembled at the City of Austin on the Fourth of July, 1845 ... (Austin, 1845)

An Ordinance in Relation to Colonization Contracts (Houston, 1845)

Constitution of the State of Texas (Austin, 1861)

Journal of the Texas State Convention (Austin, 1866)

Constitution of the State of West Texas (Austin, 1869)

Journal of the Reconstruction Convention (Austin, 1870)

Constitution of the State of Texas, Adopted by the Constitutional Convention Under the Reconstruction Acts of Congress ... (Austin, 1869)

Constitution of Texas (Houston, 1872)

McKay, S.S., ed., Debates in the Texas Constitutional Convention of 1875 (Austin, 1930)

Journal of the Constitutional Convention (Galveston, 1875)

Constitution of the State of Texas (Houston, 1876)

Sayles, John, ed., Constitutions of the State of Texas (St. Louis, 1884)

Keeton, Page, "Methods of Constitutional Revision in Texas," 35 Texas L. Rev. 901 (October 1957)

Keith, John P., Methods of Constitutional Revision (Austin, 1949)

McKay, S.S., Making the Texas Constitution of 1876 (Philadelphia, 1924)

----- Seven Decades of the Texas Constitution of 1876 (Lubbock, 1942)

Note, "Equity in Taxation -- Houston's Constitutional Dilemma," 10 Houston L. Rev. 656 (March 1973)

----- "History of the Constitutionality of Local Laws in Texas," 13 Baylor L. Rev. 155 (Summer 1961)

----- "New Look at Texas' Equal Rights Amendment," 55 Texas L. Rev. 323 (January 1977)

Stewart, Frank Mann, The Constitution and Government of Texas (Boston, 4th ed., 1949)

Story, Robert G., "Does Texas Need a New Constitution?" 31 Texas L. J. 363 (May 1968)

Urecht, E. M., "Changing Homestead: When the City Meets the Farm," 18 South Texas L. J. 145 (1977)

TEXAS INDEX

Utah

Forty-Fifth State

January 4, 1896

EDITORIAL NOTE

Utah was first organized as the Mormon state
of Deseret, but because of strong Victorian prejudice against Mormonism and particularly its
practice of polygamy, the constitution and petition
for statehood by the State of Deseret, as well as
subsequent draft constitutions and petitions, were
rejected by Congress. The Supreme Court, in the
so-called Mormon Cases, finally closed the door on
any hope of admission so long as polygamy was
practiced; but upon the renunciation of the doctrine by the church, Congress reopened the door.

UTAH CONTENTS

SOURCES OF DOCUMENTS

No. 1   31st Cong., 1st Sess. H. Misc. Doc.
         No. 18

No. 2   9 Stat. 453

No. 3   36th Cong., 2d Sess. H. Misc. Doc.
         No. 10

No. 4   42nd Cong., 2d Sess. H. Misc. Doc.
         No. 105

No. 5   47th Cong., 1st Sess., H. Misc. Doc.
         No. 43

No. 6   116 U.S. 55

No. 7   9 Richardson, Compilation of Messages
         and Papers of the Presidents, 368

No. 8   28 Stat. 107

No. 9   6 Thorpe, 3700

No.10   29 Stat. 876

UTAH CONSTITUTIONS: COMPARATIVE PROVISIONS

SUBJECT MATTER BY ARTICLES

	1849	1872	1895
Declaration of Rights	VIII	I	1
State Boundaries		XIV	2
Ordinance			3
Elections and Right of Suffrage	V	II	4
Distribution of Powers	I	III	5
Legislative Department	II	IV	6
Executive	III	V	7
Judicial Department	IV	VI	8
Congressional and Legislative Apportionment			9
Education		XI	10
Counties, Cities and Towns			11
Corporations		VIII	12
Revenue and Taxation		IX,X	13
Public Debt		IX	14
Militia	VI	XII	15
Labor			16
Water Rights			17
Forestry			18
Public Buildings and State Institutions		XIII	19
Public Lands			20
Salaries			21
Miscellaneous		XV	22
Amendments	VII	XVI	23
Schedule		XVII	24

SUBJECT MATTER BY SECTIONS

PREAMBLE

DECLARATION OF RIGHTS	VIII	I	1
Inherent and inalienable right	1	1	1
All Political Power Inherent in the people	2	2	2
Utah inseparable from the Union			3
Religious liberty	3	4,21	4
Habeas Corpus	9	5	5
Right to bear arms	14	20	6
Due Process of Law			7
Offenses bailable	8	7	8
Excessive bail and fines Cruel punishments		6	9

	1849	1872	1895
Trial by jury	7	3	10
Courts open. Redress of injuries			11
Rights of accused persons			12
Prosecution by information or indictment. Grand jury.		8	13
Unreasonable searches forbidden. Issuance of warrant	6	18	14
Freedom of speech and of the press. Libel	5	9	15
No imprisonment for debt. Exception		14	16
Elections to be free. Soldiers voting			17
Attainder. Ex post facto laws. Impairing contracts	11	15	18
Treason defined. Proof	10	19	19
Military subordinate to the civil power	16	11	20
Slavery forbidden		17	21
Private property for public use	15		22
Irrevocable franchises forbidden			23
Uniform operation of laws			24
Rights retained by people	17	22	25
Provisions mandatory and prohibitory			26
Fundamental Rights			27
Duels-disqualified from office	4		
Laws shall not be suspended, etc.	12		
Right of petition	13	10	
No quartering of soldiers		12	
Representation apportioned		13	
Foreigner's rights to property		16	
STATE BOUNDARIES		XIV	Art.2
State boundaries		1	1
ORDINANCE			Art.3
Religious toleration: Polygamy forbidden			1
Right to public domain disclaimed. Taxation of lands. Exemption			2
Territorial debts assumed			3
Free, nonsectarian schools			4
ELECTIONS AND RIGHT OF SUFFRAGE	V	II	Art.4

	1849	1872	1895
Equal political rights			1
Qualifications to vote	10	1,6	2
Electors, immunity from arrest		3	3
Electors, immunity from militia duty			4
Electors to be citizens of United States			5
Idiots, insane persons and certain criminals ineligible to vote			6
Property qualification, when forbidden			7
Ballot to be secret	8	4	8
Elections, when held. Terms, when begin	1,4	XV-3	9
Oath of Office	II-13 V-3		10
Publication in both houses	2		
Organizing the polls	5		
No loss of residence by military service		2	
Registration		5	
Counting votes	6		
General System of Election	7		
DISTRIBUTION OF POWERS	I	III	Art.5
Three departments of government	I	1	1
LEGISLATIVE DEPARTMENT	II	IV	Art.6
Power vested in Senate, House and People	1	1	1
Time of sessions	2	2,22	2
Members of House, how and when chosen	3	3	3
Senators, how and when chosen	5	4	4
Who eligible as legislator	4		5
Who ineligible as legislator	4	6	6
Ineligibility of legislator to office created at term for which elected		9	7
Legislator, privilege from arrest	10	10	8
Compensation of Legislators		23	9
Each House to be judge of election and qualification of its members. Expulsion	7	8	10
Majority is quorum. Attendance compelled	8	12	11
Rules. Choosing officers			12

	1849	1872	1895
Vacancies to be Filled		11	13
Journals. Yeas and Naip		13	14
Sessions to be public. Adjournments	11	14	15
Duration of sessions			16
Impeachment by House			17
Trial of impeachment by Senate			18
Officers liable to impeachment Judgement. Prosecution by law			19
Service of articles of impeachment			20
Removal of officers			21
Enacting Clause of law		20	
Uniform system of county and township government established by legislature		21	
Sections for representatives-elector may cost as many votes for one candidate as there are representatives to be elected			25
Appropriations by law		18	
Law takes effect after publication	15	XV-4	
General Assembly meets in seat of government	V-9		
Reading of bills. Bill to contain only one subject. Bills passed by majority	14	15,16,17	22
Regulation of income taxes			23
Presiding officers to sign bills			24
Publication of Acts. Effective dates of acts.			25
Private laws forbidden			26
Lotteries not authorized			27
Special privileges forbidden			28
Lending public credit forbidden.			29
Continuity in government			30
Additional Compensation of Legislators			31
Appointments of additional employees			32
Legislative auditor appointed			33
Number of senators	6,16	5	
Each house shall have powers necessary	9		
Oath		7	
Laws, general and uniform		19	
EXECUTIVE	III	V	Art.7
Executive Dept. Terms, residence and duties of officers	1	2	1
Election. Tie, legislature to elect		4	2

	1849	1872	1895
Qualifications of governor and other execu five officers	2	3	3
Governor commander-in-chief	3	5	4
Duties of governor	4,5	6,8	5
Convening of extra sessions of legislature	7	9	6
Adjournment of legislature by governor	9	11	7
Bills presented to governor. Veto Appropriation bills	II-14	IV-24	8
Supreme executive power vested in governor		1	
Governor may fill certain vacancies	6	7	9
Governor's appointive power Vacancies			10
Vacancy in office of governor	16	3	11
Board of pardons. Respites and reprieves	11	12	12
State prison commissioners. Board of examiners		18	13
Insane asylum commissioners			14
Reform School commissioners			15
Duties of secretary of state	15	19(14)17election &	16
Duties of auditor and treasurer	15	19(14)qualifica-	17
Duties of attorney general		19(14)tions(not duties)	18
Superintendent of public instruction			19
Compensation of state officers	12	XV-5	20
Grants and commissions	14	16	21
The great seal	13	15	22
United States Officials ineligible Governor not eligible for senate			23
Invalid			24
Governors message-condition of state	8	10	
Person holding other office-not to be governor	10		
JUDICIAL DEPARTMENT	IV	VI	Art.8
Judicial powers, how vested	1	1	1
Supreme court, how constituted. Quorum. Qualifications of judges. Chief justice	2	3,4,5 12	2
Selection of judges. Method. Basis of selection	3	2	3
Jurisdiction of supreme court. Terms		7	4

	1849	1872	1895
District courts, how constituted Terms, Jurisdiction, Judge protempore			5
Judicial district. Power of legislature with restect to		6	6
Jurisdiction of district courts			7
Justices of the peace. Jurisdiction		9	8
Appeals from district courts. From justices' courts.			9
County attorneys. Election, term, appointment protempore			10
Removal of judges from office			11
Diminution of judges' salaries forbidden			12
Disqualification of judges			13
Clerks of courts. Reporter			14
Judges shall not appoint relatives to office			15
Judicial districts, how constituted		6	16
Courts of record			17
Style of process: "The State of Utah"	4	15	18
Butone form of civil action			19
Salary of judges		13	20
Judges to be conservators of peace			21
Judges to report defects in law			22
Publication of decisions			23
Effect of extending judges' terms			24
Decisions of supreme court to be in writing			25
Court to prepare syllabus			26
Judge forfeits office by absence			27
Mandatory retirement and removal of judges from office			28
Probate judge		8	
Jurisdiction of circuit and inferior courts.		10	
Judges ineligible for another judicial office		11	
Terms of Circuit Courts	14		
CONGRESSIONAL AND LEGISLATIVE APPORTIONMENT			Art.9
Election of congressman			1
Decennial census to be taken			2
Number of members of legislature	II-12		3
Senatorial districts, how formed			4
EDUCATION	XI	Art.10	
Free nonsectarian schools			1

	1849	1872	1895
Defining what shall constitute the public school system			2
Proceeds of lands and other property. Percent of proceeds. Perpetual fund			3
University and agricultural college located. Rights and immunities confirmed			4
Proceeds of land grants to constitute permanent funds			5
Separate control of city schools			6
School funds guaranteed by state			7
State board of education			8
Text books			9
Institutions for deaf, dumb and blind. Property. Fund			10
Metric system			11
No religious or partisan tests in schools			12
Public aid to church schools forbidden			13
Legislature to encourage education		1	
Education guaranteed to all		2	
COUNTIES, CITIES AND TOWNS			Art.11
Existing counties, precincts, and school districts recognized			
Removal of county seats			2
Changing of county seats			3
Optional forms of County government			4
Municipal corporations. To Be created by general law. Right and manner of adopting charter for own government. Powers included.		VIII-2	5
Municipalities for bidden to sell water works or rights			6
CORPORATIONS		VIII	Art.12
Corporations. Formation. Control			1
Existing corparations to accept constitution			2
Legislature not to extend or validate franchises			3
"Corporation" defined. Suits			4

	1849	1872	1895
Corporate stock. Issuance, increase, fictitious increase			5
Privileges of foreign corporations			6
Limitations on alienation of franchise			7
Consent of local authorities necessary to use of streets			8
Places of business, process agent, filing of certified copy of articles			9
Corporations limited to authorized business			10
Franchises may be taken for public use			11
State not to be interested in corporation		5	
Common carriers			12
Competing railroads not to consolidate			13
Rolling stock considered personal property			14
Legislature to prescribe maximum rates. Discriminations			15
Armed bodies not to enter state			16
Employee of corporation ineligible to municipal office			17
Liability of stockholders of banks			18
Blacklisting forbidden			19
Trusts and combinations prohibited			20
No special act relating to corporate powers		1	
Corporators not individually liable		4	
REVENUE AND TAXATION		IX,X	Art.13
Fiscal year		IX-1	1
Langible property to be taxed. Value ascertained. Properties exempt. Legislature to provide annual tax for state		IX-2,X-1	2
Assessment and taxation of tangible property. Exemptions. Personal income tax. Disposition of revenues		X-1	3
Mines and claims to be assessed. Basis and multiple. What to be assessed as tangible property.			4
Local authorities to buy local taxes.			5
Annual statement to be published			6
Rate of taxation. State contribution and allocation of state's			7

	1849	1872	1895
contribution			
Officer not to make profit out of public monies			8
State expenditure to be Kept within revenues			9
All property taxable where situated			10
Creation of state tax commission Governor to appoint. Terms. Duties. County boards. Duties			11
Stamp, income, license or franchise tax permissible			12
Revenue from highway user and motor fuel taxes to be used for highway purposes			13
Property of corporation subject to tax		3	
PUBLIC DEBT		IX	Art.14
Fixing the limit of the State indebtedness			1
Debts for public defense			2
Debts of counties, cities, towns and school districts not to exceed revenue. Exception		3	3
Limit of indebtedness of counties, cities towns and school districts			4
Borrowed money to be applied to authorized use			5
State not to assume county, city, town or school district debts			6
Existing indebtedness not impaired			7
MILITIA	VI	XII	Art.15
How constituted	1	1	1
Organization and equipment			2
Commissioned officers	2	2	
LABOŔ			Art.16
Rights of labor to be protected			1
Board of labor			2
Certain employment and practices to be prohibited			3
Exchange of blacklists prohibited			4
Injuries resulting in death Damages			5
Eight hour day on public works.			6

	1849	1872	1895
Health and safety laws.			
Legislature to enforce this article.			7
Minimum wage for women and minors.			8
Comfort and safety laws.			
WATER RIGHTS			Art.17
Existing rights confirmed			1
FORESTRY			Art.18
Forests to be preserved			1
PUBLIC BUILDINGS AND STATE INSTITUTIONS		XIII	Art.19
Property of territory becomes property of state			1
Charitable and penal institutions, how maintained		1,2	2
Location of public institutions and disposition of lands			3
Counties shall provide for those infirm, etc.		3	
PUBLIC LANDS			Art.20
Land Grants Accepted on Terms of Trust			1
SALARIES			Art.21
Public officers to be paid salaries. Exceptions.			1
Legislature to provide fees. Accounting			2
MISCELLANEOUS			Art.22
Homestead exemption			1
Property rights of married women			2
Prohibition of intoxicating liquors			3
Seat of Government - Salt Lake City		XV-1	
Eligibility for office - qualified voter		XV-2	

	1849	1872	1895
Executive offices at seat of government		XV-6	
Plurality of votes constitutes a choice		XV-7	
Holding two government offices		XV-8	
AMENDMENTS	VII	XVI	Art.23
Amendments: Proposal, election	1	1	1
Revision of the Constitution	1	2	2
Submission to electors	1		3
SCHEDULE		XVII	Art.24
Actions, contract to continue			1
Territorical laws continued			2
Prisoners to be held			3
Fines, penalties and forfeitures due the territory. Debts of the territory			4
Recognizances. Judgments. Records Fines due counties, municipalities, school districts			5
Criminal prosecution begun and crimes committed before state road			6
Transfer of causes, records			7
Seals of courts			8
Transfer of probate causes to district courts			9
Officers to hold office until superseded			10
Election for adoption or rejection of Constitution and for state officers. Voters			1
Officers to be Elected			12
Contest for district judgeship, how determined			13
Constitution to be submitted to voters. Ballot			14
Election of officers not provided for herein			15
When Constitution in force			16
On Impeachment and Removal From Office		VII §1-9	

BACKGROUND NOTE

The saga of the Mormon pioneers dominates the constitutional history of Utah, which before their arrival in 1847 was little more than a crossroads of overland trails. Spanish priests had explored the region in 1776, and in 1824 frontiersman Jim Bridger discovered the Great Salt Lake; but of more significance than such events was the Church of Jesus Christ of Latter Day Saints in Fayette, New York in April 1830. Two years later, and more than two thousand miles away, Antoine Roubidoux established a trading post in the Uintah Basin. By 1839 the Mornons, harrassed from New York and other states, migrated to Nauvoo, Illinois.

The fated jointure of the Mormons and the distant desert area drew closer with exploration of northern Utah by John C. Fremont, in 1843, and the revelation to Joseph Smith, in the same year, of the dogma of plural marriage. Polygamy was the final spark for the mob powder keg; in 1844 Smith and his brother were murdered by mob in Carthage, Illinois, and Brigham Young became leader of the church. That year another trading post, near present-day Ogden, was opened by Miles Goodyear. In 1846 the great migration from Nauvoo began.

"This is the place," said Young when the advance parties came to the Great Salt Lake Valley in 1847. They called it Deseret, the Land of the Honey Bee, and in 1849 organized a government with a constitution (Doc. No. 1). Congress was directly behind them, and in 1850 created the Territory of Utah, an enormous intermountain tract from western Nebraska to the California border (Doc. No. 2). Brigham Young became the territorial governor, rendering somewhat anomalous his continuing status as governor of the state of Deseret. However, that might be, the Mormons did indeed make the desert bloom like a rose. Irrigation brought out the high productivity of the land; the first university west of the Missouri River was now founded; and colonies of the faithful were springing up throughout the region.

But persecution was to begin anew when the doctrine of polygamy was proclaimed on a world-

wide basis for the church in 1852. A long political, legal and military stuggle, in the name
of the orthodox Victorian views of social morality, would delay statehood for forty years.   In 1857
an American army, on allegations of a "rebellion"
in Utah, was sent west, and in an infamous incident a raiding party of irregulars slaughtered
more than one hundred Arkansas immigrants in the
Mountain Meadows Massacre. The "Utah War" ended
the next year, but not the hostility; in 1860
a petition for admission to the Union, accompanied
by a draft constitution was rejected by Congress
(Doc. No. 3). In 1868 Congress enacted its first
statute against polygamy, thus identifying the
root of the opposition.

Meantime the territory was being reduced to
more practical geographic dimensions, with separate organization of territories of Nevada and
Wyoming, and the removal of western Colorado, at
various dates throughout the 1860s. By 1870 the
population had doubled, Salt Lake City was a thri-
ving metropolis, railroading and mining were rapid-
ly developing. In 1872 another petition for
admission to the Union, accompanied by a new draft
constitution (Doc. No. 4), was sent to Congress,
which rejected the bid and in 1874 adopted a second anti-polygamy statute.

Ten years later the same process was repeated, with the Edmunds act disfranchising polygamists and stepping up official harrassment of the
Mormons. A redraft of an 1882 constitution was
submitted in 1887 (Doc. No. 5), provoking Congress
to pass still another statute, this time confis-
cating church property and authorizing the arrest
of church leaders. An appeal to the courts in the
"Mormon Cases" (Doc. No. 6) failed, and under the
universal pressure Church President Wilford Wood-
ruff at length began efforts to rescind the doctrine of plural marriages, and in 1890 issued a
manifesto abandoning the practice.

Satisfied that polygamy had been abolished,
President Benjamin Harrison in 1893 proclaimed a
general amnesty and the return of confiscated
church property (Doc. No. 7). The next year Congress passed an enabling act (Doc. No. 8) and in
May 1895 a constitution for the state of Utah was
approved by the people (Doc. No. 9). The end of a,
long and dubious government policy came with Presidents Cleveland's proclamation of statehood on
January 4, 1896 (Doc. No. 10).

[Doc. No. 1]

Constitution of the State of Deseret

Preamble and constitution:

Whereas a large number of citizens of the United States, before and since the treaty of peace with the republic of Mexico, emigrated to and settled in that portion of the territory of the United States lying west of the Rocky mountains, and in the great interior basin of Upper California; and

Whereas, by reason of said treaty, all civil organization originating from the republic of Mexico became abrogated; and

Whereas the Congress of the United States has failed to provide a form of civil government for the territory so acquired, or any portion thereof; and

Whereas civil government and laws are necessary for the security, peace, and prosperity of society; and

Whereas it is a fundamental principle in all republican governments, that all political power is inherent in the people; and governments instituted for their protection, security, and benefit should emanate from the same: Therefore,

Your committee beg leave to recommend the adoption of the following constitution, until the Congress of the United States shall otherwise provide for the government of the territory hereinafter named and described:

We, the people, grateful to the Supreme Being for the blessings hitherto enjoyed, and feeling our dependence on Him for a continuation of those blessings, do ordain and establish a free and independent government, by the name of the State of Deseret, including all the territory of the United States within the following boundaries, to wit: Commencing at the 33d degree of north latitude, where it crosses the 108th degree of longitude west of Greenwich; thence, running south and west, to the northern boundary of Mexico; thence west to, and down the main channel of the Gila river, on the northern line of Mexico, and on the northern boundary of Lower California, to the Pacific ocean; thence along the coast northwesterly to 118 degrees 30 minutes of west longitude; thence north to where said line intersects the dividing ridge of the Sierra Nevada mountains; thence north, along the summit of the Sierra Nevada mountains, to the dividing range of mountains that separates the waters flowing into the Columbia river from the waters running into the Great basin; thence easterly, along the dividing range of mountains that separates said waters flowing into the Columbia river on the north from the waters flowing into the Great basin on the south, to the summit of the Wind River chain of mountains; thence southeast and south, by the dividing range of mountains that separates the waters flowing into the Gulf of Mexico, from the waters flowing into the Gulf of California, to the place of beginning; as set forth in a map drawn by Charles Preuss, and published by order of the Senate of the United States, in 1848.

ARTICLE I.

The powers of government of the State of Deseret shall be divided into three distinct departments, viz: legislative, executive, and Judiciary

ARTICLE II.—*Of the Legislative.*

SEC. 1. The legislative authority of this State shall be vested in a General Assembly, consisting of a Senate and House of Representatives, both to be elected by the people.

SEC. 2. The session of the General Assembly shall be annual, and the first session be held on the first Monday of July next; and thereafter, on the first Monday of December, unless the governor of the State shall convene the Assembly in the interim by proclamation.

SEC. 3. The members of the House of Representatives shall be chosen biennially, by the qualified electors of their respective districts, on the first Monday in August, whose term of office shall continue two years from the day of the general election.

SEC. 4. No person shall be a member of the House of Representatives who has not attained the age of twenty-five years; the same to be a free white male citizen of the United States, and an inhabitant of this State one year preceding the time of his election, and a resident of the district or county thirty days next preceding his election, and have at his election an actual residence in the district he may be chosen to represent.

SEC. 5. Senators shall be chosen for the term of four years, at the same time and place of representatives; they shall be thirty years of age, and possess the qualifications of representatives as to residence and citizenship.

SEC. 6. The number of senators shall not be less than one-third nor more than one-half of the representatives; and at the first session of the General Assembly after this costitution takes effect the Senate shall be divided by lot, as equal as may be, into two classes; the seats of the senators of the first class shall be vacated at the expiration of two years, so that one-half of the Senate shall be elected biennially.

SEC. 7. Each house shall choose its own officers, and judge of the qualification, election, and return of its own members, and contested elections shall be determined in such manner as shall hereafter be determined by law.

SEC. 8. A majority in each house shall constitute a quorum to do business, but a smaller number may adjourn from day to day, and compel the attendance of absent members, in such manner and under such penalty as each house may provide.

SEC. 9. Each house shall have all powers necessary for a branch of the General Assembly of a free and independent government.

SEC. 10. Each member of the Assembly shall be privileged from civil arrest during any session, and in going to and returning from the same.

SEC. 11. Neither house shall without the consent of the other adjourn for more than three days, nor to any other place than that in which they may be sitting.

SEC. 12. The Assembly shall at its first session provide for an enumeration of the white inhabitants, and an apportionment for the senators and representatives.

SEC. 13. Each member of the Assembly shall take an oath or affirmation to support the constitution of the United States and of this State; and members shall and are hereby empowered to administer said oath or affirmation to each other.

SEC. 14. The veto power of the governor shall be allowed by the Assembly, except on bills which, when reconsidered, shall be again passed by a majority of two-thirds of those present; and any bill vetoed by the governor shall be returned within ten days, (Sundays excepted) with his objections; otherwise it shall become a law; unless the Assembly, by adjournment, prevent its return.

SEC. 15. Every law passed by the Assembly shall take effect from and after due publication by authority.

SEC. 16. The voters of this State may elect at the first election not exceeding seventeen senators, and thirty-five representatives.

ARTICLE III.—*Of the Executive.*

SEC. 1. The executive power shall be vested in a governor, who shall hold his office for four years. A lieutenant governor shall be elected at the same time, and for the same term, who shall be the president of the Senate.

SEC. 2. No person shall be eligible to the office of governor or lieutenant governor who has not been a citizen of the United States and a resident of this State two years next preceding his election, and attained the age of thirty-five years at the time of his election.

SEC. 3. The governor shall be commander-in-chief of the militia, navy, and all the armies of this State.

SEC. 4. He shall transact all executive business with the officers of government, civil and military, and may require information in writing from the officers of the Executive department upon any subject relating to the duties of their respective offices.

SEC. 5. He shall see that the laws are faithfully executed.

SEC. 6. When any office shall from any cause become vacant, and no mode is prescribed by the constitution and laws for filling such vacancy, the governor shall have power to fill such vacancy, by granting a commission, which shall expire when such vacancy shall be filled by due course of law.

SEC. 7. He shall also have power to convene the General Assembly by proclamation, when in his opinion the interests of the State require it.

SEC. 8. He shall communicate by message to the General Assembly at every session the condition of the State, and recommend such matters as he shall deem expedient.

SEC. 9. In case of disagreement in the General Assembly, with regard to the time of adjournment, the governor shall have power to dissolve the session by proclamation.

SEC. 10. No person shall, while holding any lucrative office under the United States, or this State, execute the office of governor, except as shall be prescribed by law.

SEC. 11. The governor shall have power to grant reprieves and pardons, and commute punishments after convictions, except in cases of impeachment.

SEC. 12. The governor shall receive for his services such compensation as shall hereafter be provided by law.

SEC. 13. There shall be a seal of this State, which shall be kept by the governor, and used by him officially; and shall be called the Great Seal of the State of Deseret.

Sec. 14. All grants and commissions shall be in the name and by the authority of the people of the State of Deseret; sealed with the great seal of this State, signed by the governor, and countersigned by the secretary of state.

Sec. 15. A secretary of state, auditor of public accounts, and treasurer shall be elected by the qualified electors, who shall continue in office for the term of four years. The secretary of state shall keep a fair register of all the official acts of the governor, and shall, when required, lay the same, together with all papers, minutes, and vouchers relative thereto, before either branch of the General Assembly, and shall perform such other duties as shall be assigned him by law.

Sec. 16. In case of the impeachment of the governor, his removal from office, death, resignation, or absence from the State, the powers and duties of the office shall devolve upon the lieutenant governor until such disability shall cease, or the vacancy be filled.

Article IV.—*Of the Judiciary.*

Sec. 1. The judicial power shall be vested in a supreme court and such inferior courts as the General Assembly shall, from time to time, establish.

Sec. 2. The supreme court shall consist of a chief justice and two associates, either two of whom shall be a quorum to hold courts.

Sec. 3. The judges of the supreme court shall be elected by joint vote of both houses of the General Assembly, and shall hold their courts at such time and place as the General Assembly shall direct; and hold their office for the term of four years, and until their successors are elected and qualified. The judges of the supreme court shall be conservators of the peace throughout the State, and shall exercise such other jurisdictions and appellate powers as shall be prescribed by law.

Sec. 4. The style of all process shall be *the State of Deseret;* and all prosecutions shall be in the name and by the authority of the State.

Article V.—*Of Elections.*

Sec. 1. The governor, lieutenant governor, auditor of accounts, treasurer, and secretary of state shall be elected by the qualified electors, as provided for members of the General Assembly, and at the time and place appointed for holding the same.

Sec. 2. The returns of every election for governor, lieutenant governor, auditor, treasurer, and secretary of state shall be sealed up and transmitted forthwith to the seat of government, directed to the speaker of the House of Representatives, who shall, during the first week of the session, open and publish them in the presence of both houses of the General Assembly; and the persons receiving a majority of all the legal votes cast for their respective offices shall be declared duly elected.

Sec. 3. The governor, lieutenant governor, auditor, treasurer, and secretary of state shall, before entering upon the duties of their respective offices, take an oath, or affirmation, to support the constitution of the United States and of this State; which oath, or affirmation, shall be administered by the speaker of the House of Representatives.

Sec. 4. The first election for members of the General Assembly, and other officers under this constitution, shall be held on the first Monday of May next at the usual places of holding public meetings in the different districts and settlements; at which time and place, the qualified voters shall vote for or against the adoption of this constitution; and if a majority of all the legal votes shall be in favor of its adoption, the same shall take effect from and after said election.

SEC. 5. At the time and place of holding the elections, the qualified electors shall organize the polls by appointing two judges, who shall be authorized to qualify each other, and appoint two suitable persons as clerks; and said judges shall, at the close of said election, seal up the number of votes so cast, and forthwith transmit them to the president of this convention.

SEC. 6. The returns of the first election herein provided for shall be made to the chairman of this convention, who, together with the two secretaries, shall proceed immediately to open said returns, and count the votes; upon ascertaining the persons receiving a majority of votes, they shall forthwith notify them of their election.

SEC. 7. The General Assembly shall, at its first session, provide by law a general system of election for officers under this constitution, and such other officers as may be hereafter created by law.

SEC. 8. The manner of voting shall be by ballot.

SEC. 9. The General Assembly shall meet at Great Salt Lake city; which place shall be the seat of government, until otherwise provided by law.

SEC. 10. All white male residents of this State over the age of twenty-one years shall have the privilege of voting at the first election, and at the adoption of this constitution; provided that no person in the military, naval, or marine service of the United States shall be considered a resident of this State by being stationed in any garrison, barrack, military or naval place or station within this State, unless otherwise provided for by law.

ARTICLE VI.—*Of Militia.*

SEC. 1. The militia of this State shall be composed of all able-bodied white male citizens between the ages of eighteen and forty-five years, except such as are, or may hereafter be, exempt by the laws of the United States, or of this State, and shall be armed, equipped, and trained as the General Assembly may provide by law.

SEC. 2. All commissioned officers of the militia (staff officers excepted) shall be elected by the persons liable to perform military duty, in their respective divisions, and all commissioned officers shall be commissioned by the governor.

ARTICLE VII.—*Amendments of the Constitution.*

SEC. 1. If at any time the General Assembly shall deem it necessary, and for the best interest of the State, that this constitution should be revised, altered, or amended, the Assembly shall cause such revisions, alterations, or amendments to be published in the same manner as shall be provided for the publication of the statutes, and appoint a day, not less than thirty days thereafter, for the electors of the commonwealth to assemble in their several precincts and vote for or against said revisions, alterations, or amendments; and if a majority of said electors shall vote in favor of said revisions, alterations, or amendments, the same shall thereafter become parts and parcels of this constitution; otherwise, this constitution shall remain unaltered.

ARTICLE VIII.—*Declaration of Rights.*

SEC. 1. In republican governments, all men should be born equally free and independent, and possess certain natural, essential, and inalienable rights, among which are those of enjoying and defending their life and liberty; acquiring, possessing, and protecting property, and of seeking and obtaining their safety and happiness.

SEC. 2. All political power is inherent in the people, and all free governments are founded in their authority, and instituted for their benefit; therefore, they have an inalienable and indefeasible right to institute government, and to alter, reform, and totally change the same when their safety, happiness, and the public good shall require it.

SEC. 3. All men shall have a natural and inalienable right to worship God according to the dictates of their own consciences, and the General Assembly shall make no law respecting an establishment of religion, or of prohibiting the free exercise thereof, or disturb any person in his religious worship or sentiments, provided he does not disturb the public peace, nor obstruct others in their religious worship; and all persons demeaning themselves peaceably, as good members of the State, shall be equally under the protection of the laws; and no subordination or preference of any one sect or denomination to another shall ever be established by law, nor shall any religious test be ever required for any office of trust under this State.

SEC. 4. Any citizen of this State who may hereafter be engaged, either directly or indirectly, in a duel, either as principal or accessory before the fact, shall be disqualified from holding any office under the constitution and laws of this State.

SEC. 5. Every person may speak, write, and publish his sentiments on all subjects, being responsible for the abuse of that right, and no law shall be passed to abridge the liberty of speech or of the press.

SEC. 6. The people shall be secure in their persons, houses, papers, and possessions from unreasonable searches and seizures.

SEC. 7. The right of trial by jury shall remain inviolate, and all criminals shall be heard by self or counsel, at their own election.

SEC. 8. All penalties and punishments shall be in proportion to the offence, and all offences before conviction shall be bailable, except capital offences, where the proof is evident or the presumption great.

SEC. 9. The writ of habeas corpus shall not be suspended, unless in case of rebellion or invasion, or the public safety shall require it.

SEC. 10. Treason against this State shall consist only in levying war against it, or adhering to its enemies, or giving them aid and comfort.

SEC. 11. The General Assembly shall pass no bill of attainder or *ex post facto* laws, or law impairing the obligation of contracts, to hinder the execution of justice.

SEC. 12. The laws shall not be suspended but by the legislative or executive authority.

Sec. 13. The right of petition by the people shall be preserved inviolate.

Sec. 14. The right of citizens to keep and bear arms for common defence shall not be questioned.

Sec. 15. Private property shall not be taken for public use without just compensation.

Sec. 16. No standing army shall be kept up in time of peace, and the military shall at all times, and in all places, be in strict subordination to the civil power.

Sec. 17. The enumeration of certain rights shall not be construed to impair nor deny others retained by the people.

[Doc. No. 2]

Territorial Act of September 9, 1850

CHAP. LI. — *An Act to establish a Territorial Government for Utah.* Sept. 9, 1850

Be it enacted by the Senate and House of Representatives of the United States of America in Congress assembled, That all that part of the territory of the United States included within the following limits, to wit: bounded on the west by the State of California, on the north by the Territory of Oregon, and on the east by the summit of the Rocky Mountains, and on the south by the thirty-seventh parallel of north latitude, be, and the same is hereby, created into a temporary government, by the name of the Territory of Utah; and, when admitted as a State, the said Territory, or any portion of the same, shall be received into the Union, with or without slavery, as their constitution may prescribe at the time of their admission: *Provided,* That nothing in this act contained shall be construed to inhibit the government of the United States from dividing said Territory into two or more Territories, in such manner and at such times as Congress shall deem convenient and proper, or from attaching any portion of said Territory to any other State or Territory of the United States *The boundary of the Territory of Utah defined*

Proviso.

SEC. 2. *And be it further enacted,* That the executive power and authority in and over said Territory of Utah shall be vested in a governor, who shall hold his office for four years, and until his successor shall be appointed and qualified, unless sooner removed by the President of the United States. The governor shall reside within said Territory, shall be commander-in-chief of the militia thereof, shall perform the duties and receive the emoluments of superintendent of Indian affairs, and shall approve all laws passed by the legislative assembly before they shall take effect: he may grant pardons for offences against the laws of said Territory, and reprieves for offences against the laws of the United States, until the decision of the President can be made known thereon; he shall commission all officers who shall be appointed to office under the laws of the said Territory, and shall take care that the laws be faithfully executed. *Executive power vested in a governor: his duties defined.*

SEC. 3. *And be it further enacted,* That there shall be a secretary of said Territory, who shall reside therein, and hold his office for four years, unless sooner removed by the President of the United States: he shall record and preserve all the laws and proceedings of the legislative assembly hereinafter constituted, and all the acts and proceedings of the governor in his executive department; he shall transmit one copy of the laws and one copy of the executive proceedings, on or before the first day of December in each year, to the President of the United States, and, at the same time, two copies of the laws to the Speaker of the House of Representatives, and the President of the Senate, for the use of Congress. And in the case of the death, removal, resignation, or other necessary absence of the governor from the Territory, the secretary shall have, and he is hereby authorized *Secretary: his duties defined.*

To act as governor in certain contingencies.

and required to execute and perform, all the powers and duties of the governor during such vacancy or necessary absence, or until another governor shall be duly appointed to fill such vacancy.

Legislative power: how vested.
The legislative assembly to consist of a Council and House of Representatives.
The Council shall consist of thirteen members, and the House of Representatives of twenty-six.

SEC. 4. *And be it further enacted,* That the legislative power and authority of said Territory shall be vested in the governor and a legislative assembly. The legislative assembly shall consist of a Council and House of Representatives. The Council shall consist of thirteen members, having the qualifications of voters as hereinafter prescribed, whose term of service shall continue two years. The House of Representatives shall consist of twenty-six members, possessing the same qualifications as prescribed for members of the Council, and whose term of service shall continue one year. An apportionment shall be made, as nearly equal as practicable, among the several counties or districts, for the election of the Council and House of Representatives, giving to each section of the Territory representation in the ratio of its population, Indians excepted, as nearly as may be. And the members of the Council and of the House of Representatives shall reside in, and be inhabitants of, the district for which they may be

Previous to the first election, a census to be taken.

elected respectively. Previous to the first election, the governor shall cause a census or enumeration of the inhabitants of the several counties and districts of the Territory to be taken, and the first election shall be held at such time and places, and be conducted in such manner, as the governor shall appoint and direct; and he shall, at the same time, declare the number of members of the Council and House of Representatives to which each of the counties or districts shall be entitled

Elections: how conducted.

under this act. The number of persons authorized to be elected having the highest number of votes in each of said Council districts for members of the Council, shall be declared by the governor to be duly elected to the Council; and the person or persons authorized to be elected having the highest number of votes for the House of Representatives, equal to the number to which each county or district shall be entitled, shall be declared by the governor to be duly elected members of the House of Representatives:

Proviso.

Provided, That in case of a tie between two or more persons voted for, the governor shall order a new election to supply the vacancy made by such a tie. And the persons thus elected to the legislative assembly shall meet at such place, and on such day, as the governor shall appoint; but thereafter, the time, place, and manner of holding and conducting all elections by the people, and the apportioning the representation in the several counties or districts to the Council and House of Representatives, according to population, shall be prescribed by law, as well as the day of the commencement of the regular sessions of the legislative assembly:

Further proviso.

Provided, That no one session shall exceed the term of forty days.

Qualifications of voters.

SEC. 5. *And be it further enacted,* That every free white male inhabitant above the age of twenty-one years, who shall have been a resident of said Territory at the time of the passage of this act, shall be entitled to vote at the first election, and shall be eligible to any office within the said Territory; but the qualifications of voters and of holding office, at all subsequent elections, shall be such as shall be prescribed by the legislative assembly:

Proviso.

Provided, That the right of suffrage and of holding office shall be exercised only by citizens of the United States, including those recognized as citizens by the treaty with the republic of Mexico, concluded February second, eighteen hundred and forty-eight.

Legislative power of the Territory defined.

SEC. 6. *And be it further enacted,* That the legislative power of said Territory shall extend to all rightful subjects of legislation, consistent with the Constitution of the United States and the provisions of this act; but no law shall be passed interfering with the primary disposal of the soil; no tax shall be imposed upon the property of the

United States; nor shall the lands or other property of non-residents be taxed higher than the lands or other property of residents. All the laws passed by the legislative assembly and governor shall be submitted to the Congress of the United States, and, if disapproved, shall be null and of no effect.

SEC. 7. *And be it further enacted,* That all township, district, and county officers, not herein otherwise provided for, shall be appointed or elected, as the case may be, in such manner as shall be provided by the governor and legislative assembly of the territory of Utah. The governor shall nominate, and, by and with the advice and consent of the legislative Council, appoint all officers not herein otherwise provided for; and in the first instance the governor alone may appoint all said officers, who shall hold their offices until the end of the first session of the legislative assembly, and shall lay off the necessary districts for members of the Council and House of Representatives, and all other offices. *[marginal note: How township, district, and county officers are to be appointed.]*

SEC. 8. *And be it further enacted,* That no member of the legislative assembly shall hold or be appointed to any office which shall have been created, or the salary or emoluments of which shall have been increased while he was a member, during the term for which he was elected, and for one year after the expiration of such term; and no person holding a commission or appointment under the United States, except postmasters, shall be a member of the legislative assembly, or shall hold any office under the government of said Territory. *[marginal note: No member of legislative assembly to hold certain offices during his term of election, or for one year thereafter. Officers of the United States, except postmasters, not to be members of assembly, or hold office.]*

SEC. 9. *And be it further enacted,* That the judicial power of said Territory shall be vested in a Supreme Court, District Courts, Probate Courts, and in justices of the peace. The Supreme Court shall consist of a chief justice and two associate justices, any two of whom shall constitute a quorum, and who shall hold a term at the seat of government of said Territory annually, and they shall hold their offices during the period of four years. The said Territory shall be divided into three judicial districts, and a District Court shall be held in each of said districts by one of the justices of the Supreme Court, at such time and place as may be prescribed by law; and the said judges shall, after their appointments, respectively, reside in the districts which shall be assigned them. The jurisdiction of the several courts herein provided for, both appellate and original, and that of the Probate Courts and of justices of the peace, shall be as limited by law: *Provided,* That justices of the peace shall not have jurisdiction of any matter in controversy when the title or boundaries of land may be in dispute, or where the debt or sum claimed shall exceed one hundred dollars; and the said Supreme and District Courts, respectively, shall possess chancery as well as common law jurisdiction. Each District Court, or the judge thereof, shall appoint its clerk, who shall also be the register in chancery, and shall keep his office at the place where the court may be held. Writs of error, bills of exception, and appeals shall be allowed in all cases from the final decisions of said District Courts to the Supreme Court, under such regulations as may be prescribed by law; but in no case removed to the Supreme Court shall trial by jury be allowed in said court. The Supreme Court, or the justices thereof, shall appoint its own clerk, and every clerk shall hold his office at the pleasure of the court for which he shall have been appointed. Writs of error, and appeals from the final decisions of said Supreme Court, shall be allowed, and may be taken to the Supreme Court of the United States, in the same manner and under the same regulations as from the Circuit Courts of the United States, where the value of the property or the amount in controversy, to be ascertained by the oath or affirmation of either party, or other competent witness, shall exceed one thousand dollars, except only that, in all *[marginal note: The judicial power: in whom vested, and how to be exercised. District Courts. Jurisdiction of courts and justices of the peace, etc. Proviso. Clerk. Writs of error, &c. Clerk. Writs of error and appeals shall be allowed, &c.]*

Exceptions.	cases involving title to slaves, the said writs of error or appeals shall be allowed and decided by the said Supreme Court, without regard to the value of the matter, property, or title in controversy; and except, also, that a writ of error or appeal shall also be allowed to the Supreme Court of the United States, from the decisions of the said Supreme Court created by this act, or of any judge thereof, or of the District Courts created by this act, or of any judge thereof, upon any writ of habeas corpus involving the question of personal freedom; and each of the said District Courts shall have and exercise the same jurisdiction in all cases arising under the Constitution and laws of the United States as is vested in the Circuit and District Courts of the United States; and the said Supreme and District Courts of the said Territory, and the respective judges thereof, shall and may grant writs of habeas corpus in all cases in which the same are granted by the judges of the United States in the District of Columbia; and the first six days of every term of said courts, or so much thereof as shall be necessary, shall be appropriated to the trial of causes arising under the said Constitution and laws; and writs of error and appeal, in all such cases, shall be made to the Supreme Court of said Territory, the same as in
Fees of clerk.	other cases. The said clerk shall receive in all such cases the same fees which the clerks of the District Courts of Oregon Territory now receive for similar services.
Attorney and marshal: their fees and duties.	SEC. 10. *And be it further enacted;* That there shall be appointed an attorney for said Territory, who shall continue in office for four years, unless sooner removed by the President, and who shall receive the same fees and salary as the attorney of the United States for the present Territory of Oregon. There shall also be a marshal for the Territory appointed, who shall hold his office for four years, unless sooner removed by the President, and who shall execute all processes issuing from the said courts, when exercising their jurisdiction as Circuit and District Courts of the United States: he shall perform the duties, be subject to the same regulation and penalties, and be entitled to the same fees as the marshal of the District Court of the United States for the present Territory of Oregon; and shall, in addition, be paid two hundred dollars annually as a compensation for extra services.
Governor, secretary, chief justice and associate justices, attorney and marshal: how to be appointed. Oaths.	SEC. 11. *And be it further enacted,* That the governor, secretary, chief justice and associate justices, attorney and marshal, shall be nominated, and, by and with the advice and consent of the Senate, appointed by the President of the United States. The governor and secretary to be appointed as aforesaid shall, before they act as such, respectively, take an oath or affirmation, before the district judge, or some justice of the peace in the limits of said Territory, duly authorized to administer oaths and affirmations by the laws now in force therein, or before the chief justice or some associate justice of the Supreme Court of the United States, to support the Constitution of the United States, and faithfully to discharge the duties of their respective offices; which said oaths, when so taken, shall be certified by the person by whom the same shall have been taken, and such certificates shall be received and recorded by the said secretary among the executive proceedings; and the chief justice and associate justices, and all other civil officers in said Territory, before they act as such, shall take a like oath or affirmation, before the said governor or secretary, or some judge or justice of the peace of the Territory who may be duly commissioned and qualified, which said oath or affirmation shall be certified and transmitted, by the person taking the same, to the secretary, to be by him recorded as aforesaid; and afterwards, the like oath or affirmation shall be taken, certified, and recorded, in such manner and form as may be prescribed by law. The governor shall re-
Salary of governor.	ceive an annual salary of fifteen hundred dollars as governor, and one

thousand dollars as superintendent of Indian affairs. The chief jus- Salary of chief
tice and associate justices shall each receive an annual salary of eigh- justice and asso-
teen hundred dollars. The secretary shall receive an annual salary ciate justices.
of eighteen hundred dollars. The said salaries shall be paid quarter- retary.
yearly, at the treasury of the United States. The members of the Compensation
legislative assembly shall be entitled to receive three dollars each per of members of
day during their attendance at the sessions thereof, and three dollars assembly.
each for twenty miles' travel, in going to and returning from the said
sessions, estimated according to the nearest usually travelled route.
There shall be appropriated annually the sum of one thousand dollars, Contingent ex-
to be expended by the governor, to defray the contingent expenses of penses provided
the Territory. There shall also be appropriated, annually, a sufficient for.
sum, to be expended by the secretary of the Territory, and upon an estimate to be made by the Secretary of the Treasury of the United
States, to defray the expenses of the legislative assembly, the printing of the laws, and other incidental expenses; and the secretary of
the Territory shall annually account to the Secretary of the Treasury
of the United States for the manner in which the aforesaid sum shall
have been expended.

SEC. 12. *And be it further enacted*, That the legislative assembly Legislative as-
of the Territory of Utah shall hold its first session at such time and sembly to hold
place in said Territory as the governor thereof shall appoint and direct; as directed by
and at said first session, or as soon thereafter as they shall deem expe- the governor.
dient, the governor and legislative assembly shall proceed to locate
and establish the seat of government for said Territory at such place Seat of gov-
as they may deem eligible; which place, however, shall thereafter be ernment.
subject to be changed by the said governor and legislative assembly.
And the sum of twenty thousand dollars, out of any money in the treas- Appropriation
ury not otherwise appropriated, is hereby appropriated and granted to for public build-
said Territory of Utah to be applied by the governor and legislative ings.
assembly to the erection of suitable public buildings at the seat of
government.

SEC. 13. *And be it further enacted*, That a delegate to the House A delegate to
of Representatives of the United States, to serve during each Congress be elected to
of the United States, may be elected by the voters qualified to elect United States.
members of the legislative assembly, who shall be entitled to the same
rights and privileges as are exercised and enjoyed by the delegates from
the several other Territories of the United States to the said House of
Representatives. The first election shall be held at such time and
places, and be conducted in such manner, as the governor shall appoint and direct; and at all subsequent elections, the times, places,
and manner of holding the elections shall be prescribed by law. The
person having the greatest number of votes shall be declared by the
governor to be duly elected, and a certificate thereof shall be given accordingly : *Provided*, That said delegate shall receive no higher sum Proviso.
for mileage than is allowed by law to the delegate from Oregon.

SEC. 14. *And be it further enacted*, That the sum of five thousand Appropriation
dollars be, and the same is hereby, appropriated out of any moneys in for the purchase
the treasury not otherwise appropriated, to be expended by and un- of a library.
der the direction of the said governor of the territory of Utah, in the
purchase of a library, to be kept at the seat of government for the use
of the governor, legislative assembly, judges of the Supreme Court,
secretary, marshal, and attorney of said Territory, and such other persons, and under such regulations, as shall be prescribed by law.

SEC. 15. *And be it further enacted*, That when the lands in the said Lands to be
Territory shall be surveyed under the direction of the government of surveyed, how to
the United States, preparatory to bringing the same into market, sec- be disposed of.
tions numbered sixteen and thirty-six in each township in said Territory shall be, and the same are hereby, reserved for the purpose of

being applied to schools in said Territory, and in the States and Territories hereafter to be erected out of the same.

Judicial district: how defined.

SEC. 16. *And be it further enacted,* That temporarily, and until otherwise provided by law, the governor of said Territory may define the judicial districts of said Territory, and assign the judges who may be appointed for said Territory to the several districts, and also appoint the times and places for holding courts in the several counties or subdivisions in each of said judicial districts, by proclamation to be issued by him; but the legislative assembly, at their first or any subsequent session, may organize, alter, or modify such judicial districts, and assign the judges, and alter the times and places of holding the courts, as to them shall seem proper and convenient.

The Constitution and laws of the U. States to extend over the Territory of Utah so far as applicable.

SEC. 17. *And be it further enacted,* That the Constitution and laws of the United States are hereby extended over and declared to be in force in said Territory of Utah, so far as the same, or any provision thereof, may be applicable.

APPROVED, September 9, 1850.

[Doc. No. 3]

Draft Constitution of 1860

PREAMBLE.

Whereas, all citizens of the United States have the right guaranteed by the Constitution to make those laws by which they are governed; and

Whereas, it appears from a census report, made pursuant to an act of the late legislature, that the Territory of Utah possesses a population sufficiently numerous to justify them in asserting their claims to this inestimable privilege;

Therefore we, the people, grateful to the Supreme Being for the enjoyment of life and mercy, and feeling our dependence on Him for a continuation of those blessings, do ordain and establish the following constitution:

ARTICLE I.

Boundary and Name.

SECTION 1. All that part of the territory of the United States now known as Utah Territory, and bounded as follows, viz: on the west by the State of California, on the north by the Territory of Oregon, on the east by the summit of the Rocky Mountains, and on the south by the thirty-seventh (37th) parallel of north latitude, is hereby formed into a free and sovereign State, and named Deseret.

ARTICLE II.

Declaration of Rights.

SECTION. 1. In republican governments all men should possess their natural rights, among which are those of enjoying and defending their life and liberty; acquiring, possessing, and protecting property, and of seeking and obtaining their safety and happiness.

SECTION 2. All political power is inherent in the people, and all free governments are founded in their authority and instituted for their benefit; therefore they have an inalienable and indefeasible right to institute government, and to alter, reform, or totally change the same when their safety, happiness, and the public good shall require it.

SECTION 3. All men shall have a natural and inalienable right to worship God according to the dictates of their own consciences; and the general assembly shall make no law respecting an establishment of religion or prohibiting the free exercise thereof, or to disturb any person in his religious worship or sentiments; and all persons demeaning themselves peaceably as good members of this State shall be equally under the protection of the laws; and no subordination or preference of any one sect or denomination to another shall ever be established by law; nor shall any religious test be ever required for any office of trust under this constitution.

SECTION 4. Any person of this State who may hereafter be engaged directly or indirectly in a duel, either as principal or accessory before the fact, shall be disqualified from holding any office under the constitution and laws of this State.

SECTION 5. Every person may speak, write, and publish his sentiments on all subjects, being responsible for the abuse of that right; and no law shall be passed to abridge the liberty of speech or of the press.

SECTION 6. The people shall be secure in their persons, houses, papers, and possessions from unreasonable searches and seizures.

SECTION 7. The right of trial by jury shall remain inviolate; and all prisoners shall be heard by self or counsel at their own election; and no person shall be held to answer a capital or otherwise infamous crime, unless on presentment or indictment of a grand jury; nor shall any person be subject for the same offence to be twice put in jeopardy of life or limb, nor be compelled in any criminal case to be a witness against himself.

SECTION 8. All penalties and punishments shall be in proportion to the offence; and all offences before conviction shall be bailable, except capital offences where the proof is evident or the presumption great; excessive bail shall not be required.

SECTION 9. The writ of habeas corpus shall not be suspended, unless in case of rebellion, or invasion, or the public safety shall require it.

SECTION 10. Treason against this State shall consist only in levying war against it, or adhering to its enemies, or giving them aid or comfort.

SECTION 11. The general assembly shall pass no bill of attainder, or ex post facto law, or law impairing the obligation of contracts.

SECTION 12. The law shall not be suspended but by legislative authority.

SECTION 13. The right of petition by the people shall be preserved inviolate.

SECTION 14. The right of citizens to keep and bear arms for common defence shall not be questioned.

SECTION 15. Private property shall not be taken for public use without just compensation.

SECTION 16. No standing army shall be kept up in this State in time of peace; and the military shall at all times, and in all places, be in strict subordination to civil power.

SECTION 17. The enumeration of certain rights shall not be construed to impair or deny others retained by the people.

ARTICLE III.

The powers of government of the State of Deseret shall be divided into three distinct departments, viz: legislative, executive, and judicial.

ARTICLE IV.

Of the Legislative.

SECTION 1. The legislative authority shall be vested in a general assembly, consisting of a senate and house of representatives, the members of which shall be elected by the people.

SECTION 2. The sessions of the general assembly shall be annual, until otherwise provided by legislative enactment ; and the first session shall be as hereinafter provided.

SECTION 3. The members of the house of representatives shall be chosen biennially, by the qualified electors of their respective districts, whose term of office shall continue two years from the day of their election.

SECTION 4. Senators shall be chosen in the same manner as the representatives, whose term of office shall continue four years from the day of their election.

SECTION 5. No person shall be a member of the general assembly except he be a free, white, male citizen of the United States, and an inhabitant of this State one year preceding the time of his election, and has at his election an actual residence in the district he may be chosen to represent.

SECTION 6. The general assembly shall have power to prescribe the number and make the apportionment of senators and representatives: *Provided,* the number of senators shall not be less than one-third, nor more than one-half of the representatives ; and at its first session the general assembly shall be divided by lot, as equally as may be, into two classes ; the seats of the representatives of the first class shall be vacated at the expiration of one year, and of the senators of the first class, at the expiration of two years.

SECTION 7. Each house shall choose its own officers, and judge of the qualification, election, and return of its own members.

SECTION 8. A majority in each house shall constitute a quorum to do business, but a smaller number may adjourn from day to day, and compel the attendance of absent members, in such manner and under such penalty as each house may provide.

SECTION 9. Each house shall have all powers necessary for a branch of the general assembly of a free and independent government.

SECTION 10. Each member of the general assembly shall be privileged from civil arrest during any session, and in going to and returning from the same.

SECTION 11. Neither house shall, without the consent of the other, adjourn for more than three days, nor to any other place than that in which they may be sitting.

SECTION 12. The members of the general assembly shall take an oath or affirmation to support the Constitution of the United States and of this State, which may be administered by each other, or by any person qualified to administer oaths.

SECTION 13. The veto power of the governor shall be allowed by the general assembly, except on bills which, when reconsidered, shall be again passed by a majority of two-thirds ; and any bill vetoed by the governor shall be returned within ten days (Sundays excepted) with his objections, otherwise it shall become a law, unless the general assembly, by adjournment, prevent its return.

SECTION 14. Every law passed by the general assembly shall take effect from and after its publication, unless otherwise provided at the time of its enactment.

SECTION 15. At the first election, after this constitution takes effect, the voters of this State shall elect the same number of senators and representatives as are now elected to the legislative assembly of the Territory of Utah, and according to the present apportionment.

SECTION 16. The legislative power of the general assembly of this State shall extend to all rightful subjects of legislation consistent with the Constitution of the United States and of this State.

ARTICLE V.

Of the Executive.

SECTION 1. The executive power shall be vested in a governor, whose term of office shall be four years. A lieutenant governor shall be elected at the same time, and for the same term, who shall be the president of the senate.

SECTION 2. No person shall be eligible to the office of governor or lieutenant governor who has not been a citizen of the United States six years, and a resident of this State four years next preceding his election.

SECTION 3. The governor shall be commander-in-chief of the militia, navy, and all the armies of this State.

SECTION 4. He shall transact all executive business with the officers of government, civil and military, and may require information in writing from the officers of the executive department upon any subject relating to the duties of their respective offices.

SECTION 5. He shall see that the laws are faithfully executed.

SECTION 6. When any office shall from any cause become vacant, and no mode is prescribed by the constitution and laws for filling such vacancy, the governor shall have power to fill such vacancy by appointment and commission, which shall expire when such vacancy shall be filled by due course of law.

SECTION 7. He shall also have power to convene the general assembly by proclamation, when in his opinion the interests of the State require it.

SECTION 8. He shall communicate, by message, to the general assembly at every session the condition of the State, and recommend such measures as he in his wisdom shall deem expedient.

SECTION 9. In case of disagreement in the general assembly with regard to the time of adjournment, the governor shall have power to dissolve the session by proclamation.

SECTION 10. No person shall, while holding any lucrative office under the United States or this State, execute the office of governor, except as shall be prescribed by law.

SECTION 11. The governor shall have power to grant reprieves and pardons, and commute punishments after conviction, except in cases of impeachment.

SECTION 12. There shall be a seal of this State, which shall be kept by the governor and used by him officially, and be called "Great Seal of the State of Deseret."

SECTION 13. All grants and commissions shall be in the name and by the authority of the people of the State of Deseret, sealed with the great seal of State, signed by the governor, and countersigned by the secretary of state.

SECTION 14. A secretary of state, treasurer, auditor of public accounts, and attorney general, shall be elected by the general assembly, who shall continue in office for the term of four years, and shall perform such duties as may be assigned them by law.

SECTION 15. In case of impeachment of the governor, his removal from office, death, resignation, or absence from the State, the powers and duties of the office shall devolve upon the lieutenant governor, until such disability shall cease or the vacancy be filled.

ARTICLE VI.

Of the Judicial.

SECTION 1. The judicial power shall be vested in a supreme court, district courts, and such inferior courts as the general assembly may from time to time establish.

SECTION 2. The supreme court shall consist of a chief justice and two associates, two of whom shall be a quorum to hold courts.

SECTION 3. The supreme judges shall be elected by the general assembly for the term of six years after the first election under this constitution. At said first election one shall be elected for two years, one for four years, and one for six years.

SECTION 4. The judges of the supreme court shall be conservators of the peace throughout the State, and shall exercise such other jurisdiction and appellate powers as shall be prescribed by law.

SECTION 5. Until otherwise provided by the general assembly, the State is hereby divided into eleven judicial districts, as follows:

Great Salt Lake and Summit counties shall compose the first judicial district.

Utah and Cedar counties shall compose the second judicial district.

Juab and San Pete	"	third	"
Millard and Beaver	"	fourth	"
Iron and Washington	"	fifth	"
Carson county	"	sixth	"
Humboldt, St. Mary's, Greasewood and Malad } counties	"	seventh	"
Cache and Box Elder	" "	eighth	"
Weber and Davis	" "	ninth	"
Green River county	"	tenth	"

Tooele, Shambip and Desert counties shall compose the eleventh judicial district.

SECTION 6. The judges of the district courts shall be elected by the electors of their respective districts, whose term of office shall be two years, and shall have such jurisdiction as may be prescribed by the general assembly.

SECTION 7. The style of all process shall be "State of Deseret," and all criminal prosecutions shall be in the name and by the authority of the people of the State.

ARTICLE VII.
Of Elections.

SECTION 1. All male persons over twenty-one years of age, having a residence of six months in this State, being citizens of the United States, shall be entitled to vote.

SECTION 2. Electors shall in all cases, except treason, felony or breach of the peace, be privileged from arrest on the days of election, during their attendance at such election, going to and returning therefrom.

SECTION 3. No elector shall be obliged to perform military duty on the day of election, except in time of war or public danger.

SECTION 4. No person in the military, naval, or marine service of the United States, by being stationed in any garrison, barrack, military or naval place or station within this State, shall be entitled to vote, unless otherwise provided for by law.

SECTION 5. No idiot or insane person, or person guilty of any infamous crime shall be entitled to the privilege of an elector.

SECTION 6. The first general election under this constitution shall be held at such time as the acting governor of this Territory, by proclamation, shall appoint, for the election of a governor, lieutenant governor, representatives in the Congress of the United States, members of the general assembly, and all other officers of this State, as provided for in this constitution. Said election shall be conducted and returns made in accordance with the existing laws of the Territory of Utah, at the time when said election shall be called.

SECTION 7. That first meeting of the general assembly shall be as directed by proclamation by the governor elect, and subsequent sessions shall be held as provided by law.

ARTICLE VIII.
Of the Militia.

SECTION 1. The militia of this State shall be composed of all able-bodied male citizens between the ages of 18 and 45 years, except such as are or may hereafter be exempt by the laws of the United States or of this State, and shall be armed, equipped, and trained, as the general assembly may provide by law.

SECTION 2. All commissioned officers of the militia shall be elected as the general assembly shall prescribe, and shall be commissioned by the governor of the State.

ARTICLE IX.

Amendments of the Constitution.

SECTION 1. If at any time the general assembly deem it necessary, and for the best interest of the State, that this constitution be revised, altered, or amended, they shall cause such proposed revisions, alterations, or amendments, to be published in the same manner as provided for notices of elections, and submitted to the votes of the electors of the commonwealth at their next general election ; and if a majority of said electors shall vote in favor of such proposed revisions, alterations, or amendments, the same shall thereafter become parts of this constitution ; otherwise, this constitution shall remain unaltered.

ARTICLE X.

Miscellaneous provisions.

SECTION 1. In order that no inconvenience may arise in passing from a territorial to a State government, it is hereby declared that the present organization, laws, and everything pertaining to the territorial government of Utah shall remain in full force and virtue in law until superseded by the action of the State government under the provisions of this constitution.

SECTION 2. The compensation of the governor, lieutenant governor, judges, members of the general assembly, and all other officers shall be as may be prescribed by law.

SECTION 3. All officers of this State may continue in office until superseded by their successors.

SECTION 4. The officers created by virtue of this constitution shall take an oath or affirmation to support the Constitution of the United States and of this State, and to faithfully perform the duties of their office.

SECTION 5. The general assembly shall encourage education.

J. M. Grant,
Daniel H. Wells,
Albert Carrington,
Edwin D. Wooley,
A. W. Babbitt,
John F. Kinney,
William Bell,
Garland Hunt,
W. H. Hooper,
S. M. Blair,
Orson Pratt, senior,
Parley P. Pratt,
J. C. Little,
Samuel W. Richards,

George P. Stiles,
T. S. Williams,
    Great Salt Lake county.

Lorin Farr,
Chauncey W. West,
Lorenzo Snow,
Jonathan C. Wright,
    Weber county.

Joseph Holbrook,
James Leithead,
J. D. Parker,
    Davis county

George A. Smith,
J. C. Haight,
Iron county.

John D. Lee,
Washington county.

Ezra T. Benson,
Tooele county.

Leonard E. Harrington,
James C. Snow,
B. F. Johnson,
Joseph A. Kelting,

Aaron Johnson,
Utah county.

Madison D. Hambleton,
Juab county.

Isaac Morley,
George Peacock,
San Pete county.

Samuel P. Hoyt,
Reuben McBride,
Millard county.

Enoch Reese,
Carson county.

[Doc. No. 4]

Draft Constitution of 1872

ORDINANCE.

We, the people of the Territory of Utah, do ordain as follows, and this ordinance shall be irrevocable, without the consent of the United States and the people of the State of Deseret:

First. That we adopt the Constitution of the United States.

Second. That there shall be in this State neither slavery nor involuntary servitude, otherwise than in the punishment of crimes whereof the party shall be duly convicted.

Third. That perfect toleration of religion shall be secured, and no inhabitant of said State shall ever be molested, in person or property, on account of his or her mode of religious worship.

Fourth. That the people inhabiting said Territory do agree and declare, that they forever disclaim all right and title to the unappropriated public lands lying within said Territory, and that the same shall be and remain at the sole and entire disposition of the United States; and that lands belonging to citizens of the United States residing without the said State shall never be taxed higher than the land belonging to residents thereof, and that no taxes shall be imposed by said State on lands or property therein belonging to, or which may hereafter be purchased by, the United States.

Fifth. That such terms, if any, as may be prescribed by Congress as a condition *as a condition* for the admission of the said State into the Union, shall, if ratified by a majority vote of the people thereof, at such time and under such regulations as may be prescribed by this convention, thereupon be embraced within and constitute a part of this ordinance.

PREAMBLE.

We, the people of the State of Deseret, grateful to Almighty God for our freedom, in order to secure its blessings, insure domestic tranquillity, and form a more perfect government, do establish this

CONSTITUTION.

ARTICLE I.—DECLARATION OF RIGHTS.

SECTION 1. In republican governments all men should possess their natural rights, among which are those of enjoying and defending their lives and liberty, acquiring, possessing, and protecting property, and of seeking and obtaining their safety and happiness.

SEC. 2. All political power is inherent in the people, and all free governments are founded in their authority and instituted for their benefit; therefore they have an inalienable right to institute government, and to alter, reform, or change the same, when their safety, happiness, and the public good require it. But the paramount allegiance of every citizen is due to the Federal Government in the exercise of all its constitutional powers.

SEC. 3. The right of trial by jury shall be secured to all and remain inviolate forever; but a jury trial may be waived by the parties in all civil cases, in the manner to be prescribed by law; and in civil cases, if three-fourths of the jurors agree upon a verdict, it shall stand and have the same force and effect as a verdict by the whole jury: *Provided,* The legislature, by a law passed by a two-third vote of all the members elected to each branch thereof, may require a unanimous verdict notwithstanding this provision.

SEC. 4. The free exercise and enjoyment of religious profession and worship shall, without discrimination or preference, forever be allowed in this State; and no person shall be rendered incompetent to be a witness or juror on account of opinions of matters of religion; but the liberty of conscience hereby secured shall not be so construed as to excuse acts of licentiousness or other crimes, or justify practices inconsistent with the peace or safety of this State.

SEC. 5. The privilege of the writ of *habeas corpus* shall not be suspended, unless when, in cases of rebellion or invasion, the public safety may require its suspension.

SEC. 6. Excessive bail shall not be required, nor excessive fines imposed, nor shall cruel or unusual punishments be inflicted; nor shall witnesses be unreasonably detained.

SEC. 7. All persons shall be bailable by sufficient sureties; unless for capital offenses, when the proof is evident or the presumption great.

SEC. 8. No person shall be tried for a capital or other infamous crime, (except in cases of impeachment, and in cases of the militia when in actual service, and the land and naval forces in time of war, and in cases of petit larceny, under the regulation of the legislature,) except on presentment or indictment of a grand jury: *Provided*, That the legislature may, by a two-third vote of all the members elected to each house thereof, abolish the grand jury system, anything in this section to the contrary notwithstanding; and in any trial in any court whatever, the party accused shall be allowed to appear and defend in person, and with counsel, as in civil actions. No person shall be subject to be twice put in jeopardy for the same offense, nor shall he be compelled, in any criminal case, to be a witness against himself; nor be deprived of life, liberty, or property, without due process of law; nor shall private property be taken for public use without just compensation having been first made or secured, except in cases of war, riot, fire, or great public peril, in which case compensation shall be afterward made.

SEC. 9. Every person may freely speak, write, and publish his sentiments on all subjects, being responsible for the abuse of that right, and no law shall be passed to restrain or abridge the liberty of speech or of the press. In all criminal prosecutions and civil actions for libels, the truth may be given in evidence to the jury, and if it shall appear to the jury that the matter charged as libelous is true, and was published with good motives, and for justifiable ends, the party shall be acquitted or exonerated.

SEC. 10. The people shall have the right freely to assemble together to consult for the common good, to instruct their representatives, and to petition for redress of grievances.

SEC. 11. The military shall be subordinate to the civil power, and no standing army shall be maintained by this State in time of peace.

SEC. 12. No soldier shall, in time of peace, be quartered in any house without the consent of the owner, nor in time of war, except in the manner to be prescribed by law.

SEC. 13. Representation shall be apportioned according to population.

SEC. 14. The privilege of the debtor to enjoy the necessary comforts of life shall be recognized by wholesome laws exempting a reasonable amount of property from seizure or sale for payment of any debts or liabilities hereafter contracted; and there shall be no imprisonment for debt, except in cases of fraud, libel, or slander, and no person shall be imprisoned for a militia fine in time of peace.

SEC. 15. No bill of attainder, *ex post facto* law, or law impairing the obligation of contracts, shall ever be passed.

SEC. 16. Foreigners who are, or who may hereafter become, *bona fide* residents of this State, shall enjoy the same rights in respect to the possession, enjoyment and inheritence of property as native-born citizens.

SEC. 17. Neither slavery nor involuntary servitude, unless for the punishment of crimes, shall ever be tolerated in this State.

SEC. 18. The right of the people to be secure in their persons, houses, papers, and effects, against unreasonable seizure and searches, shall not be violated; and no warrant shall issue but on probable cause, supported by oath or affirmation, particularly describing the place or places to be searched, and the person or persons and thing or things to be seized.

SEC. 19. Treason against the State shall consist only in levying war against it, adhering to its enemies, or giving them aid and comfort. And no person shall be convicted of treason unless on the testimony of two witnesses to the same overt act, or on confession in open court.

SEC. 20. The right of citizens to keep and bear arms, for common defense, shall not be questioned.

SEC. 21. No religious test shall ever be required as a qualification for holding any office of honor, trust, or profit under this State.

SEC. 22. This enumeration of rights shall not be construed to impair or deny others retained by the people.

ARTICLE II.—RIGHT OF SUFFRAGE.

SECTION 1. Every citizen of the United States, male and female, (not laboring under the disabilities named in this constitution,) of the age of twenty-one years and over, who shall have resided in the State six months, and in the county thirty days, next preceding any election, shall be entitled to vote for all officers that now are, or hereafter may be, elected by the people, and upon all questions submitted to the electors at such elections: *Provided,* That no person who has been or may be convicted of treason or felony in any State or Territory of the United States, unless restored to civil rights, and no idiot or insane person, shall be entitled to the privilege of an elector.

SEC. 2. For the purpose of voting, no person shall be deemed to have gained or lost a residence by reason of presence or absence while employed in the service of the United States, nor while engaged in the navigation of the waters of the United States or of the high seas, nor while a student of any seminary of learning, nor while kept at any almshouse or other asylum, nor while confined in any public prison.

SEC. 3. During the day on which any general election shall be held no qualified elector shall be arrested by virtue of any civil process; and no elector shall be obliged to perform military duty on the day of such election, except in time of war or public danger.

SEC. 4. All elections by the people shall be by ballot; and all elections by the legislature, or by either branch thereof, shall be *viva voce.*

SEC. 5. Provision shall be made by law for the registration of the names of the electors within the counties of which they may be residents, and for the ascertainment, by proper proofs, of the persons who shall be entitled to the right of suffrage, as hereby established, to preserve the purity of elections, and to regulate the manner of holding and making returns of the same; and the legislature shall have power to prescribe by law any other or further rules or oaths as may be deemed necessary, as a test of electoral qualification.

SEC. 6. All persons qualified by law to vote for representatives to the legislative assembly of the Territory of Utah at the date of the submission of this constitution, shall be entitled to vote upon the question of adopting or rejecting the same.

ARTICLE III.—DISTRIBUTION OF POWERS.

SECTION 1. The powers of the government of the State of Deseret shall be divided into three separate departments: the legislative, the executive, and the judicial; and no person charged with the exercise of powers properly belonging to one of these departments, shall exercise any functions appertaining to either of the others, except in the cases herein expressly directed or permitted.

ARTICLE IV.—LEGISLATIVE DEPARTMENT.

SECTION 1. The legislative authority of this State shall be vested in a legislature, which shall consist of a senate and house of representatives, and the sessions thereof shall be held at the seat of government.

SEC. 2. The sessions of the legislature shall be biennial, and, except at the first session thereof, shall commence on the second Monday in January next ensuing the election of members of the house of representatives, unless the governor shall convene the legislature by proclamation.

SEC. 3. The members of the house of representatives shall, except at the first election, be chosen biennially, by the qualified electors of their respective counties, or districts, on the first Monday in August, and their term of office shall be two years from the day next after their election.

SEC. 4. The senators shall be chosen at the same time and places as the members of the house of representatives, by the qualified electors of their respective counties or districts, and their term of office shall be four years from the day next after their election: *Provided, however,* That the senators elect at the first session of the legislature shall be divided equally into two classes as nearly as may be; and the seats of senators of the first class shall be vacated at the expiration of two years, those of the second class at the expiration of four years, so that one-half, as nearly as possible, shall be chosen biennially thereafter. And in case of increase in the number of senators, they shall be so annexed by lot to one or the other of the two classes as to keep them as equal as practicable.

SEC. 5. The first legislature shall consist of thirteen senators and twenty-six representatives, and shall be apportioned as prescribed by law. The number of senators and representatives may be increased from time to time: *Provided,* The number of representatives shall never be less than twice that of the senators: *And provided further,* That the senators shall never exceed thirty in number. The apportionment of the members of both houses shall be as prescribed by law.

SEC. 6. No person shall be a senator who shall not have attained the age of twenty-five years, or a representative who shall not have attained the age of twenty-one years. No person shall be a senator or representative who shall not be a citizen of the United States, and who, except at the first election, shall not have been two years a resident of this State, and for one year next preceding his election a resident of the county or district in which he is elected. No person holding any office of profit or trust under authority of the United States, or of this State, shall have a seat in the legislature: *Provided,* That appointments in the State militia, and the offices of notary public, justice of the peace, United States commissioner, commissioner of deeds, and postmasters, (whose annual compensation does not exceed five hundred dollars,) shall not, within the meaning of this section, be considered offices of profit or trust.

SEC. 7. The members of the legislature shall, before entering upon their official duties, take and subscribe the following oath or affirmation: "I do solemnly swear (or affirm) that I will support the Constitution of the United States and of the State of Deseret, and will faithfully discharge the duties of senator (or representative) according to the best of my ability, (if on oath,) so help me God; (if an affirmation,) under the pain and penalty of perjury."

SEC. 8. Each house shall judge of the qualifications, elections, and returns of its own members, and may punish its members for disorderly conduct, and, with the concurrence of two-thirds of all the members elected, expel a member.

SEC. 9. No member of the legislature shall, during the term for which he shall have been elected, be appointed to any civil office of profit under this State, which shall have been created, or the emoluments of which shall 'have been increased, during such term, except such office as may be filled by elections by the people.

SEC. 10. Members of the legislature shall be privileged from arrest on civil process during the session thereof, and for fifteen days next before the commencement of each session.

SEC. 11. When a vacancy occurs in either house the governor shall order an election to fill such vacancy.

SEC. 12. A majority of all the members elected to each house shall constitute a quorum to transact business, but a smaller number may adjourn from day to day, and compel the attendance of absent members, in such manner and under such penalties as such house may prescribe.

SEC. 13. Each house shall keep a journal of its own proceedings, which shall be published, and the yeas and nays of the members of either house on any question shall, at the desire of any five members present, be entered on the journal.

SEC. 14. The door of each house shall be kept open during its session, except the senate, while sitting in executive session; and neither shall, without the consent of the other, adjourn for more than three days, nor to any other place than that in which they may be holding their session.

SEC. 15. Any bill may originate in either house of the legislature, and all bills passed by one may be amended or rejected by the other.

SEC. 16. Each law enacted by the legislature shall embrace but one subject and matter properly connected therewith, which subject shall be briefly expressed in the title; and no law shall be revised or amended by reference to its title only; but in such case, the act as revised, or section as amended, shall be re-enacted and published at length.

SEC. 17. A majority of all the members elected to each house shall be necessary to pass every bill or joint resolution, and all bills or joint resolutions so passed, shall be signed by the presiding officers of the respective house.

SEC. 18. No money shall be drawn from the treasurer except as appropriated by law.

SEC. 19. In all cases where a general law can be made applicable, the law shall be general and of uniform operation, and provision shall be made by law for bringing suit against the State.

SEC. 20. The enacting clause of every law shall be as follows: "Be it enacted by the legislature of the State of Deseret;" and no law shall be enacted except by bill.

SEC. 21. The legislature may establish a uniform system of county and township government.

SEC. 22. The first regular session of the legislature may extend to ninety days, but no subsequent regular session shall exceed sixty days, nor shall any session convened by the governor exceed twenty days.

SEC. 23. The members and officers of the legislature shall receive for their services a compensation to be fixed by law, and no increase of such compensation shall take effect during the term for which the members and officers of either house shall have been elected.

SEC. 24. Every bill passed by the legislature shall be presented to the governor. If he approve it, he shall sign it, whereupon it shall become a law; but if not, he shall return it, with his objections, to the house in which it originated, which house shall cause such objection to be entered upon its journal, and proceed to reconsider it. If, after such reconsideration, it again pass both houses, by a vote of two-thirds of the members elected to each house, it shall become a law, notwithstanding the governor's objections. If any bill shall not be returned within five days after it shall have been presented to him, (Sunday excepted,) exclusive on which he received it, the same shall be a law in like manner as if he had signed it, unless the legislature, by its final adjournment, prevent such return, in which case it shall not become a law unless the governor, within five days after the adjournment, shall file such bill, with his approval thereof, in the office of the secretary of state.

SEC. 25. At all elections for representatives each qualified elector may cast as many votes for one candidate as there are representatives to be elected in the county or district, or may distribute the same among any or all the candidates, and the candidates receiving the highest number of votes shall be declared elected.

ARTICLE V.—EXECUTIVE DEPARTMENT.

SECTION 1. The supreme executive power of the State shall be vested in a governor.

SEC. 2. The governor shall be elected by the qualified electors at the time and places of voting for the members of the legislature, and shall hold his office for the term of two years, and until his successor shall be qualified.

SEC. 3. No person shall be eligible to the office of governor who is not a qualified elector, and who at the time of such election has not attained the age of twenty-five years; and who, except at the first election under this constitution, shall not have been a citizen, resident of this State, for two years next preceding the election.

SEC. 4. The returns of every election for governor and other State officers, voted for at the general election, shall be sealed up and transmitted to the seat of government, directed to the secretary of state, and on the third Monday of September next, succeeding such election, the chief justice of the supreme court, and the associate justices, or a majority thereof, shall meet at the office of the secretary of state, and open and canvass the election returns for governor, and all other State officers, and forthwith declare and publish the result, and notify the officers-elect of their election. The persons having the highest number of votes for the respective offices shall be declared elected; but in case two or more have an equal, and the highest number of votes for the same office, the legislature shall, by joint vote of both houses, elect one of said persons to said office.

SEC. 5. The governor shall be commander-in-chief of the military forces of this State, and may call out the same to execute the laws, suppress insurrection, and repel invasion; when the governor shall, with the consent of the legislature, be out of the State in time of war, and at the head of a military force thereof, he shall continue commander-in-chief of the military forces of the State.

SEC. 6. He shall transact all executive business with the officers of the government, civil and military, and may require information in writing from the officers of the executive department upon any subject relating to the duties of their respective offices.

SEC. 7. When any office shall from any cause become vacant, and no mode prescribed by the constitution or laws for filling such vacancy, the governor shall have power to fill such vacancy by appointment, which shall expire when such vacancy shall be filled by due course of law.

SEC. 8. He shall see that the laws are faithfully executed.

SEC. 9. The governor may, on extraordinary occasions, convene the legislature by proclamation, and shall state to both houses, when organized, the purpose for which they have been convened.

SEC. 10. He shall communicate, by message, to the legislature, at every regular session, the condition of the State, and recommend such measures as he may deem expedient.

SEC. 11. In case of a disagreement between the two houses with respect to the time of adjournment, the governor may, on the same being certified to him by the house for moving the adjournment, adjourn the legislature, by proclamation, to such time as he thinks proper, not beyond the first day of the next regular session.

SEC. 12. The governor shall have power to grant reprieves, commutations, and pardons, after conviction of all offenses except impeachment, subject to such regulations as may be provided by law.

SEC. 3. A lieutenant governor shall be elected at the same time and places, and in the same manner as the governor, and his term of office and his eligibility shall also be the same. He shall be the president of the senate; but shall only have a casting vote therein. In case of impeachment of the governor, or his removal from office, death, inability to discharge the duties of said office, resignation, or absence from the State, the powers and duties of the office shall devolve upon the lieutenant governor for the residue of the term, or until the disability shall cease; and in case of the disability of both the governor and lieutenant governor, the powers and duties of the executive shall devolve upon the secretary of state, until such disability shall cease or the vacancy be filled.

SEC. 14. A secretary of state, a treasurer, an auditor of public accounts, a surveyor general, a superintendent of public instruction, and an attorney general shall be elected at the same time and places, and in the same manner as the governor; the term of office of each shall be the same as is prescribed for the governor. And an elector shall be eligible to any of said offices except the secretary of state, whose qualifications shall be the same as those of the governor.

SEC. 15. There shall be a seal of the State, which shall be called the "great seal of the State of Deseret," which shall be kept by the secretary of state.

SEC. 16. All grants and commissions shall be in the name and by the authority of the State of Deseret, and shall be signed by the governor and countersigned by the secretary of state, who shall affix the great seal of State thereto.

SEC. 17. The secretary of state shall be the custodian of the official acts of the legislature, and shall keep a true record of the proceedings of the executive department of the government, and shall, when required, lay the same, and all matters relative thereto, before either branch of the legislature.

SEC. 18. The governor, secretary of state, and the attorney general shall constitute a board of State prison commissioners, which board shall have supervision of all matters connected with the State prison as may be provided by law. They shall also constitute a board of examiners, with power to examine all claims against the State, (except salaries or compensations of officers fixed by law,) and perform such other duties as may be prescribed by law.

SEC. 19. The secretary of state, State treasurer, auditor of public accounts, surveyor general, superintendent of public instruction, and attorney general, shall perform such other duties as may be prescribed by law.

ARTICLE VI.—JUDICIAL DEPARTMENT.

SECTION 1. The judicial power of this State shall be vested in a supreme court, circuit courts, probate courts, municipal courts of incorporated cities, and in justices of the peace.

SEC. 2. At the first general election there shall be elected, by the qualified electors of this State, four circuit judges, who shall continue in office two, four, six, and eight years respectively, from and including the first Monday in January next succeeding their elections and until their successors are elected and qualified. They shall meet as soon as practicable after their election and qualification, and at their first meeting shall determine by lot the term of office each shall fill, and circuit in which each shall travel, and thereafter, when vacancies occur, the same shall be filled at the general election: *Provided*, That the legislature may provide by law that the judges shall alternate in the various circuits.

SEC. 3. The circuit judges shall, until otherwise provided by law; constitute the supreme court. When a case is appealed from the decision of a circuit court, the judge thereof shall not sit for the hearing of that case as a justice of the supreme court, but said case shall be heard and determined by the other three, and the concurrence of two of them shall be necessary to render a decision. The legislature at any time shall have power to increase the number of circuits in this State, and provide for the election of judges to fill them, and also to reorganize the supreme court, and provide for the election and tenure of office of the justices thereof, who shall not be required to perform the duties of circuit judges.

SEC. 4. The supreme court, whenever it shall be organized, as provided for in section three, shall consist of a chief justice and two associate justices, a majority of whom shall constitute a quorum. The legislature, by a majority of all the members elected to each branch thereof, may provide for the election of two additional associate justices, and if so increased, three shall constitute the quorum. The concurrence of a majority of the whole court shall be necessary to render a decision.

SEC. 5. For the purpose of organizing the supreme court, as contemplated in section three, the circuit judges shall meet as soon as practicable after their election and qualification, and at their first meeting shall determine, by lot, the term of office each shall fill, and the justice drawing the shortest term shall be chief justice, and after the expiration of his term, the one having the next shortest term shall be chief justice, after which the senior justice in commission shall be chief justice. And in case the commissions of any two or more of said justices shall bear the same date, they shall determine by lot who shall be chief justice.

SEC. 6. The State shall be divided into four judicial districts; the first to be composed of the counties of Washington, Kane, Iron, Beaver, Piute, Sevier, Millard, and San Pete; the second, of the counties of Juab, Utah, Tooele, Wasatch, and Summit; the third, of the counties of Salt Lake, Davis, and Weber; the fourth, of the counties of Box Elder, Cache, Rich, and Morgan; and the legislature may provide by law for an alteration of the boundaries of the judicial circuits, as herein prescribed, and for the election of the judges therein, by the qualified electors of the respective circuits.

SEC. 7. The supreme court shall have appellate jurisdiction in all cases of *quo warranto, mandamus, prohibition, certiorari*, and *habeas corpus*, and in all civil cases, both in law and equity, where the amount in controversy exceeds three hundred dollars; and in all criminal cases where the fine exceeds fifty dollars or the imprisonment is sixty days or upward; and in all cases in which is involved the title or right of possession to, or the possession of, real estate or mining claims, or the legality of any tax, impost, assessment, toll, or municipal fine. The court shall also have power to issue all writs necessary or proper to the complete exercise of its appellate jurisdiction; and each of the justices shall have power to issue writs of *habeas corpus* to any part of the State, upon petition by, or on behalf of, any person held in actual custody, and may make such writs returnable before himself or the supreme court.

SEC. 8. There shall be a probate judge elected by the qualified electors of each county at the general election, whose term of office shall be four years, and until his successor is elected and qualified.

SEC. 9. The legislature shall determine the number of justices of the peace to be elected in each precinct of the State, and fix by law their term of office, their duties and responsibilities.

SEC. 10. The jurisdiction, both original and appellate, of the circuit and all inferior courts, shall be as prescribed by law.

SEC. 11. The judges of the supreme and circuit courts shall be meligible to any office, other than a judicial office, during the term for which they shall have been elected.

SEC. 12. No person shall be eligible to the office of supreme or circuit judge who is not a citizen of the United States, and has not attained to the age of twenty-five years, and who, except at the first election, has not been a resident of this State at least two years next preceding his election.

SEC. 13. The judges of the supreme and circuit courts shall each receive quarterly for their services a compensation to be fixed by law, which shall not be increased or diminished during the term for which they shall have been elected.

SEC. 14. There shall be one or more terms of the circuit courts held annually at the county-seat in each county, at such times as shall be provided by law, and there shall be not less than two terms of the supreme court held annually, which terms shall be held at the seat of government.

SEC. 15. The style of all process shall be " The State of Deseret," and all prosecutions shall be conducted in the name and by the authority of the same.

ARTICLE VII.—ON IMPEACHMENT AND REMOVAL FROM OFFICE.

SECTION 1. The house of representatives shall have the sole power of impeachment, and a majority of all the members elected must concur therein. All impeachments shall be tried by the senate, and when sitting as a court of impeachment, the senators shall be upon oath or affirmation to do justice according to law and evidence. When the governor or lieutenant governor is tried, the chief justice of the supreme court shall preside.

SEC. 2. No person shall be convicted without the concurrence of two-thirds of all the senators elected. But judgment in such cases shall not extend further than removal from office, and disqualification to hold any office of honor, trust, or profit under the government of this State.

SEC. 3. When an impeachment is directed, the house of representatives shall elect from their own body three members, whose duty it shall be to prosecute such impeachment. No impeachment shall be tried until the final adjournment of the legislature, when the senate shall proceed to try the same.

SEC. 4. The party, whether convicted or acquitted, shall nevertheless be liable to prosecution, trial, judgment, and punishment according to law.

SEC. 5. In all impeachment trials the accused shall have the right to appear and defend in person and by counsel, to demand the nature and cause of the accusation, and to have a copy thereof, to meet the witnesses face to face, and to have process to compel the attendance of witnesses in his behalf.

SEC. 6. All civil officers shall be liable to impeachment for corrupt conduct in office, or for crimes or misdemeanors.

SEC. 7. No judicial officer shall exercise his office after an impeachment is directed, until he is acquitted.

SEC. 8. The governor may make a provisional appointment to fill a vacancy occasioned by the suspension of such officer until he shall be acquitted, or until the election and qualification of a successor.

SEC. 9. The legislature shall provide by law for the removal of any officer elected by a county, township, mining or school district, in such manner and for such cause as to them shall be deemed just and proper.

ARTICLE VIII.—MUNICIPAL AND OTHER CORPORATIONS.

SECTION 1. The legislature shall pass no special act in any manner relating to corporate powers, except for municipal purposes.

SEC. 2. The legislature shall provide for the organization of cities and towns, and other corporations, by general laws, and restrict their power of taxation, assessment, borrowing money, contracting debts, and loaning their credit, except for procuring supplies of water and assisting in the construction of railroads.

SEC. 3. All real property and possessory rights to the same, as well as personal property in this State, belonging to corporations now existing, or hereafter created, shall be subject to taxation, the same as property of individuals: *Provided*, That the property of corporations formed for municipal, charitable, religious, or educational purposes may be exempted by law.

SEC. 4. Dues from corporations shall be secured by such means as may be prescribed by law: *Provided*, That corporators in corporations formed under the laws of this State shall not be individually liable for the debts or liabilities of such corporation, unless by their articles of incorporation they may so elect.

SEC. 5. This State shall not donate or loan money, or its credit, subscribe to, or be interested in the stock of any company, association, or corporation, except corporations formed for educational, charitable, irrigation, or railroad purposes within this State.

ARTICLE IX.—FINANCE AND STATE DEBT.

SECTION 1. The fiscal year shall commence January first.

SEC. 2. The legislature shall provide by law for an annual tax, sufficient to defray the estimated expenses of the State for each fiscal year, and whenever the expenses of any year shall exceed the income, the legislature shall provide for levying a tax sufficient, with other sources of income, to pay the deficiency, as well as the estimated expenses of such ensuing year or two years.

SEC. 3. The State shall never assume or guarantee the debts of any county, town, city, or other corporation whatever, unless such debts may have been created to repel invasion, suppress insurrection, or to provide for the public defense.

ARTICLE X.—TAXATION.

SECTION 1. The legislature shall, by law, provide for uniform and equal rates of assessment and taxation, and shall prescribe such regulations as shall secure a just valuation for taxation of all property, real, personal, and possessory, except mines and mining claims, the proceeds of which shall be taxed, as regulated by law; and, also, excepting such property as may be exempted by law for municipal, educational, literary, scientific, religious, or charitable purposes.

ARTICLE XI.—EDUCATION.

SECTION 1. The legislature shall protect and encourage education.

SEC. 2. All legislation in regard to education shall be impartial, guaranteeing to males and females, to citizens and foreigners, and to persons of all races, colors, and religions, equal rights and privileges.

ARTICLE XII.—MILITIA.

SECTION 1. The militia of the State shall be composed of all ablebodied male citizens between the ages of eighteen and forty-five years, except such as are or may hereafter be exempt by the laws of the United States, or of this State, and shall be organized, armed, equipped, and trained as the legislature may provide by law.

SEC. 2. All commissioned officers of the militia (staff officers excepted) shall be elected by persons liable to military duty, in such manner as the legislature may provide, and shall be commissioned by the governor.

ARTICLE XIII.—PUBLIC INSTITUTIONS.

SECTION 1. Institutions for the benefit of the insane, blind, deaf, and dumb, and such other benevolent institutions as the public good may require, shall be fostered and supported by the State, subject to such regulations as may be prescribed by law.

SEC. 2. A State prison shall be established and maintained in such manner as may be prescribed by law, and provisions made be made by law for the establishment and maintenance of a house of refuge for juvenile offenders.

SEC. 3. The respective counties of the State shall provide, as may be prescribed by law, for those inhabitants who, by reason of age or infirmity, or misfortunes, may have claim upon the sympathy and aid of society.

ARTICLE XIV.—BOUNDARY.

SECTION 1. The boundary of the State of Deseret shall be as follows: Commencing at point formed by the intersection of the thirty-second degree of longitude west from Washington with the thirty-seventh degree of north latitude; thence due west along said thirty-seventh degree of north latitude to the intersection of the same with the thirty-seventh degree of longitude west from Washington; thence due north along said thirty-seventh degree of west longitude to the intersection of the same with the forty-second degree of north latitude; thence due east along said forty-second degree of north latitude to the intersection of the same with the thirty-fourth degree of longitude west from Washington; thence due south along said thirty-fourth degree of west longitude to the intersection of the same with the forty-first degree of north latitude; thence due east along said forty-first degree of north latitude to the intersection of the same with the thirty-second degree of longitude west from Washington; thence due south along said thirty-second degree west longitude to the place of beginning. And whenever Congress shall authorize the addition to the Territory of Utah or State of Deseret of any portion of the territory on the northerly or southerly boundaries of the foregoing defined limits, the same shall thereupon be embraced within and become a part of this State.

ARTICLE XV.—MISCELLANEOUS PROVISIONS.

SECTION 1. The seat of government shall be at Salt Lake City, or such place as the legislature may determine.

SEC. 2. No person shall be eligible to any office who is not a qualified elector.

SEC. 3. The general election shall be held on the first Monday in August of each year, unless otherwise provided for by law.

SEC. 4. The legislature shall provide for the speedy publication of all laws of a general nature.

SEC. 5. The compensation of all State officers shall be as prescribed by law: *Provided*, No change of salary or compensation shall apply to any officer during the term for which he may have been elected.

SEC. 6. All executive officers of the State shall keep their respective offices at the seat of government.

SEC. 7. A plurality of votes given at any election by the people shall constitute a choice, where not otherwise provided by this constitution.

SEC. 8. No person holding any office of honor or profit under the Government of the United States shall hold office under the government of this State, except postmasters, whose annual compensation does not exceed five hundred dollars, and except as otherwise provided in this constitution.

ARTICLE XVI.—AMENDMENTS.

SECTION 1. Any amendment or amendments to this constitution, if agreed to by a majority of all the members elected to each of the two houses of the legislature, shall be entered on their respective journals, with the yeas and nays taken thereon, and referred to the legislature then next to be chosen, and shall be published for three months next preceding the time of making such choice. And if, in the legislature next chosen, as aforesaid, such proposed amendment or amendments shall be agreed to by a majority of all the members elected to each house, then it shall be the duty of the legislature to submit such proposed amendment or amendments to the people, in such manner and at such time as the legislature shall prescribe; and if the people shall approve and ratify such amendment or amendments, by a majority of the electors qualified to vote for members of the legislature voting thereon, such amendment or amendments shall become a part of the voting constitution.

SEC. 2. If at any time the legislature, by a vote of two-thirds of the members elected to each house, shall determine that it is necessary to cause a revision of this entire constitution, they shall recommend to the electors, at the next election for members of the legislature, to vote for or against a convention; and if it shall appear that a majority of the electors voting at such election shall have voted in favor of calling a convention, the legislature shall, at its next session, provide by law for calling a convention, to be holden within six months after the passage of such law; and such convention shall consist of a number of members not less than that of the two branches of the legislature.

ARTICLE XVII.—SCHEDULE.

SECTION 1. That no inconvenience may arise by reason of a change from a territorial to a State government, it is declared that all rights, actions, prosecutions, judgments, claims, and contracts, as well of individuals as of bodies-corporate, including counties, towns, and cities, shall continue as if no change had taken place; and all process which may issue under the authority of the Territory of Utah previous to its admission into the Union shall be as valid as if issued in the name of the State of Deseret.

SEC. 2. All laws of the Territory of Utah in force at the time of the admission of this State not repugnant to this constitution shall remain in force until they expire by their own limitations, or be altered or repealed by the legislature.

SEC. 3. All fines, penalties, and forfeitures accruing to the Territory of Utah, or to the people of the United States in the Territory of Utah, shall inure to the State of Deseret.

SEC. 4. All recognizances heretofore taken, or which may be taken before the change from a territorial to a State government, shall remain valid, and shall pass to, and may be prosecuted in, the name of the State; and all bonds executed to the governor of the Territory, or to any other officer or court in his or their official capacity, or to the people of the United States in the Territory of Utah, shall pass to the governor or other officer or court, and his or their successors in office, for the uses therein respectively expressed, and may be sued on, and recovery had accordingly; and all revenue, property, real, personal, or mixed: and all judgments, bonds, specialties, choses in action, claims, and debts, of whatsoever description; and all records and public archives of the Territory of Utah, shall issue and vest in the State of Deseret, and may be used for and recovered in the same manner and to the same extent, by the State of Deseret, as the same could have been by the Territory of Utah. All criminal prosecutions and penal actions which may have arisen, or which may arise before the change from a territorial to a State government, and which shall then be pending, shall be prosecuted to judgment and execution in the name of the State. All offenses committed against the laws of the Territory of Utah before the change from a territorial to a State government, and which shall not be prosecuted before such change, may be prosecuted in the name and by the authority of the State of Deseret, with like effect as though such change had not taken place, and all penalties incurred shall remain the same as if this constitution had not been adopted. All actions at law, and suits in equity, and other legal proceedings which may be pending in any of the courts of the Territory of Utah at the time of the change from a territorial to a State government, may be continued and transferred to and determined by any court of the State which shall have jurisdiction of the subject-matter thereof; and all books, papers, and records relating to the same shall be transferred in like manner to such court.

SEC. 5. For the purpose of taking the vote of the electors of this Territory, for the ratification or rejection of this constitution, and for the election of members of the legislature, and a Representative in Congress, an election shall be held in the several counties of the Territory,

on the third Monday in March, anno Domini eighteen hundred and
seventy-two, and the election shall be conducted and the returns thereof
made as nearly as practiable in conformity with the existing laws of the
Territory in relation to the holding of the general election, except
that in voting for members of the House of Representatives, the
electors may cast their ballots in accordance with section twenty-five of
article four of the constitution.

SEC. 6. Each elector shall express his opinion by depositing in the
ballot-box a ticket, whereon shall be written or printed, "Constitution,
yes," or "Constitution, no," or such words as will distinctly convey the
intention of the voter.

SEC. 7. The county clerks of their respective counties shall issue to
the members of the State legislature certificates of their election, and
said clerks shall forthwith make duplicate returns of the votes cast for
and against the constitution, and the votes cast for Representative in
Congress, and transmit the same by the most safe and expeditious conveyance to R. L. Campbell, the secretary of this convention, inclosed in
an envelope, marked, "Election returns."

SEC. 8. Upon receipt of said returns, or within fourteen days after
the election, if the returns be not sooner received, it shall be the duty
of a board of canvassers, to consist of the president and secretary of
this convention, and the probate judge of Salt Lake County, or any two
of the persons herein named, to canvass the returns of said election in
presence of all who may choose to attend, and immediately publish an
abstract of the same in one or more of the newspapers of the Territory
of Utah, and forward a copy of said abstract, duly certified by them, to
the President of the United States, President of the Senate, Speaker
of the House of Representatives, and the Delegate in Congress from
Utah Territory, and said board shall, after the adoption of this constitution and canvass of said votes, issue a certificate of election to the
person receiving thereat the highest number of votes for Representative
in Congress.

SEC. 9. Until otherwise provided by law, the apportionment of senators
and representatives in the different counties shall be as follows: Salt
Lake, Tooele, and Summit Counties, four senators; Salt Lake County,
six representatives; Tooele County, one representative; Summit County,
one representative; Davis and Morgan Counties, one senator and two
representatives; Box Elder and Weber Counties, one senator; Box Elder County, one representative; Weber County, two representatives;
Cash and Rich Counties, one senator and two representatives; Utah
and Wasatch Counties, two senators; Utah County, three representatives; Wasatch County, one representative; Juab and Millard Counties, one senator; Juab County, one representative; Millard County,
one representative; Beaver and Iron Counties, one senator; Beaver
County, one representative; Iron County, one representative; Kane
and Washington Counties, one senator and one representative; San
Pete and Sevier Counties, one senator and two representatives.

SEC. 10. If this constitution be ratified by the people, the president
of this convention, or in case of his inability, the secretary of this convention, shall convene the legislature at the City Hall in Salt Lake City,
on the first Thursday of April, eighteen hundred and seventy-two, for
the purpose of electing United States Senators.

SEC. 11. A copy of this constitution, certified to be correct by the president and secretary of this convention, shall be published by them in one
or more of the newspapers of this Territory as soon as practicable after
the final adjournment of this convention. Such president and secretary
shall forward a copy of this constitution, duly certified, to the President

of the United States, President of the Senate, Speaker of the House of Representatives, and the Delegate in Congress from this Territory, and shall deliver or forward a copy, certified as aforesaid, to each of the delegates elected by this convention, in accordance with section twenty-four of this article.

SEC. 12. For the purpose of taking the vote of the electors of this Territory, for the acceptance or rejection of such terms, if any, as may be prescribed by Congress as a condition of the admission of said State into the Union, and for the election of all State officers and judges of the circuit courts, an election shall be held in the several counties of the Territory on the third Monday of the month succeeding that in which such act of Congress aforesaid, prescribing such terms, shall have become a law; and the election shall be conducted and the returns thereof made, as nearly as practicable, in conformity with the existing laws of the Territory in relation to the holding of the general election.

SEC. 13. Each elector shall express his opinion by depositing in the ballot-box a ticket, whereon shall be written or printed, "Constitution as amended, yes," or "Constitution as amended, no," or such words as will distinctly convey the intention of the voter.

SEC. 14. The county clerks of their respective counties shall forthwith make duplicate returns of the votes cast for and against the constitution as amended, and the votes cast for all State officers and circuit judges, and transmit the same, by the most safe and expeditious conveyance, to R. L. Campbell, the secretary of this convention, inclosed in an envelope, marked "Election returns."

SEC. 15. Upon receipt of said returns, or within thirty days after the election, if the returns be not sooner received, it shall be the duty of a board of canvassers, to consist of the president and secretary of this convention, the president of the State senate, the speaker of the house of representatives, and the probate judge of Salt Lake County, or any three of the persons herein named, to canvass the returns of said election, in presence of all who may choose to attend, and immediately publish an abstract of the same in one or more of the newspapers of the Territory of Utah; and said board shall, if said constitution as amended has received a majority vote of the electors voting upon the question of the acceptance or rejection of the same, thereupon make public announcement of the fact, and transmit a certificate thereof, by the most safe and expeditious conveyance, to the President of the United States, President of the Senate, and Speaker of the House of Representatives, at Washington, District of Columbia, and also issue certificates of election to such persons as were elected at said election; and thenceforth this constitution shall be ordained and established as the constitution of the State of Deseret.

SEC. 16. The term of State officers, except judicial, elected at the first election, shall continue until the Tuesday after the first Monday of January, anno Domini eighteen hundred and seventy-five, and until the election and qualification of their successors.

SEC. 17. The State senators to be elected at the first election under this constitution shall draw lots, so that the term of one-half of the number, as nearly as may be, shall expire on the day succeeding the general election in anno Domini eighteen hundred and seventy-four, and the term of the other half shall expire on the day succeeding the general election in anno Domini eighteen hundred and seventy-six: *Provided*, That in drawing lots for all senatorial terms, the senatorial representation shall be allotted so that, in the counties having two or more senators, the terms thereof shall be divided, as equally as may be, between the long and short terms.

SEC. 18. The term of members of the house of representatives elected at the first election shall expire on the day succeeding the general election in anno Domini eighteen hundred and seventy-four.

SEC. 19. The first regular session of the legislature shall commence on the third Monday of the month succeeding that in which said State shall be, by act of Congress, or by proclamation of the President of the United States, made in pursuance of an act of Congress, admitted into the Union.

SEC. 20. The State officers and circuit judges elected at the first election shall be sworn in and assume the duties of their respective offices on the third Monday of the month succeeding that in which said State shall, by act of Congress, or by proclamation of the President of the United States, made in pursuance of an act of Congress, be admitted into the Union.

SEC. 21. The governor, secretary, district judges, and other officers of the Territory of Utah may continue to discharge the duties of their respective offices, after the admission of this State into the Union, and until the time designated for the qualification of the officers to be elected under the State government: *Provided*, That the said officers shall be subject to the restrictions and conditions provided in this constitution, and none of them shall receive, to his own use, any fees or perquisites for the performance of any duty connected with his office.

SEC. 22. All county, precinct, city, and district officers under the laws of the Territory of Utah, at the time this constitution shall take effect, and whose offices are not inconsistent with the provisions of this constitution, shall continue in office until their successors are elected and qualified. The time of such election and qualification shall be as prescribed by law.

SEC. 23. After the admission of this State into the Union, and until the legislature shall otherwise provide, the several judges shall hold courts in their respective circuits at such times and places as they may respectively appoint; and until provision shall be made by law for holding the terms of the supreme court, the governor shall fix the time and place of holding such court.

SEC. 24. George Q. Cannon, Thomas Fitch, and Frank Fuller are hereby elected delegates from this convention to proceed to Washington, District of Columbia, and, with the Delegate in Congress from Utah Territory, the Hon. W. H. Hooper, are requested to present this constitution to the President of the United States, the Senate of the United States, and the United States House of Representatives, and urge the passage of an act of Congress admitting the State of Deseret into the Union.

Done in convention at Salt Lake City the second day of March, in the year of our Lord one thousand eight hundred and seventy-two, and of the Independence of the United States the ninety-sixth, and signed by the delegates.

E. M. BARNUM,
President of the Convention and
Delegate from Salt Lake County.

[Doc. No. 5]

Draft Constitution of 1887

PREAMBLE.

We, the people of the State of Utah, grateful to Almighty God for our freedom, in order to secure its blessings, insure domestic tranquillity, and form a more perfect government, do establish this

CONSTITUTION.

ARTICLE I.—BILL OF RIGHTS.

SECTION 1. All men are possessed of equal and inalienable natural rights, among which are life, liberty, and the pursuit of happiness.

SEC. 2. All free governments are founded on the authority of the people, and instituted for their equal protection and benefit.

SEC. 3. The right of trial by jury shall remain forever inviolate.

SEC. 4. The right to worship God, according to the dictates of conscience, shall never be infringed ; nor shall any person be compelled to attend or support any form of worship; nor shall any control of, or interference with the right of conscience be permitted, nor any preference be given by law to any religious establishment or mode of worship. No religious test or property qualification shall be required for any office of public trust, nor for any vote at any election, nor shall any person be incompetent to testify on account of religious belief.

SEC. 5. The privilege of the writ of *habeas corpus* shall not be suspended, unless, when in cases of rebellion or invasion, the public safety may require its suspension.

SEC. 6. Excessive bail shall not be required, nor excessive fines imposed, nor shall cruel or unusual punishment be inflicted.

SEC. 7. All persons shall be bailable by sufficient sureties; unless for capital offenses, when the proof is evident or the presumption great.

SEC. 8. No person shall be held to answer for a capital or otherwise infamous crime, unless on a presentment or indictment of a grand jury, except in cases arising in the land and naval forces, or in the militia when in actual service in time of war or public danger, nor shall any person for the same offense be twice put in jeopardy; nor be compelled in any criminal case to be witness against himself, nor be deprived of life, liberty, or property, without due process of law ; nor shall private property be taken for public use without just compensation.

SEC. 9. In all criminal prosecutions the accused shall enjoy the right to a speedy and public trial, by an impartial jury of the State and district wherein the crime shall have been committed, which district shall have been previously ascertained by law, and to be informed of the nature and cause of the accusation; to be confronted with he witnesses against him; to have compulsory process for obtaining witnesses in his favor, and to have the assistance of counsel for his defense.

Sec. 10. The State shall pass no law abridging the freedom of speech or of the press, or the right of the people peaceably to assemble, and to petition the government for the redress of grievances.

Sec. 11. The military shall be subordinate to the civil power.

Sec. 12. No soldier shall, in time of peace, be quartered in any house without the consent of the owner, nor in time of war, except in the manner to be prescribed by law.

Sec. 13. Representation shall be apportioned according to population.

Sec. 14. There shall be no imprisonment for debt, except in cases of fraud.

Sec. 15. Foreigners who are, or who may hereafter become, *bona fide* residents of this State, shall enjoy the same rights in respect to the possession, enjoyment, transmission, and inheritance of property as native-born citizens.

Sec. 16. The right of the people to be secure in their persons, houses, papers, and effects, against unreasonable searches and seizures, shall not be violated; and no warrant shall issue but on probable cause, supported by oath or affirmation, particularly describing the place or places to be searched, and the person or persons, and thing or things, to be seized.

Sec. 17. Treason against the State shall consist only in levying war against it, adhering to its enemies, or giving them aid and comfort. And no person shall be convicted of treason unless on the testimony of two witnesses to the same overt act, or on confession in open court.

Sec. 18. The right of citizens to keep and bear arms, for common defense, shall not be questioned.

Sec. 19. The blessings of free government can only be maintained by a firm adherence to justice, moderation, temperance, frugality and virtue, and frequent recurrence to fundamental principles.

Sec. 20. This enumeration of rights shall not be construed to impair or deny others retained by the people.

ARTICLE II.—RIGHT OF SUFFRAGE.

Section 1. Every citizen of the United States, not laboring under the disabilities mentioned in this constitution, of the age of twenty-one years and over, who shall have resided in the State six months, and in the county thirty days, next preceding any election, shall be entitled to vote for all officers that now are or hereafter may be elected by the people, and upon all questions submitted to the electors at such election : *Provided,* That no person who has been or may be convicted of treason or felony, in any State or Territory of the United States, unless restored to civil rights, shall be entitled to the privileges of an elector.

Sec. 2. During the day on which any general election shall be held, no elector shall be obliged to perform military duty, except in time of war or public danger.

Sec. 3. All elections by the people shall be by secret ballot.

Sec. 4. Provision shall be made by law for the registration of the names of electors within the counties of which they may be residents, and for the ascertainment, by proper proofs, of the persons who shall be entitled to the right of suffrage.

ARTICLE III.—DISTRIBUTION OF POWERS.

Section 1. The powers of the government of the State of Utah shall be divided into three separate departments—the legislative, the executive, and the judicial; and neither of said departments shall exercise any functions appertaining to either of the others, except in the cases herein expressly directed or permitted.

ARTICLE IV.—LEGISLATIVE DEPARTMENT.

Section 1. The legislative authority of this State shall be vested in a legislature' which shall consist of a senate and house of representatives, and the sessions thereof shall be held at the seat of government.

Sec. 2. The sessions of the legislature shall be biennial, and, except at the first session thereof, shall commence on the second Monday in January next ensuing the election of members of the house of representatives, unless the governor shall convene the legislature by proclamation.

Sec. 3. The members of the house of representatives shall, except at the first election, be chosen biennially, by the qualified electors of their respective districts, on the first Monday in August, and their term of office shall be two years from the day next after their election.

Sec. 4. The senators shall be chosen by the qualified electors of their respective districts, at the same time and places as the members of the house of representatives, and their term of office shall be four years from the day next after their election, except as herein otherwise provided.

SEC. 5. The first legislature shall consist of thirteen senators and twenty-six representatives; the number of senators and representatives may be increased, but the senators shall never exceed thirty in number, and the number of representatives shall never be less than twice that of the senators. The apportionment and increase of the members of both houses shall be as prescribed by law.

SEC. 6. No person shall be a senator who shall not have attained the age of twenty-five years, nor shall any person be a senator or representative who shall not be a citizen of the United States, and who, except at the first election, shall not have been two years a resident of this State, and for one year next preceding his election a resident of the district in which he is elected. No person holding any State office except officers of the State militia, commissioners of deeds and notaries public, and no executive or judicial officer shall have a seat in the legislature.

SEC. 7. The members of the legislature shall, before entering upon their official duties, take an oath or affirmation to support the Constitution of the United States and of this State, and faithfully to discharge the duties of their respective offices.

SEC. 8. Each house shall judge of the qualifications, elections, and returns of its own members, may punish them for disorderly conduct, and, with the concurrence of two-thirds of its whole number, expel a member.

SEC. 9. No member of the legislature shall, during the term for which he shall have been elected, be appointed to any civil office of profit under this State which shall have been created, or the emoluments of which shall have been increased, during such term, except such office as may be filled by election by the people.

SEC. 10. Members of the legislature, in all cases except treason, felony, or breach of the peace, shall be privileged from arrest during the session of the legislature, and for fifteen days next before the commencement and after the termination thereof.

SEC. 11. When a vacancy occurs in either house, the governor shall order an election to fill such vacancy.

SEC. 12. A majority of all the members elected to each house shall constitute a quorum to transact business, but a smaller number may adjourn from day to day, and compel the attendance of absent members in such manner and under such penalties as each house may prescribe.

SEC. 13. Each house shall establish its own rules, keep a journal of its own proceedings, and publish them, except such parts as require secrecy, and the yeas and nays of the members of either house, on any question, shall, at the desire of any three members present, be entered on the journal.

SEC. 14. The door of each house shall be kept open during its session, except the senate while sitting in executive session; and neither house shall, without the consent of the other, adjourn for more than three days, or to any other place than that in which it may be holding session.

SEC. 15. The enacting clause of every law shall be as follows: "Be it enacted by the legislature of the State of Utah."

SEC. 16. Any bill or joint resolution may originate in either house of the legislature, and shall be read three times in each house before the final passage thereof, and shall not become a law without the concurrence of a majority of all the members elected to each house. On the final passage of all bills the vote shall be by yeas and nays, which shall be entered on the journal.

SEC. 17. No law shall be revised or amended by reference to its title only, but the act as revised, or section as amended, shall be enacted and published at length.

SEC. 18. All bills or joint resolutions passed by the legislature shall be signed by the presiding officers of the respective houses.

SEC. 19. The legislature shall not grant any special privilege or bill of divorce, nor authorize any lottery, gift enterprise, or game of chance.

SEC. 20. No money shall be drawn from the treasury except as appropriated by law.

SEC. 21. Provision shall be made by law for bringing suit against the State.

SEC. 22. The first regular session of the legislature may extend to one hundred and twenty days, but no subsequent regular session shall exceed sixty days, nor shall any session convened by the governor exceed twenty days.

SEC. 23. The members and officers of the legislature shall receive for their services a compensation to be fixed by law, and no increase for such compensation shall take effect during the term for which the members and officers of either house shall have been elected.

SEC. 24. Every bill passed by the legislature shall be presented to the governor. If he approve it, he shall sign it, whereupon it shall become a law; but if not, he shall return it, with his objections, to the house in which it originated, which house shall cause such objections to be entered upon its journal, and proceed to reconsider it. If, after such consideration, it again pass both houses by a vote of two-thirds of the members elected to each house, it shall become a law, notwithstanding the governor's objections. If any bill shall not be returned within five days after it shall have been presented to him, Sunday excepted, exclusive of the day on which he received it, the same shall be law in like manner as if he had signed it, unless the legislature, by its final adjournment, prevent such return, in which case it shall not become a law unless the governor, within five days after the adjournment, shall file such bill, with his approval thereof, in the office of the secretary of state.

ARTICLE V.—EXECUTIVE DEPARTMENT.

SECTION 1. The supreme executive power of this State shall be vested in a governor.

SEC. 2. The governor shall be elected by the qualified electors at the time and places of voting for the members of the legislature, and shall hold his office for the term of two years, and until his successor shall be qualified.

SEC. 3. No person shall be eligible to the office of governor who is not a qualified male elector, and who, at the time of such election, has not attained the age of twenty-five years, and who, except at the first election under this constitution, shall not have been a citizen resident of this State for two years next preceding the election.

SEC. 4. The governor shall be commander-in-chief of the military forces of this State, and may call out the same to execute the laws, suppress insurrection, and repel invasion, and when the governor shall, with the consent of the legislature, be out of the State in time of war, and at the head of any military force thereof, he shall continue commander-in-chief of the military forces of the State.

SEC. 5. He shall transact all executive business for and in behalf of the State, and may require information, in writing, from the officers of the executive department upon any subject relating to the duties of their respective offices.

SEC. 6. When any office shall from any cause become vacant, and no mode is prescribed by the constitution and laws for filling such vacancy, the governor shall have power to fill such vacancy by appointment, which shall expire when such vacancy shall be filled by due course of law.

SEC. 7. He shall see that the laws are faithfully executed.

SEC. 8. The governor may, on extraordinary occasions, convene the legislature by proclamation, and shall state to both houses when organized the purpose for which they have been convened.

SEC. 9. He shall communicate by message to the legislature at every regular session the condition of the State, and recommend such measures as he may deem expedient.

SEC. 10. The governor shall have power to grant reprieves, commutations, and pardons, after conviction, of all offenses except impeachment, subject to such regulations as may be provided by law.

SEC. 11. A lieutenant-governor shall be elected at the same time and places and in the same manner as the governor, and his term of office and his eligibility shall also be the same. He shall be the president of the senate, but shall only have a casting vote therein. In case of impeachment of the governor, or his removal from office, death, inability to discharge the duties of said office, resignation, or absence from the State, the powers and duties of the office shall devolve upon the lieutenant-governor for the residue of the term, or until the disability shall cease; and in case of the disability of both the governor and lieutenant-governor, the powers and duties of the executive shall devolve upon the secretary of state until such disability shall cease, or the vacancy be filled.

SEC. 12. A secretary of state, a treasurer, an auditor, a surveyor-general, a superintendent of public instruction, and an attorney-general shall be elected at the same time and places and in the same manner as the governor; the term of office of each shall be the same as is prescribed for the governor. Any male elector who, except at the first election, shall have resided in this State two years next preceding such election, shall be eligible to any of said offices, except the secretary of state, whose qualifications shall be the same as those of the governor.

SEC. 13. There shall be a seal of the State, kept by the secretary of state, which shall be called the " Great Seal of the State of Utah."

SEC. 14. All grants and commissions shall be in the name and by the authority of the State of Utah, and shall be signed by the governor and countersigned by the secretary of state, who shall affix the great seal of the State thereto.

SEC. 15. The secretary of state shall be the custodian of the official acts of the legislature, and shall keep a true record of the proceedings of the executive department of the government, and shall, when required, lay the same and all other matters relative thereto before either branch of the legislature.

SEC. 16. The secretary of state, treasurer, auditor, surveyor-general, superintendent of public instruction, and attorney-general shall perform such other duties as may be prescribed by law.

SEC. 17. The governor shall not, during the term for which he is elected and qualified, be elected to the Senate of the United States.

ARTICLE VI.—JUDICIAL DEPARTMENT.

SECTION 1. The judicial power of this State shall be vested in a supreme court, circuit courts, and such inferior courts as shall be established and whose jurisdiction shall be determined by law.

SEC. 2. The supreme court shall consist of a chief justice and two associate justices, a majority of whom shall constitute a quorum.

SEC. 3. The justices of the supreme court shall be elected by the qualified electors of the State at the general election, and shall hold office for the term of six years from and including the first Monday in January next succeeding their election; the senior justice in commission shall be chief justice, and in case the commissions of any two or more of said justices shall bear the same date, they shall determine by lot who shall be chief justice.

SEC. 4. The supreme court shall have appellate jurisdiction in all cases arising under the laws of the State, including special proceedings. The court shall also have power to issue writs of mandamus, certiorari, prohibition, quo warranto, and habeas corpus, and also all writs necessary or proper to the complete exercise of its appellate jurisdiction. Each of the justices shall have power to issue writs of habeas corpus to any part of the State upon petition by or on behalf of any person held in actual custody, and may make such writs returnable before himself or the supreme court, or before any circuit court in the State, or before any judge of said courts.

SEC. 5. The State shall be divided into three or more judicial circuits, in each of which shall be elected, by the electors thereof, one judge, who shall be the judge of the circuit court therein, and whose term of office shall be four years, and until his successor shall be elected and qualified. Until otherwise provided by law, there shall be three circuits, as follows: The counties of Rich, Cache, Box Elder, Weber, Davis, Morgan, and Summit shall constitute the first circuit; the counties of Salt Lake, Tooele, Utah, Juab, Wasatch, Uintah, San Pete, and Emery shall constitute the second circuit; and the counties of Sevier, Millard, Beaver, Piute, San Juan, Garfield, Iron, Washington, and Kane shall constitute the third circuit.

SEC. 6. The circuit courts shall have both chancery and common law jurisdiction, and such other jurisdiction, both original and appellate, as may be prescribed by law: *Provided*, That nothing herein shall be so construed as to prevent the legislature from conferring limited common law or chancery jurisdiction upon inferior courts.

SEC. 7. The judges of the circuit courts may hold court for each other, and shall do so when required by law.

SEC. 8. The judges of the supreme and circuit courts shall be ineligible to election to any other than a judicial office.

SEC. 9. No person shall be eligible to the office of supreme or circuit judge who is not a male citizen of the United States, and has not attained the age of twenty-five years, and who, except at the first election, has not been a resident of this State at least two years next preceding his election.

SEC. 10. The judges of the supreme and circuit courts shall each receive for his services a salary to be fixed by law, which shall not be diminished for the term for which he shall have been elected.

SEC. 11. There shall be one or more terms of the circuit court held annually at the county seat in each county, at such times as shall be prescribed by law: *Provided*, That two or more counties may be consolidated for judicial purposes.

SEC. 12. The supreme court shall be always open for business, except in cases of adjournment, which, in no case, shall exceed thirty days, nor shall any adjournment be taken while business requires the court to be in session. Its sessions shall be held at the seat of government.

SEC. 13. The style of all process shall be "The State of Utah," and all prosecutions shall be conducted in the name and by the authority of the same.

ARTICLE VII.—IMPEACHMENT.

SECTION 1. The house of representatives shall have the sole power of impeachment, and all impeachments shall be tried by the senate. When sitting as a court of impeachment, the senators shall be upon oath or affirmation to do justice according to law and evidence, and no person shall be convicted without the concurrence of two-thirds of all the members.

SEC. 2. The governor, judges of the supreme and circuit courts, and other State officers shall be liable to impeachment. When the governor or lieutenant-governor is tried, the chief justice of the supreme court shall preside, and in all cases judgment shall extend only to removal from office and disqualification to hold any office of honor, trust, or profit under this State, but the party convicted or acquitted shall nevertheless be liable to indictment, trial, and punishment according to law.

SEC. 3. When an impeachment is directed, the house of representatives shall elect from their own body three members, whose duty it shall be to prosecute such impeachment. No impeachment shall be tried until the final adjournment of the legislature, when the senate shall proceed to try the same.

SEC. 4. In all impeachment trials the accused shall have the right to appear, and in person and by counsel to demand the nature and cause of the accusation, and to have a copy thereof; to meet the witnesses face to face, and to have process to compel the attendance of witnesses in his behalf.

SEC. 5. All State officers shall be liable to impeachment for corrupt conduct in office, for immoral conduct, for habitual drunkenness, and for any act which, by the laws of the State, may be made a felony.

SEC. 6. The legislature shall provide by law for the removal of any officer elected by a district, county, precinct, or school district.

ARTICLE VIII.—MUNICIPAL AND OTHER CORPORATIONS.

SECTION 1. The legislature shall pass no special act conferring corporate powers.

SEC. 2. The legislature shall provide for the organization of cities, towns, and villages by general laws, and restrict their powers of taxation, assessment, borrowing money, contracting debts, and loaning their credit; but for sanitary purposes and procuring supplies of water for irrigation and other purposes, municipal corporations may borrow money to such amount as may be determined by a two-thirds vote of the electors thereof.

SEC. 3. The legislature shall provide, by general laws, for the organization of private corporations.

SEC. 4. This State shall not donate or loan money or its credit, subscribe to, or be interested in, the stock of any company, association, or corporation, except corporations formed for educational, charitable, reformatory, or irrigation purposes, which are to be and remain under the patronage and control of the State.

ARTICLE IX.—FINANCE AND STATE DEBT.

SECTION 1. The legislature shall provide by law for an annual tax sufficient to defray the expenses of the State.

SEC. 2. The State shall not assume or guarantee the debts of any county, city, town, village, or private corporation, nor loan money or its credit to or in aid of any individual.

ARTICLE X.—TAXATION.

SECTION 1. The legislature shall provide by law for a uniform and equal rate of taxation, and shall prescribe such regulations as shall secure a just valuation for taxation of all property, real, personal, and possessory: *Provided*, That mines and mining claims bearing gold, silver, and other precious metals, except the net proceeds and surface improvements thereof, shall be exempt from taxation for the period of ten years from the date of the adoption of this constitution, and thereafter may be taxed as provided by law.

SEC. 2. The property of the United States and the property of this State shall be exempt from taxation, and such property as may belong to any county or municipal corporation or as may be used exclusively for agricultural, horticultural, and scientific societies, or for school, religious, cemetery, or charitable purposes may be exempt from taxation, but such exemptions shall be only by general law.

SEC. 3. The legislature shall not impose taxes for the purpose of any county, city, town, or other corporation, but may by law vest in the corporate authorities thereof, respectively, the power to assess and collect taxes for all purposes of such corporations.

SEC. 4. The property of non-residents shall never be taxed higher than that of residents.

ARTICLE XI.—EDUCATION.

SECTION 1. The legislature shall provide for a uniform system of public schools, and may establish free schools: *Provided*, That no sectarian or denominational doctrines shall be taught in any school supported in whole or in part by public funds.

SEC. 2. All legislation in regard to education shall be impartial, guaranteeing to all persons of every race, color, and religion equal rights and privileges.

SEC. 3. The proceeds of all lands that have been or may be granted by the United States to this State for the support of schools shall be and remain a perpetual fund, the interest of which, together with all the rents of the unsold lands, and such other means as the legislature may provide, shall be inviolably appropriated to the support of the public schools throughout the State.

SEC. 4. The University of Deseret shall be the University of this State, and be under the control of the legislature, and constitute a public trust. The proceeds of all lands that have been granted by Congress for university purposes shall be and remain a perpetual fund, the interest of which, together with the rents of unsold lands, shall be appropriated to the support of said university.

SEC. 5. No religious sect or denomination shall ever control or appropriate to its own use any of the public school or university funds of the State. .

ARTICLE XII.—MILITIA.

SECTION 1. The militia of the State shall be composed of all able-bodied male citizens between the ages of eighteen and forty-five years, except such as are, or may hereafter be, exempted by the laws of the United States or of this State, and shall be armed, equipped, and disciplined as the legislature may provide by law.

SEC. 2. All officers of the militia shall be elected by persons liable to military duty, in such manner as the legislature may provide. Staff officers shall be chosen from officers of the line.

ARTICLE XIII.—PUBLIC INSTITUTIONS.

SECTION 1. Institutions for the benefit of the insane, and such other benevolent institutions as the public good may require, shall be fostered and supported by the State.

SEC. 2. A State prison shall be established and maintained in such manner as may be prescribed by law.

SEC. 3. The respective counties of the State shall provide, as may be prescribed by law, for those inhabitants who, by reason of age and infirmity, or misfortunes, may have claim upon the sympathy and aid of society.

ARTICLE XIV.—BOUNDARY.

The boundary of the State of Utah shall be as follows:

Commencing at a point formed by the intersection of the thirty-second degree of longitude west from Washington with the thirty-seventh degree of north latitude; thence due west along said thirty seventh degree of north latitude to the intersection of the same with the thirty-seventh degree of longitude west from Washington; thence due north along said thirty-seventh degree; west longitude to the intersection of the same with the forty-second degree of north latitude; thence due east along said forty-second degree of north latitude to the intersection of the same with the thirty-fourth degree of longitude west from Washington; thence due south along said thirty-fourth degree of west longitude to the intersection of the same with the forty-first degree of north latitude; thence due east along said forty-first degree of north latitude to the intersection of the of the same with the thirty-second degree of longitude west from Washington; thence due south along said thirty-second degree west longitude to the place of beginning.

ARTICLE XV.—MISCELLANEOUS PROVISIONS.

SECTION 1. The seat of government shall be at Salt Lake City, or such place as the legislature may determine.

SEC. 2. No person shall be eligible to any elective office who is not a qualified elector, and no female citizen shall be eligible to serve as juror.

SEC. 3. The general election shall be held on the first Monday in August of each year, unless otherwise provided by law.

SEC. 4. The legislature shall provide for the speedy publication of all laws.

SEC. 5. The compensation of all State officers shall be as prescribed by law: *Provided*, No change of salary or compensation shall apply to any officer, except a judge of the supreme or circuit court, during the term for which he may have been elected.

SEC. 6. All executive officers of the State shall keep their respective offices at the seat of government.

SEC. 7. A plurality of votes given at any election by the people shall constitute a choice, where not otherwise provided by the constitution.

SEC. 8. No person holding any office of honor or profit under the government of the United States shall hold office under the government of this State. except postmasters whose annual compensation does not exceed three hundred dollars, and except as otherwise provided in the constitution.

SEC. 9. The returns of every election, except the first for governor and other State officers, shall be sealed up and transmitted to the seat of government by the returning officers, directed to the president of the senate, who, during the first week of the session, shall open and publish them, and declare the result in the presence of a majority of the members of each house of the legislature. The person having the highest number of votes shall be declared duly elected, but if any two or more shall be highest and equal in numbers of votes for the same office, one of them shall be chosen by the joint vote of both houses.

SEC. 10. All officers, executive, judicial, and ministerial, shall, before they enter upon the duties of their respective offices, take and subscribe to the following oath or affirmation: I, —— ——, do solemnly swear (or affirm) that I will support the Constitution of the United States, and of the State of Utah, and will faithfully discharge the duties of the office of ——, according to the best of my ability.

SEC. 11. Until otherwise provided by law, the several counties, as they now exist, are hereby recognized as legal subdivisions of this State.

SEC. 12. All property, real and personal, owned by either husband or wife before marriage, and that acquired by either of them afterwards, by purchase, gift, devise, or descent, shall be the separate property of each.

ARTICLE XVI.—AMENDMENTS.

SECTION 1. Any amendment or amendments to this constitution, if agreed to by a majority of all the members elected to each of the two houses of the legislature, shall be entered on their respective journals, with the yeas and nays taken thereon, and referred to the legislature then next to be elected, and shall be published for three months next preceding the time of such election, and if in the legislature next elected as aforesaid, such proposed amendment or amendments shall be agreed to by a majority of all the members elected to each house, then it shall be the duty of the legislature to submit such proposed amendment or amendments to the people, in such manner and at such time as the legislature shall prescribe, and if the people shall approve and ratify such amendment or amendments, by a majority of the qualified electors voting thereon, such amendment or amendments shall become a part of the constitution.

SEC. 2. If at any time the legislature, by a vote of two-thirds of the members elected to each house, shall determine that it is necessary to cause a revision of this constitution, the electors shall vote at the next election for members of the legislature, for or against a convention for that purpose, and if it shall appear that a majority of the electors voting at such election shall have voted in favor of calling a convention, the legislature shall, at its next session, provide by law for calling a convention to be held within six months after the passage of such law; and such convention shall consist of a number of members not less than that of the two branches of the legislature.

ARTICLE XVII.—SCHEDULE AND ELECTION.

SECTION 1. That no inconvenience may arise by reason of a change from a territorial to a State government, it is declared that all rights, actions, prosecutions, judgments, claims and contracts, as well of individuals as of bodies corporate, both public and private, shall continue as if no change had taken place, and all process which may issue under the authority of the Territory of Utah previous to its admission into the Union shall be as valid as if issued in the name of the State of Utah.

SEC. 2. All laws of the Territory of Utah, in force at the time of the admission of this State, not repugnant to this constitution, shall remain in force until they expire by their own limitations, or are altered or repealed by the legislature.

SEC. 3. All fines, penalties, and forfeitures accruing to the Territory of Utah, or to the people of the United States in the Territory of Utah, shall inure to this State, and all debts, liabilities and obligations of said Territory shall be valid against the State, and enforced as may be provided by law.

SEC. 4. All recognizances heretofore taken, or which may be taken before the change from a territorial to a State government, shall remain valid, and shall pass to and be prosecuted in the name of the State; and all bonds executed to the governor of the Territory, or to any other officer or court, in his or their official capacity, or to the people of the United States in the Territory of Utah, shall pass to the governor or other officer or court, and his or their successors in office, for the uses therein respectively expressed, and may be sued on and recovery had accordingly; and all revenue, property, real, personal, or mixed, and all judgments, bonds, specialties, choses in action, claims, and debts, of whatsoever description, and all records and public archives of the Territory of Utah, shall issue and vest in the State of Utah, and may be sued for and recovered in the same manner and to the same extent by the State of Utah as the same could have been by the Territory of Utah. All criminal prosecutions and penal actions which may have arisen, or which may arise before the change from a territorial to a State government, and which shall then be pending, shall be prosecuted to judgment and execution in the name of the State. All offenses committed against the laws of the Territory of Utah before the change from a territorial to a State government, and which shall not be prosecuted before such change, may be prosecuted in the name and by the authority of the State of Utah, with like effect as though such change had not taken place; and all penalties incurred shall remain the same as if this constitution had not been adopted. All actions at law and suits in equity, and other legal proceedings which may be pending in any of the courts of the Territory of Utah at the time of a change from a territorial to a State government, may be continued and transferred to and determined by any court of the State having jurisdiction; and all books, papers, and records relating to the same shall be transferred in like manner to such court.

SEC. 5. For the purpose of taking the vote of the electors of this Territory for the ratification or rejection of this constitution, a special election shall be held in the several counties of this Territory on Monday, the twenty-second day of May, A. D. 1882, which shall be conducted in the following manner: The county clerks of the several counties shall cause notices of said election to be posted up in each election precinct in said county, at least ten days before the day of said election. The senior justice of the peace of each precinct shall act as judge of said election, or in case of his absence or inability to act, a judge may be elected by the six electors first assembled at the polls. The judge shall appoint a clerk, whose duty it shall be to keep a list of the names of all persons voting, which list shall form a part of the returns of said election. All votes cast shall first be delivered by the elector to the judge, who shall deposit the same in the ballot-box in the presence of the elector and clerk. Ballot-boxes and stationery shall be furnished by the county court, and the canvassing of votes and returns of said election of the several precincts shall be as provided in an act entitled "An act providing for the registration of voters, and to further regulate the manner of conducting elections in this Territory," approved February 22, 1878, except as herein otherwise provided. The term elector, as used in this section, shall be understood to mean any citizen of the United States, over twenty-one years of age, residing in the Territory.

SEC. 6. Each elector shall vote by a ballot, whereon shall be written or printed "Constitution, yes," or "Constitution, no."

SEC. 7. The county clerks of their respective counties shall forthwith make returns of said election, and transmit the same by the most safe and most expeditious conveyance, to Arthur Stayner, the secretary of this convention, inclosed in an envelope marked "Election returns."

SEC. 8. Upon receipt of said returns, or within fourteen days after the election, if the returns be not sooner received, it shall be the duty of a board of canvassers, to consist of the president and secretary of this convention, and the probate judge of of Salt Lake County, or any two of the persons herein named, to canvass the returns of said election in presence of all who may choose to attend, and immediately publish an abstract of the same in one or more of the newspapers in the Territory of Utah, and forward a copy of said abstract, duly certified by them, to the President of the Senate, Speaker of the House of Representatives, and the Delegate in Congress from Utah Territory.

SEC. 9. Until otherwise provided by law, the apportionment of senators and representatives in the different counties shall be as follows: Cache, Rich, Box Elder, and Weber counties shall elect three senators to the legislature; Wasatch, Uintah, Summit, and Morgan counties, one; Salt Lake, Davis, and Tooele counties, four; Utah and Juab counties, two; San Pete, Sevier, and Emery counties, one; Millard, Beaver, Iron, Garfield, and Pi Ute counties, one; Washington, Kane, and San Juan counties, one; Cache and Rich counties shall elect three representatives to the legislature; Box Elder county, one; Weber county, two; Wasatch and Uintah counties, one; Summit county, one; Morgan, Salt Lake, and Davis counties, seven: Tooele county, one; Utah and Juab counties, four; San Pete, Sevier, and Emery counties, two; Millard county, one; Beaver and Pi Ute counties, one; Iron, Garfield, and San Juan counties, one; Washington and Kane counties, one.

SEC. 10. A copy of this constitution, certified to be correct by the president and secretary of this convention, shall be published by them as soon as practicable in one or more of the newspapers in this Territory. Such president and secretary shall, immediately after its ratification, forward a copy of this constitution, duly certified, to the President of the United States, President of the Senate, and Speaker of the House of Representatives, and shall deliver or forward a copy, certified as aforesaid, to each of the delegates who may hereafter be elected by this convention.

SEC. 11. The term of State officers, except judicial, elected at the first election, shall continue from the time of qualification until the expiration of two years from the first Monday in January next succeeding their election and until the election and qualification of their successors.

SEC. 12. The State senators to be elected at the first election under this constitution, shall draw lots, so that the term of one-half of the number, as nearly as may be, shall expire at the end of one year from the first Monday in August next succeeding their election, and term of the other half shall expire in three years from the first Monday in August next succeeding their election, so that one-half, as nearly as possible, shall be elected biennially thereafter: *Provided*, That in drawing lots for all senatorial terms, the senatorial representation shall be allotted so that in the counties having two or more senators the terms thereof shall be divided as equally as may be between the long and short terms, and in case of increase in the number of senators they shall be so annexed by lot to one or the other of the two classes as to keep them as nearly equal as practicable.

SEC. 13. The term of members of the house of representatives elected at the first election shall expire at the end of one year from the first Monday in August next succeeding their election.

SEC. 14. Unless otherwise provided by Congress, the first election under this constitution shall be held on the first Monday in the second month next succeeding the passage of an enabling act or the approval of this constitution by Congress, and such election shall be conducted and returns thereof made and the qualification of electors shall be as herein provided for the ratification or rejection of this consitution. The first session of the legislature shall commence, and all officers herein provided for shall enter upon the duties of their respective offices, on the first Monday of the second month next succeeding said election.

SEC. 15. There shall be elected at the first election, under this constitution, three justices of the supreme court, who shall hold office from and including the last Monday in the month next succeeding their election, and continue in office thereafter, two, four, and six years respectively, from and including the first Monday in January next succeeding their election. They shall meet as soon as practicable after their election and qualification, and, at their first meeting, shall determine by lot the term of office each shall fill, and the justice drawing the shortest term shall be chief justice, and after the expiration of his term the one having the next shortest term shall be chief justice.

SEC. 16. All officers under the laws of the Territory of Utah, at the time this constitution shall take effect, shall continue in office until their successors are elected and qualified. The time of such election and qualification shall be as prescribed by law.

SEC. 17. After the admission of this State into the Union, and until the legislature shall otherwise provide, the several judges shall hold courts in their respective circuits at such times and places as they may respectively appoint; and until provisions shall be made by law for holding the terms of the supreme court, the governor shall fix the time and place of holding such court.

We hereby certify that the foregoing constitution was adopted, in convention at Salt Lake City, the twenty-seventh day of April, in the year of our Lord one thousand eight hundred and eighty-two, and of the independence of the United States the one hundred and sixth.

JOSEPH F. SMITH,
President.

ARTHUR STAYNER,
Secretary.
SALT LAKE CITY,
April 27, 1882.

[Doc. No. 6]

The Mormon Case (Cannon v. United States)

The principal question argued at the bar was the proper construction of § 3 of the act of 1882. That question depends on the meaning of the word " cohabit" in the section. The meaning contended for by the defendant is indicated by his offer to show by Clara C. Cannon non-access, and facts to rebut the presumption of sexual intercourse with her, and the actual absence of such intercourse ; and by the requests for instructions to the jury, which are based on the view that the word " cohabit" necessarily includes the idea of having sexual intercourse. But we are of opinion that this is not the proper interpretation of the statute ; and that the court properly charged the jury that the defendant was to be found guilty if he lived in the same house with the two women, and ate at their respective tables one-third of his time or thereabouts, and held them out to the world, by his language or conduct, or both, as his wives ; and that it was not necessary it should be shown that he and the two women, or either of them, occupied the same bed or slept in the same room, or that he had sexual intercourse with either of them.

This interpretation is deducible from the language of the statute throughout. It refers wholly to the relations between men and women founded on the existence of actual marriages, or on the holding out of their existence. Section 1 makes it an offence for a man or a woman, with a living wife or husband, to marry another, and calls such offence polygamy. Section 3 singles out the man, and makes it a misdemeanor for him to cohabit with more than one woman. Section 4 provides that counts for any or all of the offences named in §§ 1 and 3 may be joined in the same information or indictment. This certainly has no tendency to show that the cohabitation referred to is one outside of a marital relation, actual or ostensible. So, in § 5, bigamy, polygamy, and unlawful cohabitation are classed together, and it is provided, that, in any prosecution for any one of such offences, it shall be sufficient cause of challenge to a juror, that he has been living in the practice of bigamy, polygamy, or unlawful cohabitation with more than one woman, or has been guilty of an offence punishable by the preceding sections, or that he believes it to be right for a man to have more than one living and undivorced wife at the same time, or to live in the practice of cohabiting with more than one woman. It is the practice of unlawful cohabitation with more than one woman that is aimed at—a cohabitation classed with polygamy and having its outward semblance. It is not, on the one hand, meretricious unmarital intercourse with more than one woman. General legislation as to lewd practices is left to the Territorial government. Nor, on the other hand, does the statute pry into the intimacies of the marriage relation. But it seeks not only to punish bigamy and polygamy when direct proof of the existence of those relations can be made, but to prevent a man from flaunting in the face of the world the ostentation and opportunities of a bigamous household, with all the outward appearances of the continuance of the same relations which existed before the act was passed; and without reference to what may occur in the privacy of those relations. Compacts for sexual non-intercourse, easily made and as easily broken, when the prior marriage relations continue to exist, with the occupation of the same house and table and the keeping up of the same family unity, is not a lawful substitute for the monogamous family which alone the statute tolerates. In like manner, bigamy, polygamy, and unlawful cohabitation are classed together in §§ 6 and 8 of the act. Section 6 authorizes the President to grant amnesty to persons guilty of bigamy, polygamy, or unlawful cohabitation before the passage of the act. Any unlawful cohabitation, under the laws of the United States, before that time, could only have been ostensibly marital cohabitation, for the only statute on the subject was § 5352 of the Revised Statutes, in regard to bigamy. Section 8 excludes from voting every polygamist, bigamist, or person cohabiting with more than one woman, and every woman cohabiting with any polygamist, bigamist, or person cohabiting with more than one woman. This section was considered by this court in *Murphy* v. *Ramsey*, 114 U. S. 15, where Mr. Justice Matthews, speaking for the court, in construing the words "bigamist" and "polygamist" in that section, says: "In our opinion, any man is a polygamist or bigamist, in the sense of this section of the act, who, having previously married one wife, still living, and having another at the time when he

presents himself to claim registration as a voter, still maintains that relation to a plurality of wives, although, from the
date of the passage of the act of March 22, 1882, until the
day he offers to register and to vote, he may not in fact have
cohabited with more than one woman. Without regard to
the question whether, at the time he entered into such relation,
it was a prohibited and punishable offence, or whether, by
reason of lapse of time since its commission, a prosecution for
it may not be barred, if he still maintains the relation, he is a
bigamist or polygamist, because that is the status which the
fixed habit and practice of his living has established. He has
a plurality of wives, more than one woman whom he recog-
nizes as a wife, of whose children he is the acknowledged
father, and whom with their children he maintains as a family,
of which he is the head. And this status as to several wives
may well continue to exist, as a practical relation, although for
a period he may not in fact cohabit with more than one; for
that is quite consistent with the constant recognition of the
same relation to many, accompanied with a possible intention
to renew cohabitation with one or more of the others when it
may be convenient. It is not, therefore, because the person
has committed the offence of bigamy or polygamy, at some
previous time, in violation of some existing statute, and as an
additional punishment for its commission, that he is disfranchised by the act of Congress of March 22, 1882; nor because
he is guilty of the offence, as defined and punished by the
terms of that act; but because, having at some time entered
into a bigamous or polygamous relation, by a marriage with a
second or third wife, while the first was living, he still maintains it, and has not dissolved it, although for the time being
he restricts actual cohabitation to but one. He might in fact
abstain from actual cohabitation with all, and be still as much
as ever a bigamist or a polygamist. He can only cease to be
such when he has finally and fully dissolved in some effective
manner, which we are not called on here to point out, the very
relation of husband to several wives, which constitutes the
forbidden status he has previously assumed. Cohabitation is
but one of the many incidents to the marriage relation. It is

not essential to it.   One man, where such a system has been
tolerated and practised, may have several establishments, each
of which may be the home of a separate family, none of which
he himself may dwell in or even visit.   The statute makes an
express distinction between bigamists and polygamists on the
one hand, and those who cohabit with more than one woman
on the other; whereas, if cohabitation with several wives
was essential to the description of those who are bigamists or
polygamists, those words in the statute would be superfluous
and unnecessary.   It follows, therefore, that any person having
several wives is a bigamist or polygamist in the sense of the
act of March 22, 1882, although since the date of its passage
he may not have cohabited with more than one of them."   p.
41.   In the spirit of this interpretation, a man cohabits with
more than one woman, in the sense of §§ 3, 5 and 8 of the act,
when, holding out to the world two women as his wives, by
his language or conduct, or both, he lives in the house with
them, and eats at the table of each a portion of his time,
although he may not occupy the same bed or sleep in the same
room with either of them, or actually have sexual intercourse
with either of them.   He holds two women out to the world
as his wives, by his conduct, when, being the recognized and
reputed husband of each, so understood to be by the two
wives, and by the son of one of them, and by the son of a
third reputed wife, he maintains the two wives and the
children of each, all in the same house with himself, and
regularly eats at the table of each, and acts as the head of the
two families.

This meaning of the phrase " cohabit with more than one
woman," in the statute, is in consonance with a recognized
definition of the word " cohabit."   In Webster " cohabit " is
defined thus: " 1. To dwell with ; to inhabit or reside in company, or in the same place or country.   2. To dwell or live together as husband and wife."   In Worcester it is defined thus:
" 1. To dwell with another in the same place.   2. To live together as husband and wife."   The word is never used in its
first meaning, in a criminal statute ; and its second meaning is
that to which its use in this statute has relation.   The context

in which it is found, and the manifest evils which gave rise to the special enactments in regard to "cohabitation," require that the word should have the meaning which we have assigned to it. Bigamy and polygamy might fail of proof, for want of direct evidence of any marriage, but cohabitation with more than one woman, in the sense proved in this case, was susceptible of the proof here given; and it was such offence as was here proved that section 3 of the act was intended to reach—the exhibition of all the indicia of a marriage, a household, and a family, twice repeated. However, in some divorce cases, and in reference to a question of the condonation of adultery, the word "cohabit" may have been used in the limited sense of sexual intercourse, or however its meaning may have been so limited by its context in other statutes, it has no such meaning in the statute before us.

[Doc. No. 7]

Proclamation of Amnesty

By the President of the United States of America.

A PROCLAMATION.

Whereas Congress by a statute approved March 22, 1882, and by statutes in furtherance and amendment thereof defined the crimes of bigamy, polygamy, and unlawful cohabitation in the Territories and other places within the exclusive jurisdiction of the United States and prescribed a penalty for such crimes; and

Whereas on or about the 6th day of October, 1890, the Church of the Latter-day Saints, commonly known as the Mormon Church, through its president issued a manifesto proclaiming the purpose of said church no longer to sanction the practice of polygamous marriages and calling upon all members and adherents of said church to obey the laws of the United States in reference to said subject-matter; and

Whereas it is represented that since the date of said declaration the members and adherents of said church have generally obeyed said laws and have abstained from plural marriages and polygamous cohabitation; and

Whereas by a petition dated December 19, 1891, the officials of said church, pledging the membership thereof to a faithful obedience to the laws against plural marriage and unlawful cohabitation, have applied to me to grant amnesty for past offenses against said laws, which request a very large number of influential non-Mormons residing in the Territories have also strongly urged; and

Whereas the Utah Commission in their report bearing date September 15, 1892, recommend that said petition be granted and said amnesty proclaimed, under proper conditions as to the future observance of the law, with a view to the encouragement of those now disposed to become law-abiding citizens; and

Whereas during the past two years such amnesty has been granted to individual applicants in a very large number of cases, conditioned upon the faithful observance of the laws of the United States against unlawful cohabitation, and there are now pending many more such applications:

Now, therefore, I, Benjamin Harrison, President of the United States, by virtue of the powers in me vested, do hereby declare and grant a full amnesty and pardon to all persons liable to the penalties of said act by reason of unlawful cohabitation under the color of polygamous or plural marriage who have since November 1, 1890, abstained from such unlawful cohabitation, but upon the express condition that they shall in the future faithfully obey the laws of the United States hereinbefore named, and not otherwise. Those who shall fail to avail themselves of the clemency hereby offered will be vigorously prosecuted.

In witness whereof I have hereunto set my hand and caused the seal of
the United States to be affixed.

[SEAL.]   Done at the city of Washington, this 4th day of January,
A. D. 1893, and of the Independence of the United States the
one hundred and seventeenth.

BENJ. HARRISON.

By the President:
JOHN W. FOSTER, *Secretary of State.*

[Doc. No. 8]

Enabling Act of July , 1894

CHAP. 138.—An Act To enable the people of Utah to form a constitution and State government, and to be admitted into the Union on an equal footing with the original States.

July 16, 1894.

Be it enacted by the Senate and House of Representatives of the United States of America in Congress assembled, That the inhabitants of all that part of the area of the United States now constituting the Territory of Utah, as at present described, may become the State of Utah, as hereinafter provided.

Utah. Admission as a State.

SEC. 2. That all male citizens of the United States over the age of twenty-one years, who have resided in said Territory for one year next prior to such election, are hereby authorized to vote for and choose delegates to form a convention in said Territory. Such delegates shall possess the qualifications of such electors; and the aforesaid convention shall consist of one hundred and seven delegates, apportioned among the several counties within the limits of the proposed State as follows: Beaver County, two delegates; Box Elder County, four delegates; Cache County, eight delegates; Davis County, three delegates; Emery County, three delegates; Garfield County, one delegate; Grand County, one delegate; Iron County, one delegate; Juab County, three delegates; Kane County, one delegate; Millard County, two delegates; Morgan County, one delegate; Piute County, one delegate; Rich County, one delegate; Salt Lake County, twenty-nine delegates, thus apportioned, to wit: Salt Lake City, first precinct, four delegates; second precinct, six delegates; third precinct, five delegates; fourth precinct, three delegates; fifth precinct, three delegates; all other precincts in said county, outside of Salt Lake City, eight delegates; San Juan County, one delegate; San Pete County, seven delegates; Sevier County, three delegates; Summit County, four delegates; Tooele County, two delegates; Uintah County, one delegate; Utah County, twelve delegates; Wasatch County, two delegates; Washington County, two delegates; Wayne County, one delegate, and Weber County, eleven delegates; and the governor of said Territory shall, on the first day of August, eighteen hundred and ninety-four, issue a proclamation ordering an election of the delegates aforesaid in said Territory to be held on the Tuesday next after the first Monday in November following. The board of commissioners known as the Utah commission is hereby authorized and required to cause a new and complete registration of voters of said Territory to be made under the provisions of the laws of the United States and said Territory, except that the oath required for registration under said laws shall be so modified as to test the qualifications of the electors as prescribed in this Act; such new registration to be made as nearly conformable with the provisions of such laws as may be; and such

Delegates to convention to be chosen.

Qualifications.

Apportionment.

Governor to issue proclamation for election.
Registration by Utah Commission.

election for delegates shall be conducted, the returns made, the result ascertained, and the certificate of persons elected to such convention issued in the same manner as is prescribed by the laws of said Territory regulating elections therein of members of the legislature. Persons possessing the qualifications entitling them to vote for delegates under this Act shall be entitled to vote on the ratification or rejection of the constitution, under such rules or regulations as said convention may prescribe, not in conflict with this Act.

Meeting of convention.   SEC. 3. That the delegates to the convention thus elected shall meet at the seat of government of said Territory on the first Monday in March, eighteen hundred and ninety-five, and, after organization, shall declare on behalf of the people of said proposed State that they adopt the Constitution of the United States, whereupon the said convention shall be, and is hereby, authorized to form a constitution and State government for said proposed State.

Adoption of constitution.
Provisions.
Civil rights.

The constitution shall be republican in form, and make no distinction in civil or political rights on account of race or color, except as to Indians not taxed, and not to be repugnant to the Constitution of the United States and the principles of the Declaration of Independence. And said convention shall provide, by ordinance irrevocable without the consent of the United States and the people of said State—

Religious freedom.

First. That perfect toleration of religious sentiment shall be secured, and that no inhabitant of said State shall ever be molested in person

Proviso.
Polygamy.

or property on account of his or her mode of religious worship: *Provided,* That polygamous or plural marriages are forever prohibited.

Renunciation of public lands.

Second. That the people inhabiting said proposed State do agree and declare that they forever disclaim all right and title to the unappropriated public lands lying within the boundaries thereof; and to all lands lying within said limits owned or held by any Indian or Indian tribes; and that until the title thereto shall have been extinguished by the United States, the same shall be and remain subject to the disposition of the United States, and said Indian lands shall remain under the absolute jurisdiction and control of the Congress of the United

Taxation of lands.

States; that the lands belonging to citizens of the United States residing without the said State shall never be taxed at a higher rate than the lands belonging to residents thereof; that no taxes shall be imposed by the State on lands or property therein belonging to or which may hereafter be purchased by the United States or reserved for its use;

Indian lands.

but nothing herein, or in the ordinance herein provided for, shall preclude the said State from taxing, as other lands are taxed, any lands owned or held by any Indian who has severed his tribal relations and has obtained from the United States or from any person a title thereto by patent or other grant, save and except such lands as have been or may be granted to any Indian or Indians under any Act of Congress containing a provision exempting the lands thus granted from taxation; but said ordinance shall provide that all such lands shall be exempt from taxation by said State so long and to such extent as such Act of Congress may prescribe.

Territorial debts.

Third. That the debts and liabilities of said Territory, under authority of the legislative assembly thereof, shall be assumed and paid by said State.

Public schools.

Fourth. That provision shall be made for the establishment and maintenance of a system of public schools, which shall be open to all the children of said State and free from sectarian control.

Submission of constitution for ratification.

SEC. 4. That in case a constitution and State government shall be formed in compliance with the provisions of this Act, the convention forming the same shall provide by ordinance for submitting said constitution to the people of said State for its ratification or rejection, at an election to be held on the Tuesday next after the first Monday in November, eighteen hundred and ninety-five, at which election the

Vote.

qualified voters of said proposed State shall vote directly for or against the proposed constitution, and for or against any provisions separately

Canvass of returns. submitted. The return of said election shall be made to the said Utah commission, who shall cause the same to be canvassed, and if a majority of the votes cast on that question shall be for the constitution, shall certify the result to the President of the United States, together with a statement of the votes cast thereon, and upon separate articles or propositions, and a copy of said constitution, articles, propositions, and ordinances.   And if the constitution and government of said proposed State are republican in form, and if all the provisions of this Act have been complied with in the formation thereof, it shall be the duty of the President of the United States to issue his proclamation announcing the result of said election, and thereupon the proposed State of Utah shall be deemed admitted by Congress into the Union, under and by virtue of this Act, on an equal footing with the original States, from and after the date of said proclamation.

Certifying result.

Proclamation of admission by President.

SEC. 5. That until the next general census, or until otherwise provided by law, said State shall be entitled to one Representative in the House of Representatives of the United States, which Representative in the Fifty-fourth Congress, together with the governor and other officers provided for in said constitution, may be elected on the same day of the election for the adoption of the constitution; and until said State officers are elected and qualified under the provisions of the constitution, and the State is admitted into the Union, the Territorial officers shall continue to discharge the duties of the respective offices in said Territory.

Representative in Congress.

Election.

SEC. 6. That upon the admission of said State into the Union, sections numbered two, sixteen, thirty-two, and thirty-six in every township of said proposed State, and where such sections or any parts thereof have been sold or otherwise disposed of by or under the authority of any Act of Congress other lands equivalent thereto, in legal subdivisions of not less than one quarter section and as contiguous as may be to the section in lieu of which the same is taken, are hereby granted to said State for the support of common schools, such indemnity lands to be selected within said State in such manner as the legislature may provide, with the approval of the Secretary of the Interior: *Provided*, That the second, sixteenth, thirty-second, and thirty-sixth sections embraced in permanent reservations for national purposes shall not, at any time, be subject to the grants nor to the indemnity provisions of this Act, nor shall any lands embraced in Indian, military, or other reservations of any character be subject to the grants or to the indemnity provisions of this Act until the reservation shall have been extinguished and such lands be restored to and become a part of the public domain.

Grant of school lands, etc.

Proviso.
Lands in reservations excepted.

SEC. 7. That upon the admission of said State into the Union, in accordance with the provisions of this Act, one hundred sections of the unappropriated lands within said State to be selected and located in legal subdivisions as provided in section six of this Act, shall be, and are hereby, granted to said State for the purpose of erecting public buildings at the capital of said State, when permanently located, for legislative, executive, and judicial purposes.

Lands for public buildings.

SEC. 8. That lands to the extent of two townships in quantity, authorized by the third section of the Act of February twenty-one, eighteen hundred and fifty-five, to be reserved for the establishment of the University of Utah, are hereby granted to the State of Utah for university purposes, to be held and used in accordance with the provisions of this section; and any portions of said lands that may not have been selected by said Territory may be selected by said State.   That in addition to the above, one hundred and ten thousand acres of land, to be selected and located as provided in the foregoing section of this Act, and including all saline lands in said State, are hereby granted to said State, for the use of the said university, and two hundred thousand acres for the use of an agricultural college therein.   That the proceeds of the sale of said lands, or any portion thereof, shall constitute permanent funds, to be safely invested and held by said State; and the income thereof to be

University lands.
Vol. 10, p. 611.
Post, p. 117.

Additional grant.

Proceeds to be invested.

used exclusively for the purposes of such university and agricultural college respectively.

Sales of lands.
Five per cent fund
for schools.

SEC. 9. That five per centum of the proceeds of the sales of public lands lying within said State, which shall be sold by the United States subsequent to the admission of said State into the Union, after deducting all the expenses incident to the same, shall be paid to the said State, to be used as a permanent fund, the interest of which only shall be expended for the support of the common schools within said State.

School fund.

SEC. 10. That the proceeds of lands herein granted for educational purposes, except as hereinafter otherwise provided, shall constitute a permanent school fund, the interest of which only shall be expended for the support of said schools, and such land shall not be subject to preëmption, homestead entry, or any other entry under the land laws of the United States, whether surveyed or unsurveyed, but shall be surveyed for school purposes only.

State to control
schools, etc.

SEC. 11. The schools, colleges, and university provided for in this Act shall forever remain under the exclusive control of said State, and no part of the proceeds arising from the sale or disposal of any lands herein granted for educational purposes, or of the income thereof, shall be used for the support of any sectarian or denominational school, college, or university.

Sectarian schools.

Lands for public improvements.
Vol. 5, p. 455.

SEC. 12. That in lieu of the grant of land for purposes of internal improvement made to new States by the eighth section of the Act of September fourth, eighteen hundred and forty-one, which section is hereby repealed as to said State, and in lieu of any claim or demand by the State of Utah under the Act of September twenty-eighth, eighteen hundred and fifty, and section twenty-four hundred and seventy-nine of the Revised Statutes, making a grant of swamp and overflowed lands to certain States, which grant it is hereby declared is not extended to said State of Utah, the following grants of land are hereby made to said State for the purposes indicated, namely:

Swamp lands.
Vol. 9, p. 520.
R. S., sec. 2479, p. 453.

Grants in lieu of former.

For the establishment of permanent water reservoirs for irrigating purposes, five hundred thousand acres; for the establishment and maintenance of an insane asylum, one hundred thousand acres; for the establishment and maintenance of a school of mines in connection with the university, one hundred thousand acres; for the establishment and maintenance of a deaf and dumb asylum, one hundred thousand acres; for the establishment and maintenance of a reform school, one hundred thousand acres; for establishment and maintenance of State normal schools, one hundred thousand acres; for the establishment and maintenance of an institution for the blind, one hundred thousand acres; for a miners' hospital for disabled miners, fifty thousand acres. The United States penitentiary near Salt Lake City and all lands and appurtenances connected therewith and set apart and reserved therefor are hereby granted to the State of Utah.

Penitentiary.

No further grants.

The said State of Utah shall not be entitled to any further or other grants of land for any purpose than as expressly provided in this Act; and the lands granted by this section shall be held, appropriated, and disposed of exclusively for the purposes herein mentioned, in such manner as the legislature of the State may provide.

Disposition.

Selection of lands.

SEC. 13. That all land granted in quantity or as indemnity by this Act shall be selected under the direction of the Secretary of the Interior, from the unappropriated public lands of the United States within the limits of said State of Utah.

Judicial district established.

SEC. 14. That the State of Utah shall constitute one judicial district, which shall be called the district of Utah, and the circuit and district courts thereof shall be held at the capital of this State for the time being. The judge of said district shall receive a yearly salary of five thousand dollars, payable monthly, and shall reside in his district. There shall be appointed clerks of said courts, who shall keep their offices at the capital of said State. There shall be appointed for said district one district judge, one United States attorney, and one United States marshal. The regular terms of said courts shall be held at the

Judge, etc.

Terms.

place aforesaid on the first Monday in April and the first Monday in November of each year. For judicial purposes, the district of Utah shall be attached to the eighth judicial circuit, and only one grand jury and one petit jury shall be summoned in both of said courts. *Attached to eighth circuit.*

SEC. 15. That the circuit and district courts for the district of Utah and the judges thereof, respectively, shall possess the same powers and jurisdiction and perform the same duties possessed and required to be performed by the other circuit and district courts and judges of the United States, and shall be governed by the same laws and regulations. *Jurisdiction.*

SEC. 16. That the marshal, district attorney, and clerks of the circuit and district courts of the said district of Utah, and all other officers and other persons performing duty in the administration of justice therein, shall severally possess the powers and perform the duties lawfully possessed and required to be performed by similar officers in other districts of the United States, and shall, for the services they may perform, receive the same fees and compensation allowed by law to other similar officers and persons performing similar duties. *Powers of officers.* *Compensation.*

SEC. 17. That the convention herein provided for shall have the power to provide, by ordinance, for the transfer of actions, cases, proceedings, and matters pending in the supreme or district courts of the Territory of Utah at the time of the admission of the said State into the Union, to such courts as shall be established under the constitution to be thus formed, or to the circuit or district court of the United States for the district of Utah; and no indictment, action, or proceeding shall abate by reason of any change in the courts, but shall be proceeded with in the State or United States courts according to the laws thereof, respectively. That all cases of appeal or writ of error heretofore prosecuted and now pending in the Supreme Court of the United States upon any record from the supreme court of said Territory, or that may hereafter lawfully be prosecuted upon any record from said court, may be heard and determined by said Supreme Court of the United States; and the mandate of execution or of further proceedings shall be directed by the Supreme Court of the United States to the circuit or district court hereby established within the said State from or to the supreme court of such State, as the nature of the case may require. And the circuit, district, and State courts herein named shall, respectively, be the successors of the supreme court of the Territory as to all such cases arising within the limits embraced within the jurisdiction of such courts, respectively, with full power to proceed with the same, and award mesne or final process therein; and that from all judgments and decrees of the supreme court of the Territory, mentioned in this Act, in any case arising within the limits of the proposed State prior to admission, the parties to such judgment shall have the same right to prosecute appeals and writs of error to the Supreme Court of the United States as they shall have had by law prior to the admission of said State into the Union. *Transfer of causes.* *Cases pending in Supreme Court.* *Final proceedings.* *Succession of State, etc., courts to supreme Territorial court.*

SEC. 18. That the sum of thirty thousand dollars, or so much thereof as may be necessary, is hereby appropriated out of any money in the Treasury not otherwise appropriated to said Territory for defraying the expenses of said convention and for the payment of the members thereof, under the same rules and regulations and at the same rates as are now provided by law for the payment of the Territorial legislature. *Appropriation for convention expenses.*

SEC. 19. That the constitutional convention may by ordinance provide for the election of officers for a full State government, including members of the legislature and Representative in the Fifty-fourth Congress, at the time for the election for the ratification or rejection of the constitution; but the said State government shall remain in abeyance until the State shall be admitted into the Union as proposed by this Act. In case the constitution of said State shall be ratified by the people, but not otherwise, the legislature thereof may assemble, organize, and elect two Senators of the United States in the manner now prescribed by the laws of the United States; and the governor *Election for full State government.* *Senators.*

and secretary of state of the proposed State shall certify the election of the Senators and Representative in the manner required by law, and when such State is admitted into the Union as provided in this Act, the Senators and Representative shall be entitled to be admitted to seats in Congress, and to all rights and privileges of Senators and Representatives of other States in the Congress of the United States; and the State government formed in pursuance of said constitution, as provided by the constitutional convention, shall proceed to exercise all the functions of State officers; and all laws in force made by said Territory at the time of its admission into the Union shall be in force in said State, except as modified or changed by this Act or by the constitution of the State; and the laws of the United States shall have the same force and effect within the said State as elsewhere within the United States.

SEC. 20. That all Acts or parts of Acts in conflict with the provisions of this Act, whether passed by the legislature of said Territory or by Congress, are hereby repealed.

Approved, July 16, 1894.

Admission to Congress.

Existing laws.

Repeal provision.

[Doc. No. 9]

Constitution of 1895

PREAMBLE

Grateful to Almighty God for life and liberty, we, the people of
Utah, in order to secure and perpetuate the principles of free government, do ordain and establish this

CONSTITUTION

ARTICLE I

DECLARATION OF RIGHTS

SECTION 1. All men have the inherent and inalienable right to enjoy
and defend their lives and liberties; to acquire, possess, and protect
property; to worship according to the dictates of their consciences;
to assemble peaceably, protest against wrongs, and petition for redress
of grievances; to communicate freely their thoughts and opinions,
being responsible for the abuse of that right.

SEC. 2. All political power is inherent in the people, and all free
governments are founded on their authority for their equal protection and benefit, and they have the right to alter or reform their
government as the public welfare may require.

SEC. 3. The State of Utah is an inseparable part of the Federal
Union, and the Constitution of the United States is the supreme law
of the land.

SEC. 4. The rights of conscience shall never be infringed. The
State shall make no law respecting an establishment of religion or
prohibiting the free exercise thereof; no religious test shall be required
as a qualification for any office of public trust or for any vote at any
election, nor shall any person be incompetent as a witness or juror on
account of religious belief or the absence thereof. There shall be no
union of church and state, nor shall any church dominate the State or
interfere with its functions. No public money or property shall be
appropriated for or applied to any religious worship, exercise, or
instruction, or for the support of any ecclesiastical establishment.
No property qualification shall be required of any person to vote or
hold office, except as provided in this constitution.

SEC. 5. The privilege of the writ of habeas corpus shall not be suspended unless, in case of rebellion or invasion, the public safety
requires it.

SEC. 6. The people have the right to bear arms for their security
and defense, but the legislature may regulate the exercise of this right
by law.

SEC. 7. No person shall be deprived of life, liberty, or property
without due process of law.

Sec. 8. All prisoners shall be bailable by sufficient sureties, except for capital offenses when the proof is evident or the presumption strong.

Sec. 9. Excessive bail shall not be required; excessive fines shall not be imposed; nor shall cruel and unusual punishments be inflicted. Persons arrested or imprisoned shall not be treated with unnecessary rigor.

Sec. 10. In capital cases the right of trial by jury shall remain inviolate. In courts of general jurisdiction, except in capital cases, a jury shall consist of eight jurors. In courts of inferior jurisdiction a jury shall consist of four jurors. In criminal cases the verdict shall be unanimous. In civil cases three-fourths of the jurors may find a verdict. A jury in civil cases shall be waived unless demanded.

Sec. 11. All courts shall be open, and every person, for an injury done to him in his person, property, or reputation, shall have remedy by due course of law, which shall be administered without denial or unnecessary delay; and no person shall be barred from prosecuting or defending before any tribunal in this State, by himself or counsel, any civil cause to which he is a party.

Sec. 12. In criminal prosecutions the accused shall have the right to appear and defend in person and by counsel, to demand the nature and cause of the accusation against him, to have a copy thereof, to testify in his own behalf, to be confronted by the witnesses against him, to have compulsory process to compel the attendance of witnesses in his own behalf, to have a speedy public trial by an impartial jury of the county or district in which the offense is alleged to have been committed, and the right to appeal in all cases. In no instance shall any accused person, before final judgment, be compelled to advance money or fees to secure the rights herein guaranteed. The accused shall not be compelled to give evidence against himself; a wife shall not be compelled to testify against her husband, nor a husband against his wife, nor shall any person be twice put in jeopardy for the same offense.

Sec. 13. Offenses heretofore required to be prosecuted by indictment shall be prosecuted by information after examination and commitment by a magistrate, unless the examination be waived by the accused with the consent of the State, or by indictment, with or without such examination and commitment. The grand jury shall consist of seven persons, five of whom must concur to find an indictment; but no grand jury shall be drawn or summoned unless, in the opinion of the judge of the district, public interest demands it.

Sec. 14. The right of the people to be secure in their persons, houses, papers, and effects against unreasonable searches and seizures shall not be violated; and no warrant shall issue but upon probable cause supported by oath or affirmation, particularly describing the place to be searched and the person or thing to be seized.

Sec. 15. No law shall be passed to abridge or restrain the freedom of speech or of the press. In all criminal prosecutions for libel the truth may be given in evidence to the jury; and if it shall appear to the jury that the matter charged as libelous is true, and was published with good motives, and for justifiable ends, the party shall be acquitted, and the jury shall have the right to determine the law and the fact.

SEC. 16. There shall be no imprisonment for debt, except in cases of absconding debtors.

SEC. 17. All elections shall be free, and no power, civil or military, shall at any time interfere to prevent the free exercise of the right of suffrage. Soldiers in time of war may vote at their post of duty, in or out of the State, under regulations to be prescribed by law.

SEC. 18. No bill of attainder, ex post facto law, or law impairing the obligation of contracts shall be passed.

SEC. 19. Treason against the State shall consist only in levying war against it, or in adhering to its enemies, or in giving them aid and comfort. No person shall be convicted of treason unless on the testimony of two witnesses to the same overt act.

SEC. 20. The military shall be in strict subordination to the civil power, and no soldier in time of peace shall be quartered in any house without the consent of the owner; nor in time of war, except in a manner to be prescribed by law.

SEC. 21. Neither slavery nor involuntary servitude, except as a punishment for crime, whereof the party shall have been duly convicted, shall exist within this State.

SEC. 22. Private property shall not be taken or damaged for public use without just compensation.

SEC. 23. No law shall be passed granting irrevocably any franchise, privilege, or immunity.

SEC. 24. All laws of a general nature shall have uniform operation.

SEC. 25. This enumeration of rights shall not be construed to impair or deny others retained by the people.

SEC. 26. The provisions of this constitution are mandatory and prohibitory, unless by express words they are declared to be otherwise.

SEC. 27. Frequent recurrence to fundamental principles is essential to the security of individual rights and the perpetuity of free government.

ARTICLE II

STATE BOUNDARIES

SECTION 1. The boundaries of the State of Utah shall be as follows: Beginning at a point formed by the intersection of the thirty-second degree of longitude west from Washington with the thirty-seventh degree of north latitude; thence due west along said thirty-seventh degree of north latitude to the intersection of the same with the thirty-seventh degree of longitude west from Washington; thence due north along said thirty-seventh degree of west longitude to the intersection of the same with the forty-second degree of north latitude; thence due east along said forty-second degree of north latitude to the intersection of the same with the thirty-fourth degree of longitude west from Washington; thence due south along said thirty-fourth degree of west longitude to the intersection of the same with the forty-first degree of north latitude; thence due east along said forty-first degree of north latitude to the intersection of the same with the thirty-second degree of longitude west from Washington; thence due south along said thirty-second degree of west longitude to the place of beginning.

ARTICLE III

ORDINANCE

The following ordinance shall be irrevocable without the consent of the United States and the people of this State:

First. Perfect toleration of religious sentiment is guaranteed. No inhabitant of this State shall ever be molested in person or property on account of his or her mode of religious worship; but polygamous or plural marriages are forever prohibited.

Second. The people inhabiting this State do affirm and declare that they forever disclaim all right and title to the unappropriated public lands lying within the boundaries hereof, and to all lands lying within said limits owned or held by any Indian or Indian tribes, and that until the title thereto shall have been extinguished by the United States the same shall be and remain subject to the disposition of the United States, and said Indian lands shall remain under the absolute jurisdiction and control of the Congress of the United States. The lands belonging to citizens of the United States residing without this State shall never be taxed at a higher rate than the lands belonging to residents of this State; nor shall taxes be imposed by this State on lands or property herein belonging to or which may hereafter be purchased by the United States or reserved for its use; but nothing in this ordinance shall preclude this State from taxing, as other lands are taxed, any lands owned or held by any Indian who has severed his tribal relations and has obtained from the United States or from any person, by patent or other grant, a title thereto, save and except such lands as have been or may be granted to any Indian or Indians under any act of Congress containing a provision exempting the land thus granted from taxation, which last-mentioned lands shall be exempt from taxation so long, and to such extent, as is or may be provided in the act of Congress granting the same.

Third. All debts and liabilities of the Territory of Utah, incurred by authority of the legislative assembly thereof, are hereby assumed and shall be paid by this State.

Fourth. The legislature shall make laws for the establishment and maintenance of a system of public schools, which shall be open to all the children of the State and be free from sectarian control.

ARTICLE IV

ELECTIONS AND RIGHT OF SUFFRAGE

SECTION 1. The rights of citizens of the State of Utah to vote and hold office shall not be denied or abridged on account of sex. Both male and female citizens of this State shall enjoy equally all civil, political, and religious rights and privileges.

SEC. 2. Every citizen of the United States of the age of 21 years and upward, who shall have been a citizen for ninety days, and shall have resided in the State or Territory one year, in the county four months, and in the precinct sixty days next preceding any election, shall be entitled to vote at such election except as herein otherwise provided.

SEC. 3. In all cases except those of treason, felony, or breach of the peace, electors, shall be privileged from arrest on the days of election, during their attendance at elections, and going to and returning therefrom.

SEC. 4. No elector shall be obliged to perform militia duty on the day of election except in time of war or public danger.

SEC. 5. No person shall be deemed a qualified elector of this State unless such person be a citizen of the United States.

SEC. 6. No idiot, insane person, or person convicted of treason or crime against the elective franchise, unless restored to civil rights, shall be permitted to vote at any election or be eligible to hold office in this State.

SEC. 7. Except in elections levying a special tax or creating indebtedness, no property qualification shall be required for any person to vote or hold office.·

SEC. 8. All elections shall be by secret ballot. Nothing in this section shall be construed to prevent the use of any machine or mechanical contrivance for the purpose of receiving and registering the votes cast at any election: *Provided*, That secrecy in voting be preserved.

SEC. 9. All general elections, except for municipal and school officers, shall be held on the Tuesday next following the first Monday in November of the year in which the election is held. Special elections may be held as provided by law. The terms of all officers elected at any general election shall commence on the first Monday in January next following the date of their election. Municipal and school officers shall be elected at such time as may be provided by law.

SEC. 10. All officers made elective or appointive by this constitution or by the laws made in pursuance thereof, before entering upon the duties of their respective offices, shall take and subscribe the following oath or affirmation: " I do solemnly swear (or affirm) that I will support, obey, and defend the Constitution of the United States and the constitution of this State, and that I will discharge the duties of my office with fidelity."

ARTICLE V

DISTRIBUTION OF POWERS

SECTION 1. The powers of the government of the State of Utah shall be divided into three distinct departments, the legislative, the executive, and the judicial; and no person charged with the exercise of powers properly belonging to one of these departments shall exercise any functions appertaining to either of the others, except in the cases herein expressly directed or permitted.

ARTICLE VI

LEGISLATIVE DEPARTMENT

a SECTION 1. The legislative power of this State shall be vested in a senate and house of representatives, which shall be designated the legislature of the State of Utah.

---

a See amendment, November 6, 1900.

SEC. 2. Regular sessions of the legislature shall be held biennially at the seat of the government, and, except the first session thereof, shall commence on the second Monday in January next after the election of members of the house of representatives.

SEC. 3. The members of the house of representatives, after the first election, shall be chosen by the qualified electors of the respective representative districts on the first Tuesday after the first Monday in November, 1896, and biennially thereafter. Their term of office shall be two years from the first day of January next after their election.

SEC. 4. The senators shall be chosen by the qualified electors of the respective senatorial districts at the same times and places as members of the house of representatives, and their term of office shall be four years from the first day of January next after their election: *Provided*, That the senators elected in 1896 shall be divided by lot into two classes as nearly equal as may be; seats of senators of the first class shall be vacated at the expiration of two years, those of the second class at the expiration of four years; so that one-half, as near as possible, shall be chosen biennially thereafter. In case of increase in the number of senators, they shall be annexed by lot to one or the other of the two classes, so as to keep them as nearly equal as practicable.

SEC. 5. No person shall be eligible to the office of senator or representative who is not a citizen of the United States, twenty-five years of age, a qualified voter in the district from which he is chosen, a resident for three years of the State, and for one year of the district from which he is elected.

SEC. 6. No person holding any public office of profit or trust under authority of the United States or of this State shall be a member of the legislature: *Provided*, That appointments in the State militia and the offices of notary public, justice of the peace, United States commissioner, and postmaster of the fourth class shall not, within the meaning of this section, be considered offices of profit or trust.

SEC. 7. No member of the legislature, during the term for which he was elected, shall be appointed or elected to any civil office of profit under this State which shall have been created, or the emoluments of which shall have been increased, during the term for which he was elected.

SEC. 8. Members of the legislature, in all cases except treason, felony, or breach of peace, shall be privileged from arrest during each session of the legislature, for fifteen days next preceding each session, and in returning therefrom; and for words used in any speech or debate in either house they shall not be questioned in any other place.

SEC. 9. The members of the legislature shall receive such per diem and mileage as the legislature may provide, not exceeding four dollars per day and ten cents per mile for the distance necessarily traveled going to and returning from the place of meeting on the most usual route, and they shall receive no other pay or perquisite.

SEC. 10. Each house shall be the judge of the election and qualifications of its members, and may punish them for disorderly conduct, and, with the concurrence of two-thirds of all the members elected, expel a member for cause.

SEC. 11. A majority of the members of each house shall constitute a quorum to transact business, but a smaller number may adjourn

from day to day, and may compel the attendance of absent members
in such manner and under such penalties as each house may prescribe.

SEC. 12. Each house shall determine the rules of its proceedings,
and choose its own officers and employees.

SEC. 13. The governor shall issue writs of election to fill vacancies
that may occur in either house of the legislature.

SEC.. 14. Each house shall keep a journal of its proceedings, which,
except in case of executive sessions, shall be published, and the yeas
and nays on any question, at the request of five members of such
house, shall be entered upon the journal.

SEC. 15. All sessions of the legislature, except those of the senate
while sitting in executive session, shall be public; and neither house,
without the consent of the other, shall adjourn for more than three
days, nor to any other place than that in which it may be holding
session.

SEC. 16. No regular session of the legislature (except the first,
which may sit ninety days) shall exceed sixty days, except in cases
of impeachment. No special session shall exceed thirty days, and in
such special session, or when a regular session of the legislature trying cases of impeachment exceeds sixty days, the members shall receive for compensation only the usual per diem and mileage.

SEC. 17. The house of representatives shall have the sole power of
impeachment, but in order to impeach two-thirds of all the members
elected must vote therefor.

SEC. 18. All impeachments shall be tried by the senate, and senators, when sitting for that purpose, shall take oath or make affirmation to do justice according to the law and the evidence. When the
governor is on trial the chief justice of the supreme court shall preside. No person shall be convicted without the concurrence of two-
thirds of the senators elected.

SEC. 19. The governor and other State and judicial officers, except
justices of the peace, shall be liable to impeachment for high crimes,
misdemeanors, or malfeasance in office; but judgment in such cases
shall extend only to removal from office and disqualification to hold
any office of honor, trust, or profit in the State. The party, whether
convicted or acquitted, shall, nevertheless, be liable to prosecution,
trial, and punishment according to law.

SEC. 20. No person shall be tried on impeachment unless he shall
have been served with a copy of the articles thereof at least ten days
before the trial, and after such service he shall not exercise the duties
of his office until he shall have been acquitted.

SEC. 21. All officers not liable to impeachment shall be removed for
any of the offenses specified in this article, in such manner as may be
provided by law.

ᵃ SEC. 22. The enacting clause of every law shall be: " Be it enacted
by the legislature of the State of Utah," and no bill or joint resolution shall be passed except with the assent of a majority of all the
members elected to each house of the legislature, and after it has been
read three times. The vote upon the final passage of all bills shall
be by yeas and nays; and no law shall be revised or amended by reference to its title only; but the act as revised, or section as amended,
shall be reenacted and published at length.

ᵃ See amendment, November 6, 1900.

SEC. 23. Except general appropriation bills, and bills for the codification and general revision of laws, no bill shall be passed containing more than one subject, which shall be clearly expressed in its title.

SEC. 24. The presiding officer of each house, in the presence of the house over which he presides, shall sign all bills and joint resolutions passed by the legislature, after their titles have been publicly read immediately before signing, and the fact of such signing shall be entered upon the journal.

SEC. 25. All acts shall be officially published, and no act shall take effect until so published, nor until sixty days after the adjournment of the session at which it passed, unless the legislature by vote of two-thirds of all the members elected to each house shall otherwise direct.

SEC. 26. The legislature is prohibited from enacting any private or special laws in the following cases:

First. Granting divorce.

Second. Changing the names of persons or places, or constituting one person the heir at law of another.

Third. Locating or changing county seats.

Fourth. Regulating the jurisdiction and duties of justices of the peace.

Fifth. Punishing crimes and misdemeanors.

Sixth. Regulating the practice of courts of justice.

Seventh. Providing for a change of venue in civil or criminal actions.

Eighth. Assessing and collecting taxes.

Ninth. Regulating the interest on money.

Tenth. Changing the law of descent or succession.

Eleventh. Regulating county and township affairs.

Twelfth. Incorporating cities, towns, or villages; changing or amending the charter of any city, town, or village; laying out, opening, vacating, or altering town plats, highways, streets, wards, alleys, or public grounds.

Thirteenth. Providing for sale or mortgage of real estate belonging to minors or others under disability.

Fourteenth. Authorizing persons to keep ferries across streams within the State.

Fifteenth. Remitting fines, penalties, or forfeitures.

Sixteenth. Granting to an individual, association, or corporation any privilege, immunity, or franchise.

Seventeenth. Providing for the management of common schools.

Eighteenth. Creating, increasing, or decreasing fees, percentages, or allowances of public officers during the term for which said officers are elected or appointed.

The legislature may repeal any existing special law relating to the forgoing subdivisions.

In all cases where a general law can be applicable no special law shall be enacted.

Nothing in this section shall be construed to deny or restrict the power of the legislature to establish and regulate the compensation and fees of county and township officers; to establish and regulate the rates of freight, passage, toll, and charges of railroads, toll roads, ditch, flume, and tunnel companies incorporated under the laws of the State or doing business therein.

SEC. 27. The legislature shall have no power to release or extinguish, in whole or in part, the indebtedness, liability, or obligation of any corporation or person to the State, or to any municipal corporation therein.

SEC. 28. The legislature shall not authorize any game of chance, lottery, or gift enterprise under any pretense or for any purpose.

SEC. 29. The legislature shall not delegate to any special commission, private corporation, or association any power to make, supervise, or interfere with any municipal improvement, money, property, or effects, whether held in trust or otherwise, to levy taxes, to select a capitol site, or to perform any municipal functions.

SEC. 30. The legislature shall have no power to grant, or authorize any county or municipal authority to grant, any extra compensation, fee, or allowance to any public officer, agent, servant, or contractor, after service has been rendered or a contract has been entered into and performed in whole or in part, nor pay or authorize the payment of any claim hereafter created against the State, or any county or municipality of the State, under any agreement or contract made without authority of law: *Provided*, That this section shall not apply to claims incurred by public officers in the execution of the laws of the State.

SEC. 31. The legislature shall not authorize the State, or any county, city, town, township, district, or other political subdivision of the State, to lend its credit or subscribe to stock or bonds in aid of any railroad, telegraph, or other private individual or corporate enterprise or undertaking.

ARTICLE VII

EXECUTIVE

SECTION 1. The executive department shall consist of governor, secretary of state, State auditor, State treasurer, attorney-general, and superintendent of public instruction, each of whom shall hold his office for four years, beginning on the first Monday of January next after his election, except that the terms of office of those elected at the first election shall begin when the State shall be admitted into the Union, and shall end on the first Monday in January, A. D. 1901. The officers of the executive department, during their terms of office, shall reside at the seat of government, where they shall keep the public records, books, and papers. They shall perform such duties as are prescribed by this constitution and as may be prescribed by law.

SEC. 2. The officers provided for in section one of this article shall be elected by the qualified electors of the State at the time and place of voting for members of the legislature, and the persons respectively having the highest number of votes cast for the office voted for shall be elected; but if two or more shall have an equal and highest number of votes for any one of said offices, the two houses of the legislature, at its next regular session, shall elect forthwith by joint ballot one of such persons for said office.

SEC. 3. No person shall be eligible to the office of governor or secretary of state unless he shall have attained the age of thirty years at the time of his election, nor to the office of attorney-general unless he shall have attained the age of twenty-five years at the time of his election and have been admitted to practice in the supreme court of the Territory or of the State of Utah, nor unless he shall be in good standing at the bar at the time of his election. No person shall be eligible to any of the offices provided for in section one of this article unless at the time of his election he shall be a qualified elector and shall have been a resident citizen of the State or Territory for five years next preceding his election. The State auditor and State treasurer shall be ineligible to election as their own successors.

SEC. 4. The governor shall be commander in chief of the military forces of the State, except when they shall be called into the service of the United States. He shall have the power to call out the militia to execute the laws, to suppress insurrection, or to repel invasion.

SEC. 5. The governor shall see that the laws are faithfully executed; he shall transact all executive business with the officers of the government, civil and military, and may require information in writing from the officers of the executive department, and from the officers and managers of State institutions upon any subject relating to the condition, management, and expenses of their respective offices and institutions, and at any time when the legislative assembly is not in session may, if he deem it necessary, appoint a committee to investigate and report to him upon the condition of any executive office or State institution. He shall communicate by message the condition of the State to the legislature at every regular session, and recommend such measures as he may deem expedient.

SEC. 6. On extraordinary occasions the governor may convene the legislature by proclamation, in which shall be stated the purpose for which the legislature is to be convened, and it shall transact no legislative business except that for which it was especially convened, or such other legislative business as the governor may call to its attention while in sesion. The legislature, however, may provide for the expenses of the session and other matters incidental thereto. The governor may also by proclamation convene the senate in extraordinary session for the transaction of executive business.

SEC. 7. In case of a disagreement between the two houses of the legislature at any special session with respect to the time of adjournment, the governor shall have power to adjourn the legislature to such time as he may think proper: *Provided*, That it be not beyond the time fixed for the convening of the next legislature.

SEC. 8. Every bill passed by the legislature, before it becomes a law, shall be presented to the governor. If he approve, he shall sign it, and thereupon it shall become a law; but if he do not approve, he shall return it with his objections to the house in which it originated, which house shall enter the objections at large upon its journal and proceed to reconsider the bill. If, after such reconsideration, it again passes both houses by a yea-and-nay vote of two-thirds of the members elected to each house, it shall become a law, notwithstanding the governor's objections. If any bill be not returned within five days after it shall have been presented to him (Sunday and the day on which he received it excepted), the same shall be a law in like manner as if he had signed it, unless the legislature by its final adjournment prevent such return, in which case it shall be filed with his objections in the office of the Secretary of State within ten days after such adjournment (Sundays excepted) or become a law. If any bill presented to the governor contains several items of appropriations of money, he may object to one or more such items while approving other portions of the bill.   In such case he shall append to the bill at the time of signing it a statement of the item or items which he declines to approve, together with his reasons therefor, and such item or items shall not take effect unless passed over the governor's objection as in this section provided.

SEC. 9. When any State or district office shall become vacant and no mode is provided by the constitution and laws for filling such vacancy, the governor shall have the power to fill the same by granting a commission, which shall expire at the next election and upon qualification of the person elected to such office.

SEC. 10. The governor shall nominate, and by and with the consent of the senate appoint, all State and district officers whose offices are established by this constitution, or which may be created by law, and whose appointment or election is not otherwise provided for.   If, during the recess of the senate, a vacancy occur in any State or district office, the governor shall appoint some fit person to discharge the duties thereof until the next meeting of the Senate, when he shall nominate some person to fill such office.   If the office of justice of the supreme or district court, secretary of state, State auditor, State treasurer, attorney-general, or superintendent of public instruction be vacated by death, resignation, or otherwise it shall be the duty of the governor to fill the same by appointment, and the appointee shall hold his office until his successor shall be elected and qualified, as may be by law provided.

SEC. 11. In case of the death of the governor, or his impeachment, removal from office, inability to discharge the duties of his office, resignation, or absence from the State, the powers and duties of said office shall devolve upon the secretary of state until the disability shall cease, or until the next general election, when the vacancy shall befilled by election.   If, during a vacancy in the office of the governor, the secretary of state resign, die, or become incapable of performing the duties of the office, or be displaced, or be absent from the State, the president pro tempore of the senate shall act as governor until the vacancy be filled or the disability cease.   While performing the duties of the governor as in this section provided, the secretary of state or the president pro tempore of the senate, as the case may be, except in cases of temporary disability or absence from the State, shall be entitled to the salary and emoluments of the governor.

SEC. 12. Until otherwise provided by law, the governor, justices of the supreme court, and attorney-general shall constitute a board of pardons, a majority of whom, including the governor, upon such conditions and with such limitations and restrictions as they deem proper, may remit fines and forfeitures, commute punishments, and grant pardons after convictions in all cases except treason and impeachments, subject to such regulations as may be provided by law relative to the manner of applying for pardons; but no fine or forfeiture shall be remitted and no commutation or pardon granted except after a full hearing before the board, in open session, after previous notice of the time and place of such hearing has been given. The proceedings and decisions of the board, with the reasons therefor in each case, together with the dissent of any member who may disagree, shall be reduced to writing and filed, with all the papers used upon the hearing, in the office of the secretary of state.

The governor shall have power to grant respites or reprieves in all cases of convictions for offenses against the State, except treason or conviction on impeachment; but such respites or reprieves shall not extend beyond the next session of the board of pardons; and such board, at such session, shall continue or determine such respite or reprieve, or they may commute the punishment or pardon the offense as herein provided. In case of conviction for treason, the governor shall have the power to suspend execution of the sentence until the case shall be reported to the legislature at its next regular session, when the legislature shall either pardon or commute the sentence or direct its execution; he shall communicate to the legislature at each regular session each case of remission of fine or forfeiture, reprive, commutation, or pardon granted since the last previous report, stating the name of the convict, the crime for which he was convicted, the sentence and its date, the date of remission, commutation, pardon, or reprieve, with the reasons for granting the same, and the objections, if any, of any member of the board made thereto.

SEC. 13. Until otherwise provided by law, the governor, secretary of state, and attorney-general shall constitute a board of State prison commissioners, which board shall have such supervision of all matters connected with the State prison as may be provided by law. They shall also constitute a board of examiners, with power to examine all claims against the State except salaries or compensation of officers fixed by law, and perform such other duties as may be prescribed by law, and no other claim against the State, except for salaries and compensation of officers fixed by law, shall be passed upon by the legislature without having been considered and acted upon by the said board of examiners.

SEC. 14. Until otherwise provided by law, the governor, State treasurer, and state auditor shall constitute a board of insane asylum commissioners. Said board shall have such supervision of all matters connected with the State insane asylum as may be provided by law.

SEC. 15. Until otherwise provided by law, the governor, attorney-general, and superintendent of public instruction shall constitute a board of reform-school commissioners. Said board shall have such supervision of all matters connected with the State reform school as may be provided by law.

SEC. 16. The secretary of state shall keep a record of the official acts of the legislature and executive department of the State, and, when required, shall lay the same and all matters relative thereto before either branch of the legislature, and shall perform such other duties as may be provided by law.

SEC. 17. The auditor shall be auditor of public accounts, and the treasurer shall be the custodian of public moneys, and each shall perform such other duties as may be provided by law.

SEC. 18. The attorney-general shall be the legal adviser of the State officers, and shall perform such other duties as may be provided by law.

SEC. 19. The superintendent of public instruction shall perform such duties as may be provided by law.

SEC. 20. The governor, secretary of state, auditor, treasurer, attorney-general, superintendent of public instruction, and such other

State and district officers as may be provided for by law shall receive
for their services quarterly a compensation as fixed by law, which
shall not be diminished or increased so as to affect the salary of any
officer during his term, or the term next ensuing after the adoption
of this Constitution, unless a vacancy occur, in which case the successor of the former incumbent shall receive only such salary as may be
provided by law at the time of his election or appointment.   The
compensation of the officers provided for by this article, until otherwise provided by law, is fixed as follows:
    Governor, two thousand dollars per annum.
    Secretary of state, two thousand dollars per annum.
    State auditor, fifteen hundred dollars per annum.
    State treasurer, one thousand dollars per annum.
    Attorney-general, fifteen hundred dollars per annum.
    Superintendent of public instruction, fifteen hundred dollars per
annum.
    The compensation for said officers as prescribed in this section, and
in all laws enacted pursuant to this constitution, shall be in full for
all services rendered by said officers, respectively, in any official capacity or employment during their respective terms of office.   No
such officer shall receive for the performance of any official duty any
fee for his own use, but all fees fixed by law for the performance by
either of them of any official duty shall be collected in advance and
deposited with the State treasurer quarterly to the credit of the
State.   The legislature may provide for the payment of actual and
necessary expenses of said officers while traveling in the State in the
performance of official duty.
    SEC. 21. All grants and commissions shall be in the name and by
the authority of the State of Utah, sealed with the great seal of the
State, signed by the governor, and countersigned by the secretary of
state.
    SEC. 22. There shall be a seal of the State, which shall be kept by
the secretary of state, and used by him officially.   Said seal shall be
called "the great seal of the State of Utah."   The present seal of
the Territory of Utah shall be the seal of the State until otherwise
provided by law.
    SEC. 23. No person while holding any office under the United States
Government shall hold any office under the State government of
Utah, and the governor shall not be eligible for election to the Senate of the United States during the term for which he shall have
been elected governor.

ARTICLE VIII

JUDICIAL DEPARTMENT

    SECTION 1. The judicial power of the State shall be vested in the
senate sitting as a court of impeachment, in a supreme court, in district courts, in justices of the peace, and such other courts inferior
to the supreme court as may be established by law.
    SEC. 2. The supreme court shall consist of three judges; but after
the year A. D. 1905 the legislature may increase the number thereof
to five.   A majority of the judges constituting the court shall be
necessary to form a quorum or render a decision.   If a justice of the
supreme court shall be disqualified from sitting in a cause before said

court the remaining judges shall call a district judge to sit with them on the hearing of such cause. The judges of the supreme court shall be elected by the electors of the State at large. The term of office of the judges of the supreme court, excepting as in this article otherwise provided, shall be six years. The judges of the supreme court, immediately after the first election under this constitution, shall be selected by lot, so that one shall hold office for the term of three years, one for the term of five years, and one for the term of seven years. The lots shall be drawn by the judges of the supreme court, who, for that purpose, shall assemble at the seat of government; and they shall cause the result thereof to be certified by the secretary of state, and filed in his office. The judge having the shortest term to serve, not holding his office by appointment or election to fill a vacancy, shall be the chief justice and shall preside at all terms of the supreme court, and in case of his absence the judge having, in like manner, the next shortest term shall preside in his stead.

SEC. 3. Every judge of the supreme court shall be at least thirty years of age, and before his election shall be a member of the bar, learned in the law, and a resident of the Territory or State of Utah for five years next preceding his election.

SEC. 4. The supreme court shall have original jurisdiction to issue writs of mandamus, certiorari, prohibition, quo warranto, and habeas corpus. Each of the justices shall have power to issue writs of habeas corpus, to any part of the State, upon petition by or on behalf of any person held in actual custody, and may make such writs returnable before himself or the supreme court, or before any district court or judge thereof in the State. In other cases the supreme court shall have appellate jurisdiction only, and power to issue writs necessary and proper for the exercise of that jurisdiction. The supreme court shall hold at least three terms every year, and shall sit at the capital of the State.

SEC. 5. The State shall be divided into seven judicial districts, for each of which at least one, and not exceeding three, judges shall be chosen by the qualified electors thereof. The term of office of the district judges shall be four years, except that the district judges elected at the first election shall serve until the first Monday in January, A. D. 1901, and until their successors shall have qualified. Until otherwise provided by law a district court at the county seat of each county shall be held at least four times a year. All civil and criminal business arising in any county must be tried in such county, unless a change of venue be taken in such cases as may be provided by law. Each judge of the district court shall be at least twenty-five years of age, a member of the bar, learned in the law, a resident of the Territory or State of Utah three years next preceding his election, and shall reside in the district for which he shall be elected. Any district judge may hold a district court in any county at the request of the judge of the district, and upon a request of the governor it shall be his duty to do so. Any cause in the district court may be tried by a judge pro tempore, who must be a member of the bar, sworn to try the cause, and agreed upon by the parties or their attorneys of record.

SEC. 6. The legislature may change the limits of any judicial district, or increase or decrease the number of districts, or the judges thereof. No alteration or increase shall have the effect of removing a judge from office. In every additional district established a judge shall be elected by the electors thereof, and his term of office shall continue as provided in section five of this article.

SEC. 7. The district court shall have original jurisdiction in all matters civil and criminal not excepted in this constitution and not prohibited by law, appellate jurisdiction from all inferior courts and tribunals, and a supervisory control of the same. The district courts or any judge thereof shall have power to issue writs of habeas corpus, mandamus, injunction, quo warranto, certiorari, prohibition, and other writs necessary to carry into effect their orders, judgments, and decrees, and to give them a general control over inferior courts and tribunals within their respective jurisdictions.

SEC. 8. The legislature shall determine the number of justices of the peace to be elected, and shall fix by law their powers, duties, and compensation. The jurisdiction of justices of the peace shall be as now provided by law, but the legislature may restrict the same.

SEC. 9. From all final judgments of the district courts there shall be a right of appeal to the supreme court. The appeal shall be upon the record made in the court below, and under such regulations as may be provided by law. In equity cases the appeal may be on questions of both law and fact; in cases at law the appeal shall be on questions of law alone. Appeals shall also lie from the final orders and decrees of the court in the administration of decedent estates, and in cases of guardianship, as shall be provided by law. Appeals shall also lie from the final judgment of justices of the peace in civil and criminal cases to the district courts on both questions of law and fact, with such limitations and restrictions as shall be provided by law; and the decision of the district courts on such appeals shall be final, except in cases involving the validity or constitutionality of a statute.

SEC. 10. A county attorney shall be elected by the qualified voters of each county, who shall hold his office for a term of two years. The powers and duties of county attorneys, and such other attorneys for the State as the legislature may provide, shall be prescribed by law. In all cases where the attorney for any county or for the State fails or refuses to attend and prosecute according to law the court shall have power to appoint an attorney pro tempore.

SEC. 11. Judges may be removed from office by the concurrent vote of both houses of the legislature, each voting separately; but two-thirds of the members to which each house may be entitled must concur in such vote. The vote shall be determined by yeas and nays, and the names of the members voting for or against a judge, together with the cause or causes of removal, shall be entered on the journal of each house. The judge against whom the house may be about to proceed shall receive notice thereof, accompanied with a copy of the cause alleged for his removal, at least ten days before the day on which either house of the legislature shall act thereon.

SEC. 12. The judges of the supreme and district courts shall receive at stated times compensation for their services, which shall not be increased or diminished during the time for which they are elected.

SEC. 13. Except by consent of all the parties, no judge of the supreme or inferior courts shall preside in the trial of any cause where either of the parties shall be connected with him by affinity or consanguinity within the degree of first cousin, or in which he may have been of counsel, or in the trial of which he may have presided in any inferior court.

SEC. 14. The supreme court shall appoint a clerk and a reporter of its decisions, who shall hold their offices during the pleasure of the court. Until otherwise provided county clerks shall be ex officio clerks of the district courts in and for their respective counties, and shall perform such other duties as may be provided by law.

SEC. 15. No person related to any judge of any court by affinity or consanguinity within the degree of first cousin shall be appointed by such court or judge to or employed by such court or judge in any office or duty in any court of which such judge may be a member.

SEC. 16. Until otherwise provided by law, the judicial districts of the State shall be constituted as follows:

First district.—The counties of Cache, Boxelder, and Rich.

Second district.—The counties of Weber, Morgan, and Davis.

Third district.—The counties of Summit, Salt Lake, and Tooele, in which there shall be elected three district judges.

Fourth district.—The counties of Utah, Wasatch, and Uinta.

Fifth district.—The counties of Juab, Millard, Beaver, Iron, and Washington.

Sixth district.—The counties of Sevier, Piute, Wayne, Garfield, and Kane.

Seventh district.—The counties of Sanpete, Carbon, Emery, Grand, and San Juan.

SEC. 17. The supreme and district courts shall be courts of record, and each shall have a seal.

SEC. 18. The style of all process shall be " The State of Utah," and all prosecutions shall be conducted in the name and by the authority of the same.

SEC. 19. There shall be but one form of civil action, and law and equity may be administered in the same action.

SEC. 20. Until otherwise provided by law, salaries of supreme and district judges shall be three thousand dollars per annum and mileage, payable quarterly out of the State treasury.

SEC. 21. Judges of the supreme court, district court, and justices of the peace shall be conservators of the peace, and may hold preliminary examinations in cases of felony.

SEC. 22. District judges may at any time report defects and omissions in the law to the supreme court, and the supreme court, on or before the first day of December of each year, shall report in writing to the governor any seeming defect or omission in the law.

SEC. 23. The legislature may provide for the publication of decisions and opinions of the supreme court, but all decisions shall be free to publishers.

SEC. 24. The terms of office of supreme and district judges may be extended by law, but such extension shall not affect the term for which any judge was elected.

SEC. 25. When a judgment or decree is reversed, modified, or affirmed by the supreme court the reasons therefor shall be stated concisely in writing, signed by the judges concurring, filed in the office of the clerk of the supreme court, and preserved with a record of the case. Any judge dissenting therefrom may give the reasons of his dissent in writing over his signature.

SEC. 26. It shall be the duty of the court to prepare a syllabus of all the points adjudicated in each case, which shall be concurred in by a majority of the judges thereof, and it shall be prefixed to the published reports of the case.

SEC. 27. Any judicial officer who shall absent himself from the State or district for more than ninety consecutive days shall be deemed to have forfeited his office: *Provided*, That in case of extreme necessity the governor may extend the leave of absence to such time as the necessity therefor shall exist.

ARTICLE IX

CONGRESSIONAL AND LEGISLATIVE APPORTIONMENT

SECTION 1. One representative in the Congress of the United States shall be elected from the State at large on the Tuesday next after the first Monday in November, A. D. 1895, and thereafter at such times and places and in such manner as may be prescribed by law. When a new apportionment shall be made by Congress, the legislature shall divide the State into Congressional districts accordingly.

SEC. 2. The legislature shall provide by law for an enumeration of the inhabitants of the State A. D. 1905, and every tenth year thereafter, and at the session next following such enumeration, and also at the session next following an enumeration made by the authority of the United States, shall revise and adjust the apportionment for senators and representatives on the basis of such enumeration, according to ratios to be fixed by law.

SEC. 3. The senate shall consist of eighteen members and the house of representatives of forty-five members. The legislature may increase the number of senators and representatives, but the senators shall never exceed thirty in number, and the number of representatives shall never be less than twice nor greater than three times the number of senators.

SEC. 4. When more than one county shall constitute a senatorial district, such counties shall be contiguous, and no county shall be divided in the formation of such districts unless such county contains sufficient population within itself to form two or more districts, nor shall a part of any county be united with any other county in forming any district.

REPRESENTATIVE DISTRICTS

Until otherwise provided by law, representatives shall be apportioned among the several counties of the State as follows: *Provided*, That in any future apportionment made by the legislature each county shall be entitled to at least one representative:

The county of Boxelder shall constitute the first representative district, and be entitled to one representative.

The county of Cache shall constitute the second representative district, and be entitled to three representatives.

The county of Rich shall constitute the third representative district, and be entitled to one representative.

The county of Weber shall constitute the fourth representative district, and be entitled to four representatives.

The county of Morgan shall constitute the fifth representative district, and be entitled to one representative.

The county of Davis shall constitute the sixth representative district, and be entitled to one representative.

The county of Tooele shall constitute the seventh representative district, and be entitled to one representative.

The county of Salt Lake shall constitute the eighth representative district, and be entitled to ten representatives.

The county of Summit shall constitute the ninth representative district, and be entitled to one representative.

The county of Wasatch shall constitute the tenth representative district, and be entitled to one representative.

The county of Utah shall constitute the eleventh representative district, and be entitled to four representatives.

The county of Uinta shall constitute the twelfth representative district, and be entitled to one representative.

The county of Juab shall constitute the thirteenth representative district, and be entitled to one representative.

The county of Sanpete shall constitute the fourteenth representative district, and be entitled to two representatives.

The county of Carbon shall constitute the fifteenth representative district, and be entitled to one representative.

The county of Emery shall constitute the sixteenth representative district, and be entitled to one representative.

The county of Grand shall constitute the seventeenth representative district, and be entitled to one representative.

The county of Sevier shall constitute the eighteenth representative district, and be entitled to one representative.

The county of Millard shall constitute the nineteenth representative district, and be entitled to one representative.

The county of Beaver shall constitute the twentieth representative district, and be entitled to one representative.

The county of Piute shall constitute the twenty-first representative disrtict, and be entitled to one representative.

The county of Wayne shall constitute the twenty-second represetative district, and be entitled to one representative.

The county of Garfield shall constitute the twenty-third representative district, and be entitled to one representative.

The county of Iron shall constitute the twenty-fourth representative district, and be entitled to one representative.

The county of Washington shall constitute the twenty-fifth representative district, and be entitled to one representative.

The county of Kane shall constitute the twenty-sixth representative district, and be entitled to one representative.

The county of San Juan shall constitute the twenty-seventh representative district, and be entitled to one representative.

SENATORIAL DISTRICTS

Until otherwise provided by law, the senatorial districts shall be constituted and numbered as follows

The counties of Boxelder and Tooele shall constitute the first district, and be entitled to one senator.

The county of Cache shall constitute the second district, and be entitled to one senator.

The counties of Rich, Morgan, and Davis shall constitute the third district, and be entitled to one senator.

The county of Weber shall constitute the fourth district, and be entitled to two senators.

The counties of Summit and Wasatch shall constitute the fifth district, and be entitled to one senator.

The county of Salt Lake shall constitute the sixth district, and be entitled to five senators.

The county of Utah shall constitute the seventh district, and be entitled to two senators.

The counties of Juab and Millard shall constitute the eighth district, and be entitled to one senator.

The county of Sanpete shall constitute the ninth district, and be entitled to one senator.

The counties of Sevier, Wayne, Piute, and Garfield shall constitute the tenth district, and be entitled to one senator.

The counties of Beaver, Iron, Washington, and Kane shall constitute the eleventh district, and be entitled to one senator.

The counties of Emery, Carbon, Uinta, Grand, and San Juan shall constitute the twelfth district, and be entitled to one senator.

ARTICLE X

EDUCATION

SECTION 1. The legislature shall provide for the establishment and maintenance of a uniform system of public schools, which shall be open to all the children of the State and free from sectarian control.

a SEC. 2. The public school system shall include kindergarten schools; common schools, consisting of primary and grammar grades; high schools, an agricultural college, a university, and such other schools as the legislature may establish. The common school shall be free. The other departments of the system shall be supported as provided by law: *Provided*, That high schools may be maintained free in all cities of the first and second class now constituting school districts, and in such other cities and districts as may be designated by the legislature. But where the proportion of school moneys apportioned or accruing to any city or district shall not be sufficient to maintain all the free schools in such city or district, the high schools shall be supported by local taxation.

SEC. 3. The proceeds of all lands that have been or may be granted by the United States to this State for the support of the common schools, the proceeds of all property that may accrue to the State by escheat or forfeiture, and all unclaimed shares and dividends of any corporation incorporated under the laws of this State, the proceeds of the sale of timber, minerals, or other property from school and State lands other than those granted for specific purposes, and the five per centum of the net proceeds of the sales of public lands lying within the State, which shall be sold by the United States subsequent to the admission of this State into the Union, shall be and remain a perpetual fund, to be called the State school fund; the interest of which only, together with such other means as the legislature may provide, shall be distributed among the several school districts according to the school population residing therein.

---

a See amendment.

Sec. 4. The location and establishment by existing laws of the University of Utah and Agricultural College are hereby confirmed, and all the rights, immunities, franchises, and endowments heretofore granted or conferred are hereby perpetuated unto said university and agricultural college, respectively.

Sec. 5. The proceeds of the sale of lands reserved by an act of Congress approved February 21, 1855, for the establishment of the University of Utah, and all the lands granted by an act of Congress approved July 16, 1894, shall constitute permanent funds, to be safely invested and held by the State; and the income thereof shall be used exclusively for the support and maintenance of the different institutions and colleges, respectively, in accordance with the requirements and conditions of said acts of Congress.

a Sec. 6. In cities of the first and second class the public school system shall be maintained and controlled by the board of education of such cities, separate and apart from the counties in which said cities are located.

Sec. 7. All public school funds shall be guaranteed by the State against loss or diversion.

Sec. 8. The general control and supervision of the public school system shall be vested in a State board of education, consisting of the superintendent of public instruction and such other persons as the legislature may provide.

Sec. 9. Neither the legislature nor the State board of education shall have power to prescribe text-books to be used in the common schools.

Sec. 10. Institutions for the deaf and dumb and for the blind are hereby established. All property belonging to the school for the deaf and dumb, heretofore connected with the University of Utah, shall be transferred to said institution for the deaf and dumb. All the proceeds of the lands granted by the United States for the support of a deaf and dumb asylum and for an institution for the blind shall be a perpetual fund for the maintenance of said institutions. It shall be a trust fund, the principal of which shall remain inviolate, guaranteed by the State against loss or diversion.

Sec. 11. The metric system shall be taught in the public schools of the State.

Sec. 12. Neither religious nor partisan test or qualification shall be required of any person as a condition of admission, as teacher or student, into any public educational institution of the State.

Sec. 13. Neither the legislature nor any county, city, town, school district, or other public corporation shall make any appropriation to aid in the support of any school, seminary, academy, college, university, or other institution controlled in whole or in part by any church, sect, or denomination whatever.

Article XI

COUNTIES, CITIES, AND TOWNS

Section 1. The several counties of the Territory of Utah existing at the time of the adoption of this constitution are hereby recognized as legal subdivisions of this State, and the precincts and school dis-

---

a See amendment, adopted November 6, 1900.

tricts now existing in the said counties as legal subdivisions thereof, and they shall so continue until changed by law in pursuance of this article.

SEC. 2. No county seat shall be removed unless two-thirds of the qualified electors of the county, voting on the proposition at a general election, shall vote in favor of such removal, and two-thirds of the votes cast on the proposition shall be required to relocate a county seat. A proposition of removal shall not be submitted in the same county more than once in four years.

SEC. 3. No territory shall be stricken from any county unless a majority of the voters living in such territory, as well as of the county to which it is to be annexed, shall vote therefor, and then only under such conditions as may be prescribed by general law.

SEC. 4. The legislature shall establish a system of county government, which shall be uniform throughout the State, and by general laws shall provide for precinct and township organizations.

SEC. 5. Corporations for municipal purposes shall not be created by special laws; the legislature, by general laws, shall provide for the incorporation, organization, and classification of cities and towns in proportion to population; which laws may be altered, amended, or repealed.

SEC. 6. No municipal corporation shall directly or indirectly lease, sell, alien, or dispose of any waterworks, water rights, or sources of water supply now or hereafter to be owned or controlled by it, but all such waterworks, water rights, and sources of water supply now owned or hereafter to be acquired by any municipal corporation shall be preserved, maintained, and operated by it for supplying its inhabitants with water at reasonable charges: *Provided*, That nothing herein contained shall be construed to prevent any such municipal corporation from exchanging water rights or sources of water supply for other water rights or sources of water supply of equal value, and to be devoted in like manner to the public supply of its inhabitants.

ARTICLE XII

CORPORATIONS

SECTION 1. Corporations may be formed under general laws, but shall not be created by special acts. All laws relating to corporations may be altered, amended, or repealed by the legislature, and all corporations doing business in this State may, as to such business, be regulated, limited, or restrained by law.

SEC. 2. All existing charters, franchises, special or exclusive privileges under which an actual and bona fide organization shall not have taken place and business been commenced in good faith at the time of the adoption of this constitution shall thereafter have no validity; and no corporation in existence at the time of the adoption of this constitution shall have the benefit of future legislation without first filing in the office of the secretary of state an acceptance of the provisions of this constitution.

SEC. 3. The legislature shall not extend any franchise or charter, nor remit the forfeiture of any franchise or charter of any corporation now existing or which shall hereafter exist under the laws of this State.

SEC. 4. The term "corporation," as used in this article, shall be construed to include all associations and joint stock companies having any powers or privileges of corporations not possessed by individuals or partnerships, and all corporations shall have the right to sue, and shall be subject to be sued, in all courts in like cases as natural persons.

SEC. 5. Corporations shall not issue stock except to bona fide subscribers thereof or their assignee, nor shall any corporation issue any bond or other obligation for the payment of money except for money or property received or labor done. The stock of corporations shall not be increased except in pursuance of general law, nor shall any law authorize the increase of stock without the consent of the person or persons holding the larger amount in value of the stock, or without due notice of the proposed increase having previously been given in such manner as may be prescribed by law. All fictitious increase of stock or indebtedness shall be void.

SEC. 6. No corporations organized outside of this State shall be allowed to transact business within the State on conditions more favorable than those prescribed by law to similar corporations organized under the laws of this State.

SEC. 7. No corporation shall lease or alienate any franchise so as to relieve the franchise or property held thereunder from the liabilities of the lessor or grantor, lessee or grantee, contracted or incurred in operation, use, or enjoyment of such franchise or any of its privileges.

SEC. 8. No law shall be passed granting the right to construct and operate a street railroad, telegraph, telephone, or electric-light plant within any city or incorporated town without the consent of the local authorities who have the control of the street or highway proposed to be occupied for such purposes.

SEC. 9. No corporation shall do business in this State without having one or more places of business, with an authorized agent or agents upon whom process may be served, nor without first filing a certified copy of its articles of incorporation with the secretary of state.

SEC. 10. No corporation shall engage in any business other than that expressly authorized in its charter or articles of incorporation.

SEC. 11. The exercise of the right of eminent domain shall never be so abridged or construed as to prevent the legislature from taking the property and franchises of incorporated companies and subjecting them to public use the same as the property of individuals.

SEC. 12. All railroad and other transportation companies are declared to be common carriers and subject to legislative control, and such companies shall receive and transport each other's passengers and freight without discrimination or unnecessary delay.

SEC. 13. No railroad corporation shall consolidate its stock, property, or franchises with any other railroad corporation owning a competing line.

SEC. 14. The rolling stock and other movable property belonging to any railroad company or corporation in this State shall be considered personal property, and shall be liable to taxation and to execution and sale in the same manner as the personal property of individuals, and such property shall not be exempted from execution and sale.

Sec. 15. The legislature shall pass laws establishing reasonable maximum rates of charges for the transportation of passengers and freight, for correcting abuses, and preventing discrimination and extortion in rates of freight and passenger tariffs by the different railroads and other common carriers in the State, and shall enforce such laws by adequate penalties.

Sec. 16. No corporation or association shall bring any armed person or bodies of men into this State for the preservation of the peace or the suppression of domestic troubles without authority of law.

Sec. 17. No officer, employee, attorney, or agent of any corporation, company, or association doing business under or by virtue of any municipal charter or franchise shall be eligible to or permitted to hold any municipal office in the municipality granting such charter or franchise.

Sec. 18. The stockholders in every corporation and joint stock association for banking purposes, in addition to the amount of capital stock subscribed and fully paid by them, shall be individually responsible for an additional amount equal to the amount of their stock in such corporation for all its debts and liabilities of every kind.

Sec. 19. Every person in this State shall be free to obtain employment whenever possible; and any person, corporation, or agent, servant, or employee thereof, maliciously interfering or hindering in any way any person from obtaining or enjoying employment already obtained from any other corporation or person shall be deemed guilty of a crime. The legislature shall provide by law for the enforcement of this section.

Sec. 20. Any combination by individuals, corporations, or associations having for its object or effect the controlling of the price of any products of the soil, or of any article of manufacture or commerce, or the cost of exchange or transportation, is prohibited and hereby declared unlawful and against public policy. The legislature shall pass laws for the enforcement of this section by adequate penalties, and, in case of incorporated companies, if necessary may declare a forfeiture of their franchise.

Article XIII

REVENUE AND TAXATION

Section 1. The fiscal year shall begin on the first day of January, unless changed by the legislature.

Sec. 2. All property in the State, not exempt under the laws of the United States or under this constitution, shall be taxed in proportion to its value, to be ascertained as provided by law. The word property, as used in this article, is hereby declared to include moneys, credits, bonds, stocks, franchises, and all matters and things (real, personal, and mixed) capable of private ownership; but this shall not be so construed as to authorize the taxation of the stocks of any company or corporation when the property of such company or corporation represented by such stocks has been taxed. The legislature shall provide by law for an annual tax sufficient, with other sources of revenue, to defray the estimated ordinary expenses of the State for each fiscal year. For the purpose of paying the State debt, if any there be, the legislature shall provide for levying a tax annually sufficient to pay the annual interest and principal of such debt within twenty years from the final passage of the law creating the debt.

^a SEC. 3. The legislature shall provide by law a uniform and equal rate of assessment and taxation on all property in the State according to its value in money, and shall prescribe by general law such regulations as shall secure a just valuation for taxation of all property; so that every person and corporation shall pay a tax in proportion to the value of his, her, or its property: *Provided*, That a deduction of debts from credits may be authorized: *Provided further*, That the property of the United States, of the State, counties, cities, towns, school districts, municipal corporations, and public libraries, lots with the buildings thereon used exclusively for either religious worship or charitable purposes, and places of burial not held or used for private or corporate benefit shall be exempt from taxation. Ditches, canals, and flumes owned and used by individuals or corporations for irrigating lands owned by such individuals or corporations, or the individual members thereof, shall not be separately taxed so long as they shall be owned and used exclusively for such purpose.

SEC. 4. All mines and mining claims, both placer and rock in place, containing or bearing gold, silver, copper, lead, coal, or other valuable mineral deposits, after purchase thereof from the United States, shall be taxed at the price paid the United States therefor, unless the surface ground, or some part thereof, of such mine or claim is used for other than mining purposes, and has a separate and independent value for such other purposes; in which case said surface ground, or any part thereof, so used for other than mining purposes shall be taxed at its value for such other purposes, as provided by law; and all the machinery used in mining, and all property and surface improvements upon or appurtenant to mines and mining claims, which have a value separate and independent of such mines or mining claims, and the net annual proceeds of all mines and mining claims, shall be taxed as provided by law.

SEC. 5. The legislature shall not impose taxes for the purpose of any county, city,. town, or other municipal corporation, but may by law vest in the corporate authorities thereof, respectively, the power to assess and collect taxes for all purposes of such corporation.

SEC. 6. An accurate statement of the receipts and expenditures of the public moneys shall be published annually in such manner as the legislature may provide.

SEC. 7. The rate of taxation on property for State purposes shall never exceed eight mills on each dollar of valuation; and whenever the taxable property within the State shall amount to two hundred million dollars the rate shall not exceed five mills on each dollar of valuation, and whenever the taxable property within the State shall amount to three hundred million dollars the rate shall never thereafter exceed four mills on each dollar of valuation; unless a proposition to increase such rate, specifying the rate proposed and the time during which the same shall be levied, be first submitted to a vote of such of the qualified electors of the State as, in the year next preceding such election, shall have paid a property tax assessed to them within the State, and the majority of those voting thereon shall vote in favor thereof, in such manner as may be provided by law.

---

^a See amendment, November 6, 1900.

SEC. 8. The making of profit out of public moneys, or using the same for any purpose not authorized by law, by any public officer shall be deemed a felony, and shall be punished as provided by law, but part of such punishment shall be disqualification to hold public office.

SEC. 9. No appropriation shall be made or any expenditure authorized by the legislature whereby the expenditure of the State during any fiscal year shall exceed the total tax then provided for by law and applicable for such appropriation or expenditure, unless the legislature making such appropriation shall provide for levying a sufficient tax, not exceeding the rates allowed in section seven of this article, to pay such appropriation or expenditure within such fiscal year. This provision shall not apply to appropriations or expenditures to suppress insurrections, defend the State, or assist in defending the United States in time of war.

SEC. 10. All corporations or persons in this State, or doing business herein, shall be subject to taxation for State, county, school, municipal, or other purposes on the real and personal property owned or used by them within the territorial limits of the authority levying the tax.

SEC. 11. Until otherwise provided by law, there shall be a State board of equalization, consisting of the governor, State auditor, State treasurer, secretary of state, and attorney-general; also, in each county of this State, a county board of equalization, consisting of the board of county commissioners of said county. The duty of the State board of equalization shall be to adjust and equalize the valuation of the real and personal property among the several counties of the State. The duty of the county board of equalization shall be to adjust and equalize the valuation of the real and personal property within their respective counties. Each board shall also perform such other duties as may be prescribed by law.

SEC. 12. Nothing in this constitution shall be construed to prevent the legislature from providing a stamp tax, or a tax based on income, occupation, licenses, franchises, or mortgages.

ARTICLE XIV

PUBLIC DEBT

SECTION. 1. To meet casual deficits or failures in revenue, and for necessary expenditures for public purposes, including the erection of public buildings and for the payment of all Territorial indebtedness assumed by the State, the State may contract debts, not exceeding in the aggregate at any one time the sum of two hundred thousand dollars over and above the amount of the Territorial indebtedness assumed by the State. But when the said Territorial indebtedness shall have been paid the State shall never contract any indebtedness, except as in the next section provided, in excess of the sum of two hundred thousand dollars, and all moneys arising from loans herein authorized shall be applied solely to the purposes for which they were obtained.

SEC. 2. The State may contract debts to repel invasion, suppress insurrection, or to defend the State in war, but the money arising from the contracting of such debts shall be applied solely to the purpose for which it was obtained.

Sec. 3. No debt in excess of the taxes for the current year shall be created by any county or subdivison thereof, or by any school district therein, or by any city, town, or village, or any subdivision thereof in this State, unless the proposition to create such debt shall have been submitted to a vote of such qualified electors as shall have paid a property tax therein in the year preceding such election, and a majority of those voting thereon shall have voted in favor of incudding such debt.

Sec. 4. When authorized to create indebtedness as provided in section three of this article, no county shall become indebted to an amount, including existing indebtedness, exceeding two per centum. No city, town, school district, or other municipal corporation shall become indebted to an amount, including existing indebtedness, exceeding four per centum of the value of the taxable property therein, the value to be ascertained by the last assessment for State and county purposes previous to the incurring of such indebtedness; except that in incorporated cities the assessment shall be taken from the last assessment for city purposes: *Provided*, That no part of the indebtedness allowed in this section shall be incurred for other than strictly county, city, town, or school district purposes: *Provided further*, That any city or town, when authorized as provided in section three of this article, may be allowed to incur a larger indebtedness, not exceeding four per centum additional for supplying, such city or town with water, artificial light, or sewers, when the works for supplying such water, light, and sewers shall be owned and controlled by the municipality.

Sec. 5. All moneys borrowed by or on behalf of the State, or any legal subdivision thereof, shall be used solely for the purposes specified in the law authorizing the loan.

Sec. 6. The State shall not assume the debt, or any part thereof, of any county, city, town, or school district.

Sec. 7. Nothing in this article shall be so construed as to impair or add to the obligation of any debt heretofore contracted, in accordance with the laws of Utah Territory, by any county, city, town, or school district, or to prevent the contracting of any debt, or the issuing of bonds therefor, in accordance with said laws, upon any proposition for that purpose which, according to said laws, may have been submitted to a vote of the qualified electors of any county, city, town, or school district before the day on which this constitution takes effect.

Article XV

MILITIA

Section 1. The militia shall consist of all able-bodied male inhabitants of the State between the ages of eighteen and forty-five years, except such as are exempt by law.

Sec. 2. The legislature shall provide by law for the organization, equipment, and discipline of the militia, which shall conform as nearly as practicable to the regulations for the government of the Armies of the United States.

Article XVI

LABOR

Section 1. The rights of labor shall have just protection through laws calculated to promote the industrial welfare of the State.

Sec. 2. The legislature shall provide by law for a board of labor, conciliation, and arbitration, which shall fairly represent the interests of both capital and labor. The board shall perform duties and receive compensation as prescribed by law.

Sec. 3. The legislature shall prohibit:

First. The employment of women or of children under the age of fourteen years in underground mines.

Second. The contracting of convict labor.

Third. The labor of convicts outside prison grounds, except on public works under the direct control of the State.

Fourth. The political and commercial control of employees.

Sec. 4. The exchange of black lists by railroad companies or other corporations, associations, or persons is prohibited.

Sec. 5. The right of action to recover damages for injuries resulting in death shall never be abrogated, and the amount recoverable shall not be subject to any statutory limitation.

Sec. 6. Eight hours shall constitute a day's work on all works or undertakings carried on or aided by the State, county, or municipal governments, and the legislature shall pass laws to provide for the health and safety of employees in factories, smelters, and mines.

Sec. 7. The legislature, by appropriate legislation, shall provide for the enforcement of the provisions of this article.

Article XVII

WATER RIGHTS

Section 1. All existing rights to the use of any of the waters in this State for any useful or beneficial purpose are hereby recognized and confirmed.

Article XVIII

FORESTRY

Section 1. The legislature shall enact laws to prevent the destruction of and to preserve the forests on the lands of the State and upon any part of the public domain the control of which may be conferred by Congress upon the State.

Article XIX

PUBLIC BUILDINGS AND STATE INSTITUTIONS

Section 1. All institutions and other property of the Territory upon the adoption of this constitution shall become the institutions and property of the State of Utah.

Sec. 2. Reformatory and penal institutions, and those for the benefit of the insane, blind, deaf and dumb, and such other institutions as the public good may require, shall be established and supported by the State in such manner and under such boards of control as may be prescribed by law.

Sec. 3. The public institutions of the State are hereby permanently located at the places hereinafter named, each to have the lands specifically granted to it by the United States in the act of Congress approved July 16, 1894, to be disposed of and used in such manner as the legislature may provide:

First. The seat of government and the State fair, at Salt Lake City, and the State prison in the county of Salt Lake.

Second. The institutions for the deaf and dumb and the blind and the State reform school, at Ogden City, in the county of Weber.

Third. The State insane asylum, at Provo City, in the county of Utah.

Article XX

PUBLIC LANDS

Section 1. All lands of the State that have been or may hereafter be granted to the State by Congress, and all lands acquired by gift, grant, or devise from any person or corporation, or that may otherwise be acquired, are hereby accepted and declared to be the public lands of the State, and shall be held in trust for the people, to be disposed of as may be provided by law, for the respective purposes for which they have been or may be granted, donated, devised, or otherwise acquired.

Article XXI

SALARIES

Section 1. All State, district, city, county, town, and school officers, excepting notaries public, boards of arbitration, court commissioners, justices of the peace, and constables, shall be paid fixed and definite salaries: *Provided,* That city justices may be paid by salary when so determined by the mayor and council of such cities.

Sec. 2. The legislature shall provide by law the fees which shall be collected by all officers within the State. Notaries public, boards of arbitration, court commissioners, justices of the peace, and constables paid by fees shall accept said fees as their full compensation. But all other State, district, county, city, town, and school officers shall be required by law to keep a true and correct account of all fees collected by them, and to pay the same into the proper treasury, and the officer whose duty it is to collect such fees shall be held responsible under his bond for the same.

Article XXII

MISCELLANEOUS

Section 1. The legislature shall provide by law for the selection by each head of a family an exemption of a homestead, which may consist of one or more parcels of land, together with the appurtenances and improvements thereon, of the value of at least fifteen hundred dollars, from sale on execution.

SEC. 2. Real and personal estate of every female acquired before marriage, and all property to which she may afterwards become entitled by purchase, gift, grant, inheritance, or devise, shall be and remain the estate and property of such female, and shall not be liable for the debts, obligations, or engagements of her husband, and may be conveyed, devised, or bequeathed by her as if she were unmarried.

ARTICLE XXIII

AMENDMENTS

SECTION 1. Any amendment or amendments to this constitution may be proposed in either house of the legislature, and if two-thirds of all the members elected to each of the two houses shall vote in favor thereof such proposed amendment or amendments shall be entered on their respective journals with the yeas and nays taken thereon; and the legislature shall cause the same to be published in at least one newspaper in every county of the State where a newspaper is published, for two months immediately preceding the next general election, at which time the said amendment or amendments shall be submitted to the electors of the State for their approval or rejection, and if a majority of the electors voting thereon shall approve the same, such amendment or amendments shall become part of this constitution. If two or more amendments are proposed, they shall be so submitted as to enable the electors to vote on each of them separately.

SEC. 2. Whenever two-thirds of the members elected to each branch of the legislature shall deem it necessary to call a convention to revise or amend this constitution, they shall recommend to the electors to vote at the next general election for or against a convention, and if a majority of all the electors voting at such election shall vote for a convention, the legislature at its next session shall provide by law for calling the same. The convention shall consist of not less than the number of members in both branches of the legislature.

SEC. 3. No constitution or amendments adopted by such convention shall have validity until submitted to and adopted by a majority of the electors of the State voting at the next general election.

ARTICLE XXIV

SCHEDULE

SECTION 1. In order that no inconvenience may arise by reason of the change from a Territorial to a State government, it is hereby declared that all writs, actions, prosecutions, judgments, claims, and contracts, as well of individuals as of bodies corporate, both public and private, shall continue as if no change had taken place; and all process which may issue under the authority of the Territory of Utah previous to its admission into the Union shall be as valid as if issued in the name of the State of Utah.

SEC. 2. All laws of the Territory of Utah now in force, not repugnant to this constitution, shall remain in force until they expire by their own limitations or are altered or repealed by the legislature. The act of the governor and legislative assembly of the Territory of Utah entitled "An act to punish polygamy and other kindred offenses," approved February 4, A. D. 1892, in so far as the same defines and imposes penalties for polygamy, is hereby declared to be in force in the State of Utah.

SEC. 3. Any person who, at the time of the admission of the State into the Union, may be confined under lawful commitments, or otherwise lawfully held to answer for alleged violations of any of the criminal laws of the Territory of Utah, shall continue to be so held or confined until discharged therefrom by the proper courts of the State.

SEC. 4. All fines, penalties, and forfeitures accruing to the Territory of Utah, or to the people of the United States in the Territory of Utah, shall inure to this State, and all debts, liabilities, and obligations of said Territory shall be valid against the State and enforced as may be provided by law.

SEC. 5. All recognizances heretofore taken, or which may be taken before the change from a Territorial to a State government, shall remain valid, and shall pass to and be prosecuted in the name of the State; and all bonds executed to the governor of the Territory, or to any other officer or court in his or their official capacity, or to any official board for the benefit of the Territory of Utah, or the people thereof, shall pass to the governor or other officer, court, or board, and his or their successors in office, for the uses therein respectively expressed, and may be sued on and recovered accordingly. Assessed taxes and all revenue, property—real, personal, or mixed—and all judgments, bonds, specialties, choses in action, claims, and debts of whatsoever description, and all records and public archives of the Territory of Utah, shall issue and vest in the State of Utah, and may be sued for and recovered in the same manner and to the same extent by the State of Utah as the same could have been by the Territory of Utah; and all fines, taxes, penalties, and forfeitures due or owing to any county, municipality, or school district therein at the time the State shall be admitted into the Union are hereby respectively assigned and transferred, and the same shall be payable to the county, municipality, or school district, as the case may be, and payment thereof be enforced under the laws of the State.

SEC. 6. All criminal prosecutions and penal actions which may have arisen or which may arise before the change from a Territorial to a State government, and which shall then be pending, shall be prosecuted to judgment and execution in the name of the State, and in the court having jurisdiction thereof. All offenses committed against the laws of the Territory of Utah before the change from a Territorial to a State government, and which shall not have been prosecuted before such change, may be prosecuted in the name and by the authority of the State of Utah, with like effect as though such change had not taken place, and all penalties incurred shall remain the same as if this constitution had not been adopted.

SEC. 7. All actions, cases, proceedings, and matters pending in the supreme and district courts of the Territory of Utah at the time the State shall be admitted into the Union, and all files, records, and indictments relating thereto, except as otherwise provided herein, shall be appropriately transferred to the supreme and district courts of the State, respectively; and thereafter all such actions, matters, and cases shall be proceeded with in the proper State courts. All actions, cases, proceedings, and matters which shall be pending in the district courts of the Territory of Utah at the time of the admission of the State into the Union whereof the United States circuit or district courts might have had jurisdiction had there been a State government at the time of the commencement thereof, respectively, shall be transferred to the proper United States circuit and district courts, respectively; and all files, records, indictments, and proceedings relating thereto shall be transferred to said United States courts: *Provided*, That no civil actions, other than causes and proceedings of which the said United States courts shall have exclusive jurisdiction, shall be transferred to either of said United States courts except upon motion or petition by one of the parties thereto, made under and in accordance with the act or acts of the Congress of the United States, and such motion and petition not being made, all such cases shall be proceeded with in the proper State courts.

SEC. 8. Upon a change from Territorial to State government, the seal in use by the supreme court of the Territory of Utah, until otherwise provided by law, shall pass to and become the seal of the supreme court of the State, and the several district courts of the State may adopt seals for their respective courts, until otherwise provided by law.

SEC. 9. When the State is admitted into the Union, and the district courts in the respective districts are organized, the books, records, papers, and proceedings of the probate court in each county, and all causes and matters of administration pending therein, upon the expiration of the term of office of the probate judge, on the second Monday in January, 1896, shall pass into the jurisdiction and possession of the district court, which shall proceed to final judgment or decree, order, or other determination in the several matters and causes as the Territorial probate court might have done if this constitution had not been adopted. And until the expiration of the term of office of the probate judges, such probate judges shall perform the duties now imposed upon them by the laws of the Territory. The district court shall have appellate and revisory jurisdiction over the decisions of the probate courts, as now provided by law, until such latter courts expire by limitation.

SEC. 10. All officers, civil and military, now holding their offices and appointments in this Territory by authority of law, shall continue to hold and exercise their respective offices and appointments until superseded under this constitution: *Provided*, That the provisions of this section shall be subject to the provisions of the act of Congress providing for the admission of the State of Utah, approved by the President of the United States on July 16, 1894.

SEC. 11. The election for the adoption or rejection of this constitution, and for State officers herein provided for, shall be held on the Tuesday next after the first Monday in November, 1895, and shall be conducted according to the laws of the Territory and the provisions of the enabling act; the votes cast at said election shall be canvassed and returns made in the same manner as was provided for in the election for delegates to the constitutional convention: *Provided*, That all male citizens of the United States over the age of twenty-one years, who have resided in the Territory for one year prior to such election, are hereby authorized to vote for or against the adoption of this constitution, and for the State officers herein provided for. The returns of said election shall be made to the Utah commission, who shall cause the same to be canvassed, and shall certify the result of the vote for or against the constitution to the President of the United States in the manner required by the enabling act; and said commission shall issue certificates of election to the persons elected to said offices severally, and shall make and file with the secretary of the Territory an abstract, certified to by them, of the number of votes cast for each person for each of said offices, and of the total number of votes cast in each county.

SEC. 12. The State officers to be voted for at the time of the adoption of this constitution shall be a governor, secretary of state, State auditor, State treasurer, attorney-general, superintendent of public instruction, members of the senate and house of representatives, three supreme judges, nine district judges, and a Representative to Congress.

SEC. 13. In case of a contest of election between candidates at the first general election under this constitution for judges of the district courts, the evidence shall be taken in the manner prescribed by the Territorial laws, and the testimony so taken shall be certified to the secretary of state, and said officer, together with the governor and the treasurer of the State, shall review the evidence and determine who is entitled to the certificate of election.

SEC. 14. This constitution shall be submitted for adoption or rejection to a vote of the qualified electors of the proposed State at the general election to be held on the Tuesday next after the first Monday in November, A. D. 1895. At the said election the ballot shall be in the following form:

For the constitution: Yes. No.

As a heading to each of said ballots there shall be printed on each ballot the following instructions to voters:

All persons desiring to vote for the constitution must erase the word "No."

All persons desiring to vote against the constitution must erase the word "Yes."

SEC. 15. The legislature at its first session shall provide for the election of all officers whose election is not provided for elsewhere in this constitution, and fix the time for the commencement and duration of their terms.

SEC. 16. The provisions of this constitution shall be in force from the day on which the President of the United States shall issue his proclamation declaring the State of Utah admitted into the Union; and the terms of all officers elected at the first election under the provisions of this constitution shall commence on the first Monday next succeeding the issue of said proclamation. Their terms of office shall expire when their successors are elected and qualified under this constitution.

Done in convention at Salt Lake City, in the Territory of Utah, this eighth day of May, in the year of our Lord one thousand eight hundred and ninety-five, and of the independence of the United States the one hundred and nineteenth.

JOHN HENRY SMITH, *President.*

Attest:

PARLEY P. CHRISTENSEN, *Secretary.*

AMENDMENTS

ARTICLE VI

SEC. 1. [*Power vested in Senate, House and People.*] The legislative power of the State shall be vested:

1. In a Senate and House of Representatives, which shall be designated the Legislature of the State of Utah.

2. In the people of the State of Utah as hereinafter stated:

The legal voters or such fractional part thereof of the State of Utah, as may be provided by law, under such conditions and in such manner and within such time as may be provided by law, may initiate any desired legislation and cause the same to be submitted to a vote of the people for approval or rejection, or may require any law passed by the Legislature (except those laws passed by a two-thirds vote of the members elected to each house of the Legislature) to be submitted to the voters of the State before such law shall take effect.

The legal voters, or such fractional part thereof, as may be provided by law, of any legal subdivision of the State, under such conditions and in such manner and within such time as may be provided by law, may initiate any desired legislation and cause the same to be submitted to a vote of the people of said legal subdivision for approval or rejection, or may require any law or odinance passed by the law-making body of said legal subdivision to be submitted to the voters thereof before such law or ordinance shall take effect. [Amendment adopted Nov. 6, 1900.]

SEC. 22. [*Enacting Clause. Passage and amendments of law.*] The enacting clause of every law 'shall be, " Be it enacted by the Legislature of the State of Utah." Except such laws as may be passed by the vote of the electors as provided in subdivision 2, section 1 of this article, and such laws shall begin as follows: " Be it enacted by the people of the State of Utah." No bill or joint resolution shall be passed, except with the assent of the majority of all the members elected to each house of the Legislature, and after it has been read three times. The vote upon the final passage of all bills shall be by yeas and nays; and no law shall be revised or amended by reference to its title only; but the act as revised, or section as amended, shall be re-enacted and published at length. [Amendment adopted Nov. 6, 1900.]

ARTICLE **X**

SEC. 2. " The Public School system shall include kindergarten schools, common schools, consisting of primary and grammar grades, High Schools, an Agricultural College, a University, and such other schools as the Legislature may establish. The common schools shall be free. The other departments of the system shall be supported as provided by law. Provided, That High Schools may be maintained free in all cities of the first and second class now constituting school districts, and in such other cities and districts as may be designated by the Legislature. But where the proportion of school monies apportioned or accruing to any city or district shall not be sufficient to maintain all the free schools in such city or district, the High Schools shall be supported by local taxation;

Provided, That when any cities or districts shall establish High Schools, the Legislature may authorize the use of State school funds to assist in supporting such schools, said funds being apportioned to the cities or districts concerned, by the State Board of Education."

SEC. 6. [*Separate control of city schools.*] In cities of the first and second class the public school system shall be controlled by the Board of Education of such cities, separate and apart from the counties in which said cities are located. [Amendment adopted Nov. 6, 1900.]

ARTICLE XIII

SEC. 3. [*Legislature to provide uniform tax. Exemptions.*] The Legislature shall provide by law a uniform and equal rate of assessment and taxation on all property in the State, according to its value in money, and shall prescribe by general law such regulations as shall secure a just valuation for taxation of all property, so that every person and corporation shall pay a tax in proportion to the value of his, her or its property: provided that a deduction of debts from credits may be authorized: Provided further, that the property of the United States, of the State, counties, cities, towns, school districts, municipal corporations and public libraries, lots with the buildings thereon used exclusively for either religious worship or charitable purposes, and places of burial not held or used for private or corporate benefit, shall be exempt from taxation. Ditches, canals, reservoirs, pipes and flumes owned and used by individuals or corporations for irrigating lands owned by such individuals or corporations, or the individual members thereof, shall not be separately taxed so long as they shall be owned and used exclusively for such purpose. Provided further, that the taxes of the indigent poor may be remitted or abated at such time and in such manner as may be provided by law. [Amendment adopted Nov. 6; 1900.]

SEC. 3. The legislature shall provide by law a uniform and equal rate of assessment and taxation on all property in the state, according to its value in money, any shall prescribe by general law such regulations as shall secure a just valuation for taxation of all property, so that every person and corporation shall pay a tax in proportion to the value of his, her or its property. Provided, that a deduction of debts from credits may be authorized; Provided, further, that the property of the United States, of the state, counties, cities, towns, school districts, municipal corporations and public libraries, lots with the buildings thereon used exclusively for either religious worship or charitable purposes, and places of burial not held or used for private or corporate benefit, shall be exempt from taxation. Ditches, canals, reservoirs, pipes and flumes owned and used by individuals or corporations for irrigating lands owned by such individuals or corporations, or the individual members thereof, shall not be separately taxed as long as they shall be owned and used exclusively for such purpose; Provided, further, that mortgages upon both real and personal property shall be exempt from taxation; Provided, further, that the taxes of the indigent poor may be remitted or abated at such time and in such manner as may be provided by law. 12. (Stamps, income, license, franchise, or mortgage tax permissible). Nothing in this Constitution shall be construed to prevent the legislature from providing a stamp tax, or a tax based on income, occupation, licenses or franchises.

[Doc. No. 10]

Proclamation of January 4, 1896

Whereas: The Congress of the United States passed an Act which was approved on the sixteenth day of July, eighteen hundred and ninety four, entitled "An Act to enable the people of Utah to form a Constitution and State Government and to be admitted into the Union on an equal footing with the original States," which Act provided for the election of delegates to a Constitutional Convention to meet, at the seat of government of the Territory of Utah, on the first Monday in March eighteen hundred and ninety-five, for the purpose of declaring the adoption of the Constitution of the United States by the people of the proposed State and forming a Constitution and State Government for such State;

And whereas, delegates were accordingly elected who met, organized and declared on behalf of the people of said proposed State their adoption of the Constitution of the United States, all as provided in said Act;

And whereas, said Convention, so organized, did, by ordinance irrevocable without the consent of the United States and the people of said State, as required by said Act, provide that perfect toleration of religious sentiment shall be secured and that no inhabitant of said State shall ever be molested in person or property on account of his or her mode of religious worship, but that polygamous or plural marriages are forever prohibited; and did also by said ordinance make the other various stipulations recited in Section Three of said Act;

And whereas, said Convention thereupon formed a Constitution and State government for said proposed State, which Constitution, including said Ordinance, was duly submitted to the people thereof at an election held on the Tuesday next after the first Monday of November, eighteen hundred and ninety five, as directed by said Act;

And whereas, the return of said election has been made and canvassed and the result thereof certified to me, together with a statement of the votes cast and a copy of said Constitution and Ordinance, all as provided in said Act, showing that a majority of the votes lawfully cast at such election was for the ratification and adoption of said Constitution and Ordinance;

And whereas the Constitution and Government of said proposed State are republican in form, said Constitution is not repugnant to the Constitution of the United States and the Declaration of Independence; and all the provisions of said Act have been complied with in the formation of said Constitution and government;

Now, therefore, I, Grover Cleveland, President of the United States of America, in accordance with the Act of Congress aforesaid and by authority thereof, announce the result of said election to be as so certified and do hereby declare and proclaim that the terms and conditions prescribed by the Congress of the United States to entitle the State of Utah to admission into the Union have been duly complied with, and that the creation of said State and its admission into the Union on an equal footing with the original States is now accomplished.

In testimony whereof, I have hereunto set my hand and caused the seal of the United States to be affixed.

Done at the city of Washington this fourth day of January in the year of our Lord one thousand eight hundred and ninety six, [SEAL.] and of the Independence of the United States of America the one hundred and twentieth.

GROVER CLEVELAND

By the President:
RICHARD OLNEY
Secretary of State.

SELECTED BIBLIOGRAPHY

Constitution of the State of Deseret, With the
    Convention That Formed It (n. p., 1849)

Constitution of the State of Utah (Salt Lake City,
    1882)

Constitution of the State of Utah (Salt Lake City,
    1887)

Official Report of the Proceedings and Debates of
the Covention (Salt Lake City, 2 vol., 1898)

Fordham, Jefferson B., "Utah Recall Proposal,"
    "1976 Utah L. Rev. 29 (1976)

Note, "State Constitutional Law Symposium,"
    1966 Utah L. Rev. 307

UTAH INDEX

Vermont

Fourteenth State

March 4, 1791

EDITORIAL NOTE

The "Hampshire grants" were the basis for a
continuing struggle between the settlers in the
Green Mountain region and the colonies and states
of Massachusetts, New Hampshire and New York; see
references under the latter two states in Volumes
VI and VII. The Vermonters insisted on declaring
their independence, citing the example of the
Declaration of 1776; and in due course the con-
tending states dropped their claims and the
Federal Congress authorized the de facto state
to be admitted to the new Union.

VERMONT CONTENTS

SOURCES OF DOCUMENTS

    No. 1   2 Poore, 1857

    No. 2   2 Poore, 1866

    No. 3   1 Stat. 191

    No. 4   2 Poore, 1875

VERMONT: COMPARATIVE PROVISIONS

Subject Matter By Sections and Chapters

		1777	1786	1793
CHAPT. I.	A DECLARATION OF THE RIGHTS OF THE INHABITANTS OF THE STATE OF VERMONT	Chapt.1 (I-XIX)	Chapt.I (I-XXIII)	I
CHAPT.II	PLAN OR FRAME OF GOVERNMENT	Chapt.2	Chapt.II	II
	Delegation and Distribution of Powers	(I-XLIV)	I-XL	1-5
	Legislative Department			6-19
	Executive Department			20-27
	Judiciary Department			28-33
	Qualifications of Freemen			34
	Elections Officers Terms of Office			35-51
	Oath of Allegiance; Oath of Office	XXXVI		52
	Impeachments	XX	XXI	53-54
	Militia			55
	General Provisions			56-67
	Amendment of the Constitution	XLIV		68
	Temporary Provisions			69-70
	Certificate of Justices			

SUBJECT MATTER BY SECTIONS
CHAPT. I BY ARTICLES: CHAPT. II BY SECTIONS

CHAPT. I.	A DECLARATION OF THE RIGHTS OF THE INHABITANTS OF THE STATE OF VERMONT	Chapt.I	Chapt.I	Chapt.I
	All men born free; natural rights	I	I	1
	Private property, public use of	II	II	2
	Religious freedom and worship	III	III	3
	Remedy at law		IV	4
	Internal police	IV	V	5
	Officers servants of the people	V	VI	6
	Government for the people, they may change it	VI	VII	7
	Elections Freeman's rights therein	VIII	IX	8
	Citizen's rights and duties in the state. Bearing arms. Taxation	IX	X	9
	Rights of accused. Personal liberty. Waiver of jury trial.	X	XI	10
	Search and seizure regulated	XI	XII	11
	Trial by jury.	XIII	XIV	12
	Freedom of speech and the press	XIV	XV	13
	Legislator's immunity in debate		XVI	14

	1777	1786	1793
Legislature only may suspend laws.		XVII	15
Right to bear arms; standing armies; civil power to govern		XVIII	16
Martial law restricted		XIX	17
Regard to fundamental principles and virtues	XVI	XX	18
Right to emigrate	XVII	XXI	19
Right assemble, instruct, and petition	XVIII	XXII	20
No transportation for trial	XIX	XXIII	21
Restraints from oppression	VII	VIII	
Writs to attach person or estate	XII	XIII	
CHAPT.II. PLAN OR FRAME OF GOVERNMENT DECLARATION AND DISTRIBUTION OF POWERS	Chapt.II	Chapt.II	Chapt.II
Governing power	I	I	1
Supreme legislative power	II	II	2
Supreme Executive power	III	III	3
Courts of Justice	IV	IV	4
Departments to be distinct.		VI	5
LEGISLATIVE DEPARTMENT			
Legislative Powers		IX	6
Biennial Sessions			7
Doors of General Assembly to be open	XII	XIII	8
Journals; yeas and nays	XIII	XIV	9
Style of laws	XV	XV	10
Governor to approve bills; veto and proceedings thereon; non-action	XIV	XVI	11
Fees for advocating bills, etc.			12
Town representation. Vacancies	XI,XVI		13
Powers of house			14
Residence of representative	VII		15
Representatives oaths			16
Oath of senators and representatives			17
Senators; number; qualifications; apportionment			18
Powers of Senate. Lieutenant governor's duties			19
Delegate may be superceded	X	XXVII	
No person declared guilty of treason by legislature		XVII	
EXECUTIVE DEPARTMENT			

	1777	1786	1793
Governor. Executive power	XVIII	XI	20
Secretary of civil and Military Affairs			21
Commissions. State seal	XVIII;XIX	XI;XX	22
Residence of governor and lieutenant-governor			23
Vacancy in office of governor, lieutenant-governor and treasurer			24
Security given by treasurer, sheriffs and high bailiffs		XXIV	25
Treasurer's accounts		XXV	26
Drawing money from treasury			27
Supreme Executive Council	XVII	X	

JUDICIARY DEPARTMENT

	1777	1786	1793
Courts, justices and judges			28
Court of Chancery	XXI	V	29
Jury trials	XXII	XXVIII	30
Form of prosecutions and indictments. Fines	XXIV		31
Imprisonment for debt restricted. Prisoners bailable	XXV XXVI		32
Habeas Corpus			33
Courts shall be open	XXIII		
Indictments		XXIX	

QUALIFICATIONS OF FREEMEN

	1777	1786	1793
Freemen's qualifications and oath	VI		34
Qualifications of civil officers	XXVIII		

ELECTIONS. OFFICERS. TERMS OF OFFICE

	1777	1786	1793
Biennial elections		(VIII)	35
Election of representatives	VII	VII	36
Elections of senators			37
Term of senators and representatives			38
Election of governor, Lieutenant governor and treasurer	XVII		39
Election of secretary of state and auditor of accounts			40
Term of governor lieutenant governor and treasurer			41
Elections by joint assembly			42

	1777	1786	1793
Term of justices of supreme court			44
Freemen to elect assistant judges, sheriffs, high bailiffs and states attorneys.	XXVII		45
Freemen to elect judges of probate	XXVII		46
Freemen to elect justices of teh peace; apportionment	XXVII		47
Terms of officers named in three preceding sections			48
Election of officers named in preceding section. Commissions			49
Incompatible offices.		XXIII	50
Freedom of elections. Bribery			51
Elections by ballot	XXIX	XXXI	
OATH OF ALLEGIANCE. OATH OF OFFICE	XXXVI	XII	
Oaths of allegiance and office		XVIII XXVI	52
IMPEACHMENTS	XX	XXI	
House may order			53
Liability to Senate to try judgment			54
MILITIA			
Militia officers	XLII	XIX	55
Freemen trained for defence	V	XIX	
GENERAL PROVISIONS			
Legislation restricted			56
Offices of profit Compensation Illegal fees			57
Record of deeds	XXXI	XXXII	58
Entails to be regulated	XXXIV	XXXIII	59
Punishment at hard labor, when	XXXV	XXXIV	60
Suicide's estate not forfeited. No deodand		XXXV	61
Citizenship		XXXVI	62
Hunting, fowling and fishing	XXXIX	XXXVI	63
Laws to encourage virtue and prevent vice. Schools Religious societies	XLI	XXXVIII	64
Charters, limit on right to grant			65

	1777	1786	1793
Workmen's compensation			66
Declaration of rights not to be violated	XLII	XXXIX	67
How fines to be paid	XXX		
Examining the proceedings of legislature	XXXII		
Establishing offices of profit	XXXIII	XXII	
Public tax	XXXVII		
Foreigner transferring land	XXXVIII		
Schools established	XL		
Debtors not kept in prison			
AMENDMENT OF THE CONSTITUTION	XLIV	XL	
Amending constitution			68
TEMPORARY PROVISIONS			
Extension of terms of certain officers			69
Revision of Chapter II			70
CERTIFICATE OF JUSTICES			

BACKGROUND NOTE

Imperfect cartographic knowledge, and casual
indifference of political leaders in England, first
left a geographic blank where Vermont was to appear, and then bred conflicts which for years were
to be identified as the "Hampshire grants." The
French had passed through the area near Lake Cham-
plain in 1666, and the Dutch established a temporary post near Chimney Rock in 1690, but English
charters were the root of the problem. In 1715 a
section of territory was ceded by Massachusetts to
Connecticut in settlement of a border dispute, and
the former then laid claim to "Equivalent Lands"
in unsettled and vaguely described areas to the
north and west. In 1724 a military detachment from
the Bay Colony set up Fort Drummer, near modern
Brattleboro, to enforce its jurisdiction.

The first of the major grants was made in 1749
when Governor Benning Wentworth of New Hampshire,
claiming authority under this colony's charter,
issued patents for lands near the site of present-
day Bennington. Wentworth followed with a number
of other grants over a twenty-year period. Then
the Crown complicated matters in 1763, as part of
the general reorganization of its American empire
after the French and Indian War, by decreeing that
New Hampshire's jurisdiction ended at the eastern
bank of the Connecticut River, giving color to the
New York claim that the 1662 grant to the Duke of
York included the disputed area west of the river.
In any case, the decree cast a cloud on scores of
titles created by the Hampshire grants.

Local settlers took matters into their own
hands, driving out New York land registrars and tax
collectors in 1770, while a local security force,
later to be the "Green Mountain Boys" of Ethan
Allen's command, harrassed settlers claiming
under New York grants. In April 1775 a petition
was set to London seeking a separate charter; but
with the outbreak of the Revolution talk immediately
shifted to statehood.

In 1777 a state constitution was drawn up and
adopted (Doc. No. 1)-- unrecognized by Massachusetts, New Hampshire and New York and challenged
in the Continental Congress. A special arbitration
group proposed by the Congress never met, and

matters dragged on indecisively until 1786, when
Massachusetts and New Hampshire gave up their
claims. A second draft constitution was prepared
(Doc. No. 2), but the now moribund Congress took
no action. Finally, under the new Federal Congress,
New York gave up its claims to the area and an
enabling act (Doc. No. 3) was adopted. A third
constitution (Doc. No. 4) was adopted, which has
served Vermont ever since.

[Doc. No. 1]

Constitution of 1777

VERMONT.*

—————

CONSTITUTION OF VERMONT—1777.†

WHEREAS, all government ought to be instituted and supported, for the security and protection of the community, as such, and to enable the individuals who compose it, to enjoy their natural rights, and the other blessings which the Author of existence has bestowed upon man; and whenever those great ends of government are not obtained, the people have a right, by common consent, to change it, and take such measures as to them may appear necessary to promote their safety and happiness.

And whereas, the inhabitants of this State have (in consideration of protection only) heretofore acknowledged allegiance to the King of Great Britain, and the said King has not only withdrawn that protection, but commenced, and still continues to carry on, with unabated vengeance, a most cruel and unjust war against them; employing therein, not only the troops of Great Britain, but foreign mercenaries, savages and slaves, for the avowed purpose of reducing them to a total and abject submission to the despotic domination of the British parliament, with many other acts of tyranny, (more fully set forth in the declaration of Congress) whereby all allegiance and fealty to the said King and his successors, are dissolved and at an end; and all power and authority derived from him, ceased in the American Colonies.

And whereas, the territory which now comprehends the State of *Vermont*, did antecedently, of right, belong to the government of *New-Hampshire;* and the former Governor thereof, viz. his Excellency *Benning Wentworth*, Esq., granted many charters of lands and corporations, within this State, to the present inhabitants and others. And whereas, the late Lieutenant Governor *Colden*, of *New York*, with others, did, in violation of the tenth command, covet those very lands; and by a false representation made to the court of Great Britain, (in the year 1764, that for the convenience of trade and administration of justice, the inhabitants were desirous of being annexed to that government,) obtained jurisdiction of those very identical lands, *ex-parte;* which ever was, and is, disagreeable to the inhabitants. And whereas, the legislature of *New-York*, ever have, and still continue to disown the good people of this State, in their landed property, which will appear in the complaints hereafter inserted, and

—————

* The State of Vermont was originally claimed by Massachusetts, New Hampshire, and New York, and at the commencement of the revolutionary struggle she not only sought independence from British rule, but from the State of New York, which claimed sovereignty over the territory to the west bank of the Connecticut River, and from New Hampshire, which contested the claims of both New York and Vermont. In March, 1781, Massachusetts assented to the independence of Vermont, which adjusted her difficulties with New Hampshire in 1782, but it was 1790 before New York consented to her admission into the Union.

† This constitution was framed by a convention which assembled at Windsor, July 2, 1777, and completed its labors July 8, 1777. It was not submitted to the people for ratification. It was affirmed by the legislature at its sessions in 1779 and 1782, and declared to be a part of the laws of the State.

in the 36th section of their present constitution, in which is established the grants of land made by that government.

They have refused to make regrants of our lands to the original proprietors and occupants, unless at the exorbitant rate of 2300 dollars fees for each township; and did enhance the quit-rent, three fold, and demanded an immediate delivery of the title derived before, from *New-Hampshire.*

The judges of their supreme court have made a solemn declaration, that the charters, conveyances, &c. of the lands included in the before described premises, were utterly null and void, on which said title was founded: in consequence of which declaration, writs of possession have been by them issued, and the sheriff of the county of Albany sent, at the head of six or seven hundred men, to enforce the execution thereof.

They have passed an act, annexing a penalty thereto, of thirty pounds fine and six months imprisonment, on any person who should refuse assisting the sheriff, after being requested, for the purpose of executing writs of possession.

The Governors, *Dunmore, Tryon* and *Colden,* have made re-grants of several tracts of land, included in the premises, to certain favorite land jobbers in the government of *New-York,* in direct violation of his Britannic majesty's express prohibition, in the year 1767.

They have issued proclamations, wherein they have offered large sums of money, for the purpose of apprehending those very persons who have dared boldly, and publicly, to appear in defence of their just rights.

They did pass twelve acts of outlawry, on the 9th day of March, A. D. 1774, impowering the respective judges of their supreme court, to award execution of death against those inhabitants in said district, that they should judge to be offenders, without trial.

They have, and still continue, an unjust claim to those lands, which greatly retards emigration into, and the settlement of, this State.

They have hired foreign troops, emigrants from *Scotland,* at two different times, and armed them, to drive us out of possession.

They have sent the savages on our frontiers, to distress us.

They have proceeded to erect the counties of Cumberland and Glocester, and establish courts of justice there, after they were discountenanced by the authority of Great Britain.

The free convention of the State of *New-York,* at *Harlem,* in the year 1776, unanimously voted, "That all quit-rents, formerly due to the King of Great Britain, are now due and owing to this Convention, or such future government as shall be hereafter established in this State."

In the several stages of the aforesaid oppressions, we have petitioned his Britannic majesty, in the most humble manner, for redress, and have, at very great expense, received several reports in our favor; and, in other instances, wherein we have petitioned the late legislative authority of *New-York,* those petitions have been treated with neglect.

And whereas, the local situation of this State, from *New-York,* at the extreme part, is upward of four hundred and fifty miles from the seat of that government, which renders it extreme difficult to continue under the jurisdiction of said State.

Therefore, it is absolutely necessary, for the welfare and safety of the inhabitants of this State, that it should be, henceforth, a free and independent State; and that a just, permanent, and proper form of government, should exist in it, derived from, and founded on, the authority of the people only, agreeable to the direction of the honorable American Congress.

We the representatives of the freemen of *Vermont,* in General Convention met, for the express purpose of forming such a government,—confessing the goodness of the Great Governor of the universe, (who alone, knows to what degree of earthly happiness, mankind may attain, by perfecting the arts of government,) in permitting the people of this State, by common consent, and without violence, deliberately to form for themselves, such just rules as they shall think best for governing their future society; and being fully convinced that it is our indispensable duty, to establish such original principles of government, as will best promote the general happiness of the people of this State, and their posterity, and provide for future improvements, without partiality for, or prejudice against, any particular class, sect, or denomination of men whatever,—do, by virtue of authority vested in us, by our constituents, ordain, declare, and establish, the following declaration of rights, and frame of government, to be the CONSTITUTION of this COMMONWEALTH, and to remain in force therein, forever, unaltered, except in such articles, as shall, hereafter, on experience, be found to require improvement, and which shall, by the same authority of the people, fairly delegated, as this frame of government directs, be amended or improved, for the more effectual obtaining and securing the great end and design of all government, herein before mentioned.

CHAPTER I.

A DECLARATION OF THE RIGHTS OF THE INHABITANTS OF THE STATE OF VERMONT.

I. THAT all men are born equally free and independent, and have certain natural, inherent and unalienable rights, amongst which are the enjoying and defending life and liberty; acquiring, possessing and protecting property, and pursuing and obtaining happiness and safety. Therefore, no male person, born in this country, or brought from over sea, ought to be holden by law, to serve any person, as a servant, slave or apprentice, after he arrives to the age of twenty-one years, nor female, in like manner, after she arrives to the age of eighteen years, unless they are bound by their own consent, after they arrive to such age, or bound by law, for the payment of debts, damages, fines, costs, or the like.

II. That private property ought to be subservient to public uses, when necessity requires it; nevertheless, whenever any particular man's property is taken for the use of the public, the owner ought to receive an equivalent in money.

III. That all men have a natural and unalienable right to worship ALMIGHTY GOD, according to the dictates of their own consciences and understanding, regulated by the word of GOD; and that no man ought, or of right can be compelled to attend any religious worship, or erect, or support any place of worship, or maintain any minister, contrary to the dictates of his conscience; nor can any man who professes the protestant religion, be justly deprived or abridged of any civil right, as a citizen, on account of his religious sentiment, or peculiar mode of religious worship, and that no authority can, or ought to be vested in, or assumed by, any power whatsoever, that shall, in any case, interfere with, or in any manner controul, the rights of conscience, in the free exercise of religious worship: nevertheless, every sect or denomination of people ought to observe the Sabbath, or the Lord's day, and keep up, and support, some sort of religious worship, which to them shall seem most agreeable to the revealed will of GOD.

IV. That the people of this State have the sole, exclusive and inherent right of governing and regulating the internal police of the same.

V. That all power being originally inherent in, and consequently, derived from, the people; therefore, all officers of government, whether legislative or executive, are their trustees and servants, and at all times accountable to them.

VI. That government is, or ought to be, instituted for the common benefit, protection, and security of the people, nation or community; and not for the particular emolument or advantage of any single man, family or set of men, who are a part only of that community; and that the community hath an indubitable, unalienable and indefeasible right to reform, alter, or abolish, government, in such manner as shall be, by that community, judged most conducive to the public weal.

VII. That those who are employed in the legislative and executive business of the State, may be restrained from oppression, the people have a right, at such periods as they may think proper, to reduce their public officers to a private station, and supply the vacancies by certain and regular elections.

VIII. That all elections ought to be free; and that all freemen, having a sufficient, evident, common interest with, and attachment to, the community, have a right to elect officers, or be elected into office.

IX. That every member of society hath a right to be protected in the enjoyment of life, liberty and property, and therefore, is bound to contribute his proportion towards the expense of that protection, and yield his personal service, when necessary, or an equivalent thereto; but no part of a man's property can be justly taken from him, or applied to public uses, without his own consent, or that of his legal representatives; nor can any man who is conscientiously scrupulous of bearing arms, be justly compelled thereto, if he will pay such equivalent; nor are the people bound by any law, but such as they have, in like manner, assented to, for their common good.

X. That, in all prosecutions for criminal offences, a man hath a right to be heard, by himself and his counsel—to demand the cause and nature of his accusation—to be confronted with the witnesses—to call for evidence in his favor, and a speedy public trial, by an impartial jury of the country; without the unanimous consent of which jury, he cannot be found guilty; nor can he be compelled to give evidence against himself; nor can any man be justly deprived of his liberty, except by the laws of the land or the judgment of his peers.

XI. That the people have a right to hold themselves, their houses, papers and possessions free from search or seizure; and therefore warrants, without oaths or affirmations first made, affording a sufficient foundation for them, and whereby any officer or messenger may be commanded or required to search suspected places, or to seize any person or persons, his, her or their property, not particularly described, are contrary to that right, and ought not to be granted.

XII. That no warrant or writ to attach the person or estate, of any freeholder within this State, shall be issued in civil action, without the person or persons, who may request such warrant or attachment, first make oath, or affirm, before the authority who may be requested to issue the same, that he, or they, are in danger of loosing his, her or their debts.

XIII. That, in controversies respecting property, and in suits between man and man, the parties have a right to a trial by jury; which ought to be held sacred.

XIV. That the people have a right to freedom of speech, and of writing and publishing their sentiments; therefore, the freedom of the press ought not be restrained.

XV. That the people have a right to bear arms for the defence of themselves and the State; and, as standing armies, in the time of peace, are dangerous to liberty, they ought not to be kept up; and that the military should be kept under strict subordination to, and governed by, the civil power.

XVI. That frequent recurrence to fundamental principles, and a firm adherence to justice, moderation, temperance, industry and frugality, are absolutely necessary to preserve the blessings of liberty, and keep government free. The people ought, therefore, to pay particular attention to these points, in the choice of officers and representatives, and have a right to exact a due and constant regard to them, from their legislators and magistrates, in the making and executing such laws as are necessary for the good government of the State.

XVII. That all people have a natural and inherent right to emigrate from one State to another, that will receive them; or to form a new State in vacant countries, or in such countries as they can purchase, whenever they think that thereby they can promote their own happiness.

XVIII. That the people have a right to assemble together, to consult for their common good—to instruct their representatives, and to apply to the legislature for redress of grievances, by address, petition or remonstrance.

XIX. That no person shall be liable to be transported out of this State for trial, for any offence committed within this State.

CHAPTER II.

PLAN OR FRAME OF GOVERNMENT.

SECTION I. THE COMMONWEALTH or STATE of VERMONT, shall be governed, hereafter, by a Governor, Deputy Governor, Council, and an Assembly of the Representatives of the Freemen of the same, in manner and form following.

SECTION II. The supreme legislative power shall be vested in a House of Representatives of the Freemen or Commonwealth or State of *Vermont.*

SECTION III. The supreme executive power shall be vested in a Governor and Council.

SECTION IV. Courts of justice shall be established in every county in this State.

SECTION V. The freemen of this Commonwealth, and their sons, shall be trained and armed for its defence, under such regulations, restrictions and exceptions, as the general assembly shall, by law, direct; preserving always to the people, the right of choosing their colonels of militia, and all commissioned officers under that rank, in such manner, and as often, as by the said laws shall be directed.

SECTION VI. Every man of the full age of twenty-one years, having resided in this State for the space of one whole year, next before the election of representatives, and who is of a quiet and peaceable behaviour, and will take the following oath (or affirmation) shall be entitled to all the privileges of a freeman of this State.

I —— —— solemnly swear, by the ever living God, (or affirm, in the presence of Almighty God,) that whenever I am called to give my vote or suffrage, touching any matter that concerns the State of Vermont, I will do it so, as in my conscience, I shall judge will most conduce to the best good of the same, as established by the constitution, without fear or favor of any man.

SECTION VII. The House of Representatives of the Freemen of this State, shall consist of persons most noted for wisdom and virtue, to be chosen by the freemen of every town in this State, respectively. And no foreigner shall be chosen, unless he has resided in the town for which he shall be elected, one year immediately before said election.

SECTION VIII. The members of the House of Representatives, shall be chosen annually, by ballot, by the freemen of this State, on the first Tuesday of September, forever, (except this present year) and shall meet on the second Thursday of the succeeding October, and shall be stiled the General Assembly of the Representatives of the Freemen of *Vermont;* and shall have power to choose their Speaker, Secretary of the State, their Clerk, and other necessary officers of the house—sit on their own adjournments—prepare bills and enact them into laws—judge of the elections and qualifications of their own members—they may expel a member, but not a second time for the same cause—They may administer oaths (or affirmations) on examination of witnesses—redress grievances—impeach State criminals—grant charters of incorporation—constitute towns, boroughs, cities and counties, and shall have all other powers necessary for the legislature of a free State: but they shall have no power to add to, alter, abolish, or infringe any part of this constitution. And for this present year, the members of the General Assembly shall be chosen on the first Tuesday of March next, and shall meet at the meeting-house, in *Windsor,* on the second Thursday of March next.

SECTION IX. A quorum of the house of representatives shall consist of two-thirds of the whole number of members elected; and having met and chosen their speaker, shall, each of them, before they proceed to business, take and subscribe, as well the oath of fidelity and allegiance herein after directed, as the following oath or affirmation, viz.

I —— —— do solemnly swear, by the ever living God, (or, I do solemnly affirm in the presence of Almighty God) that as a member of this assembly, I will not propose or assent to any bill, vote, or resolution, which shall appear to me injurious to the people; nor do or consent to any act or thing whatever, that shall have a tendency to lessen or abridge their rights and privileges, as declared in the Constitution of this State; but will, in all things, conduct myself as a faithful, honest representative and guardian of the people, according to the best of my judgment and abilities.

And each member, before he takes his seat, shall make and subscribe the following declaration, viz.

I do believe in one God, the Creator and Governor of the universe, the rewarder of the good and punisher of the wicked. And I do acknowledge the scriptures of the old and new testament to be given by divine inspiration, and own and profess the protestant religion.

And no further or other religious test shall ever, hereafter, be required of any civil officer or magistrate in this State.

SECTION X. Delegates to represent this State in Congress shall be chosen, by ballot, by the future General Assembly, at their first meeting, and annually, forever afterward, as long as such representation shall be necessary. Any Delegate may be superceded, at any time, by the General Assembly appointing another in his stead. No man shall sit in Congress longer than two years successively, nor be capable of re-election for three years afterwards; and no person who holds any office in the gift of the Congress, shall, thereafter, be elected to represent this State in Congress.

SECTION XI. If any town or towns shall neglect or refuse to elect and send representatives to the General Assembly, two thirds of the members of the towns, that do elect and send representatives, (provided they be a majority of the inhabited towns of the whole State) when met, shall have all the powers of the General Assembly, as fully and amply, as if the whole were present.

SECTION XII. The doors of the house in which the representatives of the freemen of this State, shall sit, in General Assembly, shall be and remain open for the admission of all persons, who behave decently, except only, when the welfare of this State may require the doors to be shut.

SECTION XIII. The votes and proceedings of the General Assembly shall be printed, weekly, during their sitting, with the yeas and nays, on any question, vote or resolution, where one-third of the members require it; (except when the votes are taken by ballot) and when the yeas and nays are so taken, every member shall have a right to insert the reasons of his votes upon the minutes, if he desire it.

SECTION XIV. To the end that laws, before they are enacted, may be more maturely considered, and the inconveniency of hasty determination as much as possible prevented, all bills of public nature, shall be first laid before the Governor and Council, for their perusal and proposals of amendment, and shall be printed for the consideration of the people, before they are read in General Assembly, for the last time of debate and amendment; except temporary acts, which, after being laid before the Governor and Council, may (in case of sudden necessity) be passed into laws; and no other shall be passed into laws, until the next session of assembly. And for the more perfect satisfaction of the public, the reasons and motives for making such laws, shall be fully and clearly expressed and set forth in their preambles.

SECTION XV. The style of the laws of this State shall be,—"Be it enacted, and it is hereby enacted, by the Representatives of the Freemen of the State of *Vermont*, in General Assembly met, and by the authority of the same."

SECTION XVI. In order that the Freemen of this State might enjoy the benefit of election, as equally as may be, each town within this State, that consists, or may consist, of eighty taxable inhabitants, within one septenary or seven years, next after the establishing this constitution, may hold elections therein, and choose each, two representatives; and each other inhabited town in this State may, in like manner, choose each, one representative, to represent them in General Assembly, during the said septenary or seven years; and after that, each inhabited town may, in like manner, hold such election, and choose each, one representative, forever thereafter.

SECTION XVII. The Supreme Executive Council of this State, shall consist of a Governor, Lieutenant-Governor, and twelve persons, chosen in the following manner, viz. The Freemen of each town, shall, on the day of election for choosing representatives to attend the General Assembly, bring in their votes for Governor, with his name fairly written, to the constable, who shall seal them up, and write on them, votes for the Governor, and deliver them to the representative chosen to attend the General Assembly; and, at the opening of the General Assembly, there shall be a committee appointed out of the Council and Assembly, who, after being duly sworn to the faithful discharge of their trust, shall proceed to receive, sort, and count, the votes for the Governor, and declare the person who has the major part of the votes, to be Governor, for the year ensuing. And if there be no choice made, then the Council and General Assembly, by their joint ballot, shall make choice of a Governor.

The Lieutenant Governor and Treasurer, shall be chosen in the manner above directed; and each freeman shall give in twelve votes for twelve councillors, in the same manner; and the twelve highest in nomination shall serve for the ensuing year as Councillors.

The Council that shall act in the recess of this Convention, shall supply the place of a Council for the next General Assembly, until the new Council be declared chosen. The Council shall meet annually, at the same time and place with the General Assembly; and every member of the Council shall be a Justice of the Peace for the whole State, by virtue of his office.

SECTION XVIII. The Governor, and in his absence, the Lieutenant or Deputy Governor, with the Council—seven of whom shall be a quorum—shall have power to appoint and commissionate all officers, (except those who are appointed by the General Assembly,) agreeable to this frame of government, and the laws that may be made hereafter; and shall supply every vacancy in any office, occasioned by death, resignation, removal or disqualification, until the office can be filled, in the time and manner directed by law or this constitution. They are to correspond with other States, and transact business with officers of government, civil and military; and to prepare such business as may appear to them necessary to lay before the General Assembly. They shall sit as judges to hear and determine on impeachments, taking to their assistance, for advice only, the justices of the supreme court; and shall have power to grant pardons, and remit fines, in all cases whatsoever, except cases of impeachment, and in cases of treason and murder—shall have power to grant reprieves, but not to pardon, until the end of the next session of the Assembly: but there shall be no remission or mitigation of punishment, on impeachments, except by act of legislation. They are also, to take care that the laws be faithfully executed. They are to expedite the execution of such measures as may be resolved upon by General Assembly; and they may draw upon the Treasurer for such sums as may be appropriated by the House: they may also lay embargoes, or prohibit the exportation of any commodity for any time, not exceeding thirty days, in the recess of the House only: they may grant such licences as shall be directed by law, and shall have power to call together the General Assembly, when necessary, before the day to which they shall stand adjourned. The Governor shall be commander-in-chief of the forces of the State; but shall not command in person, except advised thereto by the Council, and then, only as long as they shall approve thereof. The Governor and Council shall have a Secretary, and keep fair books of their proceedings, wherein any Councillor may enter his dissent, with his reasons to support it.

SECTION XIX. All commissions shall be in the name of the freemen of the State of *Vermont*, sealed with the State seal, signed by the Governor, and in his absence, the Lieutenant Governor, and attested by the Secretary; which seal shall be kept by the Council.

SECTION XX. Every officer of State, whether judicial or executive, shall be liable to be impeached by the General Assembly, either when in office, or after his resignation, or removal for mal-administration. All impeachments shall be before the Governor or Lieutenant Governor and Council, who shall hear and determine the same.

SECTION XXI. The supreme court, and the several courts of common pleas of this State shall, besides the powers usually exercised by such courts, have the powers of a court of chancery, so far as relates to perpetuating testimony, obtaining evidence from places not within this State, and the care of persons and estates of those who are *non compotes mentis*, and such other powers as may be found necessary by future General Assemblies, not inconsistent with this constitution.

SECTION XXII. Trials shall be by jury; and it is recommended to the legislature of this State to provide by law, against every corruption or partiality in the choice, and return, or appointment, of juries.

SECTION XXIII. All courts shall be open, and justice shall be impartially administered, without corruption or unnecessary delay; all their officers shall be paid an adequate, but moderate, compensation for their services; and if any officer shall take greater or other fees than the laws allow him, either directly or indirectly, it shall ever after disqualify him from holding any office in this State.

SECTION XXIV. All prosecutions shall commence in the name and by the authority of the freemen of the State of *Vermont*, and all indictments shall conclude with these words, "against the peace and dignity of the same." The style of all process hereafter, in this State, shall be,—The State of *Vermont*.

SECTION XXV. The person of a debtor, where there is not a strong presumption of fraud, shall not be continued in prison, after delivering up, *bona fide*, all his estate, real and personal, for the use of his creditors, in such manner as shall be hereafter regulated by law. All prisoners shall be bailable by sufficient securities, unless for capital offences, when the proof is evident or presumption great.

SECTION XXVI. Excessive bail shall not be exacted for bailable offences: and all fines shall be moderate.

SECTION XXVII. That the General Assembly, when legally formed, shall appoint times and places for county elections, and at such times and places, the freemen in each county respectively, shall have the liberty of choosing the judges of inferior court of common pleas, sheriff, justices of the peace, and judges of probates, commissioned by the Governor and Council, during good behavior, removable by the General Assembly upon proof of mal-administration.

SECTION XXVIII. That no person, shall be capable of holding any civil office, in this State, except he has acquired, and maintains a good moral character.

SECTION XXIX. All elections, whether by the people or in General Assembly, shall be by ballot, free and voluntary: and any elector who shall receive any gift or reward for his vote, in meat, drink, monies or otherwise, shall forfeit his right to elect at that time, and suffer such other penalty as future laws shall direct. And any person who shall, directly or indirectly, give, promise, or bestow, any such rewards to be elected, shall, thereby, be rendered incapable to serve for the ensuing year.

SECTION XXX. All fines, licence money, fees and forfeitures, shall be paid, according to the direction hereafter to be made by the General Assembly.

SECTION XXXI. All deeds and conveyances of land shall be recorded in the town clerk's office, in their respective towns.

SECTION XXXII. The printing presses shall be free to every person who undertakes to examine the proceedings of the legislature, or any part of government.

SECTION XXXIII. As every freeman, to preserve his independence (if without a sufficient estate) ought to have some profession, calling, trade or farm, whereby he may honestly subsist, there can be no necessity for, nor use in, establishing offices of profit, the usual effects of which are dependence and servility, unbecoming freemen, in the possessors or expectants; faction, contention, corruption and disorder among the people. But if any man is called into public service, to the prejudice of his private affairs, he has a right to a reasonable compensation; and whenever an office, through increase of fees, or otherwise, becomes so profitable as to occasion many to apply for it, the profits ought to be lessened by the legislature.

SECTION XXXIV. The future legislature of this State, shall regulate entails, in such manner as to prevent perpetuities.

SECTION XXXV. To deter more effectually from the commission of crimes, by continued visible punishment of long duration, and to make sanguinary punishments less necessary; houses ought to be provided for punishing, by hard labor, those who shall be convicted of crimes not capital; wherein the criminal shall be employed for the benefit of the public, or for reparation of injuries done to private persons; and all persons, at proper times, shall be admitted to see the prisoners at their labor.

SECTION XXXVI. Every officer, whether judicial, executive or military, in authority under this State, shall take the following oath or affirmation of allegiance, and general oath of office, before he enter on the execution of his office.

The Oath or Affirmation of Allegiance.

"I —————— ———— do solemnly swear by the ever living God, (or affirm in presence of Almighty God,) that I will be true and faithful to the State of Vermont; and that I will not, directly or indirectly, do any act or thing, prejudicial or injurious, to the constitution or government thereof, as established by Convention."

The Oath or Affirmation of Office.

"I —————— ———— do solemnly swear by the ever living God, (or affirm in presence of Almighty God) that I will faithfully execute the office of ———— for the ———— of ————; and will do equal right and justice to all men, to the best of my judgment and abilities, according to law."

SECTION XXXVII. No public tax, custom or contribution shall be imposed upon, or paid by, the people of this State, except by a law for that purpose; and before any law be made for raising it, the purpose for which any tax is to be raised ought to appear clear to the legislature to be of more service to the community than the money would be, if not collected; which being well observed, taxes can never be burthens.

SECTION XXXVIII. Every foreigner of good character, who comes to settle in this State, having first taken an oath or affirmation of allegiance to the same, may purchase, or by other just means acquire, hold, and transfer, land or other real estate; and after one years residence, shall be deemed a free denizen thereof, and intitled to all the rights of a natural born subject of this State; except that he shall not be capable of being elected a representative, until after two years residence.

SECTION XXXIX. That the inhabitants of this State, shall have liberty to hunt and fowl, in seasonable times, on the lands they hold, and on other lands (not enclosed;) and, in like manner, to fish in all boatable and other waters, not private property, under proper regulations, to be hereafter made and provided by the General Assembly.

SECTION XL. A school or schools shall be established in each town, by the legislature, for the convenient instruction of youth, with such salaries to the masters, paid by each town; making proper use of school lands in each town, thereby to enable them to instruct youth at low prices. One grammar school in each county, and one university in this State, ought to be established by direction of the General Assembly.

SECTION XLI. Laws for the encouragement of virtue and prevention of vice and immorality, shall be made and constantly kept in force; and provision shall be made for their due execution; and all religious societies or bodies of men, that have or may be hereafter united and incorporated, for the advancement of religion and learning, or for other pious and charitable purposes, shall be encouraged and protected in the enjoyment of the privileges, immunities and estates which they, in justice, ought to enjoy, under such regulations, as the General Assembly of this State shall direct.

SECTION XLII. All field and staff officers, and commissioned officers of the army, and all general officers of the militia, shall be chosen by the General Assembly.

SECTION XLIII. The declaration of rights is hereby declared to be a part of the Constitution of this State, and ought never to be violated, on any pretence whatsoever.

SECTION XLIV. In order that the freedom of this Commonwealth may be preserved inviolate, forever, there shall be chosen, by ballot, by the freemen of this State, on the last Wednesday in March, in the year one thousand seven hundred and eighty-five, and on the last Wednesday in March, in every seven years thereafter, thirteen persons, who shall be chosen in the same manner the council is chosen—except they shall not be out of the Council or General Assembly—to be called the Council of Censors; who shall meet together, on the first Wednesday of June next ensuing their election; the majority of whom shall be a quorum in every case, except as to calling a Convention, in which two-thirds of the whole number elected shall agree; and whose duty it shall be to enquire whether the constitution has been preserved inviolate, in every part; and whether the legislative and executive branches of government have performed their duty as guardians of the people; or assumed to themselves, or exercised, other or greater powers, than they are entitled to by the constitution. They are also to enquire whether the public taxes have been justly laid and collected, in all parts of this Commonwealth—in what manner the public monies have been disposed of, and whether the laws have been duly executed. For these purposes they shall have power to send for persons, papers and records; they shall have authority to pass public censures—to order impeachments, and to recommend to the legislature the repealing such laws as appear to them to have been enacted contrary to the principles of the constitution. These powers they shall continue to have, for and during the space of one year from the day of their election, and no longer. The said Council of Censors shall also have power to call a Convention, to meet within two years after their sitting, if there appears to them an absolute necessity of amending any article of this constitution which may be defective—explaining such as may be thought not clearly expressed, and of adding such as are necessary for the preservation of the rights and happiness of the people; but the articles to be amended, and the amendments proposed, and such articles as are proposed to be added or abolished, shall be promulgated at least six months before the day appointed for the election of such convention, for the previous consideration of the people, that they may have an opportunity of instructing their delegates on the subject.

[Doc. No. 2]

Constitution of 1786

WHEREAS all government ought to be instituted and supported for the security and protection of the community as such, and to enable the individuals, who compose it, to enjoy their natural rights, and the other blessings which the Author of existence has bestowed upon man: and whenever those great ends of government are not obtained, the people have a right, by common consent, to change it, and take such measures as to them may appear necessary to promote their safety and happiness.

And whereas the inhabitants of this State have (in consideration of protection only) heretofore acknowledged allegiance to the King of Great-Britain: and the said King has not only withdrawn that protection, but commenced and still continues to carry on, with unabated vengeance, a most cruel and unjust war against them; employing therein not only the troops of Great-Britain, but foreign mercenaries, savages, and slaves, for the avowed purpose of reducing them to a total and abject submission to the despotic domination of the British Parliament, with many more acts of tyranny, (more fully set forth in the Declaration of Congress) whereby all allegiance and fealty to the said King and his Successors are dissolved and at an end; and all power and authority derived from him ceased in the American Colonies. And whereas the Territory, which now comprehends the State of Vermont, did antecedently of right belong to the government of New-Hampshire, and the former Governor thereof, viz. his excellency Benning Wentworth, Esq. granted many charters of lands and corporations within this State to the present inhabitants and others. And whereas the late Lieutenant-Governor Colden, of New York, with others, did, in violation, of the tenth command, covet those very lands: and by a false representation, made to the Court of Great-Britain, (in the year 1764, that for the convenience of trade and administration of justice, the inhabitants were desirous of being annexed to that government) obtained jurisdiction of those very identical lands, *ex parte*, which ever was and is disagreeable to the inhabitants. And whereas the Legislature of New-York ever have, and still continue, to disown the good people of this State, in their landed property, which will appear in the complaints hereafter inserted, and in the 36th section of their present Constitution, in which is established the Grants of Land made by that government.

They have refused to make re-grants of our lands to the original Proprietors and Occupants, unless at the exorbitant rate of 2,300 dollars fees for each township; and did enhance the quitrent three-fold, and demanded an immediate delivery of the title derived from New-Hampshire.

The Judges of their Supreme Court have made a solemn declaration, that the charters, conveyances, &c., of the lands included in the before-described premises, were utterly null and void, on which said title was founded. In consequence of which declaration, writs of possession have been by them issued, and the Sheriff of the county of Albany sent at the head of six or seven hundred men, to enforce the execution thereof.

They have passed an act, annexing a penalty thereto, of thirty pounds' fine, and six months' imprisonment, on any person who should refuse assisting the Sheriff, after being requested, for the purpose of executing writs of possession.

The Governors Dunmore, Tryon, and Colden, have made re-grants of several tracts of land included in the premises, to certain favourite land jobbers in the government of New-York, in direct violation of his Britannic Majesty's express prohibition, in the year 1767.

They have issued proclamations, wherein they have offered large sums of money for the purpose of apprehending those very persons, who have dared boldly and publickly to appear in defence of their just rights.

They did pass twelve acts of outlawry on the ninth day of March, A. D. 1774,

---

* The original constitution of Vermont provided for the election, at intervals of seven years, commencing in 1785, of a "council of censors," who should not only inquire whether the constitution had been preserved inviolate during the last septenary, and whether the government had been faithfully exercised, but should propose such amendments to the constitution as they might deem proper, and call a convention to meet for the adoption or rejection of them. This constitution was adopted by the legislature and declared to be a part of the laws of the State, in March, 1787.

empowering the respective Judges of their Supreme Court to award execution of death against those inhabitants in said district, that they should judge to be offenders, without trial.

They have and still continue an unjust claim to those lands, which greatly retards emigration into any settlement of this State.

They have hired foreign troops, emigrants from Scotland, at two different times, and armed them to drive us out of possession.

They have sent the Savages on our frontiers to distress us.

They have proceeded to erect the counties of Cumberland and Gloucester, and establish courts of justice there, after they were discountenanced by the authority of Great-Britain.

The free Convention of the State of New-York, at Harlem, in the year 1776, unanimously voted, "That all quitrents, formerly due to the King of Great-Britain, are now due, and owing to this Convention, or such future government as shall be hereafter established in this State."

In the several stages of the aforesaid oppressions, we have petitioned his Britannic Majesty in the most humble manner for redress, and have, at very great expense, received several reports in our favour: and in other instances, wherein we have petitioned the late legislative authority of New-York, those petitions have been treated with neglect. And whereas, the local situation of this State from New-York, which, at the extreme part, is upward of four hundred and fifty miles from the seat of that government, renders it extreme difficult to continue under the jurisdiction of said State;

Therefore it is absolutely necessary, for the welfare and safety of the inhabitants of this State, that it should be henceforth a free and independent State, and that a just, permanent, and proper form of government should exist in it, derived from and founded on the authority of the people only, agreeable to the direction of the honourable American Congress.

We the Representatives of the freemen of Vermont, in General Convention met, for the express purpose of forming such a government—confessing the goodness of the great Governor of the universe (who alone knows to what degree of earthly happiness mankind may attain by perfecting the arts of government) in permitting the people of this State, by common consent, and without violence, deliberately to form for themselves such just rules as they shall think best, for governing their future society; and being fully convinced, that it is our indispensable duty to establish such original principles of government as will best promote the general happiness of the people of this State, and their posterity, and provide for future improvements, without partiality for, or prejudice against, any particular class, sect, or denomination of men whatever; do, by virtue of authority vested in us by our constituents, ordain, declare and establish the following Declaration of Rights, and Frame of Government, to be the Constitution of this Commonwealth, and to remain in force therein forever unaltered, except in such articles as shall hereafter on experience be found to require improvement, and which shall, by the same authority of the people, fairly delegated, as this Frame of Government directs, be amended or improved, for the more effectual obtaining and securing the great end and design of all government, herein before mentioned.

CHAPTER I.

A DECLARATION OF THE RIGHTS OF THE INHABITANTS OF THE STATE OF VERMONT.

I. THAT all men are born equally free and independent, and have certain natural, inherent and unalienable rights; amongst which are, the enjoying and defending life and liberty—acquiring, possessing and protecting property—and pursuing and obtaining happiness and safety. Therefore, no male person, born in this country, or brought from over sea, ought to be holden by law to serve any person, as a servant, slave, or apprentice, after he arrives to the age of twenty-one years; nor female, in like manner, after she arrives to the age of eighteen years; unless they are bound by their own consent after they arrive to such age; or bound by law for the payment of debts, damages, fines, costs, or the like.

II. That private property ought to be subservient to public uses, when necessity requires it; nevertheless, whenever any particular man's property is taken for the use of the public, the owner ought to receive an equivalent in money.

III. That all men have a natural and unalienable right to worship Almighty God according to the dictates of their own consciences and understandings, as in their opinion shall be regulated by the word of God; and that no man ought, or of right can be compelled to attend any religious worship, or erect or support any place of worship, or maintain any minister, contrary to the dictates of his conscience; nor can any man be justly deprived or abridged of any civil right as a citizen, on account of his religious sentiments, or peculiar mode of religious worship; and that no authority can, or ought to be vested in, or assumed by any power whatsoever, that shall in any case interfere with, or in any manner control the rights of conscience, in the free exercise of religious worship: Nevertheless, every sect or denomination of Christians ought to observe the Sabbath or Lord's day, and keep up some sort of religious worship, which to them shall seem most agreeable to the revealed will of God.

IV. Every person within this Commonwealth ought to find a certain remedy, by having recourse to the laws, for all injuries or wrongs which he may receive in his person, property, or character: he ought to obtain right and justice freely, and without being obliged to purchase it—completely, and without any denial—promptly, and without delay; conformably to the laws.

V. That the people of this State, by their legal representatives, have the sole, exclusive and inherent right of governing and regulating the internal police of the same.

VI. That all power being originally inherent in, and consequently derived from the people; therefore, all officers of government, whether legislative or executive, are their trustees and servants, and at all times, in a legal way, accountable to them.

VII. That government is, or ought to be, instituted for the common benefit, protection and security of the people, nation, or community, and not for the particular emolument or advantage of any single man, family, or set of men, who are a part only of that community: and that the community hath an indubitable, unalienable, and indefeasible right, to reform or alter government, in such manner as shall be, by that community, judged to be most conducive to the public weal.

VIII. That those who are employed in the legislative and executive business of the State may be restrained from oppression, the people have a right, by their legal representatives, to enact laws for reducing their public officers to a private station, and for supplying their vacancies in a constitutional manner, by regular elections, at such periods as they may think proper.

IX. That all elections ought to be free and without corruption; and that all freemen, having a sufficient evident common interest with, and attachment to the community, have a right to elect officers, and be elected into office.

X. That every member of society hath a right to be protected in the enjoyment of life, liberty and property; and therefore is bound to contribute his proportion towards the expense of that protection, and yield his personal service, when necessary, or an equivalent thereto: but no part of a man's property can be justly taken from him, or applied to public uses, without his own consent, or that of the representative body of the freemen; nor can any man, who is conscientiously scrupulous of bearing arms, be justly compelled thereto, if he will pay such equivalent; nor are the people bound by any law, but such as they have in like manner assented to, for their common good. And previous to any law being made to raise a tax, the purpose, for which it is to be raised ought to appear evident to the Legislature to be of more service to the community, than the money would be if not collected.

XI. That in all prosecutions for criminal offences, a man hath a right to be heard by himself and his counsel—to demand the cause and nature of his accusation—to be confronted with the witnesses—to call for evidence in his favour, and a speedy public trial by an impartial jury of the country, without the unanimous consent of which jury he cannot be found guilty—nor can he be compelled to give evidence against himself—nor can any man be justly deprived of his liberty, except by the laws of the land, or the judgment of his peers.

XII. That the people have a right to hold themselves, their houses, papers and possessions, free from search or seizure: and therefore warrants, without oaths or affirmations first made, affording sufficient foundation for them, and whereby any officer or messenger may be commanded or required to search suspected places, or to seize any person or persons, his, her or their property not particularly described, are contrary to that right, and ought not to be granted.

XIII. That no warrant or writ to attach the person or estate of any freeholder within this State, shall be issued in civil action, without the person or persons, who may request such warrant or attachment, first make oath, or affirm before the authority who may be requested to issue the same, that he or they are in danger of losing his, her, or their debts.

XIV. That when an issue in fact, proper for the cognizance of a jury, is joined in a court of law, the parties have a right to a trial by jury; which ought to be held sacred.

XV. That the people have a right of freedom of speech and of writing and publishing their sentiments, concerning the transactions of government—and therefore the freedom of the press ought not to be restrained.

XVI. The freedom of deliberation, speech, and debate, in the legislature, is so essential to the rights of the people, that it cannot be the foundation of any accusation or prosecution, action or complaint, in any other court or place whatsoever.

XVII. The power of suspending laws, or the execution of laws, ought never to be exercised, but by the Legislature, or by authority derived from it, to be exercised in such particular cases only as the Legislature shall expressly provide for.

XVIII. That the people have a right to bear arms, for the defence of themselves and the State: and as standing armies, in the time of peace, are dangerous to liberty, they ought not to be kept up; and that the military should be kept under strict subordination to, and governed by the civil power.

XIX. That no person in this Commonwealth can, in any case, be subjected to law-martial or to any penalties or pains, by virtue of that law, except those employed in the army, and the militia in actual service.

XX. That frequent recurrence to fundamental principles, and a firm adherence to justice, moderation, temperance, industry, and frugality, are absolutely necessary to preserve the blessings of liberty, and keep government free; the people ought therefore to pay particular attention to these points, in the choice of officers and representatives; and have a right, in a legal way, to exact a due and constant regard to them, from their legislators and magistrates, in the making and executing such laws as are necessary for the good government of the State.

XXI. That all people have a natural and inherent right to emigrate from one State to another, that will receive them; or to form a new State in vacant countries, or in such countries as they can purchase, whenever they think that thereby they can promote their own happiness.

XXII. That the people have a right to assemble together, to consult for their common good—to instruct their representatives, and to apply to the Legislature for redress of grievances, by address, petition or remonstrance.

XXIII. That no person shall be liable to be transported out of this State, for trial for any offence committed within the same.

CHAP. II.

PLAN OR FRAME OF GOVERNMENT.

SECT. I. THE Commonwealth or State of Vermont, shall be governed hereafter by a Governor, (or Lieutenant-Governor) Council, and an Assembly of the Representatives of the freemen of the same, in manner and form following:

II. The supreme legislative power shall be vested in a House of Representatives of the freemen, or Commonwealth, or State of Vermont.

III. The supreme executive power shall be vested in a Governor, (or, in his absence, a Lieutenant-Governor) and Council.

IV. Courts of justice shall be maintained in every county in this State, and also in new counties when formed; which courts shall be open for the trial of all causes proper for their cognizance, and justice shall be therein impartially administered, without corruption, or unnecessary delay. The Judges of the Supreme Court shall be Justices of the Peace throughout the State; and the several Judges of the County Courts, in their respective counties, by virtue of their offices, except in the trial of such causes as may be appealed to the County Court.

V. A future legislature may, when they shall conceive the same to be expedient and necessary, erect a Court of Chancery, with such powers as are usually exercised by that Court, or as shall appear for the interest of the Commonwealth: Provided they do not constitute themselves the Judges of the said Court.

VI. The legislative, executive and judiciary departments shall be separate and distinct, so that neither exercise the powers properly belonging to the other.

VII. In order that the freemen of this State may enjoy the benefit of election, as equally as may be, each town within this State, that consists or may consist of eighty taxable inhabitants, within one septenary or seven years next after the establishing this Constitution, may hold elections therein, and choose each two representatives; and each other inhabited town in this State may, in like manner, choose each one representative to represent them in General Assembly, during the said septenary or seven years; and after that, each inhabited town may, in like manner, hold such election, and choose each one representative forever thereafter.

VIII. The House of Representatives of the freemen of this State shall consist of persons most noted for wisdom and virtue, to be chosen by ballot by the freemen of every town in this State respectively, on the first Tuesday of September annually forever.

IX. The representatives, so chosen, (a majority of whom shall constitute a quorum for transacting any other business than raising a State tax, for which two thirds of the members elected shall be present) shall meet on the second Thursday of the succeeding October, and shall be styled, *The General Assembly of the State of Vermont:* they shall have power to choose their Speaker, Secretary of the State, their Clerk and other necessary officers of the house—sit on their own adjournments—prepare bills, and enact them into laws—judge of the elections and qualifications of their own members: they may expel members, but not for causes known to their constitutents antecedent to their election; they may administer oaths, or affirmations, in matters depending before them—redress grievances—impeach State criminals—grant charters of incorporation—constitute towns, boroughs, cities and counties: they may annually, in their first session after their election, and at other times when vacancies happen, choose Delegates to Congress: and shall also, in conjunction with the Council, annually, (or oftener if need be) elect Judges of the Supreme and several County and Probate Courts, Sheriffs and Justices of the Peace: and also with the Council, may elect Major-Generals and Brigadier-Generals, from time to time, as often as there shall be occasion; and they shall have all other powers necessary for the Legislature of a free and sovereign State: but they shall have no power to add to, alter, abolish, or infringe, any part of this Constitution.

X. The Supreme Executive Council of this State shall consist of a Governor, Lieutenant-Governor, and twelve persons, chosen in the following manner, viz. The freemen of each town shall, on the day of election for choosing representatives to attend the General Assembly, bring in their votes for Governor, with his name fairly written, to the Constable, who shall seal them up, and write on them, *Votes for the Governor,* and deliver them to the representative chosen to attend the General Assembly: and at the opening of the General Assembly, there shall be a committee appointed out of the Council and Assembly, who, after being duly sworn to the faithful discharge of their trust, shall proceed to receive, sort and count the votes for the Governor, and declare the person who has the major part of the votes to be Governor, for the year ensuing. And if there be no choice made, then the Council and General Assembly, by their joint ballot, shall make choice of a Governor.

The Lieutenant-Governor and Treasurer shall be chosen in the manner above directed. And each freeman shall give in twelve votes for twelve counsellors, in the same manner: and the twelve highest in nomination shall serve for the ensuing year as counsellors.

XI. The Governor, and in his absence, the Lieutenant-Governor, with the Council, (a major part of whom, including the Governor or Lieutenant-Governor, shall be a quorum to transact business) shall have power to commissionate all officers—and also to appoint officers, except where provision is or shall be otherwise made by law, or this frame of government; and shall supply every vacancy in any office occasioned by death or otherwise, until the office can be filled in the manner directed by law or this Constitution. They are to correspond with other States—transact business with officers of government, civil and military, and to prepare such business as may appear to them necessary to lay before the General Assembly. They shall sit as Judges to hear and determine on impeachments, taking to their assistance, for advice only, the Judges of the Supreme Court; and shall have power to grant pardons, and remit fines in all cases whatsoever, except in treason and murder, in which they shall have power to grant reprieves but not to pardon, until after the end of the next session of Assembly, and except in cases of impeachment, in which there shall be no remission or mitigation of punishment, but by act of legislation. They are also to take care that the laws be faithfully executed. They are to expedite the execution of such measures as may be resolved upon by the General Assembly: and they may draw upon the Treasurer for such sums as may be appropriated by the House of Representatives. They may also lay embargoes, or prohibit the exportation of any commodity, for any time not exceeding thirty days, in the recess of the House only: they may grant such licenses as shall be directed by law, and shall have power to call together the General Assembly, when necessary, before the day to which they shall stand adjourned. The Governor shall be captain-general and commander-in-chief of the forces of the State, but shall not command in person, except advised thereto by the Council, and then only as long as they shall approve thereof: and the Lieutenant-Governor shall, by virtue of his office, be Lieutenant-General of all the forces of the State. The Governor, or Lieutenant-Governor, and the Council, shall meet at the time and place with the General Assembly: the Lieutenant-Governor shall, during the presence of the commander-in-chief, vote and act as one of the Council; and the Governor, and, in his absence, the Lieutenant-Governor, shall, by virtue of their offices, preside in Council, and have a casting, but no other vote. Every member of the Council shall be a Justice of the Peace for the whole State, by virtue of his office. The Governor and Council shall have a Secretary, and keep fair books of their proceedings, wherein any counsellor may enter his dissent, with his reasons to support it.

XII. The representatives, having met, and chosen their speaker and clerk, shall each of them, before they proceed to business, take and subscribe, as well the oath or affirmation of allegiance herein after directed (except where they shall produce certificates of their having heretofore taken and subscribed the same) as the following oath or affirmation, viz.

You ——— do solemnly swear, (or affirm) that, as a member of this Assembly, you will not propose or assent to any bill, vote, or resolution, which shall appear to you injurious to the people; nor do nor consent to any act or thing whatever, that shall have a tendency to lessen or abridge their rights and privileges as declared by the Constitution of this State; but will, in all things, conduct yourself as a faithful, honest representative and guardian of the people, according to the best of your judgment and abilities. (In case of an oath) So help you God. (And in case of an affirmation) Under the pains and penalties of perjury.

And each member, before he takes his seat, shall make and subscribe the following declaration, viz.

You do believe in one God, the Creator and Governor of the Universe, the rewarded of the good, and punisher of the wicked. And you do acknowledge the scriptures of the Old and New Testament to be given by divine inspiration; and own and profess the Protestant religion.

And no further or other religious test shall ever hereafter be required of any civil officer or magistrate, in this State.

XIII. The doors of the House, in which the General Assembly of this Commonwealth shall sit, shall be open for the admission of all persons who behave decently, except only when the welfare of the State may require them to be shut.

XIV. The votes and preceedings of the General Assembly shall be printed (when one third of the members think it necessary) as soon as conveniently may be, after the end of each session, with the yeas and nays on any question, when required by any member, (except where the votes shall be taken by ballot) in which case every member shall have a right to insert the reasons of his vote upon the minutes.

XV. The style of laws of this State, in future to be passed, shall be, *It is hereby enacted by the General Assembly of the State of Vermont.*

XVI. To the end that laws, before they are enacted, may be more maturely considered, and the inconvenience of hasty determinations as much as possible prevented, all bills which originate in the Assembly shall be laid before the Governor and Council for their revision and concurrence, or proposals of amendment; who shall return the same to the Assembly, with their proposals of amendment (if any) in writing: and if the same are not agreed to by the Assembly, it shall be in the power of the Governor and Council to suspend the passing of such bills until the next session of the Legislature. Provided, that if the Governor and Council shall neglect or refuse to return any such bill to the Assembly with written proposals of amendment, within five days, or before the rising of the Legislature, the same shall become a law.

XVII. No person ought, in any case, or in any time, to be declared guilty of treason or felony by the Legislature.

XVIII. Every man, of the full age of twenty-one years, having resided in this State, for the space of one whole year, next before the election of representatives, and is of a quiet and peaceable behaviour, and will take the following oath, (or affirmation) shall be entitled to all the privileges of a freeman of this State.

You solemnly swear, (or affirm) that whenever you give your vote or suffrage, touching any matter that concerns the State of Vermont, you will do it so as in your conscience you shall judge will most conduce to the best good of the same, as established by the Constitution, without fear or favour of any man.

XIX. The inhabitants of this Commonwealth shall be trained and armed for its defence, under such regulations, restrictions, and exceptions, as the General Assembly shall by law direct. The several companies of militia shall, as often as vacancies happen, elect their captains and other inferior officers; and the captains and subalterns shall nominate and recommend the field officers of their respective regiments, who shall appoint their staff-officers.

XX. All commissions shall be in the name of the freemen of the State of Vermont, sealed with the State seal, signed by the Governor, and in his absence the Lieutenant-Governor, and attested by the Secretary; which seal shall be kept by the Council.

XXI. Every officer of State, whether judicial or executive, shall be liable to be impeached by the General Assembly, either when in office, or after his resignation, or removal for mal-administration. All impeachments shall be before the Governor or Lieutenant-Governor, and Council, who shall hear and determine the same, and may award costs.

XXII. As every freeman, to preserve his independence, (if without a sufficient estate) ought to have some profession, calling, trade, or farm, whereby he may honestly subsist, there can be no necessity for, nor use in establishing offices of profit, the usual effects of which are dependence and servility, unbecoming freemen, in the possessors or expectants, faction, contention, corruption and disorder among the people. But if any man is called into public service, to the prejudice of his private affairs, he has a right to a reasonable compensation: and whenever an office, through increase of fees or otherwise, becomes so profitable as to occasion many to apply for it, the profits ought to be lessened by the legislature. And if any officer shall take greater or other fees than the laws allow him, either directly or indirectly, it shall ever after disqualify him from holding any office in this State.

XXIII. No person in this State shall be capable of holding or exercising more than one of the following offices at the same time, viz. Governor, Lieutenant-Governor, Judge of the Supreme Court, Treasurer of the State, member of the Council, member of the General Assembly, Surveyor-General, or Sheriff.

XXIV. The Treasurer of the State shall, before the Governor and Council, give sufficient security to the Secretary of the State, in behalf of the General Assembly;

and each High Sheriff, before the first Judge of the County Court, to the Treasurer of their respective counties, previous to their respectively entering upon the execution of their offices, in such manner, and in such sums, as shall be directed by the Legislature.

XXV. The Treasurer's accounts shall be annually audited, and a fair state thereof laid before the General Assembly, at their session in October.

XXVI. Every officer, whether judicial, executive, or military, in authority under this State, before he enter upon the execution of his office, shall take and subscribe the following oath or affirmation of allegiance to this State, (unless he shall produce evidence that he has before taken the same) and also the following oath or affirmation of office, (except such as shall be exempted by the Legislature,) viz.

The oath or affirmation of allegiance.

You do solemnly swear (or affirm) that you will be true and faithful to the State of Vermont; and that you will not, directly nor indirectly, do any act or thing injurious to the Constitution or government thereof, as established by Convention. (If an oath) So help you God. (If an affirmation) Under the pains and penalties of perjury.

The oath or affirmation of office.

You ———— ———— do solemnly swear, (or affirm) that you will faithfully execute the office of ———— for the ———— of ————; and will therein do equal right and justice to all men, to the best of your judgment and abilities, according to law. (If an oath) So help you God. (If an affirmation) Under the pains and penalties of perjury.

XXVII. Any delegate to Congress may be superseded at any time, by the General Assembly appointing another in his stead. No man shall be capable of being a delegate to represent this State in Congress for more than three years, in any term of six years;—and no person, who holds any office in the gift of Congress, shall, during the time of his holding such office, be elected to represent this State in Congress.

XXVIII. Trials of issues, proper for the cognizance of a jury, in the Supreme and County Courts, shall be by jury, except where parties otherwise agree: and great care ought to be taken to prevent corruption or partiality in the choice and return, or appointment of juries.

XXIX. All prosecutions shall commence by the authority of the State of Vermont—all indictments shall conclude with these words, *Against the peace and dignity of the State.* And all fines shall be proportionate to the offences.

XXX. The person of a debtor, where there is not strong presumption of fraud, shall not be continued in prison after delivering up and assigning over, *bona fide*, all his estate, real and personal, in possession, reversion, or remainder, for the use ofe his creditors, in such manner as shall be hereafter regulated by law. And all prisoners, unless in execution, or committed for capital offences, when the proof is evident or presumption great, shall be bailable by sufficient sureties: nor shall excessive bail be exacted for bailable offences.

XXXI. All elections, whether by the people, or in General Assembly, shall be by ballot, free and voluntary: and any elector, who shall receive any gift or reward for his vote, in meat, drink, monies or otherwise, shall forfeit his right to elect at that time, and suffer such other penalty as the laws shall direct: and any person who shall, directly or indirectly, give, promise or bestow any such rewards to be elected, shall thereby be rendered incapable to serve for the ensuing year, and be subject to such further punishment as a future Legislature shall direct.

XXXII. All deeds and conveyances of land shall be recorded in the Town Clerk's office, in their respective towns; and, for want thereof, in the County Clerk's office of the same county.

XXXIII. The Legislature shall regulate entails in such manner as to prevent perpetuities.

XXXIV. To deter more effectually from the commission of crimes, by continued

visible punishment, of long duration, and to make sanguinary punishment less necessary, means ought to be provided for punishing by hard labour, those who shall be
convicted of crimes not capital, whereby the criminal shall be employed for the benefit
of the public, or for reparation of injuries done to private persons : and all persons,
at proper times, ought to be permitted to see them at their labour.

XXXV. The estates of such persons as may destroy their own lives, shall not for that
offence be forfeited, but descend or ascend in the same manner as if such persons had
died in a natural way. Nor shall any article, which shall accidentally occasion the
death of any person, be henceforth deemed a deodand, or in anywise forfeited on
account of such misfortune.

XXXVI. Every person of good character, who comes to settle in this State, having first taken an oath or affirmation of allegiance to the same, may purchase, or by
other just means, acquire, hold and transfer land, or other real estate; and, after one
year's residence, shall be deemed a free denizen thereof, and entitled to all the rights
of a natural born subject of this State, except that he shall not be capable of being
elected Governor, Lieutenant-Governor, Treasurer, Counsellor, or Representative in
Assembly, until after two years' residence.

XXXVII. The inhabitants of this State shall have liberty, in seasonable times, to
hunt and fowl on the lands they hold, and on other lands not inclosed; and in like
manner to fish in all boatable and other waters, not private property, under proper
regulations, to be hereafter made and provided by the General Assembly.

XXXVIII. Laws for the encouragement of virtue, and prevention of vice and immorality, ought to be constantly kept in force, and duly executed; and a competent
number of schools ought to be maintained in each town for the convenient instruction
of youth; and one or more grammar schools be incorporated, and properly supported
in each county in this State. And all religious societies, or bodies of men, that may
be hereafter united or incorporated, for the advancement of religion and learning, or
for other pious and charitable purposes, shall be encouraged and protected in the
enjoyment of the privileges, immunities, and estates, which they in justice ought to
enjoy, under such regulations as the General Assembly of this State shall direct.

XXXIX. The declaration of the political rights and privileges of the inhabitants of
this State, is hereby declared to be a part of the Constitution of this Commonwealth;
and ought not to be violated on any pretence whatsoever.

XL. In order that the freedom of this Commonwealth may be preserved inviolate
forever, there shall be chosen by ballot, by the freemen of this State, on the last Wednes-.
day in March, in the year one thousand seven hundred and eighty-five, and on the last
Wednesday in March in every seven years thereafter, thirteen persons, who shall be
chosen in the same manner the Council is chosen, except that they shall not be out
of the Council or General Assembly, to be called the Council of Censors; who shall
meet together on the first Wednesday of June next ensuing their election, the majority
of whom shall be a quorum in every case, except as to calling a convention, in which
two-thirds of the whole number elected shall agree: and whose duty it shall be to
inquire whether the Constitution has been preserved inviolate in every part, during
the last septenary (including the year of their service;) and whether the legislative
and executive branches of government have performed their duty, as guardians of
the people, or assumed to themselves, or exercised other or greater powers than they
are entitled to by the Constitution : they are also to inquire, whether the public taxes
have been justly laid and collected in all parts of this Commonwealth—in what manner the public monies have been disposed of—and whether the laws have been duly
executed. For these purposes, they shall have power to send for persons, papers,
and records; they shall have authority to pass public censures—to order impeachments—and to recommend to the Legislature the repealing such laws as appear to
them to have been enacted contrary to the principles of the Constitution; these
powers they shall continue to have, for, and during the space of one year from the
day of their election, and no longer. The said Council of Censors shall also have
power to call a Convention, to meet within two years after their sitting, if there appears
to them an absolute necessity of amending any article of this Constitution which may
be defective—explaining such as may be thought not clearly expressed—and of add-

ing such as are necessary for the preservation of the rights and happiness of the people; but the articles to be amended, and the amendments proposed and such articles-as are proposed to be added or abolished, shall be promulgated at least six months before the day appointed for the election of such Convention, for the previous consideration of the people, that they may have an opportunity of instructing their delegates on the subject.

By order of Convention, July 4th, 1786.

MOSES ROBINSON, *President.*

Attest : ELIJAH PAINE, *Secretary.*

[Doc. No. 3]

Act of February 18, 1791

STATUTE III.

Feb. 18, 1791.

CHAP. VII.—*An Act for the admission of the State of Vermont into this Union.*

THE state of Vermont having petitioned the Congress to be admitted a member of the United States, *Be it enacted by the Senate and House of Representatives of the United States of America in Congress assembled, and it is hereby enacted and declared,* That on the fourth day of March, one thousand seven hundred and ninety-one, the said state, by the name and style of "The State of Vermont," shall be received and admitted into this Union, as a new and entire member of the United States of America.

APPROVED, February 18, 1791.

State of Vermont to be admitted into the Union, 4th March, 1791.

[Doc. No. 4]

Constitution of 1793/6

CONSTITUTION OF VERMONT—1793.†

CHAPTER I.

DECLARATION OF RIGHTS.

ARTICLE I. That all men are born equally free and independent, and have certain natural, inherent, and unalienable rights, amongst which are the enjoying and defending life and liberty, acquiring, possessing, and protecting property, and pursuing and obtaining happiness and safety; therefore, no male person born in this country, or brought from over sea, ought to be holden by law to serve any person as a servant, slave, or apprentice, after he arrives to the age of twenty-one years, nor female in like manner, after she arrives to the age of eighteen years, unless they are bound by their own consent after they arrive to such age, or bound by law for the payment of debts, damages, fines, costs, or the like.

ART. II. The private property ought to be subservient to public uses when necessity requires it; nevertheless, when any person's property is taken for the use of the public, the owner ought to receive an equivalent in money.

ART. III. That all men have a natural and unalienable right to worship Almighty God according to the dictates of their own consciences and understandings, as in their opinion shall be regulated by the word of God; and that no man ought to, or of right can, be compelled to attend any religious worship, or erect or support any place of worship, or maintain any minister, contrary to the dictates of his conscience;

---

* An act approved March 2, 1791, declared that " from and after the third day of March next, all the laws of the United States, which are not locally inapplicable, ought to have, and shall have, the same force and effect within the State of Vermont as elsewhere within the United States."

† The convention of 1793, instead of announcing such of the amendments which the censors had convened them to consider as received their approval, embodied them in the constitution, and promulgated the amended document as "the constitution of Vermont, adopted by the convention holden at Windsor, July 4, 1793;"—the convention finished its labors July 9, 1793. This constitution was adopted by the legislature, November 2, 1796, "as the supreme law of the State."

nor can any man be justly deprived or abridged of any civil right as a citizen, on account of his religious sentiments or peculiar mode of religious worship; and that no authority can or ought to be vested in or assumed by any power whatever, that shall in any case interfere with or in any manner control the rights of conscience in the free exercise of religious worship. Nevertheless, every sect or denomination of Christians ought to observe the Sabbath, or Lord's day, and keep up some sort of religious worship, which to them shall seem most agreeable to the revealed will of God.

ART. IV. Every person within this State ought to find a certain remedy, by having recourse to the laws for all injuries or wrongs which he may receive in his person, property, or character; he ought to obtain right and justice freely, and without being obliged to purchase it; completely, and without any denial; promptly, and without delay, comformably to the law.

ART. V. That the people of this State, by their legal representatives, have the sole, inherent, and exclusive right of governing and regulating the internal police of the same.

ART. VI. That all power being originally inherent in, and consequently derived from, the people, therefore all officers of government, whether legislative or executive, are their trustees and servants, and at all times, in a legal way, accountable to them.

ART. VII. That government is, or ought to be, instituted for the common benefit, protection, and security of the people, nation, or community, and not for the particular emolument or advantage of any single man, family, or set of men, who are a part only of that community; and that the community hath an indubitable, unalienable, and indefeasible right to reform or alter government, in such manner as shall be by that community judged most conducive to the public weal.

ART. VIII. That all elections ought to be free and without corruption, and that all freemen, having a sufficient evidence, common interest with, and attachment to the community, have a right to elect officers and be elected into office, agreeably to the regulations made in this constitution.

ART. IX. That every member of society hath a right to be protected in the enjoyment of life, liberty, and property, and therefore is bound to contribute his proportion towards the expense of that protection, and yield his personal service, when necessary, or an equivalent thereto; but no part of any person's property can be justly taken from him, or applied to public uses, without his consent, or that of the representative body of freemen; nor can any man who is conscientiously scrupulous of bearing arms be justly compelled thereto, if he will pay such equivalent; nor are the people bound by any law but such as they have in like manner assented to for their common good; and previous to any law being made to raise a tax, the purpose for which it is to be raised ought to appear evident to the legislature to be of more service to the community than the money would be if not collected.

ART. X. That in all prosecutions for criminal offences a person hath a right to be heard by himself and his counsel; to demand the cause and nature of his accusation; to be confronted with the witnesses; to call for evidence in his favor, and a speedy public trial by an impartial jury of his country; without the unanimous consent of which jury he cannot be found guilty; nor can he be compelled to give evidence against himself; nor can any person be justly deprived of his liberty, except by the laws of the land or the judgment of his peers.

ART. XI. That the people have a right to hold themselves, their houses, papers, and possessions, free from search or seizure; and, therefore, warrants without oath or affirmation first made, affording sufficient foundation for them, and whereby any officer or messenger may be commanded or required to search suspected places, or to seize any person or persons, his, her, or their property, not particularly described, are contrary to that right, and ought not to be granted.

ART. XII. That when any issue in fact, proper for the cognizance of jury, is joined in a court of law, the parties have a right to trial by jury, which ought to be held sacred.

ART. XIII. That the people have a right to freedom of speech, and of writing and publishing their sentiments, concerning the transactions of government, and therefore the freedom of the press ought not to be restrained.

ART. XIV. The freedom of deliberation, speech, and debate, in the legislature, is so essential to the rights of the people, that it cannot be the foundation of any accusation, or prosecution, action, or complaint in any other court or place whatsoever.

ART. XV. The power of suspending laws, or the execution of laws, ought never to be exercised but by the legislature, or by authority derived from it, to be exercised in such particular cases as this constitution or the legislature shall provide for.

ART. XVI. That the people have a right to bear arms for the defence of themselves and the State; and, as standing armies in time of peace are dangerous to liberty, they ought not to be kept up; and that the military should be kept under strict subordination to, and governed by, the civil power.

ART. XVII. That no person in this State can, in any case, be subjected to law-martial, or to any penalties or pains by virtue of that law, except those employed in the army, and the militia in actual service.

ART. XVIII. The frequent recurrence to fundamental principles, and firm adherence to justice, moderation, temperance, industry, and frugality, are absolutely necessary to preserve the blessings of liberty, and keep government free; the people ought, therefore, to pay particular attention to these points, in the choice of officers and representatives, and have a right, in a legal way, to exact a due and constant regard to them, from their legislators and magistrates, in making and executing such laws as are necessary for the good government of the State.

ART. XIX. That all people have a natural and inherent right to emigrate from one State to another that will receive them.

ART. XX. That the people have a right to assemble together to consult for their common good, to instruct their representatives, and apply to the legislature for redress of grievances, by address, petition, or remonstrance.

ART. XXI. That no person shall be liable to be transported out of this State for trial for any offence committed within the same.

CHAPTER II.

PLAN OR FORM OF GOVERNMENT.

SECTION 1. The commonwealth or State of Vermont shall be governed hereafter by a governor or lieutenant-governor, council, and an assembly of the representatives of the freemen of the same, in manner and form following:

SEC. 2. The supreme legislative power shall be vested in a house of representatives, of the freemen of the commonwealth or State of Vermont.

SEC. 3. The supreme executive power shall be vested in a governor, or, in his absence, a lieutenant-governor and council.

SEC. 4. Courts of justice shall be maintained in every county in this State, and also in new counties, when formed; which courts shall be open for the trial of all causes proper for their cognizance; and justice shall be therein impartially administered, without corruption or unnecessary delay. The judges of the supreme court shall be justices of the peace throughout the State; and the several judges of the county courts, in their respective counties, by virtue of their office, except in the trial of such causes as may be appealed to the county court.

SEC. 5. A future legislature may, when they shall conceive the same to be expedient and necessary, erect a court of chancery, with such powers as are usually exercised by that court, or as shall appear for the interest of the commonwealth: *Provided*, They do not constitute themselves the judges of the said court.

SEC. 6. The legislative, executive, and judiciary departments shall be separate and distinct, so that neither exercise the powers properly belonging to the other.

SEC. 7. In order that the freemen of this State might enjoy the benefit of election, as equally as may be, each town within this State, that consists or may consist of eighty taxable inhabitants, within one septenary, or seven years next after the establishing this constitution, may hold elections therein, and choose each two representatives; and each other inhabited town in this State may, in like manner, choose each one representative to represent them in general assembly, during the said septenary, or seven years; and after that, each inhabited town may, in like manner, hold such election, and choose each one representative, forever thereafter.

SEC. 8. The house of representatives of the freemen of this State shall consist of persons most noted for wisdom and virtue, to be chosen by ballot, by the freemen of every town in this State, respectively, on the first Tuesday in September annually forever.

SEC. 9. The representatives so chosen, a majority of whom shall constitute a quorum for transacting any other business than raising a State tax, for which two-thirds of the members elected shall be present, shall meet on the second Thursday of the succeeding October, and shall be styled "the general assembly of the State of Vermont;" they shall have power to choose their speaker, secretary of state, their clerk, and other necessary officers of the house, sit on their own adjournments, prepare bills, and enact them into laws, judge of the elections and qualifications of their own members; they may expel members, but not for causes known to their own constituents antecedent to their own elections; they may administer oaths and affirmations in matters depending before them, redress grievances, impeach State criminals, grant charters of incorporation, constitute towns, boroughs, cities, and counties; they may, annually, on their first session after their election, in conjunction with the council, or oftener if need be, elect judges of the supreme and several county and probate courts, sheriffs, and justices of the peace; and also with the council may elect major-generals and brigadier-generals, from time to time, as often as there shall be occasion; and they shall have all other powers necessary for the legislature of a free and sovereign State; but they shall have no power to add to, alter, abolish, or infringe any part of this constitution.

SEC. 10. The supreme executive council of this State shall consist of a governor, lieutenant-governor, and twelve persons, chosen in the following manner, viz: The freemen of each town shall, on the day of the election for choosing representatives to attend the general assembly, bring in their votes for governor, with his name fairly written, to the constable, who shall seal them up, and write on them, "Votes for the governor," and deliver them to the representatives chosen to attend the general assembly; and at the opening of the general assembly there shall be a committee appointed out of the council and assembly, who, after being duly sworn to the faithful discharge of their trust, shall proceed to receive, sort, and count the votes for the governor, and declare the person who has the major part of the votes to be governor for the year ensuing. And if there be no choice made, then the council and general assembly, by their joint ballot, shall make choice of a governor. The lieutenant-governor and treasurer shall be chosen in the manner above directed. And each freeman shall give in twelve votes, for twelve councillors, in the same manner; and the twelve highest in nomination shall serve for the ensuing year as councillors.

SEC. 11. The governor, and, in his absence, the lieutenant-governor, with the council, a major part of whom, including the governor, or lieutenant-governor, shall be a quorum to transact business, shall have power to commission all officers, and also to appoint officers, except where provision is, or shall be, otherwise made by law, or this frame of government; and shall supply every vacancy in any office, occasioned by death or otherwise, until the office can be filled in the manner directed by law or this constitution.

They are to correspond with other States, transact business with officers of government, civil and military, and to prepare such business as may appear to them necessary to lay before the general assembly. They shall sit as judges to hear and determine on impeachments, taking to their assistance, for advice only, the judges of the supreme court. And shall have power to grant pardons, and remit fines, in all cases whatsoever, except in treason and murder; in which they shall have power to grant reprieves, but not to pardon, until after the end of the next session of assembly; and except in cases of impeachment, in which there shall be no remission or mitigation of punishment, but by act of legislation.

They are also to take care that the laws be faithfully executed. They are to expedite the execution of such measures as may be resolved upon by the general assembly

And they may draw upon the treasury for such sums as may be appropriated by the house of representatives. They may also lay embargoes, or prohibit the exportation of any commodity, for any time not exceeding thirty days, in the recess of the house only. They may grant such licenses as shall be directed by law; and shall have power to call together the general assembly, when necessary, before the day to which they shall stand adjourned. The governor shall be captain-general and commander-in-chief of the forces of the State, but shall not command in person, except advised thereto by the council, and then only so long as they shall approve thereof. And the lieutenant-governor shall, by virtue of his office, be lieutenant-general of all the forces of the State. The governor, or lieutenant-governor, and the council, shall meet at the time and place with the general assembly; the lieutenant-governor shall, during the presence of the commander-in-chief, vote and act as one of the council; and the governor, and, in his absence, the lieutenant-governor, shall, by virtue of their offices, preside in council, and have a casting but no other vote. Every member of the council shall be a justice of the peace, for the whole State, by virtue of his office. The governor and council shall have a secretary, and keep fair books of their proceedings, wherein any councillor may enter his dissent, with his reasons to support it; and the governor may appoint a secretary for himself and his council.

SEC. 12. The representatives, having met and chosen their speaker and clerk, shall, each of them, before they proceed to business, take and subscribe, as well the oath or affirmation of allegiance hereinafter directed, except where they shall produce certificates of their having heretofore taken and subscribed the same, as the following oath or affirmation, viz:

"You, ——— ———, do solemnly swear [or affirm] that, as a member of this assembly, you will not propose or assent to any bill, vote, or resolution which shall appear to you injurious to the people, nor do or consent to any act or thing whatsoever that shall have a tendency to lessen or abridge their rights and privileges, as declared by the constitution of this State; but will in all things conduct yourself as a faithful, honest representative and guardian of the people, according to the best of your judgment and abilities: [in case of an oath,] So help you God; [and in case of an affirmation,] under the pains and penalties of perjury."

SEC. 13. The doors of the house in which the general assembly of this commonwealth shall sit shall be open for the admission of all persons who behave decently, except only when the welfare of the State may require them to be shut.

SEC. 14. The votes and proceedings of the general assembly shall be printed, when one-third of the members think it necessary, as soon as convenient after the end of each session, with the yeas and nays on any question, when required by any member, except where the votes shall be taken by ballot, in which case every member shall have a right to insert the reasons of his vote upon the minutes.

SEC. 15. The style of the laws of this State, in future to be passed, shall be, "*It is hereby enacted by the general assembly of the State of Vermont.*"

SEC. 16. To the end that laws, before they are enacted, may be more maturely considered, and the inconvenience of hasty determinations, as much as possible, prevented, all bills which originate in the assembly shall be laid before the governor and council, for their revision and concurrence or proposals of amendment; who shall return the same to the assembly, with their proposals of amendment, if any, in writing; and if the same are not agreed to by the assembly, it shall be in the power of the governor and council to suspend the passing of such bills until the next session of the legislature: *Provided*, That if the governor and council shall neglect or refuse to return any such bill to the assembly, with written proposals of amendment, within five days, or before the rising of the legislature, the same shall become a law.

SEC. 17. No money shall be drawn out of the treasury, unless first appropriated by act of legislation.

SEC. 18. No person shall be elected a representative until he has resided two years in this State; the last of which shall be in the town for which he is elected.

SEC. 19. No member of the council or house of representatives shall, directly or indirectly, receive any fee or reward to bring forward or advocate any bill, petition, or other business to be transacted in the legislature; or advocate any cause, as counsel, in either house of legislation, except when employed in behalf of the State.

SEC. 20. No person ought, in any case or in any time, to be declared guilty of treason or felony by the legislature.

SEC. 21. Every man, of the full age of twenty-one years, having resided in this State for the space of one whole year next before the election of representatives, and is of a quiet and peaceable behavior, and will take the following oath or affirmation, shall be entitled to all the privileges of a freeman of this State:

"You solemnly swear [or affirm] that whenever you give your vote or suffrage touching any matter that concerns the State of Vermont, you will do it so as in your conscience you shall judge will most conduce to the best good of the same, as established by the constitution, without fear or favor of any man."

SEC. 22. The inhabitants of this State shall be trained and armed for its defence, under such regulations, restrictions, and exceptions as Congress, agreeably to the Constitution of the United States, and the legislature of this State, shall direct. The several companies of militia shall, as often as vacancies happen, elect their captain and other officers, and the captains and subalterns shall nominate and recommend the field-officers of their respective regiments, who shall appoint their staff-officers.

SEC. 23. All commissions shall be in the name of the freemen of the State of Vermont, sealed with the State seal, signed by the governor, and in his absence the lieutenant-governor, and attested by the secretary; which seal shall be kept by the governor.

SEC. 24. Every officer of state, whether judicial or executive, shall be liable to be impeached by the general assembly, either when in office or after his resignation or removal, for maladministration. All impeachments shall be before the governor, or lieutenant-governor, and council, who shall hear and determine the same, and may award costs; and no trial or impeachment shall be a bar to a prosecution at law.

SEC. 25. As every freeman, to preserve his independence, if without a sufficient estate, ought to have some profession, calling, trade, or farm, whereby he may honestly subsist, there can be no necessity for nor use in establishing offices of profit, the usual effects of which are dependence and servility, unbecoming freemen, in the possessors or expectants, and faction, contention, and discord among the people. But, if any man is called into public service, to the prejudice of his private affairs, he has a right to a reasonable compensation; and whenever an office, through increase of fees or otherwise, becomes so profitable as to occasion many to apply for it, the profits ought to be lessened by the legislature. And if any officer shall wittingly and wilfully take greater fees than the law allows him, it shall ever after disqualify him from holding any office in this State, until he shall be restored by act of legislation.

SEC. 26. No person in this State shall be capable of holding or exercising more than one of the following offices at the same time, viz: governor, lieutenant-governor, judge of the supreme court, treasurer of the State, member of the council, member of the general assembly, surveyor-general, or sheriff. Nor shall any person, holding any office of profit or trust under the authority of Congress, be eligible to any appointment in the legislature, or of holding any executive or judiciary office under this State.

SEC. 27. The treasurer of the State shall, before the governor and council, give suf-ficent security to the secretary of the State, in behalf of the general assembly; and each high sheriff, before the first judge of the county court, to the treasurer of their respective counties, previous to their respectively entering upon the execution of their offices, in such manner, and in such sums, as shall be directed by the legislature.

SEC. 28. The treasurer's accounts shall be annually audited, and a fair state thereof laid before the general assembly at their session in October.

SEC. 29. Every officer, whether judicial, executive, or military, in authority under this State, before he enters upon the execution of his office, shall take and subscribe to the following oath or affirmation of allegiance to this State, unless he shall produce evidence that he has before taken the same; and also the following oath or affirmation of office, except military officers, and such as shall be exempted by the legislature:

The oath or affirmation of allegiance.

"You do solemnly swear [or affirm] that you will be true and faithful to the State of Vermont, and that you will not, directly or indirectly, do any act or thing injurious to the constitution or government thereof, as established by convention; [if an oath,] So help you God; [if an affirmation,] under the pains and penalties of perjury."

The oath or affirmation of office.

"You, ——— ———, do solemnly swear [or affirm] that you will faithfully execute the office of ——— for the ——— of ———; and will therein do equal right and justice to all men, to the best of your judgment and abilities, according to law; [if an oath,] So help you God; [if an affirmation,] under the pains and penalties of perjury."

SEC. 30. No person shall be eligible to the office of governor or lieutenant-governor until he shall have resided in this State four years next preceding the day of his election.

SEC. 31. Trials of issues, proper for the cognizance of a jury, in the supreme and county courts, shall be by jury, except where parties otherwise agree; and great care ought to be taken to prevent corruption or partiality in the choice and return or appointment of juries.

SEC. 32. All prosecutions shall commence, "by the authority of the State of Vermont;" all indicments shall conclude with these words: "against the peace and dignity of the State." And all fines shall be proportioned to the offences.

SEC. 33. The person of a debtor, where there is not strong presumption of fraud, shall not be continued in prison after delivering up and assigning over, *bona fide*, all his estate, real and personal, in possession, reversion, or remainder, for the use of his creditors, in such manner as shall be hereafter regulated by law. And all prisoners, unless in execution, or committed for capital offences, when the proof is evident or presumption great, shall be bailable by sufficient sureties; nor shall excessive bail be exacted for bailable offences.

SEC. 34. All elections, whether by the people or the legislature, shall be free and voluntary; and any elector who shall receive any gift or reward for his vote, in meat, drink, moneys, or otherwise, shall forfeit his right to elect at that time, and suffer such other penalty as the law shall direct; and any person who shall, directly or indirectly, give, promise, or bestow any such rewards to be elected, shall thereby be rendered incapable to serve for the ensuing year, and be subject to such further punishment as a future legislature shall direct.

SEC. 35. All deeds and conveyances of land shall be recorded in the town clerk's office, in their respective towns; and for want thereof, in the county clerk's office of the same county.

SEC. 36. The legislature shall regulate entails in such manner as to prevent perpetuities.

SEC. 37. To deter more effectually from the commission of crimes, by continued visible punishments of long duration, and to make sanguinary punishments less necessary, means ought to be provided for punishing by hard labor those who shall be convicted of crimes not capital, whereby the criminal shall be employed for the benefit of the public, or for the reparation of injuries done to private persons; and all persons, at proper times, ought to be permitted to see them at their labor.

SEC. 38. The estates of such persons as may destroy their own lives shall not for that offence be forfeited, but descend or ascend in the same manner as if such persons had died in a natural way. Nor shall any article which shall accidentally occasion the death of any person be henceforth deemed a deodand, or in anywise forfeited on account of such misfortune.

SEC. 39. Every person of good character, who comes to settle in this State, having first taken an oath or affirmation of allegiance to the same, may purchase, or by other acquire, hold, and transfer, land, or other real estate; and, after one year's be deemed a free denizen thereof, and entitled to all rights of a natural his State, except that he shall not be capable of being elected governor, lieutenant-governor, treasurer, councillor, or representative in assembly, until after two years' residence.

SEC. 40. The inhabitants of this State shall have liberty, in seasonable times, to hunt and fowl on the lands they hold, and on other lands not inclosed; and in like manner to fish in all boatable and other waters, not private property, under proper regulations, to be hereafter made and provided by the general assembly.

SEC. 41. Laws for the encouragement of virtue and prevention of vice and immorality ought to be constantly kept in force and duly executed; and a competent number of schools ought to be maintained in each town, for the convenient instruction of youth, and one or more grammar-schools be incorporated, and properly supported, in each county in this State. And all religious societies or bodies of men that may be hereafter united or incorporated for the advancement of religion and learning, or for other pious and charitable purposes, shall be encouraged and protected in the enjoyment of the privileges, immunities, and estates which they in justice ought to enjoy, under such regulations as the general assembly of this State shall direct.

SEC. 42. The declaration of the political rights and privileges of the inhabitants of this State is hereby declared to be a part of the constitution of this commonwealth, and ought not to be violated on any pretence whatsoever.

SEC. 43. In order that the freedom of this commonwealth may be preserved inviolate forever, there shall be chosen, by ballot, by the freemen of this State, on the last Wednesday in March, in the year one thousand seven hundred and ninety-nine, and on the last Wednesday in March in every seven years thereafter, thirteen persons, who shall be chosen in the same manner the council is chosen, except they shall not be out of the council or general assembly, to be called the council of censors; who shall meet together on the first Wednesday in June next ensuing their election, the majority of whom shall be a quorum in every case, except as to calling a convention, in which two-thirds of the whole number elected shall agree, and whose duty it shall be to inquire whether the constitution has been preserved inviolate in every part during the last septenary, including the year of their service, and whether the legislative and executive branches of government have performed their duty, as guardians of the people, or assumed to themselves, or exercised, other or greater powers than they are entitled to by the constitution. They are also to inquire whether the public taxes have been justly laid and collected in all parts of this commonwealth; in what manner the public moneys have been disposed of; and whether the laws have been duly executed. For these purposes, they shall have power to send for persons, papers, and records; they shall have authority to pass public censures, to order impeachments, and to recommend to the legislature the repealing such laws as shall appear to them to have been passed contrary to the principles of the constitution. These powers they shall continue to have for and during the space of one year from the day of their election, and no longer. The said council of censors shall also have power to call a convention, to meet within two years after their sitting, if there appears to them an absolute necessity of amending any article of this constitution which may be defective, explaining such as may be thought not clearly expressed, and of adding such as are necessary for the preservation of the rights and happiness of the people; but the articles to be amended, and the amendments proposed, and such articles as are proposed to be added or abolished, shall be promulgated at least six months before the day appointed for the election of such convention, for the previous consideration of the people, that they may have an opportunity of instructing their delegates on the subject.

By order of convention, July 9, 1793.

THOMAS CHITTENDEN, *President.*

LEWIS R. MORRIS, *Secretary.*

AMENDMENTS TO THE CONSTITUTION OF 1793.*

ADOPTED 1828.

ARTICLE I. No person, who is not already a freeman of this State, shall be entitled to exercise the privilege of a freeman, unless he be a natural-born citizen of this or some one of the United States, or until he shall have been naturalized agreeably to the acts of Congress.

ADOPTED 1836.

ART. II. The most numerous branch of the legislature of this State shall hereafter be styled the house of representatives.

ART. III. The supreme legislative power of this State shall hereafter be exercised by a senate and the house of representatives, which shall be styled "the general assembly of the State of Vermont." Each shall have and exercise the like powers in all acts of legislation ; and no bill, resolution, or other thing, which shall have been passed by the one, shall have the effect of, or be declared to be a law, without the concurrence of the other: *Provided*, That all revenue bills shall originate in the house of representatives, but the senate may propose or concur with amendments, as on other bills. Neither house, during the session of the general assembly, shall, without the consent of the other, adjourn for more than three days, nor to any other place than that in which the two houses shall be sitting, and in case of disagreement between the two houses, with respect to adjournment, the governor may adjourn them to such time as he shall think proper.

ART. IV. The senate shall be composed of thirty senators, to be of the freemen of the county for which they are elected respectively, who are thirty years of age or upwards, and to be annually elected by the freemen of each county respectively. Each county shall be entitled to one senator, at least, and the remainder of the senators shall be apportioned to the several counties, according to their population, as the same was ascertained by the last census, taken under the authority of the United States ; regard being always had, in such apportionment, to the counties having the greatest fraction. But the several counties shall, until after the next census of the United States, be entitled to elect and have their senators in the following proportion, to wit:

Bennington County, two ; Windham County, three ; Rutland County, three ; Windsor County, four ; Addison County, three ; Orange County, three ; Washington County, two ; Chittendon County, two ; Caledonia County, two ; Franklin County, three ; Orleans County, one ; Essex County, one ; Grand Isle County, one.

The legislature shall make a new apportionment of the senators, to the several counties, after the taking of each census of the United States, or census taken for the purpose of such apportionment, by order of the government of this State, always regarding the above provisions in this article.

ART. V. The freemen of the several towns in each county shall annually give their votes for the senators apportioned to such county, at the same time and under the same regulations as are now provided for the election of councillors. And the person or persons, equal in number to the number of senators apportioned to such county, having the greatest number of legal votes in such county respectively, shall be the senator or senators of such county. At every election of senators, after the votes shall have been taken, the constable or presiding officer, assisted by the selectmen and civil authority present, shall sort and count the said votes, and make two lists of the names of each person, with the number of votes given for each annexed to his name, a record of which shall be made in the town clerk's office, and shall seal up said lists, separately, and write on each the name of the town, and these words: "Votes for senator," or "Votes for senators," as the case may be, one of which lists shall be delivered by the presiding officer to the representative of said town, (if any,) and if none be chosen,

---

* These amendments are those proposed by the councils of censors at their septennial sessions, and adopted by the conventions called to consider them. A much larger number have been proposed at different times and rejected by the successive conventions.

to the representative of an adjoining town, to be transmitted to the president of the senate; the other list the said presiding officer shall, within ten days, deliver to the clerk of the county court for the same county, and the clerk of each county court, respectively, or in case of his absence or disability, the sheriff of such county, or in case of the absence or disability of both, the high bailiff of such county, on the tenth day after such election, shall publicly open, sort, and count said votes, and make a record of the same in the office of the clerk of such county court, a copy of which he shall transmit to the senate; and shall also, within ten days thereafter, transmit to the person or persons elected a certificate of his or their election: *Provided, however,* That the general assembly shall have power to regulate, by law, the mode of balloting for senators within the several counties, and to prescribe the means, and the manner by which the result of the balloting shall be ascertained, and through which the senators chosen shall be certified of their election, and for filling all vacancies in the senate, which shall happen by death, resignation, or otherwise. But they shall not have power to apportion the senators to the several counties otherwise than according to the population thereof, agreeably to the provisions hereinbefore ordained.

ART. VI. The senate shall have the like powers to decide on the election and qualifications of, and to expel any of its members, make its own rules, and appoint its own officers, as are incident to, or are possessed by the house of representatives. A majority shall constitute a quorum. The lieutenant-governor shall be president of the senate, except when he shall exercise the office of governor, or when his office shall be vacant, or in his absence; in which cases the senate shall appoint one of its own members to be president of the senate *pro tempore.* And the president of the senate shall have a casting vote, but no other.

ART. VII. The senate shall have the sole power of trying and deciding upon all impeachments; when sitting for that purpose, they shall be on oath or affirmation; and no person shall be convicted without the concurrence of two-thirds of the members present. Judgment, in cases of impeachment, shall not extend further than removal from office, and disqualification to hold or enjoy any office of honor, or profit, or trust, under this State. But the party convicted shall, nevertheless, be liable, and subject to indictment, trial, judgment, and punishment according to law.

ART. VIII. The supreme executive power of the State shall be exercised by the governor, or, in case of his absence or disability, by the lieutenant-governor, who shall have all the powers and perform all the duties vested in and enjoined upon the governor and council by the eleventh and twenty-seventh sections of the second chapter of the constitution, as at present established, excepting that he shall not sit as a judge in case of impeachment, nor grant reprieve or pardon in any such case; nor shall he command the forces of the State in person, in time of war or insurrection, unless by the advice and consent of the senate, and no longer than they shall approve thereof. The governor may have a secretary of civil and military affairs, to be by him appointed during pleasure, whose services he may at all times command, and for whose compensation provision shall be made by law.

ART. IX. The vote for governor, lieutenant-governor, and treasurer of the State shall be sorted and counted, and the result declared by a committee, appointed by the senate and house of representatives. If at any time there shall be no election, by the freemen, of governor, lieutenant-governor, and treasurer of the State, the senate and house of representatives shall, by joint ballot, elect to fill the office, not filled by the freemen as aforesaid, one of the three candidates for such office, (if there be so many,) for whom the greatest number of votes shall have been returned.

ART. X. The secretary of state and all officers whose elections are not otherwise provided for, and who, under the existing provisions of the constitution, are elected by the council and house of representatives, shall, hereafter, be elected by the senate and house of representatives, in joint assembly, at which the presiding officer of the senate shall preside, and such presiding officer, in such joint assembly, shall have a casting vote, and no other.

ART. XI. Every bill which shall have passed the senate and house of representatives shall, before it become a law, be presented to the governor; if he approve, he shall sign it; if not, he shall return it, with his objections in writing, to the house in which it shall have originated, and which shall proceed to reconsider it. If, upon such reconsideration, a majority of the house shall pass the bill, it shall, together with the objections, be sent to the other house, by which it shall likewise be reconsidered, and if approved by a majority of that house, it shall become a law. But in all such cases the votes of both houses shall be taken by yeas and nays, and the names of the persons voting for or against the bill shall be entered upon the journal of each house, respectively. If any bill shall not be returned by the governor, as aforesaid, within five days (Sunday excepted) after it shall have been presented to him, the same shall become a law, in like manner as if he had signed it; unless the two houses by their adjournment, within three days after the presentment of such bill, shall prevent its return, in which case it shall not become a law.

ART. XII. The writ of *habeas corpus* shall, in no case, be suspended. It shall be a writ issuable of right, and the general assembly shall make provision to render it a speedy and effectual remedy in all cases proper therefor.

ART. XIII. Such parts and provisions only of the constitution of this State, established by convention on the ninth day of July, one thousand seven hundred and ninety-three, as are altered or superseded by any of the foregoing amendments, or are repugnant thereto, shall hereafter cease to have effect.

ADOPTED 1850.

ART. XIV. The assistant judges of the county court shall be elected by the freemen of their respective counties.

ART. XV. Sheriffs and high bailiffs shall be elected by the freemen of their respective counties.

ART. XVI. State's attorneys shall be elected by the freemen of their respective counties.

ART. XVII. Judges of probate shall be elected by the freemen of their respective districts.

ART. XVIII. Justices of the peace shall be elected by the freemen of their respective towns; and towns having less than one thousand inhabitants may elect any number of justices of the peace not exceeding five; towns having one thousand and less than two thousand inhabitants, may elect seven; towns having two thousand and less than three thousand inhabitants, may elect ten; towns having three thousand and less than five thousand inhabitants, may elect twelve; and towns having five thousand or more inhabitants, may elect fifteen justices of the peace.

ART. XIX. All the officers named in the preceding articles of amendment (Articles XIV to XVIII) shall be annually elected by ballot, and shall hold their offices for one year, said year commencing on the first day of December next after their election.

ART. XX. The election of the several officers mentioned in the preceding articles (Articles XIV to XVIII,) excepting town representatives, shall be made at the times and in the manner now directed in the constitution for the choice of senators. And the presiding officer of each freemen's meeting, after the votes shall have been taken, sorted, and counted, shall, in open meeting, make a certificate of the names of each person voted for, with the number of votes given for each annexed to his name and designating the office for which the votes were given, a record of which shall be made in the town clerk's office, and he shall seal up said certificate, and shall write thereon the name of the town and the words " Certificate of votes for —— ——," and add thereto, in writing, the title of the office voted for, as the case may be, and shall deliver such certificate to some representative chosen as a member of the general assembly, whose duty it will be to cause such certificate of votes to be delivered to the committee of the general assembly, appointed to canvass the same. And at the sitting of the general assembly, next after such balloting for the officers aforesaid, there shall be a committee appointed of and by the general assembly, who shall be sworn to the faithful discharge of their duty, and whose duty it shall be to examine such certificates, and ascertain the number of votes given for each candidate, and the persons receiving the largest number of votes for the respective offices shall be declared duly elected, and by such committee be reported to the general assembly, and the officers so elected shall be commissioned by the governor. And if two or more persons designated for any one of said offices shall have received an equal number of votes, the general assembly shall elect one of such persons to such office.

ART. XXI. The term of office of the governor, lieutenant-governor, and treasurer of the State, respectively, shall commence when they shall be chosen and qualified, and shall continue for the term of one year, or until their successors shall be chosen and qualified, or to the adjournment of the session of the legislature, at which, by the constitution and laws, their successors are required to be chosen, and not after such adjournment. And the legislature shall provide, by general law, declaring what officer shall act as governor whenever there shall be a vacancy in both the offices of governor and lieutenant-governor, occasioned by a failure to elect, or by the removal from office, or by the death, resignation, or inability of both governor and lieutenant-governor, to exercise the powers and discharge the duties of the office of the governor; and such officer so designated shall exercise the powers and discharge the duties appertaining to the office of governor, accordingly, until the disability shall be removed or a governor shall be elected. And in case there shall be a vacancy in the office of treasurer, by reason of any of the causes enumerated, the governor shall appoint a treasurer for the time being, who shall act as treasurer until the disability shall be removed, or a new election shall be made.

ART. XXII. The treasurer of the State shall, before entering upon the duties of his office, give sufficient security to the secretary of state, in behalf of the State of Vermont, before the governor of the State, or one of the judges of the supreme court. And sheriffs and high bailiffs, before entering upon the duties of their respective offices, shall give security to the treasurer of their respective counties, before one of the judges of the supreme court, or the two assistant judges of the county court of their respective counties, in such manner and in such sums as shall be directed by the legislature.

ART. XXIII. The senate shall be composed of thirty senators, to be of the freemen of the county for which they are elected, respectively, who shall have attained the age of thirty years, and they shall be elected annually by the freemen of each county respectively.

The senators shall be apportioned to the several counties, according to the population as ascertained by the census taken under the authority of Congress in the year 1840, regard being always had in such apportionment to the counties having the largest fraction, and giving to each county at least one senator.

The legislature shall make a new apportionment of the senators to the several counties, after the taking of each census of the United States, or after a census taken for the purpose of such apportionment, under the authority of this State, always regarding the above provisions of this article.

ADOPTED IN 1870.

ART. XXIV. SECTION 1. The general assembly shall meet on the first Wednesday of October, biennially; the first election shall be on the first Tuesday of September, A. D. 1870; the first session of the general assembly on the first Wednesday of October, A. D. 1870.

SEC. 2. The governor, lieutenant-governor, treasurer of the State, senators, town representatives, assistant judges of the county court, sheriffs, high bailiffs, State's attorneys, judges of probate, and justices of the peace shall be elected biennially, on the first Tuesday of September, in the manner prescribed by the constitution of the State.

SEC. 3. The term of office of the governor, lieutenant-governor, and treasurer of the State, respectively, shall commence when they shall be chosen and qualified, and shall continue for the term of two years, or until their successors shall be chosen and qualified, or to the adjournment of the session of the legislature at which, by the constitution and laws, their successors are required to be chosen, and not after such adjournment.

SEC. 4. The term of office of senators and town representatives shall be two years, commencing on the first Wednesday of October following their election.

SEC. 5. The term of office of the assistant judges of the county courts, sheriffs, high bailiffs, State's attorneys, judges of probate, and justices of the peace shall be two years, and shall commence on the first day of December next after their election.

ART. XXV. SECTION 1. At the session of the general assembly of this State, A. D. 1880, and at the session thereof every tenth year thereafter, the senate may, by a vote of two-thirds of its members, make proposals of amendment to the constitution of the State, which proposals of amendment, if concurred in by a majority of the members of the house of representatives, shall be entered on the journals of the house and referred to the general assembly then next to be chosen, and be published in the principal newspapers of the State; and if a majority of the members of the senate and of the house of representatives of the next following general assembly shall respectively concur in the same proposals of amendment, or any of them, it shall be the duty of the general assembly to submit the proposals of amendment so concurred in to a direct vote of the freemen of the State; and such of said proposals of amendment as shall receive a majority of the votes of the freemen voting thereon shall become a part of the constitution of this State.

SEC. 2. The general assembly shall direct the manner of voting by the people upon the proposed amendments, and enact all such laws as shall be necessary to procure a free and fair vote upon each amendment proposed, and to carry into effect all the provisions of the preceding section.

SEC. 3. The house of representatives shall have all the powers now possessed by the council of censors to order impeachments, which shall in all cases be by a vote of two-thirds of its members.

SEC. 4. The forty-third section of the second part of the constitution of this State is hereby abrogated.

ART. XXVI. The judges of the supreme court shall be elected biennially, and their term of office shall be two years.

SELECTED BIBLIOGRAPHY

The Constitution of the State of Vermont, as Established by the General Convention Elected for that Purpose (Hartford, 1777)

The Constitution of Vermont, as ... Revised by Convention in June 1786 (Windsor, 1786)

The Constitution of Vermont, as Revised and Amended by the Council of Censors ... October 1792 (Rutland, 1792)

The Constitution of Vermont (Windsor, 1793)

Journal of the Convention of Vermont (Danville, Vt., 1814)

Journal of the Convention of Vermont (Burlington, 1822)

Journal of the Convention of Vermont (Royalton, Vt., 1828)

Journal of the Convention of Montpelier (St. Albans, Vt. 1836)

Journal of the Convention of Montpelier (Montpelier, 1843)

Journal of the Convention of Montpelier (Burlington, 1850)

Journal of the Proceedings of the Constitutional Convention (Burlington, 1857)

Journal of the Proceedings of the Constitutional Convention (Burlington, 1870)

Chipman, Daniel, Memoir of Thomas Chittenden, the First Governor of Vermont, With a History of the Constitution During his Administration (Middlebury, Vt., 1849)

VERMONT INDEX